Textbook on
TORT

David Howarth
Clare College, Cambridge

Butterworths
London, Dublin, Edinburgh
1995

United Kingdom	Butterworths a Division of Reed Elsevier (UK) Ltd, Halsbury House, 35 Chancery Lane, LONDON WC2A 1EL and 4 Hill Street, EDINBURGH EH2 3JZ
Australia	Butterworths, SYDNEY, MELBOURNE, BRISBANE, ADELAIDE, PERTH, CANBERRA and HOBART
Canada	Butterworths Canada Ltd, TORONTO and VANCOUVER
Ireland	Butterworth (Ireland) Ltd, DUBLIN
Malaysia	Malayan Law Journal Sdn Bhd, KUALA LUMPUR
New Zealand	Butterworths of New Zealand Ltd, WELLINGTON and AUCKLAND
Puerto Rico	Butterworth of Puerto Rico, Inc, SAN JUAN
Singapore	Butterworths Asia, SINGAPORE
South Africa	Butterworths Publishers (Pty) Ltd, DURBAN
USA	Butterworth Legal Publishers, CARLSBAD, California and SALEM, New Hampshire

A CIP Catalogue record for this book is available from the British Library.

ISBN 0 406 03504 0

Printed in England by Clays Ltd, St Ives Plc

Preface

This book is intended for first degree students of law in England and Wales. It may hold some interest for law students from other jurisdictions and may be an object of curiosity for legal academics. It is not primarily aimed at the legal profession, although it may be of use for practising lawyers who are wondering how the overall shape of the subject they once learned is changing.

Its aim is to introduce and, from time to time, to explain tort law as it now stands in England. It does not aim to be a repository in its footnotes for all the known cases on tort, but only for those which seem to have some inherent interest. It contains some comparative material not just from the traditional sources in the Commonwealth and the United States, although, inevitably, there is much from those jurisdictions, but also from continental European sources, especially from France and Germany.

There is, to be sure, not enough French and German material even to start to give an understanding of the equivalent to tort law in those legal systems, but it is hoped that there is enough to cause the curious to want to know more. There is no common law of Europe yet, and there is much divergence in methods of working and fundamental assumptions among lawyers from the different traditions in Europe, but the practical results reached by the courts are often surprisingly similar and the underlying social, economic and political questions that European legal systems face are very much alike.

A textbook is not supposed to have themes, but there are some recurrent phrases that seem to emerge from the mass of the material. One is that much of tort law is in a state of rapid change, and, perhaps, on the verge of a new era of intellectual vigour after a decade and a half of inaction and the formulaic rejection of new ideas. Another is that in a time of change, the fundamental unit of the law is not the rule but the argument. Often one cannot say what the courts will do in the next case or what the rules are that they are applying, but one can say something interesting about which arguments are being used and how they are developing from case to case.

Tort cases use arguments from a surprisingly wide range of sources. An economic argument here and a constitutional argument there can be followed by pure pragmatism or a flight of jurisprudential principle before the argument retreats into the staid authority of the cases of the late nineteenth century. There is no pattern to this making of new arguments, nor should there be. The law, especially tort law, is a constant battle of the legal imagination to keep up with new social patterns and new technologies.

The law is not a system of thought, but it is not a predictable exercise in power politics either. The rationality of the law is a conversational rationality—the rationality of listening and responding rather than an abstract construction. It is hoped that this book has caught some of that spirit.

A book such as this is an amalgam of many different influences and is the result of help and assistance from many different sources. It is impossible to acknowledge them all, and invidious to single out particular contributions. But, at the risk of offending those whose help I have relied on just as much, I would like to mention a few names. Guido Calabresi inspired my interest in tort law many years ago. Malcom Grant and Colin Turpin exercised their considerable organisational talents to give me the time to do the work for this book. Simon Deakin took on a large chunk of my teaching responsibilities. Diane Dawson kept my scepticism about the economic analysis of law from falling into cynicism. Kurt Lipstein was a constant source of support and inspiration during the long hours in the Squire Law Library, as well as being a mine of useful linguistic and bibliographical information. The Squire Librarian Keith McVeigh and his staff were constantly helpful and resourceful. My wife, Edna Murphy, as well as enduring by proxy the agonies of authorship, read the text with her professional eye and prevented many errors. But above all, I would like to thank the undergraduate law students of Clare, Corpus Christi and, latterly, Sidney Sussex Colleges for putting up with their supervisor's eccentricities, for correcting his wilder flights of fantasy and for making perspicacious comments on earlier drafts of the text.

David Howarth
February 1995

Contents

Chapter 6

Economic loss and negligence   267

Chapter 9

Intentional torts—(1) physical interference 441

Chapter 10

Intentional torts—(2) economic and moral interests 471

Chapter 11

Nuisance and Rylands v Fletcher 495

Chapter 13

Damages　591

Table of statutes

List of cases

PAGE

Chapter 1

What is tort law?

Introduction

Many textbooks on torts begin with an attempt to define either 'tort' or 'torts' or 'the law of torts'. The attempt usually ends up as a list of the differences between tort law and other areas of the law, such as contract, trusts and criminal law. It is important to understand these differences, but more important to start further back, and to ask what sort of legal action a tort action is.

The first point to note is that a tort action is a kind of civil action. It is not a criminal prosecution. The difference between a civil action and a criminal prosecution is not simply, as some people think, that the point of civil actions is to compensate whereas the point of criminal prosecutions is to punish. Such a distinction does account for much of the difference, but there are many significant exceptions. For example, judges in criminal cases often have the power to grant compensation orders against the defendant. Similarly, judges in civil cases, although rather more infrequently, have the power to award punitive damages. Furthermore, civil court judges may threaten to imprison for contempt those who defy their orders.

But neither is the difference merely, as Glanville Williams once claimed, that civil claims are pursued in civil courts whereas criminal prosecutions are carried on in the criminal courts.[1] Such a distinction would fail to explain why there are two separate court systems in the first place.

The real difference between the civil law and the criminal law is that in a civil claim the case is about whatever it is that the plaintiff wants the court to do to the defendant (for example, to order damages, to impose an injunction, or to make a declaration of who is legally in the right) whereas in a criminal prosecution the case is not about what the victim wants, or even what anyone with a contractual relationship with the victim wants,[2] but about what the state prosecuting authorities want. Even for those criminal offences in which the law allows private citizens to bring

---

1   *Textbook on Criminal Law* (1st ed, London; 1978).
2   Eg insurance companies with rights of subrogation.

prosecutions, the Director of Public Prosecutions and the Attorney-General have the power to step in and to stop the proceedings, regardless of the views of the victim.

Another way of stating the same point is that if in a civil case the defendant offers to pay the plaintiff a sum of money in exchange for dropping the case, it is called a settlement, but if the defendant did the same thing in a criminal case it would be called a bribe. The civil case concerns private law, in the sense that whether to proceed with the action and how to proceed with it are matters for the individual or organisation bringing the claim. Criminal prosecutions are brought, or at least are supposed to be brought, not for the benefit of any particular individual, but for the good of the public at large or for the good of the state.

The significance of this seemingly obvious point is that it means that it is inherently implausible to define 'tort law' in terms of a general objective such as 'compensation for the victims of accidents'. Tort law, like all civil law, concerns the interaction between such general objectives, which the courts may or may not endorse, and the very particular objectives of the individual plaintiff. Some plaintiffs may want compensation. Others may want their property back. Others may want the defendant to stop carrying on some activity. Others may want the world to know that they are in the right and that the defendant is in the wrong. Others still may just want the defendant to suffer public humiliation or to suffer financially. And as long as plaintiffs may ask the court for remedies other than compensatory damages—remedies such as injunctions and declarations—even exclusively from the point of view of the court, tort law must be about more than compensation.

The second point about what kind of legal action a tort action is concerns how the different 'torts' get their names. In England plaintiffs do not have to insert legal theories into their claims. All they strictly have to do is to state the facts that, they allege, entitle them to the remedy they claim against the defendant. If the defendant says that even if the facts were true the plaintiff still should not win, the court has to rule on whether the facts alleged by the plaintiff, or a sub-set of them, are capable of entitling the plaintiff to win. If the court rules in favour of the plaintiff, the result is that the pattern of facts alleged gives the plaintiff a 'cause of action' against the defendant. If that 'cause of action' comes up in a number of cases, it becomes tempting to give that pattern of facts a shorthand name, for example 'malicious falsehood' or 'the Rule in *Rylands v Fletcher*'. Plaintiffs are then said by lawyers, for the sake of convenience, to sue 'in' or 'for' the shorthand name, for example 'in negligence' or 'for defamation'. But this is only shorthand. In a subsequent case, a plaintiff may be able to prove only some of the facts described by the shorthand name. The defendant will say that the plaintiff's facts are insufficient. The plaintiff will say that the missing facts are not relevant. If the court agrees with the plaintiff, one can describe the situation in two ways. First one can say that the requirements of the 'tort' known by the shorthand name have changed, and have become less onerous for plaintiffs. Or, secondly, one can say that there is a new 'tort' to be known by a new shorthand name.

Usually, if the change is simply a matter of saying that some of the facts previously believed to be necessary to establish liability are not necessary, the same shorthand name continues to be used. Take for example the case of *Emerald Construction Co Ltd v Lowthian*.[3] There is a tort with the shorthand name of 'inducing a breach of contract' between the plaintiff and a third party. In *Emerald* the question arose whether the defendant had to know about the exact terms of the contract in question and whether the defendant had to intend specifically that the contract was to be breached. The Court of Appeal decided that specific knowledge and specific intention were not necessary. It sufficed if the defendant knew about the contract's existence and did not care one way or the other whether the demands that he was making would result in a breach of the contract. *Emerald* thus relaxes previously imagined conditions for liability but does not make more radical changes. It therefore had no effect on the shorthand name given to the tort.

In contrast, when the range of the tort is expanded in a way that makes the original shorthand inadequate, name changes take place. For example, *Torquay Hotel Co Ltd v Cousins*[4] also supposedly involved 'inducement to breach a contract'. But the question raised was whether the defendant could be liable when, because of loopholes built into the contract itself, the defendant's conduct did not technically lead to a breach of the contract. The Court of Appeal again found in favour of the plaintiff. But here the shorthand name had to change. There was no breach of contract, so that the cause of action could not be 'inducing a breach of contract'. Instead it came to be called 'interference in the performance of a contract'.[5]

These changes of name and the invention of new names cause great confusion. But it is important to realise that they are only shorthand names, and stand for decisions, some clear, some not clear, about the facts the plaintiff must establish to obtain judgment.

One interesting side issue is that there used to be a lively though obscure debate about whether one should speak of the 'law of tort' or the 'law of torts'. The answer is that neither is entirely satisfactory. 'Tort' implies that there is something other than being civil actions for damages that all such cases have in common. But this is too much to expect. On the other hand, 'torts' implies that the fact patterns that give rise to liability are more fixed than they really are. The best compromise is therefore probably 'tort law', which takes a neutral stance on the question.

But notice that not only are 'torts' shorthand names for fact patterns that give rise to liability but so are 'breach of contract', 'breach of trust', 'restitution' and every other civil action. There are two possible conclusions that one might draw from this. One, the conventional conclusion, is that tort law is a residual category. It is what is left when the more easily

---

3   [1966] 1 All ER 1013, [1966] 1 WLR 691, 1 KIR 200.
4   [1969] 2 Ch 106, [1969] 1 All ER 522, [1969] 2 WLR 289, 6 KIR 15.
5   Later the cause of action was further extended and brought into being the tort of 'interference with trade by unlawful means.' See *Hadmor v Hamilton* [1983] 1 AC 191, [1982] 1 All ER 1042, [1982] 2 WLR 322.

defined categories of fact pattern giving rise to liability have been removed.
Thus, liability for breach of contract includes all those fact patterns in
which it is necessary for the plaintiff to allege that there was a valid contract
between the parties, and breach of trust includes all those fact patterns in
which it is necessary for the plaintiff to allege that the defendant was a
trustee. On this interpretation, 'torts' are any fact patterns which give
rise to liability but which are not otherwise categorised.

The other interpretation is that all forms of civil liability are in a sense
'torts'. They are fact patterns that give rise to liability. The sub-categories
into which the fact patterns may be placed are all equally shorthand names,
so that 'breach of contract' is on the same level as 'negligence' or 'inducement
to breach a contract'. Just as, because of changes in their underlying fact
patterns, both the content and the shorthand names of the traditional
'torts' can change over time, so in principle could 'breach of contract' and
'breach of trust'. This is how, for example, the field of liability known as
'restitution' has been able to emerge out of a concern with a particular
form of remedy—that what is the plaintiffs' should be restored to them—
with its concomitant concerns with some forms of breach of trust and
liability for 'quasi-contract'. Moreover, the fact patterns that now give rise
to the existence of contracts and trusts in the first place, and which are
necessary conditions of liability for breach of contract or trust, may
themselves change over time.

The first, more conventional, interpretation has the effect of drawing
attention to one particular aspect of the difference between breach of
contract and breach of trust on the one hand and negligence, defamation,
nuisance and so on on the other hand—namely that breaches of contract
and trust involve accusations that the defendant has voluntarily undertaken a specific obligation which he has failed to perform, whereas liability
for negligence, defamation, nuisance and so on seems not to depend on
specific prior undertakings by the defendant but on obligations that, prima
facie, everyone is subject to. This observation leads in turn to the idea that
'tort' liability is a 'general' or 'primary' liability that arises out of the general
law, in contrast with contract- or trust-based liability which is 'particular'
or 'secondary' liability that arises out of the will of the defendant rather
than directly out of the general law.[6]

The second interpretation tends to play down the differences between
'tort', 'contract' and 'trust' and tends to support the view that they are all
part of a grand legal category called, after the Roman and French usage,
'the law of obligations', which stands on a par with 'the law of property'
and 'the law of persons'. Within 'the law of obligations' there may be
different bases for liability, and the agreement of the parties or the will of
the defendant may certainly constitute a necessary condition of liability
in many cases. But, just as in other fact patterns that give rise to liability,
it is open to plaintiffs to argue that there may be acceptable substitutes

---

6   See RMW Dias, [1967] CLJ 62. The idea of 'secondary' obligations derives in the first
instance from HLA Hart *The Concept Of Law* 2nd ed (Oxford; Clarendon Press, 1994)
and more distantly from Wn Hohfeld *Fundamental Legal Conceptions*.

for the established requirements, for example that the status or occupation of the defendant or the reasonable expectations of the plaintiff could serve to justify liability just as well as the prior agreement of the parties or the voluntary consent of the defendant. Thus, the second interpretation leads to less strict ideas about the boundaries between, for example, tort and contract and to an easier acceptance of hybrid forms of liability.[7]

The choice between these two interpretations is of great importance for the future development of the law. Strict separation of tort and contract and of tort and trusts will mean that if the law is to change to meet changing circumstances it will have to do so by heroic leaps, by reclassifying entire problems—as tort questions rather than as contract questions, for example—rather than by the more gradual process of developing mixed forms of liability. Heroic leaps of reclassification have happened in the past. The famous case of *Donoghue v Stevenson*[8] for example worked its magic precisely by reclassifying a problem (that of the liability of a manufacturer of a product that does harm to a user of the product who has no contract with the manufacturer) as a 'tort' question rather than a 'contract' question. But the inherently conservative nature of law, especially in a system of law openly committed to case law and the doctrine of precedent, means that heroic leaps of this sort are rare.

How can one choose between the two interpretations? This is a complex question well beyond the scope of this introduction, but there is one central issue to think about: how big a difference to legal responsibility should prior agreement and voluntary consent make? Some think that the law should impose as little as possible on people, but they also think that it is an important principle that the law should enforce the bargains people voluntarily enter into. On this view, voluntary consent makes a very big difference. In a great number of cases, it says, there ought not to be legal liability without it. On the other hand, others believe that there is nothing wrong with imposing extensive duties on people to reflect the respons–ibilities that people have as citizens to their fellow citizens. Those of this view often also believe that truly voluntary consent is rare, because, for example, many people are forced to act in the way that they do because of poverty or other forms of dependence, or, they believe, more radically, that voluntary consent is impossible because people's actions are completely conditioned by their circumstances, whether social, economic or psycho–logical. For these others, therefore, prior agreement and voluntary consent either make little difference or no difference at all to where the law ought to impose liability.

Of course, a large number of intermediate positions are possible between the 'consent is all' school of thought and the 'consent does not exist' school. For example, one might say: that (a) there is at least one person whom it is impossible in reality to treat as completely irrational and lacking the

---

7   See below ch 6 on economic loss and especially Lord Goff in *Spring v Guardian Assurance plc* [1994] 3 All ER 129 and *Henderson v Merrett Syndicates, Arbuthnott v Feltrim* [1994] 3 All ER 506.

8   [1932] AC 562.

capacity to choose—namely oneself—although one also knows of situations in which choice seemed very limited, especially situations in which other people had much more information about the possible choices than one did oneself; (b) it would be extraordinarily arrogant to presume that all or most other people are irrational or lacking the capacity to choose, but that nevertheless there must be some people in that position, and, more importantly, that many people are in a worse position to choose than others because of lack of information; (c) to treat others as slaves to circumstance when one knows that one is not such a slave oneself is an invitation to play the tyrant with other people's lives or at least to act in a very patronising way, but it is not tyrannical or patronising to impose respons–ibilities on those with more information rather than on those with less; and so (d) it is important to treat people as if they were rational and able to choose even when one is unsure whether they really are.[9] But in doing so one can also accept that such rationality is bounded by the information available and the ability of humans to process it.[10] In consequence, there is room for consent and voluntary agreement to help determine liability, but evidence of overwhelming external influences should be accepted and evidence of imbalance in access to information is a ground in itself for imposing responsibility.

The legal consequence of these intermediate positions is clearest in the way in which judges are increasingly interpreting contracts, which are voluntary, as containing implied terms that reflect the imbalance in the availability of information to the two sides and which impose respons–ibility on the side that is in the better position to know.[11] But, as we shall see in some detail in the chapter on negligently caused economic loss, there is a distinct parallel between these cases on implied terms in contracts and cases on the application of the 'tort' of negligence to cases in which the defendant has harmed the plaintiff by providing the plaintiff with inaccurate information. The tendency is therefore towards the second view, and towards the development of hybrid forms of liability. But the emphasis is not only on the unimportance of consent in 'contract' cases, but also on the importance of consent in 'tort' cases. There is still a boundary between 'tort', in which consent is relatively less important, and 'contract' in which it is relatively more important, but there are areas of convergence and overlap as well.

The functions of tort law

We turn now to the question 'what does tort law do?' or, more precisely, 'what difference would it make if civil legal liability could only exist on the basis of prior agreement or consent?'[12]

9   Cf LT Hobhouse *Liberalism* (London, Williams and Novgate, 1911).
10 Cf H Simon *Models Of Man* (New York, 1957); O Williamson *Economic Institutions Of Capitalism* (New York, Free Press, 1985).
11 *Scally v Southern Health and Social Services Board* [1992] 1 AC 294.
12 Note this way of putting the question brings the law of restitution into tort law.

In the light of the previous section it ought to be said that abolishing the law of torts may not make a very great difference at all. In theory a great deal of it could be reinvented through implied terms in contracts, constructive (ie made-up) trusts and orders to restore the plaintiff's property. One might remark that in countries where attempts have been made greatly to restrict the scope of tort law, in New Zealand and Sweden for example, such developments do not seem yet to have happened. But that might have as much to do with the limits of legal imagination and the will of the judiciary as with the theoretical possibilities.

But assuming that tort law is not reinvented immediately by other means, what would be lost if it were abolished?

Compensation mechanism

Tort law acts as a way of channelling compensation payments from those who cause losses to those who suffer them. As we have seen, compensation is not the only function of tort law, and plaintiffs may have motives other than compensation when deciding whether to sue. The process may be further complicated by victims, deciding to blame a particular person for the accident because lawyers have said that the person in question may have to pay damages to the victim.[13]

But the fact remains that, both through cases that reach the courts[14] and, far more importantly, through cases that are settled out of court or which never even reach the stage at which the victim has to threaten legal action at all, tort liability is a major source of compensation for the victims of various accidents—whether at work, in the home, in the hospital or on the road—and for those whose property is damaged. The total liability insurance payouts of insurance companies in Britain may amount to less than 1% of GNP[15] but state social security payments for injury, disable—ment and sickness amount in total to a roughly similar sum.[16] Donald Harris[17] said in 1984 that sick pay and social security were 'much more important' in total than the tort system in providing compensation, but this is, and always was, an exaggeration. Harris' own figures imply that personal injury liability amounted to 0.6% of GNP in his period of study, the middle 70s, whereas at that time the entire social security budget for sickness and injury amounted to around 0.9% of GNP. When one remembers that the tort system covers property damage as well as personal injury, which the social security system does not, the gap begins to look even

13 S Lloyd-Bostock 'Common sense morality and accident compensation' [1980] Ins LJ 881.
14 See eg B Markesinis 'Litigation-Mania in England, Germany and the USA: Are We So Very Different?' [1990] CLJ 233 and Peter Vincent-Jones ' The litigation explosion' (1990) 140 NLJ 1602.
15 See 'Order in the tort' The Economist (18 July 1992) (Survey: The Legal Profession p 8).
16 See *Annual Abstract of Statistics 1995* (HMSO) p 46.
17 *Compensation and Support for Illness and Injury* (Oxford; Clarendon, 1984) at p328.

smaller. Furthermore, there has been a striking increase in the amount of personal injury litigation since the middle 70s[18] combined with a reduction in the generosity of the social security system. Even the more moderately expressed idea that the tort system is, in the words of the Pearson Commission,[19] a 'junior partner' to the social security system is therefore open to question. The tort system may not be the most important source of help for victims of misfortune (that, surely, is the National Health Service) but it is an important source of compensation.

If tort law did not exist, these compensation costs would either fall on the victims themselves or, via their own private insurance, on the clients of the insurance industry as a whole, or, via additional social security payments, on the taxpayer.

But those who would like to see the reduction of the importance of the tort system and the introduction of either private insurance or additional social security argue that the problem with the tort system is not the total amount of claims but the cost of transferring that compensation through the courts. Would not additional private insurance or additional social security payments achieve the same ends but at lower administrative cost?

It is true that a disputed tort claim that reaches the courts can be ruinously expensive. But the costs of administering a claim in which both liability and the amount of the compensation to be paid are obvious are minimal. And litigation between private insurers and their clients and between the social security authorities and their claimants can be just as expensive.

The difference between a tort system and a non-tort system comes down largely to the costs of running different sorts of insurance system. In a tort system, people will want to insure themselves against being sued. They will take out 'liability' or 'third party' insurance. Indeed, as in the case of drivers in Britain, the law may oblige them to have such insurance. In a non-tort system, it is the potential victims who need the insurance, namely 'first party' insurance. Such insurance may be provided either through the market or by the state.

Each system has its costs. In general, waste comes from over-insurance, from not knowing how risky one's situation is and taking out too much insurance against it, or from under-insurance, not knowing how risky one's situation is and taking out too little insurance against it. Over-insurance is wasteful because it leads to the insurance industry's taking up too much of the economy's resources. Under-insurance is wasteful because of the disruption caused by trying to find the uninsured amounts and because if it is known that under-insurance is widespread, people may decide to insure against the chance that other people's insurance will not be enough, thus producing duplication of effort. But equally there are two forms of not knowing enough about the risks. First, one may not know how likely it is that an accident will happen, and so either overestimate or underestimate

18 139% between 1975 and 1989 alone, according to Vincent-Jones (1990) 140 NLJ 1602.
19 Royal Commission on Civil Liability and Compensation for Personal Injury Cmnd 7054 1978.

the chances that one will need one's insurance policy. Secondly, one may not know the amount of harm that may be done by any accident that does happen, and so one may mistake the amount of loss one should insure against. The problem is that in general, people have fairly accurate information about or control of how likely they are to cause an accident to others but do not know how much harm they are likely to cause (because they do not know how much other people earn, how many people are dependent on them and so on). Equally, people know little about and have little control over how likely other people are to cause accidents but do know much about how badly they and their family would be affected if they suffered an accident themselves.

It follows that in a tort-based third party insurance system waste will arise from inaccurate estimates of the costs to others of accidents they may suffer, but in a non-tort first party insurance system waste will arise from inaccurate estimates of how likely other people are to cause accidents.

Some people, especially in the 1960s and 1970s[20], looked forward to comprehensive state-backed compensation schemes such as that introduced in New Zealand in 1972.[1] They assumed that the all-seeing, all-knowing eye of the state would be able to discern the risks more accurately than individual citizens acting by themselves. But experience has shown that the state has just as much difficulty in estimating the probable total costs of accidents as does anyone else. Moreover, the costs to the taxpayer of such schemes have proven to be politically unsustainable. There is no salvation from tort law in the state.

Deterrence mechanism

The second effect of tort law, like all law that imposes burdens on people or gives them direct orders, is to discourage some forms of conduct and to encourage others. This deterrent effect of tort law, its effect in discouraging the commission of torts, plays a central role in the economic analysis of tort law.[2] Clearly, it is unpleasant to have to pay damages or to be threatened with imprisonment for disobeying an injunction, and if the prospect of damages or injunctions has any effect at all it is in the direction of dissuading people from acting in ways which the courts would condemn. But the question is how big an incentive do they create?

Empirical evidence is lacking to answer this question. Countries such as New Zealand and Sweden have reduced the scope of tort law in areas such as accidents at work and road accidents, but it is difficult to disentangle

20 Eg Atiyah *Accidents, Compensation and the Law* (London, Weidenfeld and Nicholson, 1970). See also Jane Stapleton *Product Liability* (London, Butterworths, 1994) p 3.

1   For further discussion of the history of the New Zealand scheme see R Miller 'An Analysis And Critique of The 1992 Changes To New Zealand's Accident Compensation Scheme' (1993) 52 Md L Rev 1070.

2   See below pp 15-24.

the effect of the absence of tort remedies and other factors such as road building and the decline of manufacturing industry. It does, however, seem likely that the deterrent effect of tort law is greater in some areas than in others.

At one extreme there is car driving. The incentives to drive in a reasonably safe way are many: one's own safety, the safety of one's passengers, the protection of one's property, the criminal law, one's own sense of moral responsibility as well as tort law. It is unlikely that there would be much difference if the threat of a tort action were to be removed. The presence of compulsory third party insurance reduces incentives further, since, although losing one's no claims bonus can be expensive, it is not as expensive as having to pay out all the damages at once out of one's own pocket; otherwise one would not bother to insure.[3]

At the other extreme, there are few incentives to refrain from using one's property in a way that unreasonably annoys one's neighbours—the tort of nuisance. The criminal law takes little notice of such disputes, one's own safety is not in issue and one's own property is not in danger. The incentives, other than tort law, are the threat of an order from the local authority for statutory nuisance, the threat of retaliation from the neighbour, one's sense of moral responsibility and tort law.

In between the to two come many of the other cases covered by tort law: industrial injuries—covered by regulatory criminal law, compulsory insurance and the threat of strike action but not by any direct danger to the employer or its property; the 'economic' torts such as inducing a breach of contract—no criminal liability, often no insurance but usually restrained by the fear of retaliation; and product liability—some regulatory criminal law and usually covered by insurance but little danger to the producer.

It is also worth noting Judge Calabresi's notion of 'market deterrence'.[4] Even when there is insurance, those who cause more tortious damage have to pay more than those who do not. If the activity that gives rise to the liability is a commercial one, those who cause more damage will have higher costs than those who do not. Thus, under a tort system, in the long run, the market will tend to weed out the unsafe. If there is no tort system, and no substitute such as a tax graduated by the dangerousness of the particular taxpayer to other people (and how much more costly such a tax would be to administer and collect) those who are unsafe suffer no cost penalty in the market.

Finally, the deterrence function of tort law is at its clearest when the plaintiff asks for and gets an injunction against the defendant. The point of an injunction is precisely to prevent the recurrence of the harm. It may

---

3   The insurance company has an incentive to set premiums which differentiate between good risks and bad risks, but obtaining the information necessary to make such differentiations is costly and the insurance company is unlikely to differentiate to such an extent that each insured person simply pays a premium that represents instalment payments on the costs of accidents that they as individuals cause.

4   See eg Calabresi and Hirschoff 'Towards a test for strict liability in torts' (1972) 81 Yale LJ 1054.

also, though more rarely, require the defendant positively to put right the wrong that has been done.[5] But in either case, deterrence is not only the point of what the plaintiff has asked for but also of what the court has ordered. It is a very specific deterrent, aimed directly at the particular defendant, but knowledge that the courts may grant such remedies may have wider effects. The torts of nuisance, interference with business by unlawful means and even defamation depend for their ultimate deterrent effect not on damages but on injunctions. Note also that there is no exact criminal law equivalent of the injunction—to the extent that prosecuting authorities who find that the penalties of the criminal law are insufficient to prevent wrongdoers from repeating their crimes may turn to the injunction as a final and more drastic resort.[6]

Rectificatory justice

Another important function of the tort system is that it appeals to a basic idea of justice that wrongdoers should put right the harm they have caused to others. This form of justice, is usually called 'rectificatory' or 'corrective' justice in order to distinguish it from the broader idea of 'social' or 'distributive' justice which refers to the fairness of the overall pattern of wealth and power.[7] It is peculiarly appropriate for tort and for other civil actions since it links, as tort law often does, the defendant's wrongdoing with what the plaintiff asks for in recompense. If there was no tort law, so that, for example, people with grievances had to rely on the state, in the form of the criminal law, to bring about a just settlement between the parties, a number of difficulties would arise. First, the prosecuting authorities might decide not to prosecute for reasons of policy and expense. Secondly, the prosecuting authorities and the criminal courts may be more concerned with the future behaviour of the defendant, or the behaviour of similar possible defendants, than with the well-being of the plaintiff, so that they may, for example, decide to punish the defendant with a heavy

---

5   For the (strict) conditions for granting such positive or 'mandatory' injunctions see ICF Spry *The Principles Of Equitable Remedies: Specific Performance, Injunctions, Rectification and Equitable Damages* (4th ed) (London; Sweet & Maxwell, 1990).

6   See eg Sunday trading cases: *Chisholm v Kirklees Metropolitan Borough Council; Kirklees Metropolitan Borough Council v B&Q plc* [1993] ICR 826; *Kirklees Metropolitan Borough Council v Wickes Building Supplies Ltd* [1990] 1 WLR 1237; on appeal [1993] AC 227; [1991] 3 WLR 985; [1991] 4 All ER 240, CA; revsd [1993] AC 227, [1992] 3 WLR 170, [1992] 3 All ER 717, HL(E); *Stoke-on-Trent City Council v B & Q (Retail) Ltd* [1984] AC 754; [1984] 2 WLR 929; [1984] 2 All ER 332, HL(E); *Stoke-on-Trent City Council v B & Q plc* [1991] Ch 48, [1991] 4 All ER 221, [1991] 2 WLR 42; on appeal C-169/91 [1993] 1 All ER 481, ECJ; affd sub nom *Stoke on Trent City Council v B&Q plc* [1993] 2 All ER 297n, [1993] 2 WLR 730, HL(E).

7   These distinctions, which are the subject of controversy—some claim for example that rectificatory justice is simply a form of distributive justice, others that the two are distinct but act as limits on each other—derive from Aristotle's *Nicomachean Ethics*.

prison term as an example to others with the effect that the defendant becomes unable to pay compensation to the victim, or they may decide that the defendant should be let off because the offence is unlikely to recur, leaving the victim unsatisfied with the treatment of the incident that did occur.

It is true that the idea of 'rectificatory justice' is not easily reduced to a formula, so that it is not easy to pin down precisely what would be lost if tort law were no longer to exist. Does it mean that the wrongdoer has to 'wipe out' or 'annul' the wrong that has been done[8] or, since that is impossible in many cases of irreversible harm (for example the loss of limbs), does justice require instead that the wrongdoer offer an adequate substitute (for example the price of a holiday for the pain and suffering that has happened and cannot be removed from the record)? But if the test is that of the adequate substitute, what is adequate? What if the victim feels that the wrongdoer is not offering enough? Is justice of this sort controllable by what third parties would think to be reasonable? If so, what is reasonable? What should a reasonable person expect in recompense?

Another source of dispute is whether the duty to rectify arises simply out of the fact of harm or out of wrongdoing that causes harm. Some writers insist that no-one has the right to impose costs on other people, so that merely causing such costs raises a presumption that there is an injustice that ought to be rectified.[9] Other writers point out that the ordinary interactions of life inevitably impose costs on others but no-one believes that there is any injustice.[10] For example, if I turn up earlier than you do to queue for a ticket for a concert, I reduce your chances of getting a ticket. I have imposed a cost on you. But it would be absurd to suggest that I have done you an injustice and should hand over my ticket to you. If the system of queuing is fair, I have done nothing wrong, and your claim if successful would undermine the idea of queuing itself.

But what counts as sufficient wrongdoing is a very complex question. Some torts demand that the plaintiff show that the defendant was at fault, in the sense that the defendant could and should have acted differently. But other torts do not require fault to be proved. Does this mean that these torts do not conform to the requirements of rectificatory justice?

The answer is that it depends. Note that in many forms of breach of contract all the plaintiff has to prove is that the defendant promised to do something under a valid contract and then failed to do it. The plaintiff does not usually have to prove that the defendant was at fault in not performing the contract because the contractual promise is interpreted as meaning that the defendant guaranteed that he would perform. But this does not mean that liability for such breaches of contract goes against the tenets of rectificatory justice, for it is sufficient wrongdoing to have promised to guarantee that something would be done and for it then not to be done.

---

8   See Jules Coleman 'Tort law and the demands of justice' [1992] Indiana LJ 349 and his recantation in *Risks And Wrongs* (Cambridge; CUP 1992) at pp 307-311.
9   See eg R Epstein *A Theory of Strict Liability*.
10 *Coleman.*

Similarly, in torts in which the plaintiff does not have to prove fault, the question is whether one can say plausibly that the defendant is someone who should guarantee that harm should not occur, and that whenever harm occurs the defendant is prima facie a wrongdoer. For example, the defendant may have chosen to manufacture products that when used harm the plaintiff. The liability of such manufacturers is in many legal systems either strict, that is that fault need not be proved, or at least stricter than the usual standards of fault.[11] But such liability rules do not violate the requirements of rectificatory justice if it is plausible to say that manu-facturers of products by choosing to engage in that activity take on an obligation to guarantee that their products will be safe to use.

In some circumstances it would not be plausible to read in a guarantee of freedom from harm from the defendant's occupation, trade or status. For example, the police do not guarantee that there will be no crime, and car manufacturers do not guarantee that cars will be driven competently. But where it is plausible, the principles of rectificatory justice are not violated by liability without fault.

Note, however, that insurance does pose a problem for rectificatory justice. Insurance does not prevent the compensation from flowing to the victim but it does seem to interfere with the principle that it should flow from the wrongdoer. It is true that the wrongdoer has been paying premiums, and may well have to pay higher premiums in the future. But the problem comes in claims for very high sums, which it is unlikely that the wrongdoer has paid out or will ever have to pay out in premiums. There is a paradox that when insurance intervenes, the higher the sum claimed in relation to the premiums paid the less the requirements of rectificatory justice are fulfilled.

Another way of looking at the same set of issues is that tort law serves the function of preventing victims of accidents from feeling that those who caused the harm have got away with something, that they have acted, in Hyman Gross's phrase, 'with impunity'.[12] The criminal law may serve the same purpose, but victims of harm may not be satisfied with the penalty imposed and may believe that unless they have control of the case themselves, the chances increase of the wrongdoer escaping without being properly dealt with.

Method of testing the reasonableness of new behaviour

The final function of tort law, especially the tort of negligence, under which the court tests the actions of the defendant for 'reasonableness', is to provide a public forum in which to discuss new forms of behaviour and the consequences of new technologies.

11 The situation in Britain is the latter. See below pp 392-434.
12 See Gross 'Impunity' in Gross and Harrison *Jurisprudence: Cambridge Essays* (Oxford: Clarendon, 1991).

One form of this idea is that tort law provides a sort of ombudsman service[13] so that it serves to focus investigations into accidents and to focus public attention on wrongdoing. The problem with this idea is that because tort cases involve individual claims by individual claimants who have only one chance to get compensation, and who therefore may be very anxious to settle,[14] the cases may often disappear from public view before reaching a stage at which such a public service function comes into play. In Britain, the usual way to investigate serious accidents is therefore to hold a public inquiry. It is interesting to note, however, that such inquiries are often chaired by judges[15] and to speculate that without experience in tort cases judges may not be quite so well-qualified to act in such a capacity.

Another form of the idea is that tort law provides a way for the optimal regulation of new forms of behaviour and new technologies to be worked out on a case by case basis so that the legislature has a pattern of thought and decision about a new problem to work on before plumping for a particular set of regulations.[16] For instance, the growth of international computer information networks has produced a number of new problems in the fields of copyright and defamation. For example, should the owner of an information service which members may use to conduct public debates about current issues be liable for any defamatory statements that members make in the same way that a newspaper is liable for defamatory comments published on its letters page?[17] Is the information service more like a library, a noticeboard, a newspaper or a postal service? It would be wise to let the courts hear a number of such cases and to let the subtleties of the problem emerge, before drawing broad conclusions on which to base general legislation.

Indeed, it may be that the government and the legislature, either for reasons of pressure of time or because the issues are too politically sensitive, never get round to regulating the new behaviour or technology in a comprehensive way. If this happens, tort law is the only way, albeit incompletely and case by case, that such behaviour or technology can be challenged and regulated. If tort law were abolished, victims of new forms of behaviour and new technologies would be left to the vagaries of the political processes to have their grievances aired.

From this discussion of the place of tort law and its functions, one theme emerges strongly. Tort law provides a way of regulating and co-ordinating activities that bypasses some of the institutions of government. It allows private citizens to pursue compensation outside the social security system,

---

13 See A Linden 'Tort as Ombudsman' (1973) 51 Can Bar R 155.
14 Claimants are often 'one-shot players' in the sense used by Marc Galanter in 'Why the Haves Come Out Ahead' (1974) 9 Law and Soc Rev 95.
15 Eg Lord Donaldson on the Braer disaster off Shetland.
16 Cf Calabresi 'Concerning Cause' (1975) 43 U of Ch LR 69; 'Torts—the Law of the Mixed Society' (1978) 56 Texas LR 519 and Howarth 'Negligence After Murphy: Time to Re-think' [1991] CLJ 58.
17 See eg *Cubby Inc (t / a Skuttlebut) and Blanchard v Compuserve* 776 F Supp 135 (1991). See below.

provides incentives for potential wrongdoers to behave with due regard for the rights of others and to pursue justice without invoking the police and prosecution system and it provides a partial or fall-back system of regulation for types of conduct not otherwise regulated. It is, to be sure, a state-backed system of compensation, incentives, justice and regulation—as the whole of the law must be. But it is more in the hands of private citizens than the criminal law or the regulatory system can ever be. It may be that it is costly and that, without help to get access to it, in the form of legal aid for example, it is not particularly useful for a great number of people. But it does have a place in the legal system that cannot quite be replaced by other forms of law.[18]

The economics of tort law—a very brief introduction

The development of tort scholarship in the last three decades has been dominated by economic analysis of the law. It is possible that the dominance of economic analysis is beginning to fade as academic fashion shifts towards ethical, especially communitarian arguments. But even for the beginner student, it is essential to have at least a thumbnail sketch of some of the economic points that have influenced the last generation of those who have discussed and thought about tort law.[19]

There are two very different reasons for lawyers to be interested in economic arguments. One is simply curiosity about the economic effects of changes in legal rules and, more difficult to trace, the possible effect of economic changes on the law. The other reason, which has attracted far more attention, is a desire to use economic argument to justify the choice of one rule rather than another.

Economic argument of the second type, that is 'normative' or 'welfare' economic argument, often promises more than it delivers. There is frequently as much disagreement among economists as among lawyers about what should be done. The reasons for this are important and have to do with how economists tend to think about whether different states of the world are better or worse.

The fundamental assumption of economics is that people trade because they want to and that the result of a trade is that both parties are better off. If I have £500 and you have a TV, and I would prefer to have the TV to having the £500 whereas you would rather have the £500 than the TV, if we swap, we are both in a state that we prefer to our starting point. Because of this, welfare economists say that the best possible state to be in for everyone is one in which everyone is free to trade anything they want to but nobody wants to trade any more because there is nothing that others

---

18   Cf Calabresi 'Tort—the Law of the Mixed Society' (1978) 56 Texas LR 519.
19   NB especially G Calabresi *The Costs Of Accidents* (1970), R Posner *Torts: Cases and Economic Analysis* (1983), S Shavell *An Analysis of Accident Law* (1987), W Landes and R Posner *The Economic Structure of Tort Law* (1987).

have that they prefer to what they have now. Thus (and contrary to the shifting realities of the world) the best possible state as far as this way of thinking is concerned is an *equilibrium*—a state of balance. This state of balance is also, in the economists' rather special usage of the word 'efficient', because the allocation of goods when nobody wants to swap anymore is the allocation that squeezes the most possible value out of the goods available.

Another idea fundamental to the way most economists think is that no-one is in a better position to know what you want than you yourself. If you want to swap something you have because you prefer something someone else has, that is up to you. No-one can tell you that you do not really want what you want. In particular, economists know that they do not know more about what you want than you do.

It follows that much economic advice comes down to the simple message that the best thing to do is to let people decide for themselves what they want and what they want to swap to get what they want. This includes how much of their time and effort they are prepared to sacrifice in doing what other people want them to do, that is, in working.

But there is a snag. We are never starting from scratch. From where we start different people have different incomes. Those with higher incomes, obviously, can get more of what they want than other people can. If different people had the high incomes, they might spend them on different things. Furthermore, deciding whether you want to carrying on trading or to stop because you have reached your equilibrium position depends on how much income you have. Some swaps you just cannot do because you do not have enough income left after you have obtained the absolute essentials.

But there is no way that the economists' criterion of 'would you swap' can work to decide what would be a 'better' or 'worse' distribution of income. No-one, or so few that there would be very few swaps, would swap a higher income for a lower income. To decide what would be a better distribution of income, therefore, takes one outside the sphere in which the economists' welfare criterion works in its strict form. Everything else will include some element of somebody telling somebody else what it is that the other person really wants.

Stated formally, the distribution of income is prior to the economists' view of what counts as efficient. The most efficient allocation of goods, therefore, is only the most efficient for a particular distribution of income. Since most decisions about rules of law will affect the distribution of income more than anything else,[20] the economists' criterion of efficiency will not work in any determinate way. It is not surprising, therefore, that economists disagree. They are disagreeing, as much as anyone else, about the distribution of income.

Nevertheless, the 'swap' criterion is a very powerful one as long as we suspend argument about the distribution of income as much as we can.

20 See below.

The Coase Theorem

The idea of exchange is also built into the most powerful idea that law and economics has produced, namely the Coase Theorem.[1]

The Coase Theorem comes in many forms, and is subject to many interpretations, but its most important and usable form for lawyers is:

> **In a world in which there were no transactions costs and in which there was certainty about property rights, the law would make no difference to the economic efficiency of the allocation of resources, but it would make a difference to the distribution of wealth. In the real world, in which transactions costs exist, the law makes a difference both in terms of distribution of wealth and in terms of efficiency.**

To understand this one has to understand three things: efficiency, the distribution of wealth and transactions costs. Efficiency and the distribution of wealth we have already used. Efficiency for economists means the state of affairs in which resources are in the hands of the people who value them most, that is, at the point where there is no further advantage to be gained by further trading. The distribution of wealth means who has what proportion of the total wealth in society.

Transactions costs are the costs of moving from one economic state to another, the friction of the economic system. They are, for example, the costs of finding the person who has what you want and who wants what you have (search costs), the costs of coming to an agreement with that person (negotiation costs) and the costs of making sure that the other person keeps to the agreement (monitoring and enforcement costs).

Coase's Theorem can be illustrated by a simple nuisance case, something like *Sturges v Bridgman*.[2] Two neighbours run businesses. One runs a sweet factory, the other a dentist's practice. The sweet factory, unfortunately, interferes with the running of the dentist's practice. The sweet factory's machinery bothers the dentist's patients and puts them off going to him.

In rough terms, let us say that if there was no noise from the factory, the dentist would make £1000 per week. If, on the other hand, the sweet factory were not to use its machinery, unless it bought sound proofing equipment, it would make no money at all.

If the factory is allowed to make its noise, the factory makes £2000 per week but the dentist makes nothing. Let us also say that there is effective soundproofing equipment that costs £800 per week to run.

Let us now imagine that there is a legal action in which the dentist sues the factory for the tort of nuisance. The court has to decide whether to grant an injunction or not. What happens if the court does not grant the injunction? The dentist fails to make £1000 per week. But, assuming that it would cost the dentist much more to move out and set up somewhere

1 Coase 'The Problem of Social Cost' (1960) 3 JLE 1.
2 See below.

else, if the sound proofing equipment costs £800 per week, it is worthwhile for the dentist to pay the factory to install the equipment. The dentist then makes £200 net and the factory makes £2000.

But what if the court grants the injunction? The dentist makes £1000 per week and the factory installs the equipment itself, so that it makes £1200 per week net.

Notice what has happened. Whether the injunction is granted or not makes no difference to whether the equipment is used, for it is cost-effective in either case. Notice also that the combined profits of the two businesses added together is also the same in either case (it is £2200). This means that the granting of the injunction has made no difference to the efficiency of the resolution of the problem. Total incomes are the same and the same physical thing happens—the factory carries on using the sound-proofing equipment. But also notice that who gets what, the distribution of income, is different in the two cases. In the case in which there is an injunction, the dentist makes £1000 per week and the factory £1200, but where there is no injunction, the dentist makes only £200 and the factory makes £2000.

This is what is meant by saying that if there are no transactions costs, the law makes no difference to efficiency, but it does make a difference to the distribution of wealth. In a world without transactions costs, in other words, lawyers could concentrate solely on justice and could leave efficiency for the market to sort out for itself. There would also be no need for any further economic analysis of law.

But let us now allow in the real world, in the form of transactions costs. Let us say that for the dentist to contract with the factory to pay for the sound-proofing equipment costs the equivalent of £250 per week for paying off the lawyer's fees incurred in drawing up the agreement and for the lost time and effort spent in watching out for the factory charging more than is justified for the costs of running the equipment.

Now, if the court grants the injunction, the situation is as it was—the factory buys and runs the equipment itself. But if there is no injunction, the costs to the dentist of getting the factory to install the equipment has risen from £800 to £1050, that is more than the entire income of the practice. The effect is that the factory carries on, without the sound-proofing equipment, but the dentist closes down.

This time, if we compare the two situations, we see that they are different. If the injunction is granted, the joint profits of the two businesses added together still come to £2200. But if the injunction is not granted, the joint incomes are only £2000. One solution produces more value to the parties than the other. What has happened is that the transactions costs have prevented a trade that would otherwise have been to the parties' mutual advantage, which has prevented them from reaching the efficient solution. Notice, however, that the two solutions are also still different in their distributional consequences.

This is what is meant by saying that when there are transactions costs, the law makes a difference both to distribution and efficiency. The law, in other words, is not just about justice but efficiency too. Lawyers, or at least judges, should be worried about the consequences of their decisions.

Some people believe that the Coase Theorem also means that judges should always choose the solution to a legal problem that minimises transactions costs, since that is more likely to lead to an efficient result.[3] But such reasoning deliberately excludes the distributional side of the Coase Theorem. In our example, it so happens that the less efficient choice, to refuse an injunction, is also the one that produces the more unequal outcome. But that is not necessarily the case. There are other examples where the more efficient outcome leads to a less equal distribution. Also, there may be times when the just distributional aim is not equality but inequality, as when the court believes that a person's income is being obtained wrongfully. A better way of looking at the implications of the Coase Theorem for the law is that it cannot ignore efficiency considerations, but it will often face a choice between efficiency and justice.

The costs of accidents

The Coase Theorem, though best illustrated by tort cases, is quite general in its implications. There are, however, economic analyses that are more specifically concerned with tort law, and especially accident law. They draw upon the Coase Theorem and its basic insights but go further into the details of the law.

The most important insight of this further work is that of Guido Calabresi into the law and economics of accidents. Much of tort law is concerned with accidents and Calabresi's insights are therefore especially useful. Calabresi's fundamental insight is that not only accidents have costs but also preventing accidents has costs, and that if one were to devise an equivalent of the efficiency criterion for accidents alone, it would be to minimise not the costs of accidents but the costs of accidents and the costs of the prevention of accidents added together.[4]

The costs of accidents include the costs of repairing both people and things, and their lost productive capacities. The costs of prevention include the costs of safety devices and the costs in terms of time and effort of being more careful. But the costs of accidents and their prevention also include the costs of loss-shifting, that is the costs of setting up and running the compensation system, whether that compensation system is based on the courts or the social security system or the private insurance that people would take out if there was no state system of any sort. The running of these systems also involves transactions costs of various kinds.

Note that the costs of prevention of a particular accident can outweigh the costs of the accident. If that happens it means that, from an economic point of view, *too much* is being spent on accident prevention.[5] This is also true of prevention costs in total. For a society increasingly committed to

---

3   See eg R Posner *Economic Analysis of Law* (3d ed) (1986).
4   See *The Costs of Accidents*.
5   This is the point of Calabresi's early and seminal article 'The Decision for Accidents: An approach to no-fault allocation of costs' 78 Harv LR 713 (1965).

absolute safety all the time, it may be a shocking thing to say, but there comes a point when expenditure on safety is wasted.

The injunction to minimise the total of accident costs and their prevention is just as subject to the qualifications about the effects of different decisions and rules on the distribution of wealth and income as the Coase Theorem. And, as Calabresi always recognised, there will always be disagreement about what counts as a cost (for example, what about getting angry when you think that someone else has got away without paying compensation when you think that he ought to pay it—is your anger a cost of that compensation system?) and what counts as a cost of what (is a road accident a cost of driving a car, of travel in general or of the car industry, or even of road-building?). Nevertheless, Calabresi's basic insight has been taken up and formalised (and in the process inevitably over-simplified) by several writers. The clearest of these formal models is the 'cost of precautions' model.[6]

The cost of precautions model assumes that as society devotes more and more resources to accident prevention the number and seriousness of accidents will decline. If one separates out the costs of accidents and the costs of prevention, therefore, as the total costs of accident prevention goes up, the total costs of accidents should be coming down. But eventually a point will be reached at which putting extra resources into accident prevention will cost more than the savings obtained in the costs of accidents. This is the point at which the total costs of accidents and their prevention are at their lowest, and is therefore a point to be aimed at.

The model also assumes that people want to avoid accidents to themselves, and are prepared to pay, within reason, for safety, but that they are not particularly interested in preventing accidents to other people. This means that people will spend on preventing accidents to themselves, but not on preventing accidents to other people. Adding everyone together, we can now compare what will happen under various loss-shifting regimes compared with the best possible outcome (or at least an efficient outcome given the present distribution of wealth and income and no transactions costs).

We could have a system in which there was no state-enforced loss-shifting at all, either by tort law or by the taxation and state benefits system. What will happen in such a society? People will spend on what makes them as safe as they want to be, but they will not bother about what happens to others. In other words, the situation will be like that of the sweet factory and the dentist. Just as the factory does not care much about the harm the machinery does to the dentist's business, people will not care about the safety consequnces for others of, for example, their driving methods or the design of their car or, apart from any rules of contract, the safety of any products that they put in circulation or any machinery that they employ people to use.

As in the basic Coase model, these costs imposed on others ('external costs') would not matter much from the point of view of efficiency if people

6   See R Cooter and T Ulen *Law And Economics* (New York, HarperCollins, 1988) pp 347ff.

can trade. (It does, of course, make a difference for distribution—people who cause harm to others are better off in a regime where losses are not shifted). But the trouble with many of the situations that tort law deals with is that bargaining between those who cause harm and those who suffer it is implausible. How can you bargain, for example with the thousands of people, different every day, who might run you over? How do you persuade them, or pay them, to drive more carefully or to install equipment that makes their cars safer for you (eg rubber bumpers)? The search costs are enormous, and the monitoring costs and enforcement costs are not insignificant either (imagine trying to check that all the commuters you have paid £5 to drive at no more than 20 mph in the vicinity of your house are not reneging).

In other forms of accident, of course, the difficulties in bargaining may be less severe. In accidents at work for example, search costs are zero and there is some opportunity for monitoring and enforcement. But, at the same time, one might be concerned with the distributional consequences of giving the initial entitlement to cause harm to the employer.

On the whole, therefore, there will be comparatively little bargaining around the initial entitlement to cause accidents. The result will be, just as in the sweet factory example with transactions costs, that the best possible result may not be reached. The result will be inefficient compared with the ideal position of what would happen in a world without trans-actions costs. But one should not jump to the conclusion that this outcome is necessarily to be avoided. It may be that all other possible arrangements are worse. If there are no enforced loss-shifting arrangements, people may insure themselves against injury (take out 'first party' insurance). There is nothing necessarily bad about this, although the cost of running the first party insurance system is a cost of the system of not having state shifting of losses and should be counted as such. And in one respect first party insurance is a good thing, since there is no-one better placed to know what the losses would be of an accident than the potential victim.

Nevertheless, both the possible inefficiency of having no state-enforced loss-shifting and the distributional effects of the same system suggest that we should look at what might happen if state loss-shifting were introduced. There are two basic types of state loss-shifting, namely liability rules (tort law) and tax and benefits policies.

Let us take the tax and benefit option first. Let us say that a social security benefit is brought in, paid for out of general taxation, to compensate people for the harm they suffer as a result of accidents caused by others. What difference would such a scheme make? First, notice that it would not make any difference to whether people cause harm to others. Any inefficiency in the no-state-loss-shifting system is preserved in full. In addition, it is possible that, because they have a guaranteed income, people would take slightly less care of themselves, at least as far as accidents that are not particularly painful are concerned. Note however that if the no-state-loss-shifting system led to first party insurance, such a reduction in incentives will already have happened. In any case, the conclusion is the same. A social security compensation system does not produce any more efficient use of resources than the no-state-loss-shifting system. Indeed since there will be some cost in running the tax and benefit system itself, there will be some loss of efficiency.

The tax and benefit system may try to add some extra incentives to take care in the form of the criminal law, although this will have a cost in itself and there is a distinct risk that the regulations will be pitched at too high or too low a level of care given the extra savings in the total costs of accidents that they achieve.

The other problem, as the New Zealand no-fault scheme showed,[7] is that anywhere near full compensation is extremely expensive and the tax rates needed may themselves affect incentives, or may just be too unpopular to sustain.

Lastly there are liability regimes or tort systems. The idea is to make individuals pay the full costs of accidents they cause to other people. There are many possible liability rules,[8] but most analysis has centred on two of the possibilities. In the first rule, the individual has to pay for all the costs of accidents that his or her activities impose on other people. This rule shifts all losses caused by others and then leaves it up to the people who cause losses to negotiate with the people they harm. The advantages of such a rule are that it draws on the knowledge that those who cause accidents have of the risks they impose. Manufacturers of goods may know much more about the risks the product imposes on users than the users can. Even if the manufacturer has not done much research before the product is launched, there is no-one better placed than the manufacturer to collate the information that will come in from complainants and no-one better placed to do something about the problems. The rule also forces accident causers to take into account the likely cost to others of their activities in addition to the costs of accidents to themselves. If this works, it means that accident causers will set their activities according to the total costs of accidents and their prevention and will shift total expenditure of accident prevention to the level that minimises the total costs.

But, of course, this is too good to be true. In practice such a 'strict liability' rule will be expensive to administer because it will require a court-based case-by-case approach. There will, for example, be a constant dispute about what is a cost of what—that is about who counts as 'causing' each accident. In addition, the perfection of the level of expenditure on accident prevention depends on getting the level of compensation absolutely correct. If damages are systematically too low or too high, the 'strict liability' rule will over- or under-deter the accident causer. But the level of compensation will be for

7   See R Miller 'An Analysis And Critique of The 1992 Changes To New Zealand's Accident Compensation Scheme' (1993) 52 Md L Rev 1070. Of course, New Zealand moved from a tort system to no-fault and one of the problems of the scheme was an increase in the accident rate as incentives to be safe fell; but the inherent problem was simply the cost of full compensation. The present scheme is rather more restricted in scope and leaves room for the return of tort law.

8   See below pp 395-397.

the court to calculate case by case—again an expensive process. Moreover, although the accident causer is in the best position to find out about the frequency of accidents, the same is not true about the costs of those accidents, in terms of lost income and subjective costs such as pain and suffering, to the victims. For the amount of these costs, the victim, not the accident causer, is in the best position to know. Finally, a rule that puts all the cost on the accident causer reduces incentives on victims to take care of themselves.

This brings us to the last regime to be considered here, the second liability rule. In this rule, the accident causer pays if the costs caused by the accident were greater than the costs of taking the precautions that would have prevented the accident. If the costs of precaution would have been higher than the accident costs they would have saved, there is no liability. The result is that accident causers face steeply rising costs just at the point at which the overall costs of the accident start to outweigh the costs of prevention. If that point is correctly identified for each case, the effect will be that, on the whole, potential accident causers will not cause accidents whose prevention would have been worth it. Also, adding all accident causing and preventing activity together produces the level of accident prevention expenditure that is exactly the same as the minimum total cost point. It achieves this from the bottom up, by encouraging each accident causer to spend the optimal amount. Moreover, unlike the 'strict liability' rule, this 'negligence' rule does leave scope for incentives on victims to take care of themselves.

But again, the 'negligence' rule is not as perfect as it looks. There is still much scope for dispute, this time about whether the costs of prevention would have outweighed the costs of the accident. And instead of having to get the level of damages exactly right, the court has to get right the point at which accident prevention expenditure would save more than its own value in accident costs, which is, if anything, an even more difficult task. And again, accident causers are not in a particularly good position to know what the costs of the accident will be to victims.

Of course many subtle variations are possible in both the rules to be applied and in their expected consequences. The effects of insurance are particularly difficult to trace through.

But notice, finally, that effects on accident causers of increased costs to them may be quite small and, in any case, economists can often say which direction a change will take, but be quite unable to say how big that change will be. These two problems are often fatal to the prospect of any practical advice from economists for judges and legislators. The improvement in incentives brought about by moving from a no-liability regime to a liability regime may be wiped out completely by the new costs of running the court system necessary for the new rules to be applied.

One should not, therefore, expect too much from economic analysis. It cannot resolve the tension that frequently occurs between wealth and justice (that is, between efficiency and distribution). And it cannot often predict more than the general nature of the consequences of a particular change in the rules of law. But it is, however, a useful aid for thought, since it forces one to consider all the consequences for all parties of a proposed rule and not just the consequences for one person or group. And it is an excellent source of the new arguments on which tort law thrives.

Chapter 2

Negligence: a preface

Articles 1382 and 1383 of the French Civil Code say:

'Any act of a person which causes damage to another makes him
who by whose fault the damage occurred liable to make reparation
for the damage.
    Everyone is liable for the damage he causes not only by his acts
but also by his negligence or imprudence.'[1]

Paragraph 823(I) of the German Code says:

'A person who, wilfully or negligently, unlawfully injures the life,
body, health, freedom, property or other right of another is bound
to compensate him for any damage arising therefrom.'[2]

The law of negligence is the nearest that English law gets to such
statements of general principle such as these about the relationship
between fault, damage and the duty to pay compensation. But English
negligence law has never quite reached even the more limited level of
abstraction of the German Code, with its protected specific interests and
reference to unlawfulness, never mind the purity of the articles 1382 and
1383. It has always been hedged around with qualifications and reservations. But, whatever those restrictions and reservations, the underlying
principle is the same in English law as in the others—fault, including
both failure to act properly and acting badly, which causes legally recognised
injury, gives rise to an obligation to pay compensation to the people who
have been harmed.

This chapter sets out briefly the historical reasons why English law has
never quite managed to declare itself in such general and abstract terms,
then looks, even more briefly, at the persistent attractions of the fault
principle which the law embodies and finally lays out the structure of this
book's exposition of the law of negligence.

1   Translation in Von Mehren and Gordley *The Civil Law System* (Boston, Little Brown,
     1977).

English negligence law and the struggle against generality

Negligence originally meant in English law what it means in everyday speech, not a wrong in itself but a way of committing wrongs. Negligence is to be contrasted with maliciousness or wickedness as a state of mind that people who do harm to others may have. By the end of the nineteenth century, a study of negligence in the English law of torts would have been about the various torts that could be committed without malice (or, in more modern terms, intentionality) but by wrongful inattention, for example the actions 'on the case' arising from collisions on the street and at sea and from various accidents that result in personal injuries.[3] Furthermore, 'negligence' would have been a sufficient condition of liability when certain legal relationships went wrong—that between an innkeeper and a customer, for example, or between a bailor and a bailee (that is, a person who deposits a thing with somebody else and that somebody else).[4]

But there were various obstacles to the creation of a general principle along the lines of articles 1382 and 1383. One was that in the accident cases, the action 'on the case' alleging negligence had a rival in the action 'for trespass'—that is for the direct application of unlawful force. Confusion reigned as the courts appeared to say that for road accidents the proper action in a collision case was 'trespass', but that, exceptionally, the plaintiff had to prove fault, whether intention or negligence,[5] but in other accident cases where there was a 'direct' application of force, there could be a 'trespass' action in which it was up to the defendant to disprove fault.[6]

A second obstacle to the creation of a general principle was the notorious 'privity fallacy'. Many nineteenth century judges were impressed by the idea of the 'bargain',[7] the idea discussed above that for economists the only sure ground for saying that people want something is that they are prepared to exchange something for it. This idea was expanded in to the notion of 'privity of contract', according to which people who had not taken part in making a bargain had no legal right to sue if the bargain was not fulfilled. But it also expanded in another direction, namely that bargain

---

2   Ibid.
3   See eg *Williams v Holland* (1833) 10 Bing 112, *Holmes v Mather* (1875) LR 10 Ex Ch 261, *Stanley v Powell* [1891] 1 QB 86.
4   See Winfield 'Duties inTortious Negligence' (1934) 34 Col LR 41 and 'The History of Negligence in the Law of Torts' (1926) 42 LQR 184 (both also appear in P Winfield *Select Legal Essays*).
5   This, at least, was one explanation of Bramwell B's judgment in *Holmes v Mather* above n 3.
6   This particular set of confusions was not sorted out until *National Coal Board v Evans* [1951] 2 KB 861, *Fowler v Lanning* [1959] 1 QB 426 and *Letang v Cooper* [1965] 1 QB 232 which decided that (a) there is no difference between highway cases and others, (b) the burden of proving fault is always on the plaintiff and (c) it profits the plaintiff nothing to describe a negligence action as 'trespass'.
7   See especially Lord Bramwell's dissent in *Smith v Baker & Sons* [1891] AC 325.

and exchange should be the only basis of civil liability either in all novel cases or in all cases in which the plaintiff could have formed a bargain with the defendant but did not do so.[8]

The effect of the privity doctrine was that, for example, the ultimate consumer of a product had no legal recourse against the manufacturer of a product if it caused injury.[9] The victim would be told either that he or she should sue the retailer in contract, or, if the victim had received the product as a gift, that since there was no contractual link or bargain between the plaintiff and anyone, there was no legal liability at all. It also meant that the wife of a tenant could not sue if she was injured by the fault of the landlord. The husband had a contract with the landlord in the form of the lease, but the wife had not contracted and therefore had no rights at all.[10]

Nevertheless, as early as 1883 in *Heaven v Pender*,[11] Sir Baliol Brett MR tried to sweep away the restrictions and to announce a general principle that:

'[W]henever one person is by circumstances placed in such a position with regard to another that every one of ordinary sense who did think would at once recognise that if he did not use ordinary care and skill in his own conduct with regard to those circumstances he would cause danger of injury to the person or property of the other, a duty arises to use ordinary care and skill to avoid such danger.'

The reference to 'the person or property of the other' puts Brett's statement in to the German category of general statement, with the law limited to the protection of specific interests rather than the even more general French statement, but even so it proved too much for his colleagues at the time. They complained that it could mean that people would be held responsible for the results of long sequences of consequences. In fact, this was never the case, since Brett's formula incorporates the limitation that the 'person of ordinary sense' would have recognised at once that there would be danger not to 'another' but to 'the other', which restricts considerably the range of possible plaintiffs. In any case, the French and German formulations have no problems of this sort because they include the notion of causation, which can be used to keep liability within reasonable grounds.

Nevertheless, Brett gave way, and in *Le Lievre v Gould*[12] was driven back to the somewhat more pedestrian statement that:

'One man may owe a duty to another, even though there is no contract between them. If one man is near another or is near to

8   *Winterbottom v Wright* (1842) 10 M & W 109.
9   Ibid. Exceptions were made for things dangerous in themselves—*Langridge v Levy* (1837) 2 M & W 519.
10 *Cavalier v Pope* [1906] AC 428.
11 (1883) 11 QBD 503.
12 [1893] 1 QB 491 (nb Brett MR had become Lord Esher MR by this time).

the property of another, a duty lies upon him not to do that which may cause a personal injury to that other, or may injure his property.'

The reference to a person being 'near' to another has proved to be almost fatal for the formulation of English negligence law in terms of general principles ever since. Clearly it is absurd to limit liability to people to whom the defendant was close physically or temporally, otherwise there would not be any liability in negligence for accidentally polluting the water supply of a town several miles away by allowing chemicals to seep into the underground aquifer or negligently allowing your munitions factory to explode thus destroying life and limb for miles. But the underlying problem is an ever present source of anxiety to English lawyers. It is that if there is a general principle of liability for fault, people will be held liable for accidents that were on any reasonable view of the case nothing much to do with them. For example, if I negligently run you over and you end up in hospital have I not caused whatever the doctors subsequently inflict on you by their negligence? Or what if I accidentally knock you to the ground and a plank falls off a building and hits you on the head—am I not responsible according to any general formula?

The answer to these questions is, and was, no. In those areas in which negligence was already accepted as a basis of liability in itself without restriction, shipping collisions for example, the courts developed soph-isticated ideas of causation and the 'remoteness of damage' which excluded from the plaintiff's scope of responsibility any damage which was not 'proximate'. Intervening acts by others, especially if they were wrongful, 'broke the chain of causation'.[13] That meant that it was possible to say that the defendant should be responsible for all the 'direct' consequences of his act regardless of whether they were foreseeable, since any damage that was not really anything to do with the defendant's particular faulty act would be 'too remote' by reason of being 'indirect'. By the early 1930s, it was possible to incorporate these ideas into Brett's original formula and to produce a statement of principle that swept away the 'privity fallacy' without replacing it with liability for infinite consequences.

The case that achieved the destruction of the privity fallacy was *Donoghue v Stevenson*.[14] In *Donoghue*, alleged facts[15] were that the plaintiff went to a café in Paisley with a friend who ordered some soft drinks. The plaintiff's ginger beer arrived in the then customary opaque bottle and the plaintiff began to drink. But when the friend poured out the remainder of the contents of the bottle into her glass, a partially decomposed snail came out. The plaintiff was understandably upset and claimed that she was sick as a result. She could not sue her friend who had given her the ginger beer because a gift relationship is not a legally enforceable contract

13 Eg *The Argentino* (1888) 13 PD 191, *Weld-Blundell v Stephens* [1920] AC 956, *The San Onofre* [1922] P 243, *Harnett v Bond* [1925] AC 669, *The Paludina* [1927] AC 16.
14 [1932] AC 562.
15 *Donoghue*, like many famous tort cases, is argued out on a point of law on assumed facts before any trial takes place. *Donoghue* never came to trial.

and she had no contract herself with the café. She could not plausibly claim either that the friend or the café had been negligent, since the bottle was opaque. And so she sued the manufacturer. She had no contract with the manufacturer either, of course, but she sued in tort, alleging negligence. The manufacturer raised the privity defence. Since the plaintiff could not sue them for breach of contract, they claimed, she could not sue them in tort either.

By a three to two majority, the House of Lords rejected the privity defence and found for the plaintiff. Lord Atkin took the opportunity to restate Brett MR's original formulation of the principle that fault means an obligation to compensate, but this time with the ideas of remoteness and proximity built in. He also purged the law of the absurd notion into which Brett had been forced in *Le Lievre v Gould* that liability rested on physical proximity or 'nearness'. Lord Atkin said:

> 'You must take reasonable care to avoid acts or omissions which you can reasonably foresee would be likely to injure ... persons *who are so closely and directly affected by [your] act* that [you] ought reasonably to have them in contemplation as being so affected when [you] are directing [your] mind to the acts or omissions which are called into question.' [emphasis added]

It is the notion of 'directness' that makes Lord Atkin's formulation more acceptable than that of Brett MR. It builds 'proximity' into the abstract formulation of the law.

But note that with the development of remoteness ideas to protect the plaintiff from unreasonably extensive demands, the incorporation of directness into the idea of the plaintiff's obligation is strictly unnecessary since it can be read into the requirement that the acts or omissions 'injure' or 'affect' the plaintiff.

After *Donoghue* the main problem for English law was whether to treat *Donoghue* as stating a general principle that could transform the existing law, sweeping away restrictions on straightforward liability for fault and mandating the solving of new problems by reference to the principle rather to any analogies that the previous case law may accidentally have thrown up.

On the whole, for 50 years the courts favoured the transformative view of *Donoghue*. In cases such as *Hedley Byrne v Heller*,[16] *Home Office v Dorset Yacht Co Ltd*[17] and, ultimately, *Anns v Merton London Borough Council*[18] the House of Lords moved to the position that there should be liability for damage caused by fault unless there were good reasons why not. The much quoted *Anns* formula was:

> 'The position has now been reached that in order to establish that a duty of care arises in a particular situation, it is not necessary to

16 [1964] AC 465.
17 [1970] AC 1004.
18 [1978] AC 728.

bring the facts of that situation within those of previous situations in which a duty of care has been held to exist. Rather the question has to be approached in two stages. First, one has to ask whether as between the alleged wrongdoer and the person who has suffered damage there is a relationship of proximity ... such that in the reasonable contemplation of the former, carelessness on his part may be likely to cause damage to the latter, in which case a prima facie duty of care arises. Secondly, if the first question is answered affirmatively, it is necessary to consider whether there are any considerations which ought to negative or to reduce or limit the scope of the duty or the class of person to whom it is owed or the damages to which a breach of it may give rise.'

But along the way, two things happened which probably made some kind of reaction inevitable. The first was that the formulation of the principle changed from being in the German style, restricting its effect to the protection of certain kinds of interest, into being, especially as *Anns* was interpreted in cases such as *Junior Books v Veitchi*,[19] a French-style formula without restriction as to the type of interest protected by the law. The effect of this was that, first in the 1960s[20] but then more spectacularly in the early 1980s, the fault principle was used to undermine restrictions on suing for harm to interests other than the physical integrity of the person and of property—especially in relation to 'economic loss' (that is, mainly, the value of business deals and contracts).[1] The pace of change was beginning to get too fast.

The other thing that happened was that much of the work on remoteness and directness that made the formulation of the *Donoghue* principle acceptable was destroyed by the case that really ought to be recognised as the greatest mistake of 20th century British tort jurisprudence, namely the *Wagon Mound (No 1)* .[2] The seeds of the problem were in *Donoghue* itself. By putting the notion of directness and proximity into the abstract formulation of the defendant's obligation, and especially by associating it with the question of whether damage was foreseeable to the particular plaintiff in the case, the *Donoghue* formulation suggested that the law could do without aspects of remoteness and directness that were not associated with foreseeability, especially those to do with 'breaking the chain of causation'. It was this suggestion that the *Wagon Mound* took up. But the effect of this new formulation of remoteness was disastrous, since it could not be distinguished from the general formulation of the fault test that *Donoghue* used, namely that people should take reasonable care to avoid foreseeable harm. The effect was that the situation feared by those who disliked Brett MR's original statement of principle had apparently returned, namely that there was no separate check on the possibility of infinite liability.

19 [1983] 1 AC 520.
20 *Hedley Byrne v Heller* above n 16.
1   *Junior Books* was the high point of this development.
2   [1961] AC 388.

The two problems coalesced dangerously because 'remoteness' problems were particularly acute in the new interests that the French-style application of *Donoghue* was beginning to protect, especially economic loss. One of the original objections to protecting economic loss in negligence law was that it would lead to liability that was 'in an indeterminate amount for an indeterminate time to an indeterminate class'.[3]

The concern was probably as unjustified in the 1980s as it was in the 1880s since by the time of cases such as *Caparo*[4] in which the concern came out in the form of restrictive decisions on economic loss, the courts had largely worked out that the *Wagon Mound* was a disaster and had found ways around it to bring back the older remoteness protections of 'directness' and 'breaking the chain of causation'. But, unfortunately, since there had not been liability for any sort of economic loss in negligence when the *Wagon Mound* was decided, there were no recorded instances of the application of the older principles to economic loss. This possible route to salvation was therefore not immediately found. Instead, the courts started to turn against the French-style formulation of the fault principle as developed after *Anns*, and especially turned against its use in 'novel' cases.[5] Then, Lord Keith of Kinkel discovered that Lord Atkin in *Donoghue* had explicitly referred to the requirement of 'proximity'.[6] Originally, Lord Atkin had meant nothing more than the principle that the harm to the plaintiff had to be likely to be 'direct'. But Lord Keith, apparently not understanding the connection between this 'proximity' and the 'remoteness' of the shipping collision cases, decided that 'proximity' was a separate condition for the recognition of the defendant's obligation (or, as he confusingly put it, for the 'existence' of a duty of care).[7]

Ultimately, the House of Lords began to attack the notion of *Donoghue* as a transformative case. An almost ritual incantation developed of an obscure Australian case[8] in which Brennan J said that the law should develop 'incrementally by analogy with established categories' rather than by *Anns*-style leaps of principle.[9] Although no-one dared to say so, this approach meant a return to pre-*Donoghue* methods (though not, of course the pre-*Donoghue* law) which had led to an unacceptable jumble of decisions and 'pockets of liability'.[10] It did however lead to the formal overruling of *Anns* in *Murphy v Brentwood District Council*.[11] It was as if, since King *Donoghue* could not be criticised directly, Chief Minister *Anns* had to take the blame.

But the anti-*Anns/Donoghue* movement has eventually run into problems of its own. In particular, by not seeing the connection between

3 Cardozo J in *Ultramares v Touche* 255 NY 170, 174 NE 441 (CANY 1931).
4 *Caparo v Dickman* [1990] 2 AC 605.
5 Eg *The Aliakmon* [1986] AC 785.
6 Eg *Hill v Chief Constable of West Yorkshire* [1989] AC 53, *Yuen Kun Yeu v A-G of Hong Kong* [1988] AC 175.
7 Ibid.
8 *Sutherland Shire Council v Heyman* (1985) 157 CLR 424, 60 ALR 1.
9 See eg *Caparo v Dickman* [1990] 2 AC 605.
10 Cf Stapleton (1991) 107 LQR 249.
11 [1991] 1 AC 398.

'proximity' and old-style remoteness, the word has begun to float in a sea of meaninglessness about which even those who use it are beginning to worry.[12]

Meanwhile, some of the pre-*Donoghue* arguments that had started to make a reappearance seem to have reached their natural limits. This includes an argument that bore a very strong resemblance to the privity fallacy, namely the *Tai Hing*[13] doctrine that not making a contract counts as easily as making one as settling the matter consensually among the parties (and so they cannot sue in tort). In addition, the strength of the classic pre-*Donoghue* argument that the existing law is perfect and should not be upset in any way by inventing new fault liabilities, that is the argument against the imperialism of the fault principle, has begun to fade. In *Spring v Guardian Assurance*,[14] for example, negligence was allowed to invade the province of defamation law when the House of Lords, over Lord Keith's predictable objections, said that there could be negligence liability when one employer sends a reference to another employer that makes careless and incorrect statements about a pro–spective employee.

Where the law goes from here is unclear. There is an argument that the principle announced by articles 1382 and 1383 is so clear and appealing that its acceptance is only a matter of time. But there is also an argument that since English judges react so frequently against the principle, and on grounds that often appear to be flimsy, English law must contain a permanent distrust of abstract formulae so strong that all we can expect is for the struggle to continue for ever.

The appeal of the fault system

Before launching into the law it is worth noting that over the past 30 or so years a different sort of opponent of the fault principle has appeared, namely the person who thinks that fault is inefficient or unfair or both and should be replaced either by strict liability or by an integrated social security system of compensation for injury and illness. The fault principle was allegedly expensive to operate, produced unpredictable results and did not manage to compensate many people.[15] It was also, allegedly, based on a fiction that in, for example, road accidents or medical injuries, there had been anything other than momentary inattention whose consequences had been magnified out of all proportion by modern technology.[16] Furthermore, instead of the law responding to the moral intuitions of victims, victims

---

12 See Lord Oliver in *Alcock v Chief Constable of South Yorkshire Police* [1992] 1 AC 310.
13 [1986] AC 80 see below chs 5 and 6.
14 [1994] 3 All ER 129.
15 See eg Atiyah *Accidents Compensation and the Law* (1st ed, 1970).
16 Tunc *Responsabilité Civile* (2nd ed) (Paris: Economica 1989).

are often initially surprised by the law's choice of defendant and shift the blame to that defendant in their own mind at the law's suggestion.[17]

The fault principle has, however, survived. Some of the reasons for its survival have been mentioned above—the need for incentives on both victims and accident causers, the opportunity to consider the effects of new sorts of behaviour and the sheer cost of no-fault, social security-based schemes. Its importance for compensation, furthermore, is seriously underestimated if consideration is given only to cases brought to court or even only cases settled after a writ had been issued. All pay-outs under third party liability insurance should count as fault system compensation payments and the allegation that fault is fictitious confuses a civil law notion of fault, unreasonable behaviour judged objectively, with a criminal law notion of the guilty mind. And the fact that victims respond to the law's attribution of blame shows rather that the law is more reasonable and well-considered than many believed.

In previous decades, the introduction to a textbook section on the law of negligence might suggest that the law about to be presented was likely soon to be swept away by enlightened social reform. No such prediction can be made now. Moreover, it is no longer clear that such reform could count uncontroversially as enlightened.

Plan of the negligence chapters

It is worth mentioning at this point that the next three chapters, on fault, causation and remoteness and on the duty of care have been placed in that order for a reason, and it is hoped that at least some students will attempt to read them in the order in which they appear.

Usually, the duty of care chapter comes first (including economic loss), followed by the breach or fault chapter and then finally causation and remoteness. This order follows the formal logic of the English courts' exposition of negligence. First, there has to be a duty of care, then there has to be proof that the defendant breached that duty of care, and finally the breach has to have caused the damage.

But the formal logic of a subject is not always the best way to understand it, especially when coming across it for the first time. The order chosen here for these topics comes from the author's experience as a teacher of tort law over the last 10 years. Unless one knows what fault is about, knowing about the conditions for the recognition of a duty of care becomes meaningless and bloodless. If you don't know what care people are supposed to take, why should you be interested in or understand arguments about whether they should be required to take care in the first place? Causation and remoteness come next because their centrality to the law, especially to the way the law has developed over the whole course of the twentieth

17 Lloyd-Bostock 'Common sense morality and accident compensation' [1980] Ins LJ 331.

century, deserves to be restored. Furthermore, unless one knows which claims will never succeed anyway on causation or remoteness grounds, one gets an inflated view of the importance of duty of care arguments.

Nevertheless, no catastrophes will, I hope, befall those who choose to read the chapters in the more traditional order.

Chapter 3

Fault

KEY POINTS

* Fault is acting unreasonably.
* Defendants act unreasonably when the risk of harm caused by their conduct outweighs the costs of the effective precautions they could have taken.
* Fault concentrates on the precautions against the harm it is alleged that the defendant should have taken.
* Fault in negligence is a matter of foreseeability. Conduct is assessed by examining the situation as it would have appeared at the time.
* People with special skills are expected to use them in accordance with the standards of ordinary people having those skills.
* If professional opinion is divided, there is no fault in choosing any course of action that is professionally respectable.

The core concept in the tort of the negligence is that of fault. The underlying principle is that losses should only be shifted from the victim if the victim can show that the losses arose from faulty conduct by the defendant.

Of course, fault is not a universal requirement for loss-shifting in tort law. Even before the intervention of statute in the twentieth century, common law judges had recognised duties to compensate that arose either without any necessity to show fault (eg *Rylands v Fletcher* (1868) LR 3 HL 330) or in which fault would be inferred from the harmful consequences of the defendant's activities (eg nuisance).

Modern statutes have produced their own collection of no-fault, near no-fault or presumed fault liabilities, including the Consumer Protection Act 1987, the Civil Aviation Act 1982 and the Animals Act 1971.

Nevertheless, despite recent setbacks, negligence remains the most dynamic of torts, and, at least in principle, proof of fault remains central to the liability it creates.

Other books collect the material assembled in this chapter under the headings 'Breach of Duty' or 'Carelessness'. There is also a practice of referring to the fault element in the tort of negligence as 'negligence'.

This book does not follow any of these practices for the simple reason that, whether or not these terms are more or less technically correct than 'fault', they can be confusing and misleading.

In the case of using the word 'negligence' both to refer to the whole tort and to refer to one element of it, it should be obvious that such a usage is inherently confusing, indeed baffling.

'Breach of duty' is more widely used, and is the term used by those who favour the 'Duty-Breach-Damage' formulation of negligence (discussed in in the previous chapter). Furthermore, it has strong judicial support. For example, Lord Macmillan in *Donoghue v Stevenson* said that the law 'concerns itself with carelessness only where there is a duty to take care.'

But, even leaving aside the theoretical objections to the duty of care concept, Lord Macmillan's formulation is simply a confusing way to expound the subject from scratch. It is unlikely that someone who does not know what a duty of care entails or what its content is will be able to follow a discussion about when such a duty should apply. To know how much care is due takes one more than halfway towards understanding when the law requires due care to be taken in the first place.

Moreover, in the normal run of negligence cases, the duty of care is taken for granted. To concentrate on duty, therefore, may well distract attention away from what in practice is usually the most important question in a negligence case, namely was the defendant at fault?

'Carelessness' is a less confusing heading for the material collected in this chapter, and does not need to be avoided at all costs. But it does have the significant drawback of implying that negligence cases are necessarily about inadvertence or inattention. They are not. It is no excuse in a negligence case for the defendant to say that the harm was caused intentionally.

The key point about fault in English law is that it consists of doing what a reasonable person would not have done, or not doing what a reasonable person would have done.[1]

To know this definition, however, is only a beginning. Although every-thing one needs to know about fault is either included in it or implied by it, much careful teasing out is required before one can say that one under-stands it fully.

It is convenient to summarise the implications of the reasonableness test at the outset:

1. *The reasonableness test makes no reference to the defendant's mental state. The defendant's conduct is compared to that of the reasonable person, and if found wanting is declared to be faulty, regardless of whether the defendant caused the harm intentionally, recklessly or inadvertently.*

2. *The tense of the verbs in the definition are important—the defendant did not act as a reasonable person would have acted. 'Would have'— the conditional perfect—is crucial.*

3. *Most importantly of all, the definition offers no detail on the central*

1   See Alderson B in *Blyth v Birmingham Waterworks Co* (1856) 11 Ex Ch 781, 784.

question on which everything turns, namely: How does a reasonable person behave? Unless one knows how the courts apply the standard of reasonableness, one knows next to nothing about what fault means. These three points are now elaborated upon in reverse order.

What is reasonable behaviour?

The central question in the whole of fault is what counts as reasonable and unreasonable behaviour. Although this is a fairly straightforward area of the law, two confusions should be dealt with straight away.

Fact or law

It is often said that the question of whether the defendant acted reasonably is a question of fact, so that the decision of the trial court cannot be challenged on appeal. Indeed, the House of Lords in a trilogy of cases around 1960 starting with the *Qualcast* case seems to have said as much.[2] What these cases stand for, however, is only the proposition that the appellate courts will usually refuse to lay down detailed rules as to whether or not particular conduct amounts to fault. For example, a rule in the form 'a defendant driver who hits the rear of the car in front is always at fault' will be rejected.[3] Refusal to lay down strict rules, however, is not the same as saying that the appellate courts have nothing to say about what counts as reasonable behaviour. Appellate courts intervene in two ways.

First, they rule on whether the trial court has taken into account all that it should have taken into account, and on whether it has taken into account anything that it should not have taken into account.

So, for example, if the trial court has not taken into account how expensive it would have been for the defendant to have acted in a way that might have prevented the harm, or if the trial court has taken into account the defendant's lack of resources[4], the appellate court will decide whether or not the trial court was right to do what it did.[5]

Secondly, the appellate court may substitute its own conclusion about whether the facts as found by the trial court constitute fault on the part of the defendant.

2   *Qualcast (Wolverhampton) Ltd v Haynes* [1959] AC 743, *Cavanagh v Ulster Weaving Co Ltd* [1960] AC 145 and *Brown v Rolls-Royce Ltd* [1960] 1 WLR 210.

3   See eg *Brown & Lynn v Western Scottish Motor Traction Ltd* 1945 SC 31, adopted in *Scott v Warren* [1974] RTR 104. See also *Wooller v London Transport Board* [1976] RTR 206 and *Parnell v Metropolitan Police District Receiver* [1976] RTR 201 in which passengers failed to recover when injured in emergency stops which succeeded in avoiding a collision with the vehicle in front.

4   See below pp 49-50 and pp 58-60.

5   See eg *Kite v Nolan* [1983] RTR 253, CA.

For example, if the trial court finds that the defendant was not at fault for failing to do anything about a risk of seriously injuring one passer-by in 500, the appellate courts may take it upon themselves to say that nevertheless the defendant was at fault, an activity they distinguish from finding a fact in the sense of saying what happened. As Viscount Simonds said in *Benmax v Austin Motor Co*[6]:

> '[S]ome confusion may have arisen from the failure to distinguish between the finding of a specific fact and a finding of fact which is really an inference from facts specifically found, or as it has sometimes been said, between the perception and the evaluation of the facts... I have found, on the one hand, universal reluctance to reject a finding of specific fact, particularly where the finding could be founded on the credibility of or bearing of a witness, and, on the other hand, no less a willingness to form an independent opinion about the proper inference of fact.'[7]

But note that, although both of these methods of review are accepted appellate court practices, only the former is taken to establish any sort of usable precedent. The latter, although frequently done, is a matter solely of judging the case on its particular facts—that is, accepting the trial court's findings of fact and coming to one's own conclusions on whether or not they amount to fault, but without laying down any sort of rule for use in future cases.

There is, admittedly, a danger that whenever an appellate court gives its opinion on the relative weights that should be assigned to the various facts of a case in coming to its own conclusion on the issue of fault, it may tempt lower courts in future cases into the mistaken belief that a rule exists that whenever similar facts arise the same result should be reached. But the facts of negligence cases are so varied, and so much depends on the imaginative powers of the lawyers[8] that each conclusion thus reached must be treated as a decision on the particular facts of that case, and without precedential value. This is the real meaning of the *Qualcast* Trilogy.[9]

The reasonable man

The second point to clear up straight away is about the characteristics of the reasonable man. Although some cases give the impression that the fault issue can be clarified by further refining the law's vision of the

6   [1955] AC 370, 373-74.
7   See RSC Ord 59 r 10(3). See also *Kite v Nolan* [1983] RTR 253, 256 per Sir John Donaldson MR.
8   See below pp 67-69.
9   See *Qualcast (Wolverhampton) Ltd v Haynes* [1959] AC 743, 761-762 per Lord Denning.

character and personality of the reasonable man[10], such an exercise is usually unenlightening.[11]

There is, nevertheless, a tension in the law between the view that fault consists of taking unreasonable decisions and the view that fault consists of behaving in a way in which reasonable people would not have behaved. In most cases these two tests produce the same result, largely because there is usually some decision that the defendant has taken which it would be unreasonable even for a person with the defendant's characteristics to have taken. Indeed, the question of how to deal with defendants with unusual characteristics is often easily answered by asking whether it was reasonable for a person with these characteristics to engage in the activity in question in the first place.

Thus if a semi-blind person attempts to drive a car, and causes an accident, the question is not whether it is possible for the reasonable man to be blind, or whether the driver did his best given the impaired state of his eyesight, but rather whether it was reasonable for someone so impaired to attempt to drive a car in the first place. Similarly, it is no excuse for the alcoholic doctor who botches an operation because of drunkenness that he did quite well in the circumstances.

But in one particular set of cases, the manoeuvre of asking whether the decision to engage in the activity in the first place was reasonable does not work. These are cases involving defendants of low intelligence; for a defendant's restricted ability to process information affects all of his or her decisions, both those within the activity and those relating to taking part in the activity at all. In these cases, the court has to decide between a defendant who argues that it is unjust to criticise a person for a decision which, though wrong, represented his or her best efforts, and a plaintiff who argues that it is unjust to make the victim pay for harm caused by conduct that falls short of what should be expected from ordinary people.

The choice the law makes can been seen as early as 1837 in *Vaughan v Menlove*[12]. The defendant erected a hayrick next to his neighbour's cottages. This was careless, it was alleged, since there was a great risk of fire arising from the spontaneous heating of the hayrick's component materials. A fire did indeed break out in the hayrick and the cottages were destroyed.

The defendant lost at trial, the judge having told the jury that the defendant should be judged according to the reasonable standard of a prudent man. The defendant appealed to the Court of Common Pleas, where one of the points put forward on his behalf was that since he may not have possessed 'the highest order of intelligence'[13], he should have been judged on the basis of whether he had acted bona fide—that is, whether he had done his best given his level of understanding.

---

10 Eg Lord Macmillan's remarks in *Glasgow Corpn v Muir* [1943] AC 448, 457 that the 'reasonable man is presumed to be free both from over-apprehension and from over-confidence'.

11 See Atiyah and Cane *Accidents, Compensation and the Law* (5th edn, 1993) pp 37-39.

12 (1837) 3 Bing NC 468 (CP).

13 Ibid p 471.

But the Court of Common Pleas found for the plaintiff. According to Tindal CJ[14]:

'Instead ... of saying that the liability for negligence should be coextensive with the judgment of each individual, which would be as variable as the length of the foot of each individual, we ought rather to adhere to the rule which requires in all cases a regard to caution such as a man of ordinary prudence would observe.'

Thus, we must say that the reasonable person does at least have one important characteristic, that of being of average intelligence.

With these two preliminary points out of the way, it is now time to return to the central question of this section—how do reasonable people behave?
    There are two important questions here:
(1)   What factors does a reasonable person take into account in coming to decisions about how to act?
(2)   What is a reasonable way to weigh up the various factors identified in the answer to question (1)?
    The answer to question 2 is a good deal more difficult than the answer to question 1, but a great deal can be understood even by those who know only about the answer to question 1.

What does a reasonable person take into account?

The fundamental idea is that reasonable people take into account and weigh the consequences of their actions before deciding how to act. Consequences should be judged in terms of costs and benefits, and each cost and each benefit should be discounted by the likelihood of its occurring. Thus, a very large chance of a very small gain should be judged to have a value equal to that of a very small chance of a very large gain.[15]
    In most negligence cases, the defendant is usually being judged on whether he or she should have taken some further precaution against the accident that occurred, a precaution which, it is alleged, would have prevented the accident. The factors to be examined therefore, must refer to the probable cost of the precaution in question and the benefit to be gained by the prevention of the accident.[16] The factors to be taken into account fall into four broad categories—the chances of an accident happening, the seriousness of the accident if it does happen, the possible

14 At p 475.
15 Of course, it may be that in reality this sort of estimation of value is rare, or that people make frequent mistakes in the assessment of risks and costs. See generally S Sutherland *Irrationality*. But the standard of reasonableness represents what should be done, not what is done.
16 See *Wagon Mound (No 2)* [1967] 1 AC 617 (PC) at pp 643-44 per Lord Reid; *Watt v Hertfordshire County Council* [1954] 1 WLR 835, 838 per Lord Denning.

adverse consequences of taking the precautions in question and the chances that those adverse consequences will materialise.[17] Reasonable conduct is that which flows from considering the balance between the cost of the precaution in question and its benefits.

Chance of an accident happening

In general

It is self-evident that the greater the risk of an accident, the more a reasonable person would do to prevent it. In *Wagon Mound (No 2)*[18], for example, Lord Reid said that in a case where the risk was 'unreal' or 'fantastic' or 'far-fetched' or a 'mere possibility' the defendant could reasonably refrain from taking further precautions, but where there was a risk that was 'real' but 'small', it was reasonable to fail to act only if there was 'some valid reason for doing so, eg that it would involve considerable expense to eliminate the risk.'

It is noticeable that English judges are generally not at home with the expression of risk and probabilities in terms of numbers. Instead they attempt verbal descriptions of risk, such as 'probable', 'likely', 'possible' or 'bare possibility'. This practice should be deprecated for its imprecision, but it seems well entrenched. With regard to the evaluation of the relevant evidence, however, there are some cases which suggest a more precise approach. In *Haley v London Electricity Board*[19] for example, the House of Lords attempted to estimate the risk of injury to pedestrians of an almost completely unguarded hole in the pavement of a London street, a risk that affected, above all, blind people such as the plaintiff. The court evaluated the risk by looking at the proportion of blind people in the population of London, which they found to be 0.2 per cent. The court then decided that given the total number of people likely to pass by the hole and the low cost of effective precautions, the risk of a blind person falling into the hole was too great for nothing extra to have been done.

Threshold of risk

Perhaps as a consequence of their generally non-mathematical approach to risk, the English courts are particularly wedded to the notion that there is a threshold of risk below which doing nothing more than was done is

---

17 Cf Learned Hand J in *US v Carroll Towing* 159 F 2d 169, 173 (2d Cir. 1947) and *Conway v O'Brien* 111 F 2d 611, 612 (2d Cir 1940).
18 [1967] 1 AC 617.
19 [1965] AC 778.

perfectly acceptable. As Lord Dunedin said in *Fardon v Harcourt-Rivington*[20]:

'If the possibility of the danger emerging is reasonably apparent, then to take no precautions is negligence; but if the possibility of danger emerging is only a mere possibility which would never occur to the mind of a reasonable man, then there is no negligence in not having taken extraordinary precautions... People must guard against reasonable probabilities, but they are not bound to guard against fantastic possibilities'.

The threshold idea was taken further in *Bolton v Stone*.[1] The defendants ran a cricket club in Cheetham, Manchester. The plaintiff, Miss Stone, lived nearby in a house on a quiet suburban street. One day, when she was standing outside her house, she was struck on the head by a cricket ball which had been hit out of the cricket club's ground and over a 17 foot fence that had been erected to prevent the ball from escaping, a hit of nearly 200 yards. The defendant argued in the subsequent legal proceedings that for the ball to be hit completely out of the ground was an extremely rare event, (it had happened about six times in 28 years according to one witness and had never before caused injury) and it would have been very expensive, and perhaps impossible without closing down the cricket club, to have prevented the ball from hitting the defendant.

The House of Lords decided that the risk of the ball being hit out of the ground and then causing damage was indeed very small, so small that there was no need to anything about it at all.[2] As Lord Oaksey said:[3]

'[I]n my opinion, an ordinarily careful man does not take pre–cautions against every foreseeable risk ... He takes precautions against risks which are reasonably likely to happen.'

A difficulty with the threshold concept, however, is that it is unclear how unlikely an accident has to be before the threshold is crossed. How likely is 'reasonably likely' (per Lord Oaksey) or 'sufficient probability to lead a reasonable man to anticipate it' (per Lord Porter)?

OTHER PEOPLE'S CARELESSNESS

One particular sort of risk deserves special mention, namely the risk that other people will behave carelessly, and thus render dangerous an action of the defendant that would otherwise not be very dangerous. Does reasonable behaviour include taking such risks into account? The most everyday version of this problem was presented in *Upson v London Passenger Transport Board* [1947] KB 930 (CA), [1949] AC 155 (HL).

20 (1932) 146 LT 391, 392.
1   [1951] AC 850.
2   Eg per Lord Radcliffe at p 869.
3   At p 863.

The plaintiff attempted to cross a busy London street even though the pedestrian lights were against her and the view of oncoming traffic was being obstructed by a parked taxi. She was hit by a bus operated by the defendants. Although the case was eventually decided on the basis of breach of statutory duty, because the trial judge decided the case on the ground that the defendants had been at fault and so liable at common law, both the Court of Appeal and the House of Lords discussed the issue of whether it was reasonable for drivers to ignore the likelihood of careless behaviour by pedestrians.

There are two ways of deciding such a case. One line is to say that to make drivers responsible for failing to anticipate the carelessness of pedestrians, even taking into account the reduction in damages consequent on the inevitable finding of contributory negligence, would both seriously impair the incentive offered by the fault standard for plaintiffs to look out for their own safety and result in over-cautious driving.

The other line is to say that all that matters is the likelihood of the behaviour concerned, and if the risk of careless conduct by the plaintiff exceeded the *Bolton v Stone* threshold, no reasonable defendant would ignore it.

In the Court of Appeal in *Upson* these two views were represented by Lord Greene MR and Asquith LJ.

Lord Greene said that it was reasonable for a driver to assume that pedestrians would take ordinary care in crossing the road. He reasoned that if the law were otherwise, 'It would mean that instead of watching the road in front of him [the driver] would be under a duty to keep watch on the pavement ... for the possibility of an action being taken by a pedestrian which no reasonable or careful pedestrian can be assumed to take.' Lord Greene continued, 'If such be the standard of duty, I venture to say that there is not a driver who conforms to it ... [and moreover] one of the main purposes of traffic lights, namely, to facilitate a speedy flow of traffic, would be entirely defeated.'

Asquith LJ agreed that there was no common law negligence on the facts of the particular case, but he did so purely because of the degree of unlikelihood of the plaintiff's conduct. 'The driver of a motor vehicle is ... not entitled in all circumstances to assume that other users of the road will behave unimpeachably; but neither is he bound to anticipate and provide against every eccentricity and folly, however improbable.'

The House of Lords agreed with Asquith LJ's approach. Lord du Parcq,[4] quoting his own speech in the earlier case *Grant v Sun Shipping Co Ltd*[5] said that, 'A prudent man will guard against the possible negligence of others when experience shows such negligence to be common.'[6]

---

4   [1949] AC 155 at p 176.
5   [1948] AC 549.
6   See also Lord Wright [1949] AC 155 at p172, Lord Uthwatt at p 173 and Lord Morton at p181.

The *probability* of faulty conduct by the plaintiff is therefore now the sole determinant of its relevance.[7] But one should note that Asquith LJ's final conclusion that the plaintiff's behaviour in *Upson* was indeed improbable seems to have been against the weight of the evidence, namely that 'people in London have a habit of crossing when the lights are not in their favour'. In consequence, in the House of Lords, Lords du Parcq and Morton would have found the defendant liable at common law.

Seriousness of accident if it does happen

Reasonable people take more trouble to prevent serious accidents than trivial ones, and the more serious the accident that might happen the more a reasonable person would do to prevent it.

These propositions may seem incontrovertible, but they were not established in the law without some dispute. As late as *Paris v Stepney Borough Council*,[8] the Court of Appeal could maintain that, 'A greater risk of injury is not the same thing as a risk of greater injury; the first alone is relevant to liability.'[9]

The idea behind this odd sounding pronouncement seems to have been that no-one had a right to harm anyone else except in circumstances in which a reasonable person would have thought the chance of injury to be trivial—an idea related to the threshold idea discussed above. The degree of injury concerned was thought to be irrelevant because it was enough for the injury to be sufficiently perceptible to be actionable. A reasonable person, in other words, would act to prevent any actionable harm to another person as long as the risk of the harm occurring was above the threshold.

The rejection of this line of argument by the House of Lords in *Paris*[10] is therefore of some importance, because it establishes the support of the English courts for the proposition, not often stated openly, that negligence law does not deal only in thresholds and absolute limits but also allows for trade-offs, for example between the degree of harm to be expected from not taking a particular precaution and the costs of taking that precaution.

The main difficulty with allowing the probable seriousness of the harm to be taken into account is that, although there might often be agreement about how likely a particular event is to occur, there is often disagreement about how serious a particular sort of injury is compared either to other injuries or to the costs of taking precautions.

How serious, for example, is a momentary sharp pain, compared to a dull ache that lasts several weeks? Is the grief that people feel when a pet dies serious enough to make it unreasonable to fail to keep a look out for

---

7   Now see also *Rider v Rider* [1973] QB 505, disapproving of dicta of Lord Denning in *Bright v A-G* [1971] 2 Lloyd's Rep 68.
8   [1950] 1 KB 320; revsd [1951] AC 367.
9   Per Asquith LJ [1950] 1 KB 320 at p 324.
10 See the argument of counsel [1951] AC 367 at pp373-74, Lord Simonds at pp 375-76, Lord Normand at pp 381-82, Lord Morton at p 385, Lord MacDermott at p 389.

such pets as they dash into the road? Many of the points relevant to this question of the difficulty of the measurement of seriousness will come up for more detailed discussion in the chapter on damages.[11] At this stage one should only note that, although there are available techniques for putting a monetary value on things that are not themselves traded in a market, for example the use of limbs, general health, and even life itself, (i) the courts do not seem to use them and (ii) in any case even these techniques cannot produce conclusions that remain true for long periods of time. The result is that the measurement of the seriousness of the harm is not a very precise exercise.

Another issue raised by *Paris v Stepney Borough Council* deserves some comment. The plaintiff in *Paris* was a fitter's mate in a garage run by the defendant local authority. While working with a hammer on a rusty bolt, a metal chip flew into his eye, of which, as a consequence, he lost the sight. The defendants had not provided or required the wearing of goggles, a simple precaution that would have prevented the accident. So far so unremarkable. But the unusual, and unfortunate, aspect of the facts was that the plaintiff had already lost the sight of his other eye in the Second World War, and the result of the accident with the metal chip was that he became completely blind. The employer's defence to the claim of negligence was not only that it should not be held to be at fault only because of the extra seriousness of the harm to this particular plaintiff, but also that it should not matter that it knew of the plaintiff's special circumstances. The employer's conduct, it claimed, should be judged in the light of the risk to an average or ordinary employee. The House of Lords rejected this strand of the defendant's case. It was, said the House of Lords, indeed relevant that there were special circumstances affecting the plaintiff.

One should note that in *Paris* the evidence was that the defendant actually knew about the plaintiff's unusually vulnerable condition. Actual knowledge of vulnerability is not, however, a necessary condition for a finding of fault. It is enough that the risk of harm in question was not so low that it would have been reasonable to ignore it.[12] Extra seriousness arising from unusual vulnerability is relevant as long as it was reasonable to suspect the existence of the extra vulnerability.[13]

One should also note the following problem with the measurement of the seriousness of harm.[14] A large car manufacturer discovers that one of its models suffers from a defect, namely that if it is hit in the rear, there is a very high risk of an explosion. The manufacturer also discovers that the cost of putting the defect right in all of the cars that have already been sold, although small per car, is very large in total. In fact, the manufacturer discovers that the cost of recalling and repairing all the cars is greater than the probable damages that the company will have to pay out to victims of the explosions. The result is that, whether under the existing law, ie the

---

11 Below ch 13.
12 See eg *James v Hepworth and Grandage Ltd* [1968] 1 QB 94—extra risk caused by illiteracy of plaintiff held to be too small for finding that written safety notices insufficient. Cf *Bolton v Stone* and *Haley v London Electricity Board* above.
13 For further discussion see below pp 118-125 on the 'Thin Skull Rule'.
14 Cf the *Ford Pinto* case, *Grimshaw v Ford Motor Co* 174 Cal Rep 348 (Ct App 1981).

Consumer Protection Act 1987, which provides for liability for harm caused by defective products without further proof of fault, or at common law, the manufacturer could well decide not to recall the cars, but instead to pay out the damages as and when the need arises.

That might seem bad enough, but consider further what the position might be at common law. Would it not be possible for the manufacturer to claim that since the damages payable would total less than the costs of recall, the seriousness of the harm multiplied by the risk of harm is sufficiently low that there ought to be no finding of fault in the first place?

The answer is probably no. A court would say, surely, that it is faulty to allow cars to continue to be driven in a condition that involves a substantial risk of very serious injury. The cost of recalling all the cars may be very great, but that could not outweigh the danger to the public.

But if this is correct, note that it implies that for the purposes of assessing the seriousness of the accident if it happens, the court is not confined to using the law's own measure of damages as a measure of harm. It is at liberty to assume that the law undercompensates the victims of accidents. One might ask whether this is entirely satisfactory, and whether it suggests that the measure of damages itself might be inaccurate.

Cost of the accident—summary

It is sometimes clearer to think about the risk of the occurrence of the accident and its seriousness if it does occur together—as the total probable cost to others of the course of conduct undertaken by the defendant (as it would have appeared at the time). That is, a reasonable person in judging the dangerousness of a particular course of action will consider together each possible harmful outcome in terms of its costs and its probability of occurring. The reasonable person will then look at combined dangerousness of the totality of all the outcomes, each discounted for its probability of occurring, but ignoring those outcomes whose cost discounted for risk is trivial.

Thus, imagine a course of conduct that appears to have four possible outcomes that are harmful to others. The first outcome is extremely unlikely to happen, but would be quite nasty if it did (for example being hit by a cricket ball à la *Bolton v Stone*). The second outcome is quite likely to happen, but so trivial that a reasonable person would do nothing more to prevent it (for example, the risk of jostling someone as one tries to get onto a crowded bus). The third outcome is serious in very rare cases, but not usually (eg the risk that the person jostled in the previous example has haemophilia or brittle bone disease). And the fourth is a medium risk of medium harm. The reasonableness standard would require nothing to be done about the first two outcomes, but would require the defendant to have taken the fourth outcome seriously and may or may not, according to the precise risk involved, also require action to be taken in respect of the third outcome.[15]

15 Ie the cost of the accident is $\sum cr$ for each cr greater than the trivial, where c=cost of the accident and r=the probability of the cost being incurred.

One difficult point about assessing the likelihood and likely gravity of harm is how wide should the scope of assessment be? We have assumed so far that all the relevant risks should be considered, not just the risk of the particular accident that occurred. But how far does this principle extend?

In *Bolton v Stone*, for example, does the court consider the likelihood of cricket balls striking ladies of a particular age at a particular time of day causing particular injuries? Or does it ask about the probability as it would have appeared at the time of personal injury to anyone caused at any time by the escape of a cricket ball from the cricket ground? And what about the chances of property damage? Or damage caused by things other than the ball, for example accidents caused by the cars used by spectators to bring them to the ground?

Clearly one can make any accident sound highly unlikely if one includes a great number of specific details about the victim, the precise place, the injuries suffered and the way in which it happened. On the other hand, one can make virtually any activity sound dangerous by including all the types of accident that would be less likely if the activity were to be stopped (eg stopping cricket matches at which beer is served might reduce drunk driving accidents, or the incidence of cirrhosis of the liver).

The case law here is unclear. On the one hand there are cases such as *Bourhill v Young* [1943] AC 92, *Wagon Mound (No 1)* [1961] AC 388, and *Palsgraf v Long Island Railroad Co* 248 NY 339 (1928) that suggest that the court should concern itself solely with the unique accident which in fact occurred. On the other hand, cases such as *Hughes v Lord Advocate* [1963] AC 837 and *Smith v Leach Brain* [1962] 2 QB 405 suggest that one should look to the 'type' of damage concerned and not bother too much with exactly how the accident came about or any abnormality in the plaintiff. Both the *Wagon Mound* cases and the *Hughes v Lord Advocate* cases are conventionally categorised as cases about 'remoteness', rather than 'breach of duty' but, as Lord Denning once remarked, this distinction can become somewhat artificial.

At the moment, the *Hughes-Smith* line of cases holds sway, but, as we shall see (below ch 4), there are serious difficulties in deciding exactly how broad a 'type' of damage is, which is precisely one of the questions we need now to know the answer to.

Among those conventionally categorised as 'breach of duty' cases is *Haley v London Electricity Board* [1965] AC 778, the case in which the blind man fell into a hole marked only by two notice boards and a tool left across it. The court did not take into account when judging the risk any accidents that the precautions actually taken by the defendant would probably have prevented. They took into account the danger of what the defendant did for people suffering from the same disability as the plaintiff, namely the blind.

Haley shows that some relevant facts about the accident can be taken into account to reduce the scope of the risk, but it does not offer any advice on how to decide which characteristics are relevant and which are not. In this regard some assistance may be derived from *Glasgow Corpn v Taylor* [1922] 1 AC 44. In this case, a child died from eating berries growing on a shrub in a public garden belonging to the defendant local council. In the course of finding for the plaintiff (the boy's father), Lord Sumner said that the case did not turn on any special right or status of children, but on the fact that there was 'a measure of care appropriate to the inability or disability of those who are immature or feeble in mind or body [which] is due from others who know of or ought to anticipate the presence of such persons within the scope and hazard of their own operations.'

Thus, it is not the specific characteristic of being a child that counts, but the characteristic of being put at risk by the defendant's specific lack of precaution.

What this suggests is that assessments of fault should start not with 'likelihood of harm' in the abstract, but with the particular failing or failings of which the defendant stands accused. The court should then ask how many people would have been made safer by the precaution and by how much. The answer to these two questions should then be compared to the broad costs of the precaution.

Note that in this formulation the question of whether the plaintiff specifically would have avoided the harm had the precaution been taken is not automatically answered. It is possible for a precaution to have been worth it in general terms, but to have been undoubtedly ineffective in the particular case before the courts. The question of whether or not the precaution that the defendant failed to take would have made any difference must therefore count as a separate issue, the point being that it cannot be faulty to have failed to have done something that would have made no difference.

Adverse consequences of precaution

The third and arguably most important factor that the reasonableness standard requires to be taken into account is the cost of taking the precaution whose omission allegedly resulted in harm occurring to the plaintiff. The lower the cost of the precaution it is alleged the defendant should have taken, the less reasonable is the defendant's conduct.

The 'cost' of the precaution in question has two aspects—its cost to the defendant and its cost to others. 'Cost' also takes in not just monetary costs, but costs in the sense used by economists, namely everything, whether directly measurable in money or not, that has to be sacrificed if the precaution is taken[16]. It includes, therefore, any loss of opportunity to do good, as well as the direct costs of taking precautions against doing harm. As Lord Denning said in *Watt v Hertfordshire County Counci;*,[17] in which the employers of a fireman were held not to have been at fault for taking an extra risk of injury to the firemen themselves in order to try to arrive more quickly at the scene of a rescue attempt, '[I]n measuring due

16 Cf Learned Hand J in *Conway v O'Brien* and *US v Carroll Towing*, above n 17.
17 [1954] 1 WLR 835, 838.

care you must balance the risk against the measures eliminating the risk. To that proposition must be added this: you must balance the risk against the end to be achieved.' The cost of the extra precaution includes the end being achieved by not taking it, namely the avoidance of delay in reaching the person in danger.

Private costs

Although Lord Reid remarked in *Bolton v Stone*[18] that he did 'not think it right to take into account the difficulty of remedial measures' it is now well established that the costs to the defendant of taking precautions are a relevant consideration. For example Lord Reid himself in a later case[19] said, '[I]n considering whether some precaution should be taken against a foreseeable risk, [one should] weigh, on the one hand, the magnitude of the risk, the likelihood of an accident happening and the possible serious–ness of the consequences if an accident does happen, and, on the other hand, the difficulty and expense and any other disadvantage of taking the precaution'.

If the law were otherwise, it would mean that a whole range of activities would be declared faulty in themselves, for they are indulged in only for the pleasure or profit of the person involved and for them not to be done at all would mean no loss for anyone else. For example, in many cases, it would be faulty to drive a car without any passengers, for often no-one benefits from a journey apart from the person taking it; it would be faulty for people to employ any domestic staff, for they could easily do without; and it would be faulty for teenagers to do anything at all.

Private costs often come down to the simple question of the expensiveness of the precaution. In *Latimer v AEC Ltd*[20] for example, an employer was held not to have been at fault for failing to prevent an accident that occurred when an employee slipped on the factory floor following a flood and a partial clean-up. The court decided that the only plausible way of preventing the accident was to close the factory down while the clean-up was completed. But such a remedy, the court concluded, was to be treated, in the absence of evidence to the contrary, as too onerous.

Similarly, in *Aiken v Port of London Authority*[1] the plaintiff dock worker was injured in circumstances in which the accident would not have happened either if the employer had employed an extra full-time employee to keep a gangway clear or if the employer had provided better lighting. Paull J said that the reasonable employer would 'have to consider whether the time, trouble and expense of any precaution ... are or are not dis–proportionate to the risks involved.' Paull J found that to employ an extra

18 [1951] AC 850, 867.
19 *Morris v West Hartlepool Steam Navigation Co Ltd* [1956] AC 552, 574.
20 [1953] AC 643.
1 [1962] 2 Lloyd's Rep 30, 38.

employee would involve disproportionate expense, but that, on the other hand, providing better lighting did not involve disproportionate expense. Paull J therefore found for the plaintiff.[2]

To illustrate the same point in a case in which monetary values are less easily assigned to the private costs of taking precautions, but in which they are nevertheless highly relevant, one can turn to *Surtees v Kingston-upon-Thames Borough Council*[3].

The plaintiff, aged two, was in the care of foster parents acting for the defendant local authority. The plaintiff was left in the bathroom while the foster mother looked for a towel. Unfortunately, the child managed to turn on a hot water tap in the wash basin and as a result was very badly scalded.

The Court of Appeal ruled that although the foster mother might have been at fault if she had left the two-year-old in the vicinity of a basin full of scalding water, since the risk of injury would have been very high, it was not careless merely to have left the child alone for a few minutes in a bathroom. To hold otherwise would according to Stocker LJ 'impose an impossibly high standard' on parents.

Beldam LJ dissented on the grounds that it only required momentary thought to make it impossible for the two-year-old to reach the taps—in other words that the costs of taking the precaution in question were very low. But the majority looked to the overall level of stress in an ordinary household and decided that to require precautions by the defendant over and above those she had taken would be to ask too much.[4]

Costs to others (1)—general

More obviously, it is a relevant consideration that the precaution it is alleged the defendant should have taken might have resulted in harm to third parties (or, indeed, other harm to the plaintiff).

Watt v Hertfordshire County Council[5] provide a clear example. If the fire service had to take time to make sure that their vehicles were absolutely safe and secure for fire fighters before setting out on each rescue, the effect would be that fewer fires would be put out and more rescues would fail.

In the context of contributory negligence *Daborn v Bath Tramways*[6] stands for a similar proposition. The driver of a left-hand drive ambulance was held not to have been contributorily negligent because she had failed to stop and get out to make absolutely sure that there was no-one behind

---

2 But with a 25% reduction for contributory negligence, since the plaintiff did not keep a proper look-out and may not have benefited from the better lighting.
3 [1991] 2 FLR 559, CA.
4 Another snag with Beldam LJ's view is that if the mother had put the daughter somewhere else, there would probably have been a risk of another sort of accident.
5 [1954] 1 WLR 835.
6 [1946] 2 All ER 333.

her when she made a right turn. To do so would mean that the war-time ambulance service could not have functioned as well, to the obvious detriment of the sick and injured.

In cases involving injuries caused by the police in the course of app–rehending suspects, whether the injury is to the suspect or to third parties, a relevant consideration is the public interest in the punishment and prevention of crime. The more dangerous the criminal to public safety, the more risks the police should be entitled to take.

A case that crosses the boundary into fault, however, is *Rigby v Chief Constable of Northamptonshire*.[7] A psychopath broke into the plaintiff's gunsmith's shop and started to snipe at passers-by. The police laid siege to the shop, and brought up equipment with which they intended to fire tear gas into the shop. The police realised that there was a serious risk of fire if they launched the gas canisters into a gun shop, so they tried to arrange for the fire brigade to be in attendance. Unfortunately, the fire brigade was on strike at the time. Emergency cover was being provided by the armed forces, but their supply of fire engines was limited. The fire engine supplied by the armed forces had to be called away to tackle a fire in another part of town before the police fired their CS gas, a fact that the police failed to notice. Half an hour later, the psychopath fired shots through the roof of the shop from below in an attempt to clear his way for an escape onto the roof. The police feared that this manoeuvre might succeed, and that the psychopath would end up on top of the roof shooting at passers-by from a more advantageous position. The police therefore launched their gas canister without checking whether the fire engine was still present. A fire did indeed break out, and it quickly engulfed the building. The psychopath was safely apprehended, but the plaintiff's premises were destroyed.

In the subsequent action for negligence[8] the High Court found in favour of the plaintiff. Undoubtedly, by the time the psychopath had fired his shots through the roof, it was too late for the police to do anything apart from to fire the gas. But Taylor J decided that the police should have noticed the departure of the fire engine at the time it left and should have immediately telephoned neighbouring districts to find a replacement for it (one was indeed available). The police were therefore found liable despite the extreme dangerousness of the person they were trying to apprehend.

The cost to others (2)—dilemmas, emergencies and rescuers

If the defendant, through no fault of his own, finds himself in a situation in which he has to choose between two evils, he is not at fault merely for choosing the lesser evil.

---

7   [1985] 1 WLR 1242.
8   Inter alia. There was also discussion of liability under *Rylands v Fletcher*.

For example, in the *Frances (Ketch) v Highland Loch*[9] the defendants were about to launch a new ship when the plaintiff's ketch floated into the line of the proposed launch. The defendants, fearing that it was dangerous to their employees to postpone the launch, for preparations were by now so advanced that there was a danger that the ship would charge down the slipway of its own accord, and believing that the risk of collision with the ketch was small, went ahead anyway. A collision did, however, occur.

The House of Lords found for the defendants. Lord Loreburn explained:

'[T]he owners of the launch were placed in an extremely difficult position ... [I]t would have been a dangerous thing to the men in the yard, and also to those craft that might be in the river, if this launch had been postponed ... The owners of the launch were placed in a position in which they had to take one of two risks. It seems to me that they took the lesser risk and wisely took the lesser risk; and ... under those circumstances they did nothing to which the law can attach any blame.'

Note, however, that the court explicitly endorses the defendants' judgement that the risk that they took was the lesser risk. Does it follow that if the court disagrees with the defendant's judgement, fault will be found?

The answer to this question in principle is yes. The essence of fault is precisely whether the court agrees with the defendant's assessment, implied or actual, of the risks and costs involved in taking a particular precaution.

There is, however, a further cost the court may take into account which can tilt the balance in favour of the defendant in cases of a choice between two evils, namely the cost of delay in making a decision. In an emergency, the decision taken quickly may or may not be the right one, but to fail to make a decision at all may be much worse. The defendant is entitled to credit for making an attempt to improve a situation that left to itself would have seemed at the time to be leading to disaster.

For example, in *British School of Motoring v Simms*[10] a person who was undergoing a driving test in a dual-controlled car alleged that her examiner had been at fault in applying the dual-control brakes after she had driven through a give-way sign without stopping. She claimed that had the brakes not been applied she would have been able to accelerate out of the way of a car which, in the event, collided with the test car.

Talbot J said that the examiner was not at fault. 'Only when it became quite plain that she was going to create danger did he, in the sudden emergency, take action.' He had taken steps which were reasonable 'in the agony of the moment', even if, as it turned out, he had chosen the greater risk.

9   [1912] AC 312.
10 [1971] 1 All ER 317.

In other words, given the chances, as they would have appeared to a reasonable person in the examiner's position, of the driver being able to get out of the situation herself without causing harm, it was reasonable to decide to intervene, and the method of intervention chosen was reasonable given the amount of time available to choose it.

Talbot J based his decision in *British School of Motoring v Simms* on the famous ninteenth century case, *The Bywell Castle*.[11] 500 people lost their lives after a pleasure steamer collided with the ship the *Bywell Castle*. The pleasure steamer had foolishly navigated itself across the bows of the *Bywell Castle*, creating a danger of collision. The captain of the *Bywell Castle*, in the agony of the moment, decided at the last moment to turn his ship in what turned out to be the wrong direction. The *Bywell Castle* was found not to have been at fault since the original danger was created by the pleasure steamer and the captain of the *Bywell Castle* had acted reasonably in the emergency. Indeed, this decision goes further than was necessary for the decision in *British School of Motoring v Simms*, for it seems that if the captain had hesitated longer and had failed to make a decision about which way to turn, it is possible that the accident would have been less serious. Nevertheless, no fault was found. It is not faulty to act when delay and hesitation would have turned out to be the best policy unless it must have seemed at the time that inaction was demonstrably better than action.

The costs of delay and hesitation are also the reason behind the way the law treats the activities of rescuers who foul up their attempts at rescue. It is very rare for someone who has attempted to rescue another to be held liable to the person in danger. This is partly because of a causation point— the failed rescue must have left the person in danger in a worse position than before the attempted rescue.[12] But the main reason is that even if one is not particularly well qualified to attempt a rescue, the option of delaying in the hope of finding a more competent rescuer is usually not an attractive one.

The central case on negligence in rescue is *The Ogopogo*.[13] The defendant, the owner of the cabin cruise *The Ogopogo*, invited some friends for a Saturday cruise on Lake Ontario. They took with them 24 bottles of beer and, furthermore, put into a yacht club to drink some champagne. On the way home, one of the guests, for reasons that were never established, fell overboard. The defendant stopped the boat and reversed it towards the guest (a manoeuvre later criticised as too slow), but by the time the boat was within reach, the guest appeared to be unconscious and the rescue attempt failed.

At that point the plaintiff's husband, who had been below deck, leapt into the water to rescue the guest. This attempt, too, was unsuccessful and the guest's body slipped under the waves, never to be seen again.

---

11 *The Bywell Castle* (1879) 4 PD 219.
12 See below.
13 *Matthews v McLaren & Jones, The Ogopogo; Horsley v McLaren, The Ogopogo* [1969] 1 Lloyd's Rep 374; on appeal [1970] 1 Lloyd's Rep 257; revsd [1971] 2 Lloyd's Rep 410.

By this time, another guest, Mrs Jones, 'an experienced cold water swimmer', had also plunged in, and seemed to be in difficulties. Her husband took over the controls of the boat and brought it alongside her, from where the defendant and another guest managed to haul her on board.

The defendant then resumed control of the boat and drove it towards the plaintiff's husband. He was also hauled aboard but he was dead, not from drowning, as it turned out, but from the shock of being immersed in the bitterly cold water.

The plaintiff sued the defendant under the Ontario Fatal Accidents Act. She alleged that her husband's death had resulted from the defendant's failure to act more quickly in the original attempt to rescue the first guest to fall overboard, that the danger thus created quite naturally led the defendant's husband to attempt a rescue and that this attempt had caused his death.

Expert witnesses agreed that the rescue attempt had not been conducted well and the Ontario courts accepted that whether or not there was a duty to rescue at all, it was possible to be held liable for rescuing carelessly. But they went on to decide that even though the defendant was probably drunk at the time, because the period available for reflection and decision was so short, what was done had been reasonable. The methods adopted were not ideal, but, if anything, they saved time over the ideal method and certainly saved time over holding a discussion about the optimal method of rescue. The plaintiff's case amounted to saying that those who take out pleasure cruisers should be so highly trained that they always instinctively and immediately adopt the best rescue plan available, a view the majority of judges who heard the case did not accept.

SELFISHNESS AND THE VALUE OF OTHERS

Are people required to value their own interests less than those of others, either generally or in dilemmas and emergencies? Is it faulty to display cowardice or selfishness? There is no clear answer to these questions, but note:

1. English law, apparently as a matter of principle rather than as an inference from specific facts in specific cases, does not permit a negligence action to succeed where the basis of the accusation is that the defendant failed to rescue the plaintiff[14].

2. Furthermore, there is no longer any suggestion either that the private costs of precaution should not count at all, or that they should be discounted in any way (see above).

And so the law appears to be committed to the principle that all should count as one and as no more than one[15].

14 See below pp 171-175.
15 Cf J S Mill *Utilitarianism* ch 5 10 *Collected Works of John Stuart Mill* 157 (1967) and Bentham Plan of Parliamentary Reform in 3 *Works* 459 (Bowring edn 1838-43).

This principle is probably acceptable if all it means is that the law should not require heroic self-sacrifice. But does it have its limits? What would the courts say, for example, if a father chose to save his own son in preference to saving 50 strangers?

Social and private costs together

There is no rule that the costs to the defendant of the precaution and the costs to others have to be considered separately. Indeed in many cases it is convenient to consider them together under one heading.

For example in *Kite v Nolan*[16] the Court of Appeal had to consider whether a car driver was at fault when he drove at 15 mph past parked cars and an ice cream van, with the result that he hit a boy who dashed out from between the cars. The evidence was that if the car had been travelling at 5 mph, the accident would not have happened. Sir John Donaldson MR said that it was quite proper for trial courts to take into account the 'adverse consequences to the public and to the defendant of taking whatever precautions are under consideration.'

Indeed most precautions will involve costs both to the public at large and to the defendant.

One category of case that may be best explained as falling into the category of those in which the public and private costs of precaution are taken together is that concerning injuries suffered in the course of sport.

In *Condon v Basi* [1985] 1 WLR 866 the plaintiff suffered a broken leg as the result of a 'reckless and dangerous' tackle by the defendant in the course of an amateur football match.

The Court of Appeal agreed with the trial court that the defendant was at fault. It explained its judgment by saying, following Kitto J in *Rootes v Shelton* [1968] ALR 33, that whether or not a player followed the rules, conventions or customs of the game was a relevant consideration, but not a decisive one. Therefore, although the defendant in this case was at fault, it does not follow that every foul tackle opens up the possibility of liability for negligence.

The Court of Appeal did not elaborate any further on this point. But one may plausibly speculate that what lies in the background here is the thought that not only would a rule that every foul is tortious ruin the enjoyment of sport for the defendant individually, it would also seriously deter the organisation of sport generally.

[See also *Wooldridge v Sumner* [1963] 2 QB 43, *Simms v Leigh Rugby Football Club* [1969] 2 All ER 923, *Harrison v Vincent* [1982] RTR 8, *Wilks v Cheltenham Home Guard Motor Cycle Club* [1971] 1 WLR 668.]

---

16 [1983] RTR 253.

Illegality

The consideration together of the private costs and social costs of taking the precaution also explains the claim that it is relevant to ask whether the defendant's acts were otherwise unlawful, that is unlawful apart from the tort of negligence. For example in *Wagon Mound (No 2)*,[17] Lord Reid distinguished the case before him from *Bolton v Stone* on the basis that although in both cases the risk of harm was small, in *Bolton v Stone* the risk was created in the course of an activity that was, on the face of it, lawful—namely playing cricket, whereas the conduct under scrutiny in the *Wagon Mound* cases, pouring oil into Sydney harbour, was inherently unlawful—it was a criminal act.

The underlying idea is that if activity has been declared to be unlawful, a determination has been made that its social costs outweigh its benefits, whether to the person who engages in it or otherwise. It follows that it is necessarily the case that to refrain from such conduct must be for the public benefit, and those who engage in it must be at fault.

This is a very powerful idea, but perhaps unfortunately, it is not followed consistently by the English courts. In particular, they do not accept that there should be liability where the defendant has failed to comply with a statutory standard in circumstances in which the plaintiff would otherwise find it difficult to show fault.[18]

Knock-on effects as costs

A very effective way of countering an accusation of faulty conduct is to show that the precaution the plaintiff alleges the defendant should have taken would have produced the same or more injury to another person or, indeed, to the defendant, that is that the precaution suffers from snags and that its knock-on effects would be adverse.

The argument follows from the point that the cost of a precaution includes all the negative consequences that may flow from it for the defendant, for the plaintiff or for third parties. It is, for example, not necessarily faulty to fail to brake suddenly to avoid an accident if the probable effect of doing so would have been to cause a worse collision from behind.

The idea can also be illustrated from the advice given by the London Fire Brigade, upheld as lawful in *Buckoke v Greater London Council*,[19] to fire engine drivers about what to do if, when rushing to a fire, they came across a red light:

---

17 [1967] 1 AC 617 at 642.
18 See below ch 7 for the odd English rules preventing the easy translation of breaches of statute into actionable wrongs.
19 [1971] 1 Ch 655, 666.

'Extreme caution is to be used ... The onus of avoiding an accident ... rests entirely with the brigade driver, who is to remember that a *collision might well prevent his vehicle from reaching its destination and might also block the road for other essential services: no call is so urgent as to justify this risk.*'

The risk of preventing other rescue vehicles from reaching the scene of the accident is a good example of a knock-on effect.

Chances of adverse consequences materialising

Although the point is often overlooked, the mere possibility that the precaution the defendant is accused of omitting might have had costs is clearly not enough in itself. The cost of the precaution is its probable cost, that is, the possible cost discounted by the chance of it materialising.

Thus, if the defendant in a road accident case says that the reason he did not brake hard was that he feared being hit by the car following him, the court will need to be satisfied that it was reasonable at the time to fear such a collision. If the evidence is that the road was empty and visibility was good, the defendant's excuse may well be rejected on the ground that a reasonable estimation of the risk at the time would have been that the braking hard was fairly safe. Speculation is not enough.

The need to discount a possible cost of a precaution by its likelihood of materialising seems to lie behind Sir John Donaldson MR's reservations in *Kite v Nolan* about giving as much weight to 'general considerations' such as the effect on traffic flow of the adoption of a rule that the maximum permitted speed in the vicinity of a parked ice cream van is 5 mph as to the specific inconveniences and costs that would have occurred in the particular case had the defendant driven at 5 mph. The former is rather more speculative than the latter.[20]

The effectiveness issue

One important issue remains to be tackled. It arises out of the point often made by defendants that the precaution in question would not have prevented the injury to the defendant. It is a very powerful argument. It empties the plaintiff's accusation of fault of all content. But it must be handled with care.

---

20 Another point that may have been relevant is that the consequences of adopting a general rule and the consequences of ruling that a particular precaution should have been taken on a particular occasion are quite different. The courts are often not willing to adopt general rules not just because the outcome would be too uncertain but also because the deterrent effect might be excessive.

The argument from effectiveness works because although the defendant, according to the *Wagon Mound (No 2)*, is under a duty to 'eliminate' any substantial risk, the defendant is also entitled to ask what, precisely, should have been done instead.

The test is sometimes suggested[1] that defendants need to show merely that their conduct substantially reduced the risk of the accident's occurrence. But this test is seriously incomplete. The risk must be reduced to the level at which, under the *Bolton v Stone* threshold rule, it could reasonably be ignored. Otherwise, even after the precaution in question had been taken, the risk would still have been so great that a reasonable person would have done more to prevent injury.

IS THE DEFENDANT'S WEALTH RELEVANT?

The conventional approach to fault is that the sensitivity of the defendant to the costs of the precaution in question does not matter. Driving slowly may give me an ulcer, or looking where I am going may make my eyes ache, but nevertheless I am at fault. Similarly, defendants who cannot afford to take precautions are usually said to be in no better position than defendants who can afford to take precautions.

The standard position of the courts is that if one cannot afford to do something safely, one should not do it at all.

But there are some cases that appear to make allowances for the defendant's lack of resources.

First, public authorities appear to be able to use the spending restrictions placed on them as a reason for not taking particular precautions. In *Knight v Home Office* [1990] 3 All ER 237, in which the High Court considered whether the Prison Service had been at fault in failing to prevent a mentally ill prisoner with known suicidal tendencies from killing himself, Pill J said (at p243)

> 'Lack of funds would not excuse a public body which operated its vehicles on the public roads without any system of maintenance... [but] in making the decision as to the standard to be demanded, the court must ... bear in mind as one factor that resources available for the public service are limited and that the allocation of resources is a matter for parliament.' (Cf Lord Thankerton's reference to a public authority's 'cramped financial resources' in *East Suffolk Rivers Catchment Board v Kent* [1941] AC 74 at 96).

Secondly, where ex ante fault is relevant in nuisance (see below pp 511-515), for example where the nuisance comes about through natural causes (see *Goldman v Hargrave* [1967] 1 AC 645), it appears that the financial resources available to the defendant are relevant.

Thirdly, at common law, before the Occupiers' Liability Act 1984, it seems that the defendant's wealth was relevant to whether or not the

1   See eg *McGhee v National Coal Board* [1973] 1 WLR 1.

defendant acted properly towards trespassers (see eg *British Railways Board v Herrington* [1972] AC 877 per Lord Reid at p 899) and *Southern Portland Cement v Cooper* [1974] AC 623 per Lord Reid at p 644—'With regard to dangers of which he has knowledge but which he did not create').

In the first of these types of case, those involving public authorities, the concern of the judges may simply be that if public authorities spend beyond their authorised limits they break the law, which would count as a high cost of taking the precaution concerned. But most public authorities have some leeway in allocating resources between various budget heads, so that a lawful method of funding the required precaution may often be found. At this point, the courts' concern is not merely for 'one factor' to be borne in mind, but for an argument for exempting certain types of governmental decision from the scope of negligence law altogether, an argument that therefore falls to be discussed in the chapter on 'duty of care' (below ch 5).

As for trespassers and natural nuisances, the common factor appears to be a high valuation of land ownership and a desire to ensure that the burdens of land ownership do not fall more heavily on those on low incomes. Thus, the poor owner of dangerous land will not, according to the *Goldman* and *Herrington* approach, be obliged to sell it to someone who may be better able to keep it safe.

But why this privilege for land? Why should land owners escape liability because of lack of resources when the same point would not apply to car owners (sorry, I couldn't afford new brakes) or employers (I couldn't afford to supply a helmet/ use safer chemicals/ employ more supervisors).

On the other hand Arlen (see Jennifer H Arlen 'Should Defendants Matter?' 1992 JLS 413) argues that a general move to taking the wealth of the defendant into account in judging fault would be produce better results than not taking wealth into account, since the cost of the precaution for a poor person would be giving up necessities such as food and shelter, whereas the cost of the same precaution to a wealthy person would be trivial. Costs are therefore minimised by trying to make the wealthy bear more of the prevention costs than the poor. This can be done by setting the standard of care higher the wealthier the defendant.

But the main point to grasp is that the requirement that the pre–caution must eliminate the risk can be turned on its head and be made to assist the defendant, for the more that has to be done to reduce the risk to trivial levels, the more costly the precaution may become. One may therefore reach a point at which, although the remaining risk is far from negligible, the level of precaution needed to reduce it further has reached unreasonable levels. This, more than anything else, is the point of *AEC Ltd v Latimer*, and it may also be said to be the point of *Maloco v Littlewoods Organisations Ltd*,[2] in which the House of Lords can be read as ruling that it is not careless for an owner of empty premises to fail to mount a 24-hour guard against

2 [1987] AC 241, see below.

the possibility of a break-in by arsonous youths, since, although the risk that the youths might break in, cause a fire and destroy the property of the owner's neighbours was more than trivial, the precaution necessary to make it trivial was too burdensome for a finding of fault to be justified.

These points are very closely related to arguments that frequently make their appearance under the heading of 'causation'.[3] But in many ways, they are more clearly dealt with under the heading of fault. Consider, for example, the infamous case of *Cummings (or McWilliams) v Sir William Arrol & Co Ltd*.[4] The plaintiff, an employee of the defendant, fell off a roof and injured himself. The plaintiff complained that he had not been given any safety equipment. The defendant successfully defended itself by establishing that even if the equipment had been provided, the employee would not have used it. As a case on causation, *McWilliams* has serious problems,[5] but as a case about fault it is at least comp–rehensible, even though one might still disagree with its result. What *McWilliams* says, if interpreted as a case about fault, is that the precaution it is alleged that the defendant should have taken would not have worked—that is, it would not have reduced the risk to trivial levels. For such a reduction to have been achieved, the employer would have had to have done more—for example, the employer might have had to have taken on a large staff of supervisors, and have sent the employees on training courses about safety. The employer may even have had to close its operation down while a new work force was acquired. This, some might say, would have been too much to ask.

How does a reasonable person weigh factors?

Once assessments have been made of the risk of harm, including its degree of seriousness, and the interests that would have been sacrificed had the defendant taken sufficient precautions to have prevented the harm, the final and most difficult question remains. How does one weigh these various factors and come to a conclusion on whether or not the defendant acted unreasonably?

In many cases, the answer is clear—so clear often that the courts do not feel the need to make their reasoning clear. For example, if the defendant could have avoided a fatal accident by reducing his speed from 70 miles per hour to 60 miles per hour, and the only cost of doing so would have been that the defendant would have arrived home five minutes later, it is clear to most judges that the defendant was at fault.

Cases in which there appears to be little or no benefit attached to the defendant's acts are also fairly simple to decide. Any measurable risk of harm will usually be enough to condemn the defendant. For example in

3   See below ch 4.
4   [1962] 1 WLR 295.
5   See eg Fraser and Howarth 'More Concern for Cause' [1984] Legal Studies 131.

the *Wagon Mound (No 2)*, it was enough to seal the defendant's fate that the court found that the harm, the destruction of the plaintiff's ship in a fire that resulted from the defendant's spilling of oil into the harbour, was barely foreseeable, indeed involved a risk of fire only in 'very exceptional circumstances'. This was because 'there was no justification whatever for discharging the oil.... Not only was it an offence to do so, but it involved considerable loss financially.' In other words, the activity involved neither social benefit (at least according to the legislature—as evidenced by the fact that the discharge was criminal) nor private benefit, since the owners of the ship were losing their oil. Furthermore, this was a case in which the actions which might have been taken to eliminate the risk 'presented no difficulty, involved no disadvantage and required no expense.'

But as we have seen some cases are not so straightforward. Is it faulty for a police car to cut a corner at high speed in order to attempt to prevent a terrorist outrage? What if the crime involved were a burglary, or shoplifting? Is it faulty for parents momentarily to fail to pay attention to their children's where–abouts? Is it faulty for a government department not to spend several million pounds on setting up monitoring and accounting systems that would ensure that they could prevent fraud in the investment market? Is it faulty for a highly skilled driver not to brake hard and more effectively than an ordinary driver could, in circumstances in which to do so would mean that although the accident in front of the driver might have been avoided, the manoeuvre might have so surprised other road users that it might have caused a different accident for the vehicles following?

Many judges have imagined that the way to resolve the problem of assessment in a more objective way is to concentrate on degrees of foreseeability (ie degrees of likelihood as they would have appeared at the time).[6] But this attempt is fundamentally mistaken. If risk alone was determinative, it would be impossible to say in cases such as *Surtees v Kingston*[7] that there is a limit to what the law should require of busy parents, or in cases such as *Kite v Nolan*[8] or *Latimer v AEC Ltd*[9] that the precautions that the defendant allegedly should have implemented were excessive. The court has to come to a judgement not only on the chances, as they would have appeared at the time, of an accident's happening, but also how bad that accident would be. This involves putting a value on, for example, both readily measurable costs, such as loss of earnings, and rather

---

6 Examples of cases using the concept of variable degrees of foreseeability in this and other contexts include: *Alcock v Chief Constable of South Yorkshire Police* [1992] 1 AC 310, *Perl v Camden* [1984] 1 QB 342, *Saggers v Lewisham Borough Council* QBD 29 March 1983 LEXIS Transcript, *Topp v London Country Bus* [1992] RTR 254, *Ravenscoft v Rederiaktiebologet Transatlantic* [1991] 3 All ER 73, *Morgan Crucible v Hill Samuel* [1991] Ch 295, *Caparo v Dickman* [1990] 2 AC 605.
7 [1991] 2 FLR 559, CA (leaving two-year-old for couple of minutes too much to ask).
8 [1983] RTR 253.
9 [1953] AC 643.

less easily measurable costs such as pain and suffering.[10] Even more important, the court has to put a value on the other side of the balance, namely the interests to be sacrificed if accidents of the sort in question are to be avoided. Again, although some of these costs, especially the private costs, are fairly easily measurable, others, including many of the costs to others, are not so easily measurable.

It follows that to the extent that the costs involved are measurable on a common basis, decisions about fault may be said to be objective, or at least will be independent of judicial opinion. But to the extent that measurability is elusive, decisions on fault will be controversial.

A final point is that in some kinds of fault case, the court cannot avoid making controversial moral or political judgments.[11] One example is *Woolfall v Knowsley Borough Council*.[12]

Daniel Woolfall was 12 years old. He was walking along a road next to some land owned by the defendant, the local district council. The land was being used, partly officially and partly unofficially, as a temporary tip. It was piled high with rubbish because the council's dustmen had been on strike, and had only agreed to return to work three days previously.

Some of the rubbish on the tip was on fire, and heat from the fire seems to have caused an aerosol can to explode. The can flew through the air and hit the Daniel in the eye.

The judge found that the defendant council should have realised that there was a risk of this sort of accident. The plaintiff's case was that the defendants were at fault because they could have employed private contractors to remove the rubbish, thus reducing the danger. The defend–ants' excuse was that they did not want to cause a deterioration in industrial relations and aggravate the strike. Once the strike had ended, they did bring in private contractors to clear the rubbish, but the contractors had not reached the tip concerned.

The judge decided that the defendants' excuse was insufficient, that they should have brought in private contractors earlier and they were therefore at fault.

On appeal the defendants argued that their decision not to exacerbate the strike was reasonable. Woolf LJ, delivering the judgment of the court, rejected the defendants' argument. He said:

10 These costs can be measured indirectly by, for example, examining the prices paid for insurance against various injuries and losses. The reliability of such evidence is, however, questionable, since most people have little idea how bad the pain and suffering they are insuring against is, and they might well come to have a different view when they find out. Nevertheless, economists have even purported to calculate the value of life using similar methods, eg examining how much people pay for safer products or methods of travel that have known better chances of not killing people. See eg E Mishan *Cost-Benefit Analysis* (4th edn) 330-356.

11 That is political and moral judgments over and above those inherent in the idea that measurable costs should be measured on the basis of what people would or do pay to avoid them, as opposed to what some political process would say that they were worth.

12 (1992) Times, 26 June;. Lexis transcript 8 June 1992.

'While it is understandable that a local authority should not wish to aggravate industrial relations, they remain under a duty ... to take action [to protect the public].'

Although the court never says so explicitly, what it does in this case is to decide that it is more important to protect the public from a slight risk of physical injury than to settle public sector strikes quickly. It should be recognised that this is a view with which many people, both in trade unions and in local politics, would disagree. They would point to the grave inconveniences and public expense that flow from poor industrial relations in the public sector. That is a matter of opinion on which reasonable people may disagree.

But there is at the heart of *Woolfall v Knowsley Borough Council* another, deeper point, a point that the defendants do not seem to have argued explicitly, but which lies behind their point about industrial relations. Knowsley MBC is run by the Labour Party. The Labour Party has a long tradition of strong links with the trade unions and shares the union movement's traditions and values. One such traditional value, a value that is fiercely upheld, is that one does not indulge in strike-breaking or become involved with 'scabs' (replacement labour).

The defendants' real case in *Woolfall,* therefore, was that it is unreason–able to expect a socialist council to employ scabs and strike-breakers, and the effect of the Court of Appeal's judgment is that such traditions of the socialist and Labour movements are less important than avoiding small risks of personal injury.

Whether or not one agrees with the court in *Woolfall,*[13] it should be noted that it is impossible in this case to avoid an implicit judgment about the value of the traditions of the Labour movement. To have decided in favour of the council would have been to elevate industrial relations, and especially the relationship between Labour councillors and trade unions, to heights that those outside that particular political milieu might find puzzling.

Similar problems arise in cases involving religious convictions, although usually in the context of contributory negligence rather than that of the defendant's fault.

One striking example is the New York case *Friedman v New York,*[14] in which the plaintiff, a teenager, was trapped with her boyfriend in a ski-lift, the ski-lift having broken down because of the fault of the defendants. The plaintiff had been raised in a strict Jewish orthodox family and she believed it to be a grievous sin to stay for any length of time with a man in an enclosed place to which third parties had no access. She therefore decided, in a mental state described by the court as 'agitated, panicky and

---

13 For the sake of openness the author declares here that he does indeed agree with the Court of Appeal's judgment.

14 282 NYS 858 (1967).

... near hysteria', that she had to climb out of the ski-lift. Unfortunately, she slipped, fell 25 feet to the ground and suffered various injuries.

The plaintiff sued in negligence. The defendant alleged contributory negligence. The court found for the plaintiff and rejected the contributory negligence defence. The court accepted that the plaintiff's belief that she was under a strong moral compulsion was a good reason for her action. The fact that the belief was held only by a small ultra-orthodox minority was not relevant.

Again, the problem in this case is that to say that Miss Friedman's behaviour was unreasonable would have amounted to saying that her religious belief was unreasonable, but to find in her favour gives her a privilege, on religious grounds, to do something that, if done by someone else, might well count as careless.[15]

Legal philosophers who follow Ronald Dworkin[16] might argue that nevertheless there is a correct way to decide such cases, namely the way that fits best within our political and constitutional traditions. But it is not clear what result such a line of reasoning would bring in a country that retains both an established church and blasphemy laws.

Although these might seem to be extreme cases, they are simply the result of applying the same test that is applied in all cases in which fault is an issue. The central question is always 'was the risk worth the cost' and the answer always depends crucially on the weight the court gives to the various interests that would have to be sacrificed if accidents such as the one in issue are to be avoided. The problems raised in cases like *Woolfall* and *Friedman* arise inevitably in a fault-based tort.

Admittedly, for the lawyer with clients to advise, it is far from satisfactory to be told that the ultimate decision in the most difficult fault cases is simply a matter of the judges' values, but, as a matter of predicting what the courts will do about these disputes, there is little more that can be said of any lasting value. *Woolfall*, of course, illustrates English judges' continued adherence to the conventional, not to say conservative, values that might be expected of most people of their background and experience. But even this may pass.[17]

---

15 Cf *Ibrahim v Muhammed* QBD 21 May 1984 Lexis transcript (five-year-old boy seriously injured in religious circumcision ceremony by negligent doctor. Parents sue for nervous shock. Held: Parents entitled to full damages. Defence of contributory negligence—viz that circumcision of five-year-olds not a reasonable practice—not raised. Cf also *R v Blaue* [1975] 1 WLR 1411 (no break in chain of causation when plaintiff refuses medical treatment on religious grounds.

16 See generally *Law's Empire* (London, Fontana, 1986).

17 Note that one advantage of drawing judges, as the English system does, from a small socially homogeneous group of advocates is that bar and bench share a good many values and assumptions. Barristers may therefore be able to offer good advice about how judges might react to particular facts without exactly knowing how they do it.

The meaning of foreseeability

One of the most serious temptations for those coming across the tort of negligence for the first time is to be drawn into answering all questions with the words 'reasonable foreseeability'. Indeed, some students seem to believe that the evil necessity of detailed analysis can be kept at bay in negligence by the pious chanting of 'foreseeability' as a kind of mantra.

The courts themselves are partly responsible for this almost comical state of affairs. For example, in *Surtees v Kingston-upon-Thames Borough Council*,[18] the trial judge, Stocker LJ and Sir Nicholas Browne-Wilkinson all attempt to show that it is not 'reasonably foreseeable' at all that a child left next to a hot tap might scald itself, an intellectual enterprise so ludicrous that the two appeal judges, at least, eventually give up the attempt and slide back into admitting that the proper ground for their decision is the general knock-on effects of holding busy parents to standards of near perfection in childcare. Judges are perhaps influenced by the fact that by stressing foreseeability rather than reasonableness itself, it might be possible to give the appearance of avoiding the inherent conflicts about value that judgments about fault involve, and to concentrate solely on an issue that sounds as if it is objectively measurable. But, in reality, there is no way, in a tort based on fault, of avoiding substantive judgments of value. Foreseeability should be seen for what it is, not the philosopher's stone of the tort of negligence, but instead a shorthand way of stating a simple but important aspect of the test for fault, namely the tense of the verb to be used in judgments about fault.

That tense is the conditional perfect—*would have*. What matters is how the situation *would have* seemed to a reasonable person at the time. It would be possible[19] to construct other tests in negligence that might still be called fault-based liability but which would use a different tense. There could be, for example, a test based on the simple conditional 'would a reasonable person do this again, knowing now what the outcome would be?' Such a test would be different from foreseeability because it would allow the judgment about whether the defendant acted reasonably to take into account facts that have only come to light since the accident, including the fact that the accident happened. As Sir Nicholas Browne-Wilkinson V–C said in *Strover v Harrington*,[20] in negligence 'the question is not what [the defendant] will think is desirable in the future as a result of the perhaps bitter experience of this case, but whether on 4 March 1968 he fell below the then standards [applicable to him].'

---

18 [1991] 2 FLR 559, see above.
19 Eg Calabresi and Melamed 'Property Rules, Liability Rules and Inalienability—One View of the Cathedral' (1972) 85 Harv L Rev 1089; Calabresi and Klevorick 'Four Tests for Liability in Torts' (1985) 14 JLS 585.
20 [1988] 1 All ER 769.

EX POST TESTS

Three points might be made about ex post tests for liability (so-called because they allow into the assessment of fault information known only *after the fact*):

1. They are not the same as strict liability, although they are often classified as strict liability tests. The difference is that in the ex post test it is still possible for the defendant to avoid liability by showing that a reasonable person would indeed do it again, even knowing what we now know. Strict liability is where it does not matter whether the court agrees with what the defendant did. All that matters is that the defendant caused the harm.

2. Ex post liabilities of this sort used to be increasingly common. One example was products liability in the United States. Another was English nuisance law. But more recently, there seems to have been a reaction against them, especially in the House of Lords decision in *Cambridge Water Co Ltd v Eastern Counties Leather plc* [1994]1 All ER 53, which referred to forseeability as a 'pre-requisite of liabilty' both in nuisance and under the rule in *Rylands v Fletcher*.

3. Moreover, there may be good reason to suspect that ex post liability might be inferior in economic terms both to the ordinary negligence (so called ex ante fault liability) in cases in which defendants could have done more to find out how risky what they were doing was. The problem is that under an ex post test defendants are exposed to liability for events that they could never have predicted, so that they cannot possibly take into account other such costs, which by definition they cannot know about, in the future. See eg Stephen Shavell 'Liability and the incentive to obtain information about risks' (1992) 21 JLS 259.

Foreseeability therefore rules out anything that could not have been relevant to the defendant's decision about how to act. If, for example, technology has moved on, or scientific knowledge has accumulated, since the time of the defendant's injury-causing act, the new knowledge may not be taken into account.[1] Thus, when, as in *Doughty v Turner Manufacturing Co Ltd*,[2] a dangerous chemical reaction occurs for the first time the fact that the reaction can be readily understood and, as we know now, the accident is quite likely to happen again, the judgment of fault must remain based on how likely such an accident would have appeared before it happened.

Similarly, in *Tremain v Pike*[3] the plaintiff contracted Weil's Disease from rats. Nowadays, Weil's Disease is a well-known risk of coming into contact with rats, but at the time it appears to have been little known and the risk

1   See eg *Roe v Minister of Health* [1954] 2 QB 66 per Denning LJ: 'We must not look at [a] 1947 accident with 1954 spectacles'.
2   [1964] 1 QB 518.
3   [1969] 1 WLR 1556.

of causing the plaintiff to suffer from it would not have occurred to a reasonable person in the position of the defendant.

Note that often the reasonably foreseeable risk is no different from the risk as it seems now. Sometimes it is less. It may even be greater (if, for example, new scientific evidence shows that the event in question is very much rarer than previously believed). But it is always the risk as it *would have appeared at the time* that counts.

Note also that if the risk would have appeared at the time to be zero, or next to zero, the injury may be said to be 'unforeseeable' or 'not reasonably foreseeable'. If this is the case the defendant cannot be liable—but not for some mysterious reason to do with the magic of foreseeability, but because if the risk of injury is to be counted as zero, then there is nothing to balance against the costs of the precautions, and so the defendant cannot have been at fault.[4]

It is in this sense alone that foreseeability can be said to be a necessary element of liability in negligence. But, of course, it is clearly never sufficient by itself for liability, since a foreseeable risk may be so small that a reasonable person might ignore it (*Bolton v Stone*) or the cost of eliminating the foreseeable risk might be unreasonable (*Wagon Mound No 2*).

IMAGINATION AND THE LAW

One often hears the claim, especially from prospective undergraduates, that the quality of mind most needed by the lawyer is the ability to analyse. But reflection on the issue of fault in negligence cases suggests that there is another candidate for this title: imagination.

The essential task of the plaintiff's lawyer in a negligence case is twofold:

First, to persuade the court that the accident would have appeared at the time to have been a likely outcome of the defendant's conduct (the 'foreseeability' point), and

Secondly, to persuade the court that there were obvious, simple, cheap and effective means of preventing the damage in question, precautions which the defendant failed to implement (the 'precautions' issue).

The task of the defendant's lawyer is:

First, to play down the likelihood of harm as it would have appeared at the time (foreseeability), and

Secondly, to suggest snags, hidden costs and difficulties in all the putative precautions put forward by the plaintiff.

Note that the foreseeability issue cannot be decided without putting oneself in the position of the defendant at the time of the accident. The crucial question is one of reconstruction and imagination: What would the situation have seemed like at the time?

Imagination plays an even bigger part in the precautions issue. The more imaginative the plaintiff's lawyer, the more plausible precautions

---

4   See generally Howarth 'Negligence After Murphy' [1991] CLJ 58.

the plaintiff's lawyer places before the court, the more likely it is that the defendant will be found to have been at fault.

Similarly, the more imaginative the defendant's lawyer, the more snags and hidden costs in the plaintiff's proposals will be spotted and the more reasonable the defendant's failure to implement any of them will appears to become.

For example:

The plaintiff, who lives next to a golf club, complains that the defendant golf club tortiously failed to prevent a golf ball's being hit into her garden, where it struck the plaintiff on the head.

The defendant golf club would say not only (a) that it didn't and couldn't know that any such accident was likely (cf *Bolton v Stone*), but also (b) that there was nothing it could do, other than close down its entire operation, which would be too much to expect (cf *Latimer v AEC*).

On (a), the foreseeability issue, there would be little room for manoeuvre, except on the question of the average and maximum distances that a person experienced in running golf courses might expect that a misdirected golf ball can travel. In other words, putting oneself in the position of a golf club manager, someone experienced in the game of golf, how likely would a shot of this length and direction be?

But on (b), the precautions issue, the imagination of the lawyers would come into its own. The plaintiff might say that the golf club should have changed the course around so that the plaintiff would not have been endangered. The defendant would endeavour to show that not only would such a course of action have been prohibitively expensive, but also that to do so might well have endangered some other neighbour of the golf course or the players.

The plaintiff might also suggest that the defendant should have introduced a special rule of the game at the club severely penalising any player who hit the ball out of bounds. But the defendant would reply by saying either that such a rule would not have made the plaintiff much safer (and therefore that it cannot be said that it would have prevented the accident) because players are not competent enough to control their play sufficiently.

Or the plaintiff might say that the club should have forbidden play on the particular hole from which the shot came that caused the injury. But the defendant would reply this time that 17 hole golf courses are not a commercially viable proposition, since players strongly prefer full 18 hole courses. This course of action, according to the defendant, would amount to closing the course down.

Perhaps then, the plaintiff would suggest the defendant should have erected a fence or net, either at the boundary of the course or from near where the offending shot was likely to be played. This time the defendant would stress the expense of erecting a fence, its doubtful efficacy and, if the shot in question were a tee shot (always taken from roughly the same place) and the suggested netting was to be close to the tee itself, the defendant would mention the possible dangers of ricochets to other players.

And so on (perhaps you can think of yet more points).

Notice that first imagination depends to some extent on knowledge. The more one knows of golf, the more one can say about what might have prevented the accident.

Similarly, the more the lawyer knows about medicine, the better will be her ability to find fault with what doctors do, or to defend them. The more she knows about finance and accounting the easier she will find it to imagine what a defendant banker or auditor should or should not have done.

The consequence is that *if you want to be a great negligence lawyer you have to know about, or be very fast at finding out about, everybody else's business.*

Notice also that there are no theoretical limits on what precautions may be thought up and made plausible in any particular case. Not only does the technology of precaution change (new safety features in cars, new knowledge in medicine, computers that transform accounting) but also it is quite possible that in any particular case the plaintiff fails to raise a fairly simple precaution that the defendant might have taken but didn't. *This is the real reason why fault is open-ended and not really susceptible in detail to rules of precedent.*

Mental state of the defendant

Students of the law of tort who have already studied some criminal law are often tempted to think about the tort of negligence in terms adopted from the classifications they have learned of the mental element (mens rea) in crimes. Smith and Hogan[5] for example, distinguish 'intention', 'recklessness' and 'negligence' and define negligence as 'the inadvertent taking of a risk' or where 'D ... did consider whether or not there was a risk and concluded, wrongly or unreasonably, that there was no risk, or so small a risk that it would have been justifiable to take it.'[6] Although these definitions are not entirely beside the point in the law of tort, they are dangerously misleading and should not be used beyond the confines of the criminal law. They over-emphasise the role of mental states in determining tort liability and distract attention from the real issues.

Even more dangerous is the attempt to try to specify whether a particular test for fault is 'subjective' or 'objective'. These terms have meanings that vary too much for any sense to be made by their use. For example, 'subjective' sometimes means 'according to what was going on in this person's head' and sometimes means 'taking into account some or many of this person's traits of character'. It is much better to say precisely what one means than to attempt to use classifications that will almost certainly be misunderstood.

Three issues, however, arising from the defendant's mental state deserve separate discussion.

5 (7th ed, 1992) 53-70. Cf Card, Cross & Jones *Criminal Law* (12th edn, 1992) 57-81.
6 Ibid p 69. But see Ashworth *Principles of Criminal Law* (1991) pp168-173 for a more civil law view.

Intentional or unintentional

A key point to understand is that in English law, the fault requirement in the tort of negligence encompasses more than wrongful inadvertence or inattention. Although 'carelessness' is the most frequently alleged form of fault in negligence cases, it is equally faulty to cause harm recklessly or intentionally. As Bramwell B announced in *Emblen v Myers*,[7] 'It is said that the act of the defendant was wilful, and therefore the plaintiff cannot recover …; but the act was negligent as well as wilful.'

There should be nothing surprising in this. Fault means doing what a reasonable person would not do, and reasonable people do not, in the normal course of things, intentionally injure others.

There is some technical argument about whether 'intentional negligence' should not be spoken of, but should instead always be referred to as 'trespass' or 'battery', and it is true that there are some practical advantages for the plaintiff in the intentional torts (eg a longer limitation period). But the best way to deal with such questions is simply to say that negligence requires fault, and fault can be either intentional or unintentional, but if the fault proven is unintentional the rules dealing with, for example, remoteness[8] are slightly different from, and slightly less advantageous for the plaintiff than if the fault proven is intentional.[9] Otherwise one ends up in faintly absurd lines of argument along the lines of 'You've sued me for the wrong thing because I'm more to blame than you say'.[10]

Children and the mentally ill

It is rare that a child or a mentally ill person commits a tort, and even when they do, they are usually not worth suing, since they rarely have substantial assets or are insured. A better solution for those cases that do arise would be to hold parents and mental institutions vicariously liable, but this solution has not been adopted by English law,[11] and the only remedy against the parent or hospital is to try to find some direct negligence on their part. For example in *Gorely v Codd*[12] a parent came under scrutiny for allowing his none-too-bright 16-year-old son to have a .22 air gun after minimal training and without supervision. The son accidently (but carelessly) shot another boy and was found liable. The plaintiff also tried to allege negligence on the part of the father for allowing the situation to

7   (1860) 6 H & N 54.
8   See below ch 4.
9   This is also the result of *Emblen v Myers* (1860) 6 H & N 54 itself, in which no objection was raised to an award of exemplary damages in a negligence case in which wilfulness had been alleged and shown. Channel B (at 59-60) for example argues that there should be no difference between 'trespass' and 'wilful negligence'.
10 But see below ch 6 on the peculiar question of the Statute of Frauds Amendment Act 1828 s 6.
11 *Moon v Towers* (1860) 8 CBNS 611.
12 [1967] 1 WLR 19. See also eg *Newton v Edgerley* [1959] 1 WLR 1031.

develop, but the court found for the father, saying that although in principle it was possible for a parent to be found to have been at fault in these circumstances, on the facts of the case the father had not acted unreasonably.

Similarly, teachers may be responsible for failure to supervise children with the result that the children cause an accident which harms the plaintiff,[13] and mental hospitals may well be liable for damage done by patients whom they release unreasonably.[14]

When mentally ill people or children do, however, commit torts, two questions arise:
(1) Should these defendants be exonerated completely on the ground that they lack the capacity to tell right from wrong? and
(2) If they do have such a capacity, should their lack of experience or mental illness be taken into account in judging whether or not they acted reasonably?

Capacity

It is possible to argue that someone who is incapable of discerning right from wrong should not be held liable in tort, in the same way that such a person could not be guilty of a crime.[15] The argument for such a position is that although tort law in general and negligence in particular may have aims, such as compensating the victims of accidents, which go beyond the mere punishment of wrongdoing, the whole point of the fault principle is that losses are shifted from plaintiff to defendant only if the defendant was a wrongdoer. The force of this point is not only a moral one, but also an economic one, for if the point of tort law is to reduce the total cost of accidents, it is hardly likely to achieve that goal by attempting to deter people who cannot be deterred.

The argument against letting those who do not know the difference between right and wrong escape from liability for negligence is that the test for fault does not require that the defendant have any particular attitude towards the harm done. It is enough that a reasonable person in the same position would have, or ought to have acted differently. Whether or not the defendant either realised or ought to have realised that what he was doing was wrong is irrelevant. All that is relevant is that a reasonable person would have acted differently.

Admittedly, this second view of the fault test means that defendants will not necessarily be deterred by tort law from acting in the same way again, for they may never be able to work out for themselves what the courts' idea of reasonableness is. But an injustice will have been done to

13 *Camarthenshire County Council v Lewis* [1955] AC 549.
14 But cf *Home Office v Dorset Yacht* [1970] AC 1004. For the question of liability for the acts of third parties generally, see below ch 4.
15 *Marsh v Loader* (1863) 14 CBNS 535, 143 ER 555 (infant under seven cannot commit felony, therefore no defence to false imprisonment that seven- year-old miscreant a thief).See now *Re C* (1995) Times, 17 March.

the plaintiff, it may be claimed, if he has suffered injury as a result of an act that a reasonable person would not have carried out, an injustice which should suffice to ground a claim to compensation in a fault-based tort.

Although these issues are of great theoretical importance, the case law is too sparse to force any particular conclusion. The overall position appears to be, however, that ability to tell right from wrong is not a necessary element of liability in negligence, but consciousness that one is acting at all is.

In *Weaver v Ward*[16] the Court of Common Pleas said, 'If a lunatic kill a man or the like, because a felony must be done animo felonico, yet in trespass, which tends only to give damages according to hurt or loss, it is not so, and therefore if a lunatic hurt a man, he shall be answerable in trespass'. Thus, it appears that the capacity to tell right from wrong is not a necessary element in tort.

Conventional wisdom[17] would have it that *Weaver v Ward* was decided at a time when the courts favoured ideas of strict liability and so it has no authority in an age of fault, an age in which, despite the movement back to strict liability, we still live. But in *Morriss v Marsden*[18] Stable J decided that in a case concerning the intentional tort of battery, it was irrelevant that the defendant was a 'certifiable lunatic' who did not know what he was doing was wrong. And *Morriss v Marsden* also says that nevertheless defendants can only be liable if they are conscious of doing the act in question—that is, if they were not in a state of trance or automatism. This rule has since been applied to negligence cases in *Waugh v James Allan*[19] and *Roberts v Ramsbottom*.[20]

As for children, no-one doubts that minors can be sued in tort,[1] but the question does not yet seem to have been faced in England of whether a very young child can be sued. The best solution may be to use the concepts developed for the mentally ill. This would mean that a child's inability to realise that what it was doing was wrong would not bar liability in itself.

It should be noted, however, that even in a case of automatism, there might still be liability if the defendant should have known in advance that he might fall into a state of automatism in circumstances in which he could have taken appropriate precautions either against falling into the state in the first place or against the specific dangers that it might cause.[2] Sufferers from diseases such as epilepsy may well, therefore, find them-selves held liable in circumstances in which those suffering from serious

---

16 (1616) Hob 134.
17 See eg *Street on Torts* (8th edn) p 522.
18 [1952] 1 All ER 925.
19 [1964] 2 Lloyd's Rep 1.
20 [1980] 1 WLR 823. Cf *Hill v Baxter* [1958] 1 QB 277. See generally Wells and Morgan 'Sheer Heart Attack: The Queen of Defences?' 40 New LJ 1782.
1   See eg *Gorely v Codd* above n 12 (16-year-old).
2   Ibid.

and permanent delusions would not be liable, for sufferers from physical conditions that do not affect the judgment of the sufferer apart from during attacks might be expected to take more precautions than those for whom no judgment is possible.

To make automatism a defence at all seems to be incompatible with a very strict application of the theory that it is sufficient fault for the defendant to have acted in a way that a reasonable person would not have acted. It is not reasonable, for example, to drive a car when unconscious.

The apparent discrepancy can be overcome by concentrating on whether the defendant can be said to have 'acted' at all, and to distinguish between cases in which the defendant 'acts' but does not understand that what he is doing is wrong, and cases in which he does not 'act' in the first place. The idea is, simply, that one can never be said properly to 'drive while unconscious'. One can only be 'unconscious at the wheel.' Driving implies an act, but in unconsciousness there is no act.

It might be objected that such a manoeuvre only evades the central question. For why, it might be asked, is it necessary for liability in negligence for there to have been an 'act' at all? The answer is that at this point the economic and the moral views of negligence are for once in agreement. Deterrence can only work on those who are conscious, so that attempting to deter the unconscious is wasteful. Moreover, we do not usually think of harm caused by someone who is unconscious as unjust—indeed we tend to think of it in the same way that we think of natural disasters.

A similar point can be made for children. A child who is so young that its behaviour could not be characterised as voluntary action, a baby breaking another baby's toy, for example, would be not liable.

A different standard?

Given that it is probably the case that children and people with mental illnesses will not escape liability altogether on the grounds that they could not appreciate that what they were doing was wrong, the question arises of whether youth or mental illness should be taken into account in judging whether these defendants were at fault.

There is, again, very little authority in English law for any particular position. In *Gough v Thorne*[3] the Court of Appeal decided that age is relevant in contributory negligence,[4] but apart from some obiter remarks[5] and an unreported case[6] there are no English cases on the standard required of children, and none at all on the standard required of people with mental illnesses.

3   [1966] 3 All ER 398.
4   See below ch 15.
5   *Watkins v Birmingham City Council* (1976) 126 NLJ 442.
6   *Stanley v Suffolk County Council*—see *Clerk & Lindsell on Torts* para 10-60.

The question can still be approached, therefore, as a matter of principle.

There are arguments both from the discouragement of risky conduct and from justice for the position that youthfulness and mental illness should be taken into account.

The argument from justice is an application of the general proposition that 'ought' implies 'can'. It is difficult to see how someone could be said to be at fault if they could not possibly have reached the standard required of them.

The argument from discouraging risky conduct is that there is no point holding a child or a mentally ill person to a standard that they cannot reach and cannot understand. In order to minimise accidents, such people should be held to a standard that represents what reasonably safe people with the same characteristics could achieve.

But there are also powerful arguments the other way. Surely it is injustice enough that plaintiffs have suffered harm as a result of behaviour that no reasonable person would have indulged in. And as for deterrence, surely there are activities, such as operating machinery or vehicles, that are simply too dangerous for children or people with mental disorders to undertake at all. The imposition of a standard that such people cannot reach simply reflects the fact that they should not have been involved in the activity at all.

Other common law jurisdictions come to a variety of conclusions. In Australia, *McHale v Watson*,[7] in which the defendant was a boy of 12, holds that children are to be judged against the standard of the ordinary child of the same age. In the United States, however, a more subtle jurisprudence has arisen based on the Minnesota case *Dellwo v Pearson*.[8]

In *Dellwo*, the plaintiff was fishing from a boat on one of Minnesota's numerous lakes when the defendant, a 12-year-old boy, steered a motorboat across the plaintiff's fishing line, causing the plaintiff's tackle to break up in such a way that the plaintiff suffered an eye injury.

At trial, the defendant argued successfully that children should be judged by the standard of children of like age, mental capacity and experience, a position that would have been in line with the view expressed in the courts of several other states.[9] But there were also US decisions which took a different line. In *Hill Transport v Everett*,[10] for example, the US Court of Appeals for the First Circuit had held that a teenage bus driver ought to be held to the standard of an adult bus driver.[11]

On the plaintiff's appeal in *Dellwo*, the Supreme Court of Minnesota produced a synthesis of these apparently contradictory lines of authority

---

7   [1966] ALR 513.
8   250 Minn 452, 107 NW 2d 859 (1961) (Supreme Court of Minnesota).
9   See eg *Charbonneau v MacRury* 84 NH 501, 153 A 457 (1931) (Supreme Court of New Hampshire).
10   145 F 2d 746 (1944).
11   At least where the defendant is the youth's employer, being held responsible on the basis not of its own negligence but of vicarious liability. See below ch 14.

by declaring that children should be judged by childish standards when engaging in childish activities (such as 'play[ing] with toys, throwing balls, [or] operating tricycles or velocipedes'). But when engaging in adult activities (such as operating an 'automobile, airplane or powerboat'), since the plaintiff has no way of discerning that the operator is a youth and so has no chance of taking necessary precautions, they should be judged by adult standards.[12]

That completes the overview of what constitutes fault. The remainder of this chapter is devoted to two specialist topics on fault—the relevance of expertise (and of the lack of it), and the problems of proving fault.

The relevance of expertise

A frequent accusation by plaintiffs in negligence cases is that the defendant did not demonstrate adequate skill in the activity in which he was engaged. Cases based on such accusations often lead to perplexity among students because it is difficult to see how they fit into the general approach to fault encapsulated in the cost-benefit test.

This perplexity about fault in skill can be dispelled if the cases are divided into three categories:
(1)   cases in which the defendant lacked the training to engage at all in the activity out of which the injury arose;
(2)   cases in which the defendant did have the necessary training but failed to use it;
(3)   cases about what the necessary level of training should be.

Cases of the first type are really about whether it is worth it, in terms of risks and benefits, for untrained people to engage in the relevant activity at all.

Cases of the second type are about whether it is worth it, given the risks inherent in the defendant's failure to act with ordinary skill, to sacrifice whatever it was that was gained by the defendant's chosen course of action.

Cases of the third type are about whether or not to accept the knock-on effects of the skill being exercised at a level that would reduce the risks in question to the level of triviality. The knock-on effects of insisting on a higher standard of skill might include general considerations such as the possibility that it might cause a reduction in the number of people who enter the profession, and therefore increased prices, or particular knock-on effects, that is effects that probably would have happened immediately in the case at hand, such as any delay that might have arisen while the professionals, after having weighed up their own level of skill and concluded that it was too low, called for someone more skilled to take over.

---

12 Cf also Restatement, Second, Torts Para 283A Comment c. Adult activities include, apparently, golf (*Neumann v Shlansky* 294 NYS 2d 628).

Is specialist training necessary?

Two cases stand out on the question of whether it is faulty to engage in an activity at all without having acquired the level of skill attained by some of the other people who engage in it.

In *Philips v William Whiteley Ltd*[13] the plaintiff arranged to have her ears pierced by a jeweller acting on behalf of the defendants. The jeweller sterilised his equipment as best he could by putting it into a flame and then into disinfectant. But he did not maintain either his equipment or his premises or his clothing at the level of cleanliness that a surgeon would when undertaking a similar minor operation. The plaintiff suffered an infected ear and blamed the jeweller.

The court took notice of the fact that at the time jewellers carried out these operations every day for large numbers of people and that they rarely resulted in infection or illness.[14]

Goddard J found for the jeweller, saying that he should be judged according to the 'standard of care which you would expect from a man of his position and training', that is as a jeweller and not as a surgeon.[15]

The second case is *The Lady Gwendolen*.[16] Guinness the brewers, who ran a small fleet of ships to transport their beer from Dublin to Liverpool, failed to impress on the masters of their vessels the dangers of relying too much on radar in foggy conditions. Guinness claimed that they were in the brewing business, not the shipping business (indeed not one of their directors or senior managers had nautical experience), and that they should be judged accordingly. The Court of Appeal, however, after stressing how dangerous it was to allow over-reliance on radar and how onerous the duties of ship owners were, found against Guinness. 'It was no excuse,' said Sellers LJ, 'that ... their main business was that of brewers ... In their capacity as shipowners they must be judged by the standard of the ordinary reasonable shipowner.'[17]

On the face of it, these two cases are near to contradictory. *Philips* holds that a person need not reach the higher standards of members of another profession active in the same field, whereas *The Lady Gwendolen* says that engaging in an activity implies complying with the standards of those who specialise in it.

One might try to distinguish between the cases on the ground that doctors do not specialise in ear piercing, whereas shipowners specialise in running ships. But it is not clear why such a distinction makes any difference. If shipowners were generally companies engaged primarily in some other activity, would that reduce Guinness' obligation to ensure that radar was being properly used?

13 [1938] 1 All ER 566.
14 At p 568.
15 Goddard J, in order to make his judgment appeal-proof, also found that in any case he was not convinced that the jeweller's lack of sterility was the cause of the infection.
16 *Arthur Guinness, Son & Co (Dublin) Ltd v The Freshfield (Owners): The Lady Gwendolen* [1965] P 294.
17 At p 333.

The real difference between the two cases is simply this: the public benefit of easy access to ear piercing at jewellers' shops outweighs the risks of operating as an ear piercer in non-surgical conditions, whereas the risks of operating as a shipper without knowledge of shipping outweigh the public benefit in allowing easy access to ship ownership—especially for those who could bring experts in the field into their top management but decline to do so.

Experts who fail to meet the ordinary standards of their profession

The basic rule in the assessment of fault when the defendant is an expert is that the expert is expected to act according to the ordinary standards of a person in the same profession.[18]

The basis of this rule is quite straightforward. An expert is someone with certain skills. It should therefore be quite easy for the expert to exercise those skills. Moreover, an expert should also be able to see when he or she is no longer up to the job.

It is, however, unlikely that people with special skills simply forget to use them. When they fail to come up to the ordinary standards of their profession, it is usually for some reason other than inadvertence. And it is on that reason that attention falls in professional negligence cases.

Sometimes the reason is a good one. For example, a racing driver when driving on an ordinary road may decide not to use his special techniques for braking because to do so might give such a fright to cars following him that they might crash.

At other times, the reason is not acceptable, for example that a doctor was drunk or a lawyer wanted to go to a party rather than read another law report.

Professionals are usually quite capable of meeting the standards of their profession, but when they fail to do so for some purpose or other, the value of the purpose has to be judged against the risk involved to potential victims.

What should the level of ordinary competence for the profession be?

It is more awkward to decide what level of skill should be expected of a profession. The higher the level of skill required for a profession the fewer people will complete its selection and training process and so the more expensive the profession will become for its clients. On the other hand the higher the standards, the fewer the accidents that will occur (assuming that clients do not simply go to unauthorised practitioners). This balance is inherently difficult to strike. The trade-off between safety and the availability of professional services is often the subject of political controversy.

18 *Bolam* see above.

The difficulties for the courts are made worse by the fact that information about a profession—for example what counts as good or bad service, and what the effects of higher training levels would be—is often difficult for outsiders, even judges, to interpret.[19]

It may be that it is the difficulty in assessing expert evidence that has induced courts to adopt a further test from *Bolam v Friern Hospital Management Committee*.[20] The first test from *Bolam* is that already mentioned, that professionals should come up to the 'standard of the ordinary skilled man exercising and professing to have that special skill.'[1] The second test, however, is about what the court should do where there is more than one view in a profession about what the proper standard should be. The answer is that one should ask not whether the defendants followed the best course open to them, but 'whether the defendants in acting in the way they did were acting in accordance with a respected professional opinion.'[2] The effect of this rule, the second rule in *Bolam*, is that a conflict of expert evidence should usually be decided in favour of the defence unless it can be shown that the point of view propounded by the defence is not just a minority view, but is a view which is not even respectable.

By applying the second rule in *Bolam*, the courts may be able confine themselves to questions of the credibility of the witnesses, and may play down the importance of assessing the content of what the witnesses said.

Bolam and other professions

It is clear that the first rule in *Bolam* applies to all professions and skilled occupations.[3] But it is far from clear whether the second rule in *Bolam* equally applies to all professions. Certainly it does apply to valuers of art[4] and to auctioneers[5] and it may apply to surveyors.[6] But *Edward Wong Finance Ltd v Johnson, Stokes and Master*[7] shows that it may not apply to solicitors.

The defendants in *Edward Wong*, 'a long-established and highly res–pected firm of Hong Kong solicitors' used a technique for completing a purchase of land that was very commonly used in Hong Kong and widely

---

19 Judges nevertheless attempt to understand a wide range of topics—and not just medicine, see eg *Wimpey v Poole* [1984] 2 Lloyd's Rep 499 (civil engineering) and *Singer and Friedlander v John D Wood* (1977) 243 Estates Gazette 212 [1977] EGD 569 (surveying).
20 [1957] 1 WLR 582.
1   At p 586.
2   At p 587. See also *Hill v Potter* [1984] 1 WLR 641n and *Defreitas v O'Brien* (1995) Times, 16 February (medical opinion has to be 'substantial' but a small number of specialists can constitute an adequately substantial body of opinion).
3   See Lloyd LJ in *Gold v Haringey Health Authority* [1988] QB 481: 'The *Bolam* test is not confined to ... medicine'.
4   *Luxmoore-May v Messenger May Baverstock* [1990] 1 WLR 1009.
5   *Alchemy (International) v Tattersalls Ltd* (1985) 276 Estates Gazette 675.
6   *Singer & Friedlander v John D Wood* (1977) 243 Estates Gazette 212.
7   [1984] AC 296.

praised for its speed, efficacy and suitability for local conditions. The technique did, however, expose the buyers of the land to a risk of embezzle–ment by the seller's solicitor. One version of the Hong Kong style completion did in fact reduce the risk of embezzlement to trivial levels, but at the cost of a delay while extra checks were made. But it was not suggested that the defendants' version of the Hong Kong completion was anything apart from respectable. Very few deals went wrong and the risks seemed quite low. Nevertheless the Privy Council decided that the defendants had been at fault, on the ground that the cost of the precautions were low in view of the reduction in the risk.

Bolam was not cited in *Edward Wong*, and perhaps the case can be dismissed as having been decided per incuriam. Alternatively, a better explanation might be that since *Bolam* is a way for the courts to avoid having to understand technical issues too deeply, it should not apply in a case about lawyers, since the courts should know the law.[8]

But, even beyond fields in which the judges have more confidence in their technical abilities, there is some evidence that the second rule in *Bolam* is not altogether satisfactory. This is so even in its core field of application, namely medical negligence.

Bolam has been applied both to medical diagnosis and to treatment. Its extension to the amount of information that a doctor should give a patient before asking for consent to carry out an operation, however, has proven more controversial.

In *Sidaway v Board of Governors of the Bethlem Royal Hospital and the Maudsley Hospital*,[9] the plaintiff underwent an operation on her cervical vertebrae, an operation which, no matter how skilfully it is performed carries a risk of 1% to 2% of side effects 'ranging from the mild to the catastrophic.' The plaintiff did indeed suffer serious side effects. There was, however, no evidence of any fault on the part of the surgeon in the way he carried out the operation. What the plaintiff complained of was that she had not been fully informed of the risks by the surgeon, and that had she known of the risks she would not have given her consent. The House of Lords decided to apply both *Bolam* tests to the case.[10] The test for whether or not a doctor has given enough information to a patient is therefore whether the doctor's decision would receive the backing of a respectable body of medical opinion.

But it is noticeable that two of the judges in the House of Lords, Lords Bridge and Keith, although they did not go so far as Lord Scarman, who would have not used the second rule in *Bolam* at all, were uneasy about the prospect of accepting purely expert medical opinion on a question about which, in reality, the patient is the only real expert, namely whether the risk in question is worth taking in the light of the physical condition it is

---

8   But nb *Montriou v Jefferys* (1825) 2 C & P 113: 'God forbid that it should be imagined that an attorney, or a counsel or even a judge is bound to know all the law'.

9   [1985] AC 871.

10 Lord Scarman disagreed. He would have required the surgeon to show that the patient had received sufficient information so that a reasonable person in the patient's position could have made a rational decision about whether to have the operation —unless the particular patient could be shown to have been too irrational to come to such a decision.

meant to alleviate. Lord Bridge said that if an expert witness were to tell the court that the medical profession believed that it was all right not to inform a patient of a gross risk, for example a 10% risk of total paralysis, a judge would be right to ignore the expert and declare the doctor to have been at fault.

Similarly, there may be some doubts as to the application of the second rule in *Bolam* to surveyors. In *Singer & Friedlander* the court, admittedly with the help of experts, laid down that a surveyor whose valuation was, even in the most extraordinary of circumstances, more than 15% wrong was at fault, even though an expert witness might appear to say the opposite.

It is possible, therefore, that the second rule in *Bolam* will not, in the long run, turn out to be quite the surrender of judicial to professional opinion that it seems to be.

> **'If an actor has more than reasonable skill, he must probably exercise that which he has.'** (Harper and James *Law of Torts (1956) para 16.6. Cf Restatement, Second, Torts paras 289(b) and 299A.)*

Take the racing driver who fails to use his special skills driving on the ordinary road, with the result that an accident happens which would otherwise not have occurred. Is it the case that the racing driver is not at fault only if he can show that if he had used his special skills the surprise that such an event would have engendered in other road users would have been even more dangerous than not using them?

One argument is that the racing driver should not be made liable under any circumstances because he was not holding himself out to be a racing driver. (See eg Baker *Law of Tort* p154). Is this argument a good one?

Certainly cases such as *Wimpey Construction v Poole* [1984] 2 Lloyd's Rep 499 give the impression that it is necessary for a person explicitly to profess to have a certain skill level of before he or she can be held to it, at least if the level of skill concerned is higher than the ordinary level. And in *Bolam* itself, McNair J refers to the standard being that in professional negligence of the ordinary practitioner 'professing' to have the same skills.

And yet, this view may be profoundly mistaken. Most of the cases that adopt it are contract cases, in which the level of skill 'professed' may well be relevant to interpreting the deal between the parties, but one cannot say that therefore there can be no liability in tort without a similar act of professing. And as for *Bolam*, one should note that McNair J when talking about 'professing' is referring not to the defendant, but to the reasonable professional against whom the defendant is to be compared. The defendant does not have to profess anything. It is just that the defendant's conduct should be compared with the standard of an ordinary person who professes to have the same skills.

Consider the following example. The plaintiff drives into a ditch on a deserted country road and is knocked unconscious. The defendant, a doctor, comes across the plaintiff and proceeds to attempt to effect some first aid. The doctor, however, acts in way which, though it would be understandable for a lay person, is for a doctor incompetent, and he succeeds only in making the plaintiff's injuries worse. The plaintiff sues the doctor. Can the doctor be heard to say that there should be no liability because at no time did he make any representation to anyone, either the plaintiff or any third party, and so he should be judged not by the standards of the medical profession but as a lay person?

Learners

In *Nettleship v Weston*[11] the plaintiff gave driving lessons to the defendant. During the course of the defendant's third lesson, she panicked and steered the car into a lamppost. The plaintiff suffered a broken kneecap. The trial judge decided that the defendant had not been at fault. She had done her best and that was enough.

The Court of Appeal (Lord Denning MR, Salmon and Megaw LJJ) disagreed with the trial judge and found for the plaintiff. (Nevertheless they found that the plaintiff was half to blame and they awarded only half damages.)

Lord Denning said that the law requires the same standard of care from a learner driver as from any other driver, and he cited *Glasgow Corpn v Muir*[12] for the proposition that the reasonable man standard 'eliminates the personal equation and is independent of the idiosyncrasies of the particular person whose conduct is called into question'. Lord Denning continued 'A learner driver may be doing his best but his incompetent best is not good enough.'[13] Salmon LJ and Megaw LJ agreed that the learner driver should be held to the standard of the ordinary qualified driver.

One might wonder how someone could be said to be at fault for failing to meet a standard that she could not possibly reach. No learner driver can drive consistently with the degree of competence ordinarily achieved by qualified drivers.

Note that the usual solution to a case in which someone has attempted something that he ought to have realised was beyond his capabilities is to say that it was careless to try in the first place. If you are middle-aged and unfit, it is unreasonable even to try to run a marathon. But this solution is not available in *Nettleship v Weston*, unless one is prepared to say that it is unreasonable for perfectly ordinary people to try to learn to drive. Perhaps a judge of advanced views on the dangers of the motor car to the environ–

11 [1971] 2 QB 691.
12 [1943] AC 448, 457 per Lord Macmillan.
13 [1971] 2 QB 691 at p 699.

ment might be tempted to come to such a conclusion, but most judges would say that it is not inherently unreasonable to learn to drive.

On what argument, then, does *Nettleship v Weston* rest?

Salmon LJ said that the ordinary driver standard should apply unless there was a special relationship between the plaintiff and the defendant under which the plaintiff could be said to have agreed to a lower standard.[14] But this line of thought achieves little apart from to suggest reasons (consent, contract) why the ordinary standard of care might exceptionally be disregarded. It does not explain why the ordinary driver standard applies in the first place.

Megaw LJ said that the standard of the ordinary qualified driver was the only one available. If lower standards were applied to learner drivers, surely, Megaw LJ claimed,[15] one would have to have lower standards for newly-qualified drivers (or indeed newly-qualified surgeons), or for drivers who had taken a significant number of lessons but who had not yet passed the driving test. 'I … do not think that our legal process,' he concluded, 'could successfully or satisfactorily cope with the task of fairly assessing … such varying standards, depending on such complex and elusive factors.'[16]

But the law often deals in varying standards. The degree of skill in surgery expected of a jeweller is less than that expected of a family doctor, and in turn the standard expected of a family doctor is less than that expected of a surgeon.

It is true that in cases where varying standards are used, expert evidence has to be available to assist the court in formulating the appropriate standard, and where there is no such evidence (as, perhaps in the cases of the newly-qualified driver or doctor), no such standard could be formulated. But this point cannot explain why the court should choose, from among the standards which could be formulated, ones which are more difficult to comply with than the defendant can possibly manage, rather than ones that are less difficult to comply with. In particular, Megaw LJ's argument fails altogether to meet the point that it is possible to set a minimum standard without having to set multiple higher standards.

For example, it would be fairly simple to construct a plausible standard for learner drivers in Britain. Learner drivers in Britain must obtain a provisional driving licence, when at the wheel they must be accompanied by a suitable qualified driver, and they must not drive on motorways. One might plausibly add that no-one should attempt to learn to drive if a reasonable person in their position would have concluded, before they started, that the attempt was doomed to failure, eg where the person concerned is blind, and also that learner drivers even on their first lesson should be expected to know some very basic things, eg which side of the road we drive on.

Note that this is a perfectly understandable and easily applicable standard, pace Megaw LJ. But it does have one serious drawback: it is too

14 At p 703.
15 At pp 707-708.
16 Ibid.

easy to comply with. At the moment to obtain a provisional driving licence, for example, requires no proof of knowledge of the rules of the road or of theoretical knowledge about the controls of a motor vehicle. On the standard formulated in the last paragraph, cases in which the plaintiff would succeed would be extremely rare.

At this point we should consider Lord Denning's justification for the court's decision in *Nettleship v Weston*:

> 'The high standard ... imposed ... is, I believe, the result of the policy of the Road Traffic Acts. Parliament requires every driver to be insured against third party risks. The reason is so that a person injured by a motor car should not be left to bear the loss on his own. ... But the injured person is only able to recover if the driver is liable in law. So the judges see to it that he is liable.'[17]

Lord Denning's point is that driving is inherently a dangerous activity, but it is not one that the courts are prepared to declare faulty in itself. Learning to drive is even more inherently dangerous, but it is a necessary condition for being able to take part in the activity of driving. It is wrong, however, (whether because it is immoral or because it is economically inefficient) to make the victims of the inherently dangerous activity of learning to drive pay for the accidents it causes. The law therefore devises a sort of strict liability by imposing a duty that is too high for any real learner driver to be able to comply with it.

As Lord Denning said:

> 'Thus we are, in this branch of the law, moving away from the concept 'No liability without fault.' We are beginning to apply the test: 'On whom should the risk fall? Morally the learner driver is not at fault; but legally she is liable ... because she is insured and the risk should fall on her.'[18]

Nettleship v Weston is therefore best explained as the imposition of strict liability on learner drivers for the accidents they cause in learning to drive, the costs they bear as a whole via their own or their instructors' insurance premiums.[19]

Proof of fault

To show that the defendant was at fault it is necessary to show that there was some precaution against the accident that the defendant might easily have taken, but which the defendant unreasonably failed to take. The case

17 At p 700.
18 Ibid.
19 Does this line of reasoning also help to explain the attitude of the American courts to children who engage in adult activities?

against the defendant is a combination of what happened (how the accident happened, what the defendant did) and a hypothesis about what might have happened instead had the defendant taken proper care. These two elements are interdependent, for it is difficult to make a convincing case about what would have happened had due care been taken if it is unclear exactly what did happen. Furthermore, it is often difficult for the plaintiff to be precise about what precautions should have been taken.

This section is about short cuts that the parties, especially the plaintiff, might take in order to prove fault when more direct methods of proof seem to present difficulties.

General standards

The first short cut to a finding of fault is for the plaintiff to allege that the defendant did not act in accordance with the general standards prevailing among those engaged in the activity. The idea is to show that the defendant must have been able to act in a way that was both safe and reasonable in terms of cost, because many other people either manage to do so, or have subscribed to public standards that imply that they could manage to do so.

But although the failure of the defendant to reach the standards of common practice must be relevant to fault, the courts say that it is not decisive. This is because the precautions taken according to the common standard may be thought by the court to be unnecessarily onerous in the light of the risks. It is also possible for the common practice to be too onerous simply because it is ineffective.

In *Brown v Rolls Royce*,[20] for example, an employer had not followed a common practice of supplying barrier cream to prevent workers from contracting dermatitis. But there was no evidence that barrier cream was either effective in general against dermatitis or that it would have prevented the plaintiff in the particular case from contracting it. The employer was found not to have been at fault.

On the other hand, it is also not decisive in favour of the defence that the defendant acted in accordance with common practice or generally accepted standards. Common practice and generally accepted standards may quite easily be too lax.[1] Practices and standards are evidence of what could be done, but are not determinative of ought to be done.

20 [1960] 1 WLR 210.
1 *Cavanagh v Ulster Weaving Co Ltd* [1960] AC 145. For a horrifying illustration of what the law might be like if the common practice of employers was allowed to define reasonableness, see the nineteenth century American case *Lehigh & Wilkes-Barre Coal Corpn v Hayes* 128 Pa 294 (Supreme Court of Pennsylvania,1889).

Subsequent remedial measures

The defendant takes action after the accident to prevent the same thing happening again. Is this evidence against the defendant that he or she was at fault in allowing the accident to happen in the first place?

It would be most convenient for some plaintiffs if it were so, for then any subsequent remedial action would count as evidence against the defendant. But it is likely that such evidence would not be admitted.[2]

In the first place, it is possible that the danger only came to light because of the very accident about which the plaintiff is suing. If so, subsequent remedial measures do not show that the defendant was at fault, for fault has to be judged according to the situation as it appeared at the time of the accident.

Secondly, new information of other kinds may have come to light since the accident. Again, in such a case, evidence of subsequent remedial action is not evidence of fault.

Thirdly, if such evidence were admitted, it might mean that potential defendants would think twice about taking remedial steps, so endangering more people.

Res ipsa loquitur

Lastly, the plaintiff may lack evidence of what actually happened, but might attempt to make up for the deficiency by means of inferences from what is known. These inferences are often called instances of the application of the maxim res ipsa loquitur ('The thing itself speaks'), although the recitation of any particular Latin phrase is not necessary for the efficacy of the inference itself, nor is the res ipsa inference the only permitted inference of fault.[3]

The origin of the use of inferences to help in showing that the defendant was at fault lies in the period when negligence cases were still tried by a judge and jury. At the end of the presentation of the plaintiff's case, the defence might move that there was no case for the defendant to answer. The judge would then be required to decide whether the plaintiff had produced enough evidence for the trial to be worth continuing. If the plaintiff had not produced any evidence of fault, the proper course for the judge was not to allow the case to go to the jury, but give immediate judgment for the defendant. If, on the other hand, the judge decided that the defendant did have a case to answer, the judge would not pronounce judgment for the plaintiff, but rather would merely ask the defence to put on its case, if it had one.

2   See *Stevens v Boston Elevated Railway Co* 184 Mass 476, 69 NE 338 (1903) (Supreme Judicial Court of Massachussetts).
3   See eg *Henderson v Jenkins* [1970] AC 282.

For example, in *Scott v London and St Katherine Docks Co*,[4] the plaintiff was visiting the defendant's warehouses when a large bag of sugar fell on him. The defendant's employees had been nearby loading sugar using a hoist. But there was no evidence of what exactly had happened. The judge at trial thought that the plaintiff had not shown enough evidence for the case to go to the jury, and he directed the jury to find for the defendant. The plaintiff appealed, claiming a new trial on the ground that there was, even on the evidence presented, enough to ask a jury whether there had been carelessness. The plaintiff won both in the Court of Exchequer and the Court of Exchequer Chamber. The latter court said that, although there must be reasonable evidence of negligence, 'Where a thing is shown to be under the management of the defendant, ... and the accident is such as, in the ordinary course of things, does not happen if those who have the management of the machinery use proper care, it affords reasonable evidence, in the absence of explanation from the defendant, that the accident arose from want of care.'

In modern trials, without a jury and in which the judge decides, the motion that the defendant has no case to answer is falling into disuse. In consequence, res ipsa loquitur has now become a set of rules of thumb by which courts may be guided into concluding that the defendant was at fault even when there is no direct evidence.[5] If the conditions of res ipsa are present, an inference of fault will be made. But if they are not present, nevertheless the court may decide that such an inference is still proper.[6]

The conditions of the res ipsa inference are:

* The defendant had sole control, or probably had sole control over whatever caused the injury.
* The circumstances are such that such events do not occur unless someone is at fault.
* There is no other direct evidence of what caused the accident.

The defendant can defeat res ipsa by refuting one of the conditions. This usually comes down to putting forward a plausible explanation[7] for what happened that does not involve fault on the defendant's part.[8]

Other uses of res ipsa loquitur

Res ipsa and similar inferential techniques can be put to a variety of uses. Two deserve particular mention—overcoming the problem of impacted information, and the creation of strict liability out of fault.

---

4   (1865) 3 H & C 596.
5   See *Lloyde v West Midlands Gas Board* [1971] 1 WLR 749.
6   *Barkway v South Wales Transport Co Ltd* [1950] AC 185.
7   *Woods v Duncan* [1946] AC 401, 441.
8   *Colvilles Ltd v Devine* [1969] 1 WLR 475.

Impacted information

The problem of impacted information[9] arises when one side to a transaction has information of great relevance to the welfare of both parties but has no incentive to share the information with the other.

The legal version of impacted information is where the defendant is the only person who knows the truth about some vital piece of evidence and, of course, refuses to divulge it.

Courts on both sides of the Atlantic have responded to such situations by using res ipsa type inferences. In *Ybarra v Spangard* 25 Cal 2d 486, 154 P 2d 687 (1944), for example, the Supreme Court of California had to resolve a dispute between a patient who had undergone an operation and emerged with a mysterious frozen shoulder and the medical team he was suing, all of whom knew what had happened but were refusing to say. The court ruled that res ipsa could apply collectively, with the result that every member of the medical team would be found liable unless they revealed exactly what had happened.

Similarly, in *Henderson v Jenkins* [1970] AC 282, the defendant lorry owners were the only people in a position to know about a crucial piece of information, namely where the lorry had been and what it had been carrying, information without which it was impossible to say whether or not the defendant had carried out adequate safety inspections.

Creating strict liability

The other, perhaps less legitimate, use of res ipsa loquitur is, rather as in *Nettleship v Weston*, to create strict liability out of the material of the fault regime. In *Ward v Tesco* [1976] 1 WLR 810, for example, res ipsa was said to apply to the case of a shopper who was injured after slipping on some yoghurt that had been spilt on the floor of one of the defendants' shops. The evidence was that the floor was cleaned five or six times a day, and additionally when any spillage was noticed by staff. The court, however, refused to count Tesco's account of its cleaning procedures as an explanation of how the accident could have come about without fault. The court wanted Tesco to say exactly how the accident had occurred, something that nobody knew. By holding the defendant liable for not having information that no-one has, the *Ward* case therefore effectively creates a strict liability.

9   See O Williamson *Economic Institutions of Capitalism* (1985).

Chapter 4

Causation and remoteness

KEY POINTS

* There are two separate requirements—causation and remoteness.
* Causation concerns whether the court believes that had the defendant acted properly, the accident would not have happened.
* Remoteness is primarily about whether the presence of other causes of the accident, for example the acts of other people or the plaintiff's previous physical condition, should exonerate the defendant.
* There are two approaches to remoteness. The traditional approach stresses the magnitude of any intervening events. The *Wagon Mound* approach stresses foreseeability.
* *Wagon Mound* remoteness has become simply a requirement that the type of harm and the type of plaintiff be foreseeable. There is no need for the exact way in which the accident came about or the extent of harm to be foreseeable.
* Both forms of remoteness rule operate in modern negligence law. If the damage is too remote in either sense of remoteness, the plaintiff's case fails.

Having established that the defendant was at fault, the plaintiff in a negligence action has to go on to show that the defendant's faulty conduct was responsible for the loss that the plaintiff suffered. The law tests for responsibility in two ways and the plaintiff has to prove both in order to succeed. The first is that the defendant's fault must have caused the harm to the plaintiff in a factual sense. The second is that the harm must be morally attributable to the defendant's fault in the light of the harm's other factual causes, whether natural events or the human acts. These tests go by several names. Sometimes the first is called 'cause in fact' and the second 'legal cause'. Sometimes the first is called 'factual cause' and the second 'proximate cause'. Here, to avoid using the word 'cause' for both concepts, and to emphasise that the first test has more to do with the facts of the case whereas the latter has more to do with judgments about the facts, the first test is called simply 'causation' and the second test is called 'remoteness.'

The function of causation

In one sense, the proof of causation is inherent in the proof of fault, since one of the conditions of being found to be at fault is that the defendant, by acting differently, could have prevented the injury to the plaintiff. If there was nothing the defendant could have done to have prevented the injury to the plaintiff, the defendant could not have been at fault. And to say that the defendant was at fault is to say that the defendant could reasonably have prevented the harm. Strictly, therefore, fault implies causation.

English judges have not taken this point, however. They tend to believe that it is possible for the defendant to have been 'at fault' in circumstances in which the faulty act did not 'cause' the harm. Logically, though not explicitly, what the judges must mean by 'carelessness' or 'fault' is, therefore, something less than a full finding of fault. It is rather a provisional finding that the defendant will be found to be at fault as long as it is established that if the defendant had acted properly the plaintiff's injuries would not have occurred. This section assumes that such a finding of imperfect fault has been made.

But before we look at the detail of the ways in which the English courts tackle the notoriously difficult problems that their notion of causation produces, there is a prior question that should be asked if any sense of direction is to be maintained as we enter the maze of causal argument. It is simply this: Why should causation matter in negligence?

Notice immediately that a legal duty to compensate need not depend on a need to show that the defendant's conduct caused the plaintiff's injury. In the case of a contract of insurance, for example, the person with the duty to compensate, the insurer, does not need to have been at fault for the duty to compensate to arise. But where the duty to compensate is based on fault, it is unusual for a duty to compensate to arise without a need to show causation. This is partly because of the inherent connection between fault and causation noted above, that fault in its full sense implies causation, and partly because the duty to compensate is difficult to justify unless the plaintiff suffers actual damage; but if the plaintiff has suffered damage, it seems pointless to require the plaintiff to prove that the defendant acted badly without asking the plaintiff also to show a connection between the two.

Note, however, that there is another problem with a form of liability that requires proof of fault without proof of causation, a problem which provides a clue to the central function of causation in negligence. It is that such a form of liability would allow the plaintiff to sue anyone in the world. The plaintiff could pick on any act whose total social value was less than the cost of the plaintiff's injury and establish the liability of the actor towards the plaintiff. **One function of the causation requirement is therefore to reduce the number of potential defendants to manageable proportions**.

But why use a causation requirement rather than some other method of reducing the number of potential defendants? One might, for example, limit liability to those who can afford to pay—that is, one could establish an explicit 'deep pocket' rule. And if it is objected that such a scheme of liability would mean that the law would cease to have any deterrence value, there is another scheme that combines fault, compensation and deterrence without using causation. Such a scheme would work by providing compensation payments to accident victims out of a fund accumulated from contributions from all who have acted in a risky way, whether or not harm in fact ensued on the particular occasion when they acted riskily.

Notice, however, that the no-causation fund has in one respect an effect similar to that of the deep pocket rule, namely that the individual accident victim no longer has a claim against an individual wrongdoer, but instead against a collective fund. Another important function of the causation requirement should now be clear. Although causation has a deterrence function as well, the requirement for causation in negligence (and in torts generally) arises primarily out of the desire to maintain a system in which individual plaintiffs have rights against individual defendants. **Causation is necessary if the compensation of the victims of accidents is to remain in the realm of private law, in which individuals or organisations have rights and duties with regard to one another without further recourse to the institutions of the state.**

Cause in fact—basic concepts

The basic idea of causation is that the plaintiff has to show that if the defendant had not acted unreasonably the plaintiff would not have been injured. The simplest way of putting this is the 'but-for' test. Would the plaintiff have suffered loss but for the fault of the defendant?

Thus, in *Barnett v Chelsea and Kensington Hospital Management Committee*[1] the defendant hospital escaped liability for the death of the plaintiff's husband despite the fact that he had been abandoned uncared for in the casualty department because the court decided that he would have died anyway, even if he had been treated properly and on time.

But the 'but-for' test is not strictly adequate. This can be seen most clearly in the notorious three house fire problem. Suppose that there are three adjoining houses. At around the same time, the occupants of the two outer houses carelessly allow their houses to catch fire. The fire spreads and burns down the middle house. The owner of the middle house sues the occupants of both the other houses for negligence. The occupant of the

---

1   [1969] 1 QB 428.

first house replies: 'I may have been careless, but have I caused your loss? Let us apply the but-for test. But for my carelessness would your house have escaped being burned down? The answer is no, for the fire from the other house would still have destroyed your house.' The plaintiff then turns to the occupant of the other house, but receives the same reply: 'If I had not acted carelessly, it would have made no difference. Your house would still have burned down.'

Clearly, it would be an absurd result for both defendants in the three house fire problem to escape liability on causal grounds. It is true that it is hard to say that either of the two defendants as individuals could easily have prevented the harm to the plaintiff, since to have done so would have involved not only acting carefully with respect to their own property, but also preventing the carelessness, or the consequences of the carelessness, of the other defendant. But jointly, between them, the defendants could have prevented the harm by acting carefully.

A number of ways out of the three house fire problem could be suggested. For example, one could say that the combination of the acts of the two defendants was a but-for cause, so that the act of each should count as a cause. But although convenient, this is not really a general solution, since the combination of any other act whatsoever with a genuine but-for cause of harm would itself be a but-for cause, but it does not follow that just because the other act may in some way be faulty, that the other actor should be held liable along with the author of the but-for cause. By driving too fast, I carelessly run you down. The car travelling in front of me was also speeding, but did not hit you. It is true that the combination of my speeding and the speeding of the car in front is a but-for cause. But does it follow that the driver in front should also be held liable? Surely not.

One might say instead that where the combination of two events is a but-for cause, but each of the two events is not a but-for cause, then both events should count as causes. But this is artificial. The combination may be a cause, but does it follow that each of events making up the combination is thereby transformed into a cause? The plaintiff is not suing the combination of two defendants, but the two defendants separately.

A more satisfactory way out of the three house fire problem, and one with a more general application, is to replace but-for with the more accurate 'necessary element of a sufficient set' test (the NESS test). In the NESS test, the defendant's carelessness causes the plaintiff's injury if it was a necessary step in a series of events which were in themselves sufficient to produce the harmful result. It does not matter whether there were other sufficient sets around, as long as the set under discussion was sufficient.[2]

Thus, in the three house fire problem, one asks whether the fire started carelessly in the first defendant's house was sufficient to burn down the plaintiff's house. Clearly it was. Even if the other fire had not happened the plaintiff's house would still have been destroyed. Then one asks whether that sequence of events would still be sufficient if the defendant had not

2 See generally Wright 'Causation in Tort Law' (1985) 73 Calif L Rev 1735, improving on Fraser and Howarth 'More Concern for Cause' (1984) 4 Legal Studies 131.

been careless. The answer is probably not. The defendant's carelessness was therefore a necessary element of a set of events that was sufficient to produce the harm. Hence it caused the harm. The same analysis applies equally to the fire started by the other defendant. Both defendants are careless, both cause the harm, both are liable.

As we shall see below, NESS analysis is useful in sorting out a number of traditional problems in causation. NESS helps in the deterrence function of causation because, like but-for, it eliminates from consideration events and acts that could have made no difference at all to what happened, but it does not do so in a way that allows individuals to escape responsibility when they happen to have acted, perhaps unintentionally, in a collective way that, under but-for, would allow them to escape.

But there is a problem with the NESS test. The problem lies not so much in the notion of sufficiency, with what counts as a sequence of events sufficient to produce a certain result—which, although not absolutely clear philosophically, is usable in almost all practical cases—but in the idea of a 'necessary' element. What if something else could have happened which would have produced the same result? Is the defendant's carelessness then a 'necessary' element of the set? What is the range of other events that one is allowed to imagine to have happened instead of the defendant's careless act? Might one say, in the three house fire problem, for example, that since someone else might have come along and started a fire in the defendant's house, the defendant's carelessness was not a 'necessary' element of a set of events that was sufficient to produce the harm to the plaintiff?

Most people would answer 'no' to the last question. It is simply an implausible scenario that some complete outsider would turn up and set fire to the defendant's house. But it is difficult to say exactly why this scenario is so implausible that it should not be considered at all, whereas if, for example, it were suggested that the fire would have started even if the defendant had done nothing because of some undiscoverable electrical fault, such a scenario would be taken seriously.

The upshot of this line of argument is that, as Hart and Honoré pointed out in their celebrated analysis of causation,[3] what we think of as causation always contains an element of our expectations of normal sequences of events. What is plausible or implausible is a matter of experience and judgment rather than strict deduction.[4]

'Probability'

At this point a warning is in order on the subject of 'probability' or 'risk'. Sometimes, courts and commentators speak as if 'causation' were the same

---

3   *Causation in the Law* (2nd ed) (Oxford; Clarendon, 1985).
4   One particularly troublesome set of cases to which this insight may be profitably applied are those in which the defendant, although not otherwise at fault, injures the plaintiff at a time when the defendant did not hold a relevant licence to carry on the activity that led to the accident—eg a driving licence. See below ch 7 for further discussion.

as 'probability.' One celebrated, though now largely discredited, House of Lords opinion[5] referred to 'materially increasing the risk' of the occurrence of an event as equivalent to 'causing' it.

These kinds of remark serve largely only to confuse. Causation and probability are not the same. If something has a 10% chance of happening, and then happens, what caused it to happen was not the 10% chance that it would happen. The cause may be unknown, but whatever it was, it was not the 'chance'.

Confusion would be avoided, although it is admittedly unlikely to come to pass, if judges and commentators were to decide that 'probability' refers not to the state of the world but instead only to the state of our knowledge about the world. When we say that something is 'unlikely' to be the case, including when we say that something is 'unlikely' to have caused something else, what we mean, or at least ought to mean, is that we are uncertain about whether it is the case. We do not, or should not, mean that we think that sometimes it is true and sometimes it is not. 'The defendant materially increased the risk of harm occurring to the plaintiff' therefore refers to our beliefs about what happened, rather than to anything the defendant physically did. It means 'I would be less uncertain about saying that harm was going to happen to the plaintiff if I was told that the defendant was acting as she did than if I was not given that information.' Probability is a way of talking about our degree of certainty and about changes in our degree of certainty in response to new information.[6]

Causal puzzle cases

We now turn to the case law and to those cases on causation, small in number but significant in other ways, that have puzzled courts and commentators.

---

5   Lord Wilberforce in *McGhee v National Coal Board* [1973] 1 WLR 1.
6   The approach taken in this paragraph is that of the thorough-going Bayesian. See B Robertson and GA Vignaux 'Probability: The Logic of the Law' (1993) 13 OJLS 457, basing their analysis on Edward Jaynes 'Probability Theory: The Logic of Science' (Unpublished; fragmentary version of July 1993 on file with author). A textbook is not the place to demonstrate the superiority of Jaynes's Bayesian approach to that taken by eg Richard Eggleston in *Evidence Proof and Probability* (subjective frequentism) or by L Jonathan Cohen in *The Probable and the Provable* (barely comprehensible 'Baconianism'), but Jaynes's approach is used time and again in this chapter and its degree of success will be left to the reader to judge. It also requires some reconsideration of the author's own views, see Howarth 'O Madness of Discourse' (1987) 96 Yale LJ 1389, especially at 1416-1417, although the ability of Jaynes's approach to accommodate the possibility of a real 'probabilistic causal field' as opposed to a mere confusion between what is happening and what we know is happening may prove interesting.

Two hunter problem

The classic causation problem is that which arose in the American case *Summers v Tice*[7] and the Canadian case *Cook v Lewis*.[8] The plaintiff is minding his own business in the woods when two shots are heard. Immediately the plaintiff is hit and injured, but only by a single bullet. The shots were fired by two hunters. Both fired their guns without checking properly that it was safe to do so. Both, in that sense, were careless. But the bullet that hit the plaintiff could have come from either gun. It proves impossible to determine from which gun the bullet came. The plaintiff sues both hunters, but each hunter says that he should not be held liable because it cannot be shown that he caused the injury. The position is that, as far as the court and the plaintiff and the defendants themselves are concerned, it is equally likely that the bullet came from one gun as from the other. On the other hand, everyone also knows that only one of the defendants can possibly be responsible for the injury. One bullet, and only one bullet, hit the plaintiff. The other bullet missed.

The dilemma for the court is that if the court decides for both of the defendants, it is certain that it is making a mistake with regard to one of them. But equally, if the court decides against both defendants, it is also certainly making a mistake with regard to one of them.

Conventionally, the standard of proof in civil actions is 'the balance of probabilities'. It is far from clear what this phrase means but the best interpretation is that it tells the judge to be indifferent as between making a mistake in favour of the plaintiff and making a mistake in favour of the defendant. This is in contrast with the criminal standard of proof, which requires the jury to be 'sure' of the defendant's guilt, or traditionally, to have 'no reasonable doubt' of that guilt. The criminal standard tells the courts to care more about convicting the innocent than about acquitting the guilty. But in tort cases it is thought to be just as bad to force defendants to pay damages when they were not responsible for the harm as it is to deny plaintiffs compensation when it should have been ordered.

Over and above the standard of proof is the burden of proof. The burden of proof is like a tie-break rule in a sport such as tennis. It tells you what to do when the scores are equal. In law, it tells the court what to do when it cannot decide whether it prefers one party's account of the facts or the other party's. In general in the civil law, although there are exceptions,[9] the burden of proof is on the plaintiff. That means that if the court cannot decide between the plaintiff's account and the defendant's account, the defendant wins the case.

To return to the two hunter problem, what should the court do? The standard of proof rule tells it to be indifferent between making a mistake in favour of the plaintiff and making a mistake in favour of the defendant. The burden of proof rule tells it that when all else is equal, decide for the

7   33 Cal 2d 80, 199 P 2d 1 (1948).
8   [1952] 1 DLR 1.
9   See below ch 15 on defences.

defendant. Most people would assume that in the light of these rules, the courts would decide the two hunter cases in favour of the defendant. The court has to make either in favour of the plaintiff or a mistake in favour of the defendants. It is impossible to tell which account to believe, and so the burden of proof rule should mean victory for the defendants.[9a]

But, surprisingly, courts often find both defendants liable in these cases. It is usually said that the courts have simply reversed the burden of proof in favour of the plaintiff, and that they have done it because both defendants were faulty whereas the plaintiff was innocent.[10] The underlying argument in these cases is, however, more subtle. Everything follows from the fact that the chances of making a mistake in such a case are known. If the court finds both defendants liable, it is certain that, with respect to one defendant, a mistake will have been made. Equally, if the court decides that neither defendant should be liable, it is also certain that a mistake will have been made with regard to the other defendant. But more than that is known. If the court decides that neither defendant should be liable, the court compounds its mistake about one of the defendants with a mistake about the plaintiff. For it is certain that at least one of the defendants injured the plaintiff, so that it must be an extra mistake not to give the plaintiff damages. But clearly the same mistake about the plaintiff does not occur if the court orders both defendants to pay compensation. We know that the plaintiff should get compensation from someone, and if the court orders both defendants to pay, there is no mistake with regard to the plaintiff. Hence, the decision should be for the plaintiff, since that is the decision that minimises the number of mistakes that are certain to occur.

In other words, the balance of probabilities standard of proof requires the court to be indifferent between pro-plaintiff mistakes and pro-defendant mistakes, but it does not tell it to be indifferent about making mistakes in the first place. The burden of proof, although sometimes referred to by judges and commentators, need not enter into consideration at all, since the situation is not one in which a tie needs to be broken. There is no tie to break. To decide for the plaintiff means that one is making fewer mistakes than one would make if one decided for the defendants.

Causes that never happened—*McWilliams*

Another problem case is *McWilliams v Sir William Arrol & Co Ltd*.[11] The plaintiff was an employee of the defendant, a building contractor. The plaintiff was injured when he fell off a roof. The plaintiff's case was that the employer had been at fault in failing to supply him with a safety harness, which would have prevented the fall. The defendant's case was that the failure to supply the equipment made no difference since the

9a   This is indeed the position in criminal law: see *R v Dyos* [1979] Crim LR 660.
10   See eg *Hart and Honoré* at pp 423-24.
11   [1962] 1 WLR 295 (HL).

plaintiff was the sort of person who would not use safety equipment in the first place.

The defendant won the case, to the puzzlement of commentators ever since.[12] The point of the criticism levelled at the case is that it seems odd to say that the real cause of the plaintiff's injury was something that everyone knows never happened, namely the plaintiff's failure to use safety equipment once it had been offered.

McWilliams only makes sense in causal terms if one sticks strictly to the distinction between causes and what we know about causes. The court has to consider whether the failure to supply safety equipment made any difference to what happened to the plaintiff. The argument is that it made no difference because the plaintiff would not have used the equipment. But by failing to supply the employee with safety equipment, the defendant has robbed the court of the opportunity to know for certain whether or not the plaintiff would have used it. The decision of the court is that there is evidence, based on the plaintiff's past behaviour, that he would not have used it. This cannot be known for certain, but if the court had to say, as it does have to say, one way or the other, it would plump for saying that he would not have used it.

The reason that the result seems unsatisfactory is not that there is anything wrong in principle with the court's reasoning on causation, but that the defendant has apparently benefited from his own wrong. The defendant robbed the plaintiff of the opportunity to demonstrate that he could use safety equipment responsibly. It seems unfair to allow the defendant to take advantage of his own failure. The only solace for those who feel uneasy about the result is that it must be an exceptional one, for in most cases the court would not feel confident in saying that the plaintiff would not have used the equipment and would dismiss the point as speculative.

Increasing risks—*McGhee*

The next classic puzzle case to consider is *McGhee v National Coal Board*.[13] McGhee was employed by the NCB in a very dirty job which resulted in his being covered in brick dust at the end of every shift. McGhee contracted dermatitis and blamed his employer. The basis of McGhee's case was that the employer should have provided showers at the workplace so that he could have washed the dust off before going home. The defendant's case was that the plaintiff could not show that he would have avoided dermatitis if he had showered at the end of every shift. The dust covered his body from very soon after he started work, and it was possible that dermatitis would have ensued from these conditions even if he had washed it off at the end of the shift. The problem in the case is whether or not it was the

---

12 Eg Fraser and Howarth (1984) Legal Studies 131.
13 Above n 5.

extra time that the plaintiff had to take every day in cycling home before being able to wash off the dust that caused the disease.

The House of Lords decided in favour of the plaintiff. The most celebrated (and most reviled) speech was that of Lord Wilberforce, who said that since by not providing a workplace shower the defendants had 'materially increased the risk' of the plaintiff's contracting dermatitis, the burden of proof shifted onto the defendants to show that it was not the extra time needed before the dust could be washed off that had caused the disease.

Later cases have repudiated Lord Wilberforce's thesis about the shifting of the burden of proof[14] and have thrown some doubt on his 'materially increasing the risk' formula. But as long as 'materially increasing the risk' is properly understood, Lord Wilberforce's speech is sound enough. As explained above 'materially increasing the risk' is a statement of probability, which should be understood as referring not to some state of the world but to our level of certainty about what we know about the world. And so what Lord Wilberforce was getting at in *McGhee* was that in his view, if one were asked in advance whether McGhee would contract dermatitis as a result of his job, one's degree of certainty that he would contract it would rise if one was also told that the employer did not supply workplace showers.

The key to *McGhee*, however, is to ask how much difference to one's level of certainty the extra information would make. If, before knowing about the absence of the shower, one would have said, on balance, that McGhee would get dermatitis from his job, then the information about the absence of the shower would make no difference about one's view about what would happen. In that case, one does not, ultimately, believe that the lack of a shower made any difference and thus it was not a cause of the dermatitis. But if, on the other hand, one would have believed that, before being given the information about the absence of the shower, on balance, McGhee would not contract dermatitis from his job, then the extra information about the shower and the fact that McGhee did in reality contract dermatitis would mean that one would say that the lack of the shower did cause the disease.

The point about the burden of proof is not, or at least should not be, that the formal tie-break rule ('if you can't decide, decide for the defendant') has changed, but simply that given the court's state of knowledge, it now believes that the defendant's fault did cause the plaintiff's injury, and that unless the defendant brings in new information, the court has enough to decide for the plaintiff.

The main lesson of *McGhee*, however, lies in what it reveals about the relationship between causation and fault. If the courts had at some point decided that it was faulty of the employer to allow the employee to come into bodily contact with this amount of brick dust in the first place, instead of saying, as they did, that it was reasonable for the employee to be covered in dust during his shift, the causation problem in the case would have disappeared. The employer would have been at fault for not providing protective clothing on the job itself and there would have been no doubt

---

14 See *Wilsher v Essex Area Health Authority* [1988] AC 1074.

that the defendant's fault caused the disease. The general point is that many causal problems disappear if the court is willing to rule that more of the defendant's conduct was unreasonable in the first place.[15]

Hotson and loss of a chance

McGhee v National Coal Board brings out the interdependence of causation and fault. But there is an even more fundamental interdependence between causation and damage. Proving what damage has been suffered by the plaintiff is the practical heart of any civil action, but especially of negligence. Without provable damage there is no action in negligence.[16] If the damage is too unclear or uncertain[17] it is not recoverable. Causation must fit into this framework. The plaintiff has to show that the plaintiff's fault caused damage that is clear and certain enough to be recoverable.

Note that there are several kinds of damage which, although recoverable, by their nature verge on the speculative. For example, it is quite common for negligence plaintiffs suffering from personal injuries to claim for the income that they might have earned in the future but will not earn as a result of their injuries. It is far from certain in most cases how much these lost future earnings would have been, and because of changing patterns of work—with people expected to change their job and even their profession several times during their working lives—this uncertainty is rising. Nevertheless, the approach the courts take is that the plaintiff should receive damages for future lost earnings on the basis of present earnings together with any non-speculative expected future increments, but that the total amount should be reduced to take into account the 'vicissitudes of life', namely the ordinary risks that the plaintiff would have faced in any case—redundancy, illness, accidents and so on.

The idea that lurks behind this way of calculating damages for lost future earnings is that by including the discount for the vicissitudes, the level of damages takes into account some of the uncertainty the court must have about what the plaintiff has lost or will lose as a result of the defendant's negligence. The question arises whether one can use a similar line of reasoning where the uncertainty is not about measuring future losses but about the loss that the plaintiff is alleged to have suffered in the first place. In other words, can the plaintiff sue the defendant for loss of a chance?[18]

Other legal systems have no difficulty incorporating the idea of loss of a chance. In the USA, for example, a number of jurisdictions have developed

---

15 See Fraser and Howarth (1984) Legal Studies 131.
16 See generally Stapleton 'Damage as the Gist of Negligence' (1988) 104 LQR 213 and 389.
17 Cf the rule in French law. Viney *Les Obligations, La Responsabilité: Conditions* (Paris; LGDJ, 1982) at pp 338-341.
18 See further King 'Causation, Valuation and Chance in Personal Injury Torts involving Pre-existing Conditions and Future Consequences' (1981) 90 Yale LJ 1353.

lost chance doctrines or near equivalents.[19] And in France, the idea of 'la perte d'une chance' is not only well developed but even celebrated.[20] It is worth noting that the main function of loss of a chance in French law is to overcome objections that the damage is not clear and distinct. In many cases, although the plaintiff cannot show with certainty that the defendant caused the injury, it is beyond doubt that the defendant caused the plaintiff to lose the chance of avoiding the injury. The only question is whether the value of lost chance can be measured accurately. Thus loss of a chance solves causation problems by shifting the uncertainty into the more malleable area of valuation of the plaintiff's loss.

In England, however, the idea has not been so well received. Loss of a chance is recognised in contract,[1] but in tort although the question is still technically open, the door is rapidly closing.

The central case is *Hotson v East Berkshire Area Health Authority*.[2] In *Hotson*, a boy fell out of tree and injured his hip. He was taken to hospital where he was misdiagnosed. As a result of the misdiagnosis, he was not treated for a serious condition, and by the time the mistake was discovered it was too late to do anything about it. The boy now suffers from a permanent disability.

The hospital's defence was that the misdiagnosis, although regrettable, made no difference to the outcome. Expert witnesses disagreed on exactly what the position was, but the judge found that the boy had only a 25% chance of avoiding permanent disability when the diagnosis was made.

The choice to be made in *Hotson* appears to be a stark one. If the court does not accept the idea of loss of a chance, it has to plump for saying whether the misdiagnosis made any difference, in which case it would have to say that it did not make a difference. On the other hand, if it accepts the idea of loss of a chance, it could say that it is certain (or certain enough) that the misdiagnosis deprived the plaintiff of a 25% chance of recovery, and that the defendant should pay 25% of the full compensation.

In fact, the House of Lords tried to duck the decision by reinterpreting the facts. According to Lord Mackay, the position was that 75% of such cases that reach the hospital are inoperable—that is, on arrival, there is no chance of saving the patient from permanent disability in 75% of cases. The question, therefore, is whether, as a fact, the court believes that the plaintiff arrived at the hospital in an operable or inoperable state. Since there was no more information available other than the averages, and there was no evidence to suggest anything unusual about the plaintiff, if one had to say whether or not the patient was operable, one would have to say that probably he was not. If it is found as a fact that the plaintiff's

19 See eg *Herskovits v Group Health* 664 P 2d 474 (Wash 1983), *De Burkarte v Louvar* 393 NW 2d 131 (Iowa 1986), *Falcon v Memorial Hospital* 462 NW 2d 44 (Mich 1990), *Scafidi v Seiler* 573 A 2d 398 (NJ 1990). See generally Ellis, Note 72 Tex LR 369 (1994).

20 P Malaurie and L Aynès *Cours De Droit Civil: Les Obligations* (Paris; Editions Cujas, 1994) at pp 135-136.

1   *Chaplin v Hicks* [1911] 2 KB 786.

2   [1987] AC 750.

condition was not operable, there has been no lost chance and the question of whether lost chances are recoverable does not strictly arise for decision.

It may be observed that Lord Mackay's manoeuvre around having to decide whether lost chances are recoverable does not quite work. If in 25% of such cases the patient arrives at the hospital in an operable state, and assuming that the operation has 50-50 chance of success, the patient has still lost a 12.5% chance of recovery.

Nevertheless, the House of Lords in *Hotson* did consider that it had obviated the need to pronounce definitively on lost chances. The Court of Appeal, especially Sir John Donaldson, had made remarks generally favourable to at least a limited acceptance of loss of a chance. These remarks the House of Lords pointedly refused to endorse. But at the same time the House of Lords said that it could not rule out loss of a chance altogether, at least until it decided whether completely to overrule *McGhee*. Although subsequently in *Wilsher* the House of Lords did disapprove of much of Lord Wilberforce's contribution to *McGhee*, it did not explicitly overrule *McGhee*. Thus, the state of the law on lost chances is that although there are grounds for suspecting that the House of Lords will not support the idea, the technical position is that the House of Lords has not yet decided the point and there are strong Court of Appeal dicta in favour of the idea.

The answer to whether lost chances *should* be recoverable is con-troversial. It would help in answering it, however, if at least we were clear about what a lost chance is.

In all lost chance cases, the 'probability' associated with the lost chance is, in essence, a statement about the court's lack of certainty about some fact. That fact may be something to do with the future, future lost earnings for example, or it may be something to do with the past, for example whether the patient would have fared better if he had been treated earlier. In some cases, the uncertainties can never be fully resolved because they concern events that can now never happen—putting on the safety equipment in *McWilliams*, for example, or the 'vicissitude' of losing a job by redundancy that one can now never have.

In other cases, the uncertainties will be fully resolved at some point, but not yet—for example if you destroy my lottery ticket so that I cannot prove my entitlement to a win, whether or not I am really worse off will be resolved by the lottery itself which will in due course reveal whether or not I would have won.

From this last point it will be seen that one particular argument that is sometimes made against allowing recovery for lost chances does not stand up. This is the argument that to allow recovery for lost chances implies allowing recovery for endangering the plaintiff even when no damage in fact occurred. Even if allowing such actions might be supportable on deterrence grounds,[3] it does not follow from allowing some kinds of lost chance action that every sort of lost chance should be recoverable. Damages for endangerment without harm is the equivalent of allowing damages for the destruction of a lottery ticket now known to be a losing ticket. Lost

3   See Makdisi 'Proportional Liability' 67 NCLR 1063, 1067ff.

chances often have to do with uncertainty about whether the loss would have occurred, and not necessarily with situations in which losses are known not to have occurred.

Another objection to the recoverability of lost chances is that events in the past ought to be regarded as within the purview of causation, and an event either did or did not cause another event (assuming that we are clear what we mean by 'cause'). There is no intermediate state. The probabilities assigned to the lost chances are merely statements of uncertainty. The court should have to plump one way or the other on the basis of present information—was it a cause or wasn't it?

But it is not clear what is so special about the past. There seems to be no difference in principle between a judgment about what would have happened if the circumstances had been different (would the employee have worn the safety equipment? would the patient have been cured?) and statements about what might have happened in the future if circumstances had been different (would the plaintiff have been made redundant from this job anyway?). Both are hypothetical questions ('counterfactuals' in the parlance of specialists in this field) about situations that can never now occur. Both can either be resolved by plumping for one answer or another on the basis of the present evidence, or by expressing one's uncertainty in terms of a probability. There seems to be no reason to treat the two cases differently, so that if the 'lost chance' in the past is not accepted, neither should there be a discount on damages to take into account counterfactual 'vicissitudes' in the future.

In any case, the argument that uncertainty can be resolved by plumping on the basis of present information misses the point of damages for lost chances, which is that most people are willing to trade in their uncertainty for an up-front payment. This is the way insurance works. In lost chance cases, the plaintiff asks the court, in effect, to give damages equivalent roughly to the insurance premium a reasonable victim would take out against the occurrence of just this sort of situation. This way of looking at lost chances may be helpful in other ways. It suggests that it is right to be reluctant to apply lost chance analysis in the *McWilliams* situation. It is very difficult to estimate a reasonable premium for insurance against an event that is within the insured person's control—for example whether the victim himself would have worn the safety equipment. The person insured has a perverse incentive to take less care because of the very fact of insurance. On the other hand, where, as in *Hotson*, the uncertainty is about something outside the victim's control, for example whether or not a surgical procedure would have worked, the lost chance analysis seems more applicable, for the loss is objective and fairly easily measured.

Economic loss cases—proving there has been a loss

One special case of the lost chance is worth noting. Sometimes, the lost chance is a lost opportunity for the plaintiff to have profited from business dealings with a third party. The situation is a familiar one in contract law, in which the defendant's failure to deliver the goods robs the plaintiff of the chance of selling them on to a third party at a profit. A similar situation can arise in tort, especially in cases of professional negligence and negligent advice.[4] For example, an auditing firm fails to spot that its client's financial control system is far from perfect, so that money is being wasted. Or a valuer fails to notice that your dusty picture is a long lost Old Master until the market value of such pictures has dropped by 50%.

In cases of this sort, the plaintiff is faced with a causation/damage problem. The plaintiff has to show that had the defendant given the correct advice, the plaintiff would have acted on it. In some cases, this is easier than in others. For example, it might not be too difficult to persuade a court that had the auditors pointed out the defects in the plaintiff's financial system, the plaintiff would have done something about them. That is the normal and ordinary thing to do. But in the case of the picture valuer, the answer is not so clear, since it is quite possible that the plaintiff would not have sold the picture anyway even if its true monetary value had been known.

In reality, these are lost chance cases—the plaintiff would have liked the chance to have taken the advice—but they fall into the *McWilliams* category in which the uncertainty is about the actions of the plaintiff.

This may explain what the courts tend to say in practice in such cases that, even if the plaintiff would have acted on the better advice had that advice been given, the loss is unrecoverable because it is too remote.[5] It is too remote because the argument involves speculation about further voluntary interventions by the plaintiff.[6]

Baker v Willoughby and supervening cause

Another set of cases in which the relationship between causation and damage needs to be analysed is that concerning supervening or 'overtaking' cause. In these cases, the defendant's allegedly careless conduct precedes another event which causes even greater harm to the plaintiff, an event which is independent of the defendant's actions in the sense that it would have happened anyway regardless of what the defendant did.[7]

A central, but perplexing, case in this field is *Baker v Willoughby*.[8] In *Baker*, the defendant injured the plaintiff's leg in a car accident. Before the trial of the plaintiff's negligence action, and in circumstances which the trial court found were entirely unaffected by the plaintiff's injury, the

4   See below ch 6.
5   Eg *Galoo v Bright Grahame Murray* [1995] 1 All ER 16.
6   See below.
7   Where the second event is not independent of the first, that is when it may not have happened had the defendant not been careless, the situation is best dealt with as one of 'remoteness': see below.
8   [1970] AC 467.

plaintiff was the victim of an armed robbery, in the course of which the robbers effectively shot off the plaintiff's injured leg.

The defendant admitted carelessness, but argued that his responsibility ended when the robbers shot off the plaintiff's leg. One way of justifying the defendant's point of view is to notice that, as the facts were found, the plaintiff would have lost his leg anyway, whether or not the defendant had injured it first. The defendant's act was therefore not a 'but-for' cause of the loss of the leg. Using the NESS version of causation does not help the plaintiff either, since the defendant's bad driving was not, at least on this occasion, a necessary element in the set of events that were sufficient to produce the plaintiff's final injuries.

The House of Lords, however, although it recognised that the defendant could not be said to have caused the plaintiff to lose his leg, was worried about the fact that, were the robbers ever to be found and successfully sued, they could only be liable for making the plaintiff's condition worse than it was when they fired the shots. They could not be held responsible for the plaintiff's condition—his earning capacity, mobility and so on—when they shot him. This meant that there was a serious gap in the plaintiff's potential total damages that would leave him not completely compensated even if the robbers paid their share. The reason was that if the robbers could only be liable to the extent that they made the plaintiff's condition worse, and the defendant could only be liable for the plaintiff's injury before the robbery, the damages that the plaintiff would have received for having an injured leg after the time of the robbery would not be recovered.

The Court of Appeal was attracted by the ingenious argument, itself an example of how manipulation of the scope of fault can resolve causal problems, that they could hold the robbers responsible for the otherwise uncompensated loss on the ground that the robbers had made the plaintiff worse off by robbing him also of his right to further compensation from the defendant. The House of Lords rejected the Court of Appeal's approach as, first, artificial and, secondly, since in practice the robbers would not be found or would not be able to pay damages, as likely to lead to a situation identical to that which would subsist if the court simply accepted the defendant's case. The House of Lords then went on to decide that the defendant should pay compensation both for the injury to the time of the robbery and for the losses that would have flowed from the original injury had the robbery not intervened.

The reasoning used by the House of Lords in *Baker v Willoughby* has been much criticised. Critics include a subsequent House of Lords in *Jobling v Associated Dairies*,[9] in which a plaintiff was denied damages for a back injury for the period after he was found to be suffering, quite independently, from a disease of the back that was more disabling than the original injury. Lord Keith of Kinkel was the most outspoken of their Lordships:

'I am ... of opinion that the majority in *Baker v Willoughby* were mistaken in approaching the problems common to the case of a

9 [1981] 2 All ER 752.

supervening tortious act and to that of a supervening illness wholly from the point of view of causation ... [I]t is appropriate to keep in view that [illness] is one of the ordinary vicissitudes of life ... so that it cannot be disregarded in arriving at proper compensation, and no more than proper compensation.'

The difference in result between *Baker* and *Jobling* is difficult to justify on traditional remoteness grounds, since the 'chain of causation' that traditional remoteness invokes is usually said to be more easily broken by tortious interventions by third parties than by non-tortious interventions or natural events,[10] whereas liability is carried further in *Baker*, where the intervention was tortious, than in *Jobling*, where it was not.

A better way of analysing these cases is that they represent a clash between two views of how to calculate tort damages. On the one hand is the view that damages are awarded to compensate the plaintiff for causing reductions in his or her physical or mental capabilities. On the other is the view that damages are awarded for total future lost chances.

In *Baker*, the House of Lords views the loss incrementally, at the margin. The first injury reduces the plaintiff's capacities by a certain amount. The defendant has to pay compensation for that reduction in capacity. In order to capture its full effect, the cost of that injury to the plaintiff is measured as of the time of its infliction. The second injury reduces the plaintiff's capacities further. Those responsible for the second injury have to pay compensation for the new loss that they have caused.

In *Jobling*, the key word is 'vicissitude.' The House of Lords repeatedly says that damages for future losses have to be reduced to take into account the chances that the plaintiff would have become incapacitated anyway. In a case such as *Jobling* the court knows that the plaintiff has already become incapacitated, so that the probability of incapacitation is equal to one and the damages must consequently be reduced by 100% for the period after the supervening event.

Baker represents the view that lost chances should not be taken into account in calculating damages (hence the rejection by the House of Lords of the Court of Appeal's approach) and that the court should concentrate solely on the losses reasonably believed to have been caused by the defendant's fault. *Jobling* represents the view that lost chances are the heart of damages, but that when it can be shown that, so to speak, the plaintiff's lottery ticket has turned out to be a loser, no damages should be awarded at all.

Wilsher v Essex and multiple possibilities

Even more complex causal problems are possible. Many come about in medical cases. One example is the multiple possibility problem, best illustrated by *Wilsher v Essex Area Health Authority*.[11]

10 See below.
11 See above n 14.

Wilsher v Essex Area Health Authority brings together a version of the two hunter problem with a version of the *McGhee* problem. In *Wilsher*, the plaintiff was a premature baby who went blind after a junior doctor inserted a catheter for a blood oxygen measuring device into a vein instead of into an artery and, as a consequence, it was alleged, excess oxygen was administered to the baby. The health authority's main defence was that since there were a number of ways that the plaintiff's form of blindness could have come about anyway, even without faulty conduct on the part of the medical team, the plaintiff had failed to prove causation.

The House of Lords agreed that the defendants should win, either because the test was whether the court believed that it was more likely that the cause of the baby's blindness was excess oxygen resulting from the junior doctor's carelessness than that the cause was any of all the other possible causes put together, or because the test was that the cause was more likely than any other single possible cause.[12] Since the trial judge had not approached the question on that basis, the case was sent back for retrial.

It is not, however, entirely clear how the second trial court should approach the issue. The problem is that there was evidence that all four of the other possible causes of the baby's blindness had been present at some stage. It therefore follows that there is not a clear rule that the mere presence of other factors rules out a finding that the factor that includes the defendant's carelessness was a cause, for otherwise a retrial would not have been necessary. The result follows from the usual solution to the three house fire problem, that both fires are causes of the middle house's being burned down.

But if in cases of multiple sufficient causes, all of the sufficient causes for whose presence there is evidence count as causes, it is difficult to see exactly what new findings of fact the second trial court has to make. All five were present, so that all five should count as causes.

The House of Lords seems to be looking for evidence that would tend to show that the other candidates made no difference (as opposed to the doctor's carelessness making no difference). But that sounds like asking in the three house fire problem whether there is evidence that one of the outer fires was more likely than the other to be the cause of the destruction of the middle house. There is no new information that could make any difference here. What matters is the meaning of cause rather than any further evidence about what happened.

It also seems that *Wilsher* replaces the *McGhee* formula of 'materially contributing to the risk' by the equally mysterious phrase 'materially contributing to the injury'. How this is different from 'causing the injury' is not clear, unless it means merely that it counts as a cause to make an injury worse—although why that should count as a cause of the whole injury is itself not clear, neither its relevance to the facts of *Wilsher*.

---

12 See p 1091 citing Browne-Wilkinson VC in the Court of Appeal who uses the phrase 'more likely than any of those four candidates' in one sentence and 'excess oxygen rather than one or more than one of the four other possible agents' in the next.

One might instead analyse *Wilsher* in two steps. The first step is to apply the solution to the three house fire problem. For the junior doctor's carelessness with the catheter to count as a cause requires only that it is a necessary element in a set of events sufficient to bring about the injury. On all plausible views of what the doctor could have done instead, that is all steps that would not have been careless, the answer is that the doctor's carelessness was a NESS cause of the injury. The same analysis can also be done for the four other possible causes. They were all present and all count as NESS causes.

The second stage is to ask what happens when one has a large number of fully-qualified NESS causes? More especially, what happens when some of those NESS causes are the fault of defendants and others are natural events? The obvious step would be to apply the *McGhee* analysis. The question would be 'Would knowing about the fact that the patient had been given excessive oxygen change one's mind about whether the patient would suffer the form of blindness that he eventually did suffer from?' But there is a problem with doing this, as Browne-Wilkinson V-C pointed out in the Court of Appeal in *Wilsher*:

> 'In *McGhee* there was no doubt that the pursuer's dermatitis was physically caused by brick dust the only question was whether the continued presence of such brick dust on the pursuer's skin after the time when he should have been provided with a shower caused or materially contributed to the dermatitis which he contracted. There was only one possible agent which could have caused the dermatitis, viz brick dust, and there was no doubt that the dermatitis from which he suffered was caused by that brick dust.
>
> In the present case the question is different. There are a number of different agents which could have caused the RLF [the condition that afflicted the child]. Excess oxygen was one of them. The defendants failed to take reasonable precautions to prevent one of the possible causative agents (eg excess oxygen) from causing RLF. But no one can tell in this case whether excess oxygen did or did not cause or contribute to the RLF suffered by the plaintiff. The plaintiff's RLF may have been caused by some completely different agent or agents, eg hypercarbia, intraventricular haemorrhage, apnoea or patent ductus arteriosus. In addition to oxygen, each of those conditions has been implicated as a possible cause of RLF. This baby suffered from each of those conditions at various times in the first two months of his life. There is no satisfactory evidence that excess oxygen is more likely than any of those other four candidates to have caused RLF in this baby.'

That is, in *McGhee* it did not matter how one posed the question. In *McGhee* there are exactly two possible mutually exclusive causes. In consequence if the question asked is, 'Not knowing about the effect of the "innocent" dust, would knowing about the "guilty" dust lead one to believe that the plaintiff would suffer from dermatitis?', it leads to the same answer as the question, 'Given the presence of the "innocent" dust, would knowledge about the "guilty" dust change your mind about whether it is more likely than not that the plaintiff would get dermatitis?'

This equivalence is not present in the *Wilsher* situation, in which there are five not necessarily mutually exclusive causes. In contrast to *McGhee*, much depends on the way the question is asked and the order in which information is introduced.

For example, it might be that knowing about the presence of any of the five causes would make one certain that the injury would follow. In that case, knowing that all five were present gives one no way to distinguish between them. Or it may be that, although lacking certainty, knowing of the presence of any of the factors would make one plump, if one had to plump, for saying that the injury would follow. Again, there is no way, on purely causal grounds, of distinguishing between the five.

The second stage in *Wilsher*-type cases will often be inconclusive in this sort of way. Instead, it will often be necessary in order to achieve a result to move outside the field of factual causation altogether and into the problems of whether, and to what extent, the presence of other causes of the plaintiff's injury should exonerate the defendant even though the defendant's act was also a cause of the injury. It is a question that arises in all tort cases to some extent and goes by the name of remoteness.

MASS TORTS

The ultimate challenge for causation in negligence and in tort generally comes in so-called 'mass tort' or 'toxic tort' cases. In such cases, the problem is that there are too many defendants to choose from and they can all say that the evidence is that someone else is responsible. For example, the plaintiff develops a serious disease as an unexpected side effect of taking a prescription drug. The drug is manufactured by four different companies, which are all either liable under statute or guilty of carelessness. The plaintiff cannot prove which company made the drugs she took, since the pills all look alike and the pharmacy keeps no records of which patient is given which brand of drug. Each drug company argues that the chances are that it did not manufacture the drugs that the plaintiff took. See *Sindell v Abbott Labs* 26 Cal 3d 588, 607 P 2d 924, 163 Cal Rptr 132 (1980).

Parallel problems can arise in environmental cases. The plaintiff suffers from a disease caused by a particular pollutant. The defendant, together with 20 other similar firms, admits putting the pollutant into the environment, and admits that it should have known that the pollutant was dangerous. The defendant argues, however, that the plaintiff cannot show causation, for even if the defendant had not polluted the environment, the plaintiff might have suffered in exactly the same way.

There is an extensive literature on how the courts have approached such cases and on how they should have approached them. Suggestions include reversal of the burden of proof in favour of the plaintiff, res ipsa loquitur, liability in proportion to market share or rates of emission and the complete abandonment of the requirement of causation. Another approach is to suggest that the common law is fundamentally unsuited to such cases and that it is right that there should be no common law liability, but that criminal law and administrative measures should regulate the area instead. See generally Ball and Bell *Environmental Law* (2nd ed) (London; Blackstone, 1994) ch 8.

Remoteness

It is not sufficient for the defendant's faulty conduct to have caused harm to the plaintiff. The defendant's conduct must also be capable of being characterised as **responsible** for the harm in the light of the other factors which could also count as causes.

These factors include the conduct of third parties, natural events, the pre-existing condition of the plaintiff and the plaintiff's own conduct.

The issue in each case is whether the presence of these other causally relevant factors should allow the defendant to escape liability. If the defendant does escape liability on these grounds, the damage to the plaintiff is said to have been 'too remote' or 'not sufficiently proximate' or the other causally relevant factor is said to be a 'novus actus interveniens' (a new intervening act).[13]

The function of remoteness

The underlying justification for rules that allow the defendant to escape liability because of the presence of other factual causes is, admittedly, obscure. One thesis is that the justification for allowing defendants to escape liability on the grounds of remoteness comes from the deterrence function of negligence. The idea is that if conduct of the sort engaged in by the defendant does not usually result in harm, in contrast to the conseq‐ uences of the conduct of others or of natural events, then it may be thought to be wasteful of resources to attempt to deter what the defendant did. Why bother trying to deter someone who played only a minor role?

The problem with this suggestion is that if it is true that conduct of the kind engaged in by the defendant so rarely results in harm, the defendant will usually not have been at fault in the first place. Furthermore, if it is

13 Hart and Honoré (*Causation in the Law*) say that lack of remoteness marks 'full causation' as opposed to mere factual causation which they call 'occasioning'. They do so in order to attempt to show that the normative content in 'remoteness' is minimal and that 'remote' and 'proximate' causes can usually be distinguished without recourse to making normative judgments about the events concerned. It will be seen from what follows that the tendency of the law of England has been to move towards normative distinctions between the remote and the proximate, but that in some areas non-normative distinctions are still used.

true in a particular case that the costs associated with bringing the action outweigh any benefits that will accrue in terms of deterring future accidents, so that to allow the action to proceed is wasteful from the deterrence point of view, it does not matter whether there is anyone or anything else to blame.

Another thesis that may explain the existence of the remoteness test is one of fairness. In general, in cases in which it might be possible to sue more than one person for the same harm, English tort law uses the idea of joint and several liability. This means that any of the wrongdoers, if found liable, may be called upon to pay the whole amount of the damages awarded (subject of course to the overriding rule that the plaintiff may not recover from the defendants as a group an amount in excess of the total damages awarded). The rule is meant to make sure that if any of the defendants cannot be traced, or has no money, the plaintiff does not lose. The other defendants have to pay. The law has been modified by statute so that defendants can now proceed against other defendants to recover a part of the damages, such part being proportional to the other defendants' degree of fault.[14] But the underlying principle is still that the risk of not being able to find the other defendants, or that of finding them to be impecunious, lies on the defendant.

The effect of this rule is that, in the wrong conditions, a defendant who played only a small part in the events that led to the harm may end up being required to pay for the whole of a considerable loss. This result may be thought to be unfair. As Viscount Simonds said in the *Wagon Mound (No 1)*:[15]

> '[I]t does not seem consonant with current ideas of justice or morality that for an act of negligence, however slight or venial, which results in some trivial foreseeable damage the actor should be liable for all the consequences however foreseeable and however grave.'

In the *Wagon Mound* the defendants, for no good reason, allowed oil to spill out of their ship and into plaintiffs' dockyard. The plaintiffs' manager, fearing fire, ordered all welding work at the dockyard to stop. But he was told by the manager of a nearby oil depot that oil dispersed on the surface of the sea would not catch fire, something that he half suspected to be true himself. He therefore ordered welding work to restart. Welding continued without mishap for a day. But then disaster struck. What probably happened was that sparks from the welding work caused some debris floating in the oil to catch fire. The burning debris had the effect of heating up the oil so that it became extremely flammable. The oil itself then caught fire and destroyed the plaintiffs' dockyard.[16]

---

14 See below.
15 [1961] AC 388, 422.
16 It also destroyed a ship in the dockyard that belonged to another firm. Their claim is the basis of the *Wagon Mound (No 2)* [1967] 1 AC 388.

The defendants' argument in the *Wagon Mound (No 1)* was not that they had acted reasonably, for they were clearly at fault in spilling the oil, but that because of the occurrence of natural events that even experts did not think could happen, combined with the interventions of a variety of other actors, the loss that resulted from their carelessness was enormous in comparison with what one might normally expect in these circumstances. It would therefore, they claimed, be unfair to fix them potentially with liability for the whole loss.

But it will be noticed at once that there is a fundamental objection to the defendants' reasoning. Why should the risk of not being able to find the other defendants (or of finding that they are not worth suing, or finding that there are no other defendants since the other causes are all natural events) fall on the innocent plaintiff when the defendant was at fault? To the defendants' plea that it is unfair to make them pay so much in damages for such a little fault, the plaintiffs can reply that it is even more unfair to leave the loss on the shoulders of the innocent plaintiff. It is as if the plaintiffs' response to the defendants' moan that the punishment is unfair is the assertion of exasperated parents down the ages: 'You shouldn't have done it anyway.' This, in essence, is the position taken by the Court of Appeal in *Re Polemis*,[17] a case of which the Privy Council in the *Wagon Mound (No 1)* heartily disapproved, but whose simple appeal is still very powerful.

In *Polemis*, stevedores unloading a ship at Casablanca carelessly dropped a heavy plank into a hold in which petrol cans were stored. The plank must have produced a spark when it hit the bottom of the hold, for there was an immediate explosion which destroyed the ship. It became necessary in the ensuing legal dispute between the owners of the ship and its charterers to decide whether the ship had been destroyed in circumstances in which the stevedores might have been held liable in negligence. The argument against such a proposition was that the damage, because it was admittedly an unlikely result in the circumstances, was too remote. The Court of Appeal held that it was not too remote, since the damage flowed directly from the negligent act. As Scrutton LJ said:[18]

> 'To determine whether an act is negligent it is relevant to determine whether any reasonable person would foresee that the act would cause damage; if he would not, the act is not negligent. But if the act would or might probably cause damage, the fact that the damage it in fact causes is not the exact kind of damage one would expect is immaterial, so long as the damage is in fact directly traceable to the negligent act, and not due to the operation of independent causes having no connection with the negligent act.'

In other words, it is not unfair to require the negligent defendant to pay for the loss, no matter how large it is, as long as what happened did not

17 [1921] 3 KB 560.
18 At 577.

involve the intervention of acts or events wholly unconnected with the defendant's negligence. The defendant should not have acted carelessly in the first place, for had he not done so, the loss would not have happened.

In the *Polemis* view of remoteness, the responsibility of the defendant can only be removed if the damage is not caused 'directly' by the defendant's act. The exact meaning of directness, and the relative importance within it of factual and moral elements has always been a matter of some dispute[19] but the central idea was that the defendant's act ceased to be the direct cause of the harm if either a deliberate human act or a surprising natural event intervened that materially changed the situation.[20] The traditional example, puzzling to some and probably no longer good law, is still worth giving. If you are walking along the street and a log, thrown over a fence, lands on your head, the injury is direct. If, on the other hand, the log lands on the street in front of you and you trip over it, that is indirect, because your own voluntary act of continuing to walk has intervened.[1]

The law on remoteness is in fact largely explicable in terms of an unresolved tension between these two arguments. On the one side is the defendants' plea of unfairness that they should be required to pay so much for such a little fault. On the other is the plaintiffs' harsh reply that the defendant did wrong and should suffer the consequences, unless someone else or something else was clearly more responsible, for otherwise innocent plaintiffs would go uncompensated for something that would not have happened had defendants acted properly. The function of remoteness is to provide a space in the law for the parties to deploy these arguments.

The relationship between remoteness and the rest of negligence

Before going on to study the way in which the courts have tried to resolve the basic tension at the heart of the remoteness argument, it may help to clarify what follows to consider a number of connections that one can draw between remoteness issues and other parts of negligence law.

The consequences of joint and several liability for remoteness issues

It will be observed from the preceding section that many of the difficulties that the law faces in remoteness are largely the consequence of the joint

---

19 See *Hart & Honoré* at xli-lii.
20 Ibid at 136ff.
1   The example is probably no longer good law because although the second case involves indirect injury, it is not *sufficiently* indirect to deny liability. Directness was originally used to distinguish between different , but equally valid, forms of action (eg trespass vs case) rather than between actionable and non-actionable losses. Indeed, the difficulties that seem to dog the notion of directness in negligence may well stem from the need to introduce the inherently vague notion of *degrees* of directness when directness changed its function following the abolition of the forms of action.

and several liability rule. Matters would be very different if other rules were in place. For example, the rule might instead be that each defendant should pay only in proportion to his or her own fault, regardless of whether other defendants can be found. This principle, so-called proportional several liability, could even be extended into cases where the defendant shares liability with a natural event. There are certain difficulties with this approach, but it has been adopted from time to time by other jurisdictions, both in common law systems and in civil law systems.[2]

It is also worth noting that the issue of remoteness can arise either with regard to all the harm for which the plaintiff claims compensation (in which case it is often confused with duty issues) and sometimes with regard only to some of the harm for which compensation is claimed. Some legal systems, for example German law, treat these two forms of the remoteness issue as completely separate issues.[3]

But whether or not the two forms of remoteness should be treated separately on theoretical grounds, there is at least one more practical though less dramatic difference between them. It is that in the case of a remoteness argument that affects the whole of the plaintiff's claim there is no opportunity, as there is in a case in which remoteness applies only to some of the damage, for the loss to be shared between the plaintiff and the defendant or among defendants. In the case of partial remoteness, the defendant admits responsibility for part of the damage but disputes responsibility for the rest. If the defendant's remoteness argument is successful, responsibility for the rest of the damage comes to rest on the plaintiff or on another defendant.

Note that the way the court divides up the harm into different categories and how it describes the harm are often important. For example, loss seen in terms of what the plaintiff can no longer do is more easily divisible than loss seen in purely physical terms. If the court treats a lost leg as a physical loss, it cannot easily be treated for remoteness purposes as more than one loss. But if it is treated as if it were the same as its consequences for the plaintiff (eg disfigurement, impairment of the ability to walk, reduction in the capacity to earn a living) it may more easily be treated as more than one loss.[4]

Remoteness in the age of proportional fault

There is another connected point which explains in particular the difficulties of resolving the tension within the remoteness debate in more recent times. In modern English negligence law both the conduct of the plaintiff and the conduct of third parties are dealt with under statutes

2 See Wright 'The Logic and Fairness of Joint and Several Liability' (1992) 23 Memphis State LR 45, *Viney* paras 406-424 (pp 480-501) and Howarth 'My Brother's Keeper' [1994] Legal Studies 88.

3 See Markesinis *The German Law of Torts* 4th ed (Oxford: Clarendon 1994) at 99. Cf *Bourhill v Young* [1943] AC 92.

4 Cf *Baker v Willoughby*, discussed above.

which use the idea of proportional fault—that a person should have to pay damages in proportion to his or her relative blameworthiness for the harm. Thus if the plaintiff is also at fault, that is, if the plaintiff is contributorily negligent, the damages payable by the defendant are reduced. And if a third party is also to blame for the same damage to the plaintiff, the defendant may recover a part of the damages payable to the plaintiff from the third party in the form of a 'contribution', although, as we have seen, the risk of not being able to find the other defendants falls on the defendant not on the plaintiff. But, so far, no similar regime has been imposed on the intervention of natural events or the effect of the pre-existing condition of the plaintiff.

As a consequence, the law must still assume, despite the statutes setting up the proportional fault regimes, that it is still possible for the defendant to win outright solely on the basis of the presence of other causally relevant factors. One might have hoped that the law would have developed so that remoteness arguments came into play only when proportionality cannot be used, that is where a stark choice has to be made between no liability and unfairly heavy liability. But English law still, for the time being at least, claims to take the position that remoteness is just as relevant, and relevant in the same way, to cases where a third party or the plaintiff intervenes as to those in which the intervention is a natural event. This position is not particularly stable. There needs to be movement either to a formal recognition of the different considerations that apply when pro–portionality is relevant or to the introduction of proportionality where at present it does not apply.

Causation and remoteness—causal fade and remoteness proper

An important distinction should be made between remoteness proper and what might be called causal fade-away. Causal fade-away is a factual cause issue, although it is usually treated as remoteness because of its surface similarities to remoteness.

Causal fade-away is so called because it is about the way in which our confidence in our knowledge about what has caused what fades away in long causal sequences. Take a complex chain of events. I give X some bad advice. It is alleged that X passed the bad advice onto Y, Y passed it onto Z and Z acted on it and lost money. Am I sure that my bad advice caused the loss? Maybe Y failed to hear X but thought up the bad advice himself, or perhaps heard it from someone else. Maybe Z didn't care about Y's advice but heard the same advice from the more trustworthy Q, and only then acted on it. Perhaps Z discounted the advice completely but acted as if he had followed it for completely unrelated reasons. And so on. The longer the chain, the more maybes there are, and the more possibilities there are that the defendant's action did not cause the loss. This in turn tends to lower the judge's confidence in the proposition that the defendant's conduct did cause the harm.

In remoteness proper, on the other hand, the issue is not gradual loss of confidence in the accuracy of the statement that the defendant's act caused the harm. The issue is whether or not, despite confidence in the factual causal link, the presence of the other events inclines the judge to exonerate the defendant on the ground that his or her share in the responsibility was too small to justify legal liability.

Foreseeability cures all ills?

There has been a tendency in English law in the past half century to believe that the issue of remoteness can be dissolved into one element of the fault equation, namely the reasonable foreseeability of harm. This tendency reaches its high point in the *Wagon Mound (No 1)*. The idea is that if the harm (or, as it allegedly later became, the 'kind of harm'[5]) to the plaintiff was 'reasonably foreseeable' by the defendant, then the harm was not too remote.

But it soon became clear that the reasonable foreseeability test was not up to the job of deciding whether the degree of responsibility for the harm that might be placed at the door of other factors suffices to exonerate the defendant.

On the one hand reasonable foreseeability as the only test for remoteness would mean that plaintiffs with unusual weaknesses or with predispositions to injury or loss might be denied a remedy. The defendant would be allowed to say, for example, that if the plaintiff's precise injury came about because the plaintiff suffered from a rare brittle bone condition, there should be no liability. The result would be that the law would be saying to some of the most vulnerable citizens that they should bear the risks associated with their weaknesses when admitted wrongdoers are let off.

On the other hand, the fact that an intervention, for example by a third party, is reasonably foreseeable does not of itself shift responsibility for the third party's actions onto the defendant. The responsibility still really lies with the third party. If I live in a high crime area and I forget to lock my door properly, it is foreseeable that criminals might break in. But if these criminals then murder a house guest who surprises them, it still seems out of proportion to hold me responsible for the house guest's death when all I did was fail to lock a door. After all, the criminals committed deliberate homicide.

Remoteness and duty

The relationship between remoteness arguments and those based on lack of a 'duty of care' is difficult to pin down precisely and seems to be ever

5   See below.

shifting. Indeed, some judges have despaired of describing this relationship precisely and have resorted to saying that since the effect of a successful remoteness argument is the same as the effect of a successful lack of duty argument, namely that the defendant wins, the two arguments are indistinguishable. Thus, for example, Lord Denning in *Spartan Steel v Martin*:[6]

> 'The more I think about these cases, the more difficult I find it to put each into its proper pigeon-hole. Sometimes I say: "there was no duty." In others I say: "the damage was too remote." So much so that I think the time has come to discard these tests which have proved so elusive.'

But most judges have not followed Lord Denning's advice. In particular, they are very reluctant to take the step that Denning made and to declare that judges decide each case on the basis of 'policy',[7] probably with good reason given the vagueness of the term. But it is worth noting that a tendency to elide duty and remoteness arguments together, and to classify the result as a 'duty' argument, has become very marked in English law.

The tendency to conflate duty and remoteness arguments is most apparent in the rise of the notion of 'proximity'[8] as a necessary condition for the existence of a duty of care. 'Proximity' originally merely meant the mirror image of 'remoteness'. If an act was 'too remote' it could also be described as 'not sufficiently proximate.' And that is what it still means in most cases in which it now appears. In a case such as *Hill v Chief Constable for West Yorkshire*[9] for example, in which the claim is against the police for allowing a criminal to remain at large and to continue his murderous career, the 'proximity' issue is merely the fact that the actual harm to the plaintiff came about because of the wrongdoing both of the police and of the criminal, and, if anyone was more to blame for the injuries, it must be the criminal. This is nothing other than a classic remoteness problem. Similarly, in *Yuen Kun Yeu v A-G (Hong Kong)*,[10] in which depositors in a failed financial institution sued the government regulator of the institution for failing to protect them, the 'proximity' problem was precisely that the real culprit was the institution itself and that the plaintiffs might not be entirely free of blame themselves, so that again what is raised is the classic remoteness problem of what to do about the presence of other causes of the plaintiffs' loss. *Caparo v Dickman*[11] is another example. A company that had taken over another company found that its prey was worth rather less than expected. The plaintiff company sued the target company's auditors for negligently misleading it about the target company's value. The 'proximity' issue was that the real culprits were probably the managers of the target

6   [1973] QB 27, 37.
7   Ibid. See also *Dutton v Bognor Regis UDC* [1972] 1 QB 373.
8   See below ch 5 for an extended discussion of 'proximity'.
9   [1989] AC 53.
10 [1988] AC 175.
11 [1990] 2 AC 605.

company, who may have misled the auditors, and that in any case the plaintiff company itself could be said to have brought the disaster upon itself. These are also classic remoteness problems.

Despite the fact that there is often no difference between an old 'remoteness' point and a new 'proximity' point, judges insist, in the cases cited and elsewhere, on treating the new 'proximity' as a new idea linked intimately with 'duty', rather than as a separate question. The English judges seem to have recreated the German notion that 'remoteness' about the whole of the damage is different from 'remoteness' about part of the damage, but without realising what they have done and without articulating any reasons for doing so.

An older example of the same elision of duty and remoteness is the so-called 'foreseeable plaintiff' rule. In cases such as *Bourhill v Young*,[12] in parallel with American cases such as *Palsgraf v Long Island Railroad*,[13] the problem arises of harm being caused not to the obvious potential victim of the defendant's carelessness but to someone else. In *Palsgraf*, for example, the employees of the defendant railway company pulled a man aboard a moving train which he was about to miss. By a somewhat improbable series of events, including the fact that the man pulled on the train was carrying a package full of fireworks which he dropped and which then exploded, this act of kindness ended with injury to the plaintiff who was standing on the platform on the other side of the track. In *Bourhill*, the careless riding of a motorcycle led to a crash, but the plaintiff was not someone who was hit by the motorcycle or by anything else, but instead was a woman standing out of sight of the accident but within earshot who suffered a miscarriage allegedly as the result of hearing the crash.

In cases such as these, the tendency is to describe the problem not as remoteness but as 'duty of care to whom?' and to describe a result favourable to the defendant as a decision that there was no duty of care owed to that particular plaintiff. This is reinforced by the formulation that these cases are won by defendants because the plaintiff was 'unforeseeable'.

But a moment's thought reveals that these cases too are remoteness cases in the classical sense. The problem they present is whether to let the defendant off because of the presence of other causal factors. In the case of *Palsgraf*, the other causes of the plaintiff's injuries include the fact that a man carrying fireworks attempted to board a moving train and the fact that those fireworks exploded merely because they hit the ground.[14] In *Bourhill*, the underlying problem, as in all cases of psychological harm or 'nervous shock' is that judges have long believed that anyone who suffers from a mental illness probably has some pre-existing weakness in their personality and is therefore somehow partly responsible for their condition themselves.

12 [1943] AC 92.
13 248 NY 339, 162 NE 99, 59 ALR 1253 (1928).
14 Note that another way of seeing *Palsgraf* is as a 'causal fade' case—our confidence in the causal status of the original careless act of the railway employees declines with every link in the concatenation of events that led to the injury to the plaintiff.

The elision of remoteness points into the duty of care can be extremely confusing, since it tends to mix together the specific issue of the competing claims of 'you shouldn't have done it anyway' and 'it's unfair to blame me for all this' with all the other possible arguments for or against saying that a defendant who has admittedly acted badly should escape having to pay compensation.[15] But the temptation to do it has presumably only increased since the advent of proportional responsibility statutes and the difficulty of making sense of all or nothing arguments such as remoteness. In addition, the collapse of negligence into 'foreseeability' in the 1960s and 1970s meant first that, in the wake of the *Wagon Mound (No 1)*, 'remoteness' arguments ceased to be understood as they had previously been understood, and indeed threatened to descend into incomprehensibility, and secondly that those who knew that there was more to negligence than just foreseeability were forced to scrabble around for ways to re-introduce concepts other than foreseeability into the law. The result has been, to oversimplify but not by much, that many remoteness arguments, having been undermined by the *Wagon Mound (No 1)*'s attempt to reduce them to foreseeability, are now making a reappearance as an element of the duty of care under the guise of 'proximity.'

It is better, however, especially from the point of view of students trying to grasp negligence for the first time, and after the law has been marched up the *Wagon Mound* hill and marched back down again, to understand remoteness in its pre-*Wagon Mound* sense first, to graft on the net effect of the post-*Wagon Mound* cases, and then to understand the result both as a requirement itself and also as a way of understanding 'proximity' in the duty of care.

Another possibility would be to adopt explicitly the German distinction between remoteness about the whole of the loss, which goes to liability (and thus 'duty'), and remoteness that goes only to the extent of the loss.[16] But it would be wise to reject this distinction, even though it may underlie the present fashion for 'proximity', for it serves only to cause unnecessary confusion. 'Remoteness' can only be relevant to whether the defendant was careless in the first place if it is taken to mean either the same thing as carelessness or some element or combination of elements of carelessness (for example the chance of the accident occurring or that chance combined with the seriousness of the accident if it does occur). But if 'remoteness' or 'proximity' is used in a sense that means the same as 'carelessness' it is confusing, and if it used in a sense that refers to some part of the test for carelessness, it is both unnecessary and likely to give a false impression that the part of the test for carelessness concerned is somehow more important than the other parts. It is especially important, for example, if clarity is to be maintained in the assessment of fault, that the element of

15 This is the opposite of the conclusion drawn by Prosser, see eg *Torts* (4th ed) p 244, that ignoring the distinction between remoteness and duty would bring out the real issues in such cases with greater clarity. On the contrary, ignoring the distinction merely serves to obscure the issues.

16 See above.

the test for carelessness that draws attention to what would have been sacrificed had the harm been avoided is not obscured.

The law in detail

We can now pass on to examine the positive law in this area. The issue at all times will be whether, and if so how, the courts have resolved the tension between imposing supposedly excessive burdens on defendants and the point that the defendant should not have done what he or she did in the first place.

Pre-existing condition of the plaintiff

The most fundamental question in remoteness is the relevance of the plaintiff's own condition or circumstances. The argument for the defendant that underlies the cases is that the injury to the plaintiff should be said to be the result of plaintiff's own weaknesses and thus should count as the plaintiff's own responsibility.

The immediate difficulty the defendant faces is that any fault on the part of the plaintiff can be taken into account by a finding of contributory negligence. If the plaintiff is at fault, damages are reduced.

The defendant has to be saying that there is more at stake than contributory negligence. In fact, what the defendant is really saying is not that the defendant did anything wrong, but that the extent of the loss was greater than might have been normally expected because of circumstances beyond anyone's control. The defendant is saying in effect that those who act carelessly have a legitimate expectation that victims of accidents turn out to be near to the average in terms of vulnerability. The defendant is saying, furthermore, that forms of conduct that usually only lead to small amounts of harm to people near to that average should be judged as blameworthy only to the extent of the harm that they normally cause. To hold them responsible for harm beyond the normal range is to make them pay too much in relation to the blameworthiness of their conduct.

What has happened in practice when defendants have raised this point? The answer is simple. Especially in cases of plaintiffs with physical weaknesses, defendants have had very little success with this line of argument. The principle applied is that **tortfeasors must take their victims as they find them**, that is the courts agree with plaintiffs that the tortfeasors should not have done what they did anyway.

For example, in *Smith v Leech Brain*[17] the plaintiff, an employee of the defendants, suffered burns to his lip as the result of the inadequate safety measures in the defendants' factory. The plaintiff's lip was unfortunately

17 [1962] 2 QB 405.

in a pre-malignant state and the trauma of the accident led to the development of a cancer from which he died three years later. The defendants tried to argue that the *Wagon Mound (No 1)* meant that the court should ask only whether it was reasonably foreseeable that the plaintiff might die of cancer from being burned. Since both the pre-malignant condition and the cancer itself were quite rare, to pose the question in the manner apparently required by the *Wagon Mound* test would have meant judgment for the defendant.

But the Court refused to take the *Wagon Mound* line. Lord Parker CJ said that he did not think that the Privy Council in the *Wagon Mound* meant to undermine the traditional rule:[18]

> 'It has always been the law of this country that a tortfeasor takes his victim as he finds him.'

The rule that tortfeasors have to take their victims as they find them is also known as the 'thin skull rule.' This formulation of the rule can be illustrated from the judgment of Kennedy J in *Dulieu v White*:[19]

> 'If a man is negligently run over or otherwise negligently injured in his body, it is no answer ... that he would have suffered less injury, or no injury at all, if he had not had an unusually thin skull or an unusually weak heart.'

The reasoning that lies behind these decisions is of interest in itself, for it might be asked why the law comes out against defendants in cases like S*mith v Leech Brain*. Why should the tortfeasor 'take the victim as he finds him'?

In *Smith v Leech Brain*, Lord Parker CJ cites Kennedy J in *Dulieu v White* and Scrutton LJ in *The Arpad*.[20] Scrutton LJ said in *The Arpad*, for example, that the rule that tortfeasors take their victims as they find them is derived from the principle that tort damages compensate victims for their actual losses, not for the losses that average people might have suffered in the same circumstances.

> 'In the cases of claims in tort, damages are constantly given for consequences of which the defendant had no notice. You negligently run down a shabby looking man in the street and he turns out to be a millionaire engaged in a very profitable business which the accident disables him from carrying on; or you negligently injure the favourite for the Derby whereby he cannot run. You have to pay the damages resulting from the circumstances of which you have no notice.'[1]

18 At 414.
19 [1901] 2 KB 669 at 679.
20 [1934] P 189.
1 [1934] P 189 at 202 and 203.

In other words, the rule is that rich plaintiffs who lose a lot are compensated a lot and poor plaintiffs who lose not very much are not compensated very much. This rule, in turn, can be justified by a mixture of incentive or deterrence arguments and fairness. For if the rule were otherwise, and for example, the rich only received compensation based on average incomes, tortfeasors would be deterred less than they should be in the light of the harm that they cause. But if, to balance out this effect, compensation for poorer victims were to be set also on the basis of average incomes, not only would the situation be unfair—since the defendant would be required to pay for more harm than was actually suffered, but there might also be the perverse consequence that potential victims of accidents might have an incentive to take less care of themselves. If, for example, a person on 40% of average income were to be injured, having been half to blame for the accident, the average earnings basis of compensation would give them the equivalent of half of average income, so they would be better off to the tune of 10% of average income.

The connection between the thin skull rule and the compensation rule is simply that the compensation rule shows that the foreseeability of the plaintiff's particular circumstances is not relevant to the damages payable, even if those circumstances alter greatly the plaintiff's loss. It would be remarkable, given that the defendant cannot use the plaintiff's unusual financial circumstances to reduce the damages, if the defendant could reduce the damages by reference to the plaintiff's unusual physical circumstances.

The law of most other jurisdictions appears to follow broadly the same lines. In the USA, for example, the law of most states traces itself back to a nineteenth century case from Wisconsin, *Vosburg v Putney*[2] in which Lyon J. said:

> 'The wrongdoer is liable for all injuries resulting directly from the wrongful act, whether they could or could not have been foreseen by him.'

German law follows similar lines. In a case, for example, in which the plaintiff, who had unusually thin abdominal muscles, suffered unusually serious injuries as the result of a dog bite, the defendant was held to be responsible for the full amount of the loss. The plaintiff's unusual physical weakness did not justify reducing the damages at all.[3] In French law too, the principle is that the defendant must take the victim as he finds him, although some writers are attracted to the idea that while the plaintiff's pre-existing condition should not excuse the defendant completely, it perhaps should give rise to a partial exoneration, that is a reduction of the damages to represent the proportion of the responsibility that the plaintiff's condition should bear.[4]

---

2   50 NW 403, 80 Wis 523 (1891) (Wis).

3   See BGH NJW 1983, 168. *Markesinis* at 105ff.

4   *Viney* para 434, p.514; *Malaurie & Aynès* para 98 p 58. But note that the principle appears to have been translated directly from the English.

But 'taking the victims as you find them' is not as broadly applicable a principle of English law as one might expect. Defendants have had some success in so-called 'nervous shock' cases, for example. In these cases the plaintiff seeks compensation on the grounds that the defendant's carelessness caused the plaintiff to succumb to mental illness. The issue sometimes arises in such cases whether it matters that the victim was unusually susceptible to mental illness, perhaps to the extent of already suffering from such an illness. In *Brice v Brown*,[5] for example, Stuart-Smith J held that although it did not matter that the plaintiff ended up more seriously ill than might have been expected, the circumstances had to be such that 'a person of normal disposition and phlegm'[6] or someone 'of a normally robust constitution'[7] might have been expected to have succumbed to some recognised mental illness, albeit perhaps to a different mental illness from the one suffered by the plaintiff.[8] The effect of this rule is that in nervous shock cases, unlike physical injury cases, the defendant's point of view about the plaintiff's predisposition is respected. Liability is restricted to those cases in which average or near average victims might have been expected to suffer harm.

The reasons why nervous shock cases tend to be treated differently from physical injury cases are taken up further in chapter 5 below, but it is worth noting that in the nineteenth century, when hostility to compensation for nervous shock was at its height, the courts appeared to believe that psychiatric illnesses resulted largely from character defects. This meant two things: first, that the court thought of the illness as largely the plaintiff's own fault, since people were at that time held responsible for the development of their own characters; and, secondly, that it was far from clear in any particular case that the plaintiff would not have developed the condition anyway. This combination of a remoteness argument (the illness results from the fault of the plaintiff) and a causal fade-away problem (was the illness anything to do with the accident?) pointed clearly in the direction of no liability.

These objections to compensating psychiatric illness were partly overcome when the courts began to allow plaintiffs to recover in cases in which there had been some definite shock to the plaintiff's 'nervous system.'[9] When there was such a shock the courts felt more confident that the cause of the illness was the defendant's actions, rather than any underlying condition, and also could be persuaded that, if the shock was big enough, succumbing to mental illness could be seen as a normal reaction rather than as a sign of weakness. Neither of these points is particularly

---

5   [1984] 1 All ER 997.
6   At 1006.
7   At 1007.
8   This test cannot be taken too literally. 'Recognised' mental illnesses presumably include all the mental disorders listed in the American Psychiatric Association's Diagnostic and Statistical Manual (DSM) of Mental Disorders. But some remarkably trivial disorders have appeared in its pages, including, for example, a disorder caused by drinking too much coffee. For legal purposes, the foreseeable disorder must, it is submitted, be serious enough to count as recognisable harm.
9   Eg *Hambrook v Stokes* [1925] 1 KB 141, *Bourhill v Young* [1943] AC 92, *Dooley v Cammell Laird* [1951] 1 Lloyd's Rep 271.

convincing—why should a shock be more likely to cause mental illness than, for example, long-term exposure to stress?

The law has moved on somewhat from the shock theory[10] but some of the underlying objections to compensation for psychiatric loss persist, at least below the surface. Although the view of psychiatric illness as caused by character defects is no longer fashionable, the question of whether or not the illness would have developed anyway remains. *Brice v Brown* is an illustration of the point. If the plaintiff has a predisposition to mental illness, it is not clear whether the appearance of the illness is the result of the accident or the result of the underlying predisposition. The purpose of the 'person of normal disposition and phelgm' test is, like that of the shock theory, to help sort out the cases in which the mental illness was caused by the accident and would not have happened anyway. The idea is that circumstances in which people without mental illnesses or without predispositions to mental illnesses would have gone on to suffer from such an illness are more likely to be circumstances in which the defendant's conduct made a difference than cases in which such people would not have been affected. Whether or not this point is any more convincing than the shock theory is left to the reader to decide.[11]

The rule that defendants have to take victims as they find them does not always apply with full force where the plaintiffs' losses have been caused or worsened by their own lack of resources. The central case in this controversial area is *The Edison*.[12] In *The Edison* the defendant's ship dragged the plaintiff's ship off its moorings and out into the open sea where it sank. The plaintiff's ship was being used as a dredger, and without it the plaintiff was unable to fulfil its obligations under a contract. The plaintiff therefore hired a substitute dredger. The hire charges for the substitute were very high, and it would have been cheaper for the plaintiff to buy the dredger, but at the time they lacked the cash to buy it outright. Later the Harbour Board bought the dredger and resold it to the plaintiff on an instalment basis, the instalments being less than the hire charges.

The central question before the House of Lords was whether the plaintiff could recover in damages not just for replacing the dredger at the eventual price (including compensation for the disturbance to the contract) but also for the extra cost of the high hire charges incurred by the plaintiff before the Harbour Board stepped in to buy the dredger. The defendant's case

10 But see below ch 5 for some signs of movement back to the shock theory.

11 Note that many legal systems are affected by similar concerns about psychiatric damage, but that the rules can come out very differently. In German law, for example, the rule that the defendant must take the victim as he finds them applies to psychiatric predispositions as well. But, on the other hand, this rule is counter-balanced by a compensation neurosis rule, under which courts are apt to find that the real source of the illness is the legal process itself and to deny liability. See *Markesinis* at 106 and BGHZ 20, 137, 142. See also *Clippens Oil Co Ltd v Edinburgh and District Water Trustees* [1907] AC 291, 303.

12 [1933] AC 449 [1933] All ER Rep 144. *The Edison* was the name of the defendant's ship. Note that this case is sometimes referred to by the name of the plaintiff's ship, namely the *Liesbosch*.

was that the plaintiff's loss should be measured in terms of the cheapest reasonable method of putting the situation right, and that meant the cost of buying a new dredger immediately. The fact that the plaintiff lacked the cash to do so was no affair of the defendant.

The plaintiff's case, as put to the court by counsel,[13] was straightforward:

'One of the parties has to suffer the result of the appellants' lack of funds ... It is submitted that the wrongdoers are the proper persons to bear the misfortune. ... As the law will lay down no standard of health so it will lay down no standard of affluence for those who engage in business.'

In addition, the plaintiff pointed out that adopting the defendant's position would have adverse practical consequences:[14]

'If a firm ... may not engage in an adventure without first accumulating funds which will suffice to meet all emergencies, there would be little encouragement for enterprise.'

The defendant replied that:[15]

'When the absence of ready cash was caused entirely by their own action, by what line of argument can they visit the respondents with the consequences?'

The lack of resources, argued the defendant, should be treated as an independent extraneous cause of the loss, so that, even under *Polemis* (which was then the leading case on remoteness), the loss was indirect and therefore unrecoverable.

Lord Wright, delivering the leading judgment of the House of Lords, agreed with the defendant:[16]

'[T]he impecuniosity was not traceable to the [defendant's] acts and in my opinion was outside the legal purview of the consequences of these acts.... [It was] an independent cause, though its operative effect was conditioned by the loss of the dredger.'

Lord Wright went on to distinguish *Polemis* and the thin skull rule. On *Polemis* he agreed with the defendant's counsel that 'the [plaintiff's] want of means was ... extrinsic.' As for the thin skull rule, Lord Wright says that its effect is confined to cases concerning 'the extent of actual physical damage'.

But there are obvious difficulties with the defendant's position in *The Edison*. In the first place, the reason for treating the plaintiff's impec

13 [1933] AC 449 at 452.
14 At 453.
15 At 454.
16 At 460.

uniosity as an 'extrinsic' factor is, apparently, that it results from the actions of the plaintiff. But equally the state of the plaintiff's health in *Smith v Leech Brain* also resulted from the plaintiff's own actions, since his predisposition to cancer was thought to be connected with the chemicals he had come into contact with in his previous job. If *The Edison* is correct, the thin skull rule in physical injury cases could apply only to purely genetic preconditions.

Secondly, just as an impecunious plaintiff suffers because of his lack of ready cash, a very wealthy plaintiff is able to obtain discounts from traders hoping for future custom and from lenders who know that the risk of default is lower. But surely wealthy plaintiffs should not be allowed to recover more than their actual losses.

Doubts about whether *The Edison* was correctly decided soon set in. In *Monarch SS Co Ltd v Karlshamns*[17] Lord Wright himself admitted that:

'A different conclusion was arrived at in *Muhammed Issa el Sheikh Ahmad v Ali* [1947] AC 414 where damages consequent on impecuniosity were held not too remote, because, as I understand, the loss was such as might reasonably be expected to be in the contemplation of the parties as likely to flow from breach of the obligation... The difference in result did not depend on the differences (if any) between tort and contract in this connexion. The "reasonable contemplation" as to damages is what the court attributes to the parties.'

There are two ways of looking at this statement. It may simply be that, as in the nervous shock example, what counts is the average degree of vulnerability, so that if the average expected victim is impecunious, the defendant has to accept that fact. Or it may be that in typical English style, reasonable foreseeability has been called in to correct the effects of a decision that is thought to have gone too far.

More recently in *Dodd Properties (Kent) Ltd v Canterbury City Council*[18] the Court of Appeal distinguished *The Edison* and expressed dissatisfaction with it. In *Dodd*, the defendant's building operations damaged the plaintiff's property. The defendant denied liability until just before the trial. During this time, the plaintiff refused to carry out repairs, fearing that if the court found for the defendant, the repairs would be too expensive for its limited means. But by the time the defendant admitted liability, the cost of repairs had risen. The plaintiff claimed damages for the cost of repairs as of the time of the defendant's admission. The defendant said that it should be held responsible only for the cost of repairs at the time the damage was done. The extra loss had been incurred, according to the defendant, because of the plaintiff's impecuniosity.

As Donaldson LJ admitted:[19]

17 [1949] AC 196, 224.
18 [1980] 1 WLR 433.
19 At 458.

'Whatever the difficulties inherent in the [*Edison*] decision—and it is not at once apparent why a tortfeasor must take his victim as he finds him in terms of high or low profit-earning capacity, but not in terms of pecuniosity or impecuniosity which may be their manifestation—it binds this court … until it is reviewed by the House of Lords.'

But, having first adopted the *Muhammed Issa el Sheikh Ahmad v Ali* view that the defendant cannot plead the plaintiff's impecuniosity unless the plaintiff's lack of funds was unforeseeable, Donaldson LJ distinguishes *The Edison* on two grounds. First, the plaintiff in *Dodd* had other reasons, apart from lack of money, that kept him from taking corrective action. The main other reason, according to Donaldson LJ[20] was the plaintiff's under–standable uncertainty about the outcome of the legal action. It was, according to Donaldson LJ, ordinary prudence that caused the plaintiff to hold back. The second ground for distinguishing *The Edison* was that the plaintiff in *Dodd* was 'not impecunious in the [*Edison*] sense of one who could not afford to go to market.' The plaintiff had some funds but did not want to risk losing them in advance of the outcome of the trial.

In practice, of course, it is difficult to imagine circumstances in which pure lack of funds constitutes the only reason for the plaintiff's conduct. Whenever the plaintiff is contemplating legal action, as in *Dodd,* the uncertainties of that action must always be relevant.

Doubts about the *Edison* rule and attempts to distinguish it have continued in cases such as *Jarvis v T Richards*,[1] *Perry v Sydney Phillips*,[2] and *Archer v Brown*.[3] In *Jarvis* and *Archer*, the defendants lost because the court insisted that the impecuniosity was foreseeable, or even that the defendant had caused it. In *Perry* the Court of Appeal went further. Lord Denning MR said that *The Edison* should be restricted to its own facts[4] and Kerr LJ[5] said that 'In any event, the authority of what Lord Wright said in the [*Edison*] … is consistently being attenuated in more recent decisions of this court…'.

In *Ramwade Ltd v WJ Emson*,[6] however, the Court of Appeal gave some belated support to the *Edison* doctrine. The context of the case was a dispute about insurance contracts, but in essence the problem was that the plaintiff could not afford to replace his damaged lorry and instead had to hire one expensively. Parker and Nourse LLJ applied the *Edison* rule almost without comment.

But *Ramwade* was itself distinguished by the Court of Appeal in *Mattocks v Mann*.[7] The defendant damaged the plaintiff's car, which had to be taken

---

20 At 459-60. See also Megaw LJ at 452-3 and Browne LJ at 456.
1 (1980) 124 Sol Jo 793.
2 [1982] 1 WLR 1297.
3 [1985] QB 401.
4 [1982] 1 WLR 1297 at 1302.
5 At 1307.
6 [1987] RTR 72.
7 [1993] RTR 13.

off the road for repair. In the meantime the plaintiff hired a cheaper car. Periodically the plaintiff, who was unemployed, would run out of money and would dispense temporarily with using a car altogether. The defendant attacked the plaintiff's hiring of a car as a failure to mitigate the loss as the result of impecuniosity. The Court of Appeal disagreed. Beldam LJ explained:[8]

> 'A similar argument to that advanced in this case was advanced in *Bolton v Price* (unreported) Court of Appeal (Civil Division) Transcript no 1159 of 1989 in which I gave the judgment of the court. I there said that at the present day it is generally accepted that, in what Lord Wright termed "the varied web of affairs" that follows a sequence of events after an accident of this kind, it is only in an exceptional case that it is possible or correct to isolate impecuniosity ... as a separate cause and as terminating the consequences of the defendant's wrong. It seems to me necessary today to consider whether, having regard to all the circumstances of the case and the resources available to a plaintiff, resources known by the defendant or her representatives to be of a kind that will not be able to provide for repairs themselves, in all the circumstances the plaintiff has acted reasonably and with comm— ercial prudence.'

Beldam LJ remarked that nowadays most people rely not on their savings but on their insurance to provide the money to pay for repairs, and that lack of cash in advance of the settlement of an insurance claim should not disadvantage the plaintiff.

It can be seen from *Mattocks* that, despite the occasional brief comeback, *The Edison* is still being distinguished out of existence. It is therefore very doubtful whether the *Edison* doctrine would survive if it was challenged directly in the House of Lords.

Actions by the plaintiff

If we move from remoteness arguments based on the plaintiff's pre-existing condition to those based on acts or events, the picture begins to change. This is because it is a better reason for letting off the defendant that somebody else changed the situation than that the pre-existing situation meant that the results of the defendant's act were different from what the defendant might have expected. We begin with the acts of the plaintiff before moving on to acts of third parties.

A central case is *McKew v Holland and Hannen and Cubitts (Scotland) Ltd*,[9] in which the defendant's admitted carelessness led to an injury to

8   At 19.
9   [1969] 3 All ER 1621.

the plaintiff's leg, which in turn meant that the plaintiff was periodically very unsteady on his feet. The plaintiff subsequently went to inspect a new flat. The flat had very steep stairs and no handrail. On the way down these stairs, the plaintiff's leg gave way and he suffered further injury. The plaintiff then tried to add damages for the extra injury arising from the fall to the original damages claimed for the initial injury to his leg. The claim failed. Lord Reid in the House of Lords said that the plaintiff could not claim for the additional injury because he had acted unreasonably. He had put himself in position where he knew or should have known that an emergency of this nature might occur.

Note that another way of dealing with the plaintiff in *McKew* to produce the same result would have been to say that the defendant was responsible for the whole loss but that the plaintiff was guilty of contributory negligence, and his damages would be reduced to reflect his degree of responsibility. Indeed, in principle, it seems preferable always to use contributory negligence in cases of intervention by the plaintiff. Unfortunately, the courts have not yet accepted such a principle.

In contrast to *McKew*, in *Wieland v Cyril Lord Carpets*[10] the plaintiff's actions were considered not to exonerate the defendant. In *Wieland*, the defendant's carelessness meant that the plaintiff was injured and had to wear a surgical collar, which severely restricted her movements. The plaintiff wore bi-focal spectacles, but found that it was difficult, because of the surgical collar, to keep what she saw in focus. As a result she fell down some stairs at her son's office and was injured. The defendant claimed that the injury was too remote, but this time the court ruled in favour of the plaintiff.

The court said that two aspects of the facts of the case were important. First, the second accident happened soon after the surgical collar had been fitted. The position might well have been different, according to the court, if the plaintiff had persisted in wearing bi-focals for a long time after injury. Secondly, it was said to be important that climbing stairs is one of the ordinary activities of life.

Note that there are two ways of interpreting the importance the court placed on these facts. On the one hand, consistent with the *Wagon Mound* view of remoteness, the point may be that the plaintiff's continuing to wear bi-focals for a short time and climbing stairs are reasonably foresee–able events but that persisting in wearing them and engaging in more dangerous activities would not have been reasonably foreseeable. On the other hand, consistent with the *Polemis* view of remoteness, the point may be that persisting in wearing bi-focals for a long time, for example after having experienced difficulties caused by wearing the surgical collar, would have amounted to a deliberate intervening act by the plaintiff, and taking part in any out-of-the-ordinary activities would not count as a natural or probable consequence of the defendant's carelessness.

But on balance, the *Polemis* interpretation of *Wieland* is better than the *Wagon Mound* interpretation. For one thing, the defendant did in fact argue

10 [1969] 3 All ER 1006.

that the damage was not foreseeable under the rule in the *Wagon Mound (No 1)* but was told that the *Wagon Mound* did not apply. For another, the only foreseeability requirement the court required in *Wieland* was of a general nature.[11] The plaintiff had to prove neither that the extent of the harm was foreseeable nor that the exact way in which the injury came about was foreseeable. Indeed, courts have adopted these two rules in other cases and they have become the orthodox view of what 'foreseeability' requires in remoteness cases.[12]

Note that in the *Wagon Mound (No 1)* itself, it turned out that the plaintiff's own actions (including ordering the welding to begin again) were taken to be reasonable and not to make the damage too remote. And so the only aspects of the damage that were really unforeseeable in the *Wagon Mound* were precisely its extent and the way it came about. How the courts have made sense of this, without openly denouncing the *Wagon Mound*, is a topic fascinating in itself and is taken up in more detail below in the section on natural events. But what, in short, the courts have apparently done is to say that the *Wagon Mound* rule applies only to the 'kind' of harm, not to anything else. As long as the 'kind' of harm is reasonably foreseeable, the plaintiff's case apparently satisfies the *Wagon Mound* remoteness test. Exactly what counts as a 'kind' of harm, however, is one of the great uncertainties of English negligence law.[13]

To return to the case law on the effect of plaintiffs' acts, the question remains as to exactly what sort of behaviour on the part of the plaintiff results in the harm being declared to be too remote. An important attempt to state a principle occurs in *Emeh v Kensington and Chelsea and West-minster Area Health Authority*[14] in which the defendant doctors performed a sterilisation operation on the plaintiff incompetently. She consequently became pregnant.[15] The plaintiff discovered her condition when she was 20 weeks into her pregnancy. In principle, it would have been possible for her to have an abortion. But she refused. The defendant attempted to persuade the Court of Appeal that in refusing an abortion the plaintiff had intervened in the situation and had made the damage too remote. The

---

11 Ibid at 1011.
12 See eg *Bradford v Robinson Rentals* [1967] 1 All ER 267, [1967] 1 WLR 337, 1 KIR 486. Note, however, that in *Bradford*, as in many post-*Wagon Mound* cases, the court feels obliged to attempt to apply both the *Wieland* rules and the *Wagon Mound* principles. In *Bradford*, the effect is to produce arguments that border on the bizarre. The case concerned an employee of the defendants who drove a delivery van in the area of Brixham. The heater in the van was defective. But the employee did not only get cold: he got frostbite. Frostbite is rather unusual in the south west of England. Nevertheless, the court said that the injury was foreseeable enough to satisfy *Wagon Mound*, as well as, obviously, falling within the *Wieland* rule that the exact extent of the injury does not have to be foreseeable. If frostbite in Brixham is foreseeable, anything is.
13 See below.
14 [1985] QB 1012.
15 See below pp 619-621 for discussion of the question of whether damages are recoverable in principle in such cases for the expense involved in bringing up children.

Court refused to be moved. It was, Slade LJ said,[16] very unlikely that refusing an abortion could ever be held to break the chain of causation. The reason was, as Waller LJ said, building on a passage from the speech of Lord Reid in *McKew*, that for the plaintiff's act to break the chain of causation, 'The degree of unreasonable conduct which is required is ... very high.'[17]

This test that the plaintiff's act must be 'utterly unreasonable'[18] is clearly useful and quite easy to apply, even though its theoretical basis remains (perhaps usefully) ambiguous. In essence, it is a fault test—if the plaintiff has acted particularly badly, the chain of causation may be broken. Whether this is because utterly unreasonable acts are not reasonably foreseeable (not a particularly believable proposition) or because they tend to be conscious interventions (but then why not require intentionality?) is not clear. Perhaps its true basis is that the test is the equivalent of a finding of 100% contributory negligence.[19] That is, the idea may well be, as *Clerk & Lindsell on Torts* suggests,[20] that the plaintiff should lose if the defendant's responsibility for the harm pales into insignificance in comparison with that of the plaintiff.

Before leaving this topic, some particularly difficult problems deserve mention.

First, what should be said about plaintiffs who have committed suicide as a result, at least in part, of the defendant's fault? One example is *Pigney v Pointers Transport Services Ltd*[1] in which the plaintiff's husband, injured at work as a result of his employer's carelessness, became depressed and hanged himself. The judge found that the man was not legally insane although he did suffer from a recognised mental illness. The judge also found that the suicide was not a foreseeable result of the employer's carelessness. Nevertheless, the judge, citing the *Polemis* directness rule but not otherwise explaining his reasoning, found for the plaintiff.

As a pre-*Wagon Mound* case, the value of *Pigney* might now be doubted. But more recently in *Kirkham v Chief Constable of Greater Manchester Police*[2] the same result was reached. In *Kirkham*, the police failed to inform the prison service of the known suicidal tendencies of a prisoner who was remanded in custody. In consequence, the prison service did not put into effect their normal precautions against suicide, the result of which was that the prisoner hanged himself in his cell. The prisoner's wife sued the police under the Fatal Accidents Act and for negligence on behalf of her husband's estate. One of the various arguments advanced by the defence,

16   [1985] QB 1012 at 1024.
17   At 1019. See also *Allen v Bloomsbury Health Authority* [1993] 1 All ER 651.
18   See *Clerk & Lindsell on Torts* (15th edn) p 561.
19   Findings of 100% contributory negligence are, allegedly, not possible within the terms of the Law Reform (Contributory Negligence) Act 1945. See below ch 15. Sed quaere. But this does not affect, of course, the point being made in the text, and indeed tends to strengthen it, since there would then be no duplication in the law.
20   Ibid.
1   [1957] 2 All ER 807, [1957] 1 WLR 1121.
2   [1989] 3 All ER 882.

all of which were rejected by the court, was that the damage was too remote. Tudor Evans J rejected the remoteness argument on the grounds that:[3]

> 'Although the act of suicide was in a sense a conscious and deliberate act, the deceased's mental balance was, I am satisfied, affected at the time.'

That is, Tudor Evans J assumes that the relevant test is still something like *Polemis* directness, in which conscious and deliberate acts can break the chain of causation, but finds that, as a result of the plaintiff's mental illness, his suicide could not count as a voluntary act in the full sense. The question then becomes simply one of factual causation: if the police had passed on what they knew, would the suicide have been prevented? The answer to this question, the judge finds, is probably yes.

Whether or not the outcome of *Kirkham* is consistent with the 'utterly unreasonable' test is unclear. But one can understand why the judge did not use that test. For a court to say that a suicide was not 'utterly unreasonable' would be a remarkable thing. But equally, to say that it was 'utterly unreasonable' for the plaintiff to commit suicide seems to pass a harsh judgment on someone obviously in distress. And to admit into the judgment of reasonableness the plaintiff's state of mental health (for example to ask whether the plaintiff acted reasonably given his state of mental health) is to border on the self-contradiction of discussing whether someone who is far from capable of being reasonable has acted reasonably. It is much more convenient, since it avoids these difficult topics, to treat the mentally-ill plaintiff as an object buffeted by the causal influences of the outside world rather than as a reasoning being capable of making decisions. Whether this is philosophically or morally the right line to take is another matter.

The second difficult case concerns plaintiffs who divorce. In *Pritchard v JH Cobden*,[4] the defendant's careless driving resulted in a collision with the vehicle being driven by the plaintiff. The plaintiff suffered brain damage. Subsequently, it was alleged, the plaintiff underwent a complete change in personality with the result that his marriage broke up. The plaintiff included a claim in his action against the defendant for the extra expenses that he would have to incur as a result of the divorce, namely losses arising out of the share-out of the couple's real property, legal fees and the additional costs of running two households.

The fate of the parts of claim based on the division of the plaintiff's real property was sealed by the Court of Appeal's observation that divorce simply shares out the couple's property, it does not reduce it in value. Perhaps the plaintiff could have said that being forced to liquidate the family's assets at a time not of his own choosing must involve some loss. But he did not. Furthermore, the court claimed that it was not more expensive to run two households than one, in view of the tax advantages and social security

3 At 888-89.
4 [1988] Fam 22.

benefits then available.[5] The court also said that legal costs were 'largely speculative' (a statement that would amuse most lawyers).

But despite the fact that the Court of Appeal had successfully disposed of the plaintiff's claim by the simple but effective device of calculating the value of the loss to the plaintiff as zero, it nevertheless felt constrained to pronounce the claimed losses 'too remote' as well.[6] The plaintiff's case on remoteness seemed strong. The defendant had conceded that the divorce was a 'foreseeable' consequence of the accident and there was a previous Court of Appeal decision, *Jones v Jones*,[7] which had assumed the point in favour of the plaintiff. But the Court of Appeal, refusing to follow *Jones*, went the other way, albeit without very great clarity as to why. Sir Roger Ormrod, rather alarmingly, lumped together remoteness, 'indirect economic loss' and public policy[8] and found some unspecified subset of them established by the combination of a (rather shaky) argument based on the alleged circularity of having to decide both the amount of the divorce settlement and the loss to the plaintiff at the same time, an argument based on the inconvenience of allowing the intervention of negligence law in divorce proceedings and the fact that compensating such losses could encourage people to divorce more quickly. What any of this has to do with remoteness is extremely obscure. O'Connor LJ thought that the damage would be too remote 'owing to the special nature of the matrimonial proceedings', so that the intervening act is, presumably, not the divorce itself but the court's exercise of its various discretions under the Matrimonial Causes Act. This makes slightly more sense than Sir Roger Ormrod's judgment, but one might wonder at the jurisprudential consequences of treating the exercise of judicial discretion either as a wilful and deliberate act (as opposed to just applying the law) or as an overwhelming and coincidental natural catastrophe.[9]

Thirdly, there is the very odd series of cases, *Meah v McCreamer*,[10] *W and D v Meah*[11] and *Meah v McCreamer (No 2)*.[12] Technically, they concern intervening acts both of the plaintiff and of third parties, but it is

5   Social security support for ex-spouses is now frowned upon by the authorities, and the main purpose of the Child Support Agency is to eliminate it. See Child Support Act 1991, especially s 6.
6   [1988] Fam 22, O'Connor LJ at p 39, Sir Roger Ormrod at p 49.
7   [1985] QB 704.
8   [1988] Fam 22 at 48 and 49.
9   See now also Bingham MR in *M (a minor) v Newham London Borough Council* and *X (minors) v Bedfordshire County Council* [1994] 4 All ER 602, [1994] Fam Law 434 in a case about alleged negligence by a psychiatrist leading to court orders removing children from their parents to the effect that, 'It was argued that even on the basis of the facts pleaded the psychiatrist's acts and omissions were not the cause of the child's alleged injury, since her separation was the result of orders made by the justices and the judge which necessarily broke the chain of causation. I cannot accept this as a proposition of law. Causation is a question of fact.' Remoteness is, of course, not a simple matter of fact, although it is largely a judgment for the trial court to make.
10 [1985] 1 All ER 367.
11 [1986] 1 All ER 935.
12 [1986] 1 All ER 943.

convenient, indeed essential, to take them together. Mr Meah was a passenger in Mr McCreamer's car. Because of Mr McCreamer's careless— ness—he was drunk—an accident occurred in which Mr Meah suffered serious injury, including brain damage. The brain damage allegedly caused Mr Meah's personality completely to change. He became, in the judge's words, 'aggressive, violent and dangerous.' Mr Meah then proceeded to commit a series of extremely violent sexual assaults on women, for which he was sentenced to life imprisonment.

Meah sued McCreamer for negligence in respect of the road accident and won over £45,000 in damages.[13] Meah claimed damages, inter alia, specifically for the fact that he was now imprisoned for life. As a matter of factual causation, Woolf J, after reviewing the evidence of five expert witnesses, concluded that, on the balance of probabilities, Meah would not have attacked the women, and would not have ended up imprisoned for life, if he had not suffered the injury to his brain. Surprisingly, however, the defendants' counsel, perhaps over-impressed by the Court of Appeal decision in *Jones v Jones*, did not argue the obvious remoteness points— that the crimes had been deliberately committed by Meah, including that at least one of the attacks was clearly premeditated and planned, and that Meah was, according to the criminal law, bad rather than mad. The defence might also have argued that the life sentence was imposed by the court in the criminal case in the exercise of its considerable discretion, so that the chain of causation was broken by the sentence if not by the crime. But it did not. Consequently Woolf J awarded Meah £60,000 general damages for the fact of his imprisonment. The total award of £61,000 was reduced by 25% to reflect Meah's original contributory negligence in getting into McCreamer's car when McCreamer was obviously too drunk to drive.

Since Meah was now one of the wealthiest lifers in the country, two of his victims, prompted by remarks of Woolf J himself[14] brought actions against Meah for the intentional tort of assault or trespass to the person.[15] This case, also heard by Woolf J, became *W and D v Meah*.[16] Liability was admitted and damages were assessed at a total of £17,560.

At the same time as *W and D v Meah*, Meah sought to recover a contribution from McCreamer towards the damages about to be awarded to the victims of his crimes. This case, *Meah v McCreamer (No 2)*[17] at last turns to the remoteness arguments. This time McCreamer argued that the losses claimed, the injuries to the victims, were too remote and that Meah's crimes constituted a novus actus interveniens.

Woolf J begins with the *Wagon Mound (No 1)* and its foreseeability test, to which he adds the usual *Smith v Leech Brain* and *Wieland* riders: first, *Wagon Mound* foreseeability does not affect the applicability of the principle that the defendant must take the victim as he finds him—relevant here

---

13 *Meah v McCreamer* [1985] 1 All ER 367.
14 At [1984] 1 All ER 371-72.
15 See below.
16 [1986] 1 All ER 935.
17 [1986] 1 All ER 943.

because there was evidence that Meah was unusually susceptible to the kind of transformation in his personality that took place;[18] and secondly, that only the type of damage has to be foreseeable not its 'precise nature'. But Woolf J also adds a third, and crucial, rider that even if the type of damage is foreseeable, the damage is still too remote if the chain of causation has been broken by an intervening act. In other words, Woolf J resolves the conflict between the *Wagon Mound* foreseeability test for remoteness and the *Polemis* directness test by saying that the plaintiff has to pass both tests, a very strict position which is now widely assumed to be correct but which may well have surprised early commentators on the *Wagon Mound*,[19] especially since Viscount Simonds said in the *Wagon Mound (No 1)* that, '[E]qually it would be wrong that [the defendant] should escape liability however "indirect" the damage, if he foresaw or could reasonably foresee the intervening events...'.

As far as the *Wagon Mound* test is concerned, Woolf J says that Meah's personality changes were 'clearly foreseeable' consequences of the accident. Woolf J points out that personality change consequent on brain injury is a phenomenon well known to doctors. Whether such expert knowledge binds everyone else is a question Woolf J does not address, but one might suppose that the phenomenon is fairly widely known outside the medical profession as well.

But were the injuries to the victims the direct consequence of McCreamer's drunken driving? The answer to this question is, according to Woolf J, quite simply, no. Unfortunately, Woolf J makes heavy weather of explaining why the answer to the directness question is so clear, and resorts for support to what should be the infamous formulation of a near inarticulate Watkins LJ in *Lamb v Camden London Borough Council* that: [20]

> 'A robust and sensible approach to ... remoteness will more often than not produce ... an instinctive feeling that the event or act being weighed in the balance is too remote to sound in damages.'

Instinctive feelings are not the stuff of a rational system of law.

Woolf J's only non-instinctual argument is that there has to be a limit somewhere to McCreamer's liability. Would McCreamer, he asks rhet–orically, be held responsible for bringing up any child that a rape victim of Meah's might have had? Would he be liable for the break-up of the marriage of the defendant? Would he be responsible if in 20 years' time, Meah were to be released from prison on parole and then committed another offence? Woolf J anticipates the answer 'surely not' to all these questions. Any other answer would be contrary to common sense, he says. But the argument that there has to be a limit somewhere is not particularly relevant to the question of exactly where that limit should be placed. And in any case

18 Note that Woolf J does not use the *Brice v Brown* requirement that the accident had to be of a kind that would have affected the personality of a person of ordinary phlegm, but such a requirement is clearly satisfied in *Meah* in any case.
19 See eg Williams 'Causation in the Law' (1961) CLJ 62.
20 [1981] QB 625 at 647.

there is usually a natural limit to liability that is inherent in the phenomenon of causal fade-away—that it becomes increasingly uncertain whether the defendant's carelessness in fact caused the plaintiff's loss.

Woolf J is then immediately reduced to the 'public policy' argument that to allow Meah to recover from McCreamer for the results of Meah's own criminal acts would be 'distasteful'. Why it was not equally distasteful to give Meah damages for the fact of his own imprisonment is very unclear.

But the reason why the losses were too remote is surely obvious. Meah's crimes are so monstrous that McCreamer's drunken driving pales into insignificance. Why then does Woolf J not say so? The reason is the result of *Meah v McCreamer (No 1)*. If Meah's crimes did not constitute a novus actus interveniens with regard to his own ending up in prison, why should the same crimes count as breaking the chain of causation with regard to a parallel set of events, namely the consequences of the crimes for the victims? There is no answer to this question. If the plaintiff criminal wins in *Meah (No 1)*, which he probably should not have, it is impossible to bar the more meritorious claim of the victims of the criminal's crimes. The results of these cases are explicable, therefore, only in terms of what counsel chose to argue. In *Meah (No 1)*, the remoteness points were not raised. In *Meah (No 2)*, they were raised.

But, taking the *Meah* cases together with *Pritchard v JH Cobden* and its disapproval of *Jones v Jones,* it remains unclear how the courts will respond in future to cases in which plaintiffs allege that the defendants' carelessness led to detrimental changes in their personality. The inherent difficulty of such cases is that it is unclear what the relationship is between one's 'personality' and one's moral responsibility. If one's 'personality' is a something beyond one's control that governs one's actions, it is difficult to see how one could ever be held responsible for what it does. But if one's 'personality' merely sums up, from an outside observer's point of view, the kind of moral choices one is likely to make, it is difficult to see how outside influences could 'change' one's personality, for if they could, how would the choices one made remain one's own? The courts seem to want to treat the plaintiff's 'personality' as a cause of the plaintiff's actions, and the defendant's carelessness as being capable of causing changes in that 'personality', but at the same time they want to treat both the plaintiff and the defendant as morally responsible for their acts. It is far from clear that this is a coherent position.

Finally, there is the special case of plaintiffs who have been injured in attempting to rescue defendants who have carelessly put themselves in danger. Defendants, an ungrateful lot in these cases, argue that the harm suffered by the plaintiff rescuers was (a) not their fault, (b) too remote because it was a voluntary act of the plaintiff and (c) not recoverable anyway because the defendant can claim the benefit of the defence of consent. Arguments (a) and (c) are dealt with elsewhere,[1] but suffice it to say here that they are not usually very successful. As for argument (b) it also normally fails. It may be true that the rescue attempt is a positive act of

1   See chs 3 and 13.

the plaintiff, but whether, as a choice between two evils, it should count as fully voluntary is doubtful. As Cardozo J said in *Wagner v International Rly Co*[2] 'Danger invites rescue'. Rescues are both 'natural and probable' consequences of danger and also 'reasonably foreseeable' events. In any case, it is very rarely the case that attempting to rescue someone is utterly unreasonable. One might construct a case in which the rescuer should not have attempted the rescue because to do so interfered with a more professional rescue attempt in conditions in which it was folly for anyone other than a professional to attempt it. But even then the courts are likely to be sympathetic with the rescuer's cause.

Thus, in *Baker v TE Hopkins*[3] a claim succeeded in respect of the death of a doctor killed in an attempt to rescue two men from a polluted well. The defendant's argument that the doctor's decision to attempt the rescue, in full knowledge of risks was too remote, was dismissed by the Court of Appeal. Morris LJ quoted Greer LJ in *Haynes v Harwood*:

> 'If what is relied upon as a novus actus interveniens is the very kind of thing which is likely to happen if the want of care ... takes place, the principle embodied in the maxim is no defence.'

Willmer LJ was equally emphatic:

> 'In my judgment, it was a natural and probable result of the wrongdoing ... that ... a doctor would be called in, and that such doctor, having regard to the traditions of his profession, would, even at the risk of his own safety, descend the well.'[4]

Surprisingly, in the light of the fact the rescuer in *Baker* was a doctor, there were doubts in some quarters whether plaintiffs who were profess–ional rescuers, such as fire fighters, should be treated in the same way as other rescuers. *Ogwo v Taylor*[5] settles the point in favour of the professional rescuer.

Finally on rescuers, mention should be made, albeit reluctantly, of the first instance decision *Crossley v Rawlinson*.[6] A lorry bursts into flames after an accident caused by the admitted carelessness of the defendant. The plaintiff, a rescuer, rushes forward with a fire extinguisher. Before reaching the blaze, the rescuer trips, falls and is injured. The court holds that the defendant is not liable to the plaintiff for the injuries he sustained

2   (1921) 232 NY Rep 176, 180.
3   [1959] 1 WLR 966.
4   Willmer LJ goes on to say that the doctor's act would have amounted to a novus actus interveniens if the doctor had been 'negligent.' It is submitted that this is not correct, for if it were, every example of contributory negligence would break the chain of causation and would provide a complete defence, thus completely frustrating the intention of Parliament in the Law Reform (Contributory Negligence) Act 1945. The 'utterly unreasonable' test requires something well in excess of a bare finding of negligence.
5   [1988] AC 431.
6   [1982] 1 WLR 369.

in the fall because the exact injury suffered by the plaintiff was not the injury that one might expect, namely burns, from the dangerous situation created by the defendant. This decision, which is one of the few cases which apply the *Wagon Mound* test literally, is wholly indefensible in the light of the rest of the case law. It implies, contrary to cases such as *Hughes v Lord Advocate*[7] that burns are a different 'type' of harm from other physical injuries, and, contrary to *Wieland*, that the exact manner in which an accident comes about has to be reasonably foreseeable.

Interventions by others

We now pass on to perhaps the central problem in remoteness, namely what happens in cases where the other causally relevant fact is an intervention by a third party. Again, there are two very different approaches to this question, one (the *Polemis* approach) asks whether, despite the intervention, the loss being claimed remains the direct consequence of the defendant's carelessness. The other (the *Wagon Mound* approach) is interested in the defendant's relative blameworthiness and asks whether, despite the intervention, the loss was reasonably foreseeable by the defendant.

THE DIRECTNESS APPROACH

The best statement of the directness approach to the problem of third party interventions can be found in Hart and Honoré's *Causation in the Law*:[8]

'The general principle of the traditional doctrine is that the free, deliberate and informed act or omission of a human being, intended to exploit the situation created by the defendant, negatives causal connection.'

If the intervention meets the test, it counts as a 'new cause'[9] that breaks the chain of causation. The responsibility shifts from the defendant to the intervenor. If the intervention is not free, deliberate and informed, it is treated as the 'natural and probable' consequence of the defendant's carelessness and the defendant's responsibility remains.[10]

Note that, according to the directness approach, various sorts of involuntariness on the part of the intervenor may mean that the intervention does not break the chain of causation. For example, the defendant may not be able to claim that the chain of causation has been broken where

7 [1963] AC 837. See further below p 151.
8 (2nd edn) (Oxford; Clarendon, 1985) at p 136.
9 See eg *The Oropesa* [1943] P 32 at 39.
10 See eg Greer LJ in *Haynes v Harwood* [1935] 1 KB 146 at 153.

the intervenor technically had a choice but the choice was not a fair one. Such a case might be where the alternative for the intervenor was between intervening and suffering serious harm[11] or between intervening and breaching a legal or moral obligation.[12] Equally, if the intervenor acts on the basis of a mistake, the intervention cannot count as sufficiently voluntary.[13]

The most disputed issues for the directness view surround interventions that were accidental or negligent. The traditional orthodox view was that a negligent intervention by a third party who was attempting to deal with the dangerous situation created by the defendant's fault does not break the chain of causation.[14] But in *SS Singleton Abbey v SS Paludina*[15] Lord Sumner said that even a non-negligent but conscious intervening act, that is an accident, could be enough to break the chain. On the other hand, Hart and Honoré, admittedly without citing any authority,[16] claim that the key distinction is still voluntariness. Their view is that whereas a voluntary intervention which is carried out carelessly will result in the original defendant being relieved of liability, an involuntary intervention, for example that of a fireman, bound by legal and moral duties, who tries to put out a fire, will not have the same effect even if the intervention is carried out in a negligent manner.

THE FORESEEABILITY APPROACH

The *Wagon Mound* approach to third party interventions is to ask whether either the interventions themselves or the results of the interventions were reasonably foreseeable by a person in the position of the defendant at the time of the accident. If the intervention or its results would have been reasonably foreseeable, the loss concerned is not too remote. If it would not have been reasonably foreseeable, it is too remote.

One can see the operation of the foreseeability approach even in pre-*Wagon Mound* cases. One example is *Duncan v Cammell Laird*,[17] the once celebrated case about the pre-Second World War loss with all but four hands of the Royal Navy submarine *HMS Thetis*. The submarine sank because a torpedo tube was opened when the other end of the tube was also open.

11 See eg the classic case *Scott v Shepherd* (1773) 2 Wm Bl 892, 96 ER 525. For serious harm to property see Hart and Honoré pp 145-46.
12 For legal obligations see *Grébert-Borgnis v Nugent* (1885) 15 QBD 85, *Estes v Brewster Cigar Co* 197 P 36 (1930). (See further *Hart and Honoré* p 147). For moral obligations see the rescuer cases, above pp 134-136, eg *Haynes v Harwood* [1935] 1 KB 146 and *The Oropesa* [1943] P 32.
13 See eg *Philco Radio v Spurling* [1949] 2 All ER 882. See generally *Hart and Honoré* at pp 149-51.
14 See *Hart & Honoré* at p 152.
15 [1927] AC 16.
16 *Hart and Honoré* at p 153.
17 [1946] AC 401, aka *Woods v Duncan*.

How this came about was a matter of some dispute, and the full facts never became clear, but it was accepted that one of the indicators which would have shown the other end of the tube to have been open did not work because it had been blocked by paint. The sequence of events by which the careless painting of the torpedo tubes led to the loss of the *Thetis* was not straightforward. The submarine was on an early test run, during which torpedoes were not to be fired. The rear door was only opened because an officer decided to inspect the inside of the tubes for leaks. The same officer relied on information given by a sailor shortly before the opening of the tube that all the other indicators showed that the front end of the tube was closed. In addition, the officer could have cleared the indicator in question, but did not do so.

The House of Lords decided that neither the officer nor the other sailor had themselves acted carelessly at any point, including the officer's original decision to inspect the inside of the tube. The question was therefore whether those responsible for painting the tube, a main contractor and a sub-contractor, were to be held responsible for the entire damage. The House of Lords said that they were not. Viscount Simon said that it was not 'reasonably ... in [the defendants'] contemplation' that such a disaster would happen as a result of careless painting, because the defendants could not have foreseen the decision to open the torpedo tubes on a test run without torpedoes. Lord Russell agreed, relying first on the lack of foreseeability of the results of the intervention: 'The answer ... depends upon whether they could reasonably be expected to foresee' that their carelessness would 'endanger the lives of those on board,' and secondly on the lack of foreseeability of the interventions themselves: 'No-one could reasonably be expected to foresee ... the happening in the course of [the trial] of the only event which could make the faulty [indicator] responsible for the disaster.' Lord Macmillan also agreed, but relied only on the point about the foreseeability of the interventions themselves, commenting that: 'The chain of causation would appear to be composed of missing links.' Lord Simonds rather puzzlingly said that the case was not about remote–ness but the same considerations would apply if it were. He went on to say that 'the question is whether the assumed negligent actor ought reasonably to have foreseen the intervening act.'[18]

In the *Wagon Mound (No 1)* itself, similar issues were raised. The decision of the plaintiff to restart welding and activities of the welders were likewise non-negligent interventions. The Privy Council, going further than *Duncan v Cammell Laird*, decided that the only issue was foreseeability from the point of view of the defendant. If the loss claimed for was reasonably

18 The fifth judge, Lord Porter, also uses the concept of foreseeability, but does so in his own way. He accepts, as others did not, that the indicator used by the officer should not have been used for judging whether the front of the tube was open, but only for judging whether there was water in the tube, and that it was not foreseeable that anyone would use the indicator in the way the officer used it. He therefore claims that the only foreseeable injury from painting over the indicator was that someone in the torpedo room would be soaked by a tubeful of water, not that the whole submarine would sink.

foreseeable, it was recoverable, regardless of the intervening acts, but if it was not reasonably foreseeable, it was not recoverable. In the words of Viscount Simon:

'But if it would be wrong that a man should be held liable for damage unpredictable by a reasonable man because it was a "direct" or "natural", equally it would be wrong that he should escape liability, however "indirect" the damage, if he foresaw or could reasonably foresee the intervening events which led to its being done.'

It is worth noting that the assumption of the Privy Council that the damage in the *Wagon Mound (No 1)* was 'direct' is far from obvious. Lord Sumner in *SS Singleton Abbey v SS Paludina* [19] had said that even innocent accidental intervening acts could break the chain of causation. Even under Hart and Honoré's more exacting test there might still be a break in the chain because the decision of the plaintiff to begin welding again is not so much involuntary as a calculated risk based on misinformation. Admittedly, the intervenors did not 'intend to exploit the situation' in the sense that they thought they would be better off than they normally were, but they did 'exploit the situation' in the sense that they carried on with their normal business.

These issues are especially relevant to the *Wagon Mound (No 2)*[20] a case arising out of the same incident as the *Wagon Mound (No 1)* but in which the plaintiff was not the owner of the dock (and hence the employer of the welders) but the owner of a ship that was being repaired in the dock. This plaintiff, unlike the plaintiff in the *Wagon Mound (No 1)*, did not suffer from the handicap that if it was shown that it was foreseeable that fuel oil spilled on the surface of the sea could burn, its own case would be undermined by a claim of contributory negligence, at the time a complete defence in New South Wales where the events took place. In consequence, the plaintiff in the *Wagon Mound (No 2)* persuaded the trial judge that, although an unlikely occurrence, it was known to be a possibility at the time that the oil spillage would lead to a conflagration and that a reasonable person in the position of the defendant would have realised as much. On appeal, the Privy Council found for the plaintiff. The finding of fact that there was foreseeability was enough to distinguish the case from *Wagon Mound (No 1)*.

What about directness in the *Wagon Mound (No 2)*? If anything, the case for saying that the damage was indirect was even stronger in the *Wagon Mound (No 2)* than in the *Wagon Mound (No 1)*, for it was open to the plaintiff to claim that the decision of the dock owners to recommence welding was not just deliberate but was also culpable. But such arguments were not considered relevant in the *Wagon Mound (No 2)*. The *Wagon Mound (No 2)* therefore endorses a pure foreseeability approach to third

19 [1927] AC 16.
20 [1967] 1 AC 617.

party intervention, an approach in which directness is of no account at all. Admittedly, the Privy Council in both the *Wagon Mound* cases seemed to find the directness concept hard to grasp and imagined, because of the use by older judges of terms such as 'natural and probable consequence' that directness was concerned only with factual causation, with the operation, for example, of 'natural laws'. But the explicit intention of these judgments was to expunge the directness concept from the law of negligence.

MIXED APPROACHES AND THE SURVIVAL OF DIRECTNESS

We have already seen in the discussion of the *Meah* cases that, despite the clear intentions of the Privy Council in the *Wagon Mound* cases, directness is still relevant in cases about remoteness. It seems that the modern law is either that the plaintiff has to prove both directness and foreseeability or that the court should use a compromise concept, such as 'likelihood', that usually gives the same result as the directness test.[1]

How this situation came about is of some interest in itself, although one should bear in mind that the history of the law on third party intervention since the *Wagon Mound* is not straightforward. Some judges have wanted to make the foreseeability test work, largely because of the mistaken belief that the law would be tidier and easier to understand if the tests for remoteness, duty and breach were integrated. Other judges, backed by Hart and Honoré, have sought to reduce the effect of the *Wagon Mound* to a minimum, so that the previous law on remoteness is preserved, though sometimes in surprising guises such as 'proximity'. Others still, perhaps the majority, seem content to try to solve the cases before them with whatever materials come to hand, including both pre- and post-*Wagon Mound* case law, whether directness-based or foreseeability-based.

One key point in the post-*Wagon Mound* struggles is *Home Office v Dorset Yacht*.[2] In 1962, a group of young offenders who were serving custodial sentences[3] were taken outside their institution on a training exercise. The exercise, which was approved by the authorities, took place on a small island off the south coast of England. The three prison officers in charge of the party, in breach of their instructions, failed to supervise the youths properly and they escaped. The youths stole a yacht and in attempting to sail it away, ran it into the plaintiff's yacht, damaging it badly.

The plaintiff sued the government department responsible for the penal institution. The case reached the House of Lords on the basis that the

---

1   Note also that mixed approaches are common in other legal systems. The test in French law, for example, is that to exonerate the defendant the intervention has to be 'imprévisible et irrésistible'. See *Viney* para 393 ff, p 463ff.
2   [1970] AC 1004.
3   The sentences were being served at a 'borstal', in effect a training prison for young people. Borstals have now been abolished, or at least renamed.

defendant conceded, for the purposes of argument, both that the officers had been careless and that the government department was responsible for their actions.

One of the central issues in *Dorset Yacht* was a remoteness point: did the fact that the youths themselves caused the damage make the loss too remote?[4] The case is interesting because the situation was in one way the reverse of what was assumed to be the case in the *Wagon Mound* cases. In the *Wagon Mound* it was assumed that applying the *Polemis* directness rule would mean victory for the plaintiff and for the 'they shouldn't have done it anyway' school, whereas applying foreseeability would mean no liability and victory for the 'damages proportionate to the blameworthiness' school. But in *Dorset Yacht*, the situation was the reverse. On the basis of foreseeability alone, one might have said that the damage was not too remote. Surely reasonable people in the position of the defendants would have realised that escapers often cause damage in the course of their escape. On the other hand, unless one were to say that the escape was a kind of emergency in which the youths were not acting in a fully voluntary way—a somewhat far-fetched point—it seems clear that on the basis of the directness test, the loss to the plaintiff would be too remote. It was caused by the deliberate wrongdoing of the youths who were in the process of exploiting the situation created by the defendants' carelessness.

Four of the five Law Lords agreed on the proper result, that the plaintiff should win, but they disagreed profoundly on the right way to justify the result.

Three of the speeches, those of Lords Reid, Pearson and Diplock, merit closer attention and Lord Reid's speech is the one most often cited. Lord Reid's main point was this:

'The cases show that, where human action forms one of the links between the original wrongdoing of the defendant and the loss suffered by the plaintiff, the action must at least have been something very likely to happen if it is not to be regarded as a novus actus interveniens breaking the chain of causation. I do not think that a mere foreseeable possibility is or should be sufficient, for then the intervening human action can more properly be regarded as a new cause than as a consequence of the original wrongdoing. But if the intervening action was likely to happen I do not think that it can matter whether that action was innocent or tortious or criminal. Unfortunately tortious or criminal action by a third party is often the "very kind of thing" which is likely to happen as a result of the wrongful or careless act of the defendant.'

On this basis, Lord Reid decides that the damage was not too remote.

Note that Lord Reid appears to reject the *Wagon Mound* doctrine that foreseeability has replaced directness, but on the other hand that the result

---

4   The other central issue was whether the defendants ought to be immune from suit in this sort of case for reasons of public policy. See below ch 5.

he reaches, in favour of the plaintiff, is in this case the result that the foreseeability test, but not the directness test, would have produced. And note further that instead of returning openly to a directness test, he chooses to create a new test based on 'likelihood'. But it is unclear how, at least in this context, likelihood can differ much from 'foreseeability.' As we saw in chapter 3, the difference between foreseeability and likelihood is simply the tense of the verb involved. Reasonable foreseeability is about what would have seemed likely to a reasonable person at the time. 'Likelihood' can only be different from foreseeability if a different point of view in time is used. If, for example, the starting point is the present, 'likelihood' takes into account what we know now but did not know at the time of the accident. But it is quite rare that our view of how likely an event is will be much changed by knowledge that has come to light since. Perhaps it is only when we previously thought that an event was completely impossible that such knowledge will make a big difference, since it includes the knowledge that this type of accident has happened at least once. But except for such cases, 'likelihood' and 'foreseeability' are the same.

It is also unclear whether Lord Reid is requiring 'high' levels of likelihood and if so how high is high enough. Just as foreseeability by itself is not enough to establish fault (the foreseeable risk has to be a risk that a reasonable person would have done more about than the defendant did) so 'likelihood' is insufficient by itself because it is unclear why it is being used.

Lord Pearson agreed with Lord Reid that the remoteness issue should be decided in favour of the plaintiff. But he separates 'remoteness', which he declares to depend on foreseeability, from 'act of third party' for which his starting point is a classic statement of the directness point of view by Lord Sumner in *Weld-Blundell v Stephens*:[5]

> 'In general ... even though A is in fault, he is not responsible for injury to C which B, a stranger to him, deliberately chooses to do.'

Weld-Blundell v Stephens had been heavily criticised in the *Wagon Mound (No 1)* and Lord Pearson's separation of 'remoteness' and 'act of third party' may have something to do with attempting to confine the influence of the *Wagon Mound* doctrine

But Lord Pearson goes on to say that there is an exception to the Sumner rule if the defendant has legal control of the intervening third party, a category into which the facts of *Dorset Yacht* fall.

> 'The borstal boys were under the control of the Home Office's officers, and control imports responsibility. The boys' interference with the boats appears to have been a direct result of the Home Office's officers' failure to exercise proper control and supervision.'

Lord Pearson does not mention foreseeability and he returns to the language of directness, but, contrary to expectation, still decides for the

5   [1920] AC 956 at 986.

plaintiff. To understand what Lord Pearson has done, one has to remember the theory behind the directness approach—the defendant should not have acted badly in the first place and should only escape responsibility if someone or something else is clearly more responsible. In a case such as *Dorset Yacht*, according to Lord Pearson, the fact that the officers had a responsibility to control the youths means that when the youths do exactly what the officers are supposed to prevent, the officers are not clearly less responsible than the youths.

Lord Diplock, in contrast, accepts the foreseeability approach. The question to be asked in *Dorset Yacht* is whether 'it was reasonably foreseeable by the officers that if these particular trainees did escape they would be likely to appropriate a boat moored in the vicinity of Brownsea Island for the purpose of eluding immediate pursuit.' Lord Diplock does not mention directness and treats the question of remoteness as if it were the same as a question of the scope of the duty of care, exactly the sort of integration of duty, breach and remoteness envisaged by the *Wagon Mound* cases. Thus, Lord Diplock finds for the plaintiff.

That three senior judges could decide such an important case in three such contrasting ways shows into what confusion the law on third party interventions fell as a result of the *Wagon Mound* cases. In the subsequent decade, Lord Reid's judgment attracted the most comment and support both in England and in other jurisdictions. For example in *Taupo Borough Council v Birnie*[6] Cooke J, having discussed Lord Reid's approach at some length, concludes that the central element in his approach is the phrase 'the very sort of thing likely to happen' and then applies it with approval.

But then came *Lamb v Camden London Borough Council*[7] in which Lord Reid's approach came under heavy fire in the Court of Appeal. In *Lamb* the plaintiff blamed a local authority for the damage done to her house by squatters. The plaintiff had let her house while she was abroad, but the tenant moved out and the plaintiff removed the remainder of her own possessions after workers employed by the defendant local authority breached a water main in the street outside the house, and thereby undermined its foundations and caused it to subside. The squatters moved into the now empty and boarded-up house on two separate occasions and caused much damage.

The plaintiff argued on the basis of Lord Reid's likelihood test or, if it was different, reasonable foreseeability, that the damage done by the squatters was not too remote. But Lord Denning MR rejected both Lord Reid's test and reasonable foreseeability, and he did so using the same argument: if the test were either 'likelihood' or 'foreseeability', the scope of liability would be too large. According to Lord Denning, both tests would mean, for example, that the Home Office in *Dorset Yacht* would have been liable not just for the damage to the yacht but also for any harm done by the youths subsequent to their escape, for it is both highly likely and reasonably foreseeable that escaped prisoners will commit further offences

6   [1978] 2 NZLR 397.
7   [1981] QB 625.

while on the run. It is even 'the very sort of thing' one would expect from prisoners on the run. But, for Lord Denning, such a result would be absurd.

One might expect that Lord Denning would go on to attempt to reinstate some sort of directness test, since it is precisely in cases of the *Lamb* type that the *Polemis* test would deny liability. But instead, Lord Denning declares his support for the idea underlying the *Wagon Mound* that the test for duty, breach and remoteness should be the same. In order, therefore, to restrict liability in the way that he wants, Lord Denning has to find an argument that applies equally to duty, breach and remoteness. This he fails to do, and so instead he takes refuge in the claim that restrictions on liability all come down to 'policy', a point that is both trite, since all legal decision-making is in a sense about policy, that is about what ought to happen in the future as well as about what ought to have happened in the past, and confusing, since it conflates the particular problems of policy and moral choice with which remoteness cases are concerned with the different problems of policy and moral choice with which, for example, breach cases are concerned.

Nevertheless, Lord Denning's explanation of the particular 'policy' reason he believes justifies his decision turns out to be a thinly disguised directness point, namely that the real responsibility for letting the squatters in rests with Mrs Lamb herself, since it was she who abandoned the property by removing her own belongings and decamping to America from where she had little or no chance of protecting her property. One may dispute whether or not this intervention by the plaintiff herself would satisfy the 'utter unreasonableness' test discussed above, but the idea that the plaintiff's own responsibility clearly outweighed that of the defendant is wholly within the directness approach.

But, as in *Dorset Yacht* itself, the court in *Lamb* was not united. Watkins LJ, frankly admitting his bafflement at the whole remoteness issue,[8] comes fairly close to Lord Denning's position. He says that Lord Reid must have meant to say that reasonable foreseeability was the test, and that any attempt to talk about the degree of foreseeability required was unhelpful. 'In my view,' says Watkins LJ, 'the *Wagon Mound* test should be applied without any of the gloss which is from time to time applied to it.' But Watkins LJ goes on to say, in immediate self-contradiction, that reasonable foreseeability does not in all circumstances answer the remoteness question completely. Reasonable foreseeability is required, but so is something else.

That something else again turns out to be a fairly conventional directness point, this time claiming to be matters of instinct and public policy. The defendant wins, according to Watkins LJ, because the actions of the squatters were outrageous, anti-social and criminal—that is they delib–erately exploited the situation created by the defendant and the squatters' degree of responsibility for the damage clearly eclipses the blameworthiness of the defendant—precisely the line followed by Lord Pearson in *Dorset Yacht*.

8 Watkins LJ's descent into the realms of 'instinct' in *Lamb* must surely mark the low point of judicial thought about remoteness.

Oliver LJ, however, defends Lord Reid's position, or at least his own interpretation of it. He claims that Lord Reid was not bringing back any notion of 'nexus or direct or indirect causation' but was simply adjusting the 'reasonable foreseeability' test to take into account the fact that it was always foreseeable as a possibility that people do foolish or wicked things but that this bare foreseeability was not enough to fix the responsibility for the damage on the defendant. Oliver LJ's view was that Lord Reid's only mistake was not clearly to pitch the degree of likelihood needed at a much higher level. 'There may ... be circumstances, ' concluded Oliver LJ, 'in which the court would require a degree of likelihood amounting almost to inevitability before it fixes a defendant with responsibility for the act of a third party over whom he has and can have no control.'

The early 1980s saw one other, very different, attempt by the Court of Appeal to put the law on third party interventions into some sort of order. In *Knightley v Johns*[9] the courts faced a classic case of multiple causation. The defendant negligently overturned his car in a tunnel carrying one-way traffic. The police, including the plaintiff, arrived on the scene quickly, but the senior police officer present, realising that he had forgotten to close the entrance to the tunnel, told the plaintiff to ride back, against the traffic, to close it. The plaintiff complied, but was hit by a car being driven at normal speed coming the other way. The defendant admitted that his driving had been careless, but denied that he was responsible for the injuries to the plaintiff. After much consideration, the senior officer was declared also to have been negligent, not in ordering the plaintiff to ride back to close the tunnel but in forgetting to close it in the first place. The second driver and the plaintiff himself were held not to have been careless.

The leading judgment in *Knightley v Johns* is by Stephenson LJ. He attempts a synthesis of pre- and post-*Wagon Mound* cases based on the idea that the pre-*Wagon Mound* approach usually amounted to asking whether the damage was the 'natural and probable consequence' of the defendant's act. This allowed him to say, as is surely correct in many cases, that there is very little difference between 'probable' and 'foreseeable'. Both are about likelihood. The only real difference is that 'foreseeable' can be misinterpreted as meaning 'very unlikely but possible' whereas very unlikely events are not 'probable' at all. But even this difference can be eliminated by bearing in mind that 'foreseeable' should always be preceded by 'reasonably'. In Stephenson LJ's view, the reason *Polemis* was criticised was that it applied a version of directness that forgot that 'probable' means virtually the same as 'reasonably foreseeable'. Similarly, Lord Reid's test in *Dorset Yacht*, itself an echo of Greer LJ's judgment in the pre-*Wagon Mound* case *Hayes v Harwood*, says merely that the degree of likelihood needed to avoid a breaking of the chain is quite high.

'The question to be asked is accordingly whether the whole sequence of events is a natural and probable consequence of [the defendant's] negligence and a reasonably foreseeable consequence of it.'

9   [1982] 1 All ER 851, [1982] 1 WLR 349.

But there is a difficulty in Stephenson LJ's approach. It is not possible to reduce the pre-*Wagon Mound* view so easily into a notion of likelihood. Just as likelihood or risk forms only part of fault, so it formed only part of the idea of a 'new cause'. Whether the third party intervened deliberately intending to exploit the situation was also relevant, as was whether the intervenor acted reasonably.[10] Such considerations are inevitable if the job of deciding the remoteness issue is to be done. Consequently, when Stephenson LJ lays out his approach in detail, it turns out not to be a mere elaboration on probabilities and likelihoods:

'It is helpful but not decisive to consider which of these events were deliberate choices to do positive acts and which were mere omissions or failures to act; which acts and omissions were innocent mistakes or miscalculations and which were negligent .... Negligent conduct is more likely to break the chain of causation than conduct which is not; positive acts will more easily constitute new causes than inaction. Mistakes and mischances are to be expected when human beings, however well trained, have to cope with a crisis; what exactly they will be cannot be predicted, but if those which do occur are natural the wrongdoer cannot escape ... responsibility for them ... simply by calling them improbable or unforeseeable.'

Stephenson LJ thereby recreates the directness approach more comp‒rehensively than any judge in *Dorset Yacht* or *Lamb*, even while claiming to reject *Polemis* and to preserve reasonable foreseeability.

At the same time as *Knightley v Johns* was moving the law back towards directness, other cases were holding the line for Lord Reid's *Dorset Yacht* test. In cases such as *P Perl v Camden London Borough Council*,[11] *Paterson Zochonis v Merfarken*[12] and *King v Liverpool City Council*[13] courts supported Lord Reid's approach, especially as reinterpreted by Oliver LJ in *Lamb*.

Perl and *King* concerned defendants who carelessly allowed malicious third parties to break into their properties and then to use them as a base for activities that harmed the plaintiff's property. *Paterson* concerned a defendant who was accused of failing to check whether his customers might use his product intentionally to harm the plaintiff. None of these cases even cites *Knightley*. But it is worth asking why they do not do so. It seems that an unspoken distinction has developed between cases in which the intervention consists either of deliberately harming the plaintiff or committing a crime which results in harm to the plaintiff and cases in which the intervention is either negligent or completely innocent. In the

---

10 See eg *The Oropesa* test [1943] P 32 that the intervention has to be 'unreasonable, extraneous and extrinsic'. Hart and Honoré are often at pains to play down the normative content of the traditional test, but given its purpose, to judge relative responsibility, the importance of its normative content should not be underestimated.

11 [1984] QB 342.

12 [1986] 3 All ER 522.

13 [1986] 3 All ER 544, [1986] 1 WLR 890.

former sort of case, in which according to the traditional directness test, since the intervenor has clearly acted deliberately to exploit the situation created by the defendant's carelessness, there would be no liability, Lord Reid's test is cited only so that the plaintiff can fail it. In the latter sort of case, the situation under the traditional directness test is less clear, and so the issue has to be discussed more openly.

On the basis of this distinction a case in which the defendants carelessly allowed youths to break into their derelict cinema, whereupon the youths set fire to the cinema and the fire destroyed the plaintiffs' property, should be straightforward. The intervening acts consist of deliberate criminal acts. Surely, Lord Reid's test as interpreted by Oliver LJ of 'high likelihood' or 'the very sort of thing' would be deployed and promptly used to dismiss the plaintiff's case. But when such a case reached the House of Lords, in the form of *Maloco v Littlewoods*[14] only one judge, Lord Goff, took this line. The others, with varying degrees of clarity,[15] followed Lord Mackay of Clashfern in declaring that Lord Reid in *Dorset Yacht* did not in fact propound a 'high likelihood' test, but was merely requiring that the intervention be 'likely' or 'probable'.

Lord Mackay goes on to say that his view is that in principle there is no reason why a defendant should not be held liable for giving another person an opportunity to harm the plaintiff and that the question is in essence one of reasonable foreseeability with the emphasis on 'reasonable'. But because human actions are inherently unpredictable it is equally inherently difficult to prove that an intervention was reasonably foreseeable.

Lord Mackay in *Smith* thus attempts to do again that which the *Wagon Mound* cases tried but failed to do, namely to integrate the tests for fault and remoteness. Lord Mackay's opinion starts from 'reasonable foresee–ability' and seems to be heading down the familiar path to the position that Lord Denning found to be absurd in *Lamb v Camden*, namely that the defendant should be held liable for any 'reasonably foreseeable' harm. But instead of this, Lord Mackay brings in a new element, the rest of the test for fault and especially the difficulty and cost of taking sufficient precautions against the harm.[16] The idea appears to be that remoteness issues can be dealt with by asking whether the defendant was at fault with regard to the precise injury for which the plaintiff claims damages.

But exactly how such a test would work is unclear. Fault as an element in itself in negligence is not about the precise damage that occurred but about whether the defendant acted reasonably in not taking a precaution that would have prevented the harm from occurring, and reasonableness depends on a comparison of the costs of the precaution and how beneficial it would have seemed to have been at the time to prevent all the accidents that such a precaution would probably prevent. To concentrate on the precise damage that occurred, and even worse on the precise way the

14 [1987] AC 241.
15 See Markesinis 'Negligence, Nuisance and Affirmative Duties of Action' (1989) 105 LQR 104, Howarth 'Negligence After Murphy: Time to Re-think' [1991] CLJ 58, Howarth 'My Brother's Keeper? Liability for acts of third parties' (1994) 14 Legal Studies 88.
16 [1987] AC 241 at 268-70.

damage came about, means inevitably dealing with less probable events than the overall risks. The damage that actually happens is a subset of the damage that could have happened and its occurrence must be less probable than the occurrence of any of the damage that could have happened. Moreover, everything depends on how precisely the harm and the sequence of events are described. The more precise the description, the less likely their occurrence. But what controls the degree of precision?

It is notable that despite its majority endorsement, Lord Mackay's speech in *Smith* is less often cited than Lord Goff's more conventional minority speech. In *Topp v London Country Bus*,[17] for example, which concerned an action by the wife of a man killed by 'joyriders' against the owners of the vehicle which they had carelessly allowed to be taken away, the Court of Appeal applied Lord Goff's approach without even mentioning the existence of Lord Mackay's approach. Note that because it is very unlikely that the joyriders would ever be found or, if they were found, that they would be worth suing, to apply Lord Mackay's approach in *Topp* would mean in practice that, under the rules of joint and several liability discussed above, the vehicle owner would end up having to pay all the damages.

Therefore, although *Smith v Littlewoods* appeared at the time to mark a breakthrough for the *Wagon Mound* project of reducing remoteness to reasonable foreseeability,[18] it seems that this may not be so. The appeal of the *Wagon Mound* approach remains its elegance, but it does seem in some cases to lead to the very injustice it was supposed to avoid, namely that the defendant is left to pay a very large bill for compensation although he played a comparatively small role in the events that led to the plaintiff's injuries. On the other hand, the *Polemis* rules can also lead, in a case such as *Topp*, to the very results that they in turn were supposed to prevent, namely that a plaintiff may end up uncompensated even when there is a defendant who should not have done what he did. Both rules seem to lead to excess. These dilemmas have led at least one writer to propose that what should happen in such cases is a compromise, under which the defendant is held liable but only has to pay the proportion of the damages that represents his own fault.[19]

Intervening natural events

The final category of remoteness case is where the defendant seeks to escape liability on the ground that the plaintiff's injury came about mainly because of some natural event. There is one aspect of such cases that sets them apart from the other three categories of remoteness case. Since the defendant does not point to any other person as being responsible for the

17 [1993] 3 All ER 448, [1993] 1 WLR 976. See generally Howarth 'My Brother's Keeper? Liability for acts of third parties' (1994) 14 Legal Studies 88.
18 Or for 'occasioning' over traditional 'full causation', in the terms used by Hart and Honoré.
19 Howarth (1994) 14 Legal Studies 88.

harm, the question of comparative blameworthiness cannot arise. The defendant has to rely solely on the argument that the overwhelming nature of the intervening event reduces the significance of the defendant's own blameworthy conduct to minimal levels.

It should be obvious that the mere interposition of physical events between the defendant's act and the plaintiff's injury cannot relieve the defendant of responsibility for those injuries. Human actions have their effects in the physical world through the ordinary operations of nature—bones break, bruises form, injuries lead to other more serious dysfunctions in bodily processes and so on. On the other hand, as *Beven on Negligence* stated nearly 70 years ago, 'For the operations of Nature, purely as such, undirected by human power, it is manifest no-one can be accountable ... The ordinary and accustomed workings of Nature ... impute liability to no-one.'[20]

The traditional distinction in the law has therefore been between, again in Beven's words, 'those operations of Nature wholly unconnected with the agency of man and those which owe their injurious influence on man to the agency of man.'[1] The defendant has no chance of establishing that the chain of causation has been broken if the only natural events in question are ones that would not have happened but for the defendant's actions. Such events are not independent of the defendant's fault.

The traditional approach then goes on to say that the defendant will not be liable if the accident was 'due to natural causes directly and exclusively, without human intervention and ... could not have been prevented by any amount of foresight and pains and care reasonably to have been expected of [the defendant]'.[2]

On one side of the line is *Smith v London and South Western Rly Co.*[3] A spark from the defendant's railway landed on some dry stubble and a fire broke out which crossed 200 yards of open fields and burned down the plaintiff's cottage. The defendant said that the spread of the fire was an unusual and unforeseeable event. But the court said that the test was whether the fire was the natural and probable consequence of the defendant's carelessness.

On the other side of the line is the American case *Toledo & Ohio Central v Kibler*[4] in which the railway company carelessly delayed shipping the plaintiff's goods, with the result that they were destroyed in an unprecedented flood in the place from which they were being shipped.

Beven summarises the traditional approach thus: [5]

'Where the negligence of a person concurs with some ordinary cause, and the conjunction produces an effect injurious to some other person ... the operation of such an ordinary cause extraneous

---

20 *Beven On Negligence* (4th ed) (1928) p 80.
1   Ibid.
2   James LJ in *Nugent v Smith* (1876) 1 CPD 423, 435.
3   (1870) LR 6 CP 14.
4   119 NE 733 (1918).
5   *Beven* at p 81.

to the negligent person will not excuse his liability for the whole of the joint effect. The law is otherwise, where an extraordinary cause is the primary means of setting in motion an injurious agency, and by co-operating with the negligence of a person produces injury... In this case the negligent person is not liable; for not only would his negligence alone fail to produce the injurious effect (this circumstance, however, is common to the two cases, and, not–withstanding this, in the former case there is no immunity from liability), but the exciting cause being an "extraordinary occurr–ence" or an "act of God" was not reasonably to be anticipated, nor guarded against. The negligence is not followed by the injurious results in natural and probable sequence, but only by the occurrence of something abnormal and not to be anticipated.'

Hart and Honoré draw a similar conclusion. They say that the causal connection between the defendant's act and the plaintiff's damage may be negatived by 'abnormality', which includes highly unusual events and coincidences that are independent of the defendant's acts.[6]

Thus, if the defendant carelessly injures the plaintiff so that the plaintiff has to be taken to hospital, and on the way to the hospital the plaintiff is struck by lightning or is hit by a falling tree, the traditional approach would be to say that since the lightning or the tree was nothing to do with the defendant and the only part played by the defendant's fault in the second event was that it set up the coincidence that the plaintiff ended up in the wrong place at the wrong time, the defendant's liability should be limited to the harm suffered before the second accident.[7] Moreover, the lightning transformed the harm suffered by the plaintiff from bad into life-threatening and may even have superseded that harm, in the sense that, for example, in *Baker v Willoughby*[8] shooting off the plaintiff's gammy leg meant that the plaintiff no longer suffered physically from the gammy leg at all.

The traditional approach was, however, challenged by the *Wagon Mound (No 1)*. The Privy Council criticised cases such as *Smith v London & South Western Rly Co* which appeared to say that foreseeability was not relevant. The *Wagon Mound* view puts the emphasis on how blameworthy the defendant's conduct was rather than how unusual the natural event was.

But note that we know from the discussion above that the difference between 'foreseeable' and 'likely' is the point in time the law uses to assess the situation. 'Foreseeable' means the risks as they *would have* appeared

---

6 *Beven* at pp 162-185.
7 Cf Lord MacDermott in *Hogan v Bentinck Collieries* [1949] 1 All ER 588. Note the possibility of awarding damages for any 'continuing' loss after the pattern of *Baker v Willoughby*. See *Harwood v Wyken Colliery* [1913] 2 KB 158 (employee suffers knee injury at work, for which employer responsible. Subsequently employee suffers from heart disease. *Held*: consequences of knee injury continue after onset of heart disease, so that damages still payable). But not followed in *Jobling v Associated Dairies*.
8 See above.

at the time. 'Likely' can either mean the same thing, or it can mean the risks as they *now appear*. Often there is no difference between the two. There is only a difference in cases in which, for example, the very fact that the accident has happened at all has changed our view of the chances of such an accident happening. Thus in *Doughty v Turner Manu–facturing Co Ltd*[9] the lid of a cauldron containing molten metal was carelessly knocked into the liquid. No one was hurt by the incident until two minutes later when, because of a previously unknown chemical reaction, caused by the effect of the heat on the asbestos/cement compound in the lid, the cauldron erupted, badly burning the plaintiff. The risk of such an eruption is now known to be quite high. But the risk as it would have appeared at the time of such an eruption was minimal. The Court of Appeal decided that the damage was therefore too remote.

But notice that in *Doughty* something more has happened than the substitution of one verb tense for another. The traditional test required the intervening event to be independent of the defendant's faulty conduct. Independence means that we believe that the intervening event would have happened anyway, regardless of whether the defendant had acted. But in *Doughty*, the chemical reaction was not independent of the original carelessness, namely knocking the lid into the liquid. If the lid had not been immersed in the molten metal, the chemical reaction would never have happened. This contrasts with the traditional examples of breaking the chain of causation, such as the injured man struck by lightning, in which the intervening event would have happened anyway. The defendant's carelessness caused the plaintiff to be in the way of the lightning when it struck. It did not cause the lightning itself to strike. Thus in *Polemis* the process by which the falling plank caused the explosion may not have been foreseeable, but whatever it was, it would not have happened unless the stevedores had dropped the plank in the first place. *Doughty* seems to say, however, that if the intervening event was unforeseeable it need not be independent of the defendant's act.

But it is doubtful whether *Doughty* is correct. In the earlier House of Lords case *Hughes v Lord Advocate*[10] the House of Lords confirmed that the 'precise details leading up to the accident' do not have to be foreseeable.[11] In *Hughes* the plaintiff was a child who had been badly burned in an explosion in a manhole into which he had fallen. The child had found his way into the hole because the employees of the defendant, the Post Office, had left it unattended. The explosion happened because the employees had left lighted paraffin lamps around the hole and the boy, having taken one, had knocked it over. The violent explosion was a completely unexpected event. It was probably caused by the ignition of a mixture of air and paraffin which formed as paraffin sprayed out of the lamp as it fell. The defendant claimed that although the employees had been careless in leaving the hole unattended, the harm that befell the plaintiff was completely unforeseeable.

9   [1964] 1 QB 518.
10 [1963] 1 All ER 705.
11 Per Lord Guest.

But the House of Lords decided, in sharp contrast with *Doughty*, that the foreseeability was not the test for such details.

The position in *Hughes* and *Doughty* about the risk of the accident happening was identical. The accident came about in a way which no one would have foreseen beforehand, but which seems explicable now. But just as importantly, the two cases are also identical on the independence point. In both the cases the unexpected event would never have happened if the defendant had taken proper care. As Lord Reid said, echoing the classic *Polemis* argument: 'If [the defendants] had done as they ought to have done, there would have been no accident.'

Similarly, it is clear that if the only unforeseeable aspect about the accident is the extent of the damage, *Polemis* directness principles apply and the defendant is still held responsible for the full extent of the damage. If there is no *independent* intervening event that causes the damage to be much greater than that which would have been foreseeable, there is nothing upon which to hang a remoteness argument. Thus, in *Vacwell Engineering v BDH Chemicals Ltd*[12] the defendants carelessly failed to warn the plaintiffs that a chemical that they had supplied would explode if it was mixed with water. An employee of the plaintiffs then allowed the chemical to come into contact with water. But instead of a small bang which would have injured the employee concerned, a chain reaction ensued which caused a huge explosion which destroyed much of the plaintiffs' premises. The court held that the fact that the extent of the damage was much greater than that which would have been reasonably foreseeable was irrelevant.

The exact relationship between fault, the independence point and the foreseeability point becomes apparent as soon as one comes to study *Tremain v Pike*[13] a first instance decision, but one of considerable interest. The plaintiff worked on the defendants' farm as a herdsman. As the result of his work, he contracted a serious but then little-known disease known as Weil's disease. Weil's disease is caught from coming into contact with rats' urine, for example in stagnant water. The judge found that the defendants were (a) not at fault and (b) if they were at fault, the damage was too remote. The defendants were not at fault because the risk of the disease, at least as it seemed at the time, was very low and, by taking ordinary precautions against the normal, better-known risks associated with rats, the defendants had done enough. If, in the alternative, the defendants might be thought to have been at fault for not having taken those ordinary precautions the damage, harm to employees through Weil's disease, was 'unforeseeable and too remote to be recoverable'.

Payne J's judgment in *Tremain v Pike* is somewhat confused. For example, he frequently fails to distinguish points relevant to fault from points relevant to remoteness (for instance, he discusses the great expense of eliminating the risk of Weil's disease on a farm, a fault point, after he has begun to discuss remoteness). But what he does say is that *Tremain* is not a case in which Lord Reid's pro-*Polemis* point in *Hughes* applies. In

12 [1971] 1 QB 88.
13 [1969] 3 All ER 1303.

other words, he believes that the plaintiff's contracting the disease was independent of the defendants' fault. How is this possible? It is possible because Payne J believes that the defendants could have acted properly in all respects and still the plaintiff would have contracted the disease. Given the risks as they appeared at the time and the cost of the elimination of the risk of Weil's disease, the defendants would have been acting reasonably if the only precautions they took were against the usual risks of rat-bites and the contamination of foodstuffs. It is possible, according to the judge, that even if the defendants had taken all reasonable precautions against these risks, there would still have been a rat population high enough that the plaintiff would still have contracted Weil's disease. This in turn means that the defendants could have failed to take the ordinary precautions against rats, so that one might say that they were careless, but yet the disease would have happened anyway.

But note this. Payne J says that this argument means that the damage is too remote because it is unforeseeable. But what Payne J has really demonstrated is that the defendants' carelessness was not a *factual* cause of the disease in the first place. *Tremain v Pike* turns out on further analysis not to be a case about remoteness at all. It is about fault and factual cause.

The key point is that where the defendant would have had to take further precautions beyond those of reasonable care to prevent the accident, questions of remoteness do not arise. Remoteness arguments only apply where taking the care which the defendant ought to have taken anyway would have had the side effect of preventing the accident. This is a point that even the traditional approach did not recognise adequately, with its talk of intervening events which were 'not reasonably to be anticipated, nor guarded against'.[14] If the precautions that the defendant should have taken anyway would not have prevented the harm and it would have been unreasonable to expect the defendant to have taken the further precautions necessary to prevent the harm that did occur, the defendant is not liable simply because there is no proof of fault. Remoteness does not arise.

Cases of intervening natural events therefore only raise remoteness issues when the defendant could reasonably have taken action which would have prevented the harm. Otherwise, the case will turn not on remoteness but on fault and factual causation. It follows that if the intervening event is not independent of the defendant's fault, the remoteness issue will not arise in the first place, for if the intervening event would not have happened but for the defendant's fault, all the issues that arise are either fault or factual causation. The remoteness question itself, whether the remoteness issue should go in favour of the defendant or the plaintiff, therefore turns on the extent to which the intervening natural event transforms the defendant's situation, either by greatly increasing the degree of damage or by superseding the plaintiff's injury altogether.

14 The same point applies also to the French formula of 'imprévisible et irrésistible'.

'Type' of harm

The conclusion of the previous section that remoteness only arises when there is no doubt that the defendant was at fault and that the fault factually caused the harm, suggests a way forward with at least part of one of the great mysteries of English negligence law, that of the foreseeability of 'kinds (or types) of harm'. The accepted view is accurately reported by Markesinis and Deakin:[15]

> 'A major limitation on recovery following the decision of the Privy Council in the *Wagon Mound (No 1)* is the principle that the defendant will not be liable for a *kind of damage* which he could not reasonably have foreseen ... The difficulty here lies in knowing what is meant by the "kind of damage" which the defendant should have foreseen.'

The judges do refer to such a rule. Both in *Tremain*, in which there is judgment for the defendant, and in *Vacwell*, in which there is judgment for the plaintiff, the court remarks that damage is not too remote if the 'kind' or 'type' of damage was foreseeable. It is also true that in *Hughes*, the House of Lords takes the trouble to say that the damage was not too remote because it was foreseeable that the boy might suffer burns from the carelessly placed paraffin lamp, and that such an injury is not of a different type from the injuries that the boy did suffer from the explosion. And it is also true that it is difficult to pin down exactly what counts as a 'type' of damage. Blast injuries and burns are supposedly the same 'type', as are small explosions and big explosions. But being splashed by molten metal is apparently a different type of harm from being burned by exploding molten metal and being bitten by a rat is a different type of harm from contracting Weil's disease from a rat. Moreover, judges and commentators agree that one may not construct a 'type' of harm from the way the accident happened or from the extent of the harm, but a moment's reflection will reveal that those are the only ways in which it seems one could construct a type of harm argument for the *Wagon Mound (No 1)* itself and for *Doughty* and *Tremain*.

The situation is a mess. The time has surely come to move on and to reconstruct the law on more rational lines. The way out is suggested in *Tremain*. Payne J, after arguing that the costs involved in removing the risks of Weil's disease would be much greater than those involved in removing the risks of rat bites and contamination of food, says:

> 'I do not accept that all illness or infection arising from an infestation of rats should be regarded as of the same kind. One cannot say in this case, as was said by Lord Reid in the *Hughes* case: "... if they [the defenders] had done as they ought to have done there would have been no accident".'

15 *Tort Law* (Oxford; Clarendon Press, 1994) at p 186.

'Kind' of harm in this passage refers not to the extent of the damage or to the way in which the accident came about or to any other similar abstract classification system, but more straightforwardly to the precautions one has to take to prevent the accident. Different 'kinds' of accident need different measures to prevent them.

If the law were to adopt the definition of 'type' or 'kind' of harm as 'injuries that would be prevented by the same precautions' the effect on the law would be that cases such as *Tremain,* for which remoteness arguments are technically irrelevant and which the courts can solve solely by using fault and factual cause, would automatically disappear from the frame, leaving only those cases in which the defendant claims that the damage was too remote despite the fact that the accident would never have happened if the defendant had acted properly. This in turn would transform the troublesome concept of 'type of harm' into a useful device for sifting cases into those in which remoteness is implicated and those in which it is not. If the intervening event would not have happened but for the defendant's failure to take proper precautions, the damage will automatically be of the same type as that which occurred. Attention will then have to turn to other issues, such as the independence of the intervening event from the defendant's fault and the extent to which the harm caused by the intervening act either adds to harm caused by the defendant's fault or supersedes it altogether.

CAN REMOTENESS BE DISPENSED WITH?

Since much of what is conventionally thought to be remoteness turns out on further inspection to be fault or factual causation, the question arises as to whether the law of negligence could dispense with the remoteness concept altogether. The answer to this question is technically yes, although whether the resulting changes in the substance of the law would be acceptable is another question.

All 'faulty' interventions by third parties or plaintiff could be treated solely as contribution or contributory negligence points, with pro–portional several liability replacing the present contribution system. 'Innocent' interventions would have to be ignored, so that no non-faulty or reasonable third party intervention or plaintiff's act would ever prevent the defendant from being held liable. The pre-existing state of the plaintiff would need to be analysed into those states that have arisen from unreasonable action on the part of the plaintiff and those that have not.

A problem would arise with natural events. It is not plausible in our culture to divide natural events into 'reasonable' and 'unreasonable' or 'faulty' and 'innocent'. We could try apportioning the 'blame' attaching to the defendant with regard to the 'influence' of the natural event (as happens in French law from time to time), but this is difficult to do in the absence of a common metric. And it is not clear why natural events should reduce the damages but innocent human interventions not. We might instead say that natural events would never 'break the chain' no matter how unlikely and overwhelming. The only defence would be on factual causation—that the defendant's fault made no difference because the plaintiff would have been injured in exactly the same way anyway.

Thus, the plaintiff would win cases that the defendant wins now, but the intervention of third parties could not be a complete defence and would lead in cases where the intervention was faulty to a reduction in damages in the same way that the faulty conduct of the plaintiff leads to a reduction in damages in the form of contributory negligence.

Would such a change favour defendants on the whole or plaintiffs? Or neither?

Chapter 5

Duty

KEY POINTS

* **Duty arguments are those that say that even if the defendant was at fault and caused the harm, the defendant should still not be liable.**
* **One kind of duty argument is that the defendant should receive protection from the law of negligence.**
* **Another sort of duty argument is that the kind of loss suffered by the plaintiff should not be recoverable.**
* **Another sort of duty argument is that allowing a negligence action would disrupt another area of the law.**
* **Yet another sort of duty argument is that the imposition of a duty of care would do more harm than good.**
* **The categories both of negligence and of arguments against negligence are never closed.**

Nothing is more characteristic of English negligence law than for a case to be dismissed on the basis that 'the defendant owed no duty of care to the plaintiff'. At the same time, no argument in English law produces more puzzlement in students or confusion in the judiciary. It is clear that if the defendant was under no duty to 'take care', that is to act reasonably, the plaintiff cannot complain about lack of care or unreasonable behaviour. But it is often far from clear why the defendant owed no such duty.

Some legal systems do without the notion of a duty of care altogether. For example the French and Dutch Civil Codes get by without such a concept. They do so without any noticeable detriment either to the coherence of their law or to the well-being of their societies.

Other legal systems, although they make some use of the concept of a duty to take care, explain it in fairly straightforward and comprehensible terms. For example, German law links the duty to take care with the broader question of whether or not the law recognises or protects the type of interest interference in which forms the basis of the plaintiff's complaint.

English law, unfortunately, affords no simple or predictable explanation of the duty of care and, despite the exertions of some of the most eminent English academic lawyers of the twentieth century,[1] shows no inclination to rid itself of the concept—troublesome, confusing and probably superfluous though it may be.

Three sources of confusion

The central problem with the duty of care concept is that it strikes the non-tort lawyer as unnatural and artificial. For example, to say that it is wrong to run someone over because there was a duty not to run over that particular person sounds extremely peculiar. It is wrong to run someone over because it is wrong to do harm, not because one 'owed a duty' to the victim not to run him over.

The artificiality arises largely because the language of duty, at least in relation to duties that are said to be owed to other people rather than impersonal duties merely to behave in a particular way, sounds unnatural in the absence of a pre-existing relationship between the people involved in the dispute. One might say that to make a promise creates a duty to carry out what was promised and that to fail to do so involves a breach of a pre-existing obligation. In that case the duty forms part of a relationship between the people concerned. But to say that I breached an obligation to the complete stranger that I ran over in the street seems to presuppose a degree of intimacy with the stranger that simply did not exist. The only natural sense of duty in these circumstances is a strictly impersonal one in which there is a duty to behave properly with regard to the whole world, not to any particular person. But, as we shall see, negligence law allegedly does not deal in impersonal duties, but in 'duties' to specific people. **The consequence is that the 'duties' that negligence law alleges that defendants owe to specific plaintiffs are fictional duties, duties invented after the fact to justify a certain legal result rather than obligations that would be recognised as such by tort defendants at the time of their alleged tortious conduct.**

The second difficulty with the way the English courts talk about duties of care is that **they give the very puzzling impression that duties of care arise directly from the facts of the case,** as if the defendant should have known at the time that he was under a duty to take care or that the plaintiff should have known that the defendant was not under a duty to take care. But the reasons the courts give for denying that there was a duty of care include the most obscure facts imaginable, for example

---

1   See Winfield 'Duty in Tortious Negligence' in *Select Legal Essays* (London: Sweet and Maxwell, 1952) and Buckland 'The Duty to Take Care' (1935) 51 LQR 637. See contra Lawson 'Duty of Care in Negligence; a Comparative Study' (1947) 22 Tulane LR 111.

facts about Parliament's intention when it passed a statute 50 years previously or about whether the plaintiff was friendly with his brother.[2]

Moreover, obligations do not arise from facts but from judgments of right and wrong. In deciding whether or not harm caused by unreasonable behaviour should be actionable, some substantive normative judgment is required, painful though that may be for those who have to decide. Judgments do not follow from facts alone.

The courts, however, seem to find it hard to understand any legal duty that does not somehow arise from a promise. For in a promise the obligation does appear to arise out of a fact, the fact of the promise's having been made. But the difference is that the idea of a promise automatically includes the idea of obligation. The act of promising cannot be understood without reference to its moral content—a promise is by definition something that one ought to keep. But the same point does not apply to the acts that form the subject matter of tort cases—for example driving, manufacturing, building, or regulating. These are all activities that can be defined accurately without reference to right or wrong. It is true that one can drive, manufacture, build or regulate well or badly, and it may be easier to understand what any of these activities involves by starting with examples of when it is done well or badly. But the difference is that in the activity of promising it is automatically good to keep a promise, whereas it is not automatically good, and not automatically bad, to drive, manufacture, build or regulate.

It may be that to cause certain types of harm is generally accepted as wrong, but that to cause other types of harm is not necessarily wrong. Lord Oliver made such a claim in *Murphy v Brentwood District Council*:[3]

> 'The infliction of physical injury to the person or property of another universally requires to be justified. The causing of economic loss does not.'

But even if this claim is correct, and it is, to say the least, controversial, it does not mean that duties arise from facts, only that certain types of fact generally attract the same kinds of judgment.

In the day-to-day application of the law, however, the main source of confusion about the duty of care is not so much the use of the concept of personal duties in contexts in which the parties have no prior relationship, or the attempt to ground judgments about what ought to be done on findings of fact, but rather the apparent inability of English judges to distinguish duty from breach. **To say that what the defendant did was wrong but that this particular sort of wrongdoing has no legal conseq-**

2   See *Peabody Donation Fund v Sir Lindsay Parkinson* [1985] AC 210 (No duty because Parliament did not intend to protect economic interests of developers in the Public Health Act 1936) and *Alcock v Chief Constable of South Yorks* [1992] 1 AC 310 (no liability for psychiatric illness caused by witnessing injury to one's brother unless one can prove that one had a close relationship with him).

3   [1991] 1 AC 398.

uences is quite different from saying that what the defendant did was not wrong in the first place. Judges tend to use the phrase 'there was no duty' for both of these sorts of case. But this is both inaccurate and very confusing. Where the defendant is at fault but the fault has no legal consequences, the situation is one of 'no duty'. But where the defendant is not at fault in the first place, the situation is nothing to do with 'duty' but is one of 'no breach' or 'no fault'.[4]

For example, if one says[5] that a defendant government regulator of banks is not liable for the wrongdoing of the banks it was supposed to regulate, and one says that the reason for the lack of liability is that it would cost vast amounts of time and money to prevent the wrongdoing concerned, what one is saying is that the regulator was not at fault, that its behaviour was reasonable in the circumstances in the same way that the factory owner behaved reasonably in *AEC v Latimer*.[6] If, on the other hand, one says that even though the defendant regulator acted unreasonably, the plaintiffs should not be able to sue for purely financial losses, one is making a far more general point, a point that would apply regardless of the conduct of the defendant in this particular case and therefore a point that goes to duty rather than breach.

THE CONFUSION OF DUTY AND BREACH AND THE FEARS OF APPELLATE COURTS

The confusion of duty and breach has been endemic in the English courts for many years. Sometimes, however, senior judges break out of the confusion and reassert the importance of the distinction between the argument that the defendant did no wrong and that the defendant may have done wrong but should not be legally liable. For example in *Spring v Guardian Assurance* Lord Slynn and Lord Lowry make it clear that they see duty and breach as separate issues.[7] But it is important to note exactly what Lord Slynn says in *Spring*:

4 See generally Howarth 'Negligence After Murphy: Time to Re-think' [1991] CLJ 58.
5 Cf *Yuen Kun Yeu v A-G for Hong Kong* [1988] AC 175.
6 See above ch 3.
7 See also Sir Thomas Bingham MR's remarks in his powerful dissent in *M (a minor) v Newham London Borough Council* and *X (minors) v Bedfordshire County Council* [1994] 4 All ER 602, [1994] Fam Law 434 on why he rejected an argument against the existence of a duty of care in a case concerning careless advice about child abuse by a psychiatrist: 'The extreme difficulty and delicacy of the doctor's task in this context, and the highly judgmental nature of it, are very relevant. They present any plaintiff with a formidable task. As always, it will not be enough to show an error of judgment, or to show that other well-qualified members of the profession would have taken a different view. It would have to be shown that the doctor's opinion or conduct fell outside the bounds sanctioned by any responsible body of professional opinion. It can be assumed that few claims would succeed... The doctor's only certain protection would be sound performance of his professional duty, and that is how it should be.'.

✳ 'The courts can be trusted to set a standard which is not higher
than the law of negligence demands.'

The crucial word is 'trusted'. One explanation of why the confusion
between duty and breach arises is precisely that the appeal courts do
not trust the trial courts to make appropriate decisions on the issue of
fault. The fear can either be that the trial courts will set standards that
are too low, or, as in the case envisaged by Lord Slynn, that they will set
impossibly high standards. In either case, the problem for the appellate
court is that 'fault', 'breach' or 'carelessness' are without any doubt issues
for the trial court to determine, so that if the appellate court is to
intervene it has to do so by invoking another aspect of the law. This is
where 'duty' comes in. The appellate court is not allowed to contradict
the trial court's finding that the defendant was not at fault, but it is
allowed to say that there was 'no duty'. It is therefore extremely
convenient for appellate courts to redefine their disagreement with the
trial court on the issue of fault as an issue of 'duty'. But the only way to
do this is to say that there can be very specific duties, duties that amount
to saying that there was a 'duty' to take precisely the precaution that
the defendant failed to take, the result of which is a general confusion
in the law.

These three forms of confusion and sources of puzzlement, the artificiality
of talking about pre-existing duties to strangers, the false impression that
duties can arise in an uncomplicated way from facts and the confusion of
duty and breach, mean that to **understand** duty of care in a coherent way
means taking an approach radically different from that conventionally taken
by the courts. It means taking an approach that will explain the results the
courts reach and is true to the motivations underlying what judges say, but
which avoids the confusions and logical traps of the conventional language.
This is what the rest of this chapter attempts to do.

What duty cases are about

The first step must be to define the field of inquiry. What issue is at stake
in duty of care cases?

The answer for the purpose of this chapter will assume: (1) that cases
that are reducible to decisions on whether or not the defendant acted
reasonably are not duty of care cases but cases about fault (or 'breach' or
'carelessness'); (2) that there is no way that a duty of care can be 'shown' or
'proved' to exist on the basis of findings of fact alone; and (3) that the
phrase, 'there was no duty of care' is not so much an argument as a
conclusion of law—it says what the answer is, not how the answer was
reached.

Duty of care cases, therefore, are cases in which defendants claim that
it makes no difference whether or not they were careless, because for some

they should not be found to be liable even if they were at fault. Duty of care cases, in other words, are cases in which the defendant says, 'So what if I was at fault and you were harmed as a consequence, I win anyway.'

The analysis of the duty of care in turn requires looking at and assessing the various reasons put forward in support of the argument that the particular defendant's carelessness in the particular case does not matter.

✴THE HISTORY OF THE DUTY OF CARE CONCEPT

On the question of liability for unintentional harm, European legal systems fall broadly into two categories. There are those, such as the French system, which operate on the basis of broad principles in favour of liability, and there are those, such as the German system, which eschew broad principles and establish liability only on the basis of specifically delineated interests or circumstances. Art 1382 of the French Civil Code establishes a general principle that 'Tout fait quelconque de l'homme qui cause à autrui un dommage oblige celui par la faute duquel il est arrivé à le réparer' (ie 'Any act of a person which causes damage to another makes him by whose fault the damage occurred liable to make reparation for the damage'). In contrast, §823 of the German Code says, 'Wer vorsätzlich oder fahrlässig das Leben, den Körper, die Gesundheit, die Freiheit, das Eigentum oder ein sonstiges Recht eines anderen widerrechtlich verletzt, ist dem anderen zum Ersatze des daraus entstehenden Schadens verpflichtet' ('A person who, whether wilfully or negligently, unlawfully harms the life, body, health, freedom, property or other specific right of another is obliged to compensate the other for any damages that arise').

Of course, these are only starting points. Pressure on the general principle systems to exclude liability, by using causation and fault for example, and pressure on the specific interest systems to expand the scope of the interests, tend to bring the practical results achieved by the two sorts of system together. The conditions of life in most western European societies are fundamentally similar and their intellectual and ethical traditions are closely interrelated, and so it is not surprising that in practice the various systems have to solve very similar problems and often end up doing so in very similar ways. But the starting points do make a difference at the margin. They establish whether or not the fundamental orientation of the legal system in question is in favour of liability, so that in borderline cases, economic loss for example, general principle systems are more likely to favour the plaintiff than specific interest systems.

The English legal system has never quite decided whether it is a general principle system or a specific interest or circumstance system.[7a] In the nineteenth century, the English judges leant heavily towards the specific interest or circumstance view, although discontent with that approach produced a few notable counterblasts, most famously that of

7a   See ch 2 for an extended discussion of these ideas.

Brett MR in *Heaven v Pender* (1883) 11 QBD 503. The view appeared to be that to allow legal liability to extend beyond the bounds of contract, that is beyond the bounds of what people had subjected themselves to voluntarily, would be to impose an intolerable burden of state interference upon them. In consequence, the presumption had to be against liability, a presumption displaced only by established rules of custom and practice.

The position changed slightly with cases such as *Le Lievre v Gould* [1893] 1 QB 491 in which Brett (by then Lord Esher) carried some other judges with him as far as saying that if:

> 'One man is near to another, or is near to the property of another, a duty lies upon him not to do that which may cause a personal injury to that other or, or may injure his property.'

But this formulation is very far from the generality of art 1382. It is restricted to particular forms of harm (personal injury and property damage) and is qualified by the mysterious requirement of 'nearness', a requirement that, in the form of 'proximity' has dogged English law ever since.

The pendulum swung the other way, however, in *Donoghue v Stevenson* [1932] AC 562 in which a majority of the House of Lords, led by Lord Atkin, said that there was a duty to avoid harming by one's carelessness anyone whom one 'reasonably ought to have [had] in contemplation' at the time and Lord Macmillan opened out both the circumstance and the interest restrictions on negligence, by declaring that 'the categories of negligence are never closed'.

Donoghue comes close to establishing a general clause in the French style, although it is again restricted by an apparent limitation on who is entitled to sue—'nearness' in *Le Lievre v Gould* having been replaced by 'reasonable contemplation' of a plaintiff. This limitation, however, should have been quite unimportant, since it can only apply, on any sensible view, to very broad categories of people or, better, to people in general. One does not have to have in contemplation anyone specific as a potential victim of a road accident before one is liable for carelessly running him over. It is the dangerousness of the situation that should matter, rather than the identity of the victim.

Donoghue did not, however, meet with universal approval. In the 1940s commentators such as Landon reasserted the view that:

> 'Negligence is not actionable unless the duty to be careful exists. And the duty to be careful only exists where the wisdom of our ancestors has decreed that it shall exist.'[8]

Furthermore in cases such as *Deyong v Shenburn* [1946] KB 227 judges were still prepared to back the specific circumstance view.

8   (1941) 57 LQR at 183.

But in the 1960s and 1970s, the general principle view came to the fore. In *Hedley Byrne v Heller* [1964] AC 465, *Home Office v Dorset Yacht* [1970] AC 1004 and ultimately in *Anns v Merton London Borough Council* [1978] AC 728 the House of Lords came to the conclusion that there ought to be a presumption in favour of liability for harm caused by carelessness. The *Anns* 'two-stage' test, as formulated by Lord Wilberforce, was simply that there ought to be liability for harm caused by fault (stage 1) unless there were good reasons why not (stage 2). *Anns* inspired judges such as Lord Scarman to say in *McLoughlin v O'Brian* [1983] 1 AC 410 that principle required the application of *Donoghue* 'untrammelled by spatial, physical or temporal limits'.

But a reaction set in after *Anns* and *McLoughlin*, led by Lord Keith of Kinkel. Lord Keith believed that Lord Wilberforce in *Anns* had said that there ought to be liability whenever there was reasonably foreseeable damage. This was, in fact, not true. Lord Wilberforce had said only that there ought to be a presumption in favour of saying that liability was possible whenever there was reasonably foreseeable damage. The plaintiff still had to prove fault, that is that a reasonable person would have taken further precautions against the reasonably foreseeable damage, so that the presumption in favour of the plaintiff is only about the possibility of liability, not liability itself, and furthermore the presumption could in any case be displaced in the second stage of the test. Nevertheless, Lord Keith's reaction gathered strength as the 1980s continued. The reaction originally concentrated on widening the scope of the second stage of the test, so that it included 'proximity', which operated as a kind of super-remoteness test (see above chapter 4) and vague notions of what was 'just and reasonable'. Ultimately, however, 'proximity' was elevated to become a separate stage in itself (even though various judges admitted that it was not clear what it meant) and some judges began to go back on the *Donoghue* conclusion that there ought to be a presumption in favour of liability.

Lord Keith's favourite text in cases such as *Yuen Kun Yeu v A-G (Hong Kong)* [1988] AC 175 and *Murphy v Brentwood District Council* [1991] 1 AC 398 and Lord Bridge's favourite text in *Caparo v Dickman* [1990] 2 AC 605 and *Curran v Northern Ireland Co-ownership Housing Association* [1987] AC 718 was a passage from the judgment of the Australian judge Brennan J in *Sutherland Shire Council v Heyman* (1985) 60 ALR 1. Brennan J had said that:

'It is preferable, in my view, that the law should develop novel categories incrementally and by analogy with established categories, rather than by a massive extension of a prima facie duty of care restrained only by indefinable 'considerations which ought to negative, or to reduce or limit the scope of the duty or the class of person to whom it is owed'.

Ultimately, Lord Bridge went the whole way back to the pre-*Donoghue* circumstances and interests approach and declared in *Caparo* that:

'I think the law has now moved in the direction of attaching greater significance to the more traditional categorisation of distinct and recognisable situations as guides to the existence, scope and the limits of the varied duties of care which the law imposes.'

It seems, however, that just as *Anns* and *McLoughlin v O'Brian* marked the high point of the last upswing of the general principles approach, *Caparo* may mark the high point of the swing in the opposite direction. Cases such as *Spring v Guardian Assurance* [1994] 3 All ER 129 and *Henderson v Merrett Syndicates Ltd* [1994] 3 All ER 506 seem to point to the construction of general principles of liability that cut across the traditional categories of tort and contract and if they do not point to the return to the *Anns* approach or, even more, to a French approach, at least there is again a consciousness that it is possible to construct principles and rules that go beyond mere analogies with the existing case law.

It is easy to exaggerate the importance of these swings in English law. It ought to be emphasised again that we are talking here only about starting points, and just as in many circumstances French and German law, with their very different starting points, produce very similar practical results, so the different starting points adopted by English law over the last 100 years may not have affected the results of cases as much as most writers and judges think, and more widespread trends, such as that towards consumer protection, may have had more influence on the law over the same period.

Summary of duty arguments

There are nine lines of argument, apart from remoteness arguments (which have already been dealt with), that frequently succeed in negativing an alleged duty of care. This section summarises them. The following sections take up each in turn, giving examples both of where they have succeeded and where they have failed.

1   Pure omissions

The defendant should not be held liable for pure omissions, that is failures to act that cannot be re-construed as some form of acting unreasonably.

Pure omissions almost invariably turn out to be failures to rescue the plaintiff or to warn the plaintiff of danger.

2   No deterrence value

The imposition of liability would not lead to any improvement in the conduct of the defendant or of those similarly situated, but would lead to expense and inconvenience.

The imposition of liability in such circumstances allegedly does more harm than good.

3   Allocation of public resources

The imposition of liability implicates the courts in major decisions of public policy, especially about public expenditure, that should be decided by other organs of government.

4   Integrity of other legal rules

To allow liability in negligence would undermine or evade some other legal rule or procedure.

For example, wider liability of public authorities could undermine the safeguards for public authorities inherent in the law on judicial review.

Another example is the protection of res judicata, that liability should be denied when the plaintiff is attempting to reopen issues that the courts have already pronounced upon in other proceedings.

Yet another variant of the argument that other legal rules should be protected is that in some cases the underlying objective of negligence liability is to further the purpose of a statute. In these cases, it is often argued that the plaintiff should not succeed when liability would not further the purpose of the statute.

5   Plaintiff's interest not protected

There should be no liability because the kind of harm complained of by the plaintiff ought not to be recognised by the law.

For example, the type of harm suffered might be thought to be too easy to fake, or to be inherently trivial, or to be better borne by the victim than by anyone else, or to be really the plaintiff's responsibility.

6   Absolute public benefit

There should be no liability because the defendant's activities are of such public benefit that no matter how much harm results from them they must be allowed to continue.

In effect, the court declares the kind of activity to be reasonable in all circumstances as a matter of law.

7 Defendant immunity

No liability is possible because the defendant can claim an immunity either from legal actions in general or from negligence actions.

8 Lack of authority

There should be no liability in cases that have no resemblance to any previous case in which liability had been found.

This much-criticised ground (which amounts to saying that nothing should be done for the first time) holds great sway in the English courts.

9 Lack of special relationship—'proximity'

There would be liability if there was a special relationship between the plaintiff and the defendant, but in the absence of such a relationship, there is no liability.

This fashionable and much abused ground will be analysed to show that it concerns not so much a reason for denying liability as a combination of a reason for not making an exception in favour of liability in cases in which liability is already to be denied on other grounds using standard remoteness arguments.

⚓ THE FLOODGATES ARGUMENT

One argument that sometimes arises in duty cases is the so-called 'floodgates' argument.[9] In its simplest form, the floodgates argument asserts 'the impossibility of containing liability within any acceptable bounds if the law were to permit such claims to succeed'.[10] The courts do not refer to it very often, and, outside the specialist field of pure economic loss,[11] when they do refer to it, they usually either disapprove

---

9   See J Bell *Policy Arguments in Judicial Decisions* (1982, Clarendon Press, Oxford) at 71ff.

10 See eg *Preston v Torfaen Borough Council* (1993) 36 Con LR 48, 26 HLR 149.

11 See below ch 6.

of it, or say that it does not apply or, at the very least, say that it is not enough by itself.[12]

There are two forms of the floodgates argument as applied to negligence. In the first, the reason why the courts might believe that liability will not be kept within 'acceptable bounds' is that there will be too many cases for the courts to cope with. This version of the floodgates argument only has to be stated for its absurdity and injustice to become apparent. It cannot be a good reason for denying a right and annulling a duty that there are not enough judges to hear all the cases. The administrative arrangements of the courts and the workload of judges should not affect the substantive rights of citizens. In any case, it is very unlikely that the granting of new rights to sue would in practice have such an effect, simply because if the new rights and duties were reasonably clear, parties would quickly settle out of court. A surfeit of new cases only appears where the law is unclear, and if the judges are doing their job, those cases themselves soon clear up many of the uncertainties, so that the area of law then returns to normality.[13]

But nevertheless, even this version of the floodgates argument continues to attract adherents. For example in *M v Newham, X v Bedfordshire*, Staughton LJ, after admitting that all the justifications for this form of the floodgates argument are deficient in logic says:

> 'But I fear that the time has come to recognise that [the arguments against the floodgates point are] unsound in practice. If a new duty of local authorities is established in these appeals, I do not doubt that many claims will be brought, placing further strain in an already stretched system (which will be provided with no more resources). I do not doubt that many claims with little or no prospect of success will be financed by the legal aid fund. Nor that many will be delayed for years, perhaps until the plaintiff is 21. Nor that many claims will be settled, or even decided in favour of a plaintiff whose misfortunes attract sympathy, although there has been no more than an error of judgment.'

Admittedly, Staughton LJ's point goes beyond the normal floodgates point. He is saying that where there is legal aid, there are plaintiffs who will lose nothing if they lose the case, but it still costs the defendants much to defend themselves. The effect is that defendants will settle even cases in which there is a very small chance that the plaintiff will win.

12 See eg *White v Jones* [1993] 3 All ER 481, [1993] 3 WLR 730, *Jones v Wright* [1991] 3 All ER 88; affd sub nom *Alcock v Chief Constable of South Yorkshire Police* [1992] 1 AC 310, *Esso v Hall Russell* [1989] 1 AC 643, *McLoughlin v O'Brian* [1983] 1 AC 410 (per Lord Scarman).

13 There is also the argument that if the right is economically inefficient, it will cause more cases to be taken to court, since there will be more dissatisfied litigants. Even if this argument is true, its effect is small.

But this version of the floodgates argument is no better than the other versions. First, the legal aid scheme itself requires that the plaintiff has to have a realistic chance of success in order to qualify for support. Secondly, and more fundamentally, in Staughton LJ's scenario, defendants are still settling only those cases that there is some chance that the plaintiff will win. If there is no chance at all that the plaintiff will win, the defendant will continue to fight, since the defendant will be certain that his costs will be reimbursed. This makes the situation very different from that in the USA, where, because each party has to pay its own costs regardless of the result of the case, if the plaintiff, through a contingent fee arrangement, for example, does not have to care about costs, defendants have an incentive to settle even those cases in which plaintiffs have no chance at all of winning.

The second reason for talking about the number of cases going beyond 'acceptable bounds' is that it is unhealthy for society as whole that people spend much time and effort in litigation. Lord Templeman had this version of the floodgates argument in mind when he said in *CBS v Amstrad*:

> 'Since *Anns v Merton London Borough* [1978] AC 728, [1977] 2 All ER 492 put the floodgates on the jar, a fashionable plaintiff alleges negligence. The pleading assumes that we are all neighbours now, Pharisees and Samaritans alike, that foresee—ability is a reflection of hindsight and that for every mischance in an accident-prone world someone solvent must be liable in damages.'

That is, like his nineteenth century predecessor Bramwell B,[14] Lord Templeman believes that allowing too many plaintiffs to succeed in negligence actions means encouraging the point of view that somebody else must be to blame for whatever goes wrong in one's life.[15] In turn, such an attitude undermines the ethic of personal responsibility and transforms the culture into one where complaining replaces creativity and pursuing grievances replaces enterprise.

Whether as a matter of sociology such claims stand up must be a matter of some dispute, especially since they assume that the legal culture of a society has strong effects on its general ethical climate. But most judges, and probably most academics, students and citizens do have limits to what they believe that it is right to use the courts to complain about. The question is whether such beliefs should feed into duty of care arguments.

This question of the limits of legitimate complaint is one of the underlying issues in the consolidated appeals in *M v Newham Borough Council; X v Bedfordshire County Council; E v Dorset County Council;*

14 See generally Howarth 'Negligence After Murphy' [1991] AC 58.
15 There is a special version of this point—that negligence actions are bad for the economy—that applies in economic loss cases. This version is discussed not here but below in ch 6.

Christmas v Hampshire County Council and *Keating v Bromley London Borough Council.*[16] In all of these cases, plaintiffs complain that they have suffered as the result of carelessness by the employees of local authorities charged with supplying either social or educational services. In the *Newham* and *Bedfordshire* cases the Court of Appeal, with Sir Thomas Bingham MR dissenting, held that since the statutes conferring powers and duties on local authority social services departments to protect children from their parents were too general to give individuals a right to enforce them, there could be no negligence actions either when the powers were exercised carelessly. In the *Dorset, Hampshire* and *Bromley* cases, in contrast, a differently constituted Court of Appeal, but still including Sir Thomas Bingham, decided unanimously that if the plaintiff could prove fault, causation and damage, there was no reason why there should not be a cause of action where the defendant local authorities failed to provide adequate schooling for local children.

Is expecting the local authority to protect one from abuse, or to desist from making careless accusations of abuse going beyond 'acceptable bounds' of what one should be able to complain about in the courts? What, on the other hand, about failing to provide an adequate education?

Many people would think that the Court of Appeal had these cases the wrong way round—that expecting protection from abuse and false accusations of abuse is not too much to expect, but complaining about one's educational failure when many thousands of people overcame similar or worse disadvantages does seem unreasonable.

But notice that there is no need to make such general and abstract judgments at all. There is, for example, a remoteness aspect to many of these cases. In the social services cases the actual abuse is perpetrated by a third party. The question in such cases is really whether that person's fault should count as having eclipsed the local authority's fault. The view that it should not so count arises largely from the idea that the local authority's role is to prevent exactly that kind of damage. There is also a causation element—would the pupil really have fared better at school and in subsequent life had the local education spent a little more time and effort on his or her education, or would the same outcome have occurred anyway? And there is a fault element too—in the social services cases, social workers often have to make difficult and finely-balanced decisions quickly using fragmentary evidence. Can they be blamed for not getting it right every single time?

The law, therefore, does not have to exclude the possibility of any successful claims in order to make sure that unmeritorious claims fail. The court can choose instead from a wide range of other more finely-tuned arguments. In such circumstances, the likelihood that the rules of the common law might cause a decline in the values of self-reliance

16 Argument before the House of Lords began on 10 October 1994. Court of Appeal decisions reported at [1994] 2 WLR 554 and (1994) Times, 4 May.

and responsibility must be very low. In any case, finding for an unmeritorious defendant in such cases also carries dangers—for example the danger that people will think that the legal system is out of touch with ordinary life and values.

Pure omissions

In *Gautret v Egerton* [17] the defendants owned a dockyard. The case against them was that they had failed to keep in good repair the bridges that connected one part of the dockyard to another, with the result that the plaintiff had fallen from one of the bridges to his death. The Court of Common Pleas decided that the plaintiff's allegation did not amount to a sustainable claim. There could be no duty, according to Willes J, because the plaintiff, although lawfully present on the land, was not there for any purpose of the defendant, and so was in a position analogous to that of a recipient of a gift—namely that:[18]

'[T]he giver is not responsible for damage resulting from the insecurity of the thing unless he knew of its evil character, and omitted to caution the donee. There must be something like fraud on the part of the giver before he can be made answerable.'

In other words, negligence is not enough in such situations.

But Willes J then gave another illustration of his principle by way of further justification:

'No action will lie against a spiteful man who, seeing another running into a position of danger, merely omits to warn him. To bring the case within the category of actionable negligence, some wrongful act must be shewn, or a breach of a positive duty: otherwise a man who allows strangers to roam over his property would be held to be answerable for not protecting them against any danger which they might encounter whilst using the licence.'

Largely on the basis of this half-remembered case, it is usually said that there is no duty to take reasonable care for omissions, that is not doing something as opposed to doing something badly, unless there is some pre-existing relationship between the parties.

Indeed in the United States, the idea that there should be no liability for inaction (or 'nonfeasance') as opposed to faulty action (or 'misfeasance') has been taken to extremes, so that even intentional inaction gives rise to

17 (1867) LR 2 CP 371.
18 Ibid at p 375.

no liability. In *Osterlind v Hill*,[19] for example, where the defendant hired out pleasure boats on Lake Quannapowitt, the plaintiff hired a boat, although he was plainly very drunk at the time. Inevitably, the plaintiff fell into the lake. For half an hour, the plaintiff hung onto the boat and shouted for help. The defendant heard the calls from the bank, but chose to do absolutely nothing. The plaintiff eventually passed out, slipped under the surface of the lake and drowned. The Supreme Court of Massachusetts dismissed the claims both for negligence and intentionally caused harm.

Osterlind is clearly not particularly useful as a guide to English law— the extension of non-liability to intentional omissions is not established in England and the presence of the pre-existing relationship of hirer and customer may well be enough in England to bring the case into to realms of a positive duty to act. But hostility to liability in negligence for what are now usually called 'pure omissions' has been a feature of English law for most of the past 100 years and can be seen in many recent speeches in the House of Lords.

For example, Lord Goff in *Maloco v Littlewoods*[20] said that in general there was no duty to protect other people because, 'The common law does not impose liability for what are called pure omissions.'

Lord Goff based his remarks on a passage from a speech of Lord Diplock in *Home Office v Dorset Yacht*[1] in which Lord Diplock said:

> 'The branch of English law which deals with civil wrongs abounds with instances of acts and, more particularly, of omissions which give rise to no legal liability .... The very parable of the Good Samaritan (Luke 10:30) which was evoked by Lord Atkin in *Donoghue v Stevenson* illustrates, in the conduct of the priest and of the Levite who passed by on the other side, an omission which was likely to have as its reasonable and probable consequence damage to the health of the victim of the thieves, but for which the priest and the Levite would have incurred no civil liability in English law.'

The classic statement is perhaps that of Lord Keith in *Yuen Kun Yeu v A-G of Hong Kong*.[2] Lord Keith says that there is no liability for omissions because

> 'Otherwise there would be liability in negligence on the part of one who sees another about to walk over a cliff with his head in the air, and forbears to shout a warning.'[3]

---

19 160 NE 301, 263 Mass 73, 56 ALR 1123 (1928), Supreme Judicial Court of Mass–achussetts, per Braley J.
20 [1987] AC 241 at 271.
1   [1970] AC 1004 at 1060.
2   [1988] AC 175.
3   Ibid at 192. See also Lord Bridge in *Curran* [1987] AC 718 at 724 approving Smith and Burns (1983) 46 MLR 147 at 156 in their attempt to resurrect the distinction between nonfeasance and misfeasance from what they saw as attacks on it in cases such as *Anns*.

Of course, these remarks have to be read in the light of the exception in favour of a duty arising out of pre-existing relationships, and it may be, for reasons that are examined below, that the category of positive duties is expanding to include all situations in which the defendant can be said to have 'assumed responsibility' for the plaintiff or for the situation, and, because of the indeterminacy of that concept, to all situations in which there is no good independent reason for denying liability.[4] But the orthodox position remains one of a strong presumption against liability.

The orthodoxy is not without its critics and its doubters.[5] Logie,[6] for example, argues that the number of situations in which the courts say that there is a duty to warn another person of some impending danger is expanding rapidly. According to Logie, the list now includes not just the situation in which the defendant has given an explicit or implicit under–taking to the plaintiff to protect him or her from danger or where the parties have some special or fiduciary relationship (such as parent and child), but also when the defendant has control over a dangerous person or thing,[7] where the defendant created the danger in the first place,[8] where it is accepted practice to give a warning,[9] where the plaintiff is relying on the specialist knowledge of the defendant,[10] and where the risk is not widely known, arises inevitably out of the defendant's activities but cannot otherwise be reduced (for example a health risk arising from an industrial process).[11] Even the very situation upon which Willes J was pronouncing in *Gautret* is one in which, as a result of statute,[12] there is clearly liability not only for failure to warn, but also, if warnings would not have been effective, for omitting to carry out repairs in the first place. Logie goes so far as to say that the courts are in the process of working out a general duty to warn, which might depend, for example, on whether the defendant was in a better position to know about the danger than the plaintiff was. If true, this would mean that it would be very difficult to argue for any major difference in general between treatment of misfeasance and nonfeasance in negligence along the traditional lines.

---

4 See Lord Goff's judgments in *Spring v Guardian Assurance* [1994] 3 All ER 129 and *Henderson v Merrett Syndicates Ltd* [1994] 3 All ER 506.
5 See eg Weinrib 'The Case For a Duty to Rescue' (1980) 90 Yale LJ 247, P Atiyah and P Cane *Accidents, Compensation and the Law* (4th ed) (London: Weidenfeld and Nicholson, 1987) pp 80-93 and Logie 'Affirmative Action in the Law of Tort: The Case of the Duty to Warn' [1989] CLJ 115.
6 [1989] CLJ 115.
7 *Home Office v Dorset Yacht* [1970] AC 1004.
8 Eg *Kimber v Gas Light and Coke Co* [1918] 1 KB 439, per Scrutton LJ at 447.
9 *Buckner v Ashby and Horner* [1941] 1 KB 321.
10 See eg *Esso Petroleum v Mardon* [1976] QB 801 and *Cornish v Midland Bank* [1985] 3 All ER 513.
11 *White v Holbrook Precision Castings* [1985] IRLR 215.
12 Occupiers' Liability Act 1957 ss 1(1) 1(2), 2(2) and 2(4)(a).

OMISSIONS IN TORT AND REMOTENESS RULES IN CONTRACT—A COMMON AGENDA?

Students of contract law might note the similarity between Logie's conditions for the imposition of a duty to warn with those for the imposition of *Moorcock* implied terms and for *Hadley v Baxendale* remoteness. The rule in contract is often, 'Unless the parties have agreed otherwise, the person who was in the better position to know about special features of the situation is responsible for losses arising out of those special features.'

The extension of the res ipsa loquitur rules to cases such as *Henderson v Jenkins* and *Ybarra v Spangard* (see above ch 3) arise from similar concerns—the defendants in such cases know about what happened but have no other incentive to reveal it. The courts' response to such defendants is to tell them that they will be held liable unless they tell all.

All these rules derive ultimately from the fact that there are many situations in which one party has exclusive or near exclusive access to important information and has no interest in sharing it with anyone else, but in which it would be better for all concerned if the information were released. Their point is to provide incentives for the party with exclusive access to the information to release it. In the duty to warn situation and the contract problems there is the added objective of creating conditions in which the parties can come to rational decisions themselves on the basis of all the available information.[13] The idea is thus one that should apply generally in private law, and can be used to establish liability even where more conventional methods, for example the notion that the defendant 'assumed responsibility' for the plaintiffs' welfare do not quite work.

Furthermore, cases such as *Osterlind* have been very heavily criticised. Prosser[14] for example said that they are 'revolting to any moral sense'. It is hard to see, therefore, how the underlying presumption against liability for nonfeasance can long survive even the USA.

As for more recent English judicial pronouncements, it is noticeable that judges display less than absolute confidence in the traditional rule. Lord Goff's speech in *Smith v Littlewoods*, for example, itself the expression of a restrictive minority view, gives no reason for the rejection of liability for omissions beyond pure authority. Indeed, Lord Goff himself goes on to envisage the abrogation of the rule, saying only that if it was to be abandoned, any new rule would need to be limited in scope. As an example, Goff cites the French law limitations on duties to rescue—that the danger be 'grave, imminent, constant' and 'nécessitant une intervention imméd-

---

13 For the economic theories that support such concerns see eg O Williamson *The Economic Institutions of Capitalism* (New York; Free Press. London; Collier Macmillan,1985).

14 *Torts* (St Paul, Minn: West) (4th ed) at p 341. See also M Shapo *The Duty to Act: Tort Law, Power, & Public Policy* (Austin, Tex and London; University of Texas Press, 1977).

iate'. And similarly neither Lord Diplock in *Dorset Yacht* nor Lord Keith in *Yuen Kun Yeu* gives any lengthy or reasoned explanation or justification for their view.

Even in the Court of Appeal's judgment in the *Nicholas H*,[15] one of the most restrictive judgments on negligence in recent years, the Court's reasons for backing the orthodox view amounted to repeating that every-thing depended on the relationship between the parties and asserting without argument that liability for pure omissions was not 'fair, just or reasonable'.

It is submitted that the distinction between nonfeasance and misfeasance has become increasingly difficult for the judges to justify except by mere assertion, and that in consequence the law may be about to be reconsidered from first principles.

A reconsideration does not mean that the presumption against liability for omissions will necessarily be rejected. Nevertheless, students should be familiar with the case against the presumption.

There are several areas of serious doubt about the traditional rule. They are (1) doubts about whether the idea of prior relationship is adequate to capture the type of exception to the general rule that the judges want, (2) doubts about whether the law can adequately distinguish in the first place between acts and omissions, and (3) doubts about whether the cases justify a separate rule or merely illustrate the application of other rules.

Doubts about the concept of prior relationship

The prior relationships that have generally been taken to give rise to a duty to act are perhaps best summarised by the American Law Institute's Second Restatement of Torts.[16] They are:

> 'a common carrier ... to its passengers ..., an innkeeper ... to his guests, a possessor of land ... to members of the public who enter in response to his invitation, [and] one who is required by law to take or voluntarily takes the custody of another under circum-stances such as to deprive the other of his normal opportunities for protection [ie parents and jailers]'.

The ALI wisely says that it 'expresses no opinion as to whether there may not be other relations which impose a similar duty', but it is not the

---

15 [1994] 3 All ER 686, [1994] 1 WLR 1071, [1994] 1 Lloyd's Rep 492. See eg per Saville LJ: 'Walking down the street I see a blind person about to cross the road in front of a vehicle. It is foreseeable that he will be injured. I am under no legal duty to take care to save him from danger. But if I am in charge of a child in the street and the child starts to run in front of the traffic, I am under a legal duty to take care to save the child from danger; and indeed other road users from the danger the child may create.'.

16 Section 314A.

exact contents of the list that gives rise to anxiety, rather the question whether it is the right sort of list in the first place.

Take, for example, *Barnett v Chelsea and Kensington Hospital Management Committee*.[17] The plaintiff Barnett was one of three night watchmen who were taken violently ill after drinking tea which, it was later discovered, had been laced with arsenic. The watchmen presented themselves at the nearest hospital, where they were refused treatment. A doctor told a nurse on the telephone that she should 'Tell them to go home and go to bed and call in their own doctors, except Whittall [one of the other watchmen], who should stay because he is due for an X-ray later this morning.'

The plaintiff later died of arsenic poisoning.

Although the hospital in the end successfully defended the suit brought against it (on the ground that the plaintiff would probably have died anyway even if he had been treated immediately—that is, the element of causation was missing) the trial judge, Nield J, made it clear that the fact that the doctor's alleged fault consisted of an omission, a refusal to treat, made no difference.[18] But what was the relationship between the plaintiff and the doctor? Note that in the plaintiff's case, unlike that of the other watchman Whittall, there was no prior relationship of doctor and patient between himself and any of the hospital staff.

Nield J bases the relationship on the fact that the hospital was not refusing to treat anybody else:[19]

> 'This is not a case of a casualty department which closes its doors and says that no patients can be received.'

That is, the relationship arises because the men were able to walk into the casualty department freely and to talk to a nurse.

But there is a good deal of artificiality in the idea that a 'relationship' arises between two people when one of them refuses to help the other merely because the first person may possibly have helped someone else.[20] This is not so much a relationship as a rejection. It is only a relationship in the same sense that an invalid contract might be said to be a kind of contract.

Another example is the much earlier case *Smith v South Eastern Rly Co*.[1] The plaintiff's husband went to the house of a level-crossing keeper to see whether the plaintiff was there. The house was next to the railway line and the level-crossing keeper's job was to warn traffic of the approach

---

17 [1969] 1 QB 428, [1968] 1 All ER 1068.

18 At p 436.

19 At p 438.

20 Cf the view of the majority in *M v Newham London Borough Council; X v Bedfordshire County Council* [1994] 4 All ER 602, [1994] Fam Law 434 that there is no 'relationship' between a child or that child's parent and psychiatrists or social workers giving advice to a local authority about the child's future.

1 [1896] 1 QB 178.

of trains. The level-crossing keeper said that the plaintiff (the wife) was not there. The husband thereupon bade the level-crossing keeper good-night and tried to cross the railway line, whereupon he was hit and killed by a train. The level-crossing keeper had known of the train's approach, but had said and done nothing.

The Court of Appeal had no difficulty in finding for the plaintiff. Lopes LJ said simply that 'The railway company were bound to use reasonable care with regard to the crossing, and ... [t]heir servant failed to take [a] reasonable and proper precaution.' Kay LJ dismissed brusquely and without argument the contention that the level-crossing keeper's only duty was to the train-driver, to show him that the line was clear of vehicles. And Lord Esher MR thought that the duty of the defendant was so clear that the only important issue was that of contributory negligence.

But note that the level-crossing keeper acted in very much the same way as Lord Keith's person who 'forbears to shout a warning' to someone 'about to walk over a cliff with his head in the air.'

The crucial distinguishing point seems to be not any prior relationship between the plaintiff's husband and the level-crossing keeper, but instead merely that the husband had a legitimate expectation, based on experience and common decency, that the level-crossing keeper would tell him about oncoming trains.

It might be argued that the level-crossing keeper's duty arose from his specialised social role—that it was his job to warn people about trains. But the idea of legitimate expectations that arise from social or occupational roles is a broad one, potentially a very broad one and certainly broader than the idea of relationship, which implies some previous interaction of a specific type between the parties. If jobs can give rise to legitimate expectations, why should there not be duties based on wider social roles? For example, why should not all adults owe a duty to all children, all young people owe duties to all old people, and all able-bodied people to people with disabilities?

In order to meet concerns about the adequacy of the notion of prior relationship in this context, recent cases have shifted attention away from the idea of relationship and onto the broader notion of 'assumption of responsibility.'

The leading example is *Kirkham v Chief Constable of Greater Manchester*.[2] The plaintiff's husband was remanded in custody on charges of criminal damage. He had a known history of suicide attempts, but the police failed to advise the prison authorities that he was an exceptional risk. In consequence, the prison authorities did not take any steps to prevent his eventual suicide. The plaintiff sued the police and won.

One of the points raised by the police was that the police's failure to pass on the relevant information was a pure omission. If this was so, it would have been hard to say that there was much of a pre-existing relationship between Mr Kirkham and the police. He did have such a relationship with the prison authorities, of course, but they had not been

2 [1990] 2 QB 283.

at fault. But his relationship with the police amounted to little more than that they had arrested him and that they knew of his suicidal tendencies.

Lloyd LJ dealt with the point in the following way. He affirmed the general rule that there could be no liability for pure omissions, but stated the exception to the rule in a new way:[3]

> 'The common law imposes liability for a pure omission where the defendant is under a duty to act or, as the case may be, a duty to speak ... The question depends in each case on whether, having regard to the particular relationship between the parties, the defendant has assumed responsibility toward the plaintiff, and whether the plaintiff has relied on that assumption of responsibility.'

Note that in Lloyd LJ's test the particular relationship between the parties is relegated from being the test for liability itself to being merely the context in which the test is applied.

The test itself is whether the defendant 'assumed responsibility' for the plaintiff and then whether the plaintiff 'relied' on that assumption of responsibility.

Unfortunately, this assumption of responsibility test raises almost as many questions as it settles. For example, is it really necessary that the plaintiff 'relies' on the assumption? Did the watchmen 'rely' on the doctor in *Barnett*? Did the prisoner 'rely' on the police in *Kirkham*? Surely all that is needed here is a causal link, of which reliance is merely one possible form.

But the main problem with 'assumption of responsibility' stems from the fact that the test appears to be an objective one. That is, the court is not concerned with whether or not the defendant consciously thought to himself 'I have taken responsibility for this person' but with whether a reasonable person, in the court's opinion, would have assumed such a responsibility.

But if the test is an objective one, what exactly should the court take into account when deciding whether or not a reasonable person would have assumed responsibility? In particular, how exactly would the court's approach to deciding this question differ at all from its general approach to deciding the question of fault (size and seriousness of the risk weighed against the costs of attempting to eliminate it etc) or from its consideration of the other general reasons (allocation of public resources, maintenance of the integrity of other legal rules etc) for denying the existence of a duty of care? As Lord Griffiths said in a different context, although also one that necessitated consideration of an alleged 'assumption of responsibility' test:[4]

> 'The phrase "assumption of responsibility" can only have any real meaning if it is understood as referring to the circumstances in

3   [1990] 2 QB 283 and [1990] 3 All ER 246 at 250.
4   In *Smith v Eric Bush* [1990] 1 AC 831 at 862.

which the law will deem [the defendant] to have assumed
responsibility...'

What this means is that the court will say that there has been no
assumption of responsibility when they would have said either that the
defendant was not at fault or that there was no duty in the first place for
some other, independent, reason.

For example in *Banque Keyser Ullman SA v Skandia (UK) Insurance*[5]
the Court of Appeal said that the relationship between two parties who
were negotiating a contract did not give rise to any assumption of
responsibility by either party, so that there was no duty in negligence to
reveal important information to the other party in the course of the
negotiation. But the reason why the court refused to treat this as a situation
to be treated as one of assumption of responsibility was nothing inherently
to do with the fact that this was a case of pure omission or with the other
facts of the case, but rather because 'To hold that these factors by themselves
gave rise to a duty ... in tort would undermine basic principles of our law
of contract.'[6] In other words, the reason the court refuses to deem the
defendants to have assumed responsibility is a reason which independently
would have barred the imposition of a duty of care anyway, namely the
integrity of established legal rules in other areas of the law.[7]

Nevertheless, at least in the field of pure economic loss,[8] Lord Goff has
in several recent cases attempted to elevate 'assumption of responsibility'
to a general theory of liability. In *Henderson v Merrett*, for example, Lord
Goff said:[9]

'An assumption of responsibility by, for example, a professional
man may give rise to liability in respect of negligent omissions as
much as negligent acts of commission, as for example when a
solicitor assumes responsibility for business on behalf of his client
and omits to take a certain step, such as the service of a document,
which falls within the responsibility so assumed by him.'

It may be argued convincingly that, since 'responsibility' is deemed to
have been 'assumed' in precisely those cases in which were the case not
one of pure omission a duty of care would have been imposed anyway,
there is nothing special about omission cases except in the language used
to describe the justification for the decision.

It may well be, therefore, that the assumption of responsibility test will
eventually be seen as just one of the interim methods (along perhaps with
Logie's duty to warn principle) that paved the way for a reversal of the
general presumption against liability for pure omissions.

5   [1990] 1 QB 665, [1989] 2 All ER 952.
6   [1990] 1 QB 665 at p 798.
7   See also *Bank of Nova Scotia v Hellenic Mutual* [1990] 1 QB 818.
8   See below ch 6.
9   [1994] 3 All ER 506.

Doubts about the meaning of 'pure omission'

It is not clear when the expression 'pure omission' began to supplant the word 'nonfeasance' as preferred judicial jargon. Nevertheless, the addition of the word 'pure' is significant, for there has long been a suspicion that it is not easy to say exactly what should count as an 'omission' as opposed to an 'act'.

The difficulty is easy to describe. It is far from clear what distinguishes many 'omissions' from faulty 'acts'. A great many 'omissions' can be redescribed quite easily as someone doing something badly. For example, a driver who 'omits' to brake can be described as having 'driven badly.' An auditor who 'omits' to mention some of a company's liabilities has 'audited badly'. A level-crossing keeper who fails to give a warning about an on-coming train has 'done his job badly.'

But it is not clear that the addition of the word 'pure' to 'omission' has yet thrown much new light on the distinction. Indeed, confusion seems to be growing as judges conflate the purity of the omission with the overall question of liability. For example, at first instance in *Banque Keyser Ullman SA v Skandia (UK) Insurance*,[10] Steyn J said that the case before him was not one of pure omission because there was a prior relationship between the parties, namely an on-going business relationship involving the negotiating of contracts.[11] The Court of Appeal, however, said that where someone says nothing, as opposed to saying something misleading, it does count 'factually'[12] as a 'pure omission' and that there was no liability because there was no 'assumption of responsibility'.

Steyn J's formulation would leave us unable to distinguish between 'pure omissions' for which there is liability and those for which there is no liability—for where there was liability, the omission would automatically not be 'pure.' But although the Court of Appeal's approach does not fall into the same trap, it leaves one unable to say why the defendant in *Banque Keyser Ullmann* should be described as someone who failed to reveal something rather than as someone who negotiated in a faulty way.

Another attempt to distinguish between liability for acts and omissions comes to grief in a similar way. The idea is that there is a basic difference between doing something and letting something happen, because we may demand that others do not intervene to change the existing situation to our disadvantage, but we cannot demand that others intervene to make us better off than we were.[13] That is, liability for omission is where the plaintiff complains about not being given a benefit, as opposed to being harmed.[14]

10   [1990] 1 QB 665, [1989] 2 All ER 952.

11   At [1990] 1 QB 712.

12   At p 804.

13   See eg JC Smith *Liability in Negligence* (London, Sweet & Maxwell, 1984) at p29 fn 1, citing JG Urmson, 'Saints and Heroes' in AI Melden (ed) *Essays in Moral Philosophy* (1968) at p 13. See also Smith and Burns (1983) 46 MLR 147.

14   See also Bohlen 'The Moral Duty to Aid Others as a Basis of Tort Liability' (1908) 56 U Pa L Rev 217 at 220.

The central case for those who take this view is *East Suffolk Rivers Catchment Board v Kent*.[15] The plaintiff's land lay next to an estuary. An exceptionally high tide combined with a gale led to a breach in the sea wall that protected the plaintiff's land. The land was flooded. The water from the estuary gradually flowed away, but since the sea wall was damaged, more water flowed into the fields and they stayed flooded. The job of repairing sea walls was done by the defendants, acting under their statutory powers rather than under any contract with the plaintiff. They set to work fairly promptly, but were so incompetent that the wall broke again and the waters flooded back. Eventually the defendants managed to do the work properly, but by that time the plaintiff's fields had remained flooded for six months when competent work would have meant that they would have been under water for only two weeks. The plaintiff sued, alleging negligence.

The ESRCB, note, was in the position of a rescuer. It did not, according to the House of Lords,[16] have any duty, at least to the plaintiff as opposed to the Minister of Agriculture, to intervene to help the plaintiff. In judging what it took to be a separate question, namely, was what the Board did nevertheless actionable, the court bore in mind that the plaintiff's only right was not to be made worse off than he already was. He did not have a right to be made better off. As a result, the claim was dismissed, for the Board had not made the plaintiff's plight worse but had merely failed to make it better.[17]

But note that most of the judges in the House of Lords in *East Suffolk Rivers Catchment Board v Kent* do not say that because the damage claimed was a benefit not gained (as opposed to a harm caused), the case is one of pure omission. Rather they say that because there is no liability for pure omission, there can be no claim for benefits not gained. The reason for the lack of liability for pure omissions in the first place is crucial. And, in *East Suffolk Rivers Catchment Board v Kent* as in so many other cases, that reason is nothing to do with the nature of omissions but instead concerns the integrity of another area of the law. In this case it is administrative law, more particularly the procedure by which the Minister of Agriculture was permitted to direct the Board to act.

There is also a more fundamental problem with the distinction between harm done and gain not received. How does one tell the difference? The view that all one has to do is to ask whether the incident in question made the plaintiff worse off is naive. One's present wealth, crucially, includes everything that one has a legitimate expectation of receiving, not just what one has now. Furthermore, tort law often recognises that one can do 'harm' even to interests which have not yet materialised. The best example (because it is the least controversial) is that a victim of tortiously inflicted personal injuries can sue not only for the losses that have already occurred by the time of the trial, but also for those that he or she will probably

15 [1941] AC 74.
16 At p 83.
17 See eg Viscount Simon LC at pp 84-85.

suffer in the future. Most important of all, this includes lost future wages or salary. The law might say that future earnings that will never be received are not 'harm', but are instead future benefits that will not now be realised. But it does not. Lost future earnings, which plainly in one sense are benefits that will not be received, are a fully recognised head of damage.

The central question, therefore, is not 'what is a benefit not received and what is harm done', but rather 'did the plaintiff have a legitimate expectation that the defendant would act to protect the plaintiff from harm?'

This is a difficult topic and one well beyond the scope of a textbook. But one part of the answer may lie in more sophisticated notions of causation than those implied in the 'harm' vs 'benefit' debate. The assumption cannot be sustained that if left to themselves, things remain the same. A more dynamic view is required, based on the simple observation that most of the time, a predictable and normal course of events produces predictable and normal results. Expectations are formed on the basis of the normal course of events.

Thus in *Smith v South Eastern Rly Co* the normal course of events was that if a train was due, the level-crossing keeper got out of his chair and gave a warning. That he remained in his house gave rise to the expectation that no train was coming and thus that the plaintiff would come to no harm as he crossed the line.

Lord Atkin in his dissent in *East Suffolk Rivers Catchment Board v Kent*,[18] later approved in *Anns v Merton London Borough Council*[19], summed up the argument when he said that there should be no distinction between harm caused and benefits not received in a case in which 'the damage [is] such as would flow in the ordinary and usual course of things.'

Admittedly, knowing what expectations are based on and knowing that loss of expectation is both harm done and a benefit not received, do not tell us whether the expectation was 'legitimate'. In *Smith*, the expectation was that if a train was coming the level-crossing keeper would give a warning. But was it legitimate of the plaintiff's husband to rely on that expectation to the extent that the level-crossing keeper should be blamed for his death?

And although the normal course of events is that I will fall off a cliff if I walk close to its edge without looking where I am going, and normally people who see other people about to walk over cliffs do indeed attempt to warn them, should I be able to count on the fact that you do not shout a warning to me as I proceed as an indication that what I am doing is safe?

But whatever the answer to the question 'was the expectation legit— imate?' it does not depend on whether the loss of expectation amounted to harm done or to a benefit not received. It depends instead on what counts as reasonable conduct, and on the same independent reasons for denying a duty of care such as the integrity of other rules of law that control the rest of the law of negligence.

18 At pp 92-93.

19 [1978] AC 728. Note that this aspect of *Anns* was not subsequently questioned in *Murphy v Brentwood Borough Council* [1991] 1 AC 398, which overruled *Anns* on other points.

Doubts about whether there is a separate rule

To these well-established doubts one may add one more. It was noted above that neither Lord Goff in *Smith* nor Lord Keith in *Yuen Kun Yeu* showed any great inclination to explain or justify the rule as they saw it. It may well be that the reason for this reluctance is that many of the reasons put for the rule are plainly inadequate because they justify not a separate rule but merely the careful application of other established rules.

In particular, a great number of the reasons put forward for a general reluctance to impose a duty of care for omissions are not reasons of a general character at all, but are specific points to do with fault or remoteness.

One such reason is that liability for omissions puts an extra and intolerable burden on defendants. It is said that it is very burdensome to expect people to be on the look-out constantly for ways in which they could help others, and that to expect them to rescue others from danger or to prevent harm from befalling them frequently involves not just incon– venience but danger to themselves. But note that these points go not to whether there should ever be a duty of care in these situations, but rather to the question of fault. Is it reasonable to expect people to spend their time on the look-out for opportunities to rescue others rather than getting on with their own business?[20] And is it unreasonable of someone to take into account danger to themselves when deciding whether to launch a rescue attempt?

Similarly, the argument that it is wrong to pick on just one of the people who could have helped the plaintiff by acting positively is not a strong point when the ease with which the defendant could have helped the plaintiff was much greater than that for other people.

Also, in many omission cases the defendant's case comes down to a simple remoteness point—that the accident was somebody else's fault or com– pletely the plaintiff's own fault. This point is clearest in what might be called the 'regulatory rescue cases' such as *Minories Finance v Arthur Young*,[1] in which the plaintiff claims that the defendant regulatory body (for example the Bank of England) should have stepped in to prevent the plaintiff from being ripped off by a rogue. The claim does not succeed because the plaintiff has failed, due to its own incompetence, to notice that it is being ripped off. There is never a point at which the regulatory body is in a better position to find out what is going on than the plaintiff itself. The plaintiff's utterly unreasonable behaviour thus breaks the chain of causation.

---

20 One might note here the suggestion that when people have opportunities to prevent dangers to others thrust upon them they should be judged on a more subjective standard of care, one which takes into account their particular skills and resources. Cf *Goldman v Hargrave* [1967] 1 AC 645.

1 [1989] 2 All ER 105.

Arguments for the tradfitional rule

In the light of these doubts, the case in favour of retaining the presump–
tion against liability for pure omissions is difficult to make. But it is not
entirely without counter-arguments.

Indeed, the real problem for the courts may not be that good or even
interesting reasons to distinguish between acts and omissions in negligence
do not exist, but instead that those interesting reasons are difficult to
deploy openly because they depend on unfashionable ideological under–
pinnings.

The basic argument is this. Many omissions can be redescribed as faulty
acts. But it should be noticed that, given a certain view of the origins of
how people should behave, it is not true that all omissions can be so redescribed. If one believes that there are moral obligations that one has
simply because one is a human being, as opposed to obligations that arise
from one's role or status in life (e.g. as a parent, or a lawyer, or citizen) or
from one's promises, then there will be omissions that do not count as
doing something badly, but can only be described as 'acting badly' or, better,
'being a bad person.'

For example, if one fails to warn a stranger who is about to walk off a
cliff, one is simply acting badly. There is no activity which one can be said
to be doing badly, or any promise that one can be said to have broken, and,
more importantly, there is no role or status whose expectations one can be
said to have failed to meet apart from that of responsible human being.

The objection to liability in negligence in such cases is simply that some
people think that the state has no business telling people that they are
bad people, that they are immoral or wicked. On this view, the state may
tell one to pay compensation if one's activities result in harm, but not if
one's character results in harm to others. The fear that lies behind this
idea is that for the state to take upon itself the right to judge people's
characters, as opposed to their activities, is to invite the state to act in an
authoritarian or even totalitarian manner.

The usual way, though perhaps a less enlightening way, in which this
idea is expressed is that liability for pure omissions leads to a breakdown
of the distinction between law and morality. Liability for omissions is said
to involve the state in the enforcement of a particular moral view.[2] Put
this way, the point is easily countered by pointing out that the whole of
negligence law, because of the fault requirement, involves the making of
moral or political judgments. To judge the defendant's conduct to be
unreasonable involves making a substantive judgment. To object to such
judgments amounts therefore to objecting to the fault standard itself,[3] and

2   See eg JC Smith *Liability in Negligence* pp 29–47.
3   This is indeed the position taken by those commentators, such as Richard Epstein, for
    whom the very fact that the fault system requires the imposition of state-sponsored
    moral and political judgments condemns it, and requires its replacement with a system
    of strict liability or no liability: see 'A Theory of Strict Liability' (1973) 2 JLS 151. A
    similar point applies to the objection to liability for *negligent* as opposed to intentional
    nonfeasance (ie not realising what the consequences of inaction would be in circumstances
    in which a reasonable person would have realised and would have acted) that it requires

so cannot be considered to be a reasonable interpretation of the existing law.

But restated as an objection not to the making of moral judgments by the courts in negligence cases but as an objection to the scope and depth of such judgments when they involve assessments of the defendant's char-acter, the objection has more force. Whether or not this underlying objection to liability for pure omissions is ultimately convincing is left to the reader to decide. One may decide that the fear of the totalitarian tendency of liability for pure omission is exaggerated, and that legal recognition of the desirability of such character traits as mild altruism and willingness to help is unlikely to herald the return of Stalinism. On the other hand, one might decide that the line is better drawn before the law even starts to consider the defendant's character, rather to have to decide which traits of character are desirable enough to warrant legal reinforcement and which are not.

No deterrence value

The second reason for the exclusion of the duty of care is more pragmatic. It is based on a largely utilitarian calculation of the probable effects of imposing liability. One of the reasons for imposing tort liability is that it may act as a deterrent, either directly or via the price mechanism, against harmful conduct. In this way, if the cost of taking precautions against the accident is less than the costs imposed by the accident, tort law may reduce the overall cost of accidents to society as a whole. This deterrent is, however, bought at a price, namely the cost of bringing legal actions, the costs of winning them or of negotiating settlements to them and the costs of monitoring their outcome. These costs, the administrative or transactions costs involved in shifting the costs of accidents to the defendant from the plaintiff, may be considerable and it may be that, given a sufficiently low deterrent effect, the resources expended on shifting the loss outweigh the resources saved by imposing the deterrent.

The second argument against the imposition of a duty of care is the argument from the insufficiency of deterrents—that the resources used in shifting the loss outweigh the resources saved by imposing the duty of care.

The argument comes in two main forms. In the first, it is argued that in the situation at hand, the law of negligence adds nothing to what might be called the 'natural' deterrents—the defendants' sense of morality and social duty and their inclination towards self-preservation. In the second, more

---

people to guess what standard of intervention in others' affairs the court might require. The point is that all negligence-based liability has this effect. Fault-based liability inevitably discriminates against the stupid and the asocial. But note that all normative judgment requires basic intelligence—one cannot act morally unless one can imagine what effects one's actions may have on others or unless one can remember one's promises. See Friedrich Nietzsche *Human, All Too Human* (Hollingdale trans, Cambridge: Cambridge University Press, 1986) p 42 at para 59.

sophisticated, version, it is argued that the imposition of a duty of care adds nothing to the sum of the natural deterrents and the deterrents imposed by the rest of the legal system—for example by the criminal law and the law of contract.

In addition to the two main variants of the argument, there is a third theme, namely the avoidance of perverse incentives. According to this point, the problem is not so much the ineffectiveness of the incentives provided by the duty of care but their effectiveness in producing undesirable effects either alongside or instead of the reduction of accident causing behaviour.

Natural deterrents

The clearest example of the deployment of the natural deterrent argument is to be found in the speech of Lord Keith of Kinkel in *Hill v Chief Constable of West Yorkshire*.[4] In *Hill*, the plaintiff was the estate of the last victim of the serial killer Peter Sutcliffe, known as the Yorkshire Ripper. The defendants were the police officers responsible for tracking down and arresting the killer. The accusation of negligence against them was that they failed to cross-reference information and failed to appreciate the importance of evidence available to them, so that they failed to apprehend Sutcliffe in time to prevent him from killing Miss Hill.

Among the police's many arguments that the action for negligence against them should fail was the following point:

'The general sense of public duty which motivates police forces is unlikely to be appreciably reinforced by the imposition of such liability so far as concerns their function in the investigation and suppression of crime. From time to time they may make mistakes ... but it is not to be doubted that they apply their best endeavours to the performance of [their duty] ... [Furthermore a] great deal of police time, trouble and expense might be expected to have to be put into the preparation of the defence to the action.... The result would be a significant diversion of police manpower and attention from their most important function, that of the suppression of crime.'[5]

This passage contains all the elements of a successful natural deterrent defence—(1) the existence of incentives more powerful than tort law, (2) the alleged unlikelihood of any improvement in conduct if a duty of care were imposed, and (3) the likelihood of significant costs if actions of this type were allowed.

The powerful alternative incentive is provided by the police's 'sense of public duty', the probable lack of improvement in behaviour is asserted on the basis that the police always do their best and the costs of defending

4   [1989] AC 53, [1988] 2 All ER 238.
5   Per Lord Keith [1989] AC 53 at 63.

actions are identified not just in financial terms to the police but also in terms of the reduced protection that could be offered to the public.

But *Hill* also illustrates the potential weaknesses of the natural deterrent argument. Although the costs of litigation may be taken as obvious, the other points seem to require evidence. What exactly motivates the police? Is it not possible that the threat of tort actions would act as a deterrent at least against senior officers with budgets and promotion prospects to protect? And is it really true that the police always do their very best, so that no general improvement is possible? Others are of a different opinion. For example the Audit Commission recently reported that very great improvements in efficiency could be made by the police.[6] One is drawn to the conclusion that the House of Lords' assertions about the effects of the imposition of liability on the police in *Hill* would be interesting if they were true, but without specific evidence to support them, such arguments should have been regarded with more scepticism.

Another problem with the natural deterrent argument is that it may end up proving too much. Take the case of motor car accidents. Although specific research seems to be lacking, it would be surprising if tort law had a very big effect either on the care taken by drivers or on the number of miles that they drive, compared with, for example, the effects of the threats to their own safety, the safety of their passengers, the habits inculcated by their training and experience and the safety features built into the roads they travel on.[7] And what effects there are will be diluted by the effects of compulsory insurance. And yet it would be a very brave judge indeed who set out to deny the existence of a duty of care in road accident cases on the basis of the *Hill* natural deterrent argument.

Natural deterrents plus the existing law—adequate remedies elsewhere

Even more common than the natural deterrents argument is the argument that the imposition of tort liability would be harmful because it would add nothing to the deterrents imposed on the defendant by other areas of the law, for example contract law and criminal law.

This argument has a long pedigree, but it may be illustrated by the modern case *Gran Gelato v Richcliff*.[8] The plaintiff rented some commercial property for its ice cream business. The lease made it clear that the people from whom the plaintiff was renting the property were not the owners of the property, but were themselves tenants of the real owner. A general principle of English property law is that no one can sell or give away more than they have themselves. That means that any rights of the plaintiff under its lease would be subject to the rights of the owner against the intermediaries, the people from whom the plaintiff was renting. It was

6 *Helping With Enquiries: Tackling Crime Effectively* (London; HMSO, 1993).
7 Plus the effects of the criminal law—see below.
8 [1992] 1 All ER 865.

therefore vitally important for the plaintiff to know what was in the agreement between the owner and the intermediaries, the head lease. The plaintiff made inquiries, in the customary form, about the contents of the head lease with the intermediaries and their solicitors. Unfortunately, the intermediaries' solicitors botched the job. They omitted to tell the plaintiff about the owners' right to bring the head lease to an end prematurely (a 'break clause'), the exercise of which would, and in the event did, bring the plaintiff's lease to an end as well.

The plaintiff sued the intermediaries for breach of contract and misrepresentation, but it also sued the solicitors in tort.

The solicitors admitted carelessness but argued that there should be no duty of care imposed upon them because, given the existing legal relationships between the parties, it would do no additional good. The solicitors were bound in contract to the intermediaries, and the intermediaries were bound in contract to the plaintiff. Moreover, the solicitors were the intermediaries' agents, so that detrimental conduct by the solicitors would normally result in liability on the part of the intermediary. In consequence, said the solicitors, the mistake they had made resulted in the intermediary's being responsible in contract to the plaintiff, but the solicitor, in turn, had to make good any loss to the intermediary. It followed that the solicitors were fully accountable for any mistakes that they made to the intermediary, and that any extra liability in negligence to the plaintiff would be superfluous (and, by implication, a costly exercise in loss shifting for no additional deterrence).

The court agreed with the solicitors. As Sir Donald Nicholls V-C said:[9]

> '[I]n general, in a case where the principal [the intermediary] himself owes a duty of care to the third party, the existence of a further duty of care, owed by the agent to the third party, is not necessary for the reasonable protection of the latter. Good reason, therefore, should exist before the law imposes a duty when the agent already owes to his principal a duty which covers the same ground and the principal is responsible to the third party for his agent's shortcomings. I do not think there is good reason for such a duty in normal conveyancing transactions.'

The immediate objection to Sir Donald Nicholls's point is that if the intermediary has gone bust, the plaintiff ends up with no one to sue and the solicitor escapes any liability. In response Sir Donald merely said:

> 'I do not think that is sufficient reason for adding onto the solicitor-client relationship a duty owed directly to the non-client in normal conveyancing transactions. That those with whom one deals may become insolvent is an ordinary risk of everyday life.'

9 At p 873.

As it stands, this argument is unsatisfactory. Many events may be described as 'ordinary risks of everyday life', being hit by a car or being injured at work for example, but no one now believes that the mere ordinariness of a risk excludes the possibility of legal protection against it.

But there is still a point in favour of the result of the case as reached by the Court of Appeal. Sir Donald might have said instead that the degree to which people in the position of the solicitors would take less care because of the chance that their client might become insolvent is so small that the law should ignore it. The improvement in conduct to be gained by imposing liability would not be zero, but it would be so small that it would never be significant in comparison with the costs of litigation, negotiation and enforcement.

Another case in which the deterrent value of the rest of the law appears to have been decisive is *O'Leary v Islington London Borough Council*.[10] The plaintiffs were tenants of the defendant local authority. They were the victims of serious nuisances committed by a neighbour—who was also a tenant of the defendant. Instead of suing the neighbour or the defendant landlord for nuisance, the plaintiffs chose to sue the defendants in negligence, alleging that the local authority had been at fault in not taking effective action to stop the neighbour's activities. The Court of Appeal, upholding the decision at first instance, dismissed the plaintiffs' claim. As Dillon LJ said:

> 'The whole implication of this duty of care seems to me to be unnecessary, because, as I have already said, the plaintiffs have a remedy available to them in that they can sue Miss Robinson [the other tenant] in nuisance or they could sue the council in nuisance if they really felt that they could make out that the council was tortiously liable for continuing the nuisance for which Miss Robinson was initially responsible.'

The council was, according to Dillon LJ, adequately deterred by the law of nuisance. Additional liability in negligence added nothing.

In contrast, the lack of adequate deterrent in the rest of the law has also been a decisive argument in favour of the imposition of a duty of care in circumstances in which the conventional wisdom was that there was no such duty. The best-known example of the deployment of such an argument is *Donoghue v Stevenson*.[11] The central problem in *Donoghue* is that the victim had no contractual relationship with anyone. She was given the ginger beer by her friend, who had bought it from the café owner, who in turn had bought it from the manufacturer. The force of contract law, given the hostility of the common law towards allowing third parties to enforce rights under contracts agreed by others, would be brought to bear on the

10 (1983) 9 HLR 81.
11 [1932] AC 562.

manufacturer only if the friend who bought the drink could maintain an adequate action against the retailer for breach of contract. But there were two problems with such a route. In the first place, it was not clear at the time that the purchaser was exempted from the general rule of 'let the buyer beware.' The Court of Appeal had only recently decided the case of *Morelli v Fitch and Gibbons*[12] in which it was decided, contrary to previous doubts, that a retail sale over the counter in a shop could count as a 'sale by description' under s 14 of the old Sale of Goods Act 1893, with the effect that the seller was subject to an implied term guaranteeing the 'merchant-able quality' of the goods. But the scope of *Morelli* would have been uncertain at the time of *Donoghue*. In particular, it would have been noticeable that both in *Morelli* and in the previous cases in which doubts had been expressed the implied term of merchantability was imposed in cases in which the buyer asked for a particular product by its brand name, and it may have been thought at the time that some sales, for example merely pointing at the required object and saying 'that one please' would not count.[13] A further complication along the same lines was that, at least according to Lord Macmillan in *Donoghue*,[14] the case of *Gordon v McHardy*[15] seemed to suggest that in Scottish law, a retailer who was in no position to inspect the goods sold could not be liable to anybody.[16] The second, and more serious problem was that of the measure of damages. Even if the buyer could maintain a successful action against the retailer, the measure of damages could only amount to, at most, the price of the ginger beer. If the eventual victim could maintain an action *against the buyer* the position might be different, but it was well recognised that as the recipient of a gift she could not—and even if such an action might be maintained on the basis of negligence, the victim would not be able to win in the *Donoghue* situation because she could not show any carelessness on the part of the buyer. The position would therefore be that the law of contract either failed to deter the manufacturer at all or would deter the manufacturer inad-equately. The imposition of a duty of care in tort might therefore be expected

---

12 [1928] 2 KB 636.

13 The subsequent case *Grant v Australian Knitting Mills* [1936] AC 85 established that such a case would be covered by the implied term. See at p 100 'It may also be pointed out that there is a sale by description even though the buyer is buying something displayed before him on the counter: a thing is sold by description, though it is specific, so long as it is sold not merely as the specific thing but as a thing corresponding to a description'.

14 [1932] AC 562 at p 622.

15 (1903) 6 F 210 (retailer sold tinned salmon, which turned out to be contaminated. Plaintiff's son died as a result. *Held*: No liability. *Per* The Lord Justice-Clerk (Macdonald): 'I am of opinion that a grocer who gets a quantity of tins of preserved food and sells them to the public as he got them, cannot be liable for the condition of the contents of the tin if he buys from a dealer of repute.').

16 Strictly, *Gordon* covered only actions 'ex delicto' and the leading textbook of the time pointed out that if the rule also applied in contract, it would point in a direction different from English cases such as *Morelli*. See WM Gloag *The Law of Contract* (Edinburgh: W. Green and Son, 2nd ed, 1929) p 313 n 2.

to have a considerable added deterrent effect and to be worthwhile even in the light of the additional administrative costs that it would impose.

As Lord Atkin said, the result of the authorities relied upon by the manufacturer were such that the plaintiff would end up unprotected, and if that were the case he

> 'should consider the result a grave defect in the law, and so contrary to principle that I should hesitate long before following any decision to that effect which had not the authority of this House.'[17]

Thus, the argument from natural deterrents plus the effect of other parts of the law, the adequate remedies argument, depends for its effectiveness on whether in the particular case the law is as the defendant says it is and there is evidence that it in fact provides a clear incentive.[18]

Perverse incentives

It is often unclear whether the imposition of a duty of care would lead to improvement in the defendants' conduct. In such cases, the defendant may fall back on a related argument—that the imposition of a duty of care would lead to incentives to do plainly harmful things. It will be noticed that such arguments frequently amount to little more than saying that what the defendant did was reasonable in the circumstances and is therefore not a duty argument at all but instead an argument about whether or not the defendant was at fault. But there are cases when it amounts to more than a disguised argument about fault.

The most well-known perverse incentive argument is again to be found in *Hill v Chief Constable of West Yorkshire*. Lord Keith, in the course of the

---

17 [1932] AC 562 at p. 582.
18 Note also Sir Thomas Bingham's dissent in *M v Newham London Borough Council* and *X v Bedfordshire County Council* [1994] 4 All ER 602, [1994] Fam Law 434. The Master of the Rolls said: 'The local authority argued that the child's claim against it was a public law claim which could be pursued only by seeking judicial review. This is not on the facts a very attractive argument. On the material available to the mother, it seems unlikely she could have obtained leave to move. Had she done so, she would have been very unlikely to succeed without access to the transcript or knowledge of what it said, and the judge's order stood in her way. By the time she had the transcript she would have been out of time and had no need of a remedy anyway. But I think the argument is also bad in law. The child is seeking to enforce a private law claim for damages. She is not seeking to impugn the legal validity of any public law act of the local authority. If she can show that the local authority owed her a duty of care, I see no reason why she should not pursue her claim as she has: *Davy v Spelthorne Borough Council* [1984] AC 262 and *Roy v Kensington and Chelsea and Westminster Family Practitioner Committee* [1992] 1 AC 624. I do not on this point share the view of the judge below. Nor was I impressed by the supplementary submission that the child should be confined to a complaint to the Local Government Ombudsman or the Criminal Injuries Compensation Board.'.

point quoted above on the pointlessness of imposing liability on the police interposes the following:

> 'In some instances the imposition of duty may lead to the exercise of a function being carried on in a detrimentally defensive frame of mind.'

In other words, not only will imposing liability on the police do no good, it will also do positive harm because it will lead to 'defensive policing', a concept developed to parallel 'defensive medicine'—that is the excessive use of expensive tests and diagnostic aids together with meticulous record-keeping undertaken by doctors whose main concern is not the patient's welfare but their own defences against potential tort actions.[19]

The point lying behind the 'defensive behaviour' argument is an interesting one, and one that perhaps the courts have not thought through. It assumes that the extra testing and record-keeping by the defendant would have little or no benefit for the plaintiff, since otherwise the imposition of liability would mean only that standards of behaviour would improve. But if that is so, it means in turn that the courts must think of themselves as very bad at deciding which tests are reasonably necessary or that they have favoured the plaintiff in cases in which the evidence based on the records is unclear, or both. Otherwise they would trust themselves to be able to tell reasonable from unreasonable testing on a case by case basis and to treat the evidence of the case on its merits. The first point goes to the very heart of the courts' ability to set standards in any negligence case, and the second contradicts the formal position that the burden of proof lies on the plaintiff. Both points are ones which courts should find very awkward—since they imply their own incompetence. But such potential embarrassment has not deterred the courts from resorting to the point at frequent intervals.[20]

---

19 See also the cases which purport to follow *Hill*, eg *Alexandrou v Oxford* [1993] 4 All ER 328, CA, *Clough v Bussan* [1990] 1 All ER 431 per Kennedy J, and *Hughes v National Union of Mineworkers* [1991] 4 All ER 278, [1991] ICR 669 per May J. But note that these cases are based on very shaky doctrinal foundations. *Alexandrou* fails to consider whether the defensive policing point would apply specifically to cases in which the accusation is not that the police failed to follow complex lines of inquiry but simply that they failed to respond to a burglar alarm. *Clough* is even worse for the *Hill* argument plainly does not apply (failure to put in traffic police on points duty at junction after traffic lights failed—either they did or they didn't, no amount of cross-referencing or record-keeping would make any difference). The judge relies instead on an extremely nebulous 'proximity' point. And *Hughes* amounts only to saying that it is not enough to make general complaints of incompetence against the police—one must say precisely what should have been done instead. See also *Elguzouli-Daf v Metropolitan Police Comr* [1995] 2 WLR 173, CA, extending the perverse incentive argument to the Crown Prosecution Service.

20 Note that one problem here is the 'defensive medicine' idea comes from the USA, home of the civil jury—whose judgments on fault the courts may not trust—and the 'pay your own costs' rule and the contingent fee, under which a losing plaintiff does not have to pay the legal costs of the defendant or his own legal costs, and so may be encouraged to try his luck more often.

But the 'defensive behaviour' argument[1] does not always succeed. In *Lonrho v Tebbit*,[2] one of the defendant's arguments was that to allow negligence actions against the Secretary of State for Trade and Industry for careless exercise of his statutory powers to release companies from undertakings not to attempt particular take-over bids would lead to unnecessary delays and over-caution in regulation. Sir Nicholas Browne-Wilkinson V-C took the view that there would be no such perverse incentive. He agreed with the basic point made by the defendant that:[3]

> 'The question is whether, as a matter of public policy, the imposition of liability in negligence on a public officer will make him so cautious in the exercise of his statutory functions as to lead to unnecessary delay in the discharge of those functions contrary to the public interest.'

But he went on to say that since the point would in practice only arise rarely, and it would usually be fairly obvious whether or not the Secretary of State had acted with due care, there was no reason to believe, on the facts, that unnecessary delays would be caused. Indeed, he might have added that it would be too perverse even for the British government to respond to a ruling that a minister had acted too slowly by delaying future decisions even more.

Other versions of the perverse incentive arguments exist that also go beyond the 'overkill' point, but which take the debate on the existence of a duty of care into some of the fundamental difficulties of negligence law. One example may be found in *Spartan Steel v Martin*.[4] A manufacturing company claimed damages against a contractor who, in the course of digging up the road, severed the electricity power cable to the plaintiff's factory. Lord Denning, denying the claim for the 'pure economic loss' part of damages said:[5]

> 'Such a hazard is regarded by most people as a thing they must put up with—without seeking compensation from anyone. Some

1   Sometimes known as the 'overkill' argument. See Lord Keith in *Murphy v Brentwood District Coucil* [1991] 1 AC 398, 472, referring to *Rowling v Takaro Properties* [1988] AC 473, 501. See also Staughton LJ in *M v Newham London Borough Council, X v Bedfordshire County Council*, referring to '[T]he exercise of a function being carried on in a detrimentally defensive frame of mind.' See *Hill v Chief Constable of West Yorkshire* [1989] AC 53, 63: Lord Keith said: 'But the other disadvantages which I have described can also in my view be called overkill. A further problem mentioned in *Hill*'s case is that time, trouble and expense will be required for the investigation of claims, to the prejudice of the defendants' budget for their proper functions — policing in that case, caring for children in this. Again the purist would say, they must be given more money. And again I say that very probably they will not be, this time with less fear of being accused of scepticism. The claims may, I suspect, on occasion be for six-figure sums.'.
2   [1991] 4 All ER 973; affd [1992] 4 All ER 280 (CA).
3   [1991] 4 All ER at p 983.
4   [1973] QB 27. See below ch 6.
5   At p 38.

there are who install a stand-by system. Others seek refuge by taking out an insurance policy against breakdown in the supply. But most people are content to take the risk on themselves. When the supply is cut off, they do not go running round to their solicitor. They just put up with it. They try to make up the economic loss by doing more work the next day. This is a healthy attitude which the law should encourage.'

The point is that suing people for the losses one makes in business may be profitable for oneself, but it is not necessarily very productive for the economy as a whole. Economists talk about 'non-productive rent seeking' or 'paper entrepreneurialism' for activities such as lobbying and litigation whose point is not to profit by producing goods and services that others want to buy, but to profit by having the state capture and hand over part of the profits made by other people.

At the back of Lord Denning's remark lies a deep concern about the long-term consequences of encouraging litigiousness. Not only may the costs of litigation alone offset any improvement in the efficiency of the economy caused by the deterrent effect of liability, but also, and much worse, there may be catastrophic effects on productivity and innovation if many of the country's brightest young people are diverted away from careers in industry and commerce into the law.[6]

There is also a perverse incentive argument, applicable to *Hill v Chief Constable of West Yorkshire* and other cases that involve the allocation of public money, that has not yet been raised, but which may occur to the courts in the future. The argument arises out of the fact that tort damages tend to reflect victims' incomes. Because damages for personal injury include amounts for past and future lost income, the better paid the victim, the higher damages tend to be. Similarly, if the victim dies, tort damages are very high for well-paid victims with dependants, and very low for poorly-paid victims without dependants. And, obviously, damage to or loss of expensive property, a Rolls Royce for example, results in higher damages than damage to or loss of cheap property.

If, therefore, the police were required to pay negligence damages to members of the public who suffer from mistakes made in the course of investigations, in order to minimise the amount of damages they might have to pay, the police would do well to concentrate their resources on crimes that affect high earners and those who own expensive objects. Much more effort would be put into, for example, investigating an assault on a highly-paid barrister or burglaries in Mayfair than into finding a serial killer who attacked only down and outs.

No doubt if the police were to follow such a strategy of concentrating their efforts on crimes affecting the most economically productive members of society and the owners of expensive objects, they would be acting in an economically rational manner.[7] But there would be very few people who

---

6 For further discussion of these points and similar points see below ch 6 on economic loss.
7 Cf R Posner *Economics of Justice* 2nd ed (Cambridge MA and London; Harvard UP, 1983) especially pp 88-118.

consider that they would be acting justly or offering their protection to all citizens on an equal basis.

Thus, perverse incentive arguments may be persuasive in some circum–stances, but their persuasiveness is often dependent on the evidence, and on ethical and political arguments and is thus often controversial. Hence the importance of the next section.

Burden of persuasion

In *Lonrho v Tebbit* Sir Nicholas Browne-Wilkinson ended his consideration of the perverse incentive point with the rhetorical question 'What public interest is there in excluding liability in these circumstances?'[8]. He seems to be saying that there ought to be liability unless there is a good reason why not. This point of view appears to contrast sharply with Sir Donald Nicholls's remarks in *Gran Gelato*, noted above, that 'Good reason ... should exist before the law imposes a duty,' which implies that the burden of persuasion lies on the plaintiff.

It may simply be the case that these judges are disagreeing on the question of the burden of persuasion. But there is a way of reconciling them. The position may be that in natural or legal deterrents arguments the burden of persuasion lies on the plaintiff, but in perverse incentive cases it lies on the defendant. We are not talking here about the formal burden of proof, but simply about what presumptions the court may make in the course of its reasoning. In natural or legal deterrent cases, the defendant is relying only on the undisputed fact that litigation is costly and so must be justified by being offset by some positive benefits flowing from liability. In contrast, in perverse incentive cases, the positive benefits are admitted but the defendant is making a contentious claim that they should be offset by non-obvious losses to be incurred in a different way.

Court's role in the allocation of public resources

The third reason used by the courts to deny the existence of a duty of care is that the imposition of liability would have such great implications for public policy that the courts should leave the whole question to others, in particular to elected politicians.

This argument raises a wide range of questions, essentially constit–utional questions, about the role and competence of the courts and about their relationship with other organs of government. The central question, however, is what part should the courts have in the setting of levels of public spending, the priorities between different sorts of spending and the levels of taxation needed to support such spending. The position tradition–ally taken in England is that the courts should severely limit their interference in the taxing and spending decisions of central government.

8   [1991] 4 All ER 973 at p 984.

But in a society in which government undertakes a very wide range of tasks and in which government expenditure is equivalent to 40-45% of GDP, complete abstinence is probably impossible. The point is to set guidelines to limit the extent of the court's involvement.

But it must first be settled that there are reasons for restraint. There are several points of principle that can be made, and are made by the judges, in favour of restraint. Those reasons will themselves also suggest the proper extent of that restraint.

The basic idea

The fundamental point made by judges is that **the weighing of competing public interests, especially over the allocation of public resources, is not the sort of question that courts are usually capable of handling**.

Statements of this basic principle can be found in several leading cases. For example in *East Suffolk Rivers Catchment Board v Kent*[9] Viscount Simon said:

> 'Du Parq LJ in his dissenting judgment [in the Court of Appeal] points out that when Parliament has left it to the public authority to decide which of its powers it shall exercise, and when and to what extent it shall exercise them, this may raise "a question involving the consideration of matters of policy and sometimes the striking of a just balance between the rival claims of efficiency and thrift." These are matters for politicians rather than for the courts.'

More recently in *Lonrho v Tebbit*[10] Sir Nicholas Browne-Wilkinson V-C said:

> 'It is well established that in cases where the exercise of a statutory discretion involves the weighing of competing public interests, particularly financial or economic objectives, no private law duty of care arises because the matter is not justiciable by the courts. It is for the body to whom parliament has committed the discretion to weigh the competing public interest factors: the courts cannot undertake that task.'

Since arguments of this type are usually referred to as 'public policy', a term so vague that it is usually of very doubtful utility, it is worth noting further that Sir Nicholas Browne-Wilkinson went on to give a useful definition of 'policy decisions' as those which involve 'the allocation of

9 [1941] AC 74 at 86.
10 [1991] 4 All ER 973 at 981; see also [1992] 4 All ER 280 (CA).

resources or the distribution of risks'. Here we are concerned with a particular subset of policy decisions, namely those which concern the allocation of public or government resources and the distribution of risk between the government and the rest of society.

But it is obvious that negligence cases frequently have implications for public expenditure or the allocation of public resources and yet cause no doubt about whether a duty of care should be imposed. Local authorities and government departments are not exempt from liability for traffic accidents, or accidents at work or for administrative mistakes.[11] More significantly, at least in financial terms, hospitals and health authorities in the National Health Service are not exempt from responsibility for medical negligence committed by their employees. And the police, recent Court of Appeal cases notwithstanding, may be held liable not only for causing road accidents[12] but also for failing to pass on information that would have prevented a suicide.[13]

In all of these cases, not only is it possible for a public authority to be held liable in damages for negligence, it might also have to spend considerable sums in the future, for example on new technology or on training staff, to prevent a recurrence.

Moreover, the intimate connection between tort compensation and the social security system[14] means that decisions of principle about liability will often have considerable consequences for public expenditure.

The prohibition on imposing duties of care when there are competing claims on public funds is therefore not an absolute one, but it clearly does operate in some cases to restrict liability.

To answer that question and to describe the scope of prohibition, it is necessary above all to explore the reasons put forward for refusing to impose a duty of care in cases in which the argument from the allocation of public resources is raised.

Detailed reasons for prohibiting the duty of care in cases involving the allocation of public resources

Judges often say that the particular procedures and methods of reasoning used by courts are not well suited to making decisions about public expenditure. In *McLoughlin v O'Brian*,[15] for example, a case about the extent of liability for psychiatric injury, Lord Scarman said:

'Why should not the courts draw the line, as the Court of Appeal manfully tried to do in this case? Simply, because the policy issue

---

11 See *Ministry of Housing v Sharp* [1970] 2 QB 223.
12 See *Knightley v Johns* [1982] 1 WLR 349.
13 *Kirkham v Chief Constable of Greater Manchester Police* [1990] 2 QB 283.
14 See below ch 13.
15 [1983] 1 AC 410 at 431.

as to where to draw the line is not justiciable. The problem is one of social, economic and financial policy. The considerations relevant to a decision are not such as to be capable of being handled within the limits of the forensic process.'

But what is it about courts that makes them unsuitable places to make some sorts of decision, and what sort of decision are they unsuitable for? The judges make several points.

Single case

First, they point out that a single case with its own eccentric facts and, moreover, its parties who may not wish to see certain arguments deployed because of their knock-on effects on other aspects of their case, can be a bad vantage point from which to observe the full range of issues.

One notable example, is Viscount Dilhorne's dissenting speech in *Home Office v Dorset Yacht*.[16] Viscount Dilhorne was responding to some remarks of Lord Denning in the Court of Appeal in the same case. Lord Denning had said that up until then, instead of liability, people had dealt with the losses occasioned by crime caused by escaping prisoners in a particular way: 'The householder has claimed on his insurance company. The injured man can now claim on the compensation fund.' Lord Denning went on to ask, 'Should we alter all this?' What Viscount Dilhorne said was this:

'Where I differ [from Lord Denning] is in thinking that it is not part of the judicial function "to alter all this." The facts of a particular case may be a wholly inadequate basis for a far-reaching change in the law. We have not to decide what the law should be and then alter the existing law. That is the function of Parliament.'

In a similar vein, in *Hill v Chief Constable of West Yorkshire*[17] Lord Templeman gave some examples of the type of issue that he believed would not be adequately examined in the course of a trial of the particular facts of that case:

'The present action could not consider whether the training of the West Yorkshire police force is sufficiently thorough, whether the selection of candidates for appointment or promotion is defective, whether rates of pay are sufficient to attract recruits of the required calibre, whether financial restrictions prevent the provision of modern equipment and facilities, or whether the Yorkshire police is clever enough and if not, what can and ought to be done about

16 [1970] AC 1004 at 1051.
17 [1989] AC 53 at 64-65.

it. The present action could only investigate whether an individual member of the police force conscientiously carrying out his duty was negligent when he was bemused by contradictory information or overlooked significant information or failed to draw inferences which later appeared to be obvious.'

This point, therefore, is often well made, but note that it cannot be the whole story. It is similarly true that road accident cases do not consider whether the training and testing of drivers is adequate or whether accidents would be avoided by better design of cars or roads. Similarly, medical negligence cases do not, as a rule, explore whether better pay for staff in the National Health Service would attract more competent doctors and nurses or whether medical accidents could be prevented by more strict regulation of the hours worked by junior doctors. And yet the courts have no difficulty proceeding to judgment in such cases.

One might also envisage circumstances in which, given the right expert witnesses, many of the issues raised by Lord Templeman could indeed be debated in a courtroom, especially the points relating to promotion, the adequacy of training and the appropriateness of equipment.

And as for the point that an individual case may not provoke argument from the parties on the whole range of issues that would be relevant to a decision by government, by trying a substantial number of cases on similar points over time, the courts may hear a fuller range of arguments in the medium to long term than Parliament does on one or two days. It is only in cases in which neither party will ever have any incentive to make use of particular policy-relevant arguments that the 'single-case' point is decisive in itself.

Inadequacies of adversarial system

A related point is that it is claimed that the English adversarial trial procedure, in which the judge is a relatively inactive umpire whose job is to decide not what the truth is, but which side has put forward the better argument, is one that is not suited to bringing out all the relevant material. As Lord Diplock said in *Home Office v Dorset Yacht*:[18]

'The material relevant to the assessment of the reformative effect upon trainees of release under supervision or of any relaxation of control while still under detention is not of a kind which can be satisfactorily elicited by the adversary procedure and rules of evidence adopted in English courts of law.'

It is far from clear, however, why this must be so. Expert witnesses can be called and cross-examined as they are in medical negligence cases or

18 [1970] AC 1004 at 1067.

other cases that require specialists to inform the court. There may well be disagreement between, say, criminologists about the probable effects of particular policies, but the *Bolam* rule gives the courts a way through the thicket of expert disagreement in other cases, and could do so just as easily here. It may well be the case that the adversarial system is deficient as a method of arriving at the truth, and that counsel cannot always be relied on to bring out the most salient points, but such a criticism applies equally to the whole of the English legal system and has nothing special to say about the cases under scrutiny here.

No criteria by which to judge

Another point that some judges make is that in some cases the pros and cons of liability amount to comparing things that, they believe, cannot be compared. As Lord Diplock said in *Home Office v Dorset Yacht*:[19]

'If the reasonable man when directing his mind to the act or omission which has this consequence ought to have in contemplation persons in all the categories directly affected and also the general public interest in the reformation of young offenders, there is no criterion by which a court can assess where the balance lies between the weight to be given to one interest and that to be given to another.'

Lord Diplock is saying that he simply does not know how to weigh up, on the one side, the risk of physical harm and, on the other side, the benefits of rehabilitating offenders.

But, again, by itself this point is not very convincing. It cannot rest on a claim that it is impossible to compare one person's pain with another person's pleasure, since all contested negligence cases require the court to make a judgment as to whether the defendant was at fault, and that judgment inevitably involves weighing up the benefits to the defendant (and others) of not taking further precautions against the value of taking the precautions and preventing harm to the plaintiff.

It might be said instead that there are some kinds of costs of taking precautions against accidents, or of not taking them, that are so inherently controversial that no-one could say what the right answer would be to the question of fault. In these cases, it might be argued, the court, which is obliged to make an authoritative decision on behalf of the state, should not be forced to decide.

On the other hand, courts have frequently allowed themselves to decide cases on the basis of highly contestable moral or political points.[20] The judges in those cases would say that, in such circumstances, whichever

19 [1970] AC 1004 at 1067.
20 See eg *Woolfall v Knowsley Borough Council* above and *Emeh v Kensington and Chelsea and Westminster Area Health Authority*: see above ch 3.

way the case is decided, the result will be controversial and will imply a stand on a particular controversial public issue either one way or the other. If the court had decided in *Woolfall* that the council was justified in treating good industrial relations as a reason for not employing replacement labour to clear up the rubbish left uncollected by the strikers, the decision would have implied a political judgment just as controversial as the one implied by the decision that the council was not justified.

Judges and juries not trained to assess such issues

A similar reason put forward for the unsuitability of the courts for making decisions that affect the use of scarce public resources is that such decisions need specialist training that judges (and juries) do not have.[1]

Admittedly, making decisions about public expenditure is a technical matter, involving the use of cost-benefit techniques, for example, in which the training of judges leaves a lot to be desired. They lack both the skills of and the technical support given to senior civil servants. But one should note that the people to whom the judges purport to be deferring, namely ministers and members of Parliament, are themselves largely untrained. Indeed, if one had to choose between judges and members of Parliament solely on the basis of training, the training of a judge—schooled at the bar in careful thought, sharp questioning and scepticism about the statements of witnesses—would seem far more impressive and relevant than the training of the average MP, which seems to consist mostly of being told by experts in public relations about how to avoid answering embarrassing questions.

Democracy and authority

It will be observed that there are serious objections and limitations to most of the points made so far for the proposition that judges should restrain themselves from making judgments in cases that involve consequences for public expenditure. But one rather more powerful reason for restraint remains to be discussed—the undemocratic nature of courts.

This point can clearly be seen to be at work in Lord Templeman's speech in *Hill v Chief Constable of West Yorkshire*:[2]

'The efficiency of the police force can only be investigated by an inquiry instituted by the national or local authorities which are responsible to the electorate for that efficiency.'

---

1 See eg Lord Diplock in *Home Office v Dorset Yacht* [1970] AC 1004 at 1067: '[the material is not of a kind] of which judges (or juries) are suited by their training and experience to assess the probative value.'.
2 [1989] AC 53 at 64-65.

The allocation of public money to particular projects, and not to others, and the overall burden of taxation imposed to finance the programme of public expenditure are fundamental not just to policy but also to politics. Politics is expenditure and expenditure is politics.[3]

In a country that lacks a written constitution but in which parliamentary majority rule seems to be accepted as the only explicitly acknowledged form of legitimate public authority, unelected judges are in a weak position. Their entire position depends on maintaining public belief in the proposition that the courts do nothing more than enforce the law as approved of by parliamentary majorities. If they were to be seen as interfering in politics, their position would become very difficult.

Therefore, the courts strive to avoid taking decisions that would affect public expenditure to the extent that there would be a risk that their decisions might be considered to be political. Decisions that affect public expenditure only at the margin, namely most decisions in negligence cases, are all right. It is decisions that involve major shifts in spending that the courts should avoid.

Similarly, much of public spending reflects the government's political values and priorities. The balance between welfare spending and spending on the police and the prison service, for example, is not just a technical matter but is a question of political values and outlook. Similarly, the amount of public money devoted to the regulation of particular activities—financial dealings in the City as opposed to Sunday trading, for example—is a reflection not of a cool calculation of costs and benefits but of political values. Courts therefore also seek to avoid decisions that imply shifts in public spending that might be seen as motivated by a set of values and priorities different from those of parliament and the government.[4]

Hence, any decision that might seem to require significant extra public expenditure on the police or the prison service or on other regulatory and enforcement activities is generally avoided.

A different view—Lord Edmund-Davies in *McLouglin v O'Brian*

The prevailing view among the judiciary at present is certainly that judicial intervention in decisions that have major implications for public expenditure should be avoided. Even Sir Thomas Bingham MR in *M v Newham London Borough Council* said that:

> 'Save in clear cases, it is not for the courts to decide how public money is best spent nor to balance the risk that money will be

3   This oft repeated dictum of the American political scientist Aaron Wildavsky merely states the obvious to anyone who has had to set a budget,.

4   Note that in *Yuen Kun Yeu v A-G (Hong Kong)* there is an additional point, not argued at the time, that since the government of Hong Kong was not very democratic, the court should have felt less inhibition about making a decision with public spending consequences.

wasted on litigation against the hope that the possibility of suit may contribute towards the maintenance of the highest standards.'

But one should note that there is a countervailing tendency to be found in some of the cases. This tendency is not, to be sure, in favour of unlimited judicial activism, but it does promote the view that there is nothing inherently implausible about the courts being able to form opinions about public spending decisions.

The main statement of the countervailing view is to be found in the speech of Lord Edmund-Davies in *McLoughlin v O'Brian*:[5]

'In my judgment, the proposition that "the policy issue ... is not justiciable" is as novel as it is startling. So novel is it in relation to this appeal that it was never mentioned during the hearing before your Lordships. And it is startling because in my respectful judgment it runs counter to well-established and wholly acceptable law.'

Lord Edmund-Davies goes on to cite *Rondel v Worsley*[6] for the proposition the 'policy' issues in general, in the sense used by Sir Nicholas Browne-Wilkinson in *Lonrho v Tebbit*, are justiciable[7] and Lord Diplock himself in *Dorset Yacht* for the extension of that proposition to cases involving public money.[8]

He then continues:

'My Lords, in accordance with such a line of authorities, I hold that public policy issues *are* "justiciable". Their invocation calls for close scrutiny, and the conclusion may be that its nature and existence have not been established with the clarity and cogency required before recognition can be granted to any legal doctrine, and before any litigant can be properly deprived of what would otherwise be his manifest legal rights. Or the conclusion may be that the adoption of the public policy relied upon would involve the introduction of legal principles so fundamental that they are best left to the legislature: see for example *Morgans v Launchbury* [1973] AC 127, and especially per Lord Pearson at p 142G. And

5   [1983] 1 AC 410 at 427.
6   [1969] 1 AC 191.
7   Lord Reid's view was that the case depended on the answer to the question: 'Is it in the public interest that barristers and solicitors should be protected against [negligence] actions?'.
8   Lord Diplock said that he agreed with Lord Denning in the Court of Appeal when he said that the case was 'at bottom a matter of public policy which we, as judges, must resolve'. See also *Herrington v British Railways Board* [1971] 2 QB 107 (British Rail was at the time in public ownership) in which Lord Reid said about the then vexed question of the rights of juvenile trespassers to sue occupiers of land where they had been injured, 'Legal principles cannot solve the problem. How far occupiers are to be required by law to take steps to safeguard such children must be a matter of public policy,' but went on to decide the case anyway.

"public policy is not immutable" per Lord Reid in *Rondel v Worsley*
[1969] 1 AC 191, 227. Indeed, Winfield "Public Policy in the English
Common Law" (1928) 42 Harvard LR 76 described it as "*necessarily*
variable" (p 93) and wisely added, at pp 95, 96, 97:

> "this variability ... is a stone in the edifice of the doctrine, and
> not a missile to be flung at it. The march of civilization and the
> difficulty of ascertaining public policy at any given time make
> it essential ... How is public policy evidenced? If it is so variable,
> if it depends on the welfare of the community at any given
> time, how are the courts to ascertain it? Some judges have
> thought this difficulty so great, that they have urged that it
> would be solved much better by the legislature and have
> considered it to be the main reason why the courts should leave
> public policy alone ... This admonition is a wise one and judges
> are not likely to forget it. But the better view seems to be that
> the difficulty of discovering what public policy is at any given
> moment certainly does not absolve the bench from the duty of
> doing so. The judges are bound to take notice of it and of the
> changes which it undergoes, and it is immaterial that the
> question may be one of ethics rather than of law.'"

Lord Edmund-Davies's view can be broken down into the following
elements:
(i)   Issues of 'policy', that is resource and risk allocation, are relevant
       even when they involve the state.
(ii)   But such factors should only be used by the courts when there is a
       clear consensus outside the courtroom about which direction these
       factors indicate that the court should go.
(iii) Even if there is such a consensus, the court should not proceed if to
       do so would imply far-reaching changes in other aspects of the law.
Factors (ii) and (iii) themselves raise further questions. What constitutes
a broad enough consensus on what policy should be followed and on what
basis does the court know that it exists? And what constitutes legal change
that is so far-reaching that its introduction should be left to the legislature?
The judges offer very little guidance on the difficulties of factor (ii).
Indeed the difficulties involved constitute a major argument for declining
to go along Lord Edmund-Davies's route. Should the judges, for example,
consider only what appears to be the general direction of existing statute
law, the traditional method of discerning 'policy'? The problem is that given
the volume of statute law now being produced and the fact that the political
intentions and motives of the parliaments that pass it change drastically
every 20 years or so, it is far from obvious that it is reasonable to expect
any consistent policy to emerge from any area of statute law that has not
undergone a recent comprehensive reform and consolidation.[9] But does

9   See generally N Simmonds *The Decline of Juridical Reason: Doctrine and Theory in the
     Legal Order* (Manchester; Manchester UP, 1984). Of course, the fact that one should not

that mean that judges should look to the opinions of experts instead? Or perhaps, in the continuing absence of the civil jury, one of whose tasks in reality was to deal with questions such as these, should the courts look to opinions expressed in the press, or even to public opinion polls?

On factor (iii) there is more explicit debate. On the one side, it is argued that the degree of change should be measured broadly, not by the degree of intellectual disruption to the logical structure of the law, as Lord Edmund-Davies's speech would seem to imply, but instead by the degree of practical disruption to settled expectations of what legal liabilities people have.

For example, in *Yuen Kun Yeu v A-G (Hong Kong)*[10] Lord Keith gave as a reason for not extending liability to the acts of a regulatory body for banks that:

> '[T]he principles leading to ... liability would surely be equally applicable to a wide range of regulatory agencies, not only in the financial field, but also, for example, to the factory inspectorate and social workers to name only a few. If such liability were to be desirable upon any policy grounds, it would be much better that the liability were introduced by the legislature, which is better suited than the judiciary to weigh up competing policy consid–erations.'

On the other hand, one might note, at least for future reference, a point made, admittedly without success on that occasion, by the plaintiffs' counsel, Michael Beloff QC, in *Yuen Kun Yeu*.[11] Mr Beloff pointed out that:

> 'If principle moves the [court] in a certain direction it should not be overimpressed by the consequences, because the legislature can alter them.'

That is, one should look at the relationship between the court and Parliament in the round. If the introduction of a new principle seems to have inconvenient results, Parliament is at liberty to reject it or to fine-tune the law so that only those consequences believed to be beneficial remain.

But such an argument should not be taken too far. Parliamentary time is limited and to expect Parliament to spend most of its time considering the latest bizarre judicial innovation only to reject them is to enter the realms of fantasy. The court, if it wants to follow Mr Beloff's suggestion, should at least consider whether the proposed new principle has any realistic prospect of surviving parliamentary scrutiny. And even to expect Parliament to spend much time fine-tuning the more reasonable suggest–ions of a creative judiciary is to risk landing the public with a set of rules

---

expect a consistent policy to emerge does not rule out the possibility that interpretations can be made to fit if the interpreter wants them to fit. See Howarth 'Making Sense of Nonsense' in Hyman Gross and Ross Harrison *Jurisprudence: Cambridge Essays* (Oxford; Clarendon Press, 1992).

10 [1988] AC 175 at 198.
11 At p185.

that everyone knows to be inconvenient, but the degree of inconvenience of which is not quite enough to merit immediate government time in Parliament and the removal of which has to await the intervention of an interested backbencher with a private member's bill or an occasional general law reform measure.[12]

LORD KEITH AND 'POLICY'—ANY PORT IN A STORM?

Students of the styles and attitudes of the individual judges who have shaped modern English negligence law might be interested in a curious contradiction in the approach to 'policy' of the leading light of the 1980s reactionary movement in negligence, Lord Keith of Kinkel.

It can be seen both in *Yuen Kun Yeu v A-G (Hong Kong)* and in *Hill v Chief Constable of West Yorkshire*. In both cases, Lord Keith expostulates on his favourite point, namely the defensiveness point that liability in negligence will make matters worse, but then immediately launches into a defence of the view that courts should not allow themselves to take policy decisions.

If the defensive policing argument is not a policy argument, relying as it does on the notion that one consequence of liability would be to waste public money, what is?

It appears that Lord Keith allowed policy arguments against liability, but was not prepared to countenance them when they favour liability.

A clue to Lord Keith's underlying position may be seen in the words he chooses to sum up his view in *Hill*: 'Many such decisions would not be regarded by the court as appropriate to be called in question.' The language here ('called into question') is that of a challenge to authority, and it is as if Lord Keith is offended by the plaintiff's refusal to accept the judgment of that authority. It is not so much that the courts are ill-equipped to consider policy matters or that the judges lack a democratic base, but simply that Lord Keith believes that the courts should not be used by private citizens, especially by means of negligence actions, to call public authorities such as the police to account. Perhaps he wants to protect the integrity of administrative law as the only proper way for private citizens to challenge the state or perhaps he genuinely believes that private citizens have no business questioning the judgment of the state at all.

Either way, Lord Keith's pronouncements are to say the least controversial.

---

12 Note also that differences of circumstance between different sorts of regulator affected by a rule could often be taken into account more simply as part of the court's decision on fault/breach.

Excursus on the liability of public bodies

An issue related to the question of the court's role in public expenditure but which goes somewhat beyond it is the question of the general position of the public authorities in negligence actions.

The basic position was stated by Lord Blackburn in a classic piece of nineteenth century assertion in *Geddis v Bann Reservoir (Proprietors)*:[13]

> 'I take it, without citing cases, that it is now thoroughly well established that no action will lie for doing that which the Legislature has authorised, if it be done without negligence, although it does occasion damage to anyone; but an action does lie for doing that which the Legislature has authorised, if it be done negligently.'

The question, however, is: what exactly has the legislature authorised? *East Suffolk Rivers Catchment Board v Kent*[14] appeared to say that if legislation gives a public body a discretion about whether to act at all, it must have authorised the body not to act, so that inaction on the part of such a body could never give rise to liability in negligence. Thus, unless a public body can be said to have a duty to act, as opposed to power to act if it so chooses, there could be no liability in negligence.

Doubts about the *East Suffolk Rivers Catchment Board v Kent* approach appeared in the 1970s. In *Home Office v Dorset Yacht* and then *Anns v Merton London Borough Council* the House of Lords developed a distinction between 'policy decisions', for which there could be no liability either for action or inaction, and 'operational decisions', for which there could be liability for both action and inaction. The idea was to protect the govern–ment from disguised complaints about the level and allocation of public expenditure (and to authorise governmental experimentation, although, as will be argued below, that aspect could have been dealt with simply as a matter of the judgment of fault) but at the same time to compensate people who had suffered injury because of straightforward bureaucratic incompetence. The *East Suffolk Rivers Catchment Board v Kent* distinction between misfeasance and nonfeasance was superseded by the policy-operational decision in so far as a policy decision not to act would carry no liability but an operational distinction not to act, taken in the light of a policy to act, could carry liability. The idea, as expressed in *Anns*, was that the authorities were usually under no obligation to act at all, but if they did, they had to do so with due care.

The distinction between 'policy' and 'operational' levels was not a simple one. It was not merely a matter, for example, of the seniority of the person making the decision. Sometimes, depending on the wording of the statute that conferred the power in question, the 'operational' duty would extend

---

13 (1878) 3 App Cas 430, 455.
14 See above.

to having to think about whether to exercise their power at all, a decision that can only be taken near or at the top of the hierarchy. If the authority did think about it, and decided not to exercise their power, there could be no liability. But if they failed even to consider whether to exercise their power, they could be held liable just as if they had decided to exercise the power and had then done so carelessly.[15]

Nevertheless, at least it was clear what the policy-operational distinction was trying to achieve. In the 1980s, however, the policy-operational distinction came to be displaced as the courts tended to base judgments on the alleged intentions of the particular statute that conferred the power in question. By 1988, the policy-operational distinction had become indicative only, not a decisive test. According to Lord Keith, it provided a good reason to exclude liability in 'policy' cases but no reason to allow liability in 'operational' cases. [16]

In cases such as *Peabody* the new approach was probably justified. A local authority had failed to exercise a statutory power under the Public Health Act 1936 to stop the installation of an unsuitable drainage system on land that the plaintiff was developing. The plaintiff subsequently had to replace the drainage system at its own expense and it tried to recover the cost by suing the authority for negligence. The House of Lords found for the defendant on the ground that it could not have been the intention of Parliament when it conferred powers on local authorities to control drainage systems that it wanted to protect the economic interests of developers. And the notion in another House of Lords case that the intention of a statute conferring a power to give housing grants was to protect the public purse from abuse and fraud and not to ensure that the money was used to build safe buildings, although not obviously right, was not completely impossible.[17] But, since, as Professor Milsom once remarked, the history of the common law is the history of the abuse of its fundamental concepts,[18] it did not take long before the argument was taken too far, and in *Caparo v Dickman*[19] the House of Lords declared, absurdly in view of the historical record,[20] that a statute that required companies set up under the Companies Acts to deposit their accounts in a publicly available register had nothing to do with protecting investors.

In the 1990s, two different tendencies are discernible. On the one hand, Browne-Wilkinson VC in *Lonrho v Tebbit* indicated a return to the policy-operational decision. He said that if the case did not involve policy issues in the sense of the allocation of public resources or the distribution of risks, there was no reason why a public authority should receive special treatment.

15 See Lord Wilberforce in *Anns v Merton London Borough Council* [1978] AC 728 at 755.
16 *Rowling v Takaro Properties* [1988] AC 473 at 501.
17 *Curran v Northern Ireland Co-Ownership Housing Association* [1987] AC 718.
18 *Historical Foundations of the Common Law* (2nd edn) (1981: London, Butterworths).
19 [1990] 2 AC 605.
20 See Howarth 'Negligence after Murphy' [1991] CLJ 58.

On the other hand, there has been a marked tendency, discussed in more detail below, to claim that challenges to public bodies should principally be by way of judicial review, and, even more restrictively, a tendency to confuse negligence with breach of statutory duty and to claim that if there is no evidence that Parliament intended to confer a private right of action in the statute itself, it would somehow undermine the statute to allow a negligence action for incompetent exercise of the statutory powers.

The apotheosis of the restrictive approach is the argument of the majority in the Court of Appeal in *M v Newham London Borough Council*.[1] *M* concerns two sets of cases about local authority social services departments and child protection. Under various statutes, local authorities have both powers and duties to protect children from abuse and neglect. In *M*'s case, the London Borough of Newham wrongly and carelessly accused the father of a child of abusing her, causing her to be taken away from her mother. The mother and the daughter sued Newham for psychiatric illnesses that they alleged arose out of the trauma caused by these events. They also sued the psychiatrist employed by the council who made the original mistakes. In the companion case, *X v Bedfordshire County Council* in contrast, the plaintiffs were children who had been abused but whom the defendant local authority had carelessly failed to protect.

In the face of a powerful dissent from Sir Thomas Bingham MR, a majority of the Court of Appeal found in favour of both defendants. Staughton LJ said that since the statute conferring the powers and the imposing the duties were drafted in general terms, they did not in themselves establish a right of action and that consequently there could be no right to sue in negligence either. His central claim, echoed by Peter Gibson LJ, is that:

> 'The involvement of the Newham London Borough Council and of the Bedfordshire County Council comes about entirely by statute. Neither authority has by the common law any right or duty to interfere in the lives of children within its area. At common law a local authority, like a private citizen, may see a child in need but pass by on the other side. One would therefore expect that any duty of care is to be found, if at all, in the statute; if the statute on its true interpretation provides none, then none should be owed by the local authority.'

But Staughton LJ cannot possibly be right. First, simply on the facts, it is wrong for Staughton LJ to give the impression that these are cases of pure omission. In the Newham case the authority, after its social workers and psychiatrists made their mistakes, physically intervened to remove the child. That is an act, not an omission. In the Bedfordshire case, the council had intervened to remove the children temporarily but then had

1   [1994] 4 All ER 602, [1994] Fam Law 434.

sent them back. It was not a case in which the authority had decided that it would not engage in an activity it was empowered to engage in. The council had an active social services department which had acted incompetently.

Secondly, Staughton LJ's view that a council cannot be liable at common law for incompetence in the exercise of statutory powers if the statutory powers themselves establish no private rights of action is simply absurd. Local councils have, for example, a power to collect rubbish and to sweep the streets. These powers, under the Local Government Acts, plainly do not establish private rights of action of any kind. But no-one would argue that a person carelessly run over by a bin lorry or a street sweeper has no right of action against the council. The fundamental principle established by *Geddis* must still be correct. A power to do something is not the same as a right to do it negligently. The councils in *M* had chosen to exercise their statutory powers and should have been held to account for the way they exercised them.

Thirdly, *M* illustrates the continuing utility of the policy-operational distinction. These are not cases in which the mistakes that were made came about because of high level budgetary decisions. They came about because of the operational incompetence of the councils' employees. A decision in favour of the defendants means that the devastating consequences of careless errors in child protection will go uncompensated while council departments notorious for their quasi-professional arrogance will have less of an incentive to respect the rights of those whose lives they affect.

In contrast, a differently constituted Court of Appeal in *E v Dorset County Council, Christmas v Hampshire County Council and Keating v Bromley London Borough Council*[2] decided that there could be liability in the similar context of allegations of negligence against local education authorities, in which the statutes conferring the relevant powers were equally incapable of giving rise themselves to private rights. At least, the authorities failed in their claim to strike out the actions completely.

The Court of Appeal thought that although it was true that an attempt to enforce against the authority by means of a negligence action precisely the same public law duties that it was subject to under the Education Acts should not be allowed, cases in which the accusations were that specific employees of the authority committed specific acts of negligence while acting under the powers conferred by the same Acts were very different.[3]

The resolution of these issues remains one of the most important tasks of the House of Lords in the post-*Murphy* era.

2   [1994] 4 All ER 640.
3   The social services cases and the education cases were consolidated for the purposes of an appeal to the House of Lords. At the time of writing, the Lords had heard oral argument but had not yet come to any decision.

Related points that are really fault arguments in disguise.

There are also to be considered two forms of argument that look, super–ficially at least, to be variations on the theme of judicial restraint in cases involving substantial sums of public money. On closer inspection, however, both turn out to be yet further examples of arguments about whether the defendant was at fault that have been promoted, probably unjustifiably, to the rank of duty argument.

State should be allowed to experiment

The first point is that the state should be allowed to find out what would be the best policy to adopt by a process of trial and error free from the threat that the errors would result in legal liability.

To illustrate the point, one must turn yet again to *Home Office v Dorset Yacht*.[4] Counsel for the defendant, the Home Office, argued that any liability imposed upon the prison service would mean that no progress would ever be made in the direction of reducing the levels of security faced by some prisoners in the hope that they would respond positively to being given responsibility and be easier to rehabilitate. There would never be any experimentation with such 'minimum security' methods because of the threat of negligence actions. The possible benefits of such methods would, therefore, never be discovered. Counsel cited in support the celebrated New York case *Williams v State of New York*.[5]

Lord Reid, however, was not impressed:[6]

'It is argued that it would be contrary to public policy to hold the Home Office or its officers liable to a member of the public for this carelessness—or, indeed, any failure of duty on their part ... I do not think that the argument for the Home Office can be put better than it was put by the Court of Appeals of New York in *Williams v State of New York* ...

It may be that public servants of the State of New York are so apprehensive, easily dissuaded from doing their duty and intent on preserving public funds from costly claims that they could be influenced in this way. But my experience leads me to believe that Her Majesty's servants are made of sterner stuff. So I have no hesitation in rejecting this argument. I can see no good ground in public policy for giving this immunity to a government department.'

4   [1970] AC 1004 at 1016 and 1032.
5   127 NE 2d 545 (1955).
6   [1970] AC 1004 at pp 1032-33.

The basis of Lord Reid's reasoning, however, is slight and contradictory. In any particular case, public servants act either reasonably or unreasonably. If they act reasonably, then there should be no liability since the defendants are not at fault. If they act unreasonably, they should not have acted thus, and the fact that they were made of 'sterner stuff' should be deplored, not welcomed.

A better reply than Lord Reid's would be that the prospective benefits of such an experiment are part of the costs that would be incurred if the defendant public authority had taken the precaution demanded by the plaintiff and had not embarked on the experiment. They are therefore no more and no less than part of the fault equation. In any particular case, it may be that a reasonable person (or, more likely here, a reasonable expert) would say that, given what was already known at the time, the chances of the experiment's succeeding or failing was either high or low. The reasonable person would then look at the prospective risks if the experiment went wrong and the prospective benefits if the experiment worked and decide whether this was a reasonable experiment to embark on at the time.

One might argue that the court may not be able to say whether the experiment would have seemed reasonable at the time. But if so, the reason must relate to one of the points already mentioned above (lack of training, single case, democracy etc) rather than to anything special about experimentation. Otherwise the argument is simply one about fault, in the same way as any negligence defendant might be accused of choosing a novel way of doing something without proper justification.

Difficulty of judging professionals

Finally, the argument usually crops up in these cases that state officials, whether police officers or regulators, are experts in their field and their judgment should be accepted. For example in *Hill v Chief Constable of West Yorkshire* Lord Keith said:[7]

> 'The manner and conduct of such an investigation [into the general nature of police methods] must necessarily involve a variety of decisions to be made on matters of policy and discretion, for example as to which particular line of inquiry is most advantageously to be pursued and what is the most advantageous way to deploy the available resources.'

The point here, however, is no different from that which might be made of any expert judgment, whether by a state official or by anyone else—a doctor in private practice, a lawyer, a surveyor or whatever. The question

---

7   [1989] AC 53 at 63.

is not about immunity from liability but rather about how to make judgments about the conduct of experts and professionals. It may be that the presently accepted methods employed by the courts for reaching such judgments, namely the *Bolam* tests, are so favourable towards expert and professional defendants that the situation may appear to approach that of an immunity. But it is still possible for professionals to be found liable. Indeed it happens all the time. The object of the *Bolam* tests remains fundamentally to assess fault, not to exclude the possibility of any duty at all.[8]

Integrity of other legal rules

We must now turn to the argument against finding a duty of care that has developed most in the last two decades, namely the argument that **to allow the plaintiff to recover in negligence would, in certain circumstances, tend to undermine the legal position created by other legal rules**. Those legal rules establish expectations that the intrusion of negligence liability would, allegedly, upset.

For example, to allow negligence actions against public authorities eats into the territory normally covered by administrative law. To allow a negligence action for saying bad things about a prospective employee in a reference may undermine the rules of the law of defamation. And to allow a negligence action by an employer against someone who subcontracted to do the work from the person employed directly to do it, a sub-contractor with whom the employer has no direct contractual relationship, would tend to undermine the rule of English contract law against the enforceability of third party benefits.

It should be noticed that the argument from the integrity of other areas of the law depends for its force on an assumption that the legal position created by those other areas of the law is desirable, or at least not so undesirable that it is worth upsetting settled expectations in order to improve the situation.

The argument from integrity is a variation on the argument from the adequacy of other deterrents—that the imposition of negligence liability is undesirable because incentives created by other legal rules are sufficient. The difference here lies in the concentration on the legal rules that create the incentives, rather than on the incentives themselves, but the two arguments are very closely related.

It should also be noted that the argument from integrity would, if taken too seriously, close off the most important route used by common law judges over the past six centuries to avoid rigidities and mistakes in the law, namely the reclassification of a type of case from one area of the law to another. A case in which justice cannot be done as long as it is thought of

8   See further Sir Thomas Bingham's dissent in *M v Newham*.

as a contract case can be transformed by thinking about it as a case involving a trust. Procedural difficulties in property law can be evaded by treating the case as one of tort. In fact, modern contract law grew out of the reclassification of certain contractual disputes as a kind of tort ('assumpsit').[9] The crossing of boundaries between different sets of legal rules, indeed the challenging of and shifting of those boundaries, largely at the behest of plaintiffs' lawyers, is an important way in which the common law develops.

Nevertheless, the argument from the integrity of other areas of the law is now a very powerful one. We shall consider its influence by looking in turn at the various areas of the law the judges have alleged need protection from the encroachment of negligence. We begin with the most controversial relationship, namely that between negligence and contract law.

Negligence vs contract

The relationship between negligence and contract law is a troubled one.[10] The fundamental problem, however, is quite easily stated. Tort law, and negligence in particular, is built around the assumption that it is unreason–able to expect the plaintiff and the defendant to have sorted out in advance between themselves the financial consequences of the harm that occurred to the plaintiff. It is not reasonable, for example, to expect someone run down by a car in the street to have had a specific agreement with the driver of that car, an agreement covering the circumstances under which the driver would pay compensation to the victim and how much compens–ation the driver should pay. Contract law, on the other hand, is built around the assumption that it is reasonable to expect the parties concerned to have come to some kind of agreement about what should happen if one of the parties harms the other by failing to meet a contractual obligation.

The difficulty is that in practice negligence is called upon to deal with situations in which some negotiation in advance was reasonably possible (for example medical negligence cases in which the doctor worked for the National Health Service) and contract law has to deal with cases in which it is unreasonable to expect the parties to have worked out every last detail of the future relationship (eg employment contracts, long-term contracts, very simple sales transactions). The result is that the two areas of law end up dealing with very similar problems, but have a tendency to come up with different answers. This is because they come at the problems from different angles and with different presumptions—contract law presumes that if the parties have not said what is to happen in certain circumstances, the parties are content to let any losses lie where they fall. Negligence law presumes that lack of advance agreement is the normal state of affairs and that it does not preclude liability.

9   See generally *Milsom*.
10 See eg Markesinis 'An Expanding Tort Law—The Price of a Rigid Contract Law' (1987) 103 LQR 354.

What this means is that if the court believes that the situation is fundamentally governed by contract, to allow a negligence action may be to reverse the legitimate expectations of the defendant, expectations that were founded on the contract. But if the court takes the situation to be one in which it is unreasonable to expect the parties to have settled their future relationship between themselves, it follows that it is at least possible that to allow a negligence action would not be to upset any such settled legitimate expectations.

The way in which the difficulty usually presents itself is that the plaintiff's attempt to sue in negligence is said to undermine the contract rule of 'privity of contract', that is that only those who are parties to a contract can sue on it. Stated baldly, this argument sounds so odd that many students find it hard to believe that anyone could take it seriously. After all, the plaintiff is not trying to get the benefit of a contract agreed by other people, but is merely trying to get compensation for harm that the defendant has done. But the point lies not in the contracts that were made, but in those that were not made, deliberately not made as the defendant alleges, between the plaintiff and the defendant. The key to the cases is to ask whether it really is a plausible interpretation of the facts that by not contracting, the plaintiff and defendant have deliberately signalled that they intend that there should be no relevant legal obligations between them.

The classic example is *Donoghue v Stevenson* itself. The defendant makes a product which it sells to an intermediary, the intermediary sells it to the plaintiff's friend, and the plaintiff's friend gives it to the plaintiff, whom it harms. If this case is governed by contract, the plaintiff has no claim against the defendant, because English law[11] does not allow those who are not parties to a contract to sue on it. The reason for the rule is the one already stated: that it is assumed that the person who is not a party to the contract could easily have become one by negotiating directly with the other parties and that therefore the fact that there is no contract between the third party and the other parties reflects a deliberate choice on all their parts that the third party should have no legally binding rights or obligations. But if the situation in *Donoghue* is treated as governed by the tort of negligence, what is being said about the lack of a contractual relationship between the manufacturer and the final consumer? It is that the relationship cannot plausibly be interpreted as meaning that the manufacturer has a legitimate expectation that it will not be sued by the final consumer for negligently caused harm.

The majority decision in *Donoghue* was precisely that the position as established by contract law did not exhaust the legal duties of the manufacturer. As Lord Atkin said:[12]

---

11 *Donoghue* itself was, of course, a Scots law case, but although some third party rights are recognised in Scots law, they did not extend to the situation in *Donoghue v Stevenson*.

12 [1932] AC 562 at pp 593-94.

'[In *Blacker v Lake and Elliot* (1912) 106 LT 533] Hamilton J says
... that the breach of the defendants' contract with A to use care
and skill in ... the manufacture .. of an article does not itself give
any cause of action to B when injured by the article proving to be
defective in breach of that contract. He then goes on to say, "how is
the case of the plaintiffs any better when there is no contract proved
of which there could be a breach?" I think, with respect, that this
saying does not give sufficient weight to the actual issues raised
by the pleadings on which alone the older cases are an authority.
If the issue raised was an alleged duty created by a contract it
would have been irrelevant to consider duties created without
reference to contract; and contract cases cease to be authorities
for duties alleged to exist beyond or without contract.'

That is, if *Donoghue* were a case about contract alone, the defendant
should win, and that is what the older cases say. But it is not a case solely
about contract, and that is why the plaintiff should have a chance of winning
in negligence.

The basis of the *Donoghue* decision should now be easy to see. Is it
reasonable to expect a final consumer of a product to have entered into
negotiations with its manufacturer about the circumstances that would
lead to harm being done by the product and the proper amounts of
compensation if harm occurred? In modern times, given mass production
and mass distribution, the answer must be that it is not reasonable.
Therefore the absence of contract between the parties does not give rise to
any legitimate expectation of non-liability on the part of the manufacturer.[13]
Thus, negligence rules may apply, and, if the defendant was careless and
the damage not too remote, there ought to be liability.[14]

A more modern example, which goes the other way, is *Pacific Associates
v Baxter*.[15] The plaintiff contracted to do dredging and reclamation work
for the Ruler of Dubai. The Ruler of Dubai, in turn, employed the defendants
to manage the contract for him, and the contract itself specified what the
defendants' management role was to be. The defendants were not, however,
parties to the contract between the Ruler of Dubai and the plaintiffs and
there was no separate contract between the plaintiffs and the defendants.
The plaintiffs' case was that the defendants had carried out their role as
agents in a slovenly and careless manner, with the result that costly
disputes broke out between the plaintiffs and the Ruler of Dubai, disputes
that resulted in a substantial arbitration award in favour of the plaintiffs
but not substantial enough, as the plaintiffs claimed, to reimburse them

13 But note that other aspects of the situation may yet give rise to such a legitimate
    expectation—for example if the product was easy to inspect before being sold to the
    friend. In that case, it is legitimate to say that the manufacturer's responsiblity is reduced.
    This is, however, largely a point about remoteness, not a point about whether the law of
    negligence applies in the first place.
14 This precise area of the law is now, of course, covered by the Consumer Protection Act.
    See below ch 8.
15 [1990] 1 QB 993.

in full. They sued the defendants for negligence. They failed both at first instance and on appeal.

The judge at first instance[16] gave as one of his reasons for dismissing the plaintiffs' case that it was relevant to whether there should be liability in negligence that:

> '[T]he duties on which [the] plaintiff relies to found a case in tort arise out of a contract, and there would seem to be no reason why the defendant should not have been made a party to the contract if that was the intention of the parties and he had been prepared to assume a liability similar to that now sought to be attached to him in tort.'

That is, in this case it was perfectly easy for the defendants to have been made a party to the contract, so that the very fact that they were not parties was strong evidence that the intention of the parties was that the plaintiff should not be able to sue the defendant in tort for harm caused by mistakes arising out of the contract. This is not a case about mass production and distribution, so that the inference of an intention not to create legal obligations is reasonable.

A more subtle and difficult variation on the same theme arises if, instead of asking whether the defendant has a legitimate expectation of not being sued at all, one asks whether the defendant has a legitimate expectation that its liability should be limited in some way. Here, it is often the defendant who is relying on a contract to which it is not technically a party, rather than the plaintiff.

For example, in *Norwich City Council v Harvey*[17] the plaintiff employed a contractor to build an extension to a swimming pool. The contractor in turn employed various sub-contractors to do the work, including the defendant, whose job was to put the roof on the extension. In the course of carrying out the work, an employee of the sub-contractor carelessly set fire to the whole swimming pool, causing £60,000 worth of damage. The plaintiff sued the defendant for negligence.

There was no contract between the plaintiff and the defendant. The only contracts were those between the plaintiff and the main contractor and between the main contractor and the sub-contractor. Nevertheless, the defendant said that it should not be liable for what would otherwise be an obvious and straightforward case of negligently caused property damage. The reason was that both of the contracts contained clauses which said that, although the contractor would be liable for other sorts of damage caused by negligence, 'the existing structures ... and the works ... shall be at the sole risk of the [council] as regards loss or damage by fire.' The plaintiff replied that these clauses were irrelevant, since they were not contained in any contract specifically between the plaintiff and the sub-contractor. The argument for the plaintiff's position is that it would have

16 Quoted by Purchas LJ in the Court of Appeal at [1990] 1 QB 1005.
17 [1989] 1 All ER 1180, [1989] 1 WLR 828.

been very easy for the council and the sub-contractors to have entered into the same sort of a standard form contract as existed between the council and the main contractor.

The Court of Appeal, however, turned the whole argument on its head. May LJ said:[18]

> 'I do not think that the mere fact that there is no strict privity between the employer and sub-contractor should prevent the latter from relying on the clear basis on which all the parties contracted in relation to damage to the employer's building caused by fire.'

May LJ did not elaborate very much further on why the 'clear basis on which all parties contracted' should be decisive, but he did cite, without disapproval, *Welsh Health Technical Services Organisation v Haden Young (IDC, third party)*[19] in which McPherson J based a similar finding on taking into account the 'whole contractual setting' of the case. May LJ seems therefore to be making the point that one should ask whether the plaintiff has a legitimate expectation of being able to sue the defendant in this sort of case. The plaintiff would say that it did, since it only excluded its rights with regard to the main contractor. But the court would say that in reality the plaintiff had taken onto itself the whole risk of damage to the swimming pool by fire arising out of the construction of the extension.

Similarly in *Pacific Associates v Baxter*[20] the contract between the dredging contractor and the Ruler of Dubai contained a clause which said that the defendant managing engineers were not to be liable for any damage arising out of the contract, but that all claims should be directed at the Ruler himself. The Court of Appeal allowed the defendant to rely on this clause, even though it was not a party to the agreement. Purchas LJ said:[1]

> '[T]he absence of a direct contractual nexus between A and B does not necessarily exclude the recognition of a clause limiting liability to be imposed on A in a contract between B and C, when the existence of that contract is the basis of the creation of a duty of care asserted to be owed by A to B. The presence of such an exclusion clause[,] whilst not being directly binding between the parties, cannot be excluded from a general consideration of the contractual structure against which the contractor demonstrates reliance on, and the engineer accepts responsibility for, a duty in tort, arising out of the proximity established between them by the existence of that very contract.'

The theory of 'contractual structure' is very similar to the *Norwich* case's 'whole contractual setting.' The defendant has a legitimate expectation of not being held liable when the agreements made by the plaintiff indicate

18 [1989] 1 All ER at p 1187.
19 (1987) 37 BLR 130. See especially p 143.
20 [1990] 1 QB 993.
1   At p 1022.

that the plaintiff has given up the right to sue the defendant in the circumstances in question.

But it is difficult to say that the courts are being very consistent here.[2] Either the lack of a contract in a situation in which contracting would have been easy means that there is an intention not to create a legally binding relationship or contracting would have been difficult, so that no such inference can be made. But if the inference can be made, why should the defendant be allowed to rely on exemption and exclusion clauses in the contract to which it was not a party? On the other hand, if the intention to deny legal obligation cannot be inferred, the contractual position, as in *Donoghue*, is surely not particularly relevant.

In *Norwich City Council*, the inconsistency can perhaps be explained away by saying that, in comparison with any tangible benefits to the parties, the costs of the Council's having to sign up every sub-contractor to separate contracts, were high. Indeed the whole point of employing a main contractor is precisely that the Council does not have to bother with every small sub-contractor who comes and goes. Thus, perhaps, in *Norwich City Council* one cannot infer an intention to avoid any legal relationship between the parties from the absence of direct contracts with the sub-contractors.

But it is still difficult to see how *Pacific Associates* can claim any internal consistency since the Court of Appeal relies simultaneously on saying (1) that the fact that there was no contract between the parties shows an intention not to create binding legal relations and (2) that the defendant could rely on an exclusion clause in the same contract.

All one can say is that the court's reasoning in *Pacific Associates* works if it is seen as being based on an alternative—either there is an intention that there should be no legal obligations between the parties, or, if the defendant is wrong on that (because the situation is such that one would not have expected the parties to contract directly) there is still no liability because of the exemption clause.[3]

Although most of the cases in which the defendant claims that for the court to allow a negligence action would be to undermine the contractual position are about privity of contract, there are other examples. For example, in *Banque Keyser Ullman v Skandia*,[4] in the course of contractual negotiations between the plaintiff and the defendant the plaintiff complained that the defendant had not informed it of a third party's dishonesty. The defendant, in fact, had simply said nothing. The Court of Appeal said:

2   See also the hostility of the House of Lords to a similar theory, 'transferred loss', when it would help not the defendant but the plaintiff in *The Aliakmon* (*Leigh & Sillivan v Aliakmon Shipping* [1986] AC 785). See below ch 6.

3   See also Saville LJ in *The Nicholas H* [1994] 3 All ER 686, [1994] 1 WLR 1071, [1994] 1 Lloyd's Rep 492 (which concerned the relationship between cargo owners, shipowners and experts who advise shipowners and insurers on the seaworthiness of ships and the effect of exemption clauses in the contract between the cargo owners and the shipowners in an action between the cargo ownwer and the experts): 'In the present case, there is already a coherent system of internationally recognised law which places the primary burden of caring for the cargo upon the shipowners.'.

4   [1990] 1 QB 665.

'[T]here is, in our judgment, no ... exception which would enable [the court] to grant [the plaintiff] a remedy against [the defendant] in tort. To do so would be to cut across all the principles of our law of contract relating to the effect of silence in the course of pre-contractual negotiations.'

Contract law does not usually allow silence to count as a representation (for reasons that are not explored in the case), and so negligence was not allowed to undermine that rule.

Similarly, in *The Aliakmon*,[5] one of the reasons given by the House of Lords for not allowing a buyer of goods to sue a person who damages the goods before property in the goods technically passes to the buyer was that to do so would be to upset the delicately balanced, part common law part statutory system of rules that govern international sales and carriage of goods by sea.

And finally, in *Gran Gelato v Richcliff*[6] one of the reasons given for refusing to allow a buyer of real property a direct action for negligence against the seller's solicitor was that to do so would undermine the assumptions of the 'normal conveyancing transaction'.

The question which arises at this point is whether the relationship between contract and negligence can be stated in a more general way. The most prominent recent attempt[7] is a formulation of the Privy Council in *Tai Hing Cotton Mill Ltd v Liu Chong Hing Bank Ltd*.[8] In *Tai Hing*, an employee of the plaintiff, a clothing manufacturer, forged cheques, to the value of HK$5.5m, on the company's accounts with the defendant banks. The banks had paid out on the cheques and the plaintiff sued the banks in order to recover the money. The normal rule in banking law is that a forged cheque does not authorise payment, and that except in a small number of restrictively drawn circumstances—basically when the client did something that made the specific fraud more likely—the bank has to restore the money to the client's account.[9] In *Tai Hing*, however, the banks refused to reimburse the plaintiff. They argued for an extension of the exception to the rule so that clients would have to bear the loss in any case in which the client had been negligent. The trial court and the Hong Kong Court of Appeal decided for the bank. The Privy Council (delivering its opinion through Lord Scarman) reversed and confirmed the existing rule, comm-

---

5   See below ch 6 for a full discussion.
6   [1992] Ch 560, see above.
7   'Assumption of responsibility' may be seen as another such attempt.
8   [1986] AC 80, [1985] 2 All ER 947.
9   The banks' main point was that the plaintiff ought to be prevented from enforcing its normal rights by a contractual term that said that the monthly statements from the bank would be deemed to be correct if they were not challenged within a specified time. No challenge had been made because the plaintiff's internal financial control system was weak, hence the accusation of negligence.

enting that banks were in a much better position to absorb the losses involved than clients.[10]

The facts of *Tai Hing* are set out in some detail here only to illustrate that the case concerned not some general principle of contract law but instead a very particular point of banking law. Nevertheless, one of the points that arose in argument was that if the defendant banks could choose, instead of trying to extend the exception to the normal rule of banking law, to counterclaim against the plaintiff in negligence for causing the banks economic loss, the banks would be in a better position. The Privy Council denied that they could do any such thing in the first place. Lord Scarman noted that the trial judge had said:[11]

'[W]here parties are in a contractual relationship, their rights and duties as between themselves cannot be more extensive in tort than they are in contract.'

Lord Scarman agreed. He went on to say:[12]

'Their Lordships do not think that there is anything to the advantage of the law's development in searching for any liability in tort where the parties are in a contractual relationship ... [T]heir Lordships believe it to be correct in principle and necessary for the avoidance of confusion in the law to adhere to the contractual analysis: on principle because it is a relationship in which the parties have, subject to a few exceptions, the right to determine their obligations to each other, and for the avoidance of confusion because different consequences flow according to whether liability arises from contract or tort, eg in the limitation of action ... Their Lordships do not, however, accept that the parties' mutual obligations in tort can be any greater than those to be found expressly or by necessary implication in their contract.'

This passage, although produced in a very special contractual context, became something of an icon for some English judges.[13] It has, however, some inherent limitations. It cannot be literally true that 'the parties' mutual obligations in tort' cannot be 'any greater than those to be found

10 See also *Kepitigalla Rubber Estates Ltd v National Bank of India Ltd* [1909] 2 KB 1010, 1025-26 per Bray J.
11 [1986] AC 80 at p 96.
12 At pp 107ff.
13 See eg *National Bank of Greece SA v Pinios Shipping, The Maira* [1989] 1 All ER 213, *Bank of Nova Scotia v Hellenic Mutual* [1990] 1 QB 818; reversed [1992] 1 AC 233, *Blackpool and Fylde Aero Club v Blackpool Borough Council* [1990] 3 All ER 25, *Scally v Southern Health Board* [1992] 1 AC 294. But see also *Rich v Bishop Rock Marine Co Ltd: The Nicholas H* [1992] 2 Lloyd's Rep 481 at 497-8. *Tai Hing* was not referred to by the Court of Appeal in *The Nicholas H* at all.

expressly or by necessary implication in their contract.' If that were so, some absurd results would follow. Take for example, a person who orders from the defendant goods to be delivered to his house and who is run over by the defendant's carelessly driven delivery van as it enters the plaintiff's drive. No sensible interpretation of the contract between the parties, a straightforward contract of sale and carriage, would include in it an implied obligation on the seller to avoid running over the buyer. And yet no one would deny that the buyer would be able to sue the seller in tort for personal injury.

Some of the cases that attempt to follow *Tai Hing* recognise that there is a problem here. For example in *National Bank of Greece SA v Pinios Shipping, The Maira*[14] the Court of Appeal said:

> 'The position would be different if the contract and tort lay in different fields. Thus, if, to take a simple example, I give my employee a lift home and injure him by my careless driving, then obviously he will not be prevented from recovering from me in tort because of the existence between us of a contract of employment.'

The difficulty with this formulation is that it is not clear what constitutes a 'different field'. Driving an employee home may well be thought to be in a 'different field' from the contract of employment—either because driving and working are different activities, or because being hurt in a car accident is a different sort of injury from being injured at work. But it might also be thought to involve the same kind of injury (personal injury) and be thought of as an incident that occurred during a natural extension of the working day. Similarly, being injured by a delivery van might be thought of as 'in a different field' from being injured by the goods being supplied themselves, but on the other hand, since delivery was part of the deal, it might equally be said that the accident arose out of the very activity envisaged by the contract.

Indeed, another complication is that to apply the 'different field' test requires a judgment to be made about exactly what is envisaged by the contract involved, a judgment that has to be made in the light of the possible complications of the interpretation of the contract and, more particularly, various sorts of implied term.[15]

Finally, it should be noted that in several cases in which the *Tai Hing* doctrine might have been expected to play a part its influence is conspicuous by its absence,[16] and, further, that the courts have declined to extend *Tai Hing* beyond the strict confines of contractual privity as traditionally understood.[17]

14 [1989] 1 All ER 213; on appeal on other grounds [1990] 1 AC 637, [1990] 1 All ER 78.
15 See especially *Bank of Nova Scotia v Hellenic Mutual* [1990] 1 QB 818; revsd [1992] 1 AC 233.
16 Eg *Punjab National Bank v de Boinville* [1992] 1 WLR 1138 and *The Nicholas H* in the Court of Appeal.
17 Eg *The Nicholas H* at first instance.

Negligence vs other torts

Negligence is also accused of undermining the legal position established by other parts of tort law. The objection to the duty of care here is not, of course, that it upsets arrangements voluntarily entered into by the parties—for tort duties generally concern situations which it is difficult for voluntary arrangements to regulate. Nor, to be realistic, can any objection to the duty of care have much to do with the legitimate expect–ations of the defendant, for it is unlikely that many people order their affairs on the basis of the exact details of what they may or may not be liable for in tort. Rather the objection is usually based on the idea that the existing rules in other torts establish a carefully crafted balance of interests and values, a balance that allowing the plaintiff to succeed by having to prove negligence alone would destroy.

In *Smith v Scott*,[18] and *O'Leary v Islington London Borough Council*,[19] for example, plaintiffs found that the law of nuisance did not allow them to sue the landlords of their disruptive and anti-social neighbours.[20] In nuisance cases, it is the occupier, that is the tenant, who is normally liable, not the landlord. And so the aggrieved plaintiffs alleged negligence instead, either on the grounds that the landlords had acted unreasonably in selecting the disruptive neighbours as tenants or that they had neglected their duties as landlords in failing either to get the neighbours to be less disruptive or to evict them. In both cases, the plaintiffs failed.

In *Smith v Scott* Pennycuick V-C said:

> '[T]he law cannot in this respect now be reshaped by a reference to the duty of care. I should add that the relationship of landowner, tenant and neighbour is, in its nature, of the most widespread possible occurrence, and the introduction of the duty of care in this connection would have far-reaching implications in relation to business as well as to residential premises.'

In *O'Leary*, the Court of Appeal confirmed that *Smith v Scott* was rightly decided and told the plaintiff that the only recourse was to the established remedies in nuisance.[1]

One should not conclude from these two cases, however, that the law of nuisance is thought by the courts to have established an unchallengeable set of rules. The situation in *Smith v Scott* and in *O'Leary* was particularly well adapted for the application of the argument that negligence should not intervene because the point that the tort of nuisance establishes its own balance of interests could be reinforced by a contractual point about the relationship of landlord and tenant between the defendant and the disruptive neighbour. This is partly what Pennycuick V-C is referring to when he mentions the 'far-reaching implications' of allowing a negligence

18 [1973] Ch 314, [1972] 3 All ER 645.
19 (1983) 9 HLR 83.
20 See further below ch 11.
1 (1983) 9 HLR 83 at pp 86 and 90.

action against landlords. Such a move would undermine assumptions about the defendant's and the neighbour's respective responsibilities under the tenancy agreement. But in other cases where negligence and nuisance come into contact, such a contractual point may not be available.[2]

Another example of where the duty of care may be excluded because of the disruption that it would cause to the application of another tort, albeit a contested example, is the relationship between negligence and mis–feasance in public office. In *Jones v Department of Employment*[3] the plaintiff complained that an official of the Department had negligently denied the plaintiff's claim to unemployment benefit. The action was dismissed by the Court of Appeal partly on the ground that such an application of negligence would undermine the requirement of the tort of misfeasance in public office that intentional wrongdoing had to be proved against the defendant. On the other hand, negligence actions have long been maintain–able against public officials, even ones where the only damage is economic,[4] a point reaffirmed since *Jones* in *Lonrho v Tebbit*[5] and by the Court of Appeal in *E v Dorset*.[6] The resolution of the tension between these cases forms yet another strand in the tangled web of the liability of public bodies.

It is worth re-emphasising at this point the dangers inherent in pressing too far the argument from the integrity of other legal rules, especially the danger of ossification. It is also apposite to mention that its application was rejected in one of the century's leading cases, namely *Hedley Byrne v Heller*. That decision meant that a famous case, *Derry v Peek*, and the rule requiring fraud for recovery of damages in misrepresentation no longer applied in its full vigour. The argument from the integrity of the rest of tort law should only work in cases in which the court is sure that the existing balance is indeed a carefully worked out compromise of interests, and not, as it often is, a jumble of conflicting rules and one-off judgments that cannot be justified by reference to simple principles.

The clearest recent example of the rejection of the argument from undermining another tort is *Spring v Guardian Assurance*.[7] In *Spring*, the plaintiff was dismissed from his job by the defendant. The defendant considered that the plaintiff had not been competent and had been disloyal. The plaintiff attempted to set up his own business, but because of the regulations relating to the financial services industry, before he could do so, the company whose insurance policies he intended to sell had to call for a reference from the defendant. The defendant supplied a very damning reference, which made it clear that the defendant considered the plaintiff to be not just incompetent but also downright dishonest. In consequence, the plaintiff's new business failed.

2   For further discussion about the relationship betwen negligence and nuisance, see below ch 11.
3   [1989] QB 1.
4   Eg *Ministry of Housing and Local Government v Sharp* [1970] 2 QB 223.
5   [1991] 4 All ER 973 (HC) per Browne-Wilkinson V-C at 980. See also [1992] 4 All ER 280 (CA).
6   See above.
7   [1994] 3 All ER 129.

The judge at first instance found that the plaintiff was not the most brilliant or insightful employee but he was not a rogue. The judge also found that the defendant genuinely believed that the plaintiff was a rogue, but the defendant had reached that conclusion in a careless and unreasonable way.

If the plaintiff had sued the defendant for libel, the defendant would have won, since, in the absence of malice, the defendant would have been able to establish a defence of qualified privilege.[8] Furthermore, the plaintiff would also have failed if he had tried to use the tort of malicious falsehood, since he could not prove that the defendant had knowingly uttered the falsehood.[9] Knowing this, the plaintiff sued instead in negligence. The defendant said that no negligence action should lie because it would undermine the position established by defamation and malicious falsehood.

The trial judge, following the earlier case *Lawton v BOC Transhield*[10] decided in favour of the plaintiff. The Court of Appeal reversed, and in the process purported to overrule *Lawton*. Glidewell LJ said:

'If it were otherwise the defence of qualified privilege in an action for defamation where a reference was given or the necessity for the plaintiff to prove malice in an action for malicious falsehood would be bypassed. In effect, a substantial section of the law regarding these two associated torts would be emasculated.'

The Court of Appeal took its justification for its position from *Bell-Booth v A-G*[11] a decision of the New Zealand Court of Appeal. In *Bell-Booth*, a fascinating case concerning the efficacy of a fertiliser called 'Maxicrop', Cooke P said:

'The common law rules, and their statutory modifications, regarding defamation and injurious falsehood represent compromises gradually worked out by the courts over the years, with some legislative adjustments, between competing values. Personal reputation and freedom to trade on the one hand have to be balanced against freedom to speak or criticise on the other. In the result the present rules are in broad terms well known and reasonably clear ... These evolved compromises may not draw the lines in places that will always be found generally acceptable in the community. Some argue, for instance, for greater media freedom or licence ... It is a controversial area. The important point for present purposes is that the law as to injury to reputation and freedom of speech is a field of its own. To impose the law of negligence upon it by accepting that there may be common law duties of care ... would be to introduce a distorting element.'

---

8 See below ch 2.
9 Ibid.
10 [1987] ICR 7.
11 [1989] 3 NZLR 148.

It should be noted that in *Bell-Booth*, the allegations turned out to be true, and the alleged negligence referred to the timing of their publication, rather than to the fact of their publication. Nevertheless, according to Glidewell LJ the same considerations apply even when the allegations are false.

But the House of Lords reversed the Court of Appeal by a majority of 4-1 and restored the verdict of the trial court. As one might have expected, Lord Keith of Kinkel accepted all of the arguments for the defence, including the argument from the integrity of defamation. But the other law lords decisively rejected that argument, together with all the others put forward by the defendant.[12] Lords Goff, Lowry, Slynn and Woolf all agreed that the preservation of the law of defamation would not be sufficient to deny the plaintiff a remedy for a careless act that had foreseeably and directly harmed the plaintiff. Furthermore, according to the majority, the argument did not work even in its own terms because defamation deals with different issues from negligence. Defamation protects reputation—but a negligent reference can do harm without affecting the plaintiff's reputation, for example by suggesting that the plaintiff suffers from a long-term illness. And the requirement in negligence that the plaintiff has to show that the defendant was at fault is not necessarily less onerous than the complex shifting of burdens in defamation; it is just different.

The importance of *Spring* is not so much that it will mark an end to the court's use of the argument from undermining other torts—*Spring* did not purport to affect cases such as *Jones, Scott* and *O'Leary*. But it does mark an end to the knee-jerk application of the argument to any case which might be thought to be 'covered' by another tort, in the sense that someone who did not know much about the matter might suspect, wrongly, that there would be liability under that other tort. The House of Lords appears to be moving into an era of greater discernment and discrimination in its use of the argument.

Negligence vs procedural law

Another significant area of conflict between negligence law and other legal standards is procedural law. May plaintiffs sue for losses caused negligently in the course of legal proceedings by other parties and their lawyers? In one way, this attempt to extend the scope of the duty of care is merely another example of the conflict between different rules in tort law, since one of the plaintiff's problems is usually that he cannot prove that the defendant acted intentionally and so cannot establish the torts of malicious prosecution or malicious abuse of process.[13] But these cases deserve separate treatment because they bring in an extra element, namely the sanctions against wrongful conduct by a party that are inherent in

12 See below ch 6 for a full discussion.
13 See below.

procedural law itself, the threat that the wrongdoer may have his or her case thrown out, and the threat of having to pay costs. Nevertheless, the underlying argument is the same as that in the other tort cases, namely that the law has produced a delicate balance between the interests of the parties that the introduction of negligence would upset.

An early, but clear, example of negligence not being allowed to undermine the distribution of obligations established by procedural law is *Corbett v Burge, Warren and Ridgley*.[14] In *Corbett* the plaintiff owed the defendant £3 11s 4d. The plaintiff paid the debt but the defendant overlooked the payment and took legal action against the plaintiff. The plaintiff imm—ediately pointed out the defendant's mistake and the defendant apologised, saying that he would tell his solicitors to call off the action. Unfortunately, because of the defendant's carelessness, this never happened. A default judgment was entered against the plaintiff, and reported to the world in the local newspaper. After various adventures, the plaintiff managed to have the judgment against him set aside on appeal eight months later. The plaintiff then sued the defendant in negligence, alleging that the report in the newspaper had permanently affected his business.

Talbot J decided in favour of the defendant. He agreed that there was evidence that the defendant had been careless, but said that carelessness was not enough. He continued:

> 'In the view of the law, an error of this sort was dealt with
> sufficiently when the judge set aside the judgment (as he had done
> in this case) with the power either to grant or to withhold costs.'

It is hardly likely that the plaintiff would have been satisfied with this explanation, since, from his point of view, the granting of costs would be insufficient. He wanted compensation for loss of business that went beyond any sums recoverable as costs.

The point clearly also worried Talbot J, for he added:

> 'There were cases where from a judgment which should not have
> been obtained very serious consequences had resulted, such as the
> arrest of the defendant or execution on his goods. Where such
> results could be put right by damages they had been so remedied.
> But that was not the present case.'

In other words, Talbot J consoled himself that the damage complained about was only financial, and that if anything really important was at stake, such as loss of liberty or physical property, the decision might have gone the other way,[15] or, more likely, the courts might be persuaded to exercise their supervisory jurisdiction over solicitors so that they would be ordered to pay compensation.[16]

14 (1932) 48 TLR 626.
15 *Welsh v Chief Constable of the Merseyside Police* [1993] 1 All ER 692 may be seen as such a case.
16 See eg *Myers v Elman* [1940] AC 282.

But it is difficult to see how this explanation stands up. After all, the difference between seizing some of the property that the plaintiff needs to run his business (eg his stock or his cash till) would hardly be worse than the loss of his customers.

For further explanation we have to wait until *Business Computers v Registrar of Companies*.[17] In *Business Computers*, the defendant procured the winding up of the plaintiff for non-payment of a debt. Unfortunately, the whole affair came about because the defendant had the wrong address for the plaintiff. The plaintiff subsequently got the winding-up order set aside, but found that as a result of the original order, the reputation of his business was in ruins. He sued the defendant for negligence, claiming compensation for the expense of having to re-establish his business under a new name and loss of goodwill.

Scott J dismissed the plaintiff's action. He, like Talbot J 50 years earlier, concluded that:

> 'The safeguards against ineffective service of process ought to be, and I think must be, found in the rules and procedures that govern litigation.'

But, unlike Talbot J, Scott J was prepared to elaborate a little on his reasons. First, although distinguishable on the facts, there is the argument of Lord Pearce in *Rondel v Worsley*[18] that 'to remove this immunity would create a great injury to justice. Without it the honest litigant might not dare to bring an honest claim for fear that if he fails he might be sued for damages.'

Secondly, Scott J simply finds it 'conceptually odd' that a person should have a duty of care towards someone with whom he is entangled in litigation. It sounds strange to Scott J to say that one must be careful of the interests of someone on whom one wants to inflict damage through the courts.

These points are interesting, but it remains to be seen whether they will ultimately convince the highest courts. The first argument seems to prove too much, since there are many useful activities in which one can engage honestly (medicine, law, financial advice) but in which one is held to account for the consequences of carelessness. Why should the inherently dangerous and not particularly socially useful pastime of litigation be given special protection?

And as for the second point, Scott J seems to be relying on a view of litigation that would make it comparable to all-out warfare, in which there were no rights and duties owed by one side to the other because the object of the exercise was the outright annihilation of the enemy. It may be that a more civilised analogy would be with the legal position of those who engage in competitive sports,[19] where one is entitled to play to win, but not at all costs, and the rules of the game are only one factor to be taken into account when judging the reasonableness of the defendant's conduct.

17 [1988] Ch 229.
18 [1969] 1 AC 191 at 268.
19 See above ch 3.

The Court of Appeal gave general support to *Business Computers* in *Al-Kandari v Brown*[20] in which Lord Donaldson MR said that 'a solicitor acting for a party ... in "hostile" litigation ... does not normally owe any duty to his client's opponent.'[1] And Lord Donaldson reinforces his point by saying that otherwise there would be an endless relitigating of disputes as the loser sued the other side's lawyer as a way of re-opening settled issues.

But nevertheless, Lord Donaldson proceeded in *Al-Kandari v Brown* to distinguish *Business Computers* on the somewhat vague grounds that the solicitors in *Al-Kandari* were acting outside their normal responsibilities for contested litigation. The facts of the case were somewhat odd. The solicitors were holding the passports of the children of a couple who were in the middle of an acrimonious divorce. Allegedly the solicitors carelessly allowed their client, the husband, to obtain possession of the passports and to kidnap the children. The Court of Appeal decided that the solicitors could be liable to the wife.

Business Computers was again distinguished in *Welsh v Chief Constable of the Merseyside Police*,[2] in which Tudor Evans J refused to strike out an action by a criminal defendant who had been mistakenly arrested for refusal to surrender to bail because of the incompetence of the Crown Prosecution Service. Tudor Evans J said that *Business Computers* depended on the existence of an appeal procedure that could put the mistake right, plus other procedural safeguards against the making of such mistakes, safe‐guards that did not exist in *Welsh*.

Tudor Evans J's distinction is not quite convincing. True, there are more procedural safeguards against the problem that arose in the *Business Computers* situation than against the *Welsh* problem. But there are no safeguards in the *Business Computers* situation against the type of loss about which the plaintiff complains, namely the irreversible loss of reputation that flows from having a judgment entered against one, a loss which subsequent reversal of the judgment cannot put right. There is no real difference, apart from the type of harm in question, with the plight of the plaintiff in *Welsh*. He was freed when the mistake came to light, but subsequent freedom does not compensate for past imprisonment.

After having been distinguished twice, *Corbett* and *Business Computers* may now have less authority than they did. But they have yet to be overruled and the underlying idea of restricting the use of negligence in cases already governed by procedural law is still attractive to many judges.

Negligence and administrative law

The argument that the law of negligence would upset a balance established by the procedural law applies also to administrative law in general. Public officials are subject to scrutiny by way of judicial review in the exercise of their public functions. Judicial review, like appeal in civil proceedings,

---

20 [1988] QB 665.
1 At 672. See also *Gran Gelato v Richcliff* above.
2 [1993] 1 All ER 692.

operates only to undo the wrong or unlawful decision itself. It does not usually of itself give a right to damages.[3] But victims of illegal action by public officials often want monetary compensation as well as the quashing of the original decision. If, as is often the case, they cannot prove the intentional tort of misfeasance in public office, they turn naturally to negligence. When they do so the defendant public authority is often tempted to say that the only remedy against them is by way of judicial review, not negligence.

A point that ought to be distinguished from the argument about the integrity of judicial review is the argument from the integrity of the administrative process itself, especially the integrity of internal and external appeals structures. This is merely the extension to other governmental procedures of the points made in *Corbett v Burge, Warren and Ridgley* and *Business Computers v Registrar of Companies* about judicial appeal. Cases such as *Calveley v Chief Constable of Merseyside* [4] and *Mills v Winchester Diocesan Board*[5] stand for the proposition that any harm done to the plaintiff by reason of an administrative decision that was corrected through a statutory appeal system cannot be the subject of a negligence action. They rest on the same reasoning as *Business Computers*, and are subject to the same reservations.

In *Jones v Department of Employment*,[6] however, the Court of Appeal took the argument a stage further. The Court of Appeal decided that no claim in negligence would be allowed where a claimant of unemployment benefit had initially been denied benefit because of the carelessness of an official. The error had been corrected later by a higher authority. Instead of saying merely that no negligence claim would be allowed because the plaintiff had succeeded effectively on appeal, the Court of Appeal chose to make what appear to be general remarks about the place of private law rights in cases involving the exercise of public law functions. Glidewell LJ said:[7]

'Misfeasance apart, [a public officer charged with deciding whether certain payments should be made] owes no duty of care in private law. He is susceptible in public law to judicial review or to the right of appeal provided by the statute under which he makes his decision.'

But if correct at all, these remarks must be confined to the very specific circumstances of *Jones*. First, as *Lonrho v Tebbit* demonstrates, there is no general rule that the exercise of public functions that are subject to control by judicial review excludes the possibility of a negligence action. One has to show that the plaintiff has a valid claim according to the ordinary

3   See PP Craig 'Compensation and Public Law' (1980) 96 LQR 413.
4   [1989] AC 1228.
5   [1989] Ch 428.
6   [1989] QB 1.
7   At p 22.

rules of the tort—in other words the fact that the defendant is a public official does not excuse the plaintiff from showing fault, duty, causation and damage in the normal way, but, equally, the defendant's status affords no special privilege. As Dillon LJ said in *Lonrho*:

> 'The imposition of the undertaking on Lonrho in 1981 was of course a matter of public law in the public interest when the M[onopolies and] M[ergers] C[ommission] had considered that the acquisition by Lonrho of the share capital of House of Fraser might be expected to operate against the public interest. The public interest in having the undertaking released when the acquisition by Lonrho of the share capital of House of Fraser was no longer expected to operate against the public interest is considerably more remote and sophisticated. But the private interest of Lonrho in having the undertaking released as soon as it is no longer needed in the public interest is obvious. It does not therefore appall me that it should be suggested that, if the Secretary of State imposes the restrictions of the undertaking on Lonrho in the public interest, the Secretary of State should thereby assume a private law duty to Lonrho to release the undertaking when it is no longer needed and the restriction on Lonrho's freedom to conduct its business no longer has a rationale.'

Even one of the majority in the Court of Appeal in *M v Newham London Borough Council*, Peter Gibson LJ, conceded that:

> 'I accept that an action for damages for negligence differs from the assertion of a public law right by judicial review proceedings and so cannot be struck out as an abuse of the process.'

Peter Gibson LJ then cited *Davy v Spelthorne Borough Council*[8] in which the plaintiff complained that local authority officers had wrongly told him that he could not appeal against a planning enforcement order so that he lost his right. The defendant said that the plaintiff was trying to do by negligence what he ought to do by judicial review, namely to challenge the validity of the enforcement order. But the House of Lords said that a negligence action against a local authority could proceed precisely because the plaintiff was not challenging the validity of the order, but instead sought compensation for the effects of the order, effects that would only occur if the order was treated as valid.

Secondly, it should be noted that *Jones* is about a public official whose job it is to hand out public money in accordance with the rights of citizens who are entitled to receive that money. Quite apart from the floodgates arguments advanced by two Lords Justices in *Jones*,[9] there is a special

8   [1984] AC 262.
9   Slade LJ [1989] QB 1 at 25 'In the context of this legislation, under which there are likely to be many thousands of citizens who rightly or wrongly consider themselves aggrieved,

factor that applies in such a case, namely the nature of the damage. What the defendant lost in *Jones* was, in effect, the timely payment of a debt. This means that the loss is purely economic. Although the way in which the English courts treat economic loss is subject to criticism[10] a rule that ruled out negligence actions in cases in which the government merely fails to pay its debts would be perfectly consistent with the overall approach of English law.

On the other hand, there are a few cases that support the *Jones* approach. In *Cocks v Thanet District Council*[11] for example, the House of Lords struck out a civil action by a homeless person for a declaration that the local authority owed him a duty to provide him with housing under the homeless persons legislation and damages for not having provided him with accomm–odation. *Cocks* proceeds on the basis that civil actions should not be allowed against public authorities in cases in which the authority acts under statutory powers that give it discretion. The idea appears to be that unless the authority is acting beyond its statutory powers, 'ultra vires' in the jargon of administrative law, no civil action is possible. Hence, in order to begin a civil action, one first has to show that the authority acted beyond its powers, something one can only show in an action for judicial review.

Some writers have suggested that *Cocks* is simply wrong.[12] Certainly, the idea that a public body can only commit a breach of a private law duty if it is acting beyond its powers leads to some odd conclusions, for example that if a careless driver of a local authority rubbish truck runs over a pedestrian, for the few seconds when the accident was taking place the authority was acting beyond its powers. But if the authority is acting beyond its powers, it cannot pay the employee for the activity concerned. Does this mean that every time council employees are negligent, they have to pay part of their wages back to the council?

The better view is that *Cocks* is simply irrelevant to most negligence actions against public authorities.[13] In *Cocks* the plaintiff did not allege that the authority had acted unreasonably, only that it had violated a statute. It may not be very often that one can violate a statute reasonably (although it may not be impossible—is it necessarily unreasonable for a fire engine to go through a red light to save the life of a person visibly hanging from a burning building?[14]), but there are many ways in which one can act unreasonably without violating a statute. *Davy* is an example

---

it would seem to me to make no sense to hold that it is open to a disappointed citizen to challenge the decision in this particular manner.' Caulfield LJ at 26 'I conclude that it cannot be right in law that the isolated adjudicating officer should have so many hundreds, possibly thousands, of neighbours to whom the common law says he owes a duty of care when Parliament has provided a whole scheme of legislation to protect the so-called neighbours against a mistake by the adjudicating officer.'.

10 See below ch 6.
11 [1983] 2 AC 286.
12 See *Markesinis and Deakin* p 350.
13 Cf Lord Lowry in *Roy v Kensington and Chelsea Family Practitioner Committee* [1992] 1 AC 624.
14 See above ch 3.

of the latter. The accusation of unreasonable behaviour against the council officers who gave wrong information did not depend on whether they had breached a statutory duty. The same would be true in the case of accidents caused by careless drivers of council rubbish trucks. In *Cocks*, however, the plaintiff's case is only that the defendants broke the statute. If they did violate it, their behaviour was, presumably, unreasonable, but if they did not, it was not unreasonable. Thus, it may be true in *Cocks* that the private law and public law questions were the same, and that judicial review is the best way to find out whether a public authority has violated its statutory duties, but it is not true in most other cases.

Negligence vs company law and other miscellaneous provisions

Finally, mention should be made of a rag-bag of statutes whose purposes, according to the courts, are inconsistent with the imposition of negligence liability.

The cases may be divided into two groups. In the first group, the statute itself is interpreted as providing a comprehensive code covering the situation in question, so that negligence liability is taken as excluded by not being mentioned in the statute. In the second group, the purposes of the statute are used to deny that there should be an exception to another rule excluding liability.

In the first group may be found *Thorne v University of London*,[15] in which negligent marking of university examinations is said to be a matter entirely for the university's visitor; *Yuen Kun Yeu v A-G (Hong Kong)*,[16] in which Lord Keith said that, 'It would be strange that a common law duty of care should be superimposed upon such a statutory framework' about banking regulation; and, in a limited way, *Minories Finance v Arthur Young*,[17] in which Saville J said that whatever the general liability of the Bank of England for careless regulation of the banking system, it could not be held liable in cases in which the Banking Act said that there was no statutory responsibility.

But it should be noted that the argument from statutory integrity only works if the court believes that there is evidence of parliamentary intention to exclude liability. Where such evidence is lacking, and where such an exclusion would not make compelling sense on other grounds, the argument will fail.[18]

In the second category come cases such as *Caparo v Dickman*,[19] *Curran v Northern Ireland Co-ownership Housing Association*[20] and *Peabody v*

---

15 [1966] 2 QB 237.
16 [1988] AC 175.
17 [1989] 2 All ER 105.
18 See *Lonrho v Tebbit* [1991] 4 All ER 973 (HC) in which Browne-Wilkinson V-C rejects an argument based on the integrity of the Fair Trading Act.
19 [1990] 2 AC 605.
20 [1987] AC 718.

Sir Lindsay Parkinson.[1] In *Caparo*, Lord Oliver argued that the requirement for companies to have audited accounts contained in the Companies Act did not bring the plaintiff investors, who had suffered economic loss as the result of investing in a company whose accounts had been carelessly audited by the defendants, within the scope of those who could, exceptionally, sue for their economic loss in tort. Lord Oliver claimed, extremely dubiously as it happens,[2] that the requirement was intended only to help the existing shareholders in their task of holding the directors to account at the company's annual general meeting. The statutory scheme, according to Lord Oliver, did not require auditors to be held liable to investors, and so the case fell to be decided on the general principle of the non-recoverability of economic loss.[3]

Similar points, although perhaps with greater historical justification, were made in *Peabody* (about the purposes of the Public Health Acts) and *Curran* (about the functions of public bodies that make renovation grants).

Plaintiff's interest not protected

The fifth main argument used to deny that a duty of care should exist, that is to deny that the defendant should be liable even though the defendant was at fault, is that the harm to the plaintiff consists of harm for which the law should not give compensation. This section considers the interests about which this point has been raised, including those interests, for example psychological health, which initially were excluded from legal protection but which were later brought back within its scope, albeit with qualifications.

Interests/ types of harm not recognised at all

There are some interests which English law has long refused to recognise at all. The most obvious example is the plaintiff's interest in avoiding emotional distress. For example, in *Lynch v Knight*[4] Lord Wensleydale said:

> 'Mental pain or anxiety the law cannot value, and does not pretend to redress, when the unlawful act complained of causes that alone;
> … For instance, where a daughter is seduced, however deeply the feelings of the parent may be affected by the wicked act of the seducer, the law gives no redress[5].'

1   [1985] AC 210.
2   See above.
3   See below ch 6 for further discussion of this infuriating case.
4   (1861) 9 HL Cas 577 at 598, 11 ER 854 at 863.
5   Social historians might note that Lord Wensleydale says just before this passage that a husband's loss of consortium in his wife differs from a wife's loss of the same in her husband because the husband loses the equivalent of a domestic servant!

Lord Wensleydale recognised that:

> '[W]here a material damage occurs, and is connected with it, it is impossible a jury, in estimating it, should altogether overlook the feelings of the party interested.'

But, he stressed, for emotional upset alone, there is no redress.

The reason for this rule, which is not followed in other jurisdictions[6] is not entirely clear. In *Blake v Midland Rly Co*, for example,[7] Coleridge J said:

> 'If the jury were to proceed to estimate the relative degree of mental anguish of a widow and 12 children from the death of the father of the family, a serious danger might arise of damages being given to the ruin of the defendants.'

But 'the ruin of the defendants' is surely justified if the damage done is itself ruinous. The fact that damages for emotional damage might be large only justifies their exclusion if it is thought that there is something wrong with giving such damages in the first place. The question is why?

The venerable Beven says:[8]

> 'The law will not compensate cannot compensate, for mental suffering in this sense; because it is a not a consequence that in the long run has any objective symptoms, or can be submitted to any reasonable tests.'

In other words, emotional loss is not compensable because it is too subjective. But if subjectivity is a serious objection to a form of damage, it is not clear why any form of 'pain and suffering' should be compensable. And yet courts routinely give specific awards for 'pain and suffering' (and the almost as subjective 'loss of amenity').[9]

The position of English law now is, however, very different from what it was in the late ninteenth century. As we shall see, there is now some liability for causing not emotional distress alone but psychiatric illness. And doubts about the rule against the recoverability of damages for emotional harm recently surfaced in the High Court in *Whitmore v Euroways*.[10] In that case, Comyn J said that the rule was 'harsh'. But instead of declining to

---

6 See eg *Molien v Kaiser Foundation Hospitals* 27 Cal 3d 916, 616 P 2d 813 (1980) and especially *Campbell v Animal Quarantine Station* 63 Haw 587, 632 P 2d 1066 (1981) in which the plaintiffs recovered $1,000 for their anguish on learning (over the telephone) that their dog had died because the defendant had left it in an unventilated van on a very hot day. Admittedly some other jurisdictions have not been impressed by *Campbell*. See *Williams v Baker* 540 A. 2d 449 (1988 DC App).

7 (1852) 21 LJQB 233 at 238.

8 *On Negligence* (4th edn) at p 62.

9 See below ch 13.

10 (1984) Times, 4 May.

apply it, Comyn J drew a somewhat artificial distinction between 'worry, strain and distress' which was not recoverable, and the 'ordinary shock' that people suffer in accidents, which was recoverable as personal injury.[11] Note, however, that the judge's view that 'ordinary shock' is a form of physical injury has interesting consequences. If shock is a form of physical injury it is only so in the sense that it has physical symptoms. But it has to be asked whether the physical symptoms associated with 'shock' (going pale, feeling nauseous and shaky) are really distinguishable from 'emotional' injury. To allow 'ordinary shock' to count as physical injury is in many ways the first step to allowing damages for any emotional harm that has physical manifestations. If this line of argument is taken up in future cases, the rule excluding damages for pure emotional harm will be in danger. For the time being, however, the traditional rule continues.[12]

Furthermore, there has been at least one, albeit limited, statutory intervention in the direction of recognising emotional distress. The Administration of Justice Act 1982 introduced the possibility of a claim by certain of the relatives of a person killed by the fault of the defendant for 'bereavement', in addition to their long-established claims for loss of financial support under the Fatal Accidents Act.[13] Only the spouse of the deceased can claim, or the parents of a minor child, and the amount of the claim is fixed at £7,500. Note that children cannot claim for bereavement on the loss of their parents. The view of the legislature is, apparently, that children should expect to lose their parents but, oddly, that wives should not expect to lose their husbands.

Moving from personal injury to property damage, another form of damage that cannot be recovered at all is damage to a thing that the plaintiff has no right to in the first place. In other words, there can be no action if the plaintiff's allegedly harmed interest was not a legitimate one. It is obvious that one cannot sue for damage to an object that belongs in all senses to someone else. Equally one cannot sue for being robbed of the opportunity to defraud a third party.

Two points need to be made, however, about the need to establish the plaintiff's legitimate right to the property before the plaintiff can sue for damage to that property. First, the principle itself does not resolve the problem of what to do when the plaintiff has a right, for example a contractual right, to acquire the property but does not yet technically own it.[14] It is said that the fact that the plaintiff does not own the property should defeat the plaintiff's right to sue. But this is not so. The plaintiff's

---

11 It is also noteworthy that Comyn J did not require that 'ordinary shock' should be backed up by expert medical evidence, as would have been the case if 'nervous shock' or psychological harm had been in issue. In this respect his judgment is more generous to the plaintiff than that in the similar Californian case *Ochoa v Superior Court of Santa Clara* 39 Cal 3d 159; 703 P 2d 1; 216 Cal Rptr 661 (1985).

12 See eg *Ravenscroft v Rederiaktiebolaget Transatlantic* [1991] 3 All ER 73.

13 See below ch 13-.

14 See eg *The Aliakmon* [1986] AC 785.

right is plainly a legitimate one. No obvious moral outrage arises from compensating the plaintiff for harm to it. Furthermore it is not particularly uncertain what such rights are worth, since they are often tradeable, and so have a market value. It is true that in practice harm to such contractual rights is often not compensated. But this result does not flow automatically from the principle that there can be no liability for damage to interests that the plaintiff does not have, since the plaintiff clearly does have an interest. The reasons for the exclusion of liability in these cases, which are examples of 'pure economic loss', need independent explanation and justification.[15]

Secondly, in many instances the lack of legitimacy of the plaintiff's interest means that the duty point need not arise at all, since the defendant cannot be said to have been at fault in the first place. Take the example of the defendant who is accused of denying the plaintiff the opportunity to defraud a third party. In this case, although the plaintiff may have suffered, the harm to the plaintiff is offset by the benefit to the third party arising from the fact that the defendant's act prevented the fraud.

Another type of interest which English law appears to be very reluctant to protect is privacy. In *Pickering v Liverpool Daily Post*[16] a newspaper obtained and published material relating to the plaintiff's possible release from a secure unit for the mentally ill. The plaintiff had been involved in serious criminal offences and the newspaper was campaigning to prevent his release. The House of Lords found for the defendants, asserting that:

'[P]ublication of unauthorised information about proceedings on a patient's application for discharge to a mental health tribunal, though it may in one sense be adverse to the patient's interest, is incapable of causing him loss or injury of a kind for which the law awards damages.'[17]

Why this is so is unclear.[18] The best argument seems to be that protection of privacy is incompatible with freedom of expression, and especially with freedom of the press, although countries with strong constitutional protection for freedom of expression and freedom of the press such as the USA and Germany do recognise at least some forms of privacy interest as actionable in tort.[19]

---

15 See below ch 6.
16 [1991] 1 All ER 622.
17 Cf also *Kaye v Robertson* [1991] FSR 62.
18 See eg MacCormick 'A Note Upon Privacy' (1973) 89 LQR 23, Markesinis 'Our Patchy Law of Privacy' (1990) 53 MLR 802. See generally the Calcutt Report (1990 Cmnd 1102).
19 Another form of unprotected interest appears to be the ability to extract water from underground sources. See *Chasemore v Richards* (1859) 7 HL Cas 349, *Bradford Corpn v Pickles* [1895] AC 587, *Langbrook Properties v Surrey County Council* [1969] 3 All ER 1424, *Stephens v Anglian Water* [1987] 3 All ER 379, [1987] 1 WLR 1381, 55 P & CR 348, 86 LGR 48, 3 Const LJ 321.

Relational interests—plaintiff's interests partially recognised

There are two forms of harm which were formerly not recognised at all but which now are recognised but only as long as other conditions are fulfilled. The first, economic loss, will only be sketched out here, since an entire chapter is devoted to it below.[1] The other, psychological harm or 'nervous shock', has already been discussed in the chapter on remoteness, but it requires slightly more extensive treatment at this point.

Although the two issues seem at first sight to be very different, there is an underlying similarity between economic loss and nervous shock, a similarity that explains much of the development of the law in these areas. That similarity is that the controversial aspects of both economic loss and nervous shock concern losses that are in essence **relational**.

Relational losses are those that a person suffers as the result of having some relationship with another person who has also suffered loss.

Examples of (not necessarily legally recognised) relational losses include:
* I contract with you that I will spring clean your house for £50. Before I am due to start work, visitors to your house spill food and wine everywhere. I have to work a lot harder than I expected to fulfill my contract with you;
* the parents of small children are injured in an accident. The parents' income is reduced while they are in hospital so that the children's standard of living is also reduced;
* the same children are upset by their parents' distress;
* two brothers live together as one household. One brother works while the other keeps house. The working brother is killed in an accident. The other brother has no income.

Defendants have two central arguments against compensating relational losses. One applies only where the plaintiff's relationship with the third party is voluntary. The other applies equally where the relationship is voluntary or involuntary.

The first argument is that if the plaintiff entered into the relationship with the third party voluntarily, the losses suffered were results of a risk the plaintiff knew that he was taking. Thus, if you set up home with another person and voluntarily rely on their income to keep you, you must have taken the risk that the other person would for some reason no longer be able to maintain you. Similarly, if you enter into a contract to do a job and omit to negotiate the terms of the contract so that the risk of the contract's becoming more onerous would fall on the other party, you cannot complain if it does become more onerous.

The second argument is that, regardless of whether the relationship is voluntary, the plaintiff in a relational loss case is the wrong person to receive the compensation. If A is dependent on B, and B is injured, compensation should go to B, not A, and then B can support A as before. Indeed, to pay compensation direct to A is to put A in a better position

---

1   Ch 6.

than before B was injured, since it removes the disadvantage inherent in the state of dependency itself. That is, it removes the risk that B may have decided no longer to support A anyway.

These two arguments can be deployed against three of the four examples of relational loss given above. In the cleaning case, the plaintiff could have negotiated a different form of contract; in the loss of income due to dependency on a brother case, the relationship appears to be voluntary; and in the children's loss of living standards case, the appropriate plaintiffs are the parents, who, if properly compensated, could restore the living standards of the children.

But the two arguments do not appear to reach the fourth example, that of the emotional distress of the children resulting from the injury to their parents. Of course it would be possible to dismiss such a case on the ground that emotional distress itself is not a recognised form of loss. But note the property of this example that the injury is suffered directly by the plaintiff, and not by the third party, and that the relationship out of which the injury to the plaintiff arises is not a voluntary one. It is in this sort of example that the recovery of relational losses becomes more plausible.

Some relational interests, however, have been recognised for a long time. The most important, again analysed in detail in chapter 6, is the statutory recognition of the interests of dependants in the income of a deceased breadwinner. But this example only serves to confirm the importance of the two fundamental arguments against relational loss. The history of the Fatal Accidents Acts is worth noting.[2] Cases such as *Baker v Bolton*[3] decided that in fatal accident cases all claims, both for emotional damage and for loss of income or living standards, were not recoverable at common law. But from 1843, by statute, a number of relatives of the deceased person have had the right to sue in their own name for their reduced income and living standards. At that time, the law was that in personal injury cases, the plaintiff's right to sue disappeared altogether on death. The result was that the second argument against relational loss did not apply, for the proper plaintiff, the deceased, could not sue. Thus Parliament stepped in not to correct the common law but rather to apply its principles more accurately. The real move away from those principles came only later when, in 1934, a Law Reform (Miscellaneous Provisions) Act allowed the estate of the deceased to sue for personal injury in its own right. From that point on, the position has been that in fatal accidents cases the wrong plaintiffs, the dependants, have been allowed to sue. But they only became the wrong plaintiffs in 1934.[4]

Significantly, however, English law does not recognise, even now, any parallel right for the dependants of victims of non-fatal accidents. The reason is that where the breadwinner is alive, the second argument against relational loss is still as valid as it has ever been. The proper plaintiff is the breadwinner, not the dependants.

2   See Malone 'Genesis of Wrongful Death' 17 Stanford LR 1043 (1965).
3   (1808) 1 Camp 493.
4   Not surprisingly, the relationship between the Fatal Accidents Act and the 1934 Act is the source of some difficulty. See below ch 13.

Nineteenth century common lawyers also conceded, albeit sometimes reluctantly, the existence of a number of relational interests within the family. If the defendant, carelessly or intentionally, injured the plaintiff's wife or servant or child so that the plaintiff lost the valuable services of the wife, servant or child, the plaintiff could sue for damages. These rights, which were restricted by common law decisions in the twenieth century,[5] have now been abolished by statute, along with the husband's right to sue those who interfere with his right of consortium with his wife.[6] But their former existence is worth noting, for they demonstrate that in an era when domestic and employment relations were not considered to be fully voluntary, but to be matters of social obligation, and when the rights of the head of the family in his wife, servants and children were thought to be in the nature of his own property rights, so that the head of the family was always the proper plaintiff, it was possible for relational interests to be recognised which would not be recognised now, even though the arguments for not recognising relational interests remain the same now as they were then.

A more controversial development in the nineteenth century was the recognition of a relational interest in cases in which the defendant enticed the third parties to a breach of contract with the plaintiff.[7] The main argument against liability in such cases is a mirror image of the second fundamental argument against relational loss. It is not so much that the wrong plaintiff is bringing the action so much as the plaintiff is suing the wrong defendant. If A entices B to break a contract with C, C can sue B for breach of contract and receive adequate compensation. Why should C be able to sue A as well? The first fundamental argument comes in as well. Surely breach of contract by B is one of the eventualities that C would have taken into account when entering into the contract and C could have structured the remedy for breach of contract accordingly.

On the other side of the issue, the argument in favour of allowing C to sue A is that the contract remedies against B will often be insufficient to dissuade B from breaching the contract when A is offering a big incentive, so that the protection of C's interest requires a more effective remedy.

The argument for allowing C to sue A is, however, not entirely convincing. In the first place, the argument depends ultimately on a putative fault in the law of contract damages—that contract damages do not usually include the clawing back the extra profit made by the contract breacher as a result of the breach. It would be better to remedy that fault, if it is a fault, directly rather than to attempt to do it indirectly via tort. Secondly, it is not clear that it is right to protect the plaintiff's contractual expectations so absolutely, regardless of the consequences.[8] I promise to sell you my car for £1,000. X comes along and offers £3,000. You would have bought the

---

5   Eg *IRC v Hambrook* [1956] 2 QB 641.
6   See Law Reform (Miscellaneous Provisions) Act 1970 s 5 and Administration of Justice Act 1982 s 2.
7   *Lumley v Gye* (1853) 2 E & B 216; 118 ER 749, *Bowen v Hall* (1881) 6 QBD 333, *Temperton v Russell* [1893] 1 QB 715. See below ch 10 for detailed discussion.
8   See Sayre 'Inducing Breach of Contract' 36 Harv LR 663, 687.

car if I had asked £1,500, but you would have gone no further. And so, if I pay you £500 damages, you are as well off as you would have been had you bought the car for £1,000, for in both cases you would feel £500 better off than you do now. So, if I sell the car to X for £3,000 and give you £500 in damages, I am better off to the tune of £1,500, X is better off, since he would patently rather have the car than £3,000, and you are no worse off. If two people are better off and one is no worse off, it seems reasonable to say that the group as a whole is better off. Even if you would have paid £3,000 for the car, so that I pay you £2,000 damages, I am no worse off, you are no worse off, but X is better off, to the extent that he would have paid more than £3,000 for the car. Why should contract damages aim to prevent people from becoming better off?

The courts' response to these objections to the recognition of this relational interest was to say that the inducement to breach the contract had to be intentional or 'malicious'.[9] The idea is that normal commercial dealings and the ordinary operation of competition should not come within the scope of the tort. But it is unclear exactly how the defendant's intention makes it more reasonable to protect the plaintiff's contractual rights beyond the normal right to sue for breach of contract.

The recognition of a relational interest in cases of inducing a breach of contract was and remains controversial, and may have more to do with the application of the rule to the behaviour of those who organise strikes than with logic and consistency.[10] But there is less controversy when it comes to the final example of the recognition of relational interests, namely cases in which the defendant has induced the plaintiff to enter into an unprofitable relationship with a third party. In such cases, the defendant, either through carelessness or deliberately, deceives the plaintiff into believing that a relationship, usually a contract, into which the plaintiff is thinking about entering will be more profitable for the plaintiff than turns out to be the case. For example, in *Hedley Byrne v Heller*[11] a careless financial reference from the defendant induced the plaintiff to extend credit to a third party. The third party then went bust, leaving the plaintiff with a large loss. In these circumstances, note that, unless the third party is party to the deception, either intentionally or negligently,[12] there will often be very little that the plaintiff can do to get compensation from the third party. The plaintiff is therefore the right plaintiff suing the right defendant. That is, the second fundamental argument against relational loss does not apply. The first fundamental argument does not apply either, since, because of the deception, the plaintiff's actions cannot be said to be fully voluntary.

In consequence, it is not surprising that plaintiffs have often succeeded in claiming for relational losses in these circumstances. First in cases in which the deception was intentional, and then, much later, in cases in

9   See below ch 10.
10   Ibid.
11   [1964] AC 465.
12   See below ch 6.

which the deception is merely careless, tort plaintiffs have succeeded in suing defendants who caused them to enter into unprofitable relationships with third parties.[13]

It is now time to look slightly more closely at the two most controversial forms of relational loss, pure economic loss and 'nervous shock.'

Pure economic loss

Pure economic loss is that form of relational loss in which the whole of the harm to the plaintiff consists of the reduction of his or her tradable wealth.

Note that the above definition asserts that 'pure' economic loss cases are those cases in which the **only** losses suffered by the plaintiff are relational losses. Personal injury cases, therefore, although they usually involve substantial claims for relational losses of various kinds (chiefly loss of earnings and loss of earning capacity) are distinguishable from 'pure' economic loss cases because they involve matters, such as pain and suffering and loss of amenity, that are not relational.[14]

The central example of pure economic loss is where the defendant's faulty conduct reduces the value of a contractual relationship that the plaintiff has with a third party. In *Cattle v Stockton Waterworks*[15] for example, the defendant waterworks company failed properly to install a new water main with the result that the plaintiff contractor was not able to complete works that he had contracted to do for the landowner on whose land the water main had been installed. The plaintiff informed the defendant about the difficulty that he was in, but the defendant did nothing and the plaintiff was 'delayed and put to expense' with the effect that his contract with the landowner became much less profitable. The court decided that, in the absence of an intention to harm, there should be no liability.

Cattle v Stockton is about the reduction in value of an existing contractual relationship between the plaintiff and a third party. But the description 'pure economic loss' applies equally to cases in which the defendant's carelessness results in the plaintiff's entering into a new but unprofitable relationship and to cases in which the defendant's carelessness prevents the plaintiff from forming a new relationship that would have resulted in the plaintiff's being better off. An example of the former is *Smith v Eric Bush*[16] in which it was alleged that the defendant surveyor carelessly failed to spot a serious flaw in a building and overvalued it, so inducing the plaintiff to buy the property for more than it was worth. An example of the latter is *Reid v Rush & Tompkins*[17] in which the plaintiff alleged that the defendant had carelessly failed to persuade him to take out insurance

13 For details see below ch 6.
14 For an extended discussion of these points, and of the difficulties in distinguishing economic loss from property damage, see below, ch 6.
15 (1875) LR 10 QB 453.
16 [1990] 1 AC 831.
17 [1990] 1 WLR 212. See also *Van Oppen v Bedford* [1990] 1 WLR 235.

against personal injury for the period of an overseas assignment, with the result that the plaintiff was very much worse off than he otherwise would have been when he was injured in an accident while out of the country. Another example of economic loss is where the defendant's carelessness results in a failure to form a beneficial relationship between the plaintiff and a third party. For example in *Ross v Caunters*[18] and *White v Jones*[19] lawyers failed to make valid wills on behalf of clients who wanted to benefit the plaintiffs. The loss occurs in this sort of case because the defendant's conduct has permanently robbed the plaintiff of the opportunity to form the profitable relationship with the third party.

It is often said[20] that the different kinds of economic loss case should not be lumped together and treated as one. But although it is true that there are many possible distinctions between the factual situations that arise in economic loss cases, as there are in other types of case, the underlying unity of economic loss should not be ignored. They are all concerned with relational losses and the main lines of the law follow from the application of the ordinary arguments against compensating relational losses.

Thus, the underlying theme of the law is that pure economic loss should not be recoverable unless there are compelling reasons why it should. Recall the words of Lord Oliver in *Murphy*:[1]

'The infliction of physical injury to the person or property of another universally requires to be justified. The causing of economic loss does not.'

But some forms of economic loss are recognised. As mentioned above, the principal form to be recognised is that in which the complaint is that the defendant carelessly induced the plaintiff to enter into an unprofitable relationship with a third party. As explained above, the fundamental arguments against relational loss do not apply to many such cases. The recognition of pure economic loss in *Hedley Byrne* does appear nevertheless to be hedged around with conditions. For example, not only does the plaintiff

---

18 [1980] Ch 297.

19 [1995] 1 All ER 691, [1995] 2 WLR 187.

20 Eg *Markesinis and Deakin* at 86 and 95, based on Feldthusen *Economic Negligence* (2nd ed) (1989: Toronto, Carswell) and Feldthusen 'Economic Loss in the Supreme Court of Canada' (1991) 17 Can Bus LJ 556.

1   See above. See also *The Hua Lien* [1991] 1 Lloyd's Rep 309 at 328 (in cases of physical injury the question of the existence of a duty of care does not arise because it is self-evident and the contrary view is unarguable). But cf Saville LJ in *The Nicholas H* 'In recent years there have been several cases which deal with situations where no physical damage has resulted from the carelessness in question, but where the claimant has sustained financial loss or expense. To my mind the law draws no fundamental difference between such cases and those where there is damage to person or property. Whatever the nature of the loss sustained, the Court approaches the question in the same way.' See ch 6 for how these statements can be reconciled.

have to show that he relied on the defendant's careless misstatement, he also has to show that it was reasonable to do so.[2] But it is possible to exaggerate the importance of these conditions. Reliance, for example, is largely the form that factual causation must take in cases in which the loss is alleged to have been caused by words rather than by physical actions. And the requirement for the reliance to be reasonable is a built-in remoteness point—if the plaintiff was unreasonable in relying on the defendant, there is an argument that the plaintiff should be held solely responsible for his own loss.[3] The central point remains that in these cases, the fact the plaintiff's loss is purely economic is no bar in itself to recovery.

More recently, however, judges have begun to put more substantial barriers in the way of plaintiffs complaining about negligent misstatements.

In *Caparo v Dickman*[4] the plaintiff relied on the published annual accounts of a company in deciding whether to invest more in that company and eventually in deciding whether to launch a takeover bid for the company. The plaintiff launched the bid and it was successful, but the accounts turned out to be wrong, and the plaintiff was left with a large loss. The plaintiff turned on the company's accountants and blamed them for the whole episode. The plaintiff alleged that if the accountants had made proper inquiries, they would have discovered the holes in the company's balance sheet and that in turn would either have prompted the plaintiff not to invest at all, or, at least, would have meant that the price paid for shares in the company would have been much lower.

As in *Hedley Byrne*, in *Caparo* the defendant's faulty behaviour has induced the plaintiff to enter into a deal that turned out to be much less advantageous than the plaintiff expected. The question is, however, whether it is still true that the fundamental arguments against relational losses are inapplicable. In particular, the House of Lords returned to the issue of the appropriate plaintiff. The buyer's losses in *Caparo* arose not just because it entered into contracts to purchase the shares of the former owners of the target company; they also arose because it entered into a relationship with the company itself. While it may be obvious that the sellers of the shares are not appropriate plaintiffs, since they, after all, got the good end of the deal and suffered no loss, the position of the company itself is not so clear. The plaintiff's losses arose, in one sense, because the defendant failed in its duties to the company itself. The correct plaintiff may therefore on this argument be the company itself, and, just as the dependants of a living accident victim have to rely on the victim to sue the defendant and may not themselves sue the defendant directly, so the shareholders of a company that has been let down by the incompetence of its auditors may have to rely on the company to pursue the auditors and may not proceed themselves.

The idea that the company itself is the appropriate plaintiff in cases of wrongdoing about the value of the company is bolstered by its affinity to a

2 See below ch 6 for a detailed discussion of *Hedley Byrne*.
3 The only question here is why unreasonable reliance should amount to a complete defence, rather than as just contributory negligence. See below ch 6.
4 [1990] 2 AC 605.

very similar set of ideas in company law known collectively as the 'rule in *Foss v Harbottle*'.[5] But it is far from completely convincing on the facts of cases such as *Caparo*. The difficulty is that the incompetence of the auditors does not *adversely* affect the value of the company. During the period in which the market price of the company's shares is affected by the auditors' mistake, the market value of the company is above what it ought to be. When the mistakes are revealed, all that happens is that the market value of the company falls back into line with what it ought to have been all along. This cannot form the basis of any complaint by the company. The fact that the company was for a time in a better position to attract new investment than it ought to have been hardly amounts to a loss. In contrast, the buyer of shares during the period in which the market was affected by the auditors' mistake does suffer real harm if it still holds those shares when the truth comes out.

Caparo also raises objections to the idea that the other fundamental argument against relational loss does not apply in negligent misstatement cases. The idea is, remember, that the argument from voluntariness does not apply in negligent misstatement cases because, since he is deceived, the plaintiff cannot be said to enter into the relationship with the third party voluntarily. In *Caparo*, using the language of 'proximity', the House of Lords challenges this line of reasoning. The auditors do not prepare their accounts for the purposes of potential investors, says the court, rather they prepare them for the benefit of the existing shareholders as a whole.[6] As a result, if, as may be the case, the audited public accounts of a company are notoriously unreliable as a guide to the company's value, it is reasonable to suspect that, when a buyer, especially an experienced and established business, omits to take any further steps to establish the true value of the company, the buyer is voluntarily taking the risk on itself that the company will turn out to be worth less than the accounts suggest. The plaintiff has brought the loss on itself. If, on the other hand, as in *Morgan Crucible v Hill Samuel*,[7] the plaintiff specifically asks about financial assessments that have not yet been made public, so that it is signalling that it is not relying solely on the existing published material, the same considerations do not apply. By asking about a specific report the buyer indicates that it is not accepting the risk of relying on the ordinary audit. The fact that it is deceived by the report does now effectively destroy the full voluntariness of the purchase of the shares.

Note, further, that the *Caparo* point on voluntariness is a narrow one. It depends on the unusual factual background that there are good grounds for believing that the plaintiff consciously took the risk of being deceived. The point cannot be any broader than that. It cannot be, for example, that people ought to be treated as having taken the risk of being deceived, whether or not they actually did so, for if that were the law, there could no longer be any tort of deceit, that is of deliberately deceiving people, since there would never be any actionable loss.

---

5   See Farrar, Furey and Hannigan *Farrar's Company Law* (3rd ed) (London; Butterworths, 1991) ch 27.
6   As mentioned above, this is bad history as well as bad law.
7   [1991] Ch 295.

As the next chapter will discuss in detail, the courts concentrate far more on the knowledge and intentions of the defendant than on the position of the plaintiff. The question is often whether the defendant knew that the specific plaintiff would be relying on the information[8] or that the defendant was 'assuming responsibility' for the plaintiff's economic welfare.[9] But that should not divert attention from the importance of whether the plaintiff should be counted as having brought the loss on itself.

Outside negligent misstatement cases, pure economic loss is even less likely to be recoverable. If, for example, the pure economic loss arises because the defendant's carelessness makes an existing contract between the plaintiff and a third party less valuable for the plaintiff, it will not be recoverable. This is the result in *Cattle v Stockton Waterworks*.[10] It is also the result in *The Aliakmon*.[11] In *The Aliakmon* the plaintiff bought some steel springs from an overseas seller. The deal (a 'C and F' contract) was that the seller would arrange for the shipment of the goods, and would recover the cost of shipment from the buyer in the price of the goods. Under such deals, the property rights in the goods do not pass to the buyer until the buyer receives the goods along with their receipt (a bill of lading) as they are unloaded from the ship. But, on the other hand, the seller only promises that the goods are up to standard at the time they are put onto the ship. The result is that the 'risk', that is the risk that the goods may be damaged or lost in transit, lies on the buyer. The buyer thus seems to be in a vulnerable position. The buyer has no contractual rights against the carrier, because all the arrangements are made by the seller. But if anything goes wrong in transit, the buyer has no recourse against the seller, who promised only that the goods are in a fit state when they leave the seller's control. Usually, however, the buyer's position is much better than the contracts themselves appear to provide for. Under the Bills of Lading Act 1855, if the buyer gets property in the goods by means of the handing over of the receipt, the buyer automatically obtains the seller's rights to sue the carrier for any breaches of contract in the way the contract of carriage was performed. Unfortunately, in *The Aliakmon* the plaintiff's financial embarrassment meant that it did not get property in the springs immed-iately on delivery, but for a while, as it tried to collect the money to pay for them, held them on behalf of the seller. This meant that the Bills of Lading Act did not apply.[12] And so when it became clear that because of the careless way in which the springs had been stored on the ship they had gone rusty, the plaintiff found that it had no contractual rights against anyone and decided to try to sue the carrier in negligence instead. The House of Lords ruled in favour of the defendant.

The central point in *The Aliakmon*, as in *Cattle v Stockton*, was that the plaintiff had entered into a particular form of business deal, a C & F contract, when it could have chosen a quite different one in which the risks would

---

8   Eg as in *Morgan Crucible*.

9   Per Lord Goff in *Spring v Guardian Assurance, Henderson v Merrett* and *White v Jones*.

10 See above.

11 [1986] AC 785.

12 This particular aspect of the Act has subsequently been reformed. See Carriage of Goods by Sea Act 1992.

have distributed differently. The relevant risk was admittedly a very obscure one, namely the risk that the legal machinery of the Bills of Lading Act would fail at the same time as it would, exceptionally, be needed by the buyer to get redress from the carrier. And it is true that with such an obscure risk, it is not necessarily believable to say that the buyer took it consciously. Nevertheless, the courts' firm view seems to be that the buyer enters voluntarily into the machinery of the Bills of Lading Act. Furthermore, a rule in favour of liability would throw into question why buyers should bother with the Bills of Lading Act at all—since they would never need it to sue negligent carriers. One can therefore presume that buyers themselves must have expected not to be able to sue carriers directly in negligence and therefore should not complain when the courts rule against them.

The same issues seemed to be at stake in the once celebrated and now notorious case *Junior Books v Veitchi*[13]. In *Junior Books* the plaintiff hired general contractors to build a new building for him. The general contractors in turn were to employ specialists, nominated by the plaintiff, to do the more sensitive parts of the work, including the laying of a special kind of floor. Unfortunately, the floor which was installed was wholly unsatis-factory, to the extent that the building was unusable. The work needed to be redone and the plaintiff was losing money in the meantime on alternative arrangements. For reasons that are not made clear in the report, the plaintiff chose not to pursue a claim against the general contractor for breach of contract, but instead sued the specialist sub-contractor, with whom the plaintiff technically had no contract, in tort.

Junior Books therefore concerns an existing contractual relationship between the plaintiff and the general contractor which the incompetence of the sub-contractor made less valuable for the plaintiff. The plaintiff seems to have a perfectly adequate contractual claim against the general contractor, and the proper complainant against the sub-contractor is the general contractor. Furthermore, the distribution of risk was voluntary on the part of the plaintiff. Both the fundamental arguments against relational losses appear to apply and one might have expected there to be no liability.

Surprisingly, however, the plaintiff won in *Junior Books*. Even Lord Keith of Kinkel, later to become the scourge of plaintiffs in negligence, voted for liability.[14] Not so surprisingly, however, in subsequent cases[15] the

---

13 [1983] 1 AC 520.

14 Lord Keith attempts to distinguish between liability for having supplied a bad floor instead of a good one, for which only contractual remedies are available, and liability for putting the plaintiff to the expense of replacing the floor and dealing with the mess in the meantime, for which there is liability. But it will be seen at once that Lord Keith is leading us up a blind alley. There can be no distinction between his two forms of loss since the latter is merely one way of measuring the former. The cost of replacing the floor and the consequential losses of having to do without it in the meantime represent the loss the plaintiff suffers on the whole deal compared with what he expected to gain. It thus measures the difference between having a bad floor and having a good one. The plaintiff is claiming the amount by which his legitimate expectations have been disappointed, which is just what he would have claimed had the action been for breach of contract.

15 Eg especially *Greater Nottingham Co-operative v Cementation* [1989] QB 71 and *Simaan v Pilkington Glass (No 2)* [1988] QB 758.

courts at all levels backed away from *Junior Books*, declaring that it 'should be confined to its own facts'—a euphemism for 'this case is wrong'.

Very recently, *Junior Books* seems to have made something of a comeback. But it is doing so on the basis that it has more in common with *Hedley Byrne* than previously suspected. *Junior Books* may supposedly be treated as a case of negligent misstatement.[16] The justification apparently under consideration by the House of Lords for this reinterpretation of *Junior Books* arises out of ideas of 'proximity', ideas which will be discussed further below. But whatever the force of those ideas, there is a problem with this approach. *Hedley Byrne* liability rests on the fact that, because of the misrepresentation, the plaintiff does not enter into the losing relationship with the third party voluntarily. It is very difficult to see how it can be said the plaintiff in *Junior Books* was misled about the capabilities of the defendant, especially since employing the defendant was the plaintiff's idea, not the general contractor's idea.

In addition, one should ask what the plaintiff lost as a result of relying on the defendants in *Junior Books*. Unlike in *Hedley Byrne,* the plaintiff was not induced into an unprofitable relationship. The relationship with the general contractor already existed. All that the plaintiff lost was the chance to have chosen a contractor who would have done the job comp—etently, a chance the value of which it is very difficult to estimate and, if anything, especially if the defendants' specialism was rare, likely to be small.

Nervous shock or psychiatric damage

The second type of damage to which the arguments against allowing relational losses are relevant is that of psychiatric illness or 'nervous shock.'

DIRECT NON-RELATIONAL NERVOUS SHOCK

There is a direct, non-relational form of psychiatric injury which is now straightforwardly claimable.

This was not always the case. In *Victorian Railways Comrs v Coultas*[17] the Privy Council said that there should be no liability when the plaintiff suffered a miscarriage following a near miss railway accident. The classical position was, as Mr Cohen QC[18] argued in his successful presentation of the defendant's case, that:

'A mere nervous shock caused by fright of an impending event which never happens results from the constitution and circumstances of

16 See eg *Murphy v Brentwood*.
17 (1888) 13 App Cas 222.
18 At p 222.

the individual, and does not give a cause of action, to support which there must be physical injury.'

That is, such damage is too remote because it flows from the plaintiff's weak personality not from the defendant's fault. The thin skull rule did not, at this stage, help those of feeble character—largely, one suspects, because in those halcyon pre-Freudian days the courts treated one's character as the result of one's own beliefs and conduct, rather than as a ghostly presence caused by events beyond one's control in one's childhood.

Sir Richard Couch in his judgment echoes this remoteness point[19] and adds the extra objection that:[20]

'The difficulty which now often exists in cases of alleged physical injuries of determining whether they were caused by the negligent act would be greatly increased, and a wide field opened for imaginary claims.'

But by 1890, there were courts that were willing to allow actions for purely psychiatric harm. In *Bell v Great Northern Rly Co of Ireland*[1] a railway carriage in which the plaintiff was travelling became decoupled and rolled away downhill. The plaintiff was not physically injured, but she was so badly frightened that she subsequently suffered ill health. The trial judge had told the jury:

'If the injury to her health was, in your opinion, the reasonable and natural consequence of such a great fright, and was actually occasioned thereby, damages for such injury would not be too remote.'

Note that the key issue, as far as the judges at all levels were concerned, was still remoteness. Was the damage too remote? The new answer was as follows:[2]

'It is to be observed: (1) that the negligence is a cause of the injury, at least in the sense of a *causa sine qua non*; (2) that no intervening independent cause of the injury is suggested; (3) that jurors, having regard to their experience of life, may hold fright to be a natural and reasonable consequence of such negligence as occurred in the present case.

If, then, such bodily injury as we have here, may be a natural consequence of fright, the chain of reasoning is complete. But medical evidence here is such that the jury might from it reasonably arrive at the conclusion that the injury, similar to that which actually resulted to the plaintiff from the fright, might reasonably

19 At p 225.
20 At p 226.
1   (1890) 26 LR Ir 428.
2   At p 438.

have resulted to any person who had been placed in a similar position. It has not been suggested that there is anything special in the nervous organisation of the plaintiff which might render the effect of the negligence or fright upon her different in character from that which it would have produced in any other individual.'

That is, nothing particularly odd has occurred, so that there is no way of saying that the chain of causation has been broken. In another key passage, the court added[3]

'Again, it is admitted that, as the negligence caused fright, if the fright contemporaneously caused physical injury, the damage would not be too remote. The distinction insisted upon is one of time only. The proposition is that, although, if an act of negligence produces such an effect upon particular structures of the body as at the moment to afford palpable evidence of physical injury, the relation of proximate cause and effect exists between such negligence and the injury, yet such relation *cannot* in law exist in the case of a similar act producing upon the same structure an effect which, at a subsequent time—say a week, fortnight, or a month—must result, without any intervening cause, in the same physical injury. As well might it be said that a death caused by poison is not to be attributed to the person who administered it because the mortal effect is not produced contemporaneously with its administration.'

The clearest statement of principle appears in the judgment of Murphy J:[4]

'The only questions to be considered, in my opinion, are: Was the health or capacity of the plaintiff for the discharge of her duties and enjoyment of life affected by what occurred to her whilst in the carriage? next, Was this caused by the negligence of the defendants?'

The approach in *Bell* received a degree of support in the celebrated case *Dulieu v White*.[5] The defendant ran his van and horses into a pub. The plaintiff was not struck but was badly frightened and she suffered a miscarriage. The defendant said that there could be no liability in the absence of a physical impact. But the court found for the plaintiff. There was no need for physical impact if the plaintiff suffered because of a reasonable fear for her own safety. The older argument that the law should recognise no form of purely psychological injury because to accept claims for harm caused by mental processes would be to open the courts up to fraudulent claims was met by a firm rebuke:

3   At pp 438-39.
4   At p 443.
5   [1901] 2 KB 669.

'Such a course involves the denial of redress in meritorious cases, and it necessarily implies a certain degree of distrust, which I do not share, in the capacity of legal tribunals to get at the truth in this class of claim.'[6]

The only limitation is that there must be some physical manifestation of the mental state, otherwise the damage would be impossible to measure:[7]

'The use of the epithet "mental" requires caution, in view of the undoubted rule that mere mental pain unaccompanied by any injury to the person cannot sustain an action of this kind.

"Fear", as Sir Frederick Pollock has stated, "taken alone falls short of being actual damage not because it is a remote or unlikely consequence, but because it can only be measured by its physical effects".'[8]

But there is a problem with *Dulieu v White*, a problem that has dogged English law on this topic ever since. The two judges agreed on the result, but differed radically on how to reach it. Kennedy J followed the remoteness approach of *Bell*, saying that there could be liability as long as the damage came from 'a natural and continuous sequence uninterruptedly connecting the breach of duty with the damage as cause and effect.'[9] As long as the mental anguish resulted in some kind of physical illness, there was no problem. The link from the mental (the shock) to the physical (the miscarriage and other ill health) was not a puzzling one for the courts and did not involve any intervening causes that might break the chain.

Phillimore J, on the hand, said that the problem was not one of remoteness but of 'duty'[10] by which Phillimore J seemed to mean that the law should not accept claims for psychological harm because such harm was too trivial for the law to bother with and anyway was simply the result of the plaintiff's own choice:

'There are dangers sometimes from the traffic at Charing Cross which might frighten not only an inexperienced and elderly countrywoman, but an experienced and cool citizen...'

Then citing Bramwell B's notorious anti-plaintiff judgment in *Holmes v Mather*,[11] Phillimore J adds:

6   Kennedy J at p 681.
7   At p 673.
8   This is still the law. See Lord Ackner in *Alcock v Chief Constable of South Yorkshire* below.
9   [1901] 2 KB 669 at p 671.
10 At p 685 'The difficulty in these cases is to my mind not one as to the remoteness of the damage, but as to the uncertainty of there being any duty.' Later in *Bourhill v Young* Lord Wright adds to the confusion by claiming that Phillimore J was referring to breach of duty or fault.
11 (1875) LR 10 Exch 261.

'It may be (I do not say that it is so) that a person venturing into the streets takes his chances of the terrors. If not fit for the streets at hours of crowded traffic, he or she should not go there. But if a person being so unfit ... stays at home, he or she may well have a right to personal safety ... and wilfully or negligently to invade this right and so induce physical damage may give an action.'[12]

According to Phillimore J, the plaintiff wins in *Dulieu v White* only because she was indoors when the accident happened.

Kennedy J's contrasting opinion on the duty question could not be more clear:[13]

'In regard to the existence of the duty here, there can, I think, be no question. The driver of a van and horses in a highway owes a duty to use reasonable and proper care and skill so as not to injure either persons lawfully using the highway, or property adjoining the highway, or persons who, like the plaintiff, are lawfully occupying that property.'

As for Phillimore J's point that people who go out on the streets should expect to be frightened, Kennedy J replies, accurately, that it would undermine the whole of the law of negligence, which assumes that people do not consent to the risk of being injured merely by venturing out into the presence of others.

This confusion about the reasoning lying behind the acceptance of direct non-relational psychological harm persists still, although in various forms. There are three basic approaches:
(1)   the question is largely one of directness, so that as long as there is no intervening cause, there is no difficulty with liability—subject perhaps to the need for clear evidence of loss, so excluding 'pure' mental anguish; or
(2)   the question is one of 'foreseeability', so that there is liability as long as the 'type' of harm was foreseeable and the victim was a foreseeable victim of the foreseeable 'type'; or
(3)   the question is one of 'duty' in the sense that much of the time, this is a type of harm that reasonable people do not complain about but which should be recoverable in special circumstances.

Cases such as *Bourhill v Young*,[14] tended to shift about between all three views, with the foreseeability view and the duty view more prominent than the directness view. But, more recently, with a further increase in

12   Cf Lord Oliver in *Alcock v Chief Constable of South Yorkshire*: 'Grief, sorrow, deprivation and the necessity for crying for loved ones who have suffered injury or misfortune must, I think, be considered as ordinary and inevitable incidents of life which, regardless of individual susceptibilities, must be sustained without compensation ... [T]o extend liability to cover injury in such cases would be to extend the law in a direction for which there is no pressing policy need and in which there is no logical stopping point.'.
13   [1901] 2 KB 669 at 671-72.
14   [1943] AC 92.

confidence in the genuine existence of conditions such as post-traumatic stress syndrome, the tendency has been towards the directness and foreseeability views, so integrating this form of loss with ordinary personal injury. On the other hand, suspicion of the genuineness of psychiatric illness survives in the remoteness rules for nervous shock cases, where the rule is that the harm must have been such that it would have affected 'a person of normal disposition and phlegm'[15] or someone 'of a normally robust constitution',[16] instead of the ordinary rule that the foreseeability of any weakness in the plaintiff is irrelevant.

In the light of these considerations we now come to *Attia v British Gas*[17] British Gas were to install central heating at the plaintiff's house. When she returned home at around 4pm she found her house on fire. The fire had been caused by carelessness of British Gas employees.

The plaintiff suffered no physical injury. Instead she claimed that she had developed a psychiatric illness as a consequence of the shock of seeing her house burning down. The case came before the Court of Appeal on a preliminary point of law, so that it was assumed for the purpose of argument that there was a causal link between the fire and the psychiatric illness. The defence was that psychiatric illness was not foreseeable in these circumstances or even if was, the type of injury should be unrecoverable.

Dillon LJ said that it was a straightforward case. There was no reason why people should not be able to claim for psychiatric injury if that was what they could show that they suffered from. The defendants knew of the plaintiff, so she was an obvious victim of any carelessness at the house. The only question was whether the psychiatric illness was a foreseeable type of harm, which is a question of fact for the eventual trial.

Bingham LJ also follows *Bourhill* in saying that there has to be a foreseeable plaintiff before duty is established, but goes on to say that where the duty is established, as here, it is better, 'where a duty of care undeniably exists, to treat the question as one of remoteness,' by which he means *Wagon Mound* foreseeability of the type of harm rather than directness.

The significance of *Attia* is that, although as far as straight non-relational psychological injury is concerned, there is no problem about the recognition of the plaintiff's form of loss. The only question is remoteness, here in its loose *Wagon Mound* guise of foreseeability of the type of harm and of the plaintiff, but, no doubt, also, in the right case, in its more traditional directness guise.

Equally, in *Whitmore v Euroways Express Coaches*,[18] in which the plaintiff suffers shock from her own experiences (as well as from those of her husband) in a coach crash, Comyn J treats the shock simply as part of her injuries, with no distinction between shock and other personal injuries. Thus, after 100 years, the courts are coming round to the position of principle taken by Murphy J in *Bell*.

---

15 *Brice v Brown* [1984] 1 All ER 997 at 1006.
16 At p 1007. For full discussion see above ch 4.
17 [1988] QB 304.
18 (1984) Times, 4 May. Aka *Whitmore v Auto Transportes Julia* LEXIS transcript 4 May 1984.

RELATIONAL NERVOUS SHOCK

The real problems in nervous shock cases, however, come when the plaintiff suffers psychiatric illness not because of his or her direct experiences, but because of fears for the safety of others, often close relatives. For example, the mother of a child may hear about an accident in which her child has been badly injured, or a wife may see a disaster unfold on live TV when she knows that her husband is at the scene. These cases are relational because the plaintiff's suffering arises out of the relationship or emotional ties that they have with another person. Plainly one of the arguments against relational loss, that the plaintiff is the wrong plaintiff, does not apply, since the plaintiff suffers damage unique to her. And the defendant is plainly the right defendant, since it would be absurd to sue one's spouse for an illness caused by the ties of emotion and affection that one shares. But there is a problem in some cases with the argument from voluntariness. The plaintiff has made him- or herself more vulnerable to this kind of psychiatric illness by entering into such relationships. If such relationships make it more likely that this sort of illness will occur, and so make it easier to prove fault against the defendant, they also increase the scope for saying that the plaintiff is responsible for the harm that he or she suffers. The argument for the plaintiff, however, is that many relationships, especially family relationships, are not in any full sense voluntary, for they arise not from choice but from a mixture of nature and duty.

There are a number of cases that are treated as non-relational nervous shock even though at first sight they look relational. In *Dooley v Cammell Laird*[19] the plaintiff was a crane driver the load of whose crane fell, because of carelessness attributable to the defendant, into the hold of a ship and towards the plaintiff's workmates. The plaintiff's shock led to a psychiatric illness. He sued the defendant and won. The case can be read as a relational case—the plaintiff was shocked because of the danger to his workmates. But in fact the judge was right to treat it as a straightforward non-relational case, for the shock would have been the same even if the plaintiff had not known the men in the hold. The horror of the situation (plus possibly the surge of guilt that the plaintiff would feel) were sufficient explanation of the sequence of events. As Parker LJ explained in the Court of Appeal in *Alcock v Chief Constable of South Yorkshire,*[20] Dooley was entitled to win because he was an employee and was 'directly involved' in the accident.

Similarly, in *Chadwick v British Railways*[1] the plaintiff developed a psychiatric illness after taking part in rescuing victims of a horrific train accident for which the defendants were responsible. Again, the case may appear to be relational—there was no danger to the plaintiff himself—but again the court was probably right to treat the case as non-relational, for

19 [1951] 1 Lloyd's Rep 271. See also *Carlin v Helical Bar* (1970) 9 KIR 154.
20 [1992] 1 AC 310 at 351ff.
1 [1967] 1 WLR 912.

the plaintiff's illness was fully explicable by the enormity of the scene before him. His relationship with any of the victims was not relevant.[2]

The first case to allow the plaintiff to claim for a clearly relational psychiatric loss was *Hambrook v Stokes*.[3] The defendant carelessly allowed his unattended lorry to run off down a steep street. Mrs Hambrook saw the lorry and was afraid for her children whom she knew to be in the vicinity, but who were just out of her sight. She was told by another bystander that a child who might well have been one of hers had been injured by the lorry. The shock of the news eventually killed her. The Court of Appeal found the defendant liable.

Much of the discussion in the case is about whether *Dulieu v White*'s restriction that there had to be danger to the plaintiff personally should stand. The majority thought that it should not, largely, as Atkin LJ said, because it seems odd to allow damages to someone who thinks only about their own safety but to disallow damages to someone who courageously thinks about the safety of others. For this reason, Atkin LJ went much further than most judges in such cases have been prepared to go in envisaging the kinds of relationship that would give rise to liability:

'The cause of action ... appears to be created by breach of the ordinary duty to take reasonable care to avoid inflicting personal injuries, followed by damage, even though the type of damage may be unexpected—namely, shock ... but I confess that upon this view of the case I should find it difficult to explain why the duty was confined to the case of parent or guardian and child, and did not extend to other relations of life also involving intimate associations; and why it did not eventually extend to bystanders.'

But significantly Sargant LJ in his dissent said:

'It seems to me that once the requirement is relaxed that the shock is to be one caused by the plaintiff's apprehension of damage to himself, the defendant is exposed to liability for a consequence which is only reached by a new and quite unusual link in the chain of causation, and which cannot properly be held to have been within his ordinary and reasonable expectation. And the extent of this extra liability is necessarily both wide and indefinite, in as much as it may vary with the precise degree of connection between the person injured and the plaintiff, and also, perhaps, with the

2   It is submitted that these cases show the right way to treat cases in which people witness accidents as 'bystanders'. The plaintiffs have to be 'foreseeable' in the *Bourhill v Young* sense, but that should be a judgment for each case. As Lord Keith said in *Alcock*, 'The case of a bystander unconnected with the victims of an accident is difficult. Psychiatric injury to him would not ordinarily, in my view, be within the range of reasonable foreseeability, but could not perhaps be entirely excluded from it if the circumstances of a catastrophe occurring very close to him were particularly horrific.'.

3   [1925] 1 KB 141.

circumstances attending the realisation by the plaintiff of actual or apprehended injury to the third person.'

Much subsequent comment has concentrated on the second part of Sargant LJ's comment, the typical 'floodgates' fear that there might be 'wide and indefinite' liability. But the first part of Sargant LJ's comment is more important. The real objection to Atkin LJ's proposal to extend the liability to other relations and even to bystanders is that it involves, according to Sargant LJ, 'a new and quite unusual link in the chain of causation'. This link is that people will show deep concern for the welfare of strangers to the extent that they suffer mental illness if the strangers are injured.

Admittedly, as formulated in *Hambrook v Stokes*, Atkin LJ's test would not reach many cases since the majority agreed that there should only be liability where the plaintiff actually saw or heard the horrendous events with their own unaided senses.[4] The effect of this restriction is that it excludes cases which are purely relational, in which the cause of the mental illness is simply the knowledge that another person has been injured. The 'sight and sound' requirement means that in every case in which there is liability, an element remains of shock to the plaintiff which may affect them directly without their having to reflect on their relationship with the victim. But Sargant LJ's concern about 'new and quite unusual' links remains important, and it lies behind much of the debate in more recent cases.

The most important recent case is *Alcock v Chief Constable of South Yorkshire*,[5] the Hillsborough disaster case. Several relatives and friends of the people who, allegedly because of negligence by the police, were crushed and killed at the Hillsborough football stadium in Sheffield, suffered psychiatric illnesses as a result of their experiences. Some had been in other parts of the stadium and had witnessed the events. Others had seen the disaster on live television. Others still had travelled to the scene to look for their relatives only to find them dead or seriously injured. And some had suffered solely from being told the news.

The House of Lords contrived to find against all of the plaintiffs. Previous cases had indicated that parents, children or spouses who see or hear the accident itself or come across its aftermath can all recover damages.[6] In *Alcock*, brothers-in-law, grandparents, uncles and friends were told that their relationships with the deceased or injured were too distant. A brother who was present in another part of the stadium was told that he also lost because he had offered no proof that he had a close relationship with his brother who was a victim of the disaster, which was not surprising since until the Lords' judgment in *Alcock* no one had ever suspected that such proof was necessary.

---

4   Later extended to include the 'aftermath' of the accident. See *McLoughlin v O'Brian* [1983] 1 AC 410.
5   [1992] 1 AC 310.
6   *McLoughlin v O'Brian* [1983] 1 AC 410.

The defence contended in each case not that mental illness was not a recognised form of harm, or even that mental illness arising out of harm to someone with whom one had a close relationship was not a recognised form of harm. Instead, the defendant claimed that in each case the damage was too remote. It is here, however, that confusion set in. The real basis of these defences is the original *Coultas* view that if people suffer mental illness as the result of witnessing or hearing about injuries to people with whom most people do not form deep relationships, there must be some suspicion that the illness is the result of their own pathological character and their own choice to enter into unusual relationships. This is also what lies behind the widely accepted view that the thin skull rule does not apply in nervous shock cases, but instead the plaintiff has to prove that in the circumstances some form of mental illness (though not necessarily the exact form suffered by the plaintiff) would have overtaken an ordinarily strong nerved person.[7] But the House of Lords in *Alcock* failed to make clear the basis of these remoteness and relational defences and instead concentrated on whether there was 'foreseeability.'

Even Lord Keith,[8] although pointing out that foreseeability of the type of harm could not be the whole story, said that:

'As regards the class of persons to whom a duty may be owed ... I think it sufficient that reasonable foreseeability should be the guide. I would not seek to limit the class by reference to particular relationships such as husband and wife or parent and child.'

The class might even include friendships and would most likely extend to engaged couples, for:

'It is common knowledge that such ties exist, and reasonably foreseeable that those bound by them may in certain circumstances be at real risk of psychiatric illness if the loved one is injured or put in peril.'

Lord Keith's escape route into his normal conclusion that there should be no liability is, however, that:

'The closeness of the tie would, however, require to proved by a plaintiff, though no doubt being capable of being presumed in appropriate cases.'

In addition, he would maintain the sight, sound and aftermath rules, so ruling out cases in which the plaintiff merely hears the news of the accident from a third party even to the extent of ruling out claims from people who witness the accident on live TV, unless, as is unlikely, the TV shows close-ups of the close relative concerned. The sight, sound and aftermath rules

---

7   *Bourhill v Young* [1943] AC 92, *Brice v Brown* [1984] 1 All ER 997.
8   [1992] 1 AC 310 at 396-97.

uphold the result of *McLoughlin v O'Brian*, in which a wife and mother recovered for psychiatric illness that she suffered after coming across her husband and children in a very badly injured state in the hospital and after having been told that her daughter was dead. But the rule against recovery when the plaintiff did not see the results of the accident but simply heard about them from a third party, and the extension of that rule even to live TV means that *Alcock* opts for the more restrictive view of those questions than those canvassed, albeit obiter, in *McLoughlin*.

Lord Keith also maintains that there can only be liability for recognised psychiatric illnesses that result from a sudden shock, not from long term stress. This particular restriction has drawn protests both from academics and judges. The case against the shock requirement, and, incidentally against the sight and sound requirement, is well summed up by Deane J in *Jaensch v Coffey*:[9]

> '[T]he most important explanation of nervous shock resulting from injury to another is the existence of a close, constructive and loving relationship with that person (a "close relative") and that it is largely immaterial whether the close relative is at the scene of the accident or how he or she learns of it: see for example, DJ Leibson, "Recovery of Damages for Emotional Distress Caused by Physical Injury to Another" (1976-77) 15 Journal of Family Law 163 at 196; that genuine nervous shock can be caused to a person caught up in a disaster in which neither that person or any one in a pre-existing relationship with him or her is physically injured or threatened: see for example, Raphael, Singh and Bradbury "Disaster: The Helper's Perspective" (1980) 2 Medical Journal of Australia 445-447; that there is no necessary correlation between psychiatric illness caused by nervous shock and the severity of the "shock": see, for example, Parker "Accident Litigant with Neurotic Systems" (1977) 2 Medical Journal of Australia, but cf NT Sidley "Proximate Cause and Traumatic Neurosis" (1983) 11 Bulletin of the American Academy of Psychiatry and the Law 197 at 200-202 ...
>
> There is also strong expert support for the proposition that there is a real—and foreseeable—risk that psychiatric illness may result from mental stress during the period consequent upon bereavement, particularly conjugal bereavement, or during a period of constant association and care of a badly injured spouse or other close relative independent of any shock sustained at the time of the actual death or injury.'

9   (1984) 58 ALJR 426 at 448. See also Comyn J in *Whitmore*: 'I have got to be careful here, because it is well established in law that one cannot recover for distress, worry or strain of having, as the result of an accident, an injured husband or wife or child. Whatever my own personal views about the law on that are, that is the law. The distress of having day-by-day a badly injured husband or child is not a subject of claim by the wife. In the here cruel phrase, it is 'one of those things', one of those incidents of life with which one has to put up. So a sharp line has to be drawn between shock, on the one hand, and distress, worry, strain and so forth, on the other.'.

But the 'shock' requirement remains in place, at least in relational cases.[10]

The other judges in *Alcock* follow a method similar to that of Lord Keith. Foreseeability is important but so are the rules that exclude liability except for 'shocks' that insist on sight, sound or aftermath, and that insist on a physical manifestation of the psychological condition. But none of these judgments even approaches an explanation why there should be such restrictions on the ordinary principles of negligence. Even where the House of Lords says that it is following a pure foreseeability approach, in the question of which kinds of relationship qualify for protection, there are elements in their reasoning that do not fit. Why should, for example, one brother have to prove that he was fond of another brother? It makes no difference to the foreseeability of the possibility that a brother may become ill on learning of the death of a sibling that in the particular case the particular brother was fond of the particular sibling. Proof or otherwise of the strength of any particular relationship is irrelevant to how the situation would have looked to a reasonable person in the position of the defendant before the accident.

The point is that proof of the relationship has nothing at all to do with foreseeability but concerns instead factual causation (did the relationship make any difference?) and in turn, fault (would a reasonable person have taken such a risk into account?) and remoteness (was the overwhelmingly more important cause the relationship, which was the plaintiff's doing, rather than the accident?). Similarly the sight, sound and aftermath restrictions are matters of causation and fault.

The only difference between the *Alcock* cases and cases in which people suffer psychiatric illnesses because of what they experience happening to themselves is that the relationship with the relative brings an 'extra and quite unusual' link that Sargant LJ referred to in *Hambrook*. It would be better if the courts acknowledged this, and then asked the admittedly very difficult questions about whether people should have to accept the results of forming relationships with others, and if not, because some relationships are not voluntary, which relationships should be so treated and which not.

Absolute public benefit

An argument against the imposition of a duty of care that is quite often used but rarely given a name is that the judgment of fault in the case involves on the cost of the precaution side of the balance a value or interest that is so important that it is inevitable that the defendant will win. For example in *Hughes v National Union of Mineworkers*[11] the plaintiff, a junior

10 Whether it applies in non-relational cases—ie whether the plaintiff can claim extra pain and suffering because of the strain of living with their own mental illness, is quite a different question.

11 [1991] 4 All ER 278.

police officer, complained that the orders his superiors gave him during the policing of violent disorder during a miners' strike caused him to be injured. The plaintiff failed. Apart from the usual 'defensive policing' consideration, it is clear that the public interest in order is more important than the interest of an individual police officer, who is, after all a volunteer not a conscript, in his personal safety. The public benefit of policing riots will always outweigh the interests of particular police officers, so that it will never be deemed to be careless for a senior officer to order his officers to take risks with their personal safety. Thus, in such cases there will always be judgment for the defendant and the court may as well say that there is no duty of care.

But such claims of absolute public benefit should always attract a degree of scepticism. There can be no greater value than human life. But every time someone drives a car the risk of death increases. Nevertheless, the courts do not say that the very act of driving a car is always faulty.

If claims about absolute public benefit that would favour the plaintiff are difficult to make, so should similar claims made by the defence. In particular, the court must ask itself whether all the plausibly effective precautions the defendant could have taken would indeed have caused serious harm to the value or interest concerned.

One case in which a defence claim of absolute benefit failed was *Hedley Byrne v Heller*. One of the defendant's arguments was that every such case involved balancing the harm to the plaintiff against the defendant's right to free speech. But the claim was rejected. The right to free speech is already not absolute—for example many defamatory and dishonest statements already attract the attention of tort law and criminal law. And a duty to take reasonable care with the accuracy of one's statements is not such a burden as to inhibit public debate. The situation might be different if the tort expanded from causing commercial harm into making tortious any words that caused someone offence. From a purely utilitarian point of view, if someone is offended they have suffered some pain. But if the pain of pure offence were to be recognised as actionable the effect on freedom of speech would be immense. Hence offence alone is not actionable.

Defendant immunity

In one sense, all arguments that the defendant owes no duty of care are immunity arguments. They all result in the defendant's acquiring an immunity from suit in the case at hand and in some category, with great or small of future cases. But an immunity argument in the narrow sense is one that says that just because of who the defendant is, or the defendant's social role or status, no-one may sue him or her or it.

There used to be in the various common law jurisdictions a very long list of people entitled to such immunities. They included spouses when suing one another, passengers in vehicles and anyone involved in the law. The list is much shorter now. Solicitors, for example, lost their immunity in *Ross v Caunters*. Claims for new immunities are now treated with suspicion. In *IRC v Hoogstraten*[12] a claim by a sequestrator to immunity failed. In general, arbitrators still have immunity but a claim by a surveyor brought in to settle a rent review to be treated as an arbitrator has been summarily rejected.[13]

On the other hand, the Crown Prosecution Service may still have a straightforward immunity, at least according to some obiter remarks of Steyn LJ in *Elguzouli-Daf v Metropolitan Police Comr*[13a]. The Court of Appeal denied a negligence action to the victim of CPS carelessness on grounds of perverse incentives and the adequacy of other remedies, and it took care not to criticise the results of an earlier case[13b] that had refused to recognise that the CPS had immunity from negligence, but Steyn LJ said that if necessary he would have been prepared to hold that the CPS did have such immunity.

The most general claims to immunity have been those of the state, but since the Crown Proceedings Act 1947 in theory, and even before that in practice, there has been no general immunity. The state has attempted in various ways to recover its immunities in particular cases, especially by using the allocation of public resources argument, but no general return is on the cards. In *Lonrho v Tebbit* the Department of Trade and Industry attempted to establish that anything it did in regulating companies was a matter of state policy and therefore not justiciable. Both Browne-Wilkinson VC and the Court of Appeal rejected the claim, although they did accept that in some cases the state could claim a limited immunity along the lines of the 'policy/operational' distinction discussed above.

The hard core of general immunity that remains is the courts themselves. Judges still have immunity in England,[14] as do advocates for their activities in court and the immediate preparation thereof.[15] The alleged reason for this immunity is that it prevents the costly relitigation of disputes that the aggrieved plaintiff has lost and for the loss of which he now blames the lawyer or judge. This reasoning is extraordinarily unconvincing in a legal system in which the loser bears the winner's costs. The judge and advocates would be bound only by the standards of reasonable care,[16] which must include the possibility of losing the case. Anyone suing them, and thus risking having to pay the other side's legal costs, must have a very good case. And if they have, if the lawyers or judge have been grossly incompetent even to satisfy the *Bolam* test, why should they not be liable?

---

12 [1985] QB 1077.
13 [1985] 2 All ER 161, 274 Estates Gazette 143, [1985] 1 EGLR 86.
13a [1995] 1 All ER 833.
13b *Welsh v Chief Constable of Merseyside* [1993] 1 All ER 692.
14 *Sirros v Moore* [1975] QB 118. Note that they do not have general immunities in other European legal systems.
15 *Rondel v Worsley* [1969] 1 AC 191, *Saif Ali v Sydney Mitchell* [1980] AC 198.
16 See *Mathew v Maughold Life* (1988) Times, 19 February for how low a standard of care that may be for barristers. Apparently, if what the barrister says is incomprehensible, it is the fault of the solicitor. Cf *Edwin Wong* above ch 3. Whether these doctrines change as solicitors become eligible for the High Court bench remains to be seen.

Lack of authority

Another classic English reason for denying liability is that there is no precedent for liability on the precise facts of the case. The absurdity of this argument, which is solemnly brought out for inspection and worship in case after case[17] becomes clear as soon as one considers that one of the reasons given for overruling *Anns* in *Murphy* was that *Anns* lacked authority for saying what it did. But *Anns* was a House of Lords case. It was not bound by precedent. If one makes it a general rule that all new rules need support in precedent there will never be any new rules at all, and indeed no law outside statute, since every rule of the common law must have been a new rule at some point. Fortunately, the argument from precedent failed to impress the court in *Donoghue v Stevenson, Hedley Byrne v Heller* and most of the other leading cases of the century.

The real question here is how fast should the law develop? In periods when the judges are uncertain about what the purpose of negligence liability is, or are convinced that negligence liability is expanding so fast that they do not know what will happen next, there is a strong temptation to declare that the law should develop only by close analogy with existing cases. This is what happened to negligence in the 1980s. Lord Keith and his followers, uncertain about the purpose of negligence law in an age of state provided social security, turned Brennan J's dictum in the *Sutherland* case that negligence should develop slowly using analogy and the 'increm-ental' approach into a kind of mantra. In other eras, such as that of Lord Atkin, the courts have had enough self-confidence to base their decisions on what they perceive to be correct underlying principles. Those who expect to spend a lifetime in the law should treat both kinds of passing fashion with equal scepticism. Judges come and go, and the pendulum swings from confidence to hesitancy with a monotonous regularity. Those interested in the content of these predictable but uninformative expressions of judicial fashion are referred to the works of authors who take them more seriously.

Lack of relationship—'proximity'

The final ground for denying that a duty of care exists is perhaps the most fashionable but also the most difficult to understand of all. It is called 'proximity' or 'lack of relationship' and is confidently repeated in case after case. It is therefore worth quoting at the outset some revealing words of Lord Oliver in *Caparo*:

> '[T]he postulate of a simple duty to avoid any harm that is, with hindsight, reasonably capable of being foreseen becomes untenable without the imposition of some intelligible limits to keep the law of negligence within the bounds of common sense and practicality. Those limits have been found by the requirement of what has been

17 Eg *Caparo, The Aliakmon, Murphy, Smith v Scott, The Nicholas H*, and Lord Wilberforce in *McLoughlin v O'Brian*, to name but a few.

called a "relationship of proximity" between plaintiff and defendant and by the imposition of a further requirement that the attachment of liability for harm which has occurred be "just and reasonable". But although the cases in which the courts have imposed or withheld liability are capable of an approximate categorisation, one looks in vain for some common denominator by which the existence of the essential relationship can be tested. Indeed it is difficult to resist a conclusion that what have been treated as three separate requirements are, at least in most cases, in fact merely facets of the same thing, for in some cases the degree of foreseeability is such that it is from that alone that the requisite proximity can be deduced, whilst in others the absence of that essential relationship can most rationally be attributed simply to the court's view that it would not be fair and reasonable to hold the defendant responsible. "Proximity" is, no doubt, a convenient expression so long as it is realised that it is no more than a label which embraces not a definable concept but merely a description of circumstances from which, pragmatically, the courts conclude that a duty of care exists.'

The same judge, whose heroic attempts to make sense of the extraordinary inheritance that he has been landed with deserve wider recognition, said in *Murphy*:[18]

'The essential question which has to be asked in every case, given that damage which is the essential ingredient of the action has occurred, is whether the relationship between the plaintiff and the defendant is such — or, to use the favoured expression, whether it is of sufficient "proximity"—that it imposes upon the latter a duty to take care to avoid or prevent that loss which has in fact been sustained. This is essentially a question of policy.'

And in *Alcock* he added:

'The answer has, as it seems to me, to be found in the existence of a combination of circumstances from which the necessary degree of "proximity" between the plaintiff and the defendant can be deduced. And in the end, it has to be accepted that the concept of "proximity" is an artificial one which depends more upon the court's perception of what is a reasonable area for the imposition of liability than upon any logical process of analogical deduction.'

Other judges have concluded, on the basis of the same considerations, that, for example:

'Thus the three so-called requirements for a duty of care [ie foreseeability, proximity and justice and reasonableness] are not to be

18 [1991] AC at 488.

treated as wholly separate and distinct requirements but rather as convenient and helpful approaches to the pragmatic question whether a duty should be imposed in any given case. In the end whether the law does impose a duty in any particular circumstances depends upon those circumstances, though of course under our doctrine of precedent categories of cases where a duty has been held to exist (or not to exist) will build up as time goes by.'[19]

In the same case another judge, Balcombe LJ came to a slightly more radical conclusion:

'For my part I doubt whether the words "fair, just and reasonable" impose a test additional to that of "proximity"; in my judgment these are criteria to be adopted in considering whether the necess– ary degree of proximity exists.'

But Mann LJ had a different method:

'I am content to assume that the foreseeability of physical damage to the respondents' cargo was sufficient to constitute a "relationship of proximity" between them and the appellant. I regard the critical question as being whether the relationship is one in respect of which it would be "fair, just and reasonable" to impose a duty of care upon the respondent.'

Thus, in the same case, one judge thinks that 'proximity' includes what is 'fair, just and reasonable', one judge thinks that 'proximity' is irrelevant and everything turns on justice and reasonableness and one judge thinks that proximity, justice and reasonableness and foreseeability are all the same thing.

Indeed, it is inherently implausible that liability in negligence in general should depend on the existence of any sort of relationship between the parties since in the most straightforward form of negligence liability, traffic accident cases, it makes no difference at all whether the defendant had known the victim for 20 years or that the victim was a complete stranger. Prior relationship belongs in the world of contract, not of tort.

One plausible conclusion from all this might be that the talk of 'proximity' is so much nonsense and that it would be better simply to ignore it. But there is another explanation. The emphasis on 'proximity' is usually traced to Lord Atkin's speech in *Donoghue v Stevenson*, when Lord Atkin, discussing Lord Esher's judgment in the previous case *Le Lievre v Gould* says:

'I draw particular attention to the fact that Lord Esher emphasises the necessity of the goods having to be "used immediately" and "used at once before a reasonable opportunity of inspection". This

19 Saville LJ in *The Nicholas H*.

is obviously to exclude the possibility of goods having their condition altered by lapse of time, and to call attention to the proximate relationship, which may be too remote where inspection even by the person using, certainly by an intermediate person, may reasonably be interposed. With this necessary qualification of proximate relationship, as explained in *Le Lievre v Gould*, I think the judgment of Lord Esher expresses the law of England.'

The crucial words in this passage, however, are usually missed. They are 'which may be too remote where inspection ... may reasonably be interposed'. What Lord Atkin was saying in *Donoghue* was simply that negligence requires both fault (including foreseeability) and an absence of remoteness. Remoteness here takes its classical sense of 'not direct', which in turn means that the court has to investigate alleged intervening acts and events and has to ask whether the defendant's role in the accident pales into insignificance when compared with the other causes of the accident.

This gives a clue about what is going on in the rise of the use of the word 'proximity' in duty of care cases. 'Proximity' cases, where they are not simply repetitions of concerns that arise with the fault judgment (such as the degree of risk), are usually about the same concerns that used to be discussed under the rubric of 'remoteness' before *The Wagon Mound* appropriated the word 'remoteness' to mean 'foreseeability'. For example, in *Caparo* the problem was that the real culprits were not the accountants but those responsible for reducing the value of the target company in the first place and who subsequently successfully kept the facts from the defendants, the accountants. In *The Nicholas H* the problem is that the real culprit appears to be the carrier, not the classification society, and in *Alcock*, as in all nervous shock cases, there is a suspicion that the plaintiffs brought the illnesses on themselves, either because of the nature of their relationships with the victims of the physical accidents or because of their feeble characters.

In some economic loss cases, 'proximity' takes on a different meaning, namely 'near to contract'[20] and there are cases where it takes on the sense of factual cause (especially where there is a causal fade-away[1]). But for the most part, its use is very close to what used openly to be called 'remoteness'. The only important difference between remoteness and proximity is that whereas remoteness can refer either to part of the damage or to all of it, proximity applies to the whole of the damage.[2] This in turn explains how Lord Keith could easily slip 'proximity' into his discussion of 'duty', since, like duty, it referred to the whole of the damage and meant that if the plaintiff's case failed to meet its conditions, it failed completely.

---

20   See below ch 6.
1   See above ch 4.
2   Cf the German position—Markesinis *German Law of Torts* pp 92ff—and the distinction between haftungsbegründende Kausalität and haftungsausfüllende Kausalität.

Another function of 'proximity' is to explain exceptions to general rules of remoteness. Thus in cases in which the defendant allowed a third party to harm the plaintiff[3] the general rule is that the third party's intervening acts, which are usually deliberate, often criminal and almost always negligent, break the chain of causation. But in special circumstances, such as the youth custody centre in *Home Office v Dorset Yacht* and the extra powers of prison officers to control prisoners, the court may decide that the chain is not broken. The defendant's fault is not made to look insignificant by the third parties' acts in these cases because the defendant's very function is to prevent such events from happening. These exceptional conditions, under which the defendant is held liable for the acts of a third party, have also been called 'proximity.' The same usage also exists in economic loss cases in which the question is whether the general rule against liability for pure economic loss ought to be lifted for the case at hand. Thus in *Caparo*, for example, the problem was not lack of 'proximity' per se but that since the court thought that there was a presumption against pure economic loss there was not sufficient 'proximity' to displace it.[4]

It would probably be much less confusing to take Saville LJ's line in *The Nicholas H* and to say that all negligence cases require 'proximity' (presumably in the remoteness sense) not just the exceptional cases about nervous shock, economic loss and third party acts. But the danger in such a course of action is that not only would the courts be tempted to insert content in 'proximity' where, because no remoteness point arose, there would otherwise be none, but also because in most cases there are no inherent remoteness problems and it would be wrong to suggest that there were. 'He hit me', for example, needs no complex exegesis to show that there is no remoteness problem to be solved.

But 'proximity', although technically redundant since all the problems it touches on could be dealt with under remoteness, fault and causation, is likely to persist as an argument against liability precisely because it is so vague and changes its meaning periodically.

---

3   See above ch 4 and see generally Howarth 'My Brother's Keeper' [1994] Legal Studies 88.
4   See below ch 6

Chapter 6

Economic loss and negligence

KEY POINTS

* Economic loss is interference with contractual rights and potential business.
* The basic rule in English law is that the negligent infliction of economic loss is not actionable. The origin of this rule lies in the relational nature of the loss.
* There is an exception arising out of *Hedley Byrne v Heller* . The basis and scope of the exception are, however, disputed.
* One's view of the scope of the *Hedley Byrne* exception depends largely on the reasons one accepts for the rule excluding liability for economic loss. Many, but not all, of the reasons put forward for the rule are not convincing.
* One view of the *Hedley Byrne* exception is that it allows recovery for all tort cases which are 'near to contract'. Another view is that it is simply a recognition that the arguments against relational loss do not apply when there is misrepresentation.

As we saw in the last chapter, the underlying orientation of English law, in sharp contrast to the orientation of some other legal systems, is that pure economic loss is primarily the concern of the law of contract. Only in exceptional circumstances is pure economic loss recoverable in tort, and then usually only if the loss was caused intentionally. But there are exceptions.

Economic loss is notoriously difficult, especially for beginning students. Unlike most of negligence law, which concerns everyday matters such as road accidents and accidents at work, economic loss is largely about areas of life, especially shipping and international trade, which are not widely known about. It is truly said that when learning tort law, students find the facts of the cases easy to understand but the law incomprehensible, whereas in contract law it is the other way round. Economic loss cases, unfortunately, seem to combine the incomprehensible aspects of both subjects.

The reason for the difficulty of economic loss is, however, important for understanding it. Economic loss cases are usually about plaintiffs who might have expected to have contractual claims against the defendants, but who turn out not to have such claims and who in conseq–uence try to sue in negligence instead. The contract doctrines that frustrate plaintiffs, some of which we have already discussed in chapter 5, include:

(1) *The English third party benefit rule*: If A contracts with B that B will confer a benefit on C, in most legal systems, as long as there was a specific intent to benefit C, C can sue B if B fails to confer the benefit. In England, this is not so. The third party has no claim.

(2) *The consideration rule*: There is normally no binding contract between A and B if A confers a benefit on B for free. B must in some way pay for the benefit, either with a counter-promise to do something that A wants to see happen or with the transfer of something of value either to A or to someone else. It is not enough to create a contract in English law merely that A's promise to confer a benefit on B causes B to act differently in reliance on A's promise.

(3) *The indication of consent rule*: In most cases, silence does not indicate consent in English law. It follows that saying nothing cannot give rise to a contractual promise, even though the plaintiff may have relied on the silence.

(4) *The limitation rules*: Legal actions can be ruled out because the plaintiff took too long before starting the action. This limitation period is apparently the same for both tort and contract—namely six years.[1] But in contract cases, time starts to run earlier, from the breach of contract itself, than in tort, in which time runs from when the damage occurs.

In addition, there are features of particular contracts that catch the plaintiff out. Plaintiffs may discover that the obvious person to sue in contract is protected by exclusion or exemption clauses, and they have to turn to other possible defendants, defendants with whom the plaintiffs did not have contractual relations. Or the deal may have been structured so that the plaintiff expects to receive by assignment another person's rights to sue in contract, but does not receive them.

Economic loss cases are mainly about the boundary between tort and contract. There is always tension at borders. The boundaries themselves may shift from time to time. Indeed, at some point in the future the courts may even decide that economic loss cases are best classified as contract law cases rather than, as now, as tort law cases. The boundary region itself may even emerge as a distinct field in its own right.[2]

To ease understanding, this chapter looks briefly at the historical development of the law on economic loss in negligence, especially the development of the general presumption against economic loss, before turning to the exceptional cases in which pure economic loss is recoverable in negligence. It then turns to the reasons said to lie behind the law.

1 Three years in personal injury negligence cases.
2 Cf Grant Gilmore *The Death of Contract* and especially his notion of 'contorts'.

The basic principle—economic loss not recoverable

In the mid and late nineteenth century the English courts had to decide what to do about losses that were similar to those suffered by victims of breaches of contract but where the victim had no contractual rights. The approach the courts adopted was to distinguish between cases in which the losses were caused intentionally and cases in which the losses were caused unintentionally. The courts treated intentionally caused pure economic loss as, in principle, actionable. Both through the development of the tort of deceit[3] and through the invention of the tort of interference with contract[4] most intentionally caused pure economic losses became recoverable regardless of the plaintiff's rights in contract.

But the courts denied equivalent claims where the losses arose from the defendant's carelessness. In *Derry v Peek*[5] the plaintiff lost money because he relied on statements made by defendants. The defendants honestly believed in what they were saying but had not taken sufficient care. The plaintiff lost. The tort of deceit, said the House of Lords, required more than carelessness. Similarly *Cattle v Stockton Waterworks*[6] estab-lished that there was to be no liability for carelessly interfering in a contract between the plaintiff and a third party. In *Cattle v Stockton*, the defendant waterworks company failed properly to install a new water main on the property of a landowner with the result that the plaintiff contractor was not able to complete works that he had contracted to do for the landowner. The plaintiff informed the defendant about the difficulty that he was in, but the defendant did nothing and the plaintiff was 'delayed and put to expense'. As a result his contract with the landowner became much more difficult to perform and consequently less profitable.[7] The court decided that, since the defendant did not intend the harm, there should be no liability.

Whatever the underlying justification for distinguishing between intentionally and unintentionally caused pure economic loss, and it is worth noting that no equivalent distinction exists in contract, at least the position was relatively clear for over 60 years. If there was pressure for change during that period it manifested itself in the law of contract, especially in the doctrine of consideration, rather than in tort.[8] Even as the law of

3   *Peek v Gurney* (1873) LR 6 HL 377, *Edgington v Fitzmaurice* (1885) 29 Ch D 459 and *Derry v Peek* (1889) 14 App Cas 337.
4   *Lumley v Gye* (1853) 2 E & B 216, *Bowen v Hall* (1881) 6 QBD 333, *Temperton v Russell* [1893] 1 QB 715, *Allen v Flood* [1898] AC 1.
5   See above.
6   (1875) LR 10 QB 453.
7   Note that, apparently, if the defendant makes the plaintiff's contract less valuable but does so in a way that does not affect the performance of the contract itself, there is no liability even for intentional harm: *RCA v Pollard* [1983] Ch 135 (musical 'bootleggers' illicitly record concerts given by musicians under exclusive contract with plaintiff. Claim that extra competition reduces profitability of exclusive recording contracts. No liability).
8   See eg *De La Bere v Pearson Ltd* [1908] 1 KB 280.

negligence developed and expanded in the years following *Donoghue v Stevenson*,[9] it was still assumed that the new tort of negligence protected plaintiffs' interests in their physical well-being and their physical property, but not their purely economic interests.

Then came *Hedley Byrne v Heller*.[10] *Hedley Byrne* effectively reversed the result of *Derry v Peek*. Negligent misstatements causing pure economic losses to a plaintiff who had no relevant contractual rights became recoverable. Liability under the rule in *Hedley Byrne* was, however, and to some extent still is, subject to a number of conditions not usually applied in tort claims for negligence—for example that the plaintiff and the defendant had to have some kind of 'special relationship' albeit falling short of a contractual or fiduciary relationship, and that the plaintiff's reliance on the defendant's misstatement had to be 'reasonable'. But regardless of these and other restrictions, the central message of *Hedley Byrne* was that one could no longer say that English law did not allow the recovery in tort of unintentionally caused pure economic losses.

Two questions dominated the quarter century following *Hedley Byrne*. First, if the courts could reverse the effect of *Derry v Peek*, why not the effect of *Cattle v Stockton Waterworks* as well? And secondly, what exactly was the boundary between purely economic interests and interests in physical property?

The answer to the first question eventually turned out to be that *Cattle v Stockton* should not be overturned. Negligent interference in contract is still not tortious. But it was a close run thing.

In the 1970s, the House of Lords began to describe the tort of negligence in increasingly general terms. Lord Wilberforce's 'why not' principle in *Anns v Merton London Borough Council*,[11] that there should be liability in all cases in which the defendant carelessly caused the plaintiff harm unless there were clear reasons why not, gave new impetus to those who wanted to see the law on economic loss change.

The high point of the attack was *Junior Books v Veitchi*.[12] In *Junior Books*, the plaintiff had a contract with a builder to erect a new factory. The builder employed sub-contractors to do much of the work, including the installation of a special kind of floor. Although the sub-contractor was a flooring specialist and had been chosen to do the job by the plaintiff itself, the new floor was a disaster and the plaintiff had to replace it at great cost. For reasons that remain obscure, instead of proceeding against the builder for breach of contract, the plaintiff sued the sub-contractor for negligence. Under the *Cattle v Stockton* doctrine, this claim should have been doomed to failure, for the only harm caused by the defendant sub-contractor's carelessness was a reduction in the value to the plaintiff of its contract with the builder.

Admittedly there were two differences between *Cattle* and *Junior Books*, but neither should have helped the plaintiff much. First, the contract in

9   [1932] AC 562, [1932] All ER Rep 1.
10 [1964] AC 465.
11 [1978] 1 AC 728. See above ch 5.
12 [1983] 1 AC 520.

Cattle put the risk of interruption on the plaintiff, so that there was no prospect of his suing the landowner on the basis, for example, that he had not made the land available. But in *Junior Books*, the risk of interruption was on the builder, so that the plaintiff did in principle have a contractual action against the builder. But this meant only that the plaintiff's loss in *Cattle* was effectively larger than an equivalent loss in *Junior Books* because it was certain to fall on the plaintiff. In a *Junior Books* case the loss to the plaintiff may end up as nothing at all if the plaintiff manages to recover it from the builder.

The second difference between *Cattle* and *Junior Books* is that the defendant in *Cattle* had no contractual connection with the landowner, whereas there was such a connection between the defendant and the builder in *Junior Books*. But it is difficult to see how this connection helps the plaintiff, rather than simply helping the builder to recover from the sub-contractor any losses it may incur as a result of having to pay contract damages to the plaintiff.

But despite these disadvantages, by a 4-1 majority, the House of Lords found for the plaintiff in *Junior Books*. Using a line of reasoning that would later be noticed as similar to that used in *Hedley Byrne*, the majority said that although there was no contract between the plaintiff and the defend- ant, there was a special relationship between them that was near to contractual relationship. The special relationship consisted of the fact that there was a contractual chain linking the parties together and, moreover, that the plaintiff had designated the defendant as sub-contractor.

If *Junior Books* had enjoyed the same success as *Hedley Byrne*, *Cattle v Stockton* would probably have gone the same way as *Derry v Peek*. Starting with a small breach in the wall of *Cattle*'s defences, namely that there could be liability when all the parties are linked contractually and all the parties know about the obligations of the others, a large hole could have developed which eventually would have left little of the original doctrine.

But *Junior Books* had very little success. It was first misinterpreted,[13] and then denounced in the Court of Appeal as a case that applied 'only to its own facts'.[14] The House of Lords meanwhile returned to the straight and narrow of *Cattle v Stockton* in cases such as *The Mineral Transporter*[15] and *The Aliakmon*,[16] cases in which the defendant's carelessness caused loss to the plaintiff by making contracts that the plaintiffs had concluded with third parties more onerous.[17] In both of these cases the defendants won.

---

13 Eg *Tate & Lyle v Greater London Council* [1983] 2 AC 509 (*Junior Books* about damage to property, not pure economic loss).

14 See eg *Simaan v Pilkington Glass (No 2)* [1988] QB 758. The use of the formula that a case 'should be restricted to its own facts' is one of the techniques used by judges when they do not want to follow the decision of a higher court but are not permitted by the doctrine of stare decisis to disagree openly with it.

15 [1986] AC 1 (defendant damaged ship which plaintiff had contractual right to use).

16 [1986] AC 785 (defendant damaged goods in transit in which plaintiff had a contractual interest).

17 Note that the result of *RCA v Pollard* would suggest that there would have been no liability in these cases even if the defendants had acted intentionally, *sed quaere*.

Finally, in *Murphy v Brentwood District Council*[18] the House of Lords confirmed the return to orthodoxy. In the words of Lord Oliver:

> '[I]n an uninterrupted line of cases since 1875, it has consistently been held that a third party cannot successfully sue in tort for the interference with his economic expectations or advantage resulting from injury to the person or property of another person with whom he has or is likely to have a contractual relationship.'

Thus the authority of that 1875 case, namely *Cattle v Stockton*, was fully restored.

The second question to dominate the 25 years after *Hedley Byrne* was the distinction between property damage, which is recoverable, and pure economic loss, which is not. In *Spartan Steel v Martin*,[19] for example, the Court of Appeal considered the case of a maker of steel castings who suffered an interruption to production as the result of an electricity failure which had been caused in turn by the defendant's careless digging up of the street. The plaintiff claimed damages for the fact that although it had managed to reclaim the steel that was being cast when the power went off, it had recovered it in a way that meant that it was worth less than was paid for it. It also claimed for the profit over and above the cost of the materials and other costs that the plaintiff would have made had it been able to sell the castings that were in the process of being made. Finally, the plaintiff claimed for the loss of 14 hours of production that would normally have earned the plaintiff a handsome profit. The Court of Appeal character-ised the loss in value of the casting in the process of being made at the time of the power cut as a physical loss, and characterised the loss of profit from the 14 hours lost production as pure economic loss. But it decided that the lost profit on the castings that were in the process of being made at the time of the power cut was recoverable, as 'truly consequential on the physical damages'. The economic loss was recoverable because it had piggy-backed onto the physical damage.

Encouraged that some forms of loss of profit could count as recoverable as long as they were associated with physical damage, the judges began to discover other economic losses that could be associated with physical harm or at least with the threat of physical harm. The most notable moves in this direction came in cases concerning defective and disappointing houses. If A builds a house, sells it to B who then sells it to C and C discovers that A built the house carelessly so that it is worth a lot less than she paid for it, the common law position[20] would seem to be that C's only possible remedy is in contract against B, for C has no direct contract with A and for the purposes of a tort action the loss suffered by C is purely economic—she paid B more than she would otherwise have done. But in *Dutton v Bognor*

18 [1991] 1 AC 398.
19 [1973] QB 27.
20 That is before the Defective Premises Act 1972.

Regis UDC[1] and, especially, *Anns v Merton London Borough Council* the courts developed an extraordinary doctrine according to which damages became recoverable as long as and to the extent that the builder's carelessness had rendered the building unsafe, dangerous or a health risk—in other words, a threat to the physical well-being of the plaintiff.

Another attempt, perhaps even more extraordinary, to connect economic loss with physical damage occurred in *D & F Estates v Church Comrs.*[2] It was accepted that if a defect in a building caused damage to other property belonging to the plaintiff, furniture for example, that damage would be recoverable. From this, the House of Lords developed the so-called 'complex structure' theory, which said that damages for disappointing houses would be recoverable if the defect caused by the defendant's carelessness had itself caused damage to a discernibly different part of the structure, so that, for example, if a defect in the foundations caused cracks in the walls, the defect in the foundations might be economic loss but the cracks in the walls would be property damage.

Murphy v Brentwood District Council[3] ended this development. The House of Lords overruled *Dutton* and *Anns* and denounced the complex structure theory. Even the originator of the complex structure theory, Lord Bridge, joined in its denunciation. On the other hand, *Spartan Steel v Martin* appears to have survived on the ground that it is a 'borderline case' for which the courts have to find a solution 'pragmatically ... not by the application of logic.'[4]

Thus, *Murphy v Brentwood* has, at least for the time being, restored the law to a position close to that immediately following *Hedley Byrne v Heller*. English law, with the exception of negligent misstatements, operates a strong presumption against awarding compensation for negligently caused pure economic loss.

THE TORT OF DECEIT—A SUMMARY

Although the tort of deceit, as a tort based on intentional wrongdoing, belongs more appropriately in the chapter about the economic torts, it is convenient to summarise it here.

The conditions for liability in deceit are that the defendant made a false statement of fact, knowing the statement to be false or being reckless as to its truth or falsity, with the intention that the plaintiff should act on the statement and with the result that the plaintiff does act on the statement and loses because of that act.

---

1   [1972] 1 QB 373.
2   [1989] AC 177.
3   [1991] 1 AC 398.
4   Lord Oliver at p 486.

The 'statement' does not generally have to be in writing[5] and indeed can consist of conduct.[6] Silence, however, does not count unless there is some independent legal duty, under the Companies Acts for example, that obliges the defendant to speak, but telling half the truth counts as a statement about what is left unsaid.[7] Similarly, the statment should have been made by the defendant, but the defendant may be liable for failing to correct a false impression created by a third party if the defendant is under a duty to speak.[8]

The statement needs to be a statement of fact, but, as explained in Bowen LJ's famous dictum in *Edgington v Fitzmaurice*,[9] 'The state of a man's mind is as much a fact as the state of his digestion.' Thus, misleading someone as to one's intentions or as to one's opinions may count as misleading the person about a fact. But if I make a promise to you which at the time I intend to keep, but later I renege, your only remedy, if any, is in contract, for although in making the promise I made an implied statement of fact about my intentions, at the time the statement was true. Similarly if I say that I have no intention of remarrying, if I report accurately my present intentions, it is not deceit if I later change my mind.[10]

Apparently if the defendant makes a statement that is true at the time but later becomes untrue, the defendant makes an untrue state-ment by not correcting the previous false impression.[11] It should follow that if the defendant promises to do something and then changes his mind, he should have informed the plaintiff of his change of mind and thus, if he intends to mislead the plaintiff by not informing the plaintiff of his change of mind, he should be liable in deceit. Whether this is in fact the law remains to be seen. Usually when people change their minds about fulfilling promises they do not intend to deceive the promisee or the promisee has already acted.[12]

The defendant must either have known that the statement was false or have been reckless as to whether it was false or not. But as we have seen an honest but careless statement is not actionable in deceit.[13] In addition, the defendant must have intended that the plaintiff specifically, or a class of persons to which the plaintiff belongs, rely on the statement.

5 For an exception see Statute of Frauds Amendment Act 1828 (statements about creditworthiness). See *UBAF v European American Banking Corpn* [1984] QB 713. *WB Anderson v Rhodes* [1967] 2 All ER 850 holds that the Act does not apply to any liability in negligence, onlt to liability in deceit—thus setting up the absurd possibility of a defendant attempting to escape liability by claiming to have misled the plaintiff deliberately.

6 Cf *R v Barnard* (1837) 7 C & P 784.

7 *Peek v Gurney* (1873) LR 6 HL 377.

8 *Bradford Building Society v Borders* [1941] 2 All ER 205.

9 (1885) 29 Ch D 459.

10 *Wales v Wadham* [1977] 1 WLR 199.

11 *Incledon v Watson* (1862) 2 F & F 841.

12 Cf however *Briess v Woolley* [1954] AC 333.

13 *Derry v Peek* above p 269 n 3.

If someone else relies, someone outside the intended class, there is no liability.[14] On the other hand, if the defendant intends the plaintiff to rely, it is no defence that the plaintiff was stupid to do so or should have taken independent advice.[15] Moreover, according to one recent decision, contributory negligence is no defence to deceit even in its modern form of reducing the damages rather than providing a complete defence.[16]

The plaintiff must actually have relied on the statement, which means, above all, that if the plaintiff would have acted the same way anyway, there is no liability, effectively because there is no causation.

The deceit must have led to loss, which may include, and indeed usually is, economic loss. The defendant is liable for all loss, including unforeseeable loss, that flows directly from the deceit.[17]

The *Hedley Byrne* exception to the rule

The one well-established exception to the general rule against economic loss in negligence is the rule in *Hedley Byrne v Heller*. But for a landmark decision *Hedley Byrne* itself was noticeably cautious in its formulation of the new rules and careful to minimise their immediate impact. Lord Reid, for example, while agreeing that there should be a move away from *Derry v Peek*, said:[18]

> '[I]t seems to me that there is good sense behind our present law that in general an innocent but negligent misrepresentation gives no cause of action.'

Lord Reid limited liability to cases of 'special relationships':

> 'where it is plain that the party seeking information or advice was trusting the other to exercise such a degree of care as the circum–stances required, where it was reasonable for him to do that, and where the other gave the information or advice when he knew or ought to have known that the inquirer was relying on him.'[19]

Lord Morris was if anything more restrictive:[20]

> '[I]t should now be regarded as settled that if someone possessed of a special skill undertakes, quite irrespective of contract, to apply

14 *Peek v Gurney* above p 269 n 3.
15 *Dobell v Stevens* (1825) 3 B & C 623.
16 *Alliance & Leicester Building Society v Edgestop Ltd* [1994] 2 All ER 38, [1993] 1 WLR 1462. *Sed quaere*. See ch 15.
17 *Doyle v Olby* [1969] 2 QB 158.
18 [1964] AC 465 at 483.
19 At 486.
20 At 502-503.

that skill for the assistance of another person who relies on such skill, a duty of care will arise ... [I]f in a sphere in which a person is so placed that others could reasonably rely on his judgment ... a person takes it on himself to give information or advice to, or allows his information or advice to be passed on to, another person who, as he knows or should know, will place reliance on it, then a duty of care arises.'

On the other hand, Lord Devlin's formulation of the new rule was potentially more expansive. He said that the duty arose only when there was a relationship 'equivalent to contract' between plaintiff and defendant. Lord Devlin went on to explain 'equivalent to contract' in this way:[1]

'I do not understand any of your Lordships to hold that it is a responsibility imposed by law on certain types of persons or in certain types of situations. It is a responsibility that is voluntarily accepted or undertaken either generally where a general relation-ship, such as that of solicitor and client or banker and customer, is created, or specifically in relation to a particular transaction ... I regard this proposition as an application of the general conception of proximity.'

Furthermore their Lordships agreed that because the basis of liability was voluntary assumption of responsibility by the defendant, if, as happened in *Hedley Byrne* itself, the defendant gave the advice subject to a disclaimer of responsibility, no duty could arise.

The themes of the subsequent history of this form of liability are all present in the restrictions suggested in *Hedley Byrne* itself—special relationships, special skill, the degree of care required by the circumstances, reasonable reliance, voluntary assumption of responsibility and proximity. All of these issues, however, are aspects of the same question. Should *Hedley Byrne* liability be seen as a relaxation of the strict privity of contract principles of English law in favour of plaintiffs who are the victims of unreasonable behaviour in relationships that are 'equivalent to contract', or should it be seen as purely an expansion of the tort of negligence into the previously forbidden zone of economic loss? If *Hedley Byrne* is fundamentally a case about the boundaries of contract law, it does not represent a major threat to the basic principle that negligently caused pure economic loss is not recoverable in tort—all it does is shift the boundary between tort and contract and bring a few more cases within the ambit of contract law, in which, of course, economic loss is recoverable. But if *Hedley Byrne* is mainly a development within the law of negligence itself, it does represent a breakthrough, since it would mean that the tort of negligence had absorbed a clear example of the recovery of economic loss. This tension is still largely unresolved, although the pendulum is now swinging heavily in the direction of the contract view.

1   At 529.

Some frequently asked questions about *Hedley Byrne*

Hedley Byrne has given rise to a complex jurisprudence of its own. Here we list some of the most frequently raised points.

(1) Does the plaintiff have to show that the defendant was a professional advisor?

Lord Morris in *Hedley Byrne* had talked about defendants 'possessed of a special skill'. The question arises whether Hedley Byrne liability should be confined to such people, or, even more restrictively, to professional advisors.

In *Mutual Life v Evatt*[2] a bare majority of the Privy Council said that the plaintiff could not win unless he could show that the defendant carried on business as a professional advisor in the field relevant to the information the defendant gave the plaintiff. Thus, one could not say that a life assurance company had to be liable for careless advice given to a policy holder about the financial soundness of an associated company, a kind of advice the defendant was not generally in business to give. The minority, in contrast, said that there could be liability for any advice given in circumstances in which a reasonable person in the position of the defendant would realise that the plaintiff was asking for considered advice and the defendant gives advice that a reasonable person in the position of the plaintiff would take to be considered advice.

The English Court of Appeal has preferred the minority view in *Mutual Life v Evatt*. In *Esso Petroleum v Mardon*,[3] for example, the Court of Appeal said that there could be a duty of care where Esso, as petrol wholesalers, had carelessly misled the plaintiff, a potential tenant of a petrol station, about the station's likely profitability if he contracted with them. The defendants were not professional advisors, but they were in a much better position to know what the station's profitability would be than the plaintiff, and both parties would have taken the situation seriously.[4]

The present position is that Lord Morris's words are usually interpreted to mean that 'special skill' includes any special knowledge the defendant might have.[5] Indeed, the whole doctrine of the special skill may be interpreted as merely an aid in determining issues such as causation (if the defendant did not profess to have a special skill it is more likely that

---

2   [1971] AC 793.
3   *Esso Petroleum v Mardon* [1975] QB 819. One might add, however, that another interpretation of this case is rather that it undermines the contract view since it establishes that it is not necessary to show that the defendant was the sort of person with whom one might contract for advice.
4   See also *Howard Marine v Ogden* [1978] QB 574.
5   See *Spring v Guardian Assurance* 'It is, I consider, clear from the facts of *Hedley Byrne* itself that the expression "special skill" is to be understood in a broad sense, certainly broad enough to embrace special knowledge.'.

the plaintiff did not really rely on the defendant but would have acted in the same way anyway), fault (those without special skills are generally held to the standards of the ordinary person carrying out the particular task) and remoteness (a plaintiff who relies on the advice of someone who clearly lacks the skills necessary to give adequate advice is teetering on the edge of being utterly unreasonable).

(2) Can I be held liable for advice given at a party?

According to Lord Denning in *Howard Marine*, there will be no liability for 'representations made during a casual conversation in the street; or in a railway carriage; or in an impromptu opinion given offhand; or 'off the cuff' on the telephone'. But in *Chaudhry v Prabhakar*[6], where the plaintiff asked a family friend to check over a second-hand car she was about to buy and the friend failed to notice that the car had been involved in a bad accident and had been clumsily stuck back together again, the Court of Appeal was willing to countenance a duty of care between friends in a fairly informal setting.

(3) What is 'reasonable reliance'?

To show that the plaintiff has relied on what the defendant said is simply one way of showing that the defendant's carelessness caused the harm to the plaintiff. If the plaintiff would have acted in the same way anyway, and the same loss would have occurred, the defendant's carelessness has not caused the harm. But where causation is obvious anyway, reliance will not be necessary (*White v Jones* [1995] 1 All ER 691). In *Ministry of Local Government v Sharp*,[7] for example, the plaintiff suffered loss when a clerk employed by the defendant carelessly omitted to include one of the plaintiff's rights on a conclusive list of the rights pertaining to a piece of land. There was no reliance by the plaintiff on information from the defendant. The plaintiff's right was simply wiped out when the clerk issued a certificate that omitted to mention it. Nevertheless, there was clearly causation and the plaintiff won.

But it is often also said in *Hedley Byrne* cases that the plaintiff's reliance has to be reasonable.[8] Usually this turns out to mean only that if the plaintiff's reliance was unreasonable, for example where the plaintiff acts on a half-overheard remark at a noisy party, the defendant cannot be held

---

6 [1989] 1 WLR 29.

7 [1970] 1 All ER 1009.

8 See eg Lord Bridge in *Caparo*: 'So also the plaintiff, subject again to the effect of the disclaimer, would in that situation reasonably suppose that he was entitled to rely on the advice or information communicated to him for the very purpose for which he required it.' See also *Edgeworth Construction Ltd v ND Lea & Associates Ltd, Edgeworth Construction Ltd v Walji* (1991) 54 BLR 11.

to have been at fault, since the risk of harm would have seemed to have been minimal. It may also mean that there was no factual causation, since if the reliance seems to be unreasonable, it may be evidence that there was no reliance at all, but that the plaintiff would have acted in the same way anyway. Moreover, unreasonable reliance may indicate that the 'type' of harm or the plaintiff may count as 'unforeseeable' under *Wagon Mound* remoteness. Finally it may mean that the plaintiff's reliance came into the 'utterly unreasonable' category which would qualify it as a break in the chain of causation.

If the plaintiff's reliance is unreasonable, but nevertheless the defendant was still at fault, causation established, the type of harm foreseeable, the plaintiff a foreseeable plaintiff and the plaintiff's act not utterly unreasonable, the unreasonable nature of the reliance cannot defeat liability altogether, it can only reduce the damages as contributory negligence. For example, the defendant stockbroker tells the plaintiff punter that a certain share is certain to rise in value when reasonable further inquiries would have revealed that the share would probably fall. The plaintiff actually has independent inside information on the strength of which a reasonable person would not buy the shares. Nevertheless the plaintiff goes ahead and loses money. There is fault, causation, a foreseeable type of harm and a forseeable plaintiff, and the plaintiff's act, though unreasonable is not utterly unreasonable. The result should be that the plaintiff should recover but the damages should be reduced to reflect the plaintiff's contributory negligence.[9]

(4) What is the relationship between *Hedley Byrne* and the Misrepresentation Act 1967?

The Misrepresentation Act 1967 s 2(1) provides:

> 'Where a person has entered into a contract after a misrep–
> resentation has been made to him by another party thereto and as
> a result thereof he has suffered loss, then, if the person making
> the misrepresentation would be liable to damages in repect thereof
> had the misrepresentation been made fraudulently, that person
> shall be so liable notwithstanding that the misrepresentation was
> not made fraudulently, unless he proves that he had reasonable
> ground to believe and did believe up to the time the contract was
> made that the facts represented were true.'

The purpose of the section is to give a remedy in damages to a party who enters into a contract because of a wrongful but unintentional

---

9 See *Edwards v Lee* (1991) NLJR 1517. Note also that Sir Donald Nicholls V-C said in *Gran Gelato v Richcliff* [1992] Ch 560 that contributory negligence would apply also under s 2(1) of the Misrepresentation Act 1967. But see also *Alliance & Leicester Building Society v Edgestop* above n 16 (only applies where negligence, not where intentional harm).

misrepresentation by the defendant. It thus covers a subset of the cases covered by *Hedley Byrne*, namely those cases in which the plaintiff enters into a contract with the person who made the misrepresentation.

It is not the fact that the plaintiff makes a contract as a result of the misrepresentation that differentiates the cases under the Act from other *Hedley Byrne* cases, since the plaintiff in *Hedley Byrne* cases often ends up making a contract with someone as a result of the misrepresentation. In *Caparo*, for example, the plaintiff entered into contracts to buy the shares in the company. The differentiating fact is that the person with whom the plaintiff makes the contract is the defendant.

Plaintiffs have two main advantages if they can bring their case within the Act. First, the burden of proof lies on the defendant to prove that 'he had reasonable ground to believe' that what he was saying was true. This effectively reverses the burden of proof on the fault issue. It is a burden, moreover, which is difficult to discharge.[10] And secondly, at least according to the Court of Appeal, because the Act sets up an equivalence between the s 2(1) action and the notion of fraud, in other words the tort of deceit, the remoteness rules for deceit apply rather than the remoteness rules for negligence, which means that foreseeability of the type of harm and of the plaintiff are not required.[11]

(5) Does it make any difference whether the representation was one of fact, one of opinion or was a prediction of the future?

The distinction between representations of fact and representations of opinion has some significance in contract law, but it seems to make no difference in itself in *Hedley Byrne* liability.[12] On the other hand it will usually be easier to prove fault in the case of the misrepresentation of a fact than that of the misrepresentation of an opinion or a prediction.

The present debate about *Hedley Byrne*

Although *Hedley Byrne* has spawned many detailed decisions, its fundamental justification is still the subject of debate. Four particular cases are worth noting in more detail for what they show about the current state of play.

Caparo v Dickman

Caparo v Dickman[13] is an important case because it was the first House of Lords case since *Hedley Byrne* to take a markedly restrictive view of liability

---

10 *Howard Marine v Ogden.*
11 *Royscott Trust v Rogerson* [1991] 3 All ER 294, criticised by Hooley (1991) 107 LQR 547.
12 See *Midland Bank v Hett, Stubbs and Kemp* [1979] Ch 384.
13 [1990] 2 AC 605.

for negligent misstatement.[14] The essential facts of *Caparo* were that the plaintiff, a company, became interested in making a take-over bid for a company in which it already held shares. To decide whether to launch the bid and how much to offer for the shares, the plaintiff investigated the target company's accounts, to which it had access as a shareholder but which, in any case, were freely available public documents. The plaintiff, having consulted the accounts, proceeded with the bid, which was succ–essful. But the plaintiff subsequently discovered that the accounts had been seriously misleading and that the target company was worth a lot less than the plaintiff had paid for it. The accounts had been certified as a true and fair view of the target company's position by its auditors. At the time, it was a statutory requirement for all companies to submit audited accounts both to their shareholders and to the Registrar of Companies. The plaintiff claimed that the auditors had prepared the accounts carelessly and sued them for negligence. The auditors defended themselves by saying that even if they had been careless, they could not be found liable because *Hedley Byrne* could not stretch so far.

The difference between *Caparo* and *Hedley Byrne*, simply stated, is that in *Caparo*, unlike in *Hedley Byrne*, the plaintiff did not ask anyone to provide the misleading information, but instead went out and found it. From the negligence point of view, this makes little difference, since, apart from contributory negligence and, in extreme cases, remoteness, the negligence question focuses on how the defendant acted, not how the plaintiff acted. Here, one might just about argue that the plaintiff was contributorily negligent by not taking further independent advice (assum–ing there was any advice that anyone outside the target company could realistically have given), but there does not seem to be anything near the utterly unreasonable behaviour[15] by the plaintiff needed to establish remoteness or a 'break in the chain of causation.' From the 'near to contract' point of view, however, there are decisive differences between *Caparo* and *Hedley Byrne*. The plaintiff has no agreement with anyone about the relevant information. The only contract is one required by statute between the target company and the auditors. The plaintiff is not only a technical stranger to the contract, it is also a factual stranger. The defendant and the target company did not intend to confer a benefit on the plaintiff. Admittedly, some legal systems[16] recognise warranties—contractual guarantees for example of safety—that attach to objects rather than to agreements, and in such jurisdictions it might not appear so strange that the finder of information, like the recipient of a defective product, should

---

14 That is even apart from the frank admission by the highest court in England that the judges do not know what they mean by 'proximity', supposedly the key concept in Lord Keith's new dispensation in negligence, (see Lord Oliver at p 633 and Lord Roskill at p 628) and the attempt to undermine the principled approach to negligence liability established by *Donoghue v Stevenson*. See above ch 5.

15 See eg *Emeh v Kensington and Chelsea and Westminster Area Health Authority* [1985] QB 1012.

16 Eg most US jurisdictions. See Howarth 'Negligence After Murphy' [1992] CLJ 58 at 67.

be able to hold the originator of the information to account for reasonable care in research and expression. But England is not such a jurisdiction.

The House of Lords found for the defendant in *Caparo*, but not explicitly by taking the 'near to contract' route. Instead, the House followed two main lines of thought, one ingenious in conception but questionable in its application, the other clear in expression but unclear in justification.

The first line of thought was an argument based on concepts drawn from breach of statutory duty, a distinct tort separate from negligence.[17] In breach of statutory duty, the court will not grant a private right of action based on a statutory prohibition unless the type of harm suffered by the plaintiff was a type which it was a purpose of the statute to prevent.[18] In *Peabody Donation Fund v Sir Lindsay Parkinson*[19] the House of Lords under the guidance of Lord Keith had already used such an argument to deny a plaintiff a claim for economic loss which might otherwise have been recoverable under the then still valid *Anns v Merton BC*. In *Caparo*, the House of Lords claimed that the purpose of the statutory requirement to prepare, circulate and deposit audited accounts was not to protect potential investors from pure economic loss, but to assist the shareholders collectively in holding the board of directors to account. Whether this ingenious form of argument has any inherent merit is unclear, but its application to the statutory framework applicable to *Caparo* is open to serious question, for there seems little doubt that one of the purposes behind the rules in question, especially the requirement to lodge the accounts in an open, public register, was and is investor protection, that is the protection of the economic interests of those in the position of the plaintiff.[20]

The second line of thought was to announce that liability for information that the plaintiff merely finds and does not specifically call for must go too far, that there had to be a limit somewhere, that the limiting doctrine was called 'proximity', that although there were no precise criteria for what counts as sufficient proximity, in this case there was certainly not enough proximity. For there to be proximity, the defendant has to know, or according to Lord Oliver 'inferentially know', that the information is required for some specific purpose, that the defendant knew, 'either actually or inferentially', that the information would be communicated to the plaintiff or a member of an identifiable set of possible plaintiffs, and that it was (objectively) likely[1] that the plaintiff would rely on the information for the purpose specified.[2]

The House of Lords offers no clear explanation for why it chose this particular selection of requirements—some based on actual knowledge, some on objective assessments of likelihood—to govern whether a plaintiff

17 See below ch 7.
18 See eg *Gorris v Scott* (1874) LR 9 Exch 125.
19 [1985] AC 210.
20 See Howarth [1992] CLJ 58 at p 86.
1 Or 'very likely' according to Lord Bridge.
2 See eg *Morgan Crucible v Hill Samuel* [1991] Ch 295 for a case in which these criteria were allegedly satisfied.

should recover in a negligence action. But one line of thought worth pursuing is that the House of Lords was here moving towards an application of contract law notions of remoteness instead of the remoteness concepts usually used in negligence. In contract, the purpose of the remoteness rules[3] is not, as in negligence, to protect the defendant from liability when someone or something else is overwhelmingly more responsible for the damage to the plaintiff, but rather to encourage the parties to take into account unusual risks of consequential loss in the negotiations between them.[4] In contract, therefore, if there are unusual circumstances which create a risk of higher than normal losses, the risk of the extra loss lies on the party that knows about the unusual circumstances unless the parties have reached some explicit agreement about that risk.[5] In *Caparo* there was such an unusual risk, at least in the eyes of the House of Lords, namely that rather than simply using the accounts to question the directors on their running of the company, the plaintiff intended to use them in connection with a bid for the entire company. The House of Lords in *Caparo* argues, at least implicitly, that if the defendants had been told that the plaintiff intended to use the accounts as its only guide to whether or not to make a take-over bid, the defendants would have provided a more careful audit or, perhaps more likely, might have told the plaintiff that the audited accounts were not particularly trustworthy. Where the defendant knows that the plaintiff intends to take such a risk[6] the same considerations do not apply.

White v Jones

White v Jones[7] concerns a family quarrel. The father of the family fell out with his daughters. Angrily, he cut them out of his will. But later he relented and the family was reconciled. He told his solicitors to restore to his daughters their £9,000 legacies. But this suburban King Lear turned not to tragedy but to farce. After a month, the solicitors had done nothing about the father's request to restore his daughters' inheritances. He renewed his instructions. Still the solicitors failed to act. Another month passed. Then, suddenly, the father died. The daughters were surprised to find that despite the reconciliation, they had still lost their legacies. The solicitors' delay having come to light, the daughters sued the solicitors for negligence. The trial judge found against them. He said that there could be no negligence liability in these circumstances regardless of whether

---

3   See eg *Hadley v Baxendale* (1854) 9 Exch 341, *Victoria Laundry v Newman* [1949] 2 KB 528, *Koufos v Czarnikow, The Heron II* [1969] 1 AC 350.
4   See generally Bishop 'The Contract-Tort Boundary and the Economics of Insurance' (1983) 12 JLS 241.
5   Cf especially *Victoria Laundry v Newman* [1949] 2 KB 528.
6   As in *Morgan Crucible,* see above n 2.
7   [1993] 3 All ER 481.

the solicitors had been at fault. After all, the daughters had not relied on the solicitors. They were no worse off than they had been before their father's death. All they had lost was a non-legally enforceable hope that their father would leave them something in his will. The daughters, however, appealed and won.

The one precedent in the daughters' favour was *Ross v Caunters*,[8] a first instance decision by the eminent, if verbose, Sir Robert Megarry V-C. In *Ross v Caunters* a firm of solicitors had displayed breathtaking ignorance of the legal formalities necessary for making a valid will. The disappointed legatee sued the solicitors and won. Sir Robert Megarry V-C reviewed the entire case law on economic loss and concluded that since it was obvious who would be the victim of any default by a solicitor in drafting a will and it would also be obvious how much the loss would be, the fact that the plaintiff did not rely on the defendant did not matter. Reliance was merely a form taken by causation in cases in which the harm to the plaintiff came about by means of words rather than by actions. If the plaintiff could establish causation without reliance, reliance did not matter.

But *Ross v Caunters* was merely a first instance decision and, especially in the light of the contract interpretation of *Hedley Byrne* and the restrictive attitude towards liability for pure economic loss taken by the House of Lords in *Caparo* and *Murphy*, there was much doubt about whether it would survive a direct challenge such as that mounted by the defendant in *White*. But *Ross v Caunters* did survive, and received both the unanimous approval of the Court of Appeal and majority approval in the House of Lords.

White shows that English law is capable of granting a remedy where the defendant causes pure economic loss to the plaintiff even if the plaintiff does not rely on the defendant and there is nothing like a contractual relationship between them. But this does not mean that contract doctrine had no effect in *White*. Indeed the decision was rooted in the inadequacies of existing contract doctrine.

The problem in *White* arises from two lacunae in English contract law, one of which the House of Lords now appears partially to have filled. The two rules in question are the strict adherence of English law to the theory that third party beneficiaries of contracts have no enforceable rights, and the second is that there is normally no right to substantial damages for breach of contract unless the plaintiff has suffered measurable loss. The majority of the House of Lords in *White* was impressed by the fact that the combination of these two doctrines seemed to allow cases in which someone could breach a contract with impunity. If A contracts with B that B will give something to C and B reneges, C cannot sue in contract because of the third party beneficiary rule and A cannot sue for more than nominal damages since he has suffered no harm.

It was open to the House of Lords in *White* to solve the problem directly by overturning one or more of these inconvenient doctrines. Indeed, both doctrines have received a great deal of judicial criticism. Furthermore, the

8   [1980] Ch 297.

House of Lords had recently significantly weakened the second doctrine, the need for the victim of a breach of contract to show personal loss, by saying that where the plaintiff had purported to assign his rights under a contract with the defendant in contravention of a contractual agreement not to do so, the plaintiff could nevertheless sue for substantial damages if the defendant breached the contract—even though the plaintiff no longer had any rights in the subject matter of the contract.[9]

But the House of Lords declined the opportunity to take on the established contract doctrines. In the case of the privity doctrine, Lord Goff said that *White* did not provide a 'suitable occasion for the reconsideration of doctrines so fundamental as these'. In the case of the personal loss doctrine, the question did not technically arise since the beneficiaries were suing in their own names, not as the estate of the father.

That decision, however, left the House of Lords with the problem of how to justify a finding for the plaintiffs from within the law of negligence alone. For two members of the Court, this was too much to ask. Lord Keith, predictably, said that *Hedley Byrne* provided a narrow exception to the rule against recovery of economic loss, an exception that depended on the presence of reliance and a 'close relationship' of 'proximity' between plaintiff and defendant. Since there was neither reliance or 'a close relationship' between the beneficiaries and the solicitor in *White*, Lord Keith favoured the defendant.

Lord Mustill also came down on the side of the defendant. He laid down explicitly what he believes to be the rationale for the *Hedley Byrne* exception. It is, briefly put, the near to contract view. The crucial aspects of the *Hedley Byrne* exception for Lord Mustill are summed up in the words 'mutuality', 'special relationship', 'reliance' and 'undertaking of responsibility'. Their theme is that for the duty to arise, there has to be an element of reciprocity in the relationship between the parties, something close to a bilateral relationship. Even if there is not technically a contract, each side has to do something—the defendant to undertake a task for the benefit of the plaintiff, the plaintiff to rely on the defendant—for any duty to arise.

Lord Mustill pointed out that the situation under scrutiny in *White* lacks all such reciprocity. The defendant undertook to act, but the plaintiffs did nothing. It is a one-sided relationship insufficiently like a contract for there to be recoverable economic loss.

The natural line for the majority in the House of Lords, therefore, might seem to be to say that the rationale for the *Hedley Byrne* exception is not 'nearness to contract' but that the general reasons for refusing to allow pure economic loss in negligence did not apply. This, indeed, is the strategy that Lord Goff adopts. Unfortunately, he does not make very clear what he believes the basis of the rule against recoverability of economic loss in negligence to be, and his explanation for the *Hedley Byrne* exception is merely that *Hedley Byrne* involved 'assumption of responsibility', a reason which, if anything, tends to the 'nearness to contract' view. Lord Goff instead

9   *Linden Gardens v Lenesta Sludge Disposal* [1994] AC 85.

places much emphasis on the fact if the defendant wins in tort, the plaintiffs, who have clearly suffered injustice, will have no redress.

Lord Goff points out, however, that if the reason for not allowing pure economic loss is that there would be unlimited liability, that reason does not apply in *White* since the loss is limited clearly in both amount and who is liable. He also says that if the reason for the exclusion of economic loss in negligence is that otherwise there would be an unacceptable circumvention of the established principles of the law of contract, there is no such unacceptable circumvention here. But Lord Goff does not say why the obvious circumvention of the rules on third party beneficiaries that *White* involves is not 'unacceptable'.

But as we saw in chapter 5, the real reason for the denial of economic loss in negligence is that such loss is usually relational in nature and the reasons for normally not allowing the recovery of relational loss are that the plaintiff is a volunteer or that the plaintiff is the wrong plaintiff. The *Hedley Byrne* exception exists because the plaintiff is not a true volunteer where there has been misrepresentation and because the loss is the plaintiff's alone. In *White* the plaintiffs are also not volunteers, but not because of misrepresentation but because the benefits of the will are imposed on them without the need for their consent. And they are the right plaintiffs because even if the estate of the testator could sue, the money would flow to the testator's residuary legatees, not to the plaintiffs. The only question is whether the plaintiffs have suffered any loss, since they never had the money in the first place, a point that can perhaps be answered by saying that a legitimate expectation of receiving wealth is something of value and the daughters should be entitled to recover the value of that expectation, which, in the absence of any evidence that the testator was about to change his mind and cut them out of the will again, would have been equivalent to the value of their legacies.

It is submitted, therefore, that *White* is probably rightly decided, but on the wrong grounds.

Spring v Guardian Assurance

Before *White* the most significant case on the scope of the *Hedley Byrne* exception was *Spring v Guardian Assurance*.[10] *Spring* is significant in a number of ways. First, it represented a move away from the restrictive line of decisions on pure economic loss that culminated in *Caparo* and *Murphy*. Secondly, it represented the first major defeat for Lord Keith of Kinkel in an important negligence case for many years, and may even herald an era in which at long last appellate judges understand the difference between the duty of care and breach of duty and acknowledge the trial court's function in deciding the breach or fault issue.[11] Thirdly, the House of Lords stepped back from the *Peabody / Caparo* presumption that the mere presence of a statutory rule that affects the way the parties

10   [1994] 3 All ER 129.
11   See Lord Lowry at p 377, Lord Slynn at p 385.

behaved or ought to have behaved is likely to defeat a claim for pure economic loss in negligence.[12]

The facts of *Spring* are complex but may be stylised as follows. The plaintiff used to work for the defendant in the financial services industry. Following disagreements about his work, he decided to leave and work as an agent for another firm. Before he could start work, the rules of the body that regulates the industry required his old employer, the defendant, to provide a reference to the new employer. The defendant sent such a reference. It was damning. It accused the plaintiff of dishonesty. The new employer thereupon refused to allow the plaintiff to start work. But it turned out that the reference was mistaken in its accusation. The plaintiff at worst could be accused of having taken on work beyond his degree of experience. At best he was a competent employee whose employer was at fault in failing to give him proper support and training. In any case he was not dishonest.

The plaintiff's problem was that although the untruth uttered by the defendant had blighted his career, the obvious route of taking out an action for defamation was closed. The reference was defamatory but it was covered by the defence of qualified privilege, a defence that can only be defeated by proof that the defendant was malicious, proof the plaintiff did not have. But the plaintiff was able to show that the defendant had prepared the reference carelessly. So instead of suing in defamation, he sued in neg-ligence.

As we have seen, one of the standard arguments used in the English courts for denying that a duty of care exists, that is for saying that the plaintiff in a negligence action must lose regardless of whether the defendant was at fault, is that to allow a negligence action would undermine some other rule in another field of the law. Courts have denied negligence liability to protect rules in areas as diverse as contract law,[13] administrative law[14] and procedural law.[15] Here the controversy surrounded the rules of another tort.[16]

The defendant in *Spring* added another point. It claimed that if the plaintiff won, employers, fearful of liability, would either decide to write only bland references that conveyed no relevant information, or, effectively the same thing, they would write no references at all. This is an example of another standard argument in favour of denying a duty of care, namely the argument from perverse incentives or 'defensiveness'.[17]

12 See Lord Lowry at p 377.

13 *The Aliakmon* [1986] AC 785, *Banque Keyser Ullman v Skandia* [1990] 1 QB 665, CA, [1991] 2 AC 249, HL.

14 *Jones v Department of Employment* [1989] QB 1, *Calveley v Chief Constable of Merseyside Police* [1989] AC 1228, *Mills v Winchester Diocesan Board* [1989] Ch 428, but see the Court of Appeal in *Lonrho v Tebbit* [1992] 4 All ER 280 at 287.

15 *Corbett v Burge, Warren and Ridgley* (1932) 48 TLR 626, *Business Computers v Registrar of Companies* [1988] Ch 229, but see *Al-Kandari v Brown* [1988] QB 665 and *Welsh v Chief Constable of Merseyside Police* [1993] 1 All ER 692.

16 Strictly two other torts, defamation and malicious falsehood.

17 The argument originates in fears of over cautious 'defensive medicine' but the best example of the use of this argument in a House of Lords case is Lord Keith's fears of 'defensive' policing in *Hill v Chief Constable of West Yorkshire* [1989] AC 53. See above ch 5.

Unsurprisingly, Lord Keith accepted both of these points.[1] What is surprising is that Lord Keith was in a minority of one. Lords Goff, Lowry, Slynn and Woolf all agreed that the preservation of the law of defamation would not be sufficient to deny the plaintiff a remedy for a careless act that had foreseeably and directly harmed the plaintiff. In any case, the majority found, the argument did not work because defamation deals with different issues from negligence. Defamation protects reputation—but a negligent reference can do harm without affecting the plaintiff's reputation, for example by suggesting that the plaintiff suffers from a long-term illness. Furthermore the requirement in negligence that the plaintiff has to show that the defendant was at fault is not necessarily less onerous than the complex shifting of burdens in defamation; it is just different. And the argument that negligence liability will cause employers to be less frank meets a barrage of counter-arguments: that in reality it will not make very much difference; that modern management techniques are based on openness and anyway that unfair dismissal legislation requires employers to tell sacked employees the true reason for their dismissal; that 'it is by no means certain that to have more references is more in the public interest than to have careful references';[2] and most of all, that, *pace* Lord Keith, one should not confuse duty and breach—the defendant's obligation is only to take reasonable care, not to guarantee the accuracy of the reference in all details. 'The courts,' said Lord Slynn, 'can be trusted to set a standard which is not higher than the law of negligence demands.'[3]

But just as *White v Jones* is on the surface a simple extension of negligence liability but underneath is intimately connected with problems in contract doctrine, so *Spring* is also more complex than just a return to the expansive tort doctrines of the era of *Anns v Merton London Borough Council*. In the first place, two of the members of the court were also prepared to find for the plaintiff because of a duty to take care arising out of the previous contract between the plaintiff and the defendant—either because of a *Liverpool City Council v Irwin* implied term ('as a necessary incident of a definable category of contractual relationship')[4] or as an incorporation of and an interpretation of the regulatory rule that the defendant was under a duty to supply a reference to the new employer. The House of Lords thus reinforced its previous decision in *Scally v Southern Health Board*[5] that it would imply into contracts of employment, simply because of the nature of the contract, an obligation on employers to have regard for the economic welfare of employees and in particular an obligation to point out to their employees the pitfalls of the complex pension arrangements that formed part of their contract. For one of these two judges, Lord Woolf, the previous contractual relationship was crucial for

---

1   At 360-63. Note also that in this judgment Lord Keith's three-pronged test has grown yet another prong (at p 359)—the four prongs are (1) foreseeability, (2) proximity, (3) fairness justice and reasonableness, and, as a separate prong, (4) public policy. Unusually for Lord Keith, he relies solely on the fourth prong, public policy.
2   Per Lord Slynn at p 385.
3   Ibid.
4   [1977] AC 239.
5   [1992] 1 AC 294, [1991] IRLR 522.

the negligence case as well, for without it, for example in the case of references sought of a social acquaintance, Lord Woolf would doubt whether there would be sufficient 'proximity'.

This point leads naturally on to the second point that links *Spring* to contract, namely that Lords Goff and Woolf both explicitly endorse the 'equivalent to contract' test for *Hedley Byrne* liability and in Lord Goff's case there is an outright attempt to revive 'assumption of responsibility', as the theoretical basis for why *Hedley Byrne* is an exception to the general rule that pure economic loss is not recoverable in negligence. In one way *Spring* is the wrong case in which to attempt such a revival, since the assumption of responsibility was not voluntary but arose from a statutory obligation.

The assumption of responsibility approach, however, provides an arguable point of distinction between *Spring* and *Reid v Rush & Tompkins*[6] in which the Court of Appeal refused to extend the scope of an employer's responsibility for an employee's welfare to include taking positive action to protect his economic welfare, in that case giving him sufficient information to allow him to ensure that he was properly covered by insurance when working outside the United Kingdom. One of the grounds for the Court of Appeal's decision in *Reid*[7] was that there were no facts to show that the employer had assumed responsibility for the employee's economic welfare. There was only an ordinary contract of employment, and 'no reference by either side to the special risk or what might be done with reference to it'.[8]

Whether this is an adequate distinction is another matter—after all the only factual basis for saying that the defendant in *Spring* had 'assumed responsibility' for the plaintiff's economic welfare was the very act of sending a reference that ensured that the plaintiff's economic welfare would be impaired, and the only basis for saying that the employer had an implied contractual duty in *Scally* to explain the complex provisions of their pension plan to their employees was that it was a 'necessary incident' of a contract of employment. As the House of Lords argues in *Smith v Bush*[9], in the absence of explicit statements like 'leave this to me mate, I'll see you all right', a rare occurrence in real life, 'assumption of responsibility' is as much a normative concept as a factual one. It reflects as much the court's view of what a reasonable person would in the circumstances accept as his or her responsibility as what the defendant did in fact accept.[10]

Similarly any convincing distinction between *Scally* and *Reid* on the question of the implied term is difficult to discern. One might say that in *Scally* the contract already contained provisions about pensions and the question was only whether the employer, having better access to advice and information about the scheme, should be under an obligation to pass

---

6   [1990] 1 WLR 212. See also *Van Oppen v Clerk to the Bedford Charity Trustees* [1990] 1 WLR 235.
7   See Ralph Gibson LJ at p 229.
8   Ibid.
9   [1990] 1 AC 831.
10 See also Lord Oliver in *Caparo v Dickman* [1990] 2 AC 605 at 637.

on its knowledge, whereas in *Reid* the problem was that there was no provision of any sort in the contract about first party insurance. But the employer in *Reid* appears to have been in a much better position to find out about the insurance laws of foreign countries than the employee. According to the classic implied term case *The Moorcock*,[11] this should be enough for the court to imply a term. In *The Moorcock* the court found that the party to a contract who had exclusive access to knowledge relevant to the safety of the other party and to the chances of the contract being performed was subject to an implied obligation at least to take reasonable steps to find out about the danger and to warn the other party about it. The situation in *Reid* seems similar.

The only real distinction between *Scally* and *Reid* appears to be that pensions and their inevitable complexities are, for the time being, more commonly dealt with by employment contracts than are private first party insurance against accidents, so that a reasonable person would more likely accept responsibility for explaining pensions than for checking insurance liabilities. The finding of implied terms is just as much a normative exercise as finding an 'assumption of responsibility'.

To summarise: *Spring*, like *White*, shows that direct reliance by the plaintiff on the defendant, apparently required by the *Caparo* version of *Hedley Byrne* liability, is not in fact necessary. But, going beyond *White*, *Spring* also shows that the existence of such liability is not dependent on the lack of any alternative remedy—indeed it exists despite the existence of such a remedy. It is important to note that *Spring* also challenges the manoeuvre sometimes seen in the literature[12] of defining away *Ross v Caunters* and *White* as cases about some allegedly separate category of 'negligent provision of a service'. *Spring* is about the gratuitous provision of information as much as *Hedley Byrne* was. It is just that the victim of an excessively bad reference suffers if other people believe and act on it, whereas the victim of an excessively good reference only suffers if he himself believes and acts on it.

The problem with *Spring*, however, is that by endorsing the 'nearness to contract' view of *Hedley Byrne*, it made Lord Goff's task in *White v Jones* considerably harder. *White v Jones* only makes sense as an 'assumption of responsibility' case if one can 'assume responsibility' entirely unilaterally. But, then, how is the situation 'equivalent to contract'?

Henderson v Merrett

In *Henderson v Merrett*,[13] the plaintiffs were investors in the Lloyd's insurance market, known as 'names'. They were members of syndicates managed as agents by the defendant underwriters. The plaintiffs were either 'direct names', that is the syndicate to which the names belonged

11 (1889) 14 PD 64.
12 Eg B Markesinis and S Deakin *Tort Law* (1994: Oxford, OUP) at 86 and 95, based on Feldthusen *Economic Negligence* (2nd ed) (1989: Toronto, Carswell) and Feldthusen 'Economic Loss in the Supreme Court of Canada' (1991) 17 Can Bus LJ 556.
13 [1994] 3 All ER 506.

were managed by the members' agents themselves, or 'indirect names', that is the members' agents placed the names with syndicates managed by other agents and entered into agreements with the managing agents of those syndicates delegating their own responsibilities to them. The relationship between names, members' agents and managing agents was regulated by agreements which gave the agent 'absolute discretion' in respect of underwriting business conducted on behalf of the name but it was accepted that it was an implied term of the agreements that the agents would exercise due care and skill in the exercise of their functions as managing agents. The plaintiffs sued the defendants alleging that the defendants had been negligent in the management of the plaintiffs' syndicates. The plaintiffs' obvious route was to sue for breach of contract, but the limitation period for contract starts not when the damage is suffered, as in tort, but at the breach of contract itself. As a consequence the plaintiffs had run out of time for a contract action, but, since they had not yet run out of time for a tort action, they sued in negligence instead.

The defendants raised a number of issues, but they included two classic arguments against the recovery of economic loss. The defendants said first that the contracts defined the relationship between the parties exclusively, and if the plaintiffs could not sue in contract, they could not sue at all. And secondly, and somewhat contradictorily, the managing agents said that since there was no direct contract between themselves and the names, the parties had intended that there should be no legal liability of any sort, either contractual or in tort, between the managing agents and the 'indirect' names whether managing agents appointed as sub-agents by members' agents owed a duty of care to indirect names. The judge found in favour of the plaintiffs on all the issues. The defendants appealed to the Court of Appeal, which dismissed the appeal. The defendants appealed to the House of Lords, which again dismissed the appeal and found for the plaintiffs.

The principal opinion in the House of Lords is again by Lord Goff. Citing the speeches of Lord Devlin and Lord Morris in *Hedley Byrne*, Goff claims here that there is a general principle in the law that goes beyond the class–ification of cases into tort and contract to the effect that where the defendant has 'assumed responsibility' for the plaintiff's economic welfare or where the relationship between the parties is 'equivalent to contract' the defendant may be liable to the plaintiff for negligently caused economic loss. As mentioned above, the 'assumption of responsibility' theory had come in for heavy criticism in *Smith v Eric Bush*[14] on the ground that since the defendant could simply deny that he had actually assumed responsibility, what happened in practice was that the court would come to the conclusion on other grounds that the defendant should be held liable and then explain it by saying that the defendant ought to be treated *as if* he had assumed responsibility. Lord Goff's response was to accept that whether the defendant has accepted responsibility is often an 'objective' question (that is, it does not depend on whether the defendant consciously accepted

---

14 [1989] 2 All ER 514 at 536, [1990] 1 AC 831 at 864-865 per Lord Griffiths; and see also *Caparo Industries plc v Dickman* [1990] 1 All ER 568 at 582-583, [1990] 2 AC 605 at 628 per Lord Roskill.

responsibility but on whether the court believes that such an assumption of responsibility should be ascribed to the defendant) but to claim that the concept is useful because it still helps to explain why there is usually no liability for advice given informally and why disclaimers of responsibility work to negative liability, at least where the Unfair Contract Terms Act does not intervene to strike down such a disclaimer.[15]

This version of Lord Goff's defence of the assumption of responsibility theory is not entirely convincing. There is no need for it to explain non-liability in cases of informal advice or disclaimers since in such cases the defendant will usually be held to be not at fault or the harm will be too remote. In informal advice cases, the foreseeable risk of anyone taking the defendant's advice seriously enough to act on it without taking further advice will often be low, and the loss comes about because of the unreasonable actions of the plaintiff. In disclaimer cases, the disclaimer will often count in itself as a precaution taken by the defendant to signal to the plaintiff that the advice should not be relied upon and if the plaintiff does rely on it without taking further advice, that is the responsibility of the plaintiff. On the other hand, without the assumption of responsibility theory, it would at least be possible for there to be liability in a disclaimer case even if the Unfair Contract Terms Act did not apply. But there are no such cases so far.

In any case, Lord Goff's intention in *Henderson* is to use the assumption of responsibility theory not just for its own sake but also as a jumping off point from which to criticise the *Tai Hing* view of the relationship between tort and contract liability.[16] In place of the general presumption that the presence of a contract means that tort liability will usually be excluded, Goff adopts the position taken by Oliver J in the *Midland Bank Trust v Hett Stubbs and Kemp* case that: [17]

> 'A concurrent or alternative liability in tort will not be admitted if its effect would be to permit the plaintiff to circumvent or escape a contractual exclusion or limitation of liability for the act or omission that would constitute the tort.'

But where this is not the case, liability in both tort and contract is permitted and the plaintiff is allowed to choose the option that is most convenient.

That is, whereas *Tai Hing* worked by making the assumption that the parties intend there to be no tort liability where they have made no contractual provision for liability in a context in which they have made provision for contractual liability with other parties, Goff in *Henderson* says that tort liability is only excluded where it would contradict the terms of an actual contract. Goff does not go on to denounce as wrong any of the many cases, such as *Pacific Associates,* that have used the 'contractual context' argument to deny liability. But it is clear that the significance of *Henderson* is that it shows if one uses the 'equivalent to contract' theory of *Hedley Byrne* to justify liability for pure economic loss, it is inconsistent to

15 See *Smith v Bush* [1990] 1 AC 831.
16 See above ch 5.
17 [1994] 3 All ER at 521.

say that by not making an explicit contract the parties intended there to be no liability. If the parties' relationship was 'near to contract' but they did not go on to make a formal contract, there is a stark choice between saying that in consequence the situation is close enough to contract to allow a negligence action for pure economic loss and saying that the parties could easily have taken the final step of creating a formal contract and since they did not, they must have intended to create no liability at all.

Henderson also prepares the way for the acceptance of a theory that Lord Goff espoused in the Court of Appeal in *The Aliakmon* but which the House of Lords then rejected, namely that the plaintiff in a case about a contractual chain should be allowed to sue more distant links in the chain as long as the plaintiff accepts the burden of any limitations in contractual liability that the defendant has negotiated with an intermediary. This theory, called by Lord Goff the 'transferred loss' theory and which derives from the German concept of *Drittenschadensliquidation*,[18] in effect gives plaintiffs the same rights as those enjoyed by defendants under *Norwich City Council v Harvey*.[19] In *Henderson* Lord Goff is able to gloss over the point since in the cases of the indirect names there was nothing in the agreement between the members' agents and the managing agents that could plausibly protect the managing agents from liability. But the logic of the 'assumption of responsibility' approach is that if the defendant limits his liability to the intermediary, he cannot have accepted any greater responsibility to the plaintiff. And the rejection of the *Tai Hing* approach is accompanied by an assertion that tort liability will not be allowed to undermine explicit contractual promises, which is what the transferred loss theory achieves.[19a] But again, the difficulty with 'assumption of repsonsibility' is that it does not explain the result of *White v Jones*.

THE REBIRTH OF *JUNIOR BOOKS*?

One consequence of *Spring, Henderson* and *White* is that one rather mysterious aspect of *Murphy* may become clearer. Although *Murphy* restored the full authority of *Cattle v Stockton* it also purported not to overrule *Junior Books v Veitchi* but instead to reinterpret it. *Junior Books*, explained Lord Keith, would perhaps survive on the basis that it was an example of the application of the rule in *Hedley Byrne v Heller*.[20] Exactly how the defendant in *Junior Books* is supposed negligently to have misled the plaintiff was unclear, for if simply undertaking a job is a representation, virtually everything is a representation. And if the idea was that the *Junior Books* defendant may have guaranteed the success of the floor in exchange for being chosen as the sub-contractor, surely that means that there would have been a contract between the plaintiff and the sub-contractor in the first place and the problem of

18 See Markesinis *German Law of Torts* 54-56.
19 See above ch 5.
19a Goff returns to the theme of 'transferred loss' in *White v Jones*, and although not taking the German route, is clearly encouraged to reach the same practical solution.
20 See above.

economic loss in tort would not have arisen. But now, it seems, some sense can be made of Lord Keith's remark, albeit in a way of which Lord Keith himself may well disapprove. *Hedley Byrne* liability may no longer be a tightly defined exception to the restrictions on the recovery of pure economic loss in negligence, and may become a theory of liability for all cases at the boundary of contract and tort. It is fault-based, unlike contract, but, at least according to Lord Goff, the duty requires some assumption of responsibility by the defendant rather than being a duty that arises out of a general presumption of responsibility. It also operates its own peculiar remoteness or 'proximity' concepts that are closer to the remoteness rules used in contract than the remoteness rules used in negligence, with the exception that they are used to decide whether the defendant is liable at all, as in negligence, rather than, as in contract, to limit the extent of the compensation to what would normally have been expected. In this sense *Junior Books* is indeed a *Hedley Byrne* case. The claim in *Junior Books* was a fault-based one against a defendant who can plausibly be said to have assumed responsibility and in which there is nothing unusual about the extent of the loss that the parties would have taken into account in their decisions about whether to accept the deals on offer.

Anomalies

With the exception of *White v Jones*, the last section may have given the impression that English law on pure economic loss is in the process of sorting itself out by adopting the 'contractual' view of *Hedley Byrne*. But this is still far from the truth. All that is happening is a possible consolidation of the *Hedley Byrne* exception to the general rule against pure economic loss. The general rule itself still has many problems and even the consolidated exception is capable of producing anomalies. We shall look at one such anomaly before turning to three problems that arise from the general rule itself.

Surveyors vs auditors

In *Smith v Bush*[1] the plaintiffs were house buyers who had relied to their detriment on careless surveys and valuations carried out by the defendant surveyors. The surveyors had acted not for the plaintiffs themselves but for the lending institutions that were considering making loans to the plaintiffs. It was common knowledge that lending institutions show buyers the results of such surveys and that buyers rely on them. Previous cases[2] had established that surveyors could be liable in such circumstances. This liability the House of Lords confirmed in *Smith v Bush*. The defendants, however, had taken the precaution of including, on the face of their

1   [1990] 1 AC 831.
2   Eg *Yianni v Edwin Evans* [1982] QB 438.

valuations, disclaimers purporting to exclude their liability to the buyers. The House of Lords swept these disclaimers aside as contrary to the reasonableness requirements of the Unfair Contract Terms Act 1977. The House of Lords also rejected the defendants' further ingenious argument that the Unfair Contract Terms Act only applied to exclusions of liability and not to disclaimers that prevented liability from arising in the first place, a conclusion the House of Lords could only reach by rejecting the 'assumption of responsibility' theory of *Hedley Byrne* liability that Lord Goff is now assiduously trying to revive.

Two points arise. First, how is *Smith v Bush* to survive if Lord Goff succeeds in re-establishing the assumption of responsibility view of *Hedley Byrne*? If the disclaimer used by surveyors really is a denial of assumption of responsibility, why should not their argument succeed that the Unfair Contract Terms Act should not apply? But if so, how would the situation be different from one in which there was a contract between the surveyor and the buyer that included precisely the same disclaimer, a situation to which the Unfair Contract Terms Act would apply?

Secondly, compare the treatment of surveyors in *Smith* with the treatment of auditors in *Caparo*. Surveyors value houses, auditors value companies. Laying aside the question of the disclaimer and the Unfair Contract Terms Act, why should auditors receive so much more favourable treatment from the law than surveyors? The formal doctrinal answer is that the special remoteness or 'proximity' rules applicable to *Hedley Byrne* cases produce precisely this difference in result. Surveyors almost invariably carry out their task in the knowledge that there is some specific person somewhere who is interested in buying the property. But auditors carry out their task not for the purpose of any specific transaction but on an annual basis, pursuant to statutory provisions and resolutions of the company itself.

But another difference between surveyors and auditors is that the results of a surveyor's work usually remain private—they are known only to the lending institution and the buyer—whereas the results of an auditor's work are public, and potentially usable by anyone. The formal doctrinal position is that there is no liability in the auditor's case because there is a greater potential for unusual use of the information by greater numbers of people. But this, from one point of view, is very odd, for the auditor is also the potential author of much more harm than the surveyor. The House of Lords did not attempt to justify this result, although, as we shall see below, there may be good reasons for it in limited circumstances.

Piggy back loss

One of the more puzzling aspects of the English law on the recoverability of pure economic loss is one that is often taken to be straightforward or obvious,[3] namely the acceptance of the recoverability of pure economic loss

---

3   See eg *Markesinis and Deakin* at p 84.

that is the direct consequence of physical harm to property, the so-called piggy back loss doctrine.[4] In the *Edison*[5] for example, it was assumed to be self-evident that if A sinks B's ship, B can claim not just the value of the ship, but also compensation for any loss incurred by B if the loss of the ship prevented B from carrying out a contract with a third party. In *Spartan Steel v Martin*,[6] where the defendant carelessly cut the power cable supplying the plaintiff's foundry and the power cut ruined castings that were in the process of being made, the Court of Appeal compensated the plaintiff not just for the cost of replacing the materials that had been damaged but also for the profit that the plaintiff would have made if it had sold the completed casting to a customer. But at the same time, the court did not allow the plaintiff's further claim for the profit on the sale of castings that it would have made but could not even begin to make because of the power cut. In the case of the latter claim, no castings had suffered physical harm.

But these distinctions are arbitrary. Why should an act of physical destruction make any difference? There is no difference between the lost profit on the casting that was damaged and the lost profit on the castings that were not started. The plaintiff was unable to finish the first casting, so that the plaintiff could not profit from the value added to the raw materials by the process of making them into a casting. The only difference between the castings that were not finished and the castings that were not started is that the raw materials for the former were lost whereas the raw materials for the latter were not. If, therefore, the plaintiff is compensated for the loss of the materials for the first casting, the position of the plaintiff with regard to all the castings becomes identical.

Difference between economic loss and property damage

The problem of the recoverability of piggy back loss is itself only a variation on a more fundamental problem, namely the distinction between pure economic loss, presumed not to be recoverable, and property damage, presumed to be recoverable. As Stevenson J said in *Canadian National Rly v Norsk Pacific SS Co*:[7]

'Although I am prepared to recognise that a human being is more important than property and lost expectations of profit, I fail to see how property and economic losses can be distinguished.'

The crux of the problem is this. If you buy a Porsche, there is a risk that someone will damage it. If they do, the Porsche's monetary value falls. The law allows you to sue for this loss of value. The cost of repairing the

---

4   See above.
5   *Liesbosch Dredger v SS Edison* [1933] AC 449.
6   See above.
7   (1992) 91 DLR (4th) 289 at 383.

Porsche may be one measure of the loss, but the essence of your claim is loss of value.[8]

But what is the difference between the damage to your Porsche and *Cattle v Stockton*? In *Cattle* the plaintiff had something valuable, his contract with the third party, that the defendant by his careless action reduced in value. If the plaintiff's loss in *Cattle* is not recoverable, why can you recover for the reduction in value to your Porsche?

One might say that the difference is that it is easier to measure the lost value of the Porsche than the lost value of the contract. But this is not so. The market for damaged or repaired Porsches is a limited one from which to glean market information, whereas the contract may well have precise provisions about damages for breach. Furthermore, the pristine Porsche may have had a sentimental value that repairs could not restore and which will now always be diminished, a value whose magnitude will be more difficult to ascertain than the plaintiff's extra cost in *Cattle v Stockton*.

One might argue that the risk in *Cattle v Stockton* is just a risk that one has to take. But why should not the same point apply to the Porsche? Anyone who buys a Porsche knows that it may be damaged by other people's negligence. The more expensive the object you own, the greater the risk you take. Admittedly, one might have emotional attachments to objects that one will not have to contracts, but most objects do not arouse such passions, especially not objects such as the ship in *The Edison* and the semi-finished casting in *Spartan Steel*. Moreover, some contracts do potentially have emotional content—artistic commissions for example.

Finally, one might imagine that the difference between pure economic loss and property damage might be located in the non-physical nature of the loss in the former. But this is to misunderstand what pure economic loss is, and what property is. Take a case such as *The Aliakmon*.[9] The plaintiff buys goods from a third party on the basis that property in the goods will pass to the plaintiff only when they arrive, but that the risk of their being damaged in transit will rest on the plaintiff (in the sense that the seller only guarantees the quality of the goods as they are when he sends them, not as they are when they arrive). The defendant is a shipper who carelessly damages the goods in transit. Despite the fact the case is about physical damage to the goods, the plaintiff's claim is for pure economic loss. This is because his interest in the goods is contractual rather than proprietary. If the seller wanted to sue (and the case only arose because, due to a technicality, the plaintiff had not managed to acquire by assignment the seller's rights against the shipper) the seller would be claiming for property damage, not pure economic loss. The difference lies not in the physical nature of the harm but in the legal relationship between the plaintiff and the damaged object.

Even more stark is the case of *The Mineral Transporter*[10] in which a claim against a defendant who had damaged a ship chartered by the

---

8   See *The London Corpn* [1935] P 70, 77; *Payton v Brooks* [1974] RTR 169.
9   See above.
10 *Candlewood Navigation v Mitsui Lines* [1986] AC 1.

plaintiff failed because the plaintiff had the wrong sort of charter. One sort of charter gives rise to a proprietary right analogous to a leasehold, the other sort gives rise only to a contractual right. The plaintiff had only the second sort of charter, a time charter, and so the court rejected the claim as a claim for pure economic loss.

Both pure economic loss and property damage concern claims for reductions in the plaintiff's wealth. The only difference between the two appears to be the nature of the plaintiff's legal claim to that wealth. In property damage, the plaintiff is the owner of the wealth, in pure economic loss the plaintiff has only a contractual claim to the wealth or, in the case of lost business opportunities or lost legacies in wills only a non-legally enforceable hope or expectation. Admittedly there are number of difficult borderline cases between property and contract—for example beneficial interests in trusts and shares in companies—which are treated as property for many purposes but damage to which would probably count as pure economic loss.[11] But these borderline examples do not affect the point that the crucial question is the exact nature of the relationship between the plaintiff and the form of wealth whose value the defendant's carelessness has reduced, not the physicality of the harm.

There are only three ways to resolve the problem of the different treatment of property damage and pure economic loss. First, one might allow claims for pure economic loss on the same basis as claims for property damage. Second, one might disallow claims for property damage except where the equivalent pure economic loss claim would be allowed. Third one might draw the line between recoverable and non-recoverable losses in a way that cuts across the present distinction between the two. The pressure for the first solution is obvious, and has succeeded in Canada.[12] The second solution has some academic support[13] but it is the third which has most recently made its appearance in the courts in England. In *The Nicholas H*[14], for example, a ship loaded the plaintiffs' cargoes (lead and zinc) in South America for carriage to Italy and Russia. During the voyage, a crack was found in the vessel's hull and it anchored off San Juan, Puerto Rico. While at anchor further cracks developed and arrangements were made for a 'classification society' (the defendants NKK) to survey the vessel at anchor. On the surveyor's recommendation, the ship put into the nearest port for repairs. But it turned out that the recommended permanent repairs would take a very long time. The ship's owners ordered temporary repairs and asked the surveyor to recommend that the ship go to its first port of call, discharge its cargo and then undergo the permanent repairs. The surveyor agreed.

11 See *Caparo* for hints about the treatment of the value of shares—the position is of course complicated by the Rule in *Foss v Harbottle* which makes the company itself, and not the shareholders, the sole proper plaintiff when harm is caused to the company.
12 *Canadian National Rly v Norsk Pacific SS Co* (1992) 91 DLR (4th) 289.
13 Richard Abel 'Should tort law protect property against accidental loss?' in M Furmston (ed) *The Law of Tort: Policies and Trends in Liability for Damage to Property and Economic Loss* (1986; London, Duckworth) pp 155-190.
14 *Marc Rich v Bishop Rock Marine, The Nicholas H* [1994] 1 Lloyd's Rep 492.

The ship sailed from San Juan and the following day reported that the welding of the temporary repairs had cracked. Further repairs were attempted at sea but they were unsuccessful and the vessel sank with all its cargo.

The plaintiffs sued the ship's owners and NKK. The claim against the owners was settled for about $500,000, a low sum that resulted from the provisions of the Hague Visby rules, an internationally accepted set of standard conditions for the carriage of goods by sea. The plaintiffs claimed the balance of the loss, about $5.5m, from the defendants. In contrast with *The Aliakmon* and *The Mineral Transporter*, the plaintiff had property rights in the lost goods, not just contractual rights. The first instance court therefore said that there was no reason, if the facts could be proved and fault established, why the defendants should not be held liable. But the Court of Appeal said that the plaintiff could not win even if the facts and fault were proved because: (1) such a result would upset the regime established for liability for carriage of goods at sea by the Hague-Visby rules; and (2) it was the shipowners not the society who were in charge of the cargo, there was no dealing of any nature between the cargo-owners and the society and nothing to suggest that the cargo-owners were doing more than relying on the shipowners to take care of the cargo[15]—in other words the damage was too remote from the surveyor's actions and no offsetting 'equivalent to contract' relationship between the plaintiff and the defendant.

The plaintiff argued that considerations such as the effect of liability on the conclusiveness of the Hague-Visby rules and whether there was a relationship equivalent to contract were not relevant in a case that concerned property damage, not pure economic loss. But Saville LJ said:

'In recent years there have been several cases which deal with situations where no physical damage has resulted from the care-lessness in question, but where the claimant has sustained financial loss or expense. To my mind the law draws no fundamental difference between such cases and those where there is damage to person or property. Whatever the nature of the loss sustained, the court approaches the question in the same way.'

That is, all duty arguments, including the argument from the integrity of other areas of the law and arguments from 'proximity' (here meaning simply remoteness that goes to the whole of the loss), apply to property damage cases as much as to economic loss cases. As noted above, *The Nicholas H*[16] may be about property damage, but it is in a sense a case about relational damage, since the plaintiff's loss arises from the loss of potential and actual contracts with buyers of the cargo and of products that could be made out of the cargo rather than from direct harm to the plaintiff.

---

15 At p 499.
16 See above ch 5.

If the approach of *The Nicholas H* is sustained in future cases, the distinction between economic loss and property damage will continue to disappear, but not because more and more economic loss cases will give rise to liability but rather because property loss cases will not give rise to liability.

Arguments allegedly lying behind present law

We now pass from the law as it stands to the arguments that allegedly justify both the basic rule that pure economic loss is not recoverable and the *Hedley Byrne* exception. The fluidity of this area of the law means that the arguments lying behind the law will tend to be of more lasting value than the existing rules themselves. Each argument will be explained and then evaluated.[16a]

Separation of tort and contract

The first argument to consider is that economic loss should not be permitted in negligence in order to maintain the distinction between tort and contract. The separation of tort and contract is said to justify the rule against recovering pure economic loss in negligence because, since the recovery of pure economic loss is supposed to be the job of contract law, if such losses were also recoverable in negligence, contract law would allegedly lose its distinctiveness. As a consequence, some of contract law's useful and necessary principles would be undermined.

But the separation of tort and contract is not a necessary nor a necessarily beneficial state of affairs. The gradual separation of tort and contract occurred only in the eighteenth and nineteenth centuries. Before then, although there cannot be said to have been anything like a unified law of obligations in England, attention focussed on other issues, such as whether the damage had been caused directly or indirectly. The separation of tort and contract throws attention onto only one of the possible criteria for classifying legal claims, albeit a compelling one in a society based on the free exchange of goods and services, namely on whether or not the harm complained of arises from an exchange of value between the parties. Like all classification rules, it has advantages and disadvantages and tends, at its edges, to require fairly arbitrary decisions. Two of its disadvantages, however, deserve special mention. First, it fails to take into account the degree to which voluntary transactions include non-voluntary elements. Some transactions, such as marriage, have always had this characteristic, since they are package deals and subject to objective interpretation—

16a This section draws heavily on my paper 'Economic Loss in England: The Search for Coherence' delivered at the Colloquium of the UK National Committee for Comparative Law at the University of East Anglia, September 1994.

marriage itself may be voluntary but many of its legal consequences and contents have not been negotiable between the parties. Others, such as contracts between consumers and producers of goods and financial products, have more recently become increasingly subject to compulsory statutory regulation. This is why it is not satisfactory to make the application of the Unfair Contract Terms Act to the *Smith v Bush* situation depend on whether one takes the assumption of responsibility view of *Hedley Byrne* as opposed to the negligence view. The policy of the statute is to regulate the responsibilities of the suppliers of goods and services regardless of what they consent to.

Moreover the voluntariness of transactions is not always clear-cut; buying water from a monopoly supplier is a very different business from buying wine from a supermarket.

Secondly, as the discussion of *Tai Hing* has already demonstrated, it is often possible, though perhaps not as often as some judges believe, to interpret a situation in which there has been no exchange as one in which the parties have intentionally decided not to enter into a transaction, so that they may be taken to have intended the consequences of their actions as much as if they had transacted.

In any case, it is not true that allowing claims for pure economic loss in negligence would mean that contract law would lose its distinctiveness. English law has long allowed claims in tort for pure economic loss when the harm was caused intentionally, as in deceit or inducing a breach of contract or interference with business by unlawful means. None of this has reduced the distinctiveness of contract. Note especially that breach of contract in English law has nothing to do with fault. A failure to perform a contractual promise is a breach whether it is intentional or accidental, reasonable or unreasonable. Contractual rights in England can be protected without further proof of fault. Allowing negligence actions for pure economic loss does not affect that position at all.

And so the case against allowing the law of negligence into claims for pure economic loss on the grounds of keeping tort and contract separate has to rest on more specific objections. It is to these that we now turn.

Protecting the English third party benefit rule

One frequently made charge against allowing pure economic loss claims in negligence is that to do so would undermine the strictness of the English third party beneficiary rule in contract.[17] The idea is that English law gives no rights to enforce a contract to strangers to the contract, even if the parties intend the contract to benefit the stranger. Economic loss in negligence neatly side-steps the doctrine. If A contracts with B to bestow a benefit on C and then fails to perform, as long as A acted unreasonably in

---

17 See *The Aliakmon* above and *White v Jones* above.

so failing, which is likely, C's disappointment will be a foreseeable result of A's act and thus actionable.

Similarly, in a cases such as *Junior Books*,[18] *The Aliakmon*,[19] *Simaan v Pilkington (No 2)*,[20] *Greater Nottingham Co-operative v Cementation*,[1] *Gran Gelato v Richcliff*[2] and many others, the plaintiff's objective is to sue directly someone who had a contract with someone with whom the plaintiff had a contract. The basis of the plaintiff's claim is that if the defendant had properly performed its contract with the intermediary, the plaintiff would not have suffered harm or disappointment. Usually plaintiffs have little practical choice but to sue this particular defendant because the more orthodox defendant, the intermediary, has either disappeared, or gone bankrupt or benefits from some kind of impenetrable immunity. But there is no doubt that these plaintiffs are in effect complaining about failures properly to perform contracts to which they were not parties.

On the other hand, the English third party beneficiary rule is not universally applauded nor uniformly applied. To take the second point first, in several recent cases the Court of Appeal has allowed defendants to take advantage of contractual clauses placing the relevant risks on the plaintiff even though the contract in question was between the plaintiff and an intermediary, not with the defendant directly. Thus, in *Norwich City Council v Harvey* May LJ said:[3]

> 'I do not think that the mere fact that there is no strict privity between the employer and sub-contractor should prevent the latter from relying on the clear basis on which all the parties contracted in relation to damage.'

It seems that undermining the doctrine of the privity of contract is only of concern when the doctrine adversely affects plaintiffs. When applying the principle would adversely affect defendants, the courts ignore it.

As for underlying support for the rule itself, several commentators have condemned it,[4] the Law Commission has called for reform[5] and the judges themselves have long questioned it without having the boldness to institute the reform themselves.[6]

---

18 See above.
19 See above.
20 [1988] QB 758.
1   [1989] QB 71.
2   [1992] 1 All ER 865.
3   [1989] 1 All ER 1180, [1989] 1 WLR 828. See also *Pacific Associates v Baxter* [1990] 1 QB 993.
4   Eg Markesinis 'An Expanding Tort Law—the Price of a Rigid Contract Law' (1987) 103 LQR 354.
5   See Law Commission Consultation paper no 121.
6   *Woodar v Wimpey* [1980] 1 WLR 277 at 300 per Lord Scarman.

Contract about expectations and benefits, tort about harms and losses and the supposed uncertainty of economic loss

A related criticism of attempts to award pure economic loss in negligence is that it is alleged that the function of tort law is to protect one's existing health and wealth, not to protect one's expectations of future gain, which is the function of contract. But this distinction, based on the traditional distinction between *damnum emergens* and *lucrum cessans*, is not sustainable in practice. For one thing, one's present wealth, on any reasonable view, includes one's future expectations of gain, suitably discounted for the risk of those expectations not being fulfilled. That is why, for example, in negligence cases involving personal injury, plaintiffs can claim compensation for lost future earnings. Lost future earnings are expectations only, but one can lose them as much as one loses property which is destroyed. Furthermore, a contract to prevent harm (for example a contract to guard a factory) is as much a contract as a contract to bestow a benefit.

Similarly, it is not true, as is sometimes claimed,[7] that pure economic loss damages are more difficult to measure accurately than other types of tort damages. If anything, the opposite is true. Pure economic loss cases are usually about goods and services that have clear market values or about contracts at ascertained prices. Damages for pain and suffering or loss of amenity, on the other hand, are inherently uncertain and subjective.

A related claim is that although the plaintiff may know the expected profit on a deal, the defendant does not know it, and usually has no way of finding it out.[8] But the defendant in a personal injury case similarly has no way of knowing the earning capacity of the injured plaintiff, and thus has no way of knowing what damages will need to be paid.

Problems of assessing value when no exchange

There is, however, one aspect of the difference between harm or disappointment arising out of a trading relationship and similar harm or disappointment arising outside trading relationships that should be taken more seriously, and that is the added difficulty in assessing value when the parties concerned have not themselves entered into a transaction with each other. It is also another version of the uncertainty argument rehearsed above. As Lord Brandon said in his dissenting speech in *Junior Books v Veitchi*:[9]

'In any case where complaint was made by an ultimate consumer that a product made by some persons with whom he himself had no contract was defective, by what standard or standards of quality

7   See eg *Hedley Byrne* above at 536f.
8   See Stapleton 'Duty of Care and Economic Loss: A Wider Agenda' (1991) 107 LQR 249 at 255-56.
9   [1983] 1 AC 520 at 551-52.

would the question of defectiveness fall to be decided? ... [T]he question ... remains entirely at large and cannot be given any just or satisfactory answer.'

That is, contracts involve trade-offs. If there are risks involved in a deal, as there usually are, a party who wants to bear a lower share of the risk will need to offer to accept a lower price or lower quality in exchange for transferring part of the risk to the other party. Indeed, quality itself is a form of risk, since lower quality often means not lower standards of performance when the product is working but greater risks of breakdown and of complete failure over a shorter period. Because people have different preferences for risk, it follows that a deal struck by one pair of people may not be the deal that another pair might make about the same subject matter. And so, if one has not struck a deal, one cannot be certain what deal one might have struck. That others have struck a deal about the same subject matter on particular terms proves nothing.

Admittedly in many cases one can construct a near enough guess of what the parties would have agreed. Most deals arise out of a combination of market prices, explicit standard terms, accepted custom and practice, statutory presumptions and inalienable statutory rights. In particular, the courts have long been required by statute[10] to apply a set of basic minimum quality standards to many contracts. But even if one can construct most of the deal that would have been on offer, both price and quality, one cannot know for certain whether anyone other than people who have in fact accepted the deal on those terms would accept it.

One can, however, be more certain in some cases than in others. In many economic loss cases, one person is a member of both pairs of deals. A contracts with B and then B contracts with C about the same subject matter. Does it not follow that A and C would have contracted on a basis common to the A/B and B/C deals?

This certainly seems so regarding the quality of particular goods at particular prices. If A contracts with B for the supply of a car of a specific age and type, B has no incentive to ask C to supply a car of a different age and type. B has no interest in asking for a more expensive, higher quality car or a less expensive lower quality car or a car with different qualities at the same price, since B does not know whether A wants such a car. And we already know from the A/B deal that A is prepared to pay the price agreed for the car of the agreed quality.

What if B mistakenly orders the wrong car but A accepts it. Later it turns out to have a latent defect. How do we know that A would have contracted at all for a car with such defects? The answer is that we know because he already has. When the car arrived with different external characteristics, A could have rejected it, but ex hypothesi did not. A is in exactly the same situation as he would have been in if he had ordered the car that was delivered.

The position is similar if we move away from simple defects to expected special performance characteristics. For example, A contracts with B for a

10 Eg since the Sale of Goods Act 1893.

factory with certain special characteristics. B sub-contracts with C but mistakenly changes the quality requirements. C completes the work as ordered by B. A then uses the factory for a while before it becomes clear that his requirements have not been met. There is no difficulty with the value of the deal. We know what A expected from the contract with B and we know that he paid for it. That B asked C for something else may be relevant to the issue of whether C has acted unreasonably (presumably he has not) and to the issue of remoteness—should B's act and not C's count as the exclusive cause of A's disappointment (presumably it should). But none of this is a bar to measuring the extent of A's disappointment. This means that if, exceptionally, the court finds C to have acted carelessly and the damage not to be too remote, the court could be reasonably certain that there has been a loss and reasonably certain of how big it was.

On the other hand, if we focus not on quality but on other risks the picture changes. Consider the following example. A contracts with B for the supply of dry-cleaning equipment. A informs B that if the equipment arrives late A will lose a public contract to supply dry-cleaning services that offered a very high, indeed an unusual level of profit.[11] B agrees to deliver on time nevertheless, and in exchange for a slightly higher price accepts responsibility for A's expected super-profits. But B in turn has to obtain special components from C. B informs C of A's situation, but C says that it does not want to take responsibility for A's risks. B, desperate to secure the components, agrees to trade on C's standard terms, according to which C accepts no responsibility at all for any consequential losses. C fails to deliver on time, causing B to default and A to lose the public contract. B, it turns out, is insolvent. A wishes to proceed directly against C.

Lord Brandon's argument would be that we cannot know whether A would have agreed to trade directly with C either at all or on any particular terms, including the terms agreed by A and B, the terms agreed between B and C and any other possible terms. All we know is that, on the one hand, A wanted to shift the risk to B and was prepared to pay for it, and that, on the other hand, C's negotiation with B and its standard terms show that C was more unwilling than B to accept such risks. Where the risk would have ended up as between A and C, and what price they would have agreed, has to be a matter of pure speculation.

As a consequence, if A could sue C for negligence, it would indeed be unclear what damages should be claimable. C would say that on the basis of the deal it negotiated with B, it should pay nothing. But A would argue that on the basis of the deal it negotiated with B, its actual loss is the whole of the super-profit.

If C had negotiated a deal with B agreeing or impliedly agreeing to be responsible for ordinary foreseeable losses, or had agreed a deal putting a maximum figure on consequential damages, one could at least argue that C had accepted a level of responsibility of up to that level. But no such compromise is available where C explicitly contracts out of any such responsibility, and in any case it is not clear that A would have been willing

11   Cf *Victoria Laundry v Newman* [1949] 2 KB 528.

to trade at all if C insists on limiting its liability, in which case A's loss is zero since it would never have had any legitimate expectation of profit.

It seems, therefore, that Lord Brandon's argument has some force when the question raised is that of the distribution of the risk of consequential loss, but has less force when the issue is that of the quality of the goods or services to be supplied.

English law, however, does not follow any such subtleties. The fall of *Anns* and, in particular, of *Junior Books* shows that pure economic loss based on disappointment in the quality of the goods or service delivered by the defendant is not recoverable. As Lord Bridge said in *Murphy v Brentwood*:[12]

> '[I]f a manufacturer produces and sells a chattel which is merely defective in quality, even to the extent that it is valueless for the purpose for which it is intended, the manufacturer's liability at common law arises only under ... the terms of any contract to which he is a party in relation to the chattel; the common law does not impose on him any liability in tort to persons to whom he owes no duty in contract but who, having acquired the chattel, suffer economic loss because the chattel is defective in quality.'

Anthropological objections to mixing tort and contract

Finally in this section we should consider a deeper objection to the mixing of contract and tort, namely that the purpose of the distinction between the two is to keep separate and to mark out the socially important boundary between those aspects of life that are subject to trade, economic exchange and the laws of the market and those aspects of life that are not, a boundary that defines a culture and changes in which track the most important changes in the culture itself.

Tort is a culturally dangerous area of the law precisely because it is where aspects of well-being that are not usually thought of as having monetary value and as being available for exchange—for example, the use of our bodily parts and the absence of pain and distress—are, for the purposes of setting levels of compensation, given monetary values. But it is important for the moral underpinning of tort law, regardless of how economists may redescribe it, that these compensation payments are not seen as prices, as the exchange values of arms and legs and of pain and distress. Although the threat of having to pay damages can operate openly as a deterrent against causing injury, the idea, common to economic thought,[13] that damages are merely a sort of state regulated price that defendants can pay to obtain the right to cause harm is generally thought

12 [1991] 1 AC 398 at 475.
13 See generally Calabresi and Melamed 'Property Rules, Liability Rules and Inalienability: One view of the Cathedral' 85 Harv LR 1089 (1972).

to be offensive and inappropriate both by judges and by plaintiffs. In the infamous *Ford Pinto* case,[14] for example, the Ford Motor Corporation, having invested heavily in developing a new compact car, discovered that the car had a tendency to explode if hit from behind at 20 to 30 mph. Ford decided that it would cost too much money to change the design and allowed the cars onto the market, with fatal results. The California Court of Appeals upheld a judgment for $3.5m against Ford, a judgment that included a punitive element. The Court of Appeals said:

> '[I]n commerce related torts, the manufacturer may find it more profitable to treat compensatory damages as a part of the cost of doing business ... Deterrence of such "objectionable corporate policies" serves one of the principal purposes of [punitive damages].'

Lying behind these concerns is an anxiety, which one can see also in phenomena such as the banning of trade in human kidneys,[15] that the barriers between the tradable and the non-tradable should be maintained. It is an anxiety that anthropologists say affects many societies, but what appears to mark out our own society, and many western European societies, is the association of this anxiety with money itself. As the leading anthropologists in this field say:[16]

> 'One particularly prominent strand in Western discourse, which goes back to Aristotle, is the general condemnation of money and trade in the light of an ideal of household self-sufficiency and production for use ... Profit-oriented exchange is [seen as] un–natural; and is destructive of bonds between households...
>
> Our own intellectual tradition, however, also contains another very different kind of discourse about money and monetary exch–ange which sees it as a far more benign influence on social life...
>
> But what all these different strands in our cultural tradition appear to agree about is that—whether for good or ill—money acts as an incredibly powerful agent of profound social and cultural transformations. Regardless of the cultural context and the nature of existing relations of production and exchange, it is often credited with an intrinsic power to revolutionise society and culture.'

The anxiety specifically about money and exchange may therefore explain the anxiety lawyers seem to have about pure economic loss in tort, which is largely a question of monetary (or, as it is sometimes termed, 'purely pecuniary') loss. Economic loss brings negligence, which is usually about measuring the unmeasurable, into uncomfortably close contact with

---

14 *Grimshaw v Ford Motor Co* 174 Cal Rep 348 (1981). See above.
15 See Human Organ Transplants Act 1989.
16 Bloch and Parry 'Introduction: Money and the morality of exchange' in J Parry and M Bloch (eds) *Money and the Morality of Exchange* (1989: Cambridge, Cambridge University Press) at p 3.

the world of money and pure exchange values. Negligence should be kept as far away as possible from any notion that the compensation it awards has to do with money values, trade and exchange, for otherwise the law will begin to undermine fundamental ideas about the non-tradability of bodily parts and human health.

The same anxieties do not affect the intentional torts because the classification scheme for torts now widely adopted in England keeps separate the torts concerned with bodily integrity (assault, battery, false imprisonment and *Wilkinson v Downton*: see chapter 9) from the financial and business torts (deceit, interference with contract, conspiracy to injure and so on). The problem arises specifically in negligence because the central and typical example of a negligence case is about personal injury, but in which claims for pure economic loss can plausibly be made within the verbal formulae that are used to describe the tort.

But even if this anthropological explanation of legal anxiety about pure economic loss in negligence is true, which it may be, does it have any rational and persuasive force as well as explanatory force? That is, even if lawyers feel this anxiety, should they act upon it?

These are murky waters. Fundamental political questions arise about the rationality of markets and the desirability of complete openness about the trade-offs involved in the formulation and implementation of public policy. Should there be areas of life to which we should not apply rational economic analysis? How do we deal with the undoubted losses in efficiency and wealth that flow from not treating some questions in an economic or utilitarian way? Do we pretend the losses do not exist, for admitting as much would be to bring back the very kind of dialogue we want to avoid, or do we face openly the trade-offs between wealth and moral comfort?

But is also worth reflecting on the extent to which the issues raised here are purely symbolic. How many people will come to believe, for example, that safety is tradable as a result of allowing pure economic loss to be recovered in negligence? Are the classification systems of the common law really so central to our culture that if they change, our fundamental values will change with them? Or is not the reality that if there is any causal relationship between fundamental values and the classification systems of the common law, which there may not be, the direction of causality is more likely to go from the culture's fundamental values to the law rather than the other way round?

Economic incentives

We now pass on to a second set of arguments that have been put forward against allowing the recovery of pure economic loss in negligence, namely economic arguments. The underlying strategy of this form of argument is to suggest that to allow such recovery would provide incentives for people to behave in such a way that the result would be far worse than would ensue if such losses remained unrecoverable.

Protection of competitive process

The first such argument is that to allow the recovery of pure economic loss in negligence would be to undermine the will to compete and to win business away from others that lies at the heart of a market-based economy. As Goff LJ said in the Court of Appeal in *The Aliakmon*:[17]

'The philosophy of the market place presumes that it is lawful to gain profit by causing others economic loss.'

The idea is that pure economic loss is an inevitable side-effect of competition, since those traders who fail to win business will be dis—appointed in their expectations of gain. But economic loss is thus seen as beneficial, as part of the necessary reallocation of resources to their most productive uses, and thus as part of the way markets create efficiency.

There are two objections to this line of reasoning. First, the losses suffered by those who are driven out of business by competition are not the same sort of losses as those suffered by plaintiffs in pure economic loss cases. In a competitive economy no one has a legitimate expectation to an income for life. Pure economic loss is about interference in expectations that are backed by some specific form of legitimacy—for example by an already existing contract or the reasonable prospect of a specific transaction with another person, whether between the plaintiff and another or between the defendant and another. Difficulties may arise at the margins, especially in the case of contracts about to be concluded or gift relationships, but the general point is clear—it is not necessary to exclude pure economic loss from the scope of negligence to protect the functioning of competitive markets because the kind of losses suffered as a result of competition are not the kind of losses that could be recovered as pure economic loss.

Secondly, for similar reasons, in the vast majority of such cases, even if in principle the recovery of pure economic loss was admitted, the plaintiff could not be held liable because it would be impossible to show fault. Is it unreasonable behaviour, in an economy based on competitive markets, to offer one's goods at prices so low that one's competitors go out of business? It may be foreseeable that they would go out of business, but, again illustrating the difference between foreseeability and fault, it would not be unreasonable, since not to offer one's wares at the best price would deprive consumers of considerable benefits and would fail to ensure that resources reach their most valuable uses. There is, perhaps, a possible exception when the resources freed when the competitors go out of business are completely wasted because the costs of bringing them back into use are very high (retraining of old workers, costs of conversion of old properties for example) and these lost resources outweigh the gains for consumers that result from giving the business to the newcomers. But it would be very difficult for individual defendants to be able to tell apart competitors whose resources would be so wasted and those whose resources would

17 [1985] 2 All ER 44 at 73.

rapidly be redeployed, and if people were required to refrain from all competition for fear of causing the occasional such harm, the costs in lost efficiency would surely outweigh the benefits. Problems of this kind are much better dealt with by government policies on training and town and country planning than by finding defendants not to be liable in tort cases.

Waste of resources

The second economic incentive argument against pure economic loss in negligence is that it wastes resources. The charge is that it produces little improvement in economic efficiency and the costs of the legal process outweigh any benefits that it may bring.[18]

This argument depends on the following being the case:
(1) The payment of damages for pure economic loss achieves little in the way of the more efficient allocation of resources between the parties and is largely an exercise in the redistribution of wealth.
(2) The deterrent effect of the threat of having to pay damages in negligence for pure economic loss is equally ineffective in reallocating resources to their most productive uses.

Point (1) is an application of the Coase Theorem, which, when restated in its form most useful for lawyers states that, if transactions cost are zero, whether the plaintiff wins or the defendant wins makes no difference to efficiency and serves only to change the distribution of wealth between the parties in favour of the winner.[19] The reason is that as long as it costs nothing to transact, if the loser of the case is the party who puts a greater value on the resources at stake, it is always open to the loser to buy out the winner's interest.

But, of course, the corollary is that if transactions costs are present, for example the costs of finding the other party, of negotiating and drafting the agreement and of monitoring and enforcing it, the result of the case matters for efficiency as well as for distribution, for the costs of transactions may outweigh the amount by which the loser values the resources more than the winner, and so the transactions costs will prevent the resources being transferred to their most valuable use. Clearly, the greater the transactions costs, the greater the risk that this will happen.

The validity of point (1) therefore depends on showing that in pure economic loss cases potential transactions costs are very low (in real life, transactions costs are never zero). There is some possibility that this is so in some cases. In the contractual chain cases, for example, in which the plaintiff contracts with a main contractor who then sub-contracts to the defendant, the plaintiff already knows the sub-contractor, so that search

---

18 Cf Rizzo, Harris and Veljanovski 'Liability for Economic Loss in Tort' in *Furmston* pp 45-72. See also Goldberg 'Recovery for Pure Economic Loss in Tort: Another Look at *Robins Dry Dock v Flint*' 20 JLS 249 (1991).
19 Coase 'The Problem of Social Cost' 3 JLE 1 (1960) See above ch 1.

costs are zero, and the costs of negotiation and drafting, although greater than zero, are presumably small, since if they were large the sub-contractor would not have concluded a contract with the main contractor. But it is the cost of supervision and enforcement where the costs start to rise. If the case is decided in favour of the defendant in circumstances in which economic efficiency would have suggested a victory for the plaintiff, the plaintiff is required further to contract with the defendant for a different, presumably higher, standard of performance, and the plaintiff will have to monitor and enforce that performance. The problem here is that we know that the costs of such monitoring are high for the plaintiff because that presumably is why the plaintiff delegated the task of monitoring to the main contractor in the first place. Monitoring often requires specialist knowledge and skills that clients themselves do not have but main contractors, as project managers, do. Only where the tasks required of the defendant are simple and easy to monitor will monitoring costs be low, but in that case why did the plaintiff employ the main contractor? [20]

Thus, it is likely that the law on pure economic loss does make a difference to the efficiency of the allocation of resources and not just to the distribution of wealth. The next question is, if this is so, what should be the rule about liability? If, for example, the defendant is more likely to be the party that most values the resources at stake, the best course may be to have no liability at all. But to derive a rule from this consideration is very difficult. If evidence is lacking in individual cases about what deal, if any, the parties would have agreed, it is even more lacking for plaintiffs and defendants as a whole. Furthermore even if there were such evidence, any conclusions drawn from it would have to take into account the effects on the evidence of the distribution of wealth and income. If, for example, defendants were as a group much richer than plaintiffs, their willingness to offer more for the resources at stake may reflect only their greater wealth. To lay down a pro-defendant rule in such circumstances would be to reinforce existing inequalities rather than to reflect the requirements of efficiency.

We may conclude from this that the case for point (1) is inconclusive. Turning to point (2), the first question to ask is about the relative deterrent effects of the possible liability rules. The problems are the familiar ones. No liability at all leaves the losses on the victims and gives those who might cause pure economic loss no incentive to avoid it even when, as in *Spring*, *Spartan Steel* and *White*, they could do so easily. Strict liability for pure economic loss has usually been discounted because of the fear that it would indeed make ordinary competition tortious, although, as we have seen, such a result would not follow if the range of protected interests

---

20 Monitoring costs may not be quite so high if the plaintiff wins the case in circumstances in which it would have been more efficient to find for the defendant. The defendant will then negotiate for a lower standard of work at a lower price. If successful such a new contract would not be difficult to monitor from the defendant's point of view and the plaintiff would have the slightly less onerous task of checking only that the standard of the work did not fall even lower than those agreed, below the new standard.

were restricted to those where the plaintiff's expectations are backed up by specific contracts or courses of dealing. But even so strict liability is not the obvious choice since it would mean that plaintiffs would have less of an incentive to protect their own interests. If the plaintiff has to show fault, the plaintiff's case may well fail, so that it is just as well for the plaintiff to take sensible precautions. But if there is strict liability, in a *Hedley Byrne* situation the plaintiff would not have to think much about whether it was sensible to rely on the defendant, since even if the defendant had given advice that seemed reasonable to the defendant at the time but turned out to be erroneous, the plaintiff would still be entitled to compensation. Liability for intentionally caused harm alone gives the defendant no incentive to investigate or to consider the possible consequences of his acts, so that, in a *Spring* or a *White* there would be no incentive to consider the consequences for others that simple precautions might avoid. That leaves negligence liability, which has the advantage of requiring the defendant to take only such care that is justified by the risks but also requires plaintiffs to act reasonably to protect themselves.

But, assuming that negligence liability is the best rule, point (2) claims that the costs of the legal processes necessary to put it into effect would outweigh any benefits produced by the incentive to take care.

The costs of legal action are clearly high. But direct evidence is lacking either way about the other side of the balance, namely the effectiveness of the deterrent value of liability in negligence for pure economic loss. One line of thought is that since in the chain of contract cases the defendant will already be under contractual pressure to perform by the main contractor, the marginal effect of knowing that there is also the possibility of legal pressure from the plaintiff will be small. In addition, it may be the case that people are generally ignorant of the English privity rules and assume that plaintiffs can sue them anyway, so that the rule makes no difference to their conduct.

On the other hand, even in the contractual chain cases, the possibility of legal action by someone other than the main contractor may represent a real threat. There is evidence[1] that legal action is rare among people who deal with one another repeatedly. To take to court someone with whom you may want to work again in the future is risky, since the other person may reasonably interpret legal action as signalling a permanent rupture in the relationship and may refuse to deal with you ever again. Furthermore, there may be wider adverse consequences for the person who invokes the law, since no one wants a reputation for litigiousness. A litigious business partner is an expensive business partner, and such costs may end up built into the way one is assessed as a potential partner in the future.

The point is that these reputation effects restraining legal action may apply to the intermediaries in the contractual chain cases but not to the plaintiffs. A manufacturing company may require new buildings only once

---

1   Macauley 'Non-contractual relations in business' 28 ASR 55-67 (1963), Beale and Dugdale 'Contracts between businessmen' 2 BJLS 45-60 (1975).

every 25 years. A private individual may buy a newly built house once in a lifetime. Plaintiffs in these cases have fewer worries, if any, about future deals and reputations for litigiousness than intermediaries who as main contractors are constantly active in the field. The threat of legal action by the main contractor is subject to the main contractor's fear of being thought litigious, but the client may have no such fear. In consequence, the plaintiff may be the type of person who is more likely to enforce the contract vigorously than the main contractor. This in turn means that the defendant may perceive it to be potentially more costly not to perform properly if the client can sue as well as the main contractor.

In consequence, the case for point (2) is also inconclusive, so that taking the doubts about both point (1) and point (2) together, one should treat the argument from the waste of resources as a whole as interesting but unproven. It is true that the legal costs for any particular case may be very high and, because for the parties the main issue is the distribution of the spoils rather than efficiency, it may be that in those cases the costs outweigh the efficiency gains. But taking into account the effects on future cases that do not go to court, and indeed those cases that do not arise in the first place because the parties behave differently, the position becomes entirely unclear.

And note that outside the contractual chain cases, doubts should increase about whether allowing recovery for pure economic loss would encourage waste. In a case such as *Spartan Steel v Martin*, for example, in which the defendant causes the plaintiff to lose production by interfering with his electricity supply, the only contract is that between the plaintiff and the electricity company, a contract under which the electricity company refuses to take responsibility for any such risks (or indeed virtually anything else) so leaving the plaintiff with a tortious remedy against the defendant or nothing. In these cases, the potential transactions costs between plaintiff and defendant are high because in addition to the monitoring costs there are extra search costs. If the defendant has to negotiate, it would have to do so with multiple potential victims. If the plaintiff has to take the initiative in negotiating, it would have to find out about all the firms likely to dig up the highway in its vicinity. Furthermore, in such cases there is no main contractor to pressure the defendant to care about the plaintiff's interests and so the lack of a tort action, or the presence of only a partial action, surely means noticeably lower deterrents. The suggestion by Lord Denning in *Spartan Steel*[2] that the plaintiff could take out first party insurance is no answer. Not only is such insurance often difficult to obtain (because of the uncertainties of the amount of lost profit and the moral hazard problem),[3] it also does nothing to encourage either the defendant or the plaintiff to do anything to avoid such losses. Moreover, insurance itself involves considerable administrative costs.

2   [1973] QB at 38. Cf *Stapleton* pp 257 and 271.
3   More accurately, insurance for lost business opportunities is difficult to obtain. Insurance of specific contractual interests is more easily obtainable. See EW Hitcham 'Some Insurance Aspects' in *Furmston* pp 191-200.

Lord Denning, Robert Reich *and paper entrepreneurialism*

The *Spartan Steel* case obliged Lord Denning to look more widely for justifications for denying pure economic loss (other than that supposedly arising *directly* out of physical damage, whatever that might mean). One of his remarks, seemingly off the cuff, deserves further analysis, for it is associated with a serious economic problem. What Lord Denning said was:[4]

> 'Most people are content to take the risk on themselves ... [T]hey do not go running round to their solicitor. They do not try to find out whether it was anyone's fault. They just put up with it. They try to make up the economic loss by doing more work the next day. This is a healthy attitude the law should encourage.'

Behind Lord Denning's words lie an important fear. If the law is implacably pro-plaintiff, allowing plaintiffs to recover damages for any sort of harm they suffer as the result of unreasonable conduct, will not people be encouraged to spend more time looking for profitable law suits and less time on productive activities such as making steel castings? Litigation is only productive if it leads to a better allocation of resources, but its main purpose from the point of view of the plaintiff is redistributing wealth from the defendant to the plaintiff. We have already seen that, contrary to Lord Denning's assumption, allowing negligence actions for pure economic loss may improve the efficiency of the economy as a whole. But what Lord Denning's comments raise is a more long-term fear about the overall direction of economic development. One must offset the short-term improvements in the efficiency of the economy that allowing claims for pure economic loss in negligence might bring, even at the cost of paying lawyers, against the long-term losses caused by people no longer believing in creating wealth by making and selling things but instead investing their lives and creative imaginations in litigation.

The English judges' fear of litigiousness may have been fed in recent decades by a combination of anti-American xenophobia and a stereotypical view of the United States as a country dominated by litigious citizens and sharp lawyers. The basis of this America-phobia has been challenged several times[5] and perhaps should be discounted. But there are similar fears expressed in the USA itself, sometimes also on the back of prejudices, this time anti-lawyer prejudices[6] and exaggeratedly favourable stereotypes of other countries' legal habits, especially those of Japan.[7] But there are serious versions of these arguments that deserve attention.

4   [1973] QB at 38.
5   See Howarth [1992] CLJ 58 and Markesinis 'Litigation-mania in England, Germany and the USA: Are we so very different?' [1990] CLJ 233.
6   See ABA Journal (October 1991) pp 66ff. See also Jost 'Tampering with the Evidence' ABA Journal (April 1992) pp 45-51.
7   See Haley 'The Myth of the Reluctant Litigant' 4 J of Japanese Studies 359 (1978), Johnson 'Authority without Power' 27 Law and Soc Rev 619 (1993), H Oda *Japanese Law* (London, Butterworths, 1992) at pp 86-88.

One such is the contention of Robert Reich that the US economy has suffered in the past from what he calls 'paper entrepreneurialism'.[8] Reich says:[9]

> 'Managers have indeed adapted by innovating. But the innovations have not been technological or institutional. Rather they have been based on accounting, tax avoidance, financial management, mer–gers, acquisitions and litigation ... [P]aper entrepreneurialism involves little more than imposing losses on others for the sake of short-term profits... It does not create new wealth. It merely rearranges industrial assets. And it has hastened our collective decline.'

Litigation about pure economic loss is certainly an example of such paper entrepreneurialism.

One obvious objection to the problem raised by Reich is that as long as the activities concerned have an efficiency justification, the investment in them is justified. A distinction can be made between investment in tax lawyers and lobbying on the one hand and litigation on the other. When businesses are spending their time trying to squeeze money out of the state, the effect is unlikely to be improvements in the allocation of resources, unless one makes the heroic assumption that the purpose of all tax legislation and all industrial regulation is the improvement of efficiency and that the intervention of lawyers and lobbyists improves their applic–ation. But businesses who sue other businesses may, as we have seen, indirectly cause efficiency improvements by encouraging others to behave in ways that do not unreasonably impose costs on others. They may slightly over-invest in such activities because they have the incentive over and above resource allocation of capturing somebody else's wealth. But such a tendency can be counteracted by making sure that the costs of going to law are fully taken into account by litigants, for example if losers have to pay winners' costs.

But this objection does not meet the essence of Reich's point which is not about what happens in the short term but about innovation. The long-term trajectory of an economy depends, at least on one view, on human capital and innovation. If a society's most innovative and creative people are drawn into litigation rather than into industry, which they will be if firms prefer litigation to investment in research and development and to Lord Denning's hard work, there is no guarantee that their talents will move the law in the direction of producing greater efficiency. They may indeed produce the opposite result, or, most probably, like some kind of arms race in which both sides have to invest more and more just to keep up, they will make no difference at all but will siphon off more and more resources in the process.

8   R Reich *The Next American Frontier* (1983: New York, Times Books) ch 7. Another tradition within economics talks of 'non-productive rent seeking'.
9   Ibid at pp 140-41.

As Reich says:[10]

> 'Paper entrepreneurialism now preoccupies some of America's best
> minds, attracts many of its most talented graduates, employs some
> of its most creative and original thinking, and spurs some of its
> most energetic wheeling and dealing.'

The only preventative measure that the courts can take against such a
trend, apart from applying the fault standard more rigorously so that they
do not condemn defendants without proof that the overall costs of the
defendants' conduct clearly outweighed its benefits, is to view with great
suspicion all plaintiffs' innovations. In this way, the rewards of attempts
to innovate in the law will be relatively small.

The prevention of innovation would also explain why the courts obstruct
pure economic loss when one could make the same points for and against
liability for property damage. If businesses are allowed, as they are, to sue
for injury to their physical property, one could equally say that this
encourages them to blame others when they should be getting on with
their work. Acquiring physical plant for productive purposes is to take a
risk that it might be damaged in the same way as making a contract is to
take a risk that it might be interfered with.

But to allow businesses to recover for physical damage to property is
already established law, and to continue to allow it does not encourage
lawyers to spend time trying to innovate. It does not, therefore, put a
premium on innovative thinking in the law, which is what worries Reich.

On the other hand, as with the anthropological reason for not allowing
the recovery of pure economic loss in negligence, one still has to doubt
whether negligence law will much affect the level of paper entrepreneurialism. Most paper entrepreneurialism, according to Reich, consists of tax
avoidance, mergers and acquisitions and clever accountancy. And if
litigation is important, negligence actions will form only a small part of it.
Furthermore, if allowing pure economic loss in negligence has such
deleterious effects, why is there an exception for *Hedley Byrne*?

Externalities and the production of valuable information

Lord Bridge remarks in *Caparo*[11] that to allow the plaintiff to win in that
case would:

> 'confer on the world at large a quite unwarranted entitlement to
> appropriate for their own purposes the benefit of the expert
> knowledge or professional expertise attributed to the maker of the
> statement.'

10 Ibid at p 159.
11 See above.

Lord Bridge's point, which echoes academic work 10 years before *Caparo*,[12] is that the problem with information is that it is difficult for those who produce it for a living to keep from using it people who have not paid for it. Information production has 'positive externalities', that is it confers benefits on people who are not parties to its production and sale. Although this sounds like a good thing, its disadvantage is that it acts as a disincentive to the production of useful information.

It allegedly follows that the right to sue for carelessly produced inacc—urate commercial information should be limited to the same range of people who actually pay for what they get, and that those who free-load should not be able to complain. This ensures that liability does not add to the positive externality problem.

But the positive externality problem is not the end of the story. Inform—ation is a very peculiar commodity. Not only are there reasons to under-produce it, there are also reasons to over-produce it. The most important of these is that if one is well-informed one can often steal a march on those who are less well-informed. The effect of this is not to produce any new wealth, but merely to transfer the wealth of the uninformed to the informed.[13] If one takes these effects into account, the question of liability becomes slightly more complex.

Both the positive externality problem and the incentives to over-produce information are affected by the degree to which the information is likely to leak to those who do not pay for it.[14] Except where there is an intended indirect pay-off for the producer, such as in advertising, leakage increases the positive externality problem. The greater the degree of free-riding the bigger the gap between the amount of information that would be produced if the producer of the information could capture all the benefits and the amount actually produced. But the incentives to over-produce decline as leakage increases. The advantage conferred by being better informed goes down as fewer and fewer people are ill-informed.[15] It follows that Lord

12 Bishop 'Negligent Misrepresentation: An economic reformulation' in Burrows and Veljanovski *Economic Approach to Law* (London, Butterworths, 1981) 167-186. See also Bishop 'Negligent Misrepresentation through Economists' Eyes' (1980) 96 LQR 360.

13 See J Hirschleifer and J Riley *The Analytics of Uncertainty and Information* (Cambridge, Cambridge University Press, 1992) at 258-294. In addition to this 'speculative effect' Hirschleifer and Riley also point to a 'commons effect' encouraging over-production of information. New knowledge is a kind of common resource, so that new entrants can expect to gain not just the marginal return to the information but the average return. They do this by taking some of the return of those who come later. But this effect is of little relevance to the problems of economic loss since it works only where intellectual property rights can be asserted. Information as such is not really a common resource, like fishing stocks or common grazing land, because it does not have the quality that if I have it, you do not. By finding something out, I do not reduce your chances of finding it out. It only takes on this quality if I can exclude you.

14 *Hirschleifer and Riley* at 273ff.

15 Cf S Hilgartner and S Brandt-Rauf 'Data Access, Ownership and Control: Toward Empirical Studies of Access Practices' Knowledge 15(4):355-72 (1994). (As availability of an innovation grows, the competitive edge it confers falls, but its inherent usefulness remains.)

Bridge's objection applies to cases in which leakage is likely to be very high, but in cases in which leakage is very low, the problem may not be the under-production of information but over-production. Perhaps in these cases, the law should not just allow liability but move towards strict liability or a reversal of the burden of proof in favour of the plaintiff.

It is possible to see in the way the law has developed at least an echo of the result that liability should be restricted where there are likely to be very high leakage. It certainly operationalises Cardozo J's famous remark about indeterminate liability[16]—the rule should be that *when* there are likely to be indeterminate numbers of plaintiffs, *then* there is a case for restricting liability. In cases such as *Hedley Byrne*, about credit references, and *Smith v Bush*, about house valuations, the amount of leakage is likely to be low, because the parties receiving the information have no incentive to pass it on. They are in the middle of commercial negotiations and are likely to want to keep such information to themselves. Liability in such cases is therefore likely to cause no problem. But where the information is likely to leak very widely, such as in *Caparo*, the problem of under-production of information may become real. In this way, the law may be justified in reaching the otherwise very puzzling conclusion, noted above, that there should be more restrictions on liability when there is much threatened harm than when there is less threatened harm.

But one should not go so fast, at least regarding *Caparo* itself. Note that in *Caparo* one can interpret the statutory requirement that firms had to deposit audited accounts with a public official as a deliberate intervention intended to correct for the under-production of information likely to leak and to increase the amount of information produced beyond that which the market would have produced by itself. Firms were required to pay for a service that otherwise they would not necessarily have wanted and auditing firms were required to deal with the information in ways in which they otherwise would not have done. There is therefore no problem with the under-production of information. The only question is whether it is worthwhile in terms of process costs and the effectiveness of the deterrent to attempt to maintain reasonable standards of accuracy in this information by imposing a duty of care on those who produce it. The answer, one might suggest, is that, contrary to *Caparo*, since the whole point of the exercise is to produce more information than the regime of private contract would have produced, the law should admit negligence against careless auditors.

Floodgates

The third category of argument against allowing claims for pure economic loss in negligence is the so-called 'floodgates' point (see above chapter 5). Allowing any sort of negligence liability for pure economic loss, it is feared,

---

16 See below.

will lead to enormous numbers of claims for very large sums coming before the courts. As Cardozo J warned in *Ultramares v Touche*,[17] such a course of action would open up 'liability in an indeterminate amount for an indeterminate time to an indeterminate class.'

The floodgates argument is not one argument but several. We shall consider each in turn.

Flooding the courts—rights too popular to grant

The first, and worst, version of the floodgates argument is that allowing a new basis of liability would overwhelm the court system with new claims. As a result, the courts may not be able to sort out meritorious claims from non-meritorious claims.[18] This version of the argument only has to be stated for it to be refuted. To deny someone a right because many other people would also be entitled to it borders on the perverse. If many people would benefit from a new right, that speaks more for granting it than for denying it. The convenience of the courts is a minor administrative matter. In any case it is unlikely that the courts would be flooded with new cases by expanding the law in this way, since, after the first few reported cases had established the limits of the new liability, parties would be able to settle the overwhelming majority of cases out of court.

Flooding the defendant

The other versions of the floodgates argument are more serious. They concern not flooding the court system with claims but flooding the defendant with damages.[19] This is the type of floodgates argument that lies behind Cardozo J's remarks. The idea is that, whereas in cases of physical injury the effects of the defendant's act usually have an obvious natural end point and a small number of immediate victims, there is no such end point in economic loss. In pure economic loss, the plaintiff claims because the defendant's carelessness has cost him business or reduced his profit on an existing deal. But it is likely that the plaintiff in turn will have business

---

17 225 NY 170 at 179 (CANY 1931).
18 See ch 5 above. Cf J Bell *Policy Arguments in Judicial Decisions* (1982: Clarendon Press, Oxford) at 71.
19 Cf *Bell* at 71. Bell also includes as a floodgates argument the point that if a change in the law generates a large number of new claims, the change may be argued to be too great for the courts to produce themselves and to be the sort of change that only Parliament should bring in. With respect, this stretches the floodgates concept too far. The argument from the limits of the judicial role is quite a separate one. In any case, it has little relevance here for it shows only why judges should not change the existing position radically, not what position the law should take in the first place.

relationships and contracts with others, who may themselves be affected by the plaintiff's difficulties. These others in turn will also have business relationships that may be disrupted, and so on.[20] The situation in cases about inaccurate information is even worse, since bad information can be passed on and continue to do harm without the need for any business relationship between those involved.

Two types of unfortunate consequences may flow, it is alleged, from imposing such great liability on the defendant: that people will no longer be able to practise those professions that are prone to cause economic loss; and secondly that resources may be wasted in making the defendant bankrupt which would not be wasted if the market were allowed to spread the losses more widely.

The former alleged harm is prominent in the arguments of the most active lobby against negligence liability for pure economic loss, namely those professions most vulnerable to it. Auditors and other accountants, surveyors, solicitors, bankers, credit reference agencies and others who live by selling information and advice all allege that negligence liability for pure economic loss means prohibitively high insurance premiums for practitioners and, in turn, prohibitively high charges for clients—and perhaps no service at all. They therefore ask for protection. They welcome cases such as *Caparo*, which limit the number of potential plaintiffs, and cases such as *Norwich City Council v Harvey*, which allow them to limit their own liability without having to deal directly with potential plaintiffs. But they deplore cases such as *Smith v Bush*, *White v Jones* and *Henderson v Merrett* that reduce their power to limit their liability.

The objections to this lobby's complaints are fairly obvious. First, there is no evidence that the one information-based profession that has tended to fail to win the protection of the courts against *Hedley Byrne* claims, namely surveying, is about to disappear because of outrageously high liability insurance premiums. Secondly, all of these professions exist in those many countries, including France and the Netherlands, that have fewer problems in recognising liability for pure economic loss. Lastly, and most importantly, the fate of these advice professionals is entirely in their own hands. The liability they are subject to is liability for fault, that is for unreasonable behaviour. It is not a strict liability. Moreover, they are able to call in aid the *Bolam*[1] test for judging the reasonableness of professional behaviour, according to which defendants only have to show that their advice was the sort of advice that a respectable professional might have given, not that it met the standards of the best practitioners.

The second form of harm allegedly flowing from the extent of the possible liability for pure economic loss is that such losses would be more cheaply spread through the market than by dumping a potentially crushing burden on the defendant.[2] The argument relies on the following scenario: the defendant's carelessness causes pure economic loss to several primary

---

20 Cf Stapleton at pp 254-55.
1 *Bolam v Friern Hospital Management Committee* [1957] 1 WLR 582. See ch 3.
2 For 'spreading' costs see G Calabresi *The Costs of Accidents* (1970: New Haven, Yale University Press) especially chs 4 and 13.

plaintiffs, who in turn have contracts or business relationships with a group of secondary plaintiffs and so on. The loss to each plaintiff is moderate, but when added together amount to a considerable sum that is beyond the plaintiff's means. The result is that the defendant is forced into bankruptcy. Bankruptcy itself involves considerable legal and administrative costs, including the time taken by creditors in negotiations. If, as is likely, the result is not the personal bankruptcy of an individual but the liquidation of a company, even more costs result, including the costs of redeploying the company's resources, its land, equipment and employees, and the efficiency losses flowing from the break-up of an existing organisation. The argument is that if there were no liability in such cases, the defendants would absorb the moderate losses imposed upon them, raising prices or cutting costs if possible, without the disruption of bankruptcies and liquidations.

But, although the spreading argument has some force, the position is not straightforward. First, similar bankruptcies and liquidations may result from physical loss cases, especially in products liability. Secondly, the availability of liability insurance, an alternative form of spreading, means either that the risk of bankruptcy is the defendant's own choice or that the spreading objection reduces to the argument from the threat to the vulnerable professions, the argument we have just dealt with. Thirdly, the spreading argument applies to some pure economic loss cases but not to others. It should not apply where there is no threat to the defendant of bankruptcy or liquidation, and it is possible that in some cases the plaintiff faces ruin rather than the defendant. The logic of the argument dictates that in these cases the defendant should be liable. But the law would then depend on the relative poverty of the parties in relation to the size of the claim. Any party threatened with bankruptcy would win. Moreover, under such a regime the law would be unable to resolve the truly catastrophic cases in which the losses are so great that whichever side loses the case goes broke.

Apart from the specific criticisms of the two forms of the argument from flooding the defendant, there is another point that applies to the argument in both of its forms and applies to Cardozo J's *Ultramares v Touche* remark as well.[3] The idea that there is a big difference between the potential extent of physical loss and pure economic loss is not justified. First, there are some pure economic loss cases in which the number of potential victims is finite and small and the amount of the loss determinate, such as the will cases.[4] Secondly, and more significantly, the physical consequences of the defendant's carelessness are also potentially unlimited. Cases such as the *Meah v McCreamer* trilogy[5] show the possibilities. McCreamer's drunken driving led to serious injuries to Meah, including brain injuries as a result of which Meah's personality changed. Subsequently, Meah became a violent criminal who attacked a number of women including W. It is possible to

3 And to the 'fairness' argument advanced by *Bell* at 73-75.
4 Eg *Ross v Caunters* and *White v Jones* above. See also *Caltex Oil v Dredge Willemstad* (1976) 136 CLR 529.
5 *Meah v McCreamer* [1985] 1 All ER 367, *W v Meah* [1986] 1 All ER 935 and *Meah v McCreamer (No 2)* [1986] 1 All ER 943. See above ch 4 for discussion.

imagine this chain of events continuing indefinitely. But, of course, this possibility does not mean that damages are irrecoverable for the original brain injuries that cause the personality changes. Instead, the extent of liability is limited by the application of the principles of causation and remoteness. Admittedly, those principles have been obscured in England by the confusion caused by the *Wagon Mound*[6] and the tendency to over-use and over-extend the notion of foreseeability. But English law still contains two sets of rules that prevent infinite liability. First, the plaintiff has to show factual causation. As the losses become more distant from the original careless conduct, the more difficult that task becomes, since there is a steady increase in the number of ways in which the losses in question may have come about anyway. Secondly, the losses must not be too remote, which means, in essence, that the chain of causation must not have been broken by independent wilful and possibly wrongful interventions by third parties, or by utterly unreasonable actions by the plaintiff, or by over–whelming and coincidental natural events. (See chapter 4)

The recoverability of pure economic loss should equally be subject to the rules of factual causation and remoteness. Lost business opportunities unsupported by specific existing contracts are especially vulnerable to the factual causation argument that they would not have materialised anyway. And the deliberate passing on and use of inaccurate information is liable at some point to be characterised as breaking the chain of causation, so rendering all subsequent harm too remote.

There is, admittedly, a question as to what the remoteness rule should be in cases where the plaintiff had lined up an unusually profitable deal that the defendant's negligence frustrates.[7] There are two choices. First, there is the rule in *The Edison*[8] that the plaintiff's unusual financial position should count against it and that only normal losses are recoverable. This turns out to be the same as the remoteness rule in contract under which if the plaintiff intended to do something that would have brought in an unusually high profit the court limits the recoverable damages to normal profits.[9] Secondly, there is the *Smith v Leech Brain*[10] rule that the defendant 'must take the victim as he finds him' and so should pay in full. The movement in the *Hedley Byrne* cases back towards the contract theory of that case suggests that English law will plump for the former, which, being the more restrictive rule, should satisfy those with Cardozian fears.

Distance from the paradigm case of negligence, viz personal injury

The fourth main argument against the recovery of pure economic loss is, as we shall see, largely an amalgam of other arguments that we have already considered. It is that pure economic loss is conceptually too far

6 *Overseas Tankship v Morts Dock* [1961] AC 388.
7 Cf *Stapleton* at p 255.
8 See above.
9 *Victoria Laundry v Newman*.
10 [1962] 2 QB 405.

away from the central, paradigm case of negligence liability, namely personal injury.

The full form of the argument is (1) that prima facie there should be no liability for any sort of negligently caused loss unless there is special justification; (2) that such special justifications do apply to the cases of personal injury; and (3) that these considerations do not apply to pure economic loss.

Point (1) is fundamental. One view of the underlying morality of tort law is that fault of any kind raises a presumption that the wrongdoer should compensate the victim. Another view reserves the presumption for intentional harm. Yet another admits no such presumption at all. On the other hand, a fourth view is that merely causing another person harm, regardless of any kind of fault, raises a prima facie duty to compensate.

These differences of view are too deep to be easily resolved. The view that faulty action raises no presumption in favour of a duty to compensate at all derives either from a very strong commitment to self-reliance and Lord Denning's culture of not complaining, or from the almost exact opposite point of view that all that matters is the collective interest, so that individuals do not have any sort of claim on other individuals but that all interests have to be mediated through the state.

The view that only intentional harm raises a presumption in favour of compensation derives from the view that such presumptions in favour of legal intervention are only legitimate if founded on a near unanimous moral agreement. But whereas there is a wide consensus that intentional harm is wrong, there can be no similar consensus about negligence. The purportedly objective standards of conduct on which judgments of neglig–ence depend must in practice be controversial.

The view that all fault raises a presumption in favour of a duty to compensate derives from one of two lines of thought. One is the line that since fault can be recast as a cost-benefit analysis that the defendant has got wrong, it must be the case that the defendant has imposed costs on the plaintiff without justification. And so, if the law does not intervene to discourage the wrongdoer, the overall effect must be a net loss for society as a whole. The other line is that unreasonable conduct should not be allowed to continue with impunity, for otherwise it will not be seen for long as unreasonable.[11] But, because no other collective interest is involved, we should restrict the means of the prevention of impunity to compensation and not go beyond in to punishments. The result is a presumption in favour of compensation for negligently caused harm.

Finally, the view that causing any harm at all to another person raises a presumption in favour of a duty to compensate, regardless of fault or intention, derives from a strict version of libertarianism, according to which each individual has a right not to incur costs without consent. On this view, causing harm is prima facie a form of illegitimate coercion and the state is entitled to step in to prevent it.[12]

---

11 Cf Hyman Gross 'Preventing Impunity' in H Gross and R Harrison (eds) *Jurisprudence: Cambridge Essays* (1992: Oxford, Clarendon Press) pp 95-106.

12 See Richard Epstein *A Theory of Strict Liability* (1980: San Francisco, Cato Institute).

On two of these views, point (1) is established—if there is no presumption at all in favour of a duty to compensate or a presumption only if there is intentional harm, merely negligently caused harm raises no presumption that losses should be shifted. But on the other two views, point (1) is not established. Even if we exclude the two extreme views, no presumption at all and a presumption whenever anyone causes harm, we are still left with two opposing views. The difference between them is essentially whether or not one believes that the courts' judgments of what counts as negligent command general consent. In the days of the civil jury, which had some claim to be democratic, this decision would be easier to make than it is at present when reasonableness is in the hands of professional and sometimes allegedly out-of-touch judges.

Even if point (1) is established, what of points (2) and (3)?

Point (2) is that there is something special about personal injury that justifies the payment of compensation for negligently caused injuries.[13] As we have already noted, what is special about life and limb is that they are believed not to be tradable. Life and health are pearls beyond price, outside the workings of markets and exchange values. For this reason it is unreasonable to expect people to protect themselves by contract, the legal instrument of the market.

The other reason that negligently caused personal injury is alleged to be special is that if it were not punished, people would say that the defendant had been allowed to get away with something. Preventing impunity is as much a function of tort law as it is of criminal law.[14]

But it is not clear, however, that either of these arguments works.

The problem with the view of life and limb as a pearl beyond price, outside the world of exchange and money, is that it is only true on the surface. People may not like to say that life and health have market values, but they act as if they do every day. Every decision to take a physically risky job or to insure oneself against physical injury implies a trade-off between personal injury and income. Indeed, by examining such trans–actions, one can even calculate the implied price of a life.[15] Similar trade-offs are also implicit in public decisions, such as decisions on public expenditure on health care and on major construction projects such as bridges and tunnels.[16]

The issue is therefore one of openness. These choices and trade-offs between life and health on one side and money on the other happen all the time. The question is whether the law acknowledges these trade-offs, or instead gives way to the cultural taboos.

---

13 Cf Lord Oliver in *Murphy v Brentwood District Council* [1991] 1 AC 398 at 487: 'The infliction of physical injury to the person or property of another universally requires to be justified. The causing of economic loss does not.'.

14 See *Gross*.

15 For a short summary of the various techniques and their results, see 'The Price of a Life' (1993) The Economist, 4 December, p 103. The estimate for the price of a life in Britain is $1.1m.

16 See G Calabresi and P Bobbitt *Tragic Choices* (1978: New York, W W Norton).

As for the impunity argument, it applies also to property damage and pure economic loss. It is possible that there is a society in which a person who damages someone else's property or interferes with the profitability of someone else's business is not considered to have got away with something, but it is unclear whether our society is one of them.

But surely, one might say, life and limb are more important than wealth and property?[17] The problem with this point is that it does not prove that wealth and property are unimportant, or rather so unimportant that they should not be legally protected from negligent harm. The argument would have to be that allowing compensation for pure economic loss implies that economic loss is just as important as personal injury and that the only way to maintain the differential between them is to deny liability for pure economic loss. But if so, the same point would apply to property damage, which is compensable. Does the compensability of property damage imply that the law is committed to the view that things are as important as people? Some may think that it does[18] but the view more in line with the empirical reality of the relationship between law and morality is that the law is a very blunt instrument and that few people expect legal judgments to be as carefully and subtly differentiated as moral judgments.[19] Equally, the admissibility of compensation for pure economic loss does not imply that personal injury and pure economic loss are equally important.

In addition, other attempts to distinguish between the compensability of property damage and of pure economic loss are not very convincing. For example, the claim that people are somehow attached to their physical property and that it should count almost as an extension of themselves[20] seems to have some force, since it is true that individuals often value objects more than their market prices would suggest, whereas the value of a contract or a business opportunity is exactly represented by the profit it offers. But this difference is illusory. The difference between the market price of an object and the valuation put on it by the owner is the exact equivalent of the profit on a deal. It may be less easily measured than the profit on a deal, except when the market price rises to meet it, but it is not necessarily less certain than the value of a lost business opportunity. In any case, even if it were true, it would not prove that pure economic loss should not be compensable, only that property loss is more often more upsetting than pure economic loss.

Moreover, the difference between property loss and pure economic loss is not great. It has nothing to do with whether the harm involved physical damage. The harm in *The Aliakmon* was physical—the steel springs went rusty, a physical event. But the loss was purely economic—because the plaintiff had a contractual interest in the springs instead of a property

17 See *Feldthusen*.
18 Eg *Abel*.
19 See N Simmonds 'Bluntness and Bricolage' in *R Harrison and H Gross* pp 1-28.
20 Cf Coval, Smith and Coval 'Foundations of Property and Property Law' [1986] CLJ 457.

interest. It is unlikely that one can construct fundamental moral differences out of such legal distinctions.

Who benefits from the compensability of economic loss?

The fifth and final argument put forward against the recovery in negligence of pure economic loss is a distributional argument. It rests on the claim that pure economic loss claims benefit large corporations and represent a further colonisation of the legal system by powerful economic interests.

It is true that a large number of the plaintiffs in economic loss cases are powerful corporations. But then again so are a large number of the defendants. Other cases concern the conflict of interest between industry and commerce on one side and the professions and the financial institutions on the other.[1] Moreover there are many pure economic loss claims in which the plaintiffs are not economically powerful but the defendants are, in particular the negligent will cases and the cases in which house purchasers sue builders, surveyors and local authorities.

As for the objection that pure economic loss is part of the colonisation of the law by powerful economic interests, the reply is that land law, contract law and company law all have the same quality. The problem that the haves often come out ahead[2] cannot be tackled by doctrines that would deny individuals recovery against lawyers, brokers, bankers, surveyors and other professionals who carelessly harm their interests.

Relational loss

The final reason for denying recovery for pure economic loss has already been discussed in the previous chapter. It is that pure economic loss is generally a form of relational loss. The plaintiff's loss comes about because of a relationship that the plaintiff entered in to voluntarily or, in contractual chain cases, the plaintiff is the wrong plaintiff and the defendant is the wrong defendant. Where the plaintiff cannot be said to have acted in a fully voluntary way, because of misleading information, as in *Hedley Byrne* cases, there is liability, but not otherwise.

The question here is what lies behind the argument that relational economic losses should not be recoverable?

The first point to note is that much of the argument against relational loss, especially the wrong plaintiff and wrong defendant arguments, follows straightforwardly from the principle that compensation in a tort should put the plaintiff in a position no better or worse than the position the

1   Eg *Hedley Byrne, Caparo, Gran Gelato* above.
2   Cf Galanter 'Why the Haves Come Out Ahead' 9 Law and Soc Rev 95 (1974).

plaintiff enjoyed before the defendant's act. If compensation is paid directly to the plaintiff when, had not the accident happened, the plaintiff would have been dependent on the third party to fulfill an obligation or exercise a discretion, there is a risk of over-compensation. Admittedly the over-compensation is likely to be less when the third party is under an obligation to the plaintiff, but even then there is a risk that the third party will be unable to fulfill the obligations because of insolvency or physical incapacity.

The second point to make is about the argument from voluntarily accepting the risk inherent in forming relationships. The argument depends on being able to distinguish voluntary relationships (for example, contracts and friendships) from involuntary relationships (for example, close family ties). It is a distinction to which only the most dedicated determinist, whether social, psychological or economic, would object. But to what extent is this distinction drawn in the right place?

Note that marriage, which is in one sense a voluntary relationship, is placed (admittedly by statute) in the same category as the non-voluntary relationships, presumably because of its social, emotional and biological importance. But one could use similar arguments about some forms of contract, for example buying necessities or even, depending on the relative generosity of the social security system, contracts of employment. Even in a case such as *Spartan Steel v Martin* there is a lingering feeling of injustice that stems ultimately from the fact that, at least at that time, electricity was supplied by a monopoly supplier that had exempted itself from any obligation to consumers to maintain that supply, so that one of the relationships that the defendant carelessly interfered with was hardly voluntary.

This leads to further consideration of the distinction between economic loss and property damage. The central question is whether there is there an equivalence between the self-created vulnerability caused by contract and the vulnerability caused by owning property. As we have seen, the law takes the answer to be no. Vulnerability to market forces in setting the value of property is contrasted with vulnerability to the decisions of particular individuals with whom one has or might have a relationship. But note that one can in the end realise the market value of property only by entering into an exchange with a particular other person. Eventually, impersonal market forces come down to a specific act of buying and selling with ascertainable individuals. Similarly, the juridical notion of property as providing rights that are good against the world, that is against any individual who may come along, comes down to particular disputes about the property with particular individuals or ascertainable sets of individuals. Thus, the exclusion of property loss from the category of relational loss depends on distinctions between the mass and the individual and between abstract absolutes and particular instances that may not be sustainable.

This suggests that in the long term, the distinction that we may need to make is not between property and contract but between different kinds of property and different types of contract. Some kinds of property may be compared with involuntary relationships. In the same way that dependency on involuntary relationships does not mean consent to the risk of harm to the other person, so to be dependent upon some kinds of property is not evidence that one has voluntarily taken on the risk that their value or usefulness may fall. We might include in this category the necessities of life. We might also include the tools of one's trade, for although one can to some extent choose the occupation one follows, all occupations need tools of some sort. But other types of property should count as voluntary, as bringing with them the risk that their value may fall. Harm to these types of property would be subject to the arguments against relational loss and as a result may not be compensable in negligence.

Summary and conclusions

The first problem for anyone trying to justify the existing pattern of the law is that it appears to lack coherence. The most important difficulty is that the presumption against compensating pure economic loss sits unhappily with the presumption in favour of compensating property damage. Either property damage should not be compensated to the extent that it is now or the distinction between property damage and economic loss has to be redefined. This is the problem with which the Court of Appeal in *The Nicholas H* was beginning to grapple.

In addition, the basis of the one established exception to the presumption against compensating pure economic loss, *Hedley Byrne*, remains unclear. The judges have swayed back and forth between the view that the *Hedley Byrne* exception is based on equivalence to contract and the view that *Hedley Byrne* is simply an extension of negligence where the reasons for non-recoverability of economic loss do not apply.

Additionally, recent cases may herald a consensus around a compromise. Liability might rest primarily on fault and reliance by the plaintiff on the defendant is not a requirement but simply one way in which the plaintiff may show causation. But, at least according to Lord Goff, 'assumption of responsibility' is a requirement in its own right, rather than just another way of describing the result of the case, and the remoteness or 'proximity' rules are closer to those of contract than those normally used in negligence.

Nevertheless the very complexity of the developing *Hedley Byrne* compromise makes it even more difficult to describe the principles that inform it. And possible long-term developments in contract law, especially in the law of contracts that create benefits for third parties, may undermine, or at least reduce in importance, much that has happened.

The justifications that allegedly lie behind the law are also not all completely convincing.

The arguments based on the separation of tort and contract are largely without merit except for the argument from the difficulty of assessing value outside exchange relationships (Lord Brandon's argument in *Junior Books*), and even that argument seems to be applied in practice where it is intrinsically least convincing. The argument from the need to separate the tradable and the non-tradable, the anthropological argument, is capable of explaining the general principle of hostility to pure economic loss and the fact that there is constant pressure to explain the *Hedley Byrne* exception in contractual or 'equivalent to contract' terms. But it is less successful at explaining why there should be a *Hedley Byrne* exception at all. Moreover, that the desire to separate the tradable from the non-tradable may be a good explanation for the hostility to economic loss does not make it a good reason to act on that hostility.

The arguments from economic incentives fare a little better but are ultimately insufficient. The argument that allowing pure economic loss would waste resources on law suits without bringing much in the way of improvement in economic efficiency would have merit if there was convincing evidence both about the deterrent effects of liability and the costs of legal action. And even if there were such evidence, it is very unlikely that this line of reasoning would account for the *Hedley Byrne* exception—that is that the deterrent value of liability in the *Hedley Byrne* circumstances would turn out to be decisively higher than the deterrent value of liability in other pure economic loss cases. The paper entrepreneurialism argument is interesting but, like the relationship between the anthropological argument and the culture of the whole society, there have to be doubts about whether the law on economic loss is of so much practical importance for the way the economy might develop in the long term. In any case, it proves too much, for it would apply also to *Hedley Byrne* liability. The argument from the peculiarities of information as a product can explain the trends within the *Hedley Byrne* cases, but it is not a general explanation of the general hostility to pure economic cases where there is no question of information production (in *Spartan Steel* for example).

As for the floodgates arguments, they vary from the irrelevant via the contingent to the near plausible. But the nearest to plausible versions of the floodgates argument turn out on close inspection to depend on the unsustainable assumption that the remoteness rules applicable to non-economic loss cases somehow do not apply to pure economic loss cases.

The arguments from distance from the central case of personal injury and from who benefits from the recoverability of pure economic loss are too general, show only that personal injury is more important than pure economic loss not that pure economic loss should not be awarded at all and cannot explain the *Hedley Byrne* exception.

The arguments against economic loss because it is a form of relational loss, in contrast, have some force and rest on reasonable assumptions. It is an argument, however, that has the potential to change the law further.

The fact that the law on pure economic loss seems not to spring from any simple set of coherent principles but seems to be a series of ad hoc, or, as Lord Oliver said 'pragmatic', decisions has caused many writers to conclude that economic loss is not one idea but several. For example, Feldthusen[3] and Markesinis and Deakin[4] say that liability for misstatements, negligence in performance of a service, economic loss arising

3   See above.
4   See above.

from defects in buildings and products and relational losses arising from
damage to the property of a third party are distinct forms of economic loss
and have to be analysed separately.[5] Stapleton[6] takes a similar view, but,
more helpfully, suggests that the law ought to develop along new more
coherent lines.

There is, however, another approach. The search does seem fruitless for
the one unique characteristic, or even set of characteristics, of pure economic
loss that it does not share with any other form of loss and which explains
both why there is a presumption against it in negligence and a *Hedley
Byrne* exception. But instead of reacting by looking for even more particular
forms of loss, we could instead look for wider categories of case, and broader
forms of argument by which the courts deny negligence duties. This way,
we may be able to add a doctrinal underpinning to Stapleton's project of
making the law more coherent.

Recall the discussion of *Spring*. The two main arguments against liability
deployed by Lord Keith in his dissent were not arguments used exclusively
in pure economic loss cases. The argument that to allow negligence liability
would undermine the rules of defamation is a variant of a standard
argument against allowing a duty of care that to do so would interfere
with and adversely affect the operation of other areas of the law. As
mentioned above, such areas of the law have included contract, administrative law and procedural law as well as other torts.[7] Arguments based
on the supposed purposes of statutes are another example.[8] Indeed the
argument already discussed that to allow the recovery of pure economic
loss in negligence would undermine the privity and third party beneficiary
rules in contract is itself another example of the same form of argument.
Judges have used the protection of other existing contract rules to justify
denying negligence liability in a range of cases, including the rule that
silence does not mean consent,[9] the rule that risks should lie primarily
where the parties put them[10] and the caveat emptor assumptions of the
'normal conveyancing transaction' of land.[11]

The other argument used by Lord Keith in *Spring*, that liability would
reduce the degree of frankness used in references or that it would mean
that people would refuse to write references at all for fear of litigation, is
also a standard argument, namely the argument that the possibility of
litigation would encourage defensiveness, usually defensive medicine or

5   See also E Banakas *Tortious Liability for Pure Economic Loss: A Comparative Study*
     (1989: Athens, Hellenic Institute of International and Foreign Law) (two-party economic
     loss cases distinct from three-party cases).
6   Above at pp 284ff.
7   See above ch 5.
8   See above ch 5, eg *Lonrho v Shell (No 2)* [1982] AC 173, *Caparo* and *Peabody*. See also
     Stapleton at p 286.
9   See eg *Banque Keyser Ullman v Skandia* [1990] 1 QB 665 above ch 5.
10   *The Aliakmon* and, indeed, the whole of the *Tai Hing* line of cases.
11   *Gran Gelato v Richcliff*.

defensive policing.[12] It is related to the 'overkill' argument,[13] according to which either the existing law or the natural inclinations of the defendants provide adequate incentives in favour of reasonable behaviour so that adding further incentives in the form of a negligence action can only do harm.

The 'waste of resources' argument already considered is another close relative of 'overkill' and the perverse incentive argument, since its main point is that contrary to expectation, the imposition of negligence liability will not make defendants behave much better, one reason for which may be that the existing incentives are sufficient, so that the costs involved in legal action outweigh any benefits through the more efficient allocation of resources.

Above all, the argument against relational loss has a range of application well beyond economic loss, especially in relation to nervous shock.[14]

To point out that the arguments for and against liability for pure economic loss are largely simply applications of arguments that apply in negligence generally may seem to be a paradoxical conclusion to a long chapter on economic loss. But it is important to understand that the economic loss cases are not so distant from the rest of negligence law as is sometimes believed.

12 See Lord Keith in *Hill v Chief Constable of West Yorkshire* [1989] AC 53.
13 See above ch 5. Eg Lord Keith in *Murphy v Brentwood District Council* [1991] 1 AC 398 at 472 and *Rowling v Takaro Properties* [1988] AC 473 at 501. The argument was raised unsuccessfully in *Lonrho v Tebbit* in the Court of Appeal [1992] 4 All ER 280.
14 See above ch 5

Chapter 7

Breach of statutory duty— (1) in general

Introduction

There are some legal problems in which the key to understanding is to know why there is a problem in the first place. This is the case with breach of statutory duty. One might think that it is obvious that if a statute forbids people from doing certain things, for example a statute that creates a criminal offence, and as a consequence of people doing such things other people suffer, the victims should be able to sue those who breached the statute. And in most cases it is obvious, because the people who have breached the statute have usually also acted unreasonably, so that regardless of the statute they are liable in negligence. The only problems at that point are the arguments raised in chapter 5 that allowing a negligence action may have the effect of undermining a scheme of liability, or rather a scheme of non-liability, set up by the statute.[1]

The real problems come in only when, for some reason or other, the plaintiff cannot prove common law negligence against the defendant, but can nevertheless show a breach of a statute. The reasons why the plaintiff may not be able to prove negligence against the defendant are many. Some of them are permanent features of the law, others depend on doctrines that have come and gone. They include:

* The plaintiff can show damage but cannot show fault. The statute in question, however, sets up a strict liability duty.
* The action concerns forms of loss that at the time were not recoverable in negligence.
* The plaintiff and the defendant have a contract that puts the risk of what happened on the plaintiff.
* The defendant is an employer, the plaintiff an employee, and in straight negligence actions the courts follow doctrines that make it impossible for the employee to win.

---

1 Eg *M v Newham London Borough Council* [1994] 4 All ER 602 per Staughton and Peter Gibson LJJ.

In each case, the problem for the court is whether to allow the plaintiff to succeed when a negligence action would fail. In many cases, the statute itself resolves the question either by saying that the statute does set up a tort,[2] or by saying explicitly that no private rights of action arise.[3] The difficulties arise when the statute is silent.

Formally, the court's task is to establish what Parliament must have intended.[4] In reality, even now that the courts can use reports of Parliamentary debates as an aid to interpretation,[5] it is rare that there will be any direct evidence of parliamentary intent either way, even if it is coherent to talk about the 'intention' of such a large and diverse group of politicians in the first place.[6] Instead, the court has to decide the question using presumptions and arguments that displace those presumptions. But what should those presumptions be? There are three possible approaches to this question.

Negligence per se

Under this approach any breach of a statute counts as negligence. The presumption is that since Parliament has declared a certain activity to be unlawful, its intent must have been to discourage that activity. If there is no liability for breach of the statute, given that there is already no liability in common law negligence, there will be less deterrence of the activity and so more of it will happen, contrary to the intention of Parliament. It follows that there should always be liability for harm caused by breach of a statute.

Evidence of negligence

Under this approach, the court treats a breach of a statute as establishing a prima facie case of negligence, but the defendant may respond with arguments to show that the breach of the statute was justified. The presumption is that Parliament must have thought that, in most cases, the costs produced by the acts the statute forbids outweigh the benefits. But that does not mean that the costs must outweigh the benefits in every case and under all circumstances. Hence the law should give defendants an opportunity to justify their actions before they are required to pay compensation.

---

2   See below ch 8.
3   There are many examples of this. See eg reg 15 of Management of Health and Safety at Work Regulations 1992 (SI 1992/2051).
4   See eg *Cutler v Wandsworth Stadium Ltd* [1949] AC 398, *Lonrho v Shell (No 2)* [1982] AC 173.
5   *Pepper v Hart* [1993] AC 593.
6   See Dworkin *Law's Empire*.

No liability unless additional evidence of intent to protect specific group

Under this approach, the statute does not give rise to a private right of action unless there is specific evidence in the statute, albeit short of an explicit statement, that the statute was intended to protect a specific class or group of citizens rather than the public interest as a whole. The presumption is that statutes that establish criminal offences are designed to protect the public interest as a whole rather than the interests of individuals. Also, if the statute is drafted in broad vague declaratory terms, there is a presumption that the statute is designed to further the public interest as a whole, not the interests of any particular individual.[7] It is also possible, though unlikely, that the statute may contain evidence that it is meant to protect the interests of all individual citizens as individuals, as opposed to protecting a purely collective interest.

The English courts, unlike for example the Canadian courts,[8] have never discussed the choice between these three approaches openly. But the English courts invariably follow the third approach. The leading statement of the law is that of Lord Diplock for a unanimous House of Lords in *Lonrho v Shell (No 2)*:[9]

> '[O]ne starts with the presumption laid down originally by Lord Tenterden CJ in *Doe d Bishop of Rochester v Bridges* (1831) 1 B & Ad 847 at 859 ... where he spoke of the "general rule" that "where an Act creates an obligation, and enforces the performance in a specified manner ... that performance cannot be enforced in any other manner".'

Lord Diplock then says that there are two exceptions. First, 'where it is apparent that the obligation or prohibition was imposed for the benefit or protection of a particular class of individuals' and secondly, where the statute creates a statutory form of public nuisance[10] for which any one can sue as long as they suffer damage that is 'particular, direct and substantial' and 'other and different from that which was common to all the rest of the public'.

Although the English courts have not explicitly excluded the other approaches,[11] and have not therefore answered directly the question of the best approach to the civil questions of breaches of statutes, they have answered the associated question of whether breach of statutory duty is a separate tort or simply part of negligence. By saying that breach of statutory duty is a separate tort,[12] they have implicitly excluded the other approaches, both of which seek to integrate breach of statutory duty into negligence.

---

7   See *M v Newham, X v Bedfordshire* above ch 5.
8   See eg *Queen v Saskatchewan Wheat Pool* (1983) 143 DLR (3d) 9.
9   [1982] AC 173 at 185.
10 See below.
11 And note McCardie J in the Divisional Court in *Phillips v Britannia Laundry* [1923] 1 KB 539 at 548 who said, contrary to the tenor of the modern law, 'I agree however that the breach of a statutory regulation will usually afford prima facie evidence of negligence'.
12 *Bux v Slough Metals* [1974] 1 All ER 262, [1973] 1 WLR 1358, *Morris v National Coal Board* [1963] 3 All ER 644, [1963] 1 WLR 1382.

The approach taken by English law is controversial. The balance of academic opinion[13] favours either the negligence per se approach or the evidence of negligence approach or at least a presumption in favour of liability, as do most US jurisdictions. When faced with the choice, the Canadian Supreme Court chose the evidence of negligence approach, describing the English approach as 'painful'.[14] The debate has centred on three issues.

Fault

The three approaches put a different value on the importance of the fault principle. The evidence of negligence approach maintains the fault system almost in full. Breach of the statute creates a presumption that the defendant is at fault, but the defendant's ability to challenge and displace the presumption means that the court faces practically the same choice in assessing fault as it does in ordinary negligence cases. The negligence per se approach and English approach preserve fault only to the extent that the statute in question requires it. If the statute imposes liability based on intention, recklessness or negligence, the type of liability adopted con—sequentially in the tort action is the same. And so, if the statute imposes strict or absolute liability, so does the tort.

Those who favour the evidence of negligence approach often do so because it means that strict liability makes no further progress in the law. The English approach also denies further progress to strict liability in cases in which it results in no liability at all.

Notice that German law reaches a result similar to that of the evidence of negligence test by stipulating that civil liability for a breach of statute will arise if and only if the defendant was at fault in breaching the statute. Thus, if the criminal statute imposes liability without fault, civil liability will only follow if the plaintiff can prove nevertheless that the defendant was at fault.[15]

Predictability

The main criticism levelled at the English position is that it ends up being arbitrary and capricious, since it depends on a second round of statutory interpretation. How exactly does one tell whether a statute is meant to protect a specific group as opposed to society as a whole? Perhaps it is

13 See eg Williams 'The Effect of Penal Legislation in the Law of Tort' (1960) 23 MLR 233, Buckley 'Liability in Tort for Breach of Statutory Duty' (1984) 100 LQR 204, K Stanton *Breach of Statutory Duty* (Sweet and Maxwell, London, 1986). See also Law Commission, Report No 21: *The Interpretation of Statutes* (HMSO, London 1969) (calling for a statutory presumption in favour of a private right of action for breach of statutory duty).
14 Dixon J in *Queen v Sakatchewan Wheat Pool* above n 8.
15 Art 828-II BGB.

clear that statutes that protect interests that everyone has, for example bodily integrity, or that almost everyone has, for example the protection of property from theft, are not meant to protect specific groups. But the difficulties of interpretation come with interests that many but not all people have. The record of the English courts is not encouraging.[16] For example, they have usually said that employees count as a specially protected group in cases about health and safety at work legislation, but that road users do not count as such a group in cases about road traffic legislation.[17] But at any one time, except perhaps at rush hour, there are more people at work than on the roads. Admittedly, during the course of a week, more people use the roads than work as employees (at least they have done this last two centuries—if people take in very large numbers to telework and teleshopping the numbers may reverse themselves), but if the type of road-use in question is limited to the use of private motor vehicles, the question is probably a close one.[18]

The question seems to depend on aspects of social life that are subject to unpredictable change, and thus the rule itself is either unpredictable or out of date. In contrast, negligence per se is extremely predictable and the evidence of negligence test is no more or less predictable than ordinary negligence itself.

Suppression of vice

The third theme of the debate about breach of statutory duty has concerned the desired level of the activity declared illegal by the statute. The negligence per se rule assumes that the desired level is zero, otherwise the legislature would not have made it illegal. The evidence of negligence approach assumes that the desired level is the same as it would be if a negligence standard applied to it—that is that the activity is justified only when its overall benefits outweigh its costs. The English rule assumes that the desired level is usually whatever the criminal law alone produces unless there is intent to protect a specific group, when it is whatever criminal law and tort produce together.

The obvious objection to the English rule is that it is entirely lacking in principle. It takes no view at all on the question of the desired level of the activity but merely accepts whatever the imposition or the non-imposition of liability produces.

But there is one important aspect of the English rule that deserves more attention. In England, the Crown Prosecution Service, under the ultimate direction of the Director of Public Prosecutions and the Attorney-General, controls prosecutions. For some crimes, private prosecutions are

---

16 See generally Williams (1960) 23 MLR 233.

17 See *Coote v Stone* [1971] 1 WLR 279. Cf Lord Diplock in *Lonrho v Shell*.

18 Another possibility is that nineteenth and early twentieth century judges meant by a 'class' a social class. This would certainly explain why workers but not road users are a class for the purposes of breach of statutory duty, but whether such a classification is acceptable in the twenty-first century is questionable.

possible, but even they are ultimately subject to the control of the DPP and the Attorney-General.[19] Tort actions are not subject to the same control. This means that one effect of the denial of breach of statutory duty actions is to protect the discretion of the prosecuting authorities.

For example, in *Lonrho v Shell* the plaintiff accused the defendant oil companies of breaching the regulations that imposed economic sanctions on the breakaway régime in Rhodesia. The plaintiff's claim was that the defendant had supplied oil to the Rhodesians with the effect that the illegal régime had lasted much longer than it would have otherwise. This in turn meant that for that time the plaintiff lost the use of one of its assets, a pipeline for the legitimate supply of oil across Mozambique to Rhodesia. The plaintiff's claim in breach of statutory duty failed. As Fox LJ said in the Court of Appeal, with the approval of Lord Diplock in the House of Lords:

> '[The] purpose [of the orders] was the destruction, by economic pressure, of the UDI regime in Southern Rhodesia; they were instruments of state policy in an international matter.'

The enforcement of such instruments of state policy is also a matter of state policy. Indeed, this was the issue at the heart of *Lonrho v Shell*. Lonrho itself was under suspicion of busting the sanctions. Lonrho's then chief executive, Mr Rowland, was determined to show that Shell and BP, with the connivance of successive British governments were engaged in the illegal supply of oil to Rhodesia.[20] The Bingham Report,[1] which came out as Lonrho launched its action, confirmed that oil executives probably had committed criminal offences.[2] But the oil companies had not been pros-ecuted for breaching the sanctions orders although other businesses, even suppliers of petrol pumps, had been prosecuted.[3]

Two of the claims that arose out of these controversies are particularly relevant to *Lonrho v Shell*. One is the claim, by a minister in the Labour Government of the late 1960s, that the Government at that time delib-erately chose not to prosecute oil companies that breached the sanctions order and had done so as a matter of high policy.[4] The minister said that relevant considerations included the possible effect on Britain's position

---

19 See s 6(1) and s 6(2) of the Prosecution of Offences Act 1985. See eg *R v Tower Bridge Metropolitan Stipendiary Magistrate, ex p Chaudhry* [1994] QB 340.

20 See M Bailey *Oilgate: The Sanctions Scandal* (London; Hodder and Stoughton, 1969) at pp 55-61, 95-97.

1 TH Bingham *Report on the Supply of Petroleum and Petroleum Products to Rhodesia* (HMSO, 1978).

2 Bingham Report appendix III.

3 See *Bailey* at p 266. For a more measured account of the Rhodesian sanctions see H Strack *Sanctions: The Case of Rhodesia* (Syracuse NY; Syracuse Univ Press, 1978). Strack's main point is that it soon became clear that sanctions were unenforceable, so that the British government, like most governments, decided that only the symbolic value of sanctions could be salvaged. This meant that governments left the oil companies alone as long as, by acting via various intermediaries, they did not appeaar to challenge the sanctions orders directly.

4 See *Bailey* at 267f.

at the United Nations and on the Rhodesian morale if the true extent of
sanctions busting became widely known, together with the possible adverse
effect on British economic interests in South Africa. The Government, it
was claimed, preferred trying to persuade the oil companies to stop
supplying oil to prosecuting them for it. The other is the claim by Mr
Rowland that the Foreign Secretary of the time, Dr David Owen, tried to
persuade him to drop Lonrho's action against the oil companies.[5]

The importance of these claims is that they show that it is at least
possible that in some cases the decision to prosecute is a political decision
and that private tort actions can undermine such decisions. For the courts
to allow Lonrho to enforce the sanctions orders when the government found
it more convenient not to do so would be to allow Lonrho to conduct British
foreign policy.

The point is that the English rule does after all have a view on the
desired level of the activity prohibited by the statute. The English rule
commits the law to the view that the desired level of an activity may be
whatever the political authorities want it to be. It treats some statutes
that create offences not as giving rights to victims but as giving a
discretionary power to the state to prosecute if it wishes.

The law in detail

Turning to the detailed application of the English rule in the case law,
there are three issues to discuss. First, in which cases have the courts
granted a private right of action and in which not? Secondly, how do the
causation and remoteness rules work in those cases in which there is a
private right of action? Thirdly, which defences are available?

When is there a private right of action?

It is convenient and illuminating to group the cases according to the reasons
why a negligence action is not available.[6]

Plaintiff can't show fault

In *Phillips v Britannia Laundry*[7] one of the axles of the defendant's lorry
broke in two, a wheel came off, ran along the road and struck and damaged
the plaintiff's van. The reason the axle broke in two was that the manu-

5   *Bailey* p 97.
6   There are rare cases in which the courts have decided that the breach of statutory duty
     fails even though the plaintiff has a claim in negligence (*Bux v Slough Metals* [1974] 1
     All ER 262, [1973] 1 WLR 1358). But the reason for the failure of the breach of statutory
     duty here is not the unavailability of the action in principle but a failure to establish a
     breach of the statute.
7   [1923] 2 KB 832, [1923] All ER Rep 127— applied in *A-G v St Ives RDC* [1960] 1 QB 312.

facturer, to whom the defendant had sent the lorry for servicing, had carelessly failed to replace the axle even though it was showing signs of wear. The defendant, however, was not careless. He had no way of knowing about the state of the axle nor about the manufacturer's carelessness. Furthermore, his choice of the manufacturer to carry out the service was a reasonable one. But the plaintiff had another method of attack. Regulations made by the Local Government Board under powers delegated to it by an Act of 1896 required vehicles to be 'in such condition as not to cause or to be likely to cause danger to any person'. Violations of the regulation were punishable by a fine. The plaintiff claimed that the lorry had been in breach of the regulations and the breach had caused the damage. He won on this point at trial but lost on appeal both in the Divisional Court and in the Court of Appeal.

The judgment of the Court of Appeal in *Phillips* appears to be based on the same test as that Lord Diplock later propounds in *Lonrho*. Indeed Lord Diplock's rule is a synthesis of the judgments of Bankes LJ and Atkin LJ in *Phillips*.

Bankes LJ argued that although the courts should interpret statutes that provided for no punishment or remedy as setting up a private right of action by anyone injured by their violation, if the statute provided for a punishment, as in this case, there is a presumption that no private right arises unless the statute appears to be for the benefit of a particular class[8]. Bankes LJ says that the regulations in question were not passed for benefit of a particular class because 'The public using the highway is not a class; it is itself the public and not a class of the public.'[9]

Atkin LJ was, however, more circumspect:[10]

'[T]he question is not to be solved by considering whether or not the person aggrieved can bring himself within some special class of the community ... The duty may be of such paramount import–ance that it is owed to all the public. It would be strange if a less important duty, which is owed to a section of the public, may be enforced by an action, while a more important duty owed to the public at large cannot. The right of action does not depend on whether a statutory commandment ... is pronounced for the benefit of the public or for the benefit of a class. It may be conferred on anyone who can bring himself within the benefit of the Act.'

Note that each judge seems to be propounding one of Lord Diplock's exceptions.

But there is more to *Phillips* than this. Atkin LJ finds for the defendant not because of a vague impression that the statute was not intended to create a private right but because he thinks it unlikely that:[11]

8   At 838, citing Lords Halsbury and Macnaghten in *Pasmore v Oswaldtwistle Urban Council* [1898] AC 387.
9   [1923] 2 KB at 840.
10 At 841.
11 At 842.

'the Legislature, in empowering a department [of state] to make
regulations ... permitted the department to impose new duties in
favour of individuals and new causes of action ... in addition to the
obligations already well provided for and regulated by the common
law.'

He went on:

'In particular it is not likely that the Legislature intended by these
means to impose on the owners of vehicles an absolute obligation
to have them roadworthy in all events even in the absence of
negligence.'

In other words, liability for fault is the natural order of things, not strict
liability, so much so that the courts will not allow the fault principle to be
eroded by mere delegated legislation.

Bankes LJ has similar fears about the erosion of the fault system:[12]

'The Act deals with rights which have always been sufficiently
protected by the common law.'

The emphasis here is on 'sufficiently'. Fault is sufficient. Extra stricter
liability is unnecessary.

Bankes LJ also puts forward the argument that since the statute creates
absolute liability it would be possible for a plaintiff to sue simply on the
ground that the defendant's vehicle violated some regulation that was
completely irrelevant to the accident. This point may be absurd, since even
in strict liability the plaintiff has to show that the violation of the statute
caused the damage, but it illustrates clearly the judiciary's fear of strict
liability.

Scott v Green & Sons[13] shows a different approach to the same problem,
an approach that borders on the evidence of negligence view. In *Scott* the
plaintiff was walking down a street in Liverpool when a paving stone gave
way under her feet and she found herself falling into the defendant's cellar.
The trial judge found that the defendants had not been at fault in any
way. But the plaintiff claimed that there should nevertheless be liability
because the defendant was in breach of s 154(5) of the Highways Act 1959,
which said:

'Every vault, arch and cellar under a street and every opening into
any vault, arch or cellar thereunder, and every door or covering to
any such opening, and every cellar head, grating, light and coal
hole in the surface of a street, and all landings, flags or stones of
the street by which they are supported, shall be kept in good repair
by the owner or occupier of the vault, arch or cellar, or of the
premises to which it belongs.'

12 At 839.
13 [1969] 1 WLR 301.

Lord Denning MR found for the defendant. He said:[14]

'In my opinion breach of sub-s (5) does not by itself give rise to a civil action ... but forms the foundation on which the common law can build a cause of action. The statute clearly gives to the occupier a sufficient degree of control of the flagstone or grating over his cellar or basement so as to enable him to repair it, no matter whether it is [on the highway] or not. Being in control of it, the common law says ... he must use reasonable care to see that it is safe ... If the occupier has not been at fault, he is not liable.'

That is, the statute simply removes from the defendant the excuse that he could not repair the paving stone because it was on the highway. Otherwise, it has no effect. According to Lord Denning, it does not create, as it appears to, a regime of strict liability.

There is a similar pair of cases concerning the responsibility of water companies for fires that could not be put out because of lack of pressure in the mains.[14A] In *Atkinson v Newcastle Waterworks*[15] the plaintiff's premises caught fire. The fire brigade appeared quickly and prepared to put the fire out. But the firemen found that the water pressure in the fire hydrant was too low to pump water onto the fire. The blaze consequently raged on until the premises disappeared in the flames. The plaintiff claimed that the water company had failed in its duty under the Water Clauses Act 1843 to maintain the pressure to fire hydrants. The Court of Appeal found for the defendant water company. The plaintiff's case rested entirely on the statutory duty. He did not allege negligence. We do not know for certain exactly why he did not do so, but we may guess from the declaration that he had no evidence as to exactly how the failure of pressure came about. He alleges[16] only that 'the defendants were not prevented ... by frost, unusual drought, or other unavoidable cause or accident, or by the doing of necessary repairs from keeping the pressure up'. That is, the plaintiff knows what did not happen, but not what did, and so seeks to use the statute to reverse the burden of proof.

The Court of Appeal found for the defendant, apparently using the dubious argument that the statute's purpose could not be to give individuals the right to sue for compensation because it imposed a fine of £10 for breach, half of which went to the person who complained and half of which went to the local authority.[17] But the real reason for the decision appears slightly earlier in the judgment,[18] where Lord Cairns says that it is 'startling' and 'improbable' that Parliament intended to impose a liability on the water company such that the company:

14A Note that this question is now dealt with by new legislation, eg Water Act 1989 ss 45(7) and 58(7).

14 At 304.

15 (1877) 2 Ex D 441.

16 At 442.

17 Per Lord Cairns LC at 446.

18 At 445-46.

'would virtually become gratuitous insurers of the safety from fire, so far as water is capable of producing that safety, of all the houses within the district over which their powers extend.'

The other case in the pair is *Dawson v Bingley UDC*.[19] A local authority, acting under a statutory obligation, put up a sign indicating where the nearest underground fire hydrant was. The sign was wrong, and in consequence, when a fire broke out, the fire brigade could not find the hydrant. In the 15 minutes it took to find it, the fire caused much damage. The aggrieved property owners sued.

This time, the Court of Appeal found for the plaintiff householders. The Court, however, had great difficulty in explaining why it came to the opposite result to that reached in *Atkinson*. It relied mainly on unconvincing distinctions about whether the Act established penalties.[20] But the real difference between *Dawson* and *Atkinson* is that in *Dawson* the plaintiffs sued in negligence and won at trial, whereas in *Atkinson* the plaintiffs did not succeed in negligence. The trial judge in *Dawson* had asked the jury whether the defendants had been negligent, on two counts, and the jury replied that they had been negligent.[1] The relevance of the statute in *Dawson* was very much like the relevance of the statute in *Scott v Green*, namely that it removed an obvious counter-argument from the defendant, in this case that the defendant was a local authority and liable only for misfeasance not for nonfeasance.[2] Of course, there is a difference between *Dawson* and *Scott,* namely that in *Dawson* the trial court found that the defendant had been at fault, whereas in *Scott* the trial court found that the defendant had not been at fault. But the form of the argument is the same. The argument is that where allowing a breach of statutory duty action would create a strict liability tort beyond negligence, the courts are suspicious. Where the effect of the statute is only to regulate and modify negligence, then the statute may be allowed to produce a private right of action.[3]

There are, however, three House of Lords cases in which a private right of action did arise on a statutory provision in circumstances in which at least some judges were prepared to say that there was no fault on the part of the defendant. In each case, further inspection leads to the conclusion that the general presumption against strict liability and in favour of fault remains intact, but that the courts are sometimes prepared to countenance torts that modify the fault test to some degree in favour of the plaintiff.

First, in *London Passenger Transport Board v Upson*[4] a taxi obscured the view of a bus as it approached a light-controlled pedestrian crossing. The bus was travelling at only 15 mph, but that was too much to allow the

---

19 [1911] 2 KB 149.
20 See Kennedy LJ at 158.
1 See pp 151-52.
2 Vaughan Williams LJ at 154, Farwell LJ at 157, Kennedy LJ at 159.
3 Cf also *Woods v Winskill* [1913] 2 Ch 303, in which the defendant receiver knowingly dissipated a company's assets without making provision for the claims of preferential creditors. *Held*: liable.
4 [1949] AC 155.

bus to stop in time when a pedestrian appeared on the crossing. The bus hit the pedestrian and the pedestrian sued.

After much confusion in the courts below, the case reached the House of Lords with the plaintiff claiming separately for negligence and for breach of statutory duty. The statute in question was reg 3 of the Pedestrian Crossing Places (Traffic) Regulations 1941[5] which said that every driver approaching a pedestrian crossing:

> 'shall, unless he can see that there is no foot passenger thereon, proceed at such a speed as to be able if necessary to stop before reaching such crossing.'

Violation of the regulation was punishable by a fine of £2.

The negligence issue turned on whether the defendant was entitled to say that he did not have to take into account the chances that people cross the street at pedestrian crossings when the lights are in favour of the traffic. Lord du Parcq found against the defendant on this point, Lord Morton agreed and Lord Uthwatt said that, although he thought that he did not need to decide the negligence issue, in principle Lord du Parcq was correct. Lord Porter, however, disagreed and declared that the defendant had not been negligent. Lord Wright's position was similar to that of Lord Uthwatt.

The breach of statutory duty point was whether the defendant had technically breached the regulation and, although the judges did not take the point up, whether even if there was a breach, there was a causal connection between the breach and the damage. Surprisingly, counsel for the defendant seems not even to have argued the point that the regulation did not give rise to a private right of action.[6] As a result, all five of the law lords assumed that the plaintiff did have a private right of action on the statute. Only Lord Porter said explicitly that there was a breach of statutory duty even though there was no negligence. But the others, especially Lords Uthwatt and Wright who did not find it necessary to make final decisions on the question of negligence, seem prepared to find for the plaintiff whether or not the statutory test amounted to strict liability.

On the other hand, the regulation in question in *Upson* did not set up a strict liability in the sense that it defined a result or a state of affairs and then made it an offence to cause that state of affairs, regardless of intention or carelessness. Instead, it prohibited a way of behaving, namely driving too fast to stop at a pedestrian crossing. The regulation established by statutory fiat that a particular level of risk was too much. The difference between the regulation and common law negligence is that in the common law tort the court can reserve the right to disagree about precisely what level of risk is justifiable in such circumstances. The regulation does not therefore abandon fault, but simply defines a standard that is higher than that which the judges unaided may have chosen.

---

5   SI 1941/397.
6   See argument of counsel [1949] AC 155 at 158-60.

The second case is *John Summers v Frost*.[7] The House of Lords said that a duty to fence machinery under s 14(1) of the Factories Act 1937 was 'absolute', but nevertheless granted the plaintiff a private right of action on the section. Again, however, there is an explanation. Under s 14(1) liability only applied to failures to fence machinery that was 'dangerous', and 'dangerous', according to Lord Reid,[8] generally meant 'reasonably foreseeably dangerous'.[9] The effect of these two statements taken together is that the difference between liability under the statute and liability at common law was that under the statute it was not open to the defendant to argue, as it is at common law,[10] that although there was a more than trivial risk of injury, the costs of the suggested precaution, namely fencing, were too high. Once 'reasonably foreseeable danger' was established, the defendant had to choose between fencing the machine and not using it at all. Such a test is not the carelessness test in all of its glory, but this is not the same as strict liability either.

The third case is *Boyle v Kodak*.[11] The plaintiff was an employee of the defendant. He was painting a large oil storage tank when he fell off his ladder and was injured. The ladder had been tied at the bottom but not at the top, and the accident happened while the plaintiff was going up the ladder to tie it at the top. The plaintiff's first claim was that the defendant was careless because it should have ensured that the ladder was tied at the top not by someone climbing the ladder itself but by someone ascending the staircase to the top of the oil storage tank. But the trial court decided that the employer was not careless. The risk was small and would not have justified the time and effort necessary to secure the ladder in the way the plaintiff suggested. The House of Lords confirmed the judge's view. But the employee also claimed for breach of statutory duty. The regulation in question read:[12]

'Every ladder shall so far as practicable be securely fixed so that it can move neither from its top nor from its bottom points of rest.'

The House of Lords decided that a private right of action arose from this regulation and that the defendant was in breach of it. But note that, as in *John Summers v Frost*, the crime the regulation in question created was not quite one of strict liability. The words 'if practicable' meant that the plaintiff had to show some element of fault, albeit at a standard that was more favourable to the plaintiff than the ordinary negligence standard. This time, the statute deprived the defendant of the argument, available to all defendants in common law negligence, that the risk was so low that a reasonable person would have ignored it. The statute had, as in *John*

---

7   [1955] AC 740.
8   At 766.
9   See also *Close v Steel Co of Wales* [1962] AC 367, 412.
10 *AEC v Latimer* above ch 3.
11 [1969] 1 WLR 661.
12 Reg 29(4) of the Building (Health, Safety and Welfare) Regulations 1948.

Summers v Frost, taken the cost of the precaution out of the normal negligence equation.

Taking all of these cases together, the principle they apply appears to be that, if at all possible, the court should interpret the statute in question so that it does not set up a strict liability tort, but there is less difficulty in interpreting a statute so that it facilitates the application of a more pro-plaintiff fault standard than that normally used in common law negligence.[13]

Forms of loss not recoverable in negligence

The second reason to consider for the plaintiff's failure to sue in negligence and thus for the plaintiff's attempted use of breach of statutory duty is that the form or type of loss that the plaintiff suffers is not, at least at the time of the action, recoverable in negligence. Perhaps surprisingly, the judges have been more sympathetic toward the plaintiff in such cases than in cases in which plaintiffs fail to prove fault. Perhaps this indicates that judges are more attached to the fault principle than to the rules excluding various sorts of loss from the scope of negligence. There are, however, cases in which the courts refuse to allow plaintiffs to use statutory duties to make actionable types of loss that are not actionable at common law.

In *Monk v Warbey*[14] Warbey, the defendant, lent his car to one Knowles. Knowles in turn allowed a Mr May to drive the car. May then carelessly ran into the plaintiff, Monk. It turned out that neither Knowles nor May had insurance and neither could afford to pay the £70 compensation. The defendant had insurance but it did not cover other drivers. The plaintiff alleged that the defendant had thereby contravened s 35 of the Road Traffic Act 1930[15] which made it an offence for 'to cause or permit any other person to use a motor vehicle on a road unless there is in force in relation to ... that other person ... a policy of insurance in respect of third party risks.' The plaintiff claimed that the defendant's contravention of s 35 had caused him loss because if the defendant had complied with the statute, the plaintiff would have been able to obtain compensation from Knowles and May.

Although s 35 appears to set up a strict liability offence,[16] the plaintiff in *Monk v Warbey* could easily have proved fault if that had been required. The problem for the plaintiff in any equivalent negligence action would, however, have been the type of loss. The plaintiff did not suggest that the

---

13   Another example is *Nimmo v Alexander Cowan* [1968] AC 107 (reversal of burden of proof on reasonableness acceptable with breach of statutory duty).

14   [1935] 1 KB 75.

15   See now Road Traffic Act 1988 s 143.

16   See *Lyons v May* [1948] 2 All ER 1062, *Tapsell v Maslen* [1967] Crim LR 53. Its successor is not strict liability but the burden of proof lies on the defendant to prove that he neither knew or had reason to know that there was no such insurance policy: Road Traffic Act 1988 s 143(3)(c).

defendant caused the accident itself by breaching the statute[17] merely that the defendant had deprived the plaintiff of a chance of obtaining compensation. The loss was thus pure economic loss.

The Court of Appeal nevertheless allowed the plaintiff to succeed in breach of statutory duty. Greer LJ said, correctly, that if there was no private right to sue on the statute, the victims of accidents in such circumstances would have no remedy. The intention of Parliament was to protect such accident victims, and the section's penalties—imprisonment, fines and disqualification from driving—would do nothing to help them.

Critics of *Monk*[18] say that it is incompatible with *Phillips v Britannia Hygenic Laundry*. It is certainly so that *Monk* is incompatible with Bankes LJ's requirement that the statute's purpose should be to protect a particular class, and his statement that road-users are not such a class. But, on the other hand, it is not incompatible with Atkin LJ's view that there can be statutes whose purpose is to protect all members of the public individually rather than collectively, a possibility endorsed by Lord Diplock in *Lonrho*. Moreover, the element of not being able to prove fault is absent. It is true that *Monk* represents yet another turn on the winding path the judiciary have taken on the question of the effect on private rights of action of the existence of criminal penalties, but, it is submitted, this question has never really been important in deciding cases. *Monk* stands instead for the proposition that there can be statutes whose purpose is to protect the economic interests of individuals against non-intentional injury, a view once made unfashionable by Lord Keith of Kinkel[19] but now perhaps on the brink of restoration.[20]

Another example is *Cutler v Wandsworth Stadium*,[1] the plaintiff was a bookmaker whom the defendant, the operator of a stadium in which dog racing took place, had excluded from his premises. The plaintiff sued for a declaration that the defendant was under an obligation to allow him into the stadium for the purposes of bookmaking. The heart of the plaintiff's complaint was that the operator also operated its own bookmaking business, the tote, and had excluded the plaintiff to protect its own monopoly. Here, there are two reasons why the plaintiff would have had no claim in common law negligence. First, although the defendant was intentionally protecting a monopoly, it was a monopoly created by its rights as the occupier, the exercise of which to exclude others is usually taken to be reasonable. Secondly, a negligence action would have failed because the loss the plaintiff complained about was purely economic. The defendant was denying the plaintiff an opportunity to trade with others.

The statute the plaintiff hoped would allow him to improve on his common law position was the Betting and Lotteries Act 1934, which said that if operators of dog-racing tracks wanted to run their own bookmaking

17　Although that may have been a fruitful way forward, see below.
18　Eg *Markesinis and Deakin* at 317.
19　See above ch 5.
20　Ibid.
1　[1949] AC 398.

businesses (in the form of a tote), they were obliged, on pain of a hefty fine, to allow bookmakers onto their premises. Specifically, the Act prohibited dog-track operators from excluding bookmakers by reason only that they intend to carry on bookmaking, and it required the dog-track operators to 'take such steps that are necessary to secure that ... there is available for bookmaking space on the track where they can conveniently carry on bookmaking.'

The effect of the Act, the plaintiff claimed, was to cure both the defects of his common law position at once. First the Act meant that to say that exercising one's own property rights is no longer a conclusive argument for saying that the defendant was not at fault. And secondly, it meant that the bookmakers' financial interests were a legitimate object of judicial protection.

The House of Lords accepted the first point but not the second. They accepted that the defendant was in breach of the Act and that the defendant had no argument resting solely on the inherent reasonableness of exercising its rights as occupier. But they rejected the plaintiff's contention that the Act recognised his economic interests as worthy of judicial protection.

The speeches in the House of Lords in *Cutler* dealt in the usual currency of these cases, the effect of the existence of a criminal penalty (here that it made a private right of action less likely), the size of that penalty (here large enough supposedly to act as an effective deterrent without the aid of the threat of tort damages) and whether bookmakers were a class. But the most important argument the House of Lords used was that the point of the provision in question was to promote competition in bookmaking for the benefit of the dog-race-going public, not to protect the incomes of bookmakers.[2]

It seems to have occurred only to Lord Reid that these statutory provisions might have had more than one purpose, and that although the primary interest was to promote competition, a secondary object may have been to protect bookmakers' incomes from the effect of the Act itself, which allowed track operators to run totes for the first time. At this point Lord Reid uses an argument that seems only half right. He says that one can tell that Parliament intended there to be no individual rights of action because no track operator would be able to provide space for every single bookmaker who turned up, and yet the statute provides for no excuses. Thus, the statute would be absurd if it allowed private rights of action. But there are two counter-arguments against Lord Reid's position. First, Lord Reid's argument applies only to the statutory obligation to provide space, not to the right against exclusion for the reason '*only*' that the person intended to carry on bookmaking. Practical reasons would surely count as reasons other than the reason the section prohibits. Secondly, it would be a very harsh interpretation indeed of the section that it was an offence to turn away a bookmaker because there was no space left.

Regardless of the correctness of Lord Reid's position, the effect of *Cutler* appears to be that where granting a private right of action on a statute

---

2   Lord Simonds at 409, Lord Normand at 414, Lord Reid at 416-417.

would have the effect of protecting a type of interest that otherwise would not have been protected, the protection of the individual rights of people like the plaintiff has to be a primary purpose of the statute, not just a secondary purpose.

Lonrho v Shell illustrates the same test. Lonrho's claim was for economic loss, which is not normally recoverable. The sanctions orders may have had the effect of protecting the economic interests of those who wished to trade legitimately with Rhodesia and that may have been a secondary purpose of the legislation. It was not, however, the primary purpose of the legislation, which was, either in reality or symbolically, to put international pressure on the Rhodesian régime.

Yet another example is *R v Deputy Governor of Parkhurst Prison, ex p Hague*.[3] The applicant claimed that the authorities of the prison where he was held had placed him unlawfully in solitary confinement. A claim for negligence would not have succeeded because there was no physical harm beyond the fact of detention. The applicant also claimed for false imprisonment, but the House of Lords ruled that a prisoner lawfully detained under the Prison Act had no residual liberty that the defendant could take away.[4] That left a claim for breach of statutory duty arising out of alleged breaches of the rule, r 43, under which the authorities had segregated the applicant. But this claim also failed. As Lord Bridge said:[5]

'The fallacy in [the applicant's] argument is that it relies on authorities relating to statutory duties imposed for no other purpose than to protect various classes of person from the risk of personal injury ... The purpose of the rule [ie r 43], apart from the case of prisoners who need to be segregated in their own interests, is to give an obviously necessary power to segregate prisoners who are liable for any reason to disturb the orderly conduct of the prison generally. The rule is a purely preventive measure.'

Yet again, the claim is for a form of damage not recoverable in negligence. The statutory rule has the incidental effect of affording some protection to the claimant's interests but its primary purpose is something else entirely. Hence, no liability.

The House of Lords applied a much cruder version of this approach in *Pickering v Liverpool Daily Post*.[6] The plaintiff was a patient detained in a secure mental hospital. The defendant newspaper wanted to prevent the plaintiff from being released by the mental health review tribunal. To achieve this, they intended to publish, along with publicly available information such as the details of the plaintiff's criminal convictions, various other facts, including the fact that the plaintiff had applied to the tribunal for an order of release, the date of the hearing and the tribunal's

3   [1992] 1 AC 58.
4   See below.
5   At 158-60.
6   [1991] 2 AC 370, [1991] 1 All ER 622.

decision. There are no torts in England directly controlling even the intentional invasion of privacy,[7] let alone a negligence action. The plaintiff claimed, however, to have a private right of action arising either out r 21(5) of the Mental Health Review Tribunal Rules, themselves made under s 78(1) of the Mental Health Act 1983 or out of s 12(1)(b) of the Administration of Justice Act 1960. Rule 21(5) said that:

'Except in so far as the tribunal may direct, information about proceedings before the tribunal and the names of any persons concerned in the proceedings shall not be made public.'

Section 12(1) of the Administration of Justice Act 1960 says, as the House of Lords found, that it would be a contempt of court to publish information relating to the Mental Health Review Tribunal if the Tribunal had decided to sit in private.

The House of Lords, however, ruled that no private right of action arose from r 21(5) and s 12(1).[8] Lord Bridge could have said that the primary purpose of the statutory rules in question was the protection of the integrity of the judicial process so that no private right of action arose to protect a secondary purpose such as the plaintiff's privacy. But instead he simply said:[9]

'[P]ublication of unauthorised information about proceedings on a patient's application for discharge to a mental health review tribunal, though it may in one sense be adverse to the patient's interest, is incapable of causing him loss or injury of a kind for which the law awards damages.'

Lord Bridge contrasts *Pickering*'s case with cases in which the plaintiff complained of personal injury, injury to property or economic loss, which are recoverable in breach of statutory duty. Lord Bridge seems to be drawing a distinction between economic loss, a type of loss that is not normally recoverable in negligence but which is recoverable in other torts (for example deceit and conspiracy), and breach of privacy, which is not recoverable at all in tort.

But *Pickering* should be contrasted with other cases in which statutory duties have been found to protect aspects of privacy. For example, under s 2 of Dramatic and Musical Performers' Protection Act 1958[10] it was a criminal offence, punishable by a fine, to make a film out of someone else's musical or dramatic performances without their consent. In *Rickless v*

---

7   But see below chs 10 and 12.
8   They also ruled, incidentally, that what the defendants wanted to publish would not be a contempt anyway.
9   [1991] 2 AC 370 at 420.
10 Now Copyright, Designs and Patents Act 1988 Pt II ss 180 ff. These sections now give explicit private rights of action for performers against 'bootlegging', but record companies have no similar right unless they have exclusive recording contracts.

United Artists[11] the estate of the actor Peter Sellers claimed to have a private right of action under s 2 of the 1958 Act against various film companies and against the director Blake Edwards for collecting together bits and pieces of Peter Sellers' performances in old Pink Panther movies, including previously unscreened material, and cobbling them together into a new movie called 'The Trail of the Pink Panther'. The estate won.

There is no problem with fault in *Rickless* for the crime could only have been committed 'knowingly'. All that prevents the plaintiff from suing in such circumstances at common law is the recoverability of the form of loss. But the Court of Appeal had no difficulty in finding that the primary purpose of the legislation was precisely to protect performers such as Mr Sellers.

In *RCA v Pollard*,[12] in contrast, in which the plaintiffs were not the performers themselves but their record companies, the plaintiffs were only secondary beneficiaries of the statute, not its primary beneficiaries.[13] The plaintiffs' claim failed.

Pickering cannot be reconciled easily with *Rickless*, or even with *RCA v Pollard*. It is submitted that the more subtle approach of *Rickless* and *RCA v Pollard* is better than Lord Bridge's crude pronouncement in *Pickering*. That there is no general protection for privacy in English law does not rule out protection for some aspects of privacy, and, equally, it is possible for statutes to be designed to protect aspects of privacy.

The so-called 'Euro-tort' cases can be analysed in a broadly similar way. In *Garden Cottage Foods v Milk Marketing Board*[14] the House of Lords held, in an interlocutory hearing, that it was clearly arguable that a private right of action would lie at the suit of victims of those who had abused their dominant market position contrary to Art 86 of the Treaty of Rome. Article 86, which is incorporated into English law by the European Communities Act 1972, is enforced by fines imposed by the European Commission under the supervision of the European Court of Justice.

In *Garden Cottage Foods* the defendant, the Milk Marketing Board, was a statutory body that used to control the distribution of 75% of the milk produced in Britain. The plaintiff, Garden Cottage Foods, was a very small business that, among other things, bought and sold butter. The defendant used to supply butter to the plaintiffs, but in 1982 decided that in future it would supply butter only to four large distributors. The plaintiffs were cut out and their business faced serious losses. They sued, accusing the Board of violating Art 86 and, on whether they would have an arguable case, won.[15]

11 [1988] QB 40.
12 [1983] Ch 135: Elvis Presley's record company claimed against 'bootleggers'—people who surreptiously record performances and later sell copies of the recording—of Elvis Presley concerts. 'Bootlegging' was a crime under s 1 of the 1958 Act. *Held*: no cause of action in tort.
13 Note that the statutory position is now that recording companies do have a right of action if they have the performers under an exclusive contract.
14 [1984] AC 130.
15 See also *An Bord Bainne Co-operative v Milk Marketing Board* [1984] 2 CMLR 584.

Again there is no danger of creating out of Art 86 any sort of strict liability. It is true that the *Hoffman-La Roche* case[16] says that 'abuse' is 'an objective concept' but that appears to mean only that negligence is sufficient for liability, and that liability is not restricted to cases of intentional harm.[17] The difficulty is once more the form of the loss, which is, plainly, pure economic loss. The plaintiff accuses the defendant of preventing the plaintiff from making profitable deals with third parties. Nevertheless the plaintiff wins.

Admittedly there is no explicit discussion in *Garden Cottage Foods* about whether the primary purpose of Art 86 is to protect traders in the position of the plaintiff, but it is not difficult to read such a purpose into Art 86, and into Art 86(c) in particular. Article 86(c) prohibits abuse of a dominant market position by:

> 'applying dissimilar conditions to equivalent transactions with other trading parties, thereby placing them at a competitive disadvantage.'

That is, unequal treatment of, for example, small businesses such as the plaintiff in *Garden Cottage Foods* is to be an abuse of dominant market position.

In contrast in *Bourgoin v Ministry of Agriculture, Fisheries and Food*[18] the plaintiff attempted to base a breach of statutory duty case on Art 30 of the treaty, which says:

> 'Quantitative restrictions on imports and all measures having equivalent effect shall ... be prohibited between member states.'

The Court of Appeal held that no private right of action arose out of Art 30 because its purpose was less to protect individual traders in other member states than to protect the interests of the public as a whole. Any remedy was thus to be located in public law, not in private law.

It is, however, worth comparing *Garden Cottage Foods* with *Cutler v Wandsworth Stadium*. *Cutler* was also about a statutory provision that promoted competition. But the House of Lords said that the primary purpose of a statute designed to promote competition was to benefit customers, not to benefit traders. And there are parts of Art 86 that seem clearly to have the same intention. For example Art 86 (b) prohibits abuse of dominant position by:

> 'limiting production, markets or technical development to the prejudice of consumers.'

16 [1979] 3 CMLR 211.
17 See the list of considerations for judging 'abuse' at pp 616-17 of Bellamy and Child *Common Market Law of Competition* (4th ed) (1993; London, Sweet and Maxwell).
18 [1986] QB 716.

One can, however, distinguish between *Cutler* and *Garden Cottage Foods* by noticing that there are two forms of competition law. In the first form, the primary purpose of the law is by promoting competition to increase economic efficiency generally. In the second form, the purpose is to redress unfairness and to promote competition to give all producers an even chance. In the first form, the interests primarily protected are those of consumers rather than those of producers. Indeed, more competition may drive some producers out of business. But in the second form of competition law, the interests primarily protected are those of the victims of the unfairness, who may be producers not just consumers. *Cutler*, according to the House of Lords concerned an example of the first form of competition law, *Garden Cottage Foods* an example of the second.

Contract puts the risk on plaintiff

The next reason why plaintiffs may turn to breach of statutory duty is that they have debarred themselves by contract from using a common law remedy.

Such reasons lie behind the celebrated nineteenth century case *Gorris v Scott*.[19] The plaintiff contracted with the defendant for the shipment of a number of sheep from Hamburg to Newcastle. The sheep never arrived because they were washed overboard into the North Sea.

The plaintiff's difficulty with any legal action against the defendant was that the contract between them stated explicitly that the sheep would be:[20]

'On deck at [plaintiff's] risk. Not answerable for washing or throwing overboard.'

The plaintiff sought to evade this term in the contract by alleging that the defendant had breached a statutory duty against him. The statute in question was the Contagious Diseases (Animals) Act 1869, under the authority of s 75 of which there were regulations that required those who transported animals by ship to carry them in separate pens. The purpose of the regulation was plainly to reduce the chances of infection spreading from one animal to another, but the plaintiff pointed out that if the defendant had complied with the regulation, the sheep would not have fallen over the side of the ship. The plaintiff therefore said that the breach of the statutory duty had caused the loss of his sheep and that he was entitled to compensation.

Not surprisingly, the defendant won. The Court of Exchequer pointed out that since the purpose of the statute was to prevent disease, not to protect the interests of the plaintiff, there could be no action for breach of

---

19 (1874) LR 9 Exch 125, 30 LT 431, 43 LJ Ex 92.
20 See 30 LT at 432. The other reports, unfortunately, do not record the terms of the contract.

statutory duty. But the crucial point, usually missed in commentaries on the case, is that the real issue is whether the plaintiff could claim the protection of the statute when he had explicitly accepted the risk of the sheep falling overboard. Counsel for the plaintiff[1] argued that the court should interpret the contract as impliedly bringing in the statutory standard—that is that the plaintiff only accepted the risk on the understanding that the defendant would comply with all statutory standards. The argument failed. Pigott B said:

> 'The legislature never contemplated altering the relations between the owners and carriers of cattle, except for the purposes pointed out in the Act ... If, indeed, by reason of the neglect complained of, the cattle had contracted a contagious disease, the case would have been different.'

That is, it would have been plausible to say, on the basis of the statute, that there was an implied term in the contract that the defendant would take steps to protect the sheep from disease, but, especially in the light of the explicit term whereby the plaintiff accepts the risk, there was no basis anywhere for an implied term to protect the sheep from being washed overboard.

The contract point does not often arise, but it is one of the background factors in *Lonrho v Shell*. The initial claim made by Lonrho against the oil companies was one of breach of contract. Lonrho had originally built its pipeline under a contract with the oil companies. It claimed that the oil companies were in breach of an implied term in the contract that they would do nothing that was likely to contribute to the closure of the pipeline.[2] The arbitrators and every judge who heard the case agreed that there was no such implied term. It was not necessary to make the contract workable and even if it were necessary to imply a term, there was no evidence to suggest that the parties would have accepted anything like the term the plaintiff suggested.[3] The conclusion was that the risk of the closure of the pipeline because of political action should lie where it fell, in this case on the plaintiff. The breach of statutory duty claim was thus an attempt, as in *Gorris v Scott*, to evade a contractual settlement of the risk, albeit not as explicit a settlement as in *Gorris* itself.

Similarly, in *McCall v Abelesz*[4] the Court of Appeal decided that the criminal offence of harassing tenants[5] did not create a private right of action, since the plaintiff already had adequate remedies in contract and there was no evidence in the Act of an intention to alter the contractual position between the parties. The adequacy of alternative remedies is not usually a sufficient argument against creating a private right of action on

1   LR 9 Exch at 127.
2   See [1981] Com LR at 6.
3   See Parker J at 7.
4   [1976] QB 585.
5   Rent Act 1965 s 30. Now see Protection from Eviction Act 1977 s 1.

a statute,[6] so that one suspects that the underlying objection to liability was the possibility that in a future case, although not in *McCall* itself, a tenant might be able to use the statute if not to establish liability in circumstances in which the parties had agreed in advance that the tenant should go quietly, at least to expand the amount of the damages. Interest–ingly, however, Parliament has subsequently disagreed with the Court of Appeal's view of the adequacy of the remedy in contract and has intervened explicitly to give the harassed tenant a statutory right of action.[7]

In all such cases, the issue before the court is whether to interpret the statute as one which overrides the distribution of risk that the parties have explicitly agreed or that the ordinary common law rules of interpret–ation would produce. The tendency of the courts for a long time has been to presume that statutes, especially statutes that introduce a benefit for a particular class, respect the principles of freedom of contract unless the opposite is apparent—as it would be, for example, in the case of consumer protection legislation.[8] There are, however, exceptions, one of which is the topic of the next section.

An obsolete reason—evading the common employment rule

The final form of breach of statutory duty case to consider is one that most texts, to the confusion of all concerned, deal with first, namely those cases in which the reason a common law action was unavailable was the existence of the now long-abolished common employment rule, otherwise known as the fellow servant rule.[9] The effect of the common employment rule, which on one view was the result of the courts' unfortunate misinterpretation of one case, namely *Priestley v Fowler*,[10] was that, in the words of Pollock CB in *Southcote v Stanley*:[11]

> 'The master is not in general liable to a servant for injury resulting from the negligence of a fellow servant; neither can one servant maintain an action against another for negligence whilst engaged in their common employment.'

---

6 See eg *Read v Croydon Corpn* [1938] 4 All ER 631 (alternative remedy in negligence no bar where no contractual liability).

7 Housing Act 1988 ss 27 and 28. The contract remedy was thought to be insufficient because it awarded tenants the value of the tenancy to them, not the often very much higher value of the property to the landlord of vacant possession, which was a powerful incentive to harass. Section 28 of the Act awards to the tenant the whole of the extra value of the property to the landlord of vacant possession.

8 See Bennion *Statutory Interpretation* (2nd ed) (1992; London, Butterworths) at 35-40, 540 and 801-802.

9 Law Reform (Personal Injuries) Act 1948.

10 (1837) 3 M & W 1.

11 (1856) 1 H & N 247.

In the late nineteenth and early twentieth century more and more people worked for large impersonal organisations in which practically everyone with whom one was likely to come into contact was a 'fellow servant'. The result was that the common employment rule, if unchecked, would have prevented any sort of common law liability for industrial accidents. But not only was there a legislative response to the common employment doctrine, from the early Workmen's Compensation Acts to the eventual abolition of the rule, there was also a judicial response, including the invention of the idea of the employer's personal and non-delegable duties.

The judicial response also included allowing plaintiffs to bring breach of statutory duty claims based on protective statutes such as the Factories Acts. The theory behind these cases was always a little confused. One idea was that since the common employment doctrine depended on an implied acceptance of the risk of carelessness by fellow employees, there could be no such implied term if Parliament had declared the acts in question to be criminal offences. Only explicit waivers by the people intended to be protected by the statute would do. An alternative theory was that the statutes set up a personal, non-delegable duty on the employer, so that any agreement about the negligence of fellow employees was irrelevant.[12]

These were the considerations which lay behind cases such as *Groves v Lord Wimborne*,[13] *Butler (or Black) v Fife Coal Co*,[14] *Dew v United British SS Co Ltd*,[15] and *Flower v Ebbw Vale Steel*.[16] In these cases courts recognised private rights of action on statutes dealing with safety at work, statutes that created criminal sanctions only, in circumstances in which they may not have recognised such rights if the common employment doctrine had not been in operation. But note that in both *Dew* and *Flower,* which were heard as both statutory and other common law remedies were becoming available that avoided the common employment rule, the court eventually found other reasons for the plaintiff to lose. Furthermore, in one of the first industrial injury cases after the abolition of the common employment rule, *Biddle v Truvox Engineering*,[17] the High Court, although accepting the continued authority of *Groves v Lord Wimborne* for cases under the Factories Acts, refused to extend it to cases in which the defendant was the seller or manufacturer of the machine rather than the employer.

It may be worth considering whether, because the reason the courts allowed private rights of action on these statutes has now disappeared, they should no longer count as a specially privileged category of case. It turns out that in many cases such a move would make no difference to the private rights of action since they do not impose liability for a new form of loss, are not plausibly interpreted as intended to alter the contractual position between the parties and would not necessarily create strict liability.

12 See Scrutton LJ in *Dew v United British SS Co Ltd* (1928) 139 LT 628 at 631.
13 [1898] 2 QB 402.
14 [1912] AC 149.
15 (1928) 139 LT 628.
16 [1934] 2 KB 132.
17 [1952] 1 KB 101.

But in any case, the whole field of industrial safety is about to be transformed by the implementation of the EC Framework Directive on Health and Safety.[18] The implementing regulations[19] which will eventually replace the existing legislation, are all covered by explicit statements about whether or not they give rise to private rights of action.[20]

Causation and remoteness

Liability for breach of statutory duty is not exempt from the requirement that the breach should cause the plaintiff's loss.[1] Indeed, the causation question arises in breach of statutory duty in a sharper form, since the issue of causation is more clearly separate from the issue of breach than it is in common law negligence. In negligence, to say that the defendant was careless ultimately includes a finding that the carelessness caused the loss, for otherwise it would not be possible to say that the defendant could reasonably have prevented the harm to the plaintiff. But the same is not true in breach of statutory duty. It is possible for the defendant clearly to be in breach of the statute but for there to be considerable doubt about whether the breach caused the loss. If, for example, the statute requires the defendant to fence some machinery, and the defendant fails to do so, that is a breach. But it is possible that the accident in which the plaintiff was injured would have happened anyway, with the same results. For example, the plaintiff may have fallen and injured himself by hitting himself against the machine in a place at which fencing would have made no difference.

One very special problem deserves a mention, however. It concerns breaches of statutes that require defendants to obtain and hold licences for particular activities. When the law is that people commit a criminal offence if they engage in an activity without first obtaining a licence, there are always two ways in which they could obey the law. Either they refrain from the activity or they obtain the licence. But these two ways of obeying the law can profoundly affect the way the court sees the causation issue in a breach of statutory duty case.

18 Council Directive 89/391/EEC.
19 Management of Health and Safety at Work Regulations 1992 (SI 1992/2051), Workplace (Health, Safety and Welfare) Regulations 1992 (SI 1992/3004), Provision and Use of Work Equipment Regulations 1992 (SI 1992/2932), Personal Protective Equipment at Work Regulations 1992 (SI 1992/2966) amended SI 1993/3074, Manual Handling Regulations 1992 (SI 1992/2793), Health and Safety (Display Screen Equipment) Regulations 1992 (SI 1992/2792), Control of Substances Hazardous to Health (Amend‐ment) Regulations 1992 (SI 1992/2382 and 2966), and Control of Asbestos at Work Regulations 1992 (SI 1992/3068).
20 The Management of Health and Safety at Work Regulations, which deal with general matters, do not create private rights of action, all the others do. See I Smith, C Goddard and N Randall *Health and Safety: The New Legal Framework* (1993; London, Butter‐worths) at pp 25-26.
1   Eg *Cummings (or McWilliams) v Sir William Arrol* [1962] 1 All ER 623. See above.

In, for example, *The Empire Jamaica*[2] a ship commanded by a perfectly competent officer who just happened to lack the appropriate master's papers came into collision with the plaintiff's vessel. The plaintiff could show no carelessness by the officer, but said that the accident was caused by his failure to hold the correct licence. The plaintiff's point was that the owner of the ship should not have let it set sail with an unlicensed master. If the owner had not done so, the collision would not have happened. The defendant said that the officer's conduct would have been exactly the same if he had obtained a licence, so that the breach of the statute made no difference to the outcome. The court found in favour of the defendant.

The point about *The Empire Jamaica* was that the plaintiff said that the defendant should have obeyed the law by not setting sail, whereas the defendant said the officer should have obeyed the law by obtaining a licence. Normally in such cases[3] the court adopts the defendant's view. But one should not conclude that such a result is inevitable. Everything depends on what the courts believe to be the purpose of the licensing requirement. Licence requirements can exist for several reasons. Some of those purposes, for example raising revenue and providing identification, suggest that the intended mode of obeying the law is obtaining the licence rather than refraining from the activity altogether. TV licences are a good example. Similarly even licences meant to be certificates of competence are, as *The Empire Jamaica* suggests, only evidence of that competence, and are not conclusive. Their purpose is to ensure that only competent people engage in the activity concerned, so that their purpose is fulfilled if those people are indeed competent. But the purpose of some licences, for example US tradable emission licences, limited permits to pollute held by industry, is to control the number of people who engage in an activity and the amount of that activity that takes place. The intended mode of obeying the requirement to hold such a licence must be not to engage in the activity at all if one does not hold such a licence.

The ordinary rules of remoteness ought also to apply in breach of statutory duty. And indeed, there is no reason to doubt that the normal rules of novus actus interveniens concerning interventions by human beings and by natural events apply as much to breach of statutory duty as they do to negligence. But there do seem to be special rules about the foresee–ability of the type of harm and interventions by the plaintiff.

In negligence, the rule in the *Wagon Mound (No 1)* has become a rule that the type of harm the plaintiff suffers must have been a type of harm that the defendant could have reasonably foreseen. In breach of statutory duty, however, the requirement is instead that the type of harm has to be the type of harm contemplated by the statute. The case usually cited for this proposition is *Gorris v Scott*, but as we have seen above, this case is mainly about the relationship between the statute and the contract between the parties. But more recently, the *Peabody* case [4] has provided another

2   [1955] P 52.
3   See the cases cited in Hart and Honoré *Causation in the Law* (2nd edn) (1985: Oxford, Clarendon Press) at pp 119-120.
4   [1985] AC 210.

illustration. The plaintiffs were property developers. They blamed the
defendant local authority for economic loss they suffered when they
discovered that the drains under one of their developments were the wrong
type and that the local authority, acting under powers under the Public
Health Acts, had approved the installation of the drains. The defendants
lost. Lord Keith said bluntly:

> 'The purpose for which the powers ... have been conferred on [the
> local authority] is not to safeguard building developers against
> economic loss resulting from their failure to comply with approved
> plans. It is in my opinion to safeguard the occupiers of houses ...
> against dangers to their health.'

One might justify such a departure from the common law negligence
rule on the ground that since foreseeability is sometimes not a necessary
element of the duty established by statute, breach of statutory duty needs
a different test, and a test based on the contemplation of the statute is
most appropriate.

On the other hand, since the process of deciding whether or not a private
right of action arises from the statute tends to select out strict liability in
the first place, perhaps a better rule would be that the harm should be of
a type reasonably foreseeable by a defendant who knew about the statute
in question. *Gorris* is distinguishable in the way already described. *Peabody*
is explicable as a case about the liability of local authorities in common
law negligence arising out of the exercise of statutory powers rather than
a case about a private right of action arising out of a statue that creates a
public duty.

The special rule about interventions by the plaintiff appears in *Boyle v
Kodak*. The defendant employer claimed that there should be no liability
because the plaintiff himself was the means by which the defendant
allegedly breached the statute. The employer was only in breach of the
statute because the plaintiff himself had failed to secure the ladder at the
top. Instead of saying, simply, that the plaintiff's action could only be a
novus actus interveniens if it amounted to utterly unreasonable behaviour,
the House of Lords introduced the extraneous question of whether the
employer was personally responsible in any way for the employee's breach,
which, supposedly, it was because it had not proved that it took steps to
ensure that the employee knew about the regulations. The idea behind
the rule is that since remoteness is really a matter of the relative importance
of the parties' responsibility for the damage, one question that has to be
answered is the degree to which the defendant was responsible for the
harm. But note that the House of Lords in *Boyle* claims that the employer's
failure did not have to amount to fault. The test has to be whatever is the
test for liability in the statute—in *Boyle* a question of what is 'practicable'.
The test has to be adapted to the statutory context. Again, the justification
for such a departure from the common law rule is that fault in its ordinary
sense is not always necessary in breach of statutory duty. On the other

hand, it is not clear that this is sufficient justification for departing from the 'utterly unreasonable' test for the effect of interventions by the plaintiff, especially since the practical results seem not to be very different.

Defences

Boyle also illustrates a point established in cases such as *Dew v United British SS Co Ltd*,[5] and *Flower v Ebbw Vale Steel*,[6] namely that the defence of contributory negligence applies to breach of statutory duty cases in the normal way.[7] The plaintiff is judged on the ordinary fault standard for contributory negligence and the reduction of damages follows the ordinary mysteries.

The application of the defence of consent or volenti non fit injuria[8] is more controversial, since, as mentioned above, the evasion of the common employment doctrine was achieved partly by claiming that the common employment doctrine rested on implied consent whereas consent could not be given to breaches of statutory duty, which arise from a matter of public rather than private interest. But since this argument contradicts the alleged basis of liability in most breach of statutory duty cases, namely that the purpose of the statute is to protect members of a particular class, and since the common employment rule no longer exists, the better view is that volenti should apply in its ordinary, that is very restricted, way.[9] In *ICI v Shatwell*[10] two law lords said that volenti would not apply in a health and safety at work case if supervisory or managerial staff were implicated in the breach of statutory duty but could apply if the only people implicated were employees of the same level as the plaintiff. Interestingly, this is very close to the position under the common employment rule itself. In any case it is not clear how it applies outside the employment context or, even, within that context, how it can survive more modern, less hierarchical methods of organising work. Furthermore, control over contractual exclusions and contractual volenti can be exercised both through the application of the Unfair Contract Terms Act, and through interpretation of the contract. Lastly, the important point, as illustrated by *Gorris v Scott*, is whether the statute is capable of being interpreted as affecting the contractual relationship between the parties. In the case of health and safety at work legislation, an interpretation of the statute that it is intended to affect the contractual position is perhaps more plausible than in the case of animal welfare statutes.

5   (1928) 139 LT 628.
6   [1934] 2 KB 132.
7   See also *Caswell v Powell Duffryn* [1940] AC 152.
8   See below ch 15.
9   See below ch 15.
10   [1965] AC 656.

Public nuisance—breach of statutory duty without a statute

Despite the massive expansion of statute law over the past 60 years, there are still a few crimes left that arise not from statute but from the common law. Many of these are not of great interest to the tort lawyer. There are not likely to be any aggrieved individuals to sue for losses caused by crimes such as conspiracy to cheat the public revenue, escape from lawful custody or blasphemy. In other common law crimes, such as murder and man–slaughter, the appropriate tort is obvious and established by the fact of the conviction, but victims and their families rarely resort to them except where they believe that the criminal law has failed to establish guilt.[11] In others still, such as conspiracy to pervert the course of justice, there is an obvious tort to use (such as malicious prosecution) although admittedly it is possible that limitations on the tort itself restrict the victim's chances of success.[12] But there is one common law crime that frequently gives rise to private law actions, namely the crime of public nuisance.

Public nuisance usually makes its appearance in textbooks on tort as an addendum to the chapter on the tort of private nuisance. It is true that the two areas of the law are often confused,[13] and that some activities may give rise to liability in both torts. But public nuisance as a tort, unlike private nuisance, is essentially a criminal matter transformed into a civil action. It is therefore more closely related to breach of statutory duty than anything else, and indeed one might think of public nuisance as breach of statutory duty without a statute.

The first question to consider is under what circumstances does a person commit the crime of public nuisance (which, because it is a common law offence, carries a penalty of an unlimited fine and up to life imprisonment)? If there is no crime, there can be no tort either, for the tort arises out of the crime. The latest case to consider the question is *R v Shorrock*.[14] The defendant was a farmer who hired out one of his fields to a group of people who then organised a very noisy and disruptive rave party on it. In the words of the headnote:

> 'There was a great deal of noise and the police received about 275 complaints of noise and disturbance, some from people living as far as four miles away. The appellant, along with the organisers, was charged with public nuisance. He was convicted and fined £2,500 and ordered to pay £1,500 costs. He appealed on the ground that the Crown had failed to show that he had had the necessary knowledge that a public nuisance would be committed on his land.'

The Court of Appeal took the opportunity of confirming, first, that public nuisance was still a crime at common law, and secondly that a person

11 See eg *Halford v Brookes* [1991] 3 All ER 559, [1991] 1 WLR 428. But see also *Murphy v Culhane* [1977] QB 94, [1976] 3 All ER 533, [1976] 3 WLR 458.
12 See *Marrinan v Vibart* [1963] 1 QB 234; on appeal [1963] 1 QB 528.
13 Even by the House of Lords. See *Tate & Lyle v Greater London Council* [1983] 2 AC 509.
14 [1994] QB 279, [1993] 3 All ER 917, [1993] 3 WLR 698, 98 Cr App Rep 67.

committed the offence simply by causing almost any kind of serious harm to a large number of people. Rattee J quotes the three usual sources for his definition of the crime:

'It is defined in *Stephen's Digest of the Criminal Law* (9th edn, 1950) p 179 in the following terms:

"A common nuisance is an act not warranted by law or an omission to discharge a legal duty, which act or omission obstructs or causes inconvenience or damage to the public in the exercise of rights common to all His Majesty's subjects."

A similar definition is adopted in the current edition of *Archbold's Pleading Evidence and Practice in Criminal Cases* (44th edn, 1992) p 3374, para 31-40:

"Any person is guilty of an offence at common law, known as common nuisance, who (a) does an act not warranted by law, or, (b) omits to discharge a legal duty, if the effect of the act or omission is to endanger the life, health, property, morals, or comfort of the public, or to obstruct the public in the exercise or enjoyment of rights common to all Her Majesty's subjects", though the learned editors of Archbold suggest that it is doubtful whether the words "not warranted by law" should continue to be retained in the definition.

Blackstone's Commentaries (3 Bl Com (1st edn, 1768) 216) contains the following definition:

"Nusance, nocumentum, or annoyance, signifies anything that worketh hurt, inconvenience, or damage. And nusances are of two kinds; public or common nusances, which affect the public, and are an annoyance to all the King's subjects; for which reason we must refer them to the class of public wrongs, or crimes and misdemeanours: and private nusances; which are the objects of our present consideration, and may be defined, any thing done to the hurt or annoyance of the lands, tenements or hereditaments of another." '

Thus, public nuisance is a crime of astonishing breadth. It includes everything from making obscene telephone calls,[15] spreading false rumours of the death of Napoleon,[16] swimming without clothes,[17] and terrifying one's neighbours by keeping a puma and two leopards in one's garden[18] to

15 *R v Norbury* [1978] Crim LR 435.
16 *R v De Berenger* (1814) 3 M & S 67.
17 *R v Crunden* (1809) 2 Camp 89.
18 *R v Wheeler* (1971) Times, 12 December.

obstructing the highway by causing a crowd to gather,[19] causing pollution,[20] and obstructing the River Thames.[1] Indeed it is so broad and gives the state such untrammelled power that one very eminent authority in the criminal law has called for its abolition or at least a major reform that would limit its operation to the creation of major hazards to the health and safety of the public.[2]

The only substantial limitation on the scope of public nuisance is that the defendant's act must have affected a large number of people. A hoax caller who affected only a telephonist and half a dozen police officers did not therefore commit the offence.[3] On the other hand there is no require-ment that all the members of the affected group must suffer in the same way or to the same extent and the courts have been unwilling to say exactly how many people the defendant's actions have to affect before the crime is committed.[4]

Given the breadth of the crime, it is all the more alarming that in *Shorrock* the Court of Appeal found against the defendant and said that where the defendant does not actually commit the nuisance personally, but allows others to commit the crime, the defendant is guilty of the offence even if he did not know that the others would cause a nuisance, as long as he ought to have known. Moreover, the court says that we should understand 'ought to have known' 'in the sense that the means of knowledge were available to him'. That is, if the means to find out exist, the defendant is guilty even if it was unreasonable to expect the defendant to use them.

The transformation of the crime of public nuisance into a tort was a rather peculiar process.[5] During the fifteenth and sixteenth centuries, the law was very clear—no private rights arose from public nuisances, it was a crime only. But in the seventeenth century, building on some chance remarks of Fitzherbert J in a sixteenth century case and unnoticed for many years, the judges began to allow private rights of action to plaintiffs who could show that they had suffered some particular loss or damage. This became a rule that a plaintiff could sue if he showed 'special damage' and in the early nineteenth century, Lord Eldon said that the plaintiff could also obtain an injunction on proof of the same 'special damage'.[6]

The obvious question is 'what counts as special damage'? Unfortunately, as the leading commentator on the question says,[7] 'Few points in the civil

---

19 *R v Carlile* (1834) 6 C & P 636n.
20 *A-G v Cleaver* (1811) 18 Ves 211.
1 *A-G v Johnson* (1819) 2 Wils Ch 87.
2 Spencer 'Public Nuisance—A Critical Examination' [1989] CLJ 55.
3 *R v Madden* [1975] 1 WLR 1379.
4 *A-G v PYA Quarries* [1957] 2 QB 169. Note that Lord Denning's dictum in this case that the harm has to be so widespread that it would not be reasonable to expect actions for private nuisance not only puts the cart before the horse (the crime is prior to the tort) but also only works where the expected costs of bringing an action are greater than the expected compensation plus the value of any expected injunction.
5 For the definitive accounts, see J Baker *Introduction to English Legal History* (3rd ed) (London: Butterworths, 1990); *Spencer.*
6 *Crowder v Tinkler* (1816) 19 Ves 617.
7 *Spencer* at p 74. See also Kodilinye 'Public Nuisance and Particular Damage in Modern Law' (1986) 6 Legal Studies 182.

law are more obscure than the meaning of "special damage" '. There are two aspects to the question. First, what counts as the right type of loss; and secondly, what does 'special' mean? Not surprisingly, personal injury and physical harm to property count as possible types of special damage. But more surprisingly, pure economic loss also counts. Where the defendant caused the plaintiff's coffee shop to lose business because of a constant stream of wagons that visited the defendant's premises,[8] the fact that the loss was purely economic did not prevent recovery by the plaintiff. Equally the costs imposed on the plaintiff of clearing a river that has silted up because of the defendant's new wharf are not property loss because the plaintiff does not own the river. They are economic loss because they are an extra burden of cost that makes the plaintiff's business less profitable. But such losses apparently also count as possible special losses for the purposes of public nuisance.[9] Less clear is whether simply wasting someone's time counts as special damage. *Winterbottom v Lord Derby*[10] appears to say that mere inconvenience is not enough, but where the plaintiff can plausibly claim that as far as he is concerned time is money, as in *Boyd v Great Northern Rly Co*[11] in which the defendant delayed the plaintiff, a doctor, for 20 minutes, claims have succeeded.

As for what makes damage 'special', the general principle is that the plaintiff must have suffered something worse than the general public suffered. But two problems present themselves. First, does the harm the plaintiff suffers have to be of a different kind from that suffered by everyone else? And secondly, what if the harm that most people suffer as a result of the defendant's actions is as serious as that suffered by the plaintiff? The answer to the first question appears to be that a different degree of suffering is sufficient and there is no need to show a different kind of harm from that suffered by the public at large.[12] The answer to the second question has not yet appeared in the English courts, but the Canadian courts have said that if all the victims of the defendant's actions suffer the same damage, even if it is extremely serious, none of the victims has an action.[13]

In addition, the damage has to be 'direct and substantial'.[14] 'Direct' ought to mean 'not too remote', as in negligence, but the decision in *Shorrock*[15] that the owner of a field on which other people organise a rave party is liable regardless of the interventions of the party organisers and the ravers themselves suggests that the deliberate exploitation of the situation by intervening third parties does not break the chain of causation in public nuisance. Lord Reid in the *Wagon Mound (No 2)*[16] said that the meaning of

8   *Benjamin v Storr* (1874) LR 9 CP 400, but query whether this case would be classified as private nuisance now.
9   *Tate & Lyle v Greater London Council* above. See also *Gravesham Borough Council v British Rail* [1978] Ch 379.
10 (1867) LR 2 Exch 316.
11 [1895] 2 IR 555.
12 *Rose v Miles* (1815) 4 M & S 101.
13 *Hickey v Electric Reduction* (1970) 21 DLR (2d) 368.
14 Brett J in *Benjamin v Storr* (1874) LR 9 CP 400, 407.
15 See above.
16 [1967] 1 AC 617.

'direct' in public nuisance was 'narrower' than its usage in remotness, but exactly what such narrowness entails is unclear.

The requirement that the damage be 'substantial' runs into the question of the standard of behaviour that both the crime and the tort require. Again, the courts have not been very helpful. They insist that the question is one of degree, to be decided case by case, but decline to give any general guidelines.[17] Some nineteenth century cases[18] say that the defendant may not say that the public benefit of his activities outweighed or offset the harm done, a position which suggests that there must be an absolute standard of the degree of annoyance that people should not be forced to endure. But there is no evidence of any such standard in the cases. All one can do is multiply examples without much sign of principle. As Michael Jones has pointed out,[19] one case will say that a hosepipe laid across a country lane over which the plaintiff tripped was not a public nuisance[20] but another will say that a rubber pipeline on the pavement was a nuisance.[1]

In many cases, liability for public nuisance turns out to be very similar to straightforward negligence liability. *Shorrock* shows that where the immediate cause of the nuisance was the act of a third party, a defendant may be liable if the harm was foreseeable and the defendant could reasonably have prevented it. Similarly, where the nuisance consists of obstruction of the highway or causing danger to the highway, the test is usually whether the defendant acted reasonably.[2] One somewhat con–voluted exception, however, is where the obstruction or danger to the highway arises because lumps fall off a building belonging to the defendant into the street. In such a case, the liability is allegedly 'strict'—in the sense at least that foreseeability is not required—but the purity of the rule is marred by the addition of the rider that the defendant will have a defence if he can show that the harm came about because of the acts of a trespasser or the 'secret operations of nature' and that the defendant was not negligent in not preventing the trespasser or the secret operation of nature from causing the harm.[3] The net effect of this rule is to create liability without foreseeability for harm caused by third parties who are not trespassers and for discoverable defects in the building or its external fittings, and to reverse the burden of proof in almost all other cases. The result is that the defendant is in a much better position in a case in which a tree falls out of the defendant's garden into the street than in a case in which part of the defendant's building falls into the street. Why this should be so is extremely obscure.

---

17 See eg *Gillingham Borough Council v Medway Docks* [1993] QB 343.
18 *R v Train* (1862) 2 B & S 640; *R v Ward* (1836) 4 Ad &El 384.
19 *Textbook on Torts* (4th edn) (London; Blackstone, 1993) at p 242.
20 *Trevett v Lee* [1955] 1 All ER 406.
1 *Farrell v John Mowlem* [1954] 1 Lloyd's Rep 437.
2 Cf *Caminer v Northern Investment Trust* [1951] AC 88; *Dymond v Pearce* [1972] 1 QB 496.
3 *Wringe v Cohen* [1940] 1 KB 229.

If it is difficult to work out the purposes of statutes that establish crimes, it is even more difficult to work out any sort of purpose for public nuisance apart from as a reserve power for prosecutors who cannot think of a more specific crime with which to charge the defendant. Almost every case in which a plaintiff attempts to recover civil damages on a public nuisance theory would work more smoothly, justly and comprehensibly as a neglig-ence action. One set of exceptions are cases of delay on the highway and businesses adversely affected by crowds attracted by the defendant, in which economic loss is recoverable in public nuisance but not in negligence, although the problem lies more in negligence law and the artificiality of the distinction it makes between economic loss and property damage than in public nuisance. Another set of cases are those in which the plaintiff might have sued in private nuisance but was frustrated by, for example, the rule that only those with an interest in the land affected by the nuisance may sue for it.[4] But again the problem lies in the restrictive nature of the rules of private nuisance rather than in public nuisance. If public nuisance were no longer to be a recognised tort, few would mourn its passing.

4   See below ch 11

Chapter 8

Breach of statutory duty— (2) specific statutory duties

We now pass from the breaches of statutory duty in which the private right of action has to be inferred from the statute to those in which the right to sue in tort is granted explicitly by the legislation. Here there is, of course, no difficulty in establishing that there is in principle a right of action. The difficulties rather come in the form of obscurities in the language of the statute. Since each statute is different, there can be no general principles about the form and scope of the liability that they establish. But it should be noted that there is one important theme to pick out in the cases, namely the question of whether, and if so how, to use the common law that existed before the statute to interpret the statute itself.

There are many statutes and pieces of subordinate legislation that establish a right to sue in tort. To list and explain them all would be tedious in the extreme. Students are referred to the box below for a list of some of the less obscure examples. The analysis in this chapter will be devoted to four important areas of liability—that of the occupiers of land for accidents occurring on their property, that of the keepers of animals for damage done by the animals, that of the producers of goods for damage done by the products and, although we will look at common law aspects as well, that of the liability of employers for accidents to their employees.

Employers' liability was the first to receive the benefit of statutory intervention in the shape of the nineteenth century Factories Acts but, until very recently under the pressure of European integration, has not been comprehensively reformed. And even when the new European directives have all been brought into force, employers' liability will retain its basic structure of a mass of very detailed regulation overlaying a still important common law negligence liability. The other three areas have been reformed more comprehensively by statute. The Occupiers' Liability Acts 1957 and 1984 abolish the common law in the area and then bring back versions of common law standards in a renovated form. The Animals Act 1971 does not displace the whole of the common law, but does explicitly replace part of it with a reformed version of the common law. Finally, the Consumer Protection Act 1987 does not displace the common law at all, but creates for a very wide range of cases a new form of liability in addition to the common law, a form of liability that is more favourable to plaintiffs and which, therefore, the legislature expects plaintiffs will choose in preference to the common law.

SOME OTHER STATUTES ESTABLISHING CIVIL LIABILITY

Nuclear Installations Act 1965—Nuclear power station operators are under a duty 'to secure that' no one suffers personal injury or property damage as a result of their use of radioactive material. The duty is breached by the very fact of the occurrence of harm to the plaintiff. The only defences are (1) that the plaintiff contributed to the damage by an act intended to harm the person or property of another or by an act showing reckless disregard for its consequences, (2) that the harm came about through hostile action in the course of armed combat and (3) that the radioactive material causing the harm was stolen or lost more than 20 years previously. The occurrence of an unforeseeable natural disaster is not a defence. On the other hand, there is a maximum amount payable in damages for any one breach of £20m for large installations and £5m for small ones [See s 16 and the Nuclear Installations (Prescribed Sites) Regulations 1983 (SI 83/919)].

Mineral Workings (Offshore Installations) Act 1971 s 11—Operators of offshore oil and gas rigs are under a variety of duties, some requiring proof of fault, others not requiring proof of fault about the management of their installations. Section 11 of the 1971 Act provides for civil remedies for those who suffer personal injury as a result of the breach of these duties. The statutory remedy is in addition to any common law remedies and the statutory defences to the criminal offences established by the Act are not applicable in any civil claim, either under the Act itself or at common law.

Merchant Shipping (Oil Pollution Act) 1971—This Act imposes liability on oil tanker owners for personal injury and property caused by the spillage of oil, and liability for the expenses reasonably incurred in trying to clean up the mess afterwards. (See S Ball and S Bell *Environmental Law* (2nd edn) (1994; London, Pitman) at p 146.) Defences include intentional acts of third parties, war or insurrection, irresistible natural disasters and government neglect in maintaining navigational aids.

Environmental Protection Act 1990 s 73—This Act imposes civil liability whenever the defendant has caused the plaintiff personal injury or property damage by committing the criminal offences of depositing controlled waste otherwise than in accordance with a waste management licence or illegally depositing non-controlled waste. These offences, apart from the connected offence of knowingly causing or permitting such offences are, allegedly, strict liability offences. It is a defence to show that the damage was caused entirely by the fault of the plaintiff or that the plaintiff had voluntarily accepted the risk. (See *Ball and Bell* pp 335 and 352.)

Civil Aviation Act 1982 s 76(2) and (3)—If the plaintiff suffers personal injury or property damage as a result of acts of persons in an aircraft in flight or as a result of objects falling from an aircraft in flight, the owner of the aircraft is liable whether or not the plaintiff can prove negligence or intention. But it is a complete defence for the defendant to show any degree of contributory negligence by the plaintiff. Presumably, although the section does not say so explicitly, if the defendant proves contributory negligence, the liability rule reverts to being common law negligence.

Data Protection Act 1984 ss 22 and 23—'An individual who is the subject of personal data held by a data user and who suffers damage by reason of the inaccuracy of the data shall be entitled to compensation from the data user for that damage and for any distress which the individual has suffered by reason of the inaccuracy' (s 22) and anyone who suffers damage because of the loss, destruction or disclosure of personal data or from allowing unauthorised access to such data also has an action (s 23). Defendants may escape liability if they show that they took all reasonable care.

Others include: Telecommunications Act 1984 s 18, Electricity Act 1989 s 39(3) and the Water Act 1989 ss 45(7) and 58(7)

Occupiers' liability

The first common law area of liability for accidents to be reformed comprehensively by statute was the liability of the occupiers of land and buildings, the area of law that governs, for example, whether and to what extent householders are responsible for the injuries of visitors who fall down their stairs, of trespassers who impale themselves on spikes on top of the gate and of electricians who electrocute themselves repairing the wiring.

The problem with this apparently mundane and straightforward area was that nineteenth century common law judges, eager to ensure that the law did not require positive duties to act except where there was a contract, had distinguished between different kinds of visitor. Occupiers were held to a higher standard of care to people who had entered their premises in pursuance of a contract than to people who entered without a contract but in pursuance of matters of mutual interest (including making a contract) for example a customer entering a shop. And in turn, occupiers were held to a higher standard of care to people who entered in pursuance of matters of mutual interest than to people whom the occupier had given permission, including implied permission, to enter but who were here to pursue their own purposes—that is there was no chance of a contract. At the bottom of the heap were trespassers. The first group were called contractors, and to them the occupier owed an implied contractual duty to ensure that the premises were fit for the purpose of the contract. The second group, confusingly, were called invitees, and the duty owed to them was a tort duty to use reasonable care to protect them from unusual dangers which he knew or ought to have known about. The third group, called licensees, were owed only a duty to warn them of concealed dangers or traps that the occupier actually knew about. To the fourth group, trespassers, no duty was owed at all.

Sorting out the boundaries between these categories was not easy, especially that between invitees and licensees. And, as often happens, requirements of actual knowledge were subverted by deeming or presuming knowledge. Furthermore the judges distinguished between accidents caused by the state of premises, to which the graded duties applied, and accidents caused by activities carried out on the premises to which ordinary negligence applied. But this distinction between 'occupancy' and 'activity' duties only added to the confusion.

The complications became intolerable even for lawyers and the result was, first, a report from the Law Reform Committee[1] and then the Occupiers' Liability Act 1957. The 1957 Act did not deal with trespassers, however, and it was 27 years before the gap was filled by the Occupiers' Liability Act 1984.

The 1957 Act

The 1957 Act ('a little gem of a statute' according to Lord Hailsham[2]) abolished the distinction between invitees and licensees and established that each was owed a 'common duty of care' which amounted to the same as the duty to take reasonable care in negligence. The statute also abolished the difference between the activity duty and the occupancy duty. It achieved this, at least as Lord Keith[3] and the author of this book believe, by enacting in s 1(1) that the statutory rules 'shall have effect, in place of the rules of common law, to regulate the duty which an occupier of premises owes to his visitors *in respect of dangers due to the state of the premises or to things done or omitted to be done on them*' (emphasis added). Lord Goff,[4] however, believes that s 2(2) of the Act, which defines the common duty of care as 'a duty to take such care as in all the circumstances ... is reasonable to see that the visitor is reasonably safe in using *the premises for the purposes for which he is invited or permitted by the occupier to be there*' (emphasis added) implies that the Act only governs situations previously covered by the occupancy duty. But even if Lord Goff is right, his view has little practical consequence since he concedes that the standards of behaviour required by both occupancy and activity duties are the same.

1　Third Report Cmd 9305 (1954).
2　Official Report HL 443 5th col 720.
3　*Ferguson v Welsh* [1987] 1 WLR 1553.
4　Ibid.

Occupiers

The 1957 Act does not define 'occupier'. In *Wheat v Lacon*[5] the defendant brewing company were owners of a pub in Great Yarmouth. Mr Wheat was a paying guest of the manager of the pub, an employee of the defendant, who lived in a flat above the pub. One summer's evening, at around 9 pm Mr Wheat fell down the back staircase in the flat and was killed. The trial judge found that the causes of the accident were that the handrail was too short and that someone had taken the bulb out of the light at the top of the stairs. The defendants allowed the manager to occupy the flat on a licence rather than a lease and had a right to enter the flat to do repairs. The agreement between the defendant and the manager also explicitly envis–aged that the manager would take paying guests in the flat.

The House of Lords, agreeing with the trial judge, concluded that the landlord was indeed an 'occupier' of the staircase, but they went on to find that there had been no breach of duty. Unfortunately, in coming to this conclusion, the House of Lords managed thoroughly to confuse the question of occupation with that of breach.

Before *Wheat* the test for whether the defendant was an 'occupier' appeared to be whether the defendant had the power to permit or prohibit entry to the premises. Lord Denning in *Wheat* thought that this test, which has its origins in the nineteenth century view that there could be no liability for pure omissions, was too narrow. Lord Denning said that although someone with such a power would undoubtedly count as an occupier, it was possible for other people to count as occupiers as well. Indeed, Lord Denning's test was that, 'If a person has any degree of control over the state of the premises it is enough'. Lord Pearson and Lord Morris agreed that the central question was whether the defendant had 'control', although Lord Pearson seems to be more comfortable with the argument that the defendants should count as occupiers because they authorised the manager to invite in people such as the plaintiff. They also agreed with Lord Denning that since more than one person could have control over a property, it was perfectly possible for there to be more than one occupier of the property.

'Any degree of control' is, however, a very broad test. Even trespassers have some degree of control over the premises on which they trespass, since they are in a position to physically affect the state of the premises even if they have no legal right to do so. Lord Denning probably meant that anyone with any degree of legitimate control over the premises was an occupier, which would exclude trespassers, but even such a modified test would still admit as occupiers a very large number of people, including many state officials.

Partly in response to the breadth of the definition of 'occupier' that the control test implies, Lord Morris and Lord Denning both emphasised the need to consider the 'degree' of control the particular defendant had in judging whether there had been a breach of duty. In *Wheat* itself the defendant could only be expected, according to the court, to exercise its control intermittently, by means of periodic inspections and to carry out repairs when notified of the need for them by the manager. Therefore, the

5   [1966] AC 552.

defendant did not have sufficient control that it should be expected to have done something about the light-bulb and the handrail.

The trouble, however, with talking about 'degrees' of control is that it tends to confuse the question of occupation with the straightforward question of fault. If the courts want to use 'control' as the test for occupation, they should be prepared to do so without embarrassment, and to go on immediately to consider the question of fault without further reference to control or occupation.

Indeed, it may be possible to go further and for the law to operate without needing to define who is an occupier at all. One could say that the defendant's degree of control over the premises is just one aspect of how difficult it would be for the defendant to prevent the accident that occurred. If the defendant had no legal right to enter the premises, for example, the illegality of any precaution-taking activity by the defendant would count simply as one of the interests that would have to have been sacrificed if the defendant was to have prevented the harm. Thus, it is possible, by taking Lord Denning's approach only a little further, to integrate the question of occupation completely into the question of fault.

There are other consequences of the 'control test' both of which can be illustrated by *Harris v Birkenhead Corpn.*[6] A property, although in good condition, found itself in the middle of a slum clearance area. The local authority served the relevant notices on the owner who caused her tenant to leave. Before the local authority could move in to secure the property, a child got in and was injured. The court held that the local authority was the occupier, even though it had not yet taken possession, because it had the right to control the state of the property. On the other hand, the owner, although the last person to have physical control, would not have considered herself in a position to secure the premises after the tenant had moved out. Therefore the owner was not an occupier. That is, first, it is quite possible for someone to lose the status of an occupier, and, secondly, it is possible to become an occupier without taking physical control of the premises

Finally, 'control' can not only be shared, it can also be divided functionally between various occupiers, with one occupier responsible for one aspect of the safety of the property for visitors and the other occupier responsible for another aspect.[7]

Premises

The occupier is liable as an occupier of 'premises'. For the purposes of the Act, according to s 1(3), 'premises' means 'any fixed or moveable structure, including any vehicle, vessel or aircraft'. It is thus far wider than just buildings or land. A person injured in a car by being burned by the cigar lighter has as much recourse to the Act as someone injured by falling down the stairs.

6   [1976] 1 WLR 279.
7   *Collier v Anglian Water* (1983) Times, 26 March.

Visitors

Not only does the Act bring together the previous categories of invitee and licensee into one category of visitor, the old category of contractor is also incorporated by s 5(1). The implied term of fitness is replaced with an implied term of complying with the common duty of care, that is of reasonable care. The contractor's advantage is retained only to the extent that if the contract bestows a greater right, for example a right to absolute safety, the Act allows the contractor to take advantage of that greater right. Section 5(1) says that the common duty of care applies to contractors 'in so far as the duty depends on a term to be implied into the contract', which seems to exclude the possibility of an argument that the clause to be implied in, by necessary implication from the nature of the relationship between the parties for example,[8] should provide greater protection for the contractor than negligence.

Visitors have to be 'lawful' visitors. In theory, this means someone who would have counted as a contractor, invitee or licensee at common law, or someone with legal authorisation, such as a police officer with a warrant.[9] In practice it means that they must not be trespassers. One exception, however, is the position of those using public or private rights of way who are injured and try to sue adjoining owners as owners of the land over which the right of way passes. Such plaintiffs, according to the so-called rule in *Gautret v Egerton*,[10] have no rights. The rule was recently confirmed by the House of Lords in *McGeown v Northern Ireland Housing Executive*.[11] The plaintiff was injured on a footpath on land that belonged to the defendant. The footpath, although starting off as an informal route, had become a public footpath. The plaintiff argued that the rule in *Gautret v Egerton* should be overruled. The House of Lords refused to do so, and confirmed that those using rights of way, whether public or private, were neither visitors nor trespassers. Lord Keith of Kinkel said that the rule was a sound one because:

> 'Rights of way pass over many different types of terrain, and it would place an impossible burden upon landowners if they not only had to submit to the passage over them of anyone who might choose to exercise them but also were under a duty to maintain them in a safe condition. Persons using rights of way do so not with the permission of the owner ... but in the exercise of a right.'

This, of course, is a vintage Lord Keith argument. It assumes that the possibility of legal action automatically means that the defendant will be liable, and that the existence of a duty automatically implies that the defendant was at fault. None of this is correct. Breach of duty is a separate

8   *Liverpool City Council v Irwin* [1977] AC 239.
9   Section 2(6).
10 (1867) LR 2 CP 371.
11 [1994] 3 All ER 53, [1994] 3 WLR 187, 26 HLR 711, 92 LGR 629.

question from the existence of the duty and a fault question is a different
kind of question from a duty question. The expense and difficulty of
maintaining a right of way would have been taken into account in assessing
fault, of course, for the English law of negligence recognises that no one is
expected to bear 'an impossible burden'. Nevertheless only Lord Browne-
Wilkinson expressed doubts about Lord Keith's approach. Lord Browne-
Wilkinson was understandably concerned that the mysterious process
whereby an informal path becomes by repeated unchallenged usage a public
right of way should have the effect of removing the protection users of the
path would previously have had by reason of the law of negligence:

> 'It is a strange result if the duty of care owed to those using the
> path to gain access to the dwellings should have been extinguished
> (at a time which cannot be accurately identified) by reason of the
> acts of third parties ie members of the public using the path
> otherwise than to gain access to the dwellings.'

In addition, there is a general point:

> 'Moreover I am concerned that such decision may lead to an
> undesirable extinction of duties of care which public policy would
> require to exist.'

But Lord Browne-Wilkinson's proposed solution, offered only tentatively
at this point, is, it is submitted, not a happy one:

> 'But it does not necessarily follow that the existence of a public
> right of way is incompatible with the owner of the soil owing a
> duty of care to an invitee, as opposed to a licensee. In the case of
> an invitee there is no logical inconsistency between the plaintiff's
> right to be on the premises in exercise of the right of way and his
> actual presence there in response to the express or implied
> invitation of the occupier. It is the invitation which gives rise to
> the occupier's duty of care to an invitee. I do not understand your
> Lordships to be deciding that it is impossible to be an invitee (and
> therefore a visitor) on land over which there is a public right of
> way.'

In other words, Lord Browne-Wilkinson wants to bring back the distinction
between invitees and licensees. This cure is worse than the disease.

As for ordinary cases, however, an explicit invitation will put the matter
beyond doubt, although visitors who stray beyond their permission may
find themselves counted as trespassers.[12] But visitors may also have implied
permission to enter, such as the implied permission to walk up to the front
door of a house and to knock on the door.[13]

12 See ch 9 below.
13 Ibid.

There are two main problems about who counts as a lawful visitor: first, what is the scope of the implied permission people have to go onto other people's land and second the authority of non-occupiers to give permission to enter.[14]

The first problem, the implied permission to walk up to the front door of a house, for example, is dealt with in the chapter on trespass to land.[15] Here we need only deal with the special consideration that used to arise in cases in which trespassers were injured, namely that there was no liability to them at all until the late intervention of the House of Lords in *British Railways Board v Herrington*[16] and then the 1984 Act. As a result of the harsh rule against trespassers, courts in occupiers' liability cases tended to stretch the notion of implied licence beyond its natural limits, holding for example that there was an implied licence to use a path admittedly much frequented by the general public across the defendant's land, but always in the face of the owners' protests.[17] Children often received favourable treatment, as in the 'allurement' cases in which children tempted onto the defendant's property by attractive objects such as bright berries, a horse and cart and a threshing machine and thereby injured were said by the courts not to be trespassers.[18] Since the 1984 Act now gives rights to trespassers, albeit of a limited nature, there is no further need for these artificial doctrines.

The second problem is, however, still a live issue. The present answer comes from the House of Lords case *Ferguson v Welsh*[19]. In *Ferguson v Welsh* the defendant hired a contractor to demolish a wall. The contract said that the contractor was not to use subcontractors unless approved by the defendant. The contractor, however, ignored the contract and hired the plaintiff, who was then injured. The House of Lords, although finding the defendant not liable on other grounds, held that the plaintiff was not a trespasser. The contractor had 'ostensible' authority to invite the plaintiff onto the site. 'Ostensible' authority means that although the contractor did not really have authority to do what he did, in the ordinary course of dealing he would have had that authority and there was nothing in the situation that would have put the plaintiff on notice that the contractor did not have the usual authority of people in his position. Ostensible authority would not have been not applicable, of course, if the defendant had known about the contractor's lack of authority, or knew of facts which

---

14 Another problem that occasionally arises is where the defendant claims that the plaintiff could not be a visitor because the plaintiff himself had an interest in the land. This argument usually fails, For a recent example about clubs and members of clubs, see *Gesner v Wallingford & District Labour Party Supporters' Association Club Ltd* (1994) Times, 2 June.

15 See below ch 9.

16 [1972] AC 877.

17 *Lowery v Walker* [1911] AC 10, but see the later reaction in *Edwards v Railway Executive* [1952] AC 737 that 'repeated trespass itself confers no licence'.

18 Eg *Glasgow Corpn v Taylor* [1922] 1 AC 44, *Lynch v Nurdin* (1841) 1 QB 29, *Holdman v Hamlyn* [1943] KB 664.

19 [1987] 1 WLR 1553.

a reasonable person would take to mean that one should at least ask a few questions about the situation,

Finally, there is one possible source of embarrassment about the status of lawful visitors that may arise in the future. If *League Against Cruel Sports v Scott*[1] gains acceptance and trespass to land becomes a tort that requires proof of fault, there will be more cases of accidental straying onto someone else's land where there will be no precedent for saying that the person was even a licensee. In such circumstances the law of occupiers' liability should be flexible enough to incorporate developments in the law of trespass

Common duty of care

The common duty of care is a duty to 'see that the visitor will be reasonably safe'. It is, no more and no less, the duty to take reasonable care imposed by the law of negligence and explored in detail above in chapter 3. On the general issue of when there is a breach of the common duty, there is no need to repeat here more than the fundamental principle that there is fault when the defendant failed to take the precautions that a reasonable person would have taken in the light of the magnitude of the risk, the seriousness of the harm and the costs to himself and others of taking the precautions in question.

There are, however, some special features of the law under the Act which deserve special mention.

CHILDREN

Section 2(3)(a) of the Act says, 'An occupier must be prepared for children to be less careful than adults.'

This piece of common sense, it is submitted, is meant to replace the common law complexities of hidden traps and allurements, not to re-enact them, and is designed to be a flexible reminder that reasonable people when judging risks (and the seriousness of risks) take into account the habits and usual reactions of those likely to come into contact with the danger. One might mention, however, *Simkiss v Rhondda Council*[2] in which a small child fell off an unfenced steep slope belonging to the defendant local authority. The defendant pointed out that the plaintiff's own father had left her on the slope and had himself described it as not dangerous. The defendant won. The court took into account the fact that the child's own parent had considered the spot to be safe. The decision has attracted some criticism because it would mean, if applied strictly, that there would

1   [1985] 2 All ER 489.
2   (1982) 81 LGR 460.

never be liability to children, since either their parents put them in the dangerous place or the parents allowed them to wander before they came across the dangerous place. But this point is not valid if one allows children to have some will of their own and that it is unreasonable to expect parents to control their children's every movement. In *Simkiss* itself, however, there was the extra point that the father's action may have been so unreasonable that it broke the chain of causation.

Nevertheless, a better result in *Simkiss* may have been to hold the council liable but to allow the council to recover part of the damages from the father as a contribution.

VISITORS WITH SPECIAL SKILLS

Section 2(3)(b) says, 'An occupier may expect that a person, in the exercise of his calling, will appreciate and guard against any special risks ordinarily incident to it, so far as the occupier leaves him free to do so.'

This section is designed to help occupiers to argue that they have fulfilled their duty when the accident was one which one might have expected a skilled professional to avoid. It does not say that there is no duty in the first place to visitors with special skills.

Thus, if the defendant carelessly sets fire to his own house and the fire brigade arrives, the defendant cannot say to fire fighters injured in the blaze that because they are experts, there is no liability to them. Instead, if the accident was one (an explosion for example) against which no amount of skill could have protected the plaintiff, the occupier can still be liable.[3] But this rule does not absolve the plaintiff from showing that the accident was caused by the defendant's unreasonable behaviour. Thus, it is expecting too much that householders will make sure that if there is a fire, fire fighters will have safe routes in and out of the premises.[4]

An example of the kind of case the section is meant to cover is *Roles v Nathan*.[5] The defendant's central heating boiler was producing smoke, and an engineer advised the defendant to have the flues cleaned. The defendant hired two chimney sweeps to do the job. The engineer warned the sweeps of the dangers of carbon monoxide poisoning, because the boiler used coke, but the sweeps disregarded the warning and crawled about in the flues. Another expert told them of the dangers, but they ignored him too, saying that they were experts themselves. After an unknown person had relit the boiler, the sweeps carried on in the same way, failing to close vent holes that the second expert had told them to close. Eventually they were overcome by fumes and died. The case against the occupier was that he failed to prevent the relighting of the boiler. His defence was that although, as it turned out, the sweeps were extremely incompetent, he was entitled to assume that they would be competent and as competent people to have

3   *Ogwo v Taylor* [1988] AC 431, *Salmon v Seafarer Restaurants* [1983] 1 WLR 1264.
4   *Bermingham v Sher Bros* 1980 SC 67.
5   [1963] 1 WLR 1117, confirming the pre-Act case *General Cleaning Contractors v Christmas* [1953] AC 180.

avoided this kind of accident. The Court of Appeal agreed with the defendant. Lord Denning said:

> 'When a householder calls in a specialist to deal with a defective installation on his premises, he can reasonably expect the specialist to appreciate and guard against the dangers arising from the defect. The householder is not bound to watch over him to see that he comes to no harm.'

The rule applies, however, to the specialist risks themselves, not to any risks a worker might encounter. Lord Denning continued, 'If it had been a different danger, as for instance if the stairs leading to the cellar gave way, the occupier might no doubt be responsible.'

WARNINGS

Section 2(4)(a) of the Act, which is about 'determining whether the occupier ... has discharged the common duty of care', says:

> 'Where danger is caused to a visitor by a danger of which he had been warned by the occupier, the warning is not to be treated without more as absolving the occupier from liability, unless in all the circumstances it was enough to enable the visitor to be reasonably safe.'

The reason that s 2(4)(a) is phrased negatively, when one might have expected such a helpful rule for the defendant to be phrased positively is that it is meant to reverse the effect of *London Graving Dock v Horton*[6] a decision criticised by the Law Reform Committee's Report.[7] The House of Lords said in *Horton* not only that a well-placed warning could help to discharge the defendant's duty of care, but that a warning sufficient to convey full knowledge of the danger to the plaintiff would automatically absolve the defendant.

The test under the Act is whether the warning had the effect of enabling the visitor to be reasonably safe. If the circumstances are such that the warning will not improve the visitor's practical position, the defendant is still liable, no matter how clearly the plaintiff understood the dangers. In *Roles v Nathan* Lord Denning gave the example of a warning notice on the only bridge for miles across a river that the bridge was unsafe. This warning does not help to make the user of the bridge any safer. On the other hand, if there is another way across the river and the warning indicates how to find it, the warning may discharge the duty.[8]

---

6   [1951] AC 737.
7   Third Report Cmd 9305 (1954) para 77.
8   Note, however, that the defendant may not be liable in either case because of the rule in *Gautret v Egerton*.

Note that there is an important distinction between a warning and a notice that attempts to exclude liability. A warning is an attempt to fulfill one's obligations by supplementing the physical safety of one's premises with helpful information for the visitor. A exclusion notice is where the occupier is not trying to be helpful or informative but is just trying to escape from all liability by claiming that the plaintiff agreed not to sue for the risks specified in the notice. Sometimes, notices have both effects, as when an exclusion notice draws attention to a danger of which the visitor would not otherwise have known. But usually notices and warnings are very different.

Exclusion of liability

The 1957 Act explicitly preserves the defence of consent (or volenti),[9] saying explicitly that the defence is to be the same as it is elsewhere in the law. Contributory negligence also applies in the normal way. The one defence that is special to occupiers' liability, although in theory it applies elsewhere as well, is exclusion of liability by notice. Section 2(1) explicitly preserves this defence when it says that the occupier is as free to 'extend, restrict, modify or exclude his duty' as he would be otherwise.

The defence of exclusion of liability by notice arises where the defendant has expressed in a notice that people enter the premises on condition that they accept that they will not be able to sue in the circumstances specified in the notice.[10] It is said to derive from occupiers' power completely to exclude anyone from their land. The argument goes that if occupiers can exclude people completely, they should be able to admit them on terms of their own choosing.[11] The defence is 'analogous' to volenti and consent[12] but also distinct from it, since it is not necessary to show that as a result of the exclusion notice the plaintiff fully understood the risks involved.[13] Furthermore, it is possible to exclude liability by notice even though the plaintiff did not read all the notice.[14] Exclusion by notice is also separate from any contractual limitations on liability, since it applies in cases where the plaintiff has entered the premises for nothing.[15]

Since the defence is based on the power to exclude, it presumably does not apply when the occupier has no legal power to exclude the plaintiff, for example where the plaintiff has a warrant.[16] There is also an argument that the defendant cannot exclude the minimum duty owed to trespassers[17]

9   Section 2(5).
10 *Ashdown v Samuel Williams* [1957] 1 QB 409, *White v Blackmore* [1972] 2 QB 651.
11 *Ashdown v Samuel Williams* above n 10.
12 *White v Blackmore* above n 10.
13 *White v Blackmore* above n 10.
14 *Ashdown v Samuel Williams* above n 10.
15 *White v Blackmore* above n 10.
16 P North *Occupiers' Liability* pp 130-31.
17 See below.

because the 1984 Act does not allow contracting out and it would be odd if the minimum could not be excluded against trespassers but could be excluded against lawful visitors. Arguments that there can be no exclusion unless there is some minimal consciousness of the notice and its content, so that there can be no exclusion defence against the illiterate or those who cannot read English,[18] are more doubtful. In *Ashdown*, the test applied by Parker LJ, for example, was whether the defendants had 'taken all reasonable steps to bring the conditions to [the plaintiff's] notice', not whether the plaintiff had actually understood the notice. Exclusion is a unilateral defence.

The main barrier to the use of the exclusion defence is the Unfair Contract Terms Act 1977 and its successors. The Act, misnamed because it applies to non-contractual notices as well as contracts, curtails the ability of businesses to exclude their liability by notice. Section 1(3)(b) of the Act defines liability arising from the occupation of premises used for the business purposes of the occupier as a 'business liability' which, according to s 2(1) 'a person cannot by reference to any ... notice ... exclude or restrict ... for death or personal injury resulting from negligence'. Section 2(3) adds, for completeness, that such a notice does not of itself indicate either that there has been any voluntary acceptance of the risk. In the case of non-business liability (and business liability for property damage), liability for negligence cannot be excluded by notice unless the notice satisfies the requirements of reasonableness. In *Smith v Eric Bush*,[19] in the admittedly somewhat different circumstances of property valuations, Lord Griffiths said that reasonableness included the relative bargaining position of the parties, the difficulty of the task for which liability was being excluded, the relative abilities of the parties to bear any losses or to carry insurance.

'Business purposes' include professional and governmental activities,[20] but other cases are unclear, including that of charities. The 1984 Act added a curious codicil to s 1(3) that says:

> 'But liability of an occupier of premises for breach of an obligation
> or duty towards a person obtaining access to the premises for
> recreational or educational purposes, being liability for loss or
> damage suffered by reason of the dangerous state of the premises,
> is not a business liability of the occupier unless granting that person
> such access for the purposes concerned falls within the business
> purposes of the occupier.'

The point of this provision is to protect farmers who freely open their land to, for example, horse riding, but who want at the same time to exclude or restrict their liability to the riders by notice. One puzzle about it is that by referring to 'damage suffered by reason of the dangerous state of the premises' it is bringing back the confusing distinction between the

18 See *Jones* p 195.
19 [1990] 1 AC 831.
20 Section 14.

occupancy duty and the activity duty. Which aspects of a farm, for example, would be about the 'state of the premises' and which not? What about, for example, a mechanical scarecrow or a piece of farm machinery left in the corner of a field?

Independent contractors

Section 2(4)(b) of the Act says:

> 'Where damage is caused to a visitor by a danger due to the faulty execution of any work of construction, maintenance or repair by an independent contractor ... the occupier is not to be treated without more as answerable for the danger if in all the circum-stances he had acted reasonably in entrusting the work to an independent contractor and had taken such steps (if any) as he reasonably ought in order to satisfy himself that the contractor was competent and that the work had been properly done.'

There is normally no vicarious liability for the torts of independent contractors except for the special cases of the 'non-delegable duties'[1] but there can be liability for the direct negligence of the employer.[2] Section 2(4)(b) therefore adds little to the common law position. The first require-ment is somewhat odd, however, since it refers not to the obvious matters referred to in the second and third requirements about the competence of the contractor and checking the quality of the work. The first requirement is about whether it was reasonable to use an independent contractor instead, presumably, of: (a) doing it oneself; or (b) getting an employee rather than an independent contractor to do it. How the court is supposed to judge the reasonableness of such a decision is far from clear. Before the Act, in *Woodward v Mayor of Hastings*,[3] the court held an occupier (a local authority school) liable for the omission of a contractor who was employed to sweep steps, on the ground that there was no special technical knowledge necessary for that task. But technical knowledge is far from the only consideration when deciding whether to employ independent contractors. Local authorities in particular are now under legal duties to put various tasks out to competitive tender, including tasks such as cleaning buildings, construction work and even rubbish collection that do not require much technical skill. Businesses decide whether to contract out on the basis of the relative costs of having in-house or contracted-out (or 'out-sourced') operations, costs that are affected by a wide range of factors, including tax, the regularity of demand for the service, the costs of monitoring performance and so on. Individuals decide whether to contract out construction, maintenance or repair tasks on the basis not just of technical

1   See ch 14.
2   Ibid.
3   [1945] KB 174.

skill but of income levels and taste for do-it-yourself. It seems presumptuous for the law to concern itself with these decisions.

But notice that cost considerations, rather than just the technical competence of the occupier, come into decisions about the competence of the contractor and checking the work too. With enough time and money, the occupier could engage in extensive research about the competence of prospective contractors and any lack of technical knowledge by the occupier could be remedied by hiring an expert. Similarly with checking the work.[4] What is reasonable depends on what the risks are and the prospective costs. Whether the resources available to the occupier should be relevant is unclear.[5]

In *Ferguson v Welsh* the question arose of whether the occupier should have a system of inspection while the work was continuing which included checks for whether the contractors were employing a safe system of work for their employees or sub-contractors. Normally, according to the House of Lords, the answer would be no. Competent contractors could be presumed to have safe systems of work. The situation might be different if the occupier knew or had grounds to suspect that the contractor's system of work was unsafe, but depending on what exactly was unsafe, the questions of control and breach of duty could arise in the normal way.

The 1984 Act

The common law position of trespassers has already been mentioned. Until *British Railways Board v Herrington*[6] trespassers were outside the protection of occupiers' liability, although the severity of the rule was alleviated by devices such as stretching the concept of implied licence, the allurements rule and the distinction between 'occupancy' and 'activity'. In *Herrington* the House of Lords decided that occupiers should offer some minimum protection to trespassers but there was no agreement as to exactly what the extent of the occupier's liability to trespassers should be. There was more agreement that the duty to trespassers should be called the 'duty of humanity' than on what the content of the duty should be.

The common law rules were explicitly abolished by the Occupiers' Liability Act 1984 and replaced by a statutory regime that emphasises what the occupier knew or 'had reasonable grounds to believe'. The Act, according to the Lord Chancellor in the parliamentary debate[7] was meant to transpose into one rationalised set of rules the 'slightly different lines of argument' in *Herrington*.

The 1984 Act covers liability to 'persons other than visitors' and so applies to all cases to which the 1957 Act does not apply. That means that the

---

4   Cf *AMF v Magnet Bowling* [1968] 1 WLR 1028.
5   Cf *Goldman v Hargrave* [1967] 1 AC 645.
6   [1972] AC 877.
7   Lord Hailsham Official Report HL debs 5th ser vol 443 col 720.

1984 Act applies not only to the case of trespassers but also to users of public or private rights of way under the recently reaffirmed rule in *Gautret v Egerton*.[8] In the case of the highway, however, s 1(8) of the Act says that no duties arise to people using the highway as a result of the Act.

The content of the duty owed to non-visitors is 'to take such care as is reasonable in all the circumstances to see that [the non-visitor] does not suffer injury on the premises by reason of the danger' if the occupier was aware of the danger or had reasonable grounds to believe that it existed and knew or had reasonable grounds to believe the non-visitor was in or about to come into the vicinity of that danger and the risk is one 'against which in all the circumstances of the case he may reasonably be expected to offer the other some protection'. Only personal injury damage is recoverable, not property damage.

Section 1(5) establishes a warning defence, but one that it is easier to fulfill than the corresponding defence in the 1957 Act, namely that the defendant may discharge the duty by showing that he took 'such steps as are reasonable in all the circumstances of the case to give warning of the danger concerned or to discourage persons from incurring the risk'. Unlike the 1957 Act warning defence, in which the crucial question is the effectiveness of the warning for the plaintiff, this warning defence is unilateral—it turns on the defendant's efforts to warn or discourage, not on whether those efforts were effective.

On the other hand, the Act does not mention the unilateral defence that the 1957 Act does allow, namely exclusion by notice. It may be that the intention of the Act is to roll up the warning and exclusion defences by requiring the exclusion notice at least indicate what the danger is. Another view is that with a pro-defendant warning defence as compensation, the exclusion defence has been left out completely because of doubts about its fairness when applied to the most basic of standards.

Section 1(6) however, does preserve the full volenti defence in the same terms as the 1957 Act, indicating, perhaps that the concern lying behind missing out the exclusion defence was not so much that people should not be allowed to contract out of the most basic protections—otherwise volenti would have been missed out too, but instead that the notice defence goes too far because it allows the defendant to win even though the defendant need make no attempt to help the plaintiff to be safer and can work even if the defendant did not consciously agree with the terms of the notice. On this view the 1984 Act allows a defence of full consent and a defence of reasonable attempt at helping the plaintiff.

There are a number of problems with the interpretation of the Act, most of which remain untested in the courts. First, what does 'has reasonable grounds to believe' mean? This was one of the points on which *Herrington* was unclear as well, so no assistance is to be found in that quarter. The best view would seem to be that the phrase cannot mean the same as 'ought reasonably to have known' since that would mean that there would be no difference between the tests in the two Acts, and if it was intended to

8   See above ch 7.

have the same test why would the 1984 Act adopt so different a formula? Instead, it should be read literally as meaning that the occupier is put in the same position as when he knows of the danger if he knows of facts from which a reasonable person would conclude that there was a danger.[9]

Another problem is whether the fact the duty arises when it is reasonable to offer only 'some protection' means that reasonable care under s 1(4) can be less than ordinary reasonable care. In particular, does it mean that the court may take into account the resources available to the defendant. Lord Reid with the support of a majority on this point in *Herrington* supported such an approach. But it was not specifically re-enacted.

Non-occupiers' liability

Although for someone injured on someone else's property the best course is usually to pursue the occupier under the 1957 Act, sometimes, because the occupier is not worth suing, or because the occupier was not at fault, or because there is no occupier other than the plaintiff, other courses of action may be considered.

Vendors and landlords

The first possibility is to sue the vendor or the landlord of the property. If the plaintiff is the purchaser of the property, there may be an action in contract, although in sales of land the principle that the buyer takes the risk of any defects ('caveat emptor') is still stronger than it is in sales of goods. Similarly if the plaintiff is a tenant, there may be an action against the landlord under the lease if the lease includes or implies a duty on the landlord to repair whatever caused the damage. Frequently, however, the landlord will have a power to repair but not a duty.

If these contractual actions are not available the plaintiff may turn to tort. The common law position in tort was not much better than that in contract for the plaintiff. The common law position was that both vendors and landlords had immunity from tort for anything they did before letting or selling the property. The purchaser or tenant was thought to have taken on the risks and to have extinguished claims against the vendor or landlord both by himself and by future purchasers or tenants.[10]

In *Dutton v Bognor Regis UDC*[11] and then *Anns v Merton London Borough Council*[12] the courts apparently swept away these restrictions at

---

9 Cf *Harris v Birkenhead Corpn* [1976] 1 All ER 341.
10 *Cavalier v Pope* [1906] AC 428 (landlords), *Bottomley v Bannister* [1932] 1 KB 458 (vendors).
11 [1972] 1 QB 373.
12 [1978] AC 728. See also *Rimmer v Liverpool City Council* [1984] 1 All ER 930.

least for positive acts by the vendor or landlord before sale or lease (though perhaps leaving the rule as it was for omissions). But given the uncertain status of these cases following their overruling on the question of economic loss, it is safer for plaintiffs instead to rely on the provisions of the Defective Premises Act 1972.

Section 3(1) of the 1972 Act says that:

> 'Where work of construction, repair, maintenance or demolition or any other work is done on or in relation to premises any duty of care owed, because of the doing of the work, to persons who might reasonably be expected to be affected by defects in the state of the premises ... shall not be abated by the subsequent disposal of the premises by the person who owed the duty.'

This does not, however, affect the omissions rule. One probably still cannot sue intermediate purchasers for failing to put defects right. One can only sue for work that was done badly. And, of course, that in turn means that vendors are put in the same position, no better or worse, as that of builders, a position considered below.

For landlords, however, the 1972 Act is more far-reaching. Section 4(1) of the Act says that when a tenancy agreement imposes a duty on the landlord to maintain or repair the premises, the landlord owes a duty 'to take such care as is reasonable in all the circumstances' to everyone, not just the tenant,[13] who might reasonably be expected to be affected by defects in the premises. The duty is to 'see that they are reasonably safe from personal injury or from damage to their property from the relevant defect'. A 'relevant' defect, according to s 4(2) and (3) is one which the landlord knew or ought to have known about and for the repair of which the landlord was responsible. Omissions are therefore covered as well as acts. Most important of all, except for cases of injury to the tenant in which the defect arose because the tenant is in breach of the tenancy agreement, s 4(4) extends the coverage of the landlord's obligation from those cases in which the landlord has a duty to repair to those in which the landlord only has a power to enter and carry out repairs. Note the great scope of this provision. The landlord and tenant legislation implies into ordinary weekly tenancies of dwellings a power to enter to carry out structural repairs. In leases of less than seven years the legislation imposes duties on landlords to maintain the structure, exterior and major services of a dwelling, including gas, water, electricity and central heating. Moreover, it is possible that *Liverpool City Council v Irwin* implied terms[14] give the landlord other powers and duties to maintain and repair.

---

13 Note also that the section applies not just to formal tenancies but to rights of occupation given by contract or by statute: s 4(6).
14 See above.

Builders and architects

Those who actually do the physical or design work that results in defects that harm the plaintiff may also be liable. The liability is in negligence, although note that if the damage comes about through a product that the defendant has made, there may also be liability under the Consumer Protection Act 1987, even though the product has been 'comprised in land by virtue of being attached to it'.[15]

Cases such as *Dutton* and *Anns* cleared the way for negligence liability in such cases. As mentioned above, however, both *Dutton* and *Anns* were overruled by *Murphy v Brentwood District Council*[16] in so far as they purported to allow claims for pure economic loss, including economic loss in the form of physically dangerous defects that have not yet caused any harm and need to be repaired. But the law about defects that cause personal injury or damage to other property belonging to the plaintiff was left substantially unchanged.[17] It may be that if a defect becomes known before it causes harm, the plaintiff will be guilty of contributory negligence for not repairing it, although there may be circumstances in which to have expected the plaintiff to have repaired the defect by the time the accident occurred would be unreasonable. This, at least, is the result of *Targett v Torfaen Borough Council*[18] with regard to rented property (where there is the additional reason for plaintiff inaction that the tenant has asked the landlord to make repairs and the landlord had not done so before the accident). There is no reason why the same rule should not apply to builders and architects as well. There is, admittedly, an argument that such liability is based on *Donoghue v Stevenson* and for liability in that case it was necessary that the defect was a latent one not likely to be discovered before the product reached the ultimate consumer. But this is to misunderstand the requirement of latency in *Donoghue*. It was not an arbitrary rule to control liability but an expression of the operation of the ordinary rules of fault and remoteness, under which (1) products that usually undergo intermediate inspection are treated as inherently less risky than those which do not undergo inspection and (2) failure of intermediate inspection could constitute a *novus actus interveniens*. Neither of these points affects the position of the plaintiff in cases such as *Targett*, since there is usually no prospect of intermediate inspection of defects in houses and failures by the plaintiff only very rarely count as breaking the chain of causation, although they can count, and did count in *Targett*, as contributory negligence.

15 Consumer Protection Act 1987 s 45.
16 [1991] 1 AC 398.
17 Note, however, that *Murphy* did reject the 'complex structure' theory—the idea that the plaintiff could recover damage to the building itself if the case could be recast as damage done by one part of a complex structure to another, distinct part of the same structure.
18 [1992] 3 All ER 27.

Local authorities

Whether local authorities are still liable for personal injury or property damage resulting from their failure properly to inspect foundations or to examine plans was a point the House of Lords in *Murphy* explicity left open. It is possible that in such cases, there would be a relevant novus actus interveniens in the failure of the builder or vendor to take corrective action. But in principle such an intervention, foreseeable or not, does not sound wrongful enough or positive enough to constitute a novus actus.

Economic loss

For plaintiffs seeking compensation for the effect of a defect on the value of their house, the kind of plaintiff favoured by *Anns* and then sent away empty-handed by *Murphy,* there is still the possibility of using s 1 of the Defective Premises Act.[19] Section 1 provides that a person taking on work 'in relation to the provision of a dwelling' (which includes conversions and enlargements as well as new building) owes a duty both to the person who ordered the work and to everyone who subsequently acquires an interest in the dwelling, 'to see that the work ... is done in a workmanlike or ... professional manner, with proper materials and so that as regards that work the dwelling will be fit for habitation when completed'.

This liability, which apparently catches omissions as well as positive mistakes,[20] and which may extend to builders, architects, surveyors and engineers, imposes both an obligation of means akin to negligence (to carry out the work in a workmanlike or professional manner) and an obligation of result akin to a warranty (the dwelling has to be fit for habitation when completed). The question arises: what is the relationship between the two obligations? The possibilities are: that the plaintiff has to show a breach of both obligations in order to recover; that the plaintiff can show a breach of either obligation to recover; or that it is a breach of the first obligation if and only if the result of that breach will eventually be a breach of the second.

In *Alexander v Mercouris*[1] the Court of Appeal said that fulfilling the second obligation was the intended result of fulfilling the first obligation, but that the plaintiff did not have to show that the result, unfitness for habitation, had actually occurred, only that it would occur when the building was completed. This point seems to rule out the second interpretation. In *Thompson v Clive Alexander & Partners*[2] Judge Lewis went further and ruled that *Alexander v Mercouris* ruled out the first interpretation as well. It has to be said, however, that the first interpretation is the most natural reading of the clause because it says 'to see that the work is ...

---

19 *Andrews v Schooling* [1991] 3 All ER 723, [1991] 1 WLR 783, 23 HLR 316, 53 BLR 68, 26 Con LR 31.
20 Ibid.
1   [1979] 3 All ER 305, [1979] 1 WLR 1270, 252 Estates Gazette 911.
2   (1992) 28 Con LR 49, 59 BLR 77.

done in a ... professional manner and so that ... the dwelling will be fit for habitation' (emphasis added). If the second or third interpretations were intended, surely the word 'and' would have been omitted and the clause would have read simply 'so that the ... dwelling is fit'. Nevertheless, the third interpretation is at present the accepted one. For there to be liability the plaintiff has to show that the unworkmanlike quality of the work either has resulted or will result in the premises becoming unfit for habitation.

The main disadvantage with s 1, however, is the very short limitation period (six years from the time of the completion of the building). There used to be another disadvantage, that s 2 allows an opt-out into private insurance schemes such as the National House Building Council insurance scheme, but, apparently, this opt-out has not been in effect since since the late 1980s.[3]

Liability for animals

Domestic animals and pets, that is animals that belong to people, are in many ways simply a type of property to which the ordinary rules of law apply. For example, just as one can trespass on someone else's land by putting objects on it without permission, so one can trespass by allowing one's animals to enter someone else's land.[4] And whatever the special liabilities created by statute, especially by the Animals Act 1971, ordinary negligence is always in the background. If there is a foreseeable risk that the defendant's dogs would cause injury and there were reasonable precautions the defendant could have taken, there will be negligence in the ordinary way. Similarly, there will normally be negligence liability if the defendant carelessly allows the animal to escape and it causes an accident.[5]

Liability for damage caused by animals

The Animals Act 1971 attempted to reform, tidy up and codify the law on liability for damage. It is not an easy statute to interpret, and it is unfortunate that for many law students it is the first Act of Parliament they come across in its entirety. It was, however, enacted after a Law Commission report.[6]

At common law, animals were either wild (ferae naturae) or domestic (mansuetae naturae). Animals were classified purely according to their species. Elephants, for example, were defined as 'wild' no matter how docile they were in reality,[7] and camels were defined as 'domestic' no matter how vicious.[8]

3   Wallace (1991) 107 LQR 228.
4   *League Against Cruel Sports v Scott* [1985] 2 All ER 489.
5   Eg *Draper v Hodder* [1972] 2 QB 556, *Pitcher v Martin* [1937] 3 All ER 918.
6   Civil Liability for Animals (Law Commission Report no 3).
7   *Behrens v Bertram Mills Circus* [1957] 2 QB 1.
8   *McQuaker v Goddard* [1940] 1 KB 687.

There was strict liability for damage caused by wild animals. In the case of domestic animals, there was negligence liability only unless the plaintiff could show that the defendant kept the animal knowing that it was dangerous and that it had departed from the usual habits of its species.

The main reforms introduced by the Animals Act 1971 were in the classification of animals. Animals belonging to a species 'not commonly domesticated in the British Isles' and which, when fully grown, have such characteristics that they are likely, unless restrained, to cause severe damage, or any damage they do cause is likely to be severe, belong to a 'dangerous species'. The person in charge of such an animal, the 'keeper' is strictly liable for any damage the animal does.

The phrase 'commonly domesticated' is (like much else in the Act) ambiguous. It can mean 'animals that are both common in the British Isles and domesticated', and 'animals that are not common in the British Isles, but when they are here are usually domesticated'. Take the example of camels, now reclassified as 'dangerous'.[9] Whereas previously the crucial fact about camels was that they were mainly domesticated animals in the countries in which they are common, they are not common in Britain and when they are here they are mainly in zoos, which cannot count as domestication given the other sorts of animals that are kept in them. Presumably, however, elephants will stay in the 'dangerous' category for the same reason, plus the fact that although elephants are not likely to do severe damages if not restrained, if they do cause damage it is likely to be severe, especially if 'damage' includes, as it should, damage to property.

Note that creatures such as llamas are probably not 'dangerous' since although perhaps 'not commonly domesticated in the British Isles' they are not likely to do severe damage if unrestrained or to cause severe damage if they cause damage at all.

If the animal does not belong to a dangerous species, the keeper may nevertheless be strictly liable if the following, admittedly near incomprehensible section of the Act is satisfied:[10]

'(a) the damage is of a kind which the animal, unless restrained, was likely to cause or which, if caused by the animal, was likely to be severe; and

(b) the likelihood of the damage or of its being severe was due to characteristics of the animal which are not normally found in animals of the same species or are not normally so found except at particular times or in particular circumstances; and

(c) those characteristics were known to that keeper or were at any time known to a person who at that time had charge of the animal as that keeper's servant or, where that keeper is the head of a household, were known to another keeper of the animal who is a member of that household and under the age of sixteen.'

9   *Tutin v Chipperfield* (1980) 130 NLJ 807.
10 Section 2(2). Cf Lord Denning in *Cummings v Granger* [1977] QB 397 ('cumbrously worded') and Nourse LJ in *Curtis v Betts* [1990] 1 WLR 459 ('inept').

What this appears to mean, if one takes it sub-clause by sub-clause,[11] is this. Section 2(2)(a) is satisfied either if the particular animal caused the type of damage it was likely to cause—for example a goat eats a fence—or if the particular animal was likely, if it did any harm at all, to do severe harm—for example a very large though friendly dog with big teeth.[12] 'Likely', according to the Court of Appeal, means only 'might well happen' or 'a material risk', and 'type', in true *Wagon Mound* fashion, refers to the general nature of harm—personal injury, for example—rather than to its extent or the exact way it came about.[13]

Section 2(2)(b) is even more difficult to work through. It fails to make any obvious sense. How exactly can the likelihood that the animal would cause the particular kind of damage that it did cause be 'due to' a 'characteristic' of an animal. A 'characteristic' is itself no more than a likelihood that the animal will do something. The subsection seems to be fatally circular.

All the subsection can mean is that one must be able to infer the likelihood that the animal will cause the particular type of harm (or harm of the requisite severity) from some other fact about the animal which is not a fact that is true of animals of that species generally. This is how the courts, at least, have interpreted the subsection. Thus, one could not infer the likelihood that the goat will eat a fence from anything special about that goat. All goats eat fences. Therefore the subsection is not satisfied. Inference, however, is not the same as foreseeability. The subsection does not require that anyone could have made such an inference at the time.[14]

The idea, however, that some writers have of the need for a 'causal' link between the 'characteristic' and the 'likelihood' is absurd. 'Characteristics' are not physical objects, but are simply likelihoods themselves. In *Curtis*, Stuart-Smith and Nourse LJJ try to make the notion of causation work by saying that one should ignore all the words except 'the damage' at the start of section 2(2)(b), but this does not make any particular difference. 'Characteristics' do not cause damage, animals do.

The second leg of s 2(2)(b) is also obscure, but it seems to mean that 'characteristics' that animals of that species only have 'at particular times or in particular places' do not count as characteristics of the species, and so can be called in aid by the plaintiff. Thus in *Cummings v Granger* an Alsatian dog that became vicious after being allowed to roam free as a guard dog was said to satisfy s 2(2)(b) because since many Alsatians take on these characteristics when treated in this way, the characteristic is 'normal' in 'particular circumstances', and that satisfies the requirements of s 2(2)(b). *Cummings* rejected the other way of reading the subsection, namely that one should ignore characteristics the animal has at particular times and in particular circumstances when considering whether the animal had abnormal characteristics.

11 This is the judicially recommended method—see *Curtis v Betts* above n 10.
12 *Curtis* above n 10. *Cummings*, above n 10.
13 *Smith v Ainger* (1990) Times, 5 June (plaintiff knocked over by fighting dogs and broke leg—held to be likely type of damage).
14 *Curtis* above n 10.

Ormrod LJ in *Cummings* says, furthermore, that 'guard dog' is not a species of dog, so that the defendant could not argue that the dog's characteristics were normal for guard dogs. 'Species' is a biological concept, although it is possible to break species down into small categories such as 'breeds' of dog.[15] Thus in *Cummings* the court considered the characteristics of Alsatians rather than of dogs in general.

Since abnormal characteristics for the purposes of the Act include behaviours that are quite normal in the circumstances, it is not just obviously odd animals that fall within s 2(2)(b), such as the dog that attacked people carrying bags,[16] but also fairly normal animals, such as dogs that defend their territory,[17]

Section 2(2)(c) is fairly self-explanatory. The keeper (or the keeper's employees or children) have to know about the relevant characteristics, thus restoring the common law position.

Note that if the plaintiff's case falls at any point in s 2, the keeper can still be liable in negligence.

Keepers

Section 6(3) of the Act defines the keeper of the animal as the owner or possessor of the animal or the 'head of a household' in which someone under 16 has possession of the animal. To make sure that there should be no gaps in keepership, once someone is an animal's keeper that person continues to be the animal's keeper unless and until someone else becomes keeper. Section 6(4) provides that if one has taken custody of an animal only to prevent it from causing harm, or to restore it to its owner, one does not become the animal's keeper.

Defences

The defence of contributory negligence is available,[18] and if the injury is wholly due to the fault of the victim, there is no liability.[19] Consent is also a defence, although it cannot be raised against an employee who is merely doing his job.[20] In addition there is a defence specific to s 2 in s 5(3) if the plaintiff was trespassing when injured by the animal and either the animal was not a guard dog or equivalent, or, if it was a guard dog (or equivalent) keeping it there 'was not unreasonable'. This defence was made out in

15 See also *Hunt v Wallis* (1991) Times, 10 May.
16 *Kite v Napp* (1982) Times, 1 June.
17 *Curtis* above n 10.
18 Section 10.
19 Section 5(1). See *Nelmes v Chief Constable of Avon & Somerset Constabulary* Court of Appeal 9 February 1993 LEXIS transcript.
20 Section 6(5).

Cummings v Granger, where the Court of Appeal said that it was reasonable to keep a ferocious guard dog to guard a scrap yard. It is unlikely that it would now be found to be reasonable, however, to allow a guard dog to roam about without a handler, since to do so is probably a criminal offence under the Guard Dogs Act 1975.[1]

Liability for straying livestock

The ancient action of cattle trespass imposed strict liability for damage done to crops by straying livestock—even if the animals got onto the plaintiff's land because the plaintiff's own fences were broken—and established for most of England a rule that livestock farmers were expected to fence their animals in, thus confirming the dominance of the arable farmer. In parts of the USA, the fencing-in rule was one of the first parts of the common law heritage to be jettisoned, as dominant cattle farmers demanded a fencing-out rule instead,[2] and wars raged between arable farmers and cattle ranchers both in the state legislatures and on the range.[3] Nothing so dramatic has happened in England recently and the abolition of cattle trespass by the Animals Act and its replacement by a statutory strict liability action was not a matter of much note.

Section 4 of the Act says that the owner of livestock has to pay for any damage the livestock does to the land or property (but not person) of anyone onto whose land the livestock 'strays' (the word is undefined) and for the expenses reasonably incurred by such landowners in keeping the livestock while tracing the owner or while exercising their right under s 7 to detain the livestock and to sell it if the animals are not claimed within 14 days. 'Livestock' is defined by s 11 of the Act as 'cattle, horses, asses, mules, hinnies, sheep, pigs, goats and poultry, and also deer not in the wild state', a list which, the observant will notice, does not include dogs or cats.

The various defences apply, including the defence that the damage was entirely the victim's fault, but the crucial provision is, however, s 5(6), which preserves the common law position on fencing-in. Damage is not to be treated as due to the fault of the victim 'by reason only that he could have prevented it by fencing'. The defendant is only excused if someone with an interest in the land is in breach of a positive duty to fence, a duty which may arise, for example, by agreement or custom. The usual custom, however, is that there is no duty to fence cattle out.

The common law was, however, less favourable to townies than to arable farmers, and there was liability in negligence only for livestock that wandered off the highway on which they were travelling in the normal way, usually to market. Thus, in *Tillett v Ward*[4] an ox wandered into the

---

1 On criminal liability for certain types of dog, see further Dangerous Dogs Act 1991.
2 See F Harper and F James *The Law Of Torts* (1956) §14.9 and §14.10, *Delaney v Erickson* 10 Neb 492, 6 NW 600 (1880).
3 Webb *The Great Plains* (1931).
4 (1882) 10 QBD 17.

plaintiff's shop from the highway and caused much damage. There was no liability. Section 5(5) of the 1971 Act re-enacts this rule. But note that in *Matthews v Wicks*,[5] a defendant was denied the benefit of the section 5(5) defence when the livestock had wandered on to the highway in the first place and were said not to be on the highway lawfully.

One of the reasons why it was possible to say that animals wandering onto the highway were not there lawfully in *Matthews v Wicks* was that s 8(1) of the Act abolishes the common law rule that there was no duty to prevent livestock wandering onto the highway even if they caused foresee-able havoc when they got there.[6] In consequence there is now a negligence regime imposed on the owners of animals[7] that wander onto the highway,[8] subject only to s 8(2) which allows owners of animals to exercise their rights to put animals onto unfenced common land, village greens or other customary areas without fear of liability.

Dogs that worry livestock

Section 3 of the Act imposes strict liability on the keepers of dogs for any damage the dog does in injuring or killing livestock.[9] The liability is subject to contributory negligence, the defence that the damage was entirely the fault of the victim and a defence that the livestock had strayed onto land owned by the dog's keeper or land on which the dog was authorised to be.

Furthermore s 9 allows a person to kill or injure a dog to protect livestock that he was entitled to protect, as long as he reports the incident to the police within 48 hours and as long as the dog was worrying the livestock or was about to start worrying the livestock and there were no other reasonable ways of preventing the worrying, or the dog had been worrying livestock, had not left the vicinity, was not under anyone's control and there were no practicable means of finding out to whom it belonged.

Products liability

The third area of liability that Parliament has reformed extensively by statute is products liability. But this time the intention of the statute was to go further than to reform the common law and to re-introduce it in statutory form. The intention was to create a different form of liability that plaintiffs would be able to use in addition to their common law rights.

The Consumer Protection Act 1987, Part 1 of which contains all the relevant provisions, was enacted to fulfill the United Kingdom's obligations

5   (1987) Times, 25 May.
6   *Searle v Wallbank* [1947] AC 341.
7   This means all animals, not just livestock.
8   *Pike v Wallis* (1981) Times, 6 November.
9   The definition of livestock is expanded for these purposes to include game birds while in captivity.

under EC Directive 85/374 of 25 July 1985 on the approximation of the laws of member states concerning liability for defective products[10] (the product liability directive). The Act provides explicitly that it shall be construed so that it complies with the Directive.[11] This provision may become very important since, as we shall see, the Act diverges in significant detail from the Directive.

What is products liability?

Before considering the 1987 Act in detail we should first step back and consider what products liability is and what sorts of liability regime might have been chosen to regulate it.

Product liability cases are those in which one of the causes of the plaintiff's injuries is the condition, operation or design of some object. Examples include:

* The plaintiff buys a kettle from a shop. The shop bought the kettle from a wholesaler who bought it from the manufacturer. The kettle explodes on first use, injuring the plaintiff, burning down her house and causing her to miss an important business meeting which would have resulted in a very profitable contract for her business.
* The plaintiff goes to a café with a friend. The friend goes to the counter and buys two bottles of ginger beer one of which she gives to the plaintiff. The plaintiff pours the ginger beer out of its opaque bottle into her glass and out comes a decomposed snail. The plaintiff claims to have become ill as a result.
* A pharmaceutical company, having received the approval of the regulatory authorities, markets a new drug. Twenty years later the children of women who took the drug develop cancer.
* The plaintiff buys a motorised lawn mower from a garden centre. A friend asks to borrow the mower. The plaintiff agrees and decides to drive the mower three miles along the road to the friend's house. After about a mile, the mower's wheels and rotary blades, which are not adapted to travel on roads, break up. The plaintiff and a pedestrian are injured. They sue the manufacturer of the mower, who points out that the wheels and rotary blades were made by component manufacturers. The wheels were a standard off-the-shelf item. The blades were made specially to order for the manufacturer.
* The plaintiff decides to try oysters for the first time. He buys a dozen from a local fishmonger. Unfortunately, he is allergic to oysters and becomes very ill.

Note the wide variety of possible issues at stake in these examples. The plaintiff may be a person who has contractual rights against an immediate seller, or may be the recipient of a gift from such a person, or may be a bystander. The defendant may be an immediate supplier, an intermediate

---

10 OJ no L 210/29 7/8/85.
11 Section 1(1)].

supplier such as a wholesaler, or may be a manufacturer or the maker of a component part. The complaint about the object may be that it did not behave in the way that such objects usually behave, or that all such objects behaved in the same harmful way because of the way they were designed, or because of the lack of a warning to avoid particular ways of using the object or because of the inherent characteristics of that type of object. The harm may have been foreseeable by the defendant at the time the defendant made the object, or the harm may have been impossible to foresee. The factual causal link between the object and the harm may be obvious or it may be obscure. There may be remoteness issues around the type of harm and the behaviour of intermediaries and the plaintiff. The damage may be personal injury (including nervous shock), property damage or economic loss.

Conventionally, however, product liability concerns the products or objects themselves rather than the processes involved in making them. Thus, if a plant making chemicals pollutes the atmosphere, thereby injuring thousands of people, the legal liability of the factory is not usually counted as within product liability.

To some extent these classifications are arbitrary. It is not wholly clear why, for example the liability of manufacturers of products to those injured by the products themselves should be separated from the liability of manufacturers to those injured by the process of making those products, but not separated from the liability of wholesalers, importers and retailers. In fact, the reasons for this classification are purely historical. In the nineteenth century, the liability in tort of the manufacturer of products was treated as an aspect of the contractual relations, or lack of them, between the manufacturer, intermediate suppliers, customers and other users. The idea that tort liability was ruled out by the lack of a direct contract between the victim and the defendant, the 'privity fallacy', dominated the law until *Donoghue v Stevenson*.[12] Thus, the various liabilities, both contractual and tortious, of the various parties in the contractual chain that brings the product into contact with the victim, from component maker through manufacturer to retailer, tended to be treated as one topic.

The conventional classification does have one merit, however, which is that it draws attention to the importance in this field of the parties' contractual rights, which arise largely out of the law of sales. Students need to know something of the law of sales before embarking on a detailed study of the available actions in tort.

SOME POINTS FROM THE LAW OF SALES

The law of the sale of goods, and of other types of supply of goods (such as hiring or leasing), is in many ways simply the application of contract principles to one particular type of transaction. Once the parties reach agreement, the seller is under a duty to deliver the goods in accordance

12 [1932] AC 562.

with the contract and the buyer is under a duty to accept them. There are also some characteristic quirks of that result from the application of those principles. For example, since parties to a contract must take reasonable steps to mitigate their loss in the case of a breach, sales law usually assumes that there is a ready market for the goods concerned, so that a disappointed buyer can buy from someone else and a disappointed seller can find someone else to whom to sell. As a consequence, damages for failure to deliver or for refusal to accept are usually no higher than the sum of the costs of finding and dealing with a new seller or buyer and any adverse change in the market price, if any. Indeed, if the market price moves in a direction favourable to the victim of the breach (ie it goes down for a buyer victim or goes up for a seller victim), there may be no overall loss at all.

The aspect of sales law that is relevant to products liability is, however, not simply a matter of the general principles of contract law. It is the set of obligations that the law imposes on sellers by means of implied terms. These implied terms may be excluded by contrary explicit terms, as long as the exclusion does not violate the Unfair Contract Terms Act, but if not excluded they operate by dint of the Sale of Goods Act 1979 (as amended by the Sale and Supply of Goods Act 1994). These statutory implied terms include a duty that the goods are of 'satisfactory quality', which includes consideration of whether the goods are safe.

Sale of Goods Act obligations are usually obligations of result not just obligations of effort. That is, the goods will not qualify as 'satis–factory'[13] if they turn out to be unsafe even if the seller did not know and could not reasonably have known at the time of the sale that they were unsafe.

This means that sellers usually have quite onerous obligations towards buyers about safety. But the strict English application of the contract doctrine of privity by which third party beneficiaries to contracts have no legal claim means that in England, unlike in many US juris–dictions where the 'warranty' has broken free of its contractual limit–ations, only the immediate buyer benefits from the strictness of the seller's Sale of Goods Act duties. Subsequent purchasers in a contractual chain, donees of gifts from the buyer and bystanders all have no contractual, Sale of Goods Act claims against the seller, although subsequent purchasers may have such a claim against the intermediate buyer.

Possible liability regimes

The theoretical literature on products liability is almost endless.[14] There are differing economic, psychological, moral, and even philosophical schools

---

13 Sale and Supply of Goods Act 1994 s 1. Before 1995, the test was whether the goods were of 'merchantable quality'.
14 See generally J Stapleton *Product Liability* (London; Butterworths, 1994). Other relevant recent works include: J Coleman *Risks And Wrongs* (Cambridge; CUP 1992); Schwartz

of thought. But the starting point for all such discussion has to be to list the various options for liability rules that are on offer.

A large number of possible rules exist. Each can be constructed by combining the outcomes of a number of more basic choices. The choices include: (a) whether to allow liability at all; (b) whether to require fault in the full negligence sense, and if not, which parts of the fault equation to relax; (c) whether to allow defences such as contributory negligence; (d) whether to impose the ordinary rules of remoteness; (e) whether to require factual causation; and finally, (f) on whom to impose the burden of proof. Note also that different liability rules can be used for different types of defendant (for example, manufacturers as opposed to retailers) and different types of complaint against the product (for example, design errors as opposed to manufacturing errors). Here is a selection of the possible rules:

1   no liability outside contract—even negligence should be excluded;
2   ordinary negligence liability (fault, causation, remoteness, liability restricted for economic loss and nervous shock, contributory negligence and other defences available, burden of proof on plaintiff throughout);
2A   negligence with the burden of proof reversed;
3   negligence without foreseeability (ie fault using a different tense of the verb—not 'what would a reasonable person have done?' but eg 'what would a reasonable person do now if faced with the same choice?');
3A   negligence without foreseeability with the burden of proof reversed;
4   negligence without the availability to the defendant of the cost of precaution argument (ie if there is any foreseeable risk no matter how small, the plaintiff must take sufficient precautions, regardless of cost, to prevent the accident, even to the extent of not making the product)[15];
4A   negligence without the cost of precaution argument with the burden of proof reversed;
5   liability without foreseeability *and* without the cost of precaution argument, but retaining causation, remoteness and contributory negligence as in ordinary negligence;
5A   liability without foreseeability and without the cost of precaution argument, retaining causation, remoteness and contributory negligence, but with the burden of proof reversed;
6   liability without foreseeability and without the cost of precaution argument and also without contributory negligence but with a causation requirement and the ordinary remoteness rules;
6A   the same with the burden of proof reversed;
7   liability without foreseeability or the cost of precaution argument and without contributory negligence and remoteness;

'The Case Against Strict Liability' (1992) 60 Fordham LR 819, P Huber *Liability: The Legal Revolution And Its Consequences* (New York; Basic Books, 1988); Priest 'A Theory of the Consumer Product Warranty' (1987) 90 Yale LJ 1297, Weinrib 'Understanding Tort Law' (1989) 23 Val U LR 485.

15 Cf *John Summers v Frost* above.

8   liability for wrongdoing defendants without the need to prove causation (ie if the defendant acted in a reprehensible way it must act as an insurer for the plaintiff regardless of whether the defendant could have prevented the harm);

9   liability without the need to prove causation or fault (ie the defendant acts as insurer for the plaintiff, and it is irrelevant how the defendant behaved including whether the defendant could have prevented the harm from occurring);

10   the same but only the state can be sued (ie no liability rule against individuals but victims have an entitlement to compensation from the state).

   With so many possible rules (and there are more than just these 15) it is not surprising that theorists have tended to abstract and to generalise. But such generalisations have to be handled with very great care. For example the term 'strict liability' is used by some commentators to mean any of rules 3 to 9 inclusive, whereas others will use it only for rules 5 to 9. In addition some commentators prefer the term 'absolute liability' for rules 6 to 9, whereas others will use 'absolute liability' only for rules 8 and 9.

   One consequence of this confusion of terms is that great care has to be taken when interpreting statutes, cases and especially academic and political commentaries. Another consequence is that very little weight should be put on the views of commentators who think that the only choices are 'fault' and 'strict liability'.

Arguments about the best rule

Donoghue v Stevenson moved English law from rule 1 to rule 2. The 1987 Act, as we shall see, moves the law onto a position that looks as if it brings in rule 5 but, as we shall see, in reality the Act establishes an odd mixture of rules 2 to 4A inclusive. The most radical reformers argue for rule 10 or at least a state-organised version of rule 9. The latest free market approaches in the USA seem to argue for a return to rule 1. The present position in most US jurisdictions is widely believed to be something like rule 6 or even rule 7 but in fact is closer to rule 3.

   What are the arguments that motivate legislatures, commentators and, at least in the US and, perhaps also in a future European Court of Justice, judges to choose one of these rules as opposed to the others? The arguments may be divided, for convenience, into three: economic, moral and political arguments.

Economic arguments

The economic study of product liability has spawned an impressive literature.[16] Unfortunately, most of the studies have concentrated on

16   See eg R Cooter and T Ulen *Law and Economics* (Glenview Ill; Scott, Foresman, 1988) pp 421-61; Calabresi 'First Party, Third Party and Product Liability Systems' (1984) 69 Iowa LR 833; Calabresi and Hirschoff 'Towards a Test for Strict Liability' (1972) 81 Yale LJ

expanding the range of the theoretical analysis rather than on the more difficult (and expensive) task of finding out what happens in reality when new rules come in.[17] The result is that for the most part economic arguments reveal only the direction in which change will happen, not how big those changes will be, and since in most cases the analysis reveals that opposing changes will occur, the final judgment about the net result of all the changes taken together remains uncertain. In addition many economic analyses study a very limited range of possible liability rules and have been criticised for misunderstanding the rules that the courts have to deal with.[18]

But is worth stating briefly the results that most economist commentators agree on:

(1) The main difference between rules, usually thought of as 'fault' rules, that include the possibility of arguing that the costs of precautions were not justified by the magnitude of the risk and those rules that do not is that in fault rules it is the court that decides whether the costs of the defendants' activities outweighed their benefits, whereas in non-fault rules the defendant is forced to carry out a similar cost-benefit analysis itself. This is because where the defendant may not argue that the benefits of the activity outweighed the costs but instead has to pay for any costs that its activity forces onto other people (which is what harm is) the defendant is put in the position of having to take into account all the costs of the activity, not just those costs that fall on the defendant itself. The defendant is forced to 'internalise' the costs that the activity imposes on others. Of course, the producer is not the only one to lose as a result of such an internalisation of costs. Some of the costs may be passed on to consumers in the form of price rises, so that to some extent other consumers will be losers too.

(2) Negligence rules in which the court carries out the cost-benefit analysis encourage producers to take optimal precautions only as long as the court gets right the judgment about what the optimal level of precautions is. It is doubtful whether courts are very well equipped to do this. In addition, many economists claim that cost-benefit analysis is always founded on ethical judgments, such as whether to count as a cost feelings of envy or disgust created by the activity in question,[19] so that some degree of controversy is inevitable.

(3) On the other hand, even if there was a form of liability that encouraged defendants to internalise all the costs and benefits of their product, it would still not produce optimal precautions unless the compensation payable was exactly enough, no more or less, to make the plaintiff indifferent between the injury and the compensation. This is also very unlikely to happen, and indeed is exceptionally difficult to judge. In addition, some products bring benefits to people

---

1054; Priest 'A Theory of the Consumer Product Warranty' above n 14; W Landes And R Posner *The Economic Structure Of Tort Law* (Cambridge Mass; Harvard UP, 1987).

17 But see *Cooter and Ulen* at 447ff.

18 Calabresi's work is the most notable exception to this.

19 See E Mishan *Cost-Benefit Analysis* (4th ed) (London; Allen and Unwin, 1988) pp 122-23.

who do not pay for them ('positive externalities')—for example vaccinations prevent the spread of disease so that even those who are not vaccinated benefit—so that a cost-benefit exercise carried out by the defendant which internalised the costs of the accidents caused by the product would not be entirely accurate because the defendant has no reason to include such external benefits.

(4) Foreseeability often does not matter much. The difference between what a reasonable person would have done at the time and what a reasonable person would do now is the extra knowledge, including the fact of the accident itself, that has come to light in the meantime. Often no new information has come to light and, since the possibility of the harm was known before the accident, the fact of its occurring has not changed views of how likely such accidents are to occur. But sometimes there is a difference. New scientific research may reveal previously unknown dangers, and the sheer volume of claims may by itself cause one to revise previously held views on how often the type of harm concerned arises. The difference is greatest in cases in which new scientific research and large numbers of claims come together, as in the asbestosis and Thalidomide cases for example.

(5) The effect on research and development of adopting a rule that does not allow the cost of precautions argument and does not require foreseeability is unclear. On the one hand, firms may be discouraged from putting new products on the market since they will be liable for future costs that are by definition unknowable especially because they will not be able to argue that the cost of finding out about the risk was prohibitive. On the other hand, if a firm does decide to put a new product into circulation it will have very great incentives to do research into its effects and into ways of making it safer. Perhaps the best way to sum up this result is to say that to adopt such a rule encourages research but discourages development.

(6) Any rule that does not provide for some kind of contributory negligence defence (which includes points based on a novus actus interveniens by the plaintiff) will mean that in cases in which the plaintiff's safety depends in part on his or her own actions, there will be less of an incentive for the plaintiff to take appropriate precautions. The size of this reduction in incentives is, however, uncertain and if anything likely to be small, since most people do not regard money compensation as being really as good as not being injured and tend to judge the level of precautions they take without taking into account the possibility that someone else may be liable to pay them compensation if they are injured.

(7) The effect of insurance depends on how closely premiums match the riskiness of particular individuals. If they match perfectly, insurance becomes a sort of saving scheme whereby people save up over time to pay for their liabilities when they crop up. This means that insurance neither increases nor decreases the cost to the insured of carrying on the activities they want to insure against except in so far as the profits of the insurance company and the transactions costs make it slightly

more expensive to insure than to save in the normal way. On the
other hand, fear of a catastrophic loss may make the cost of not
insuring appear much higher than the cost of insuring to those
considering whether or not to buy insurance (otherwise why do people
insure?). This means that insurance does reduce the incentives to
take care overall. In practice, however, the situation is much more
complicated, for it would cost insurance companies too much to find
out, process and use all the relevant information about their customers. Insured people therefore rarely pay a premium that exactly
matches their riskiness. Instead, insurance companies charge the
same premium to individuals falling roughly within the same class
of risk. The effect is that their less risky customers end up subsidising
their more risky customers. The less risky pay more than they would
if they paid only for their own accidents and the more risky pay less.
But note that, because of new technology, the cost of data collection
and evaluation is falling and opportunities are arising to detach the
low risk customers from their high risk counterparts, leading to higher
and higher premiums for the risky.

(8)   Access to information matters. The argument for making the defendant do the cost-benefit analysis rather than having the court do it,
that is the argument for adopting rule 5 or even rule 7, is that usually
the defendant, especially the manufacturer, has more information
about the product than anyone else, especially information coming
back to it about what happens to users of the product in practice, and
can obtain new information about the product more cheaply than
anyone else. In particular it can obtain such information more cheaply
than can a judge in a hearing in the High Court. In consequence, the
cost-benefit analysis is more likely to be accurate if the defendant
does it than if anyone else does it. But in some cases, for example the
case of the allergy to oysters, it may be cheaper for individuals to
find out for themselves whether they are allergic. Furthermore, the
position of mere suppliers will often not be as good as the position of
producers.

(9)   There is such a thing as market pressure for safety in products, so
that a no-liability-outside-contract rule, such as rule 1, would not
automatically mean that all products would become less safe. Consumers will learn about and will avoid unsafe products if that is their
wish, and producers of excessively unsafe goods will develop bad
reputations that will cost them sales and may drive them out of
business. But market pressure for safety is much less for products
that are not purchased repeatedly (eg electric blankets), and for
products that are not identifiable as produced by a particular firm
(eg milk). Moreover, individual abilities can be exaggerated when it
comes to holding a mass of information about risks and reputations
and processing it successfully while, for example, wheeling a trolley
around a modern supermarket accompanied by small children with
a tendency to escape. In any case, such reputation effects do not help
bystander victims. This is an argument for rules under which the

producer has to build the costs of the harm the product will cause into its own costings, so that businesses that produce unsafe products become less profitable than those that produce safer products without consumers having to know about which producer and which product is which.

The orthodox view for many years was that the economic arguments, on the whole, point in the direction of rules 5 to 7, that is to liability rules without foreseeability and without the availability of the cost of precaution argument.

But, as we have seen, there are problems with these rules.

First, there is the problem of the loss to society of firms refusing to market new products for fear of liability. Rule 7 in particular is vulnerable to the objection that although it means that more will be known about the new products that do come onto the market, fewer new products will be marketed in the first place.[20]

One alleged example of such a problem was the refusal in 1976 of US pharmaceutical firms to release new vaccines against a virulent form of influenza known as swine flu because the firms' insurers refused to insure them against liability. The firms released the vaccine only when the US federal government agreed to accept sole responsibility for any harm that resulted from the vaccine's side effects. In the event the vaccine did cause serious side effects, and the products liability actions that victims brought against the US federal government soon caused the end of the inoculation programme.[1] Similar problems in the 1980s affected US production of vaccines against measles, mumps, polio, rabies and whooping cough and led eventually to the passing of the National Childhood Vaccine Injury Act of 1986, which set up a no-fault non-tort compensation scheme.[2]

Secondly, there is the objection that rules that force the defendant to internalise the full costs and benefits of the product only result in optimal precautions if damages are perfectly compensatory, which is not possible. One might add that in practice not all potential plaintiffs will have the necessary information, determination or income to be able to sue.

Thirdly, there is the problem of the utility of the product to people who are not purchasers of it. For example, immunisation against a contagious disease such as measles helps not only the person immunised but also everyone else in the same geographical area, because it helps to reduce the chances of the disease being passed on. It may be that liability rules that oblige producers to internalise the dangers of the product but do not make them any less indifferent about its benefits to indirect beneficiaries will lead to the underproduction of the good in question. Fault-based rules,

20 See eg Huber 'Safety and the Second Best: The hazards of public risk management in the courts' (1985) Colum LR 277.

1   Franklin and Mais 'Tort Law and Mass Immunization Programs: Lessons from the Polio and Flu Episodes' (1977) 65 Calif LR 754, *Cooter and Ulen* pp 453-54.

2   *Cooter and Ulen* at 453-54, *Stapleton* at 226. In England the Vaccine Damage Act 1979 had already set up a no-fault compensation scheme under which children and in some circumstances adults who suffer 80% disability as a result of vaccinations are entitled to up to £30,000 compensation from the state.

in contrast, although more expensive to administer, do allow for indirect benefits to be taken into account.

Nevertheless, the economic case for any of the other rules remains less than overwhelming. Negligence would produce optimal results if judges had perfect information and made perfect assessments of costs and benefits and could do so instantly at no cost. But they do not have perfect inform- ation, cannot make perfect assessments and are prevented by the parties from deciding instantly at no cost.

A return to the privity doctrine—no liability outside contract—has attracted some recent support in the USA.[3] The central economic idea is that the buyers and the manufacturers of a product will over time through the process of competition come to share out the responsibility for the various risks of losses caused by the product on the basis of comparative advantage. The manufacturers will assume responsibility for those risks of losses that manufacturers are best placed to prevent or repair, and consumers will assume responsibility for the risks of losses that they are best placed to prevent or repair. If a particular manufacturer tries to shift a risk it is best placed to deal with onto the consumer, consumers will react by not wanting to buy from that manufacturer. Equally, if a manu- facturer accepts responsibility for a risk that the consumer is best placed to deal with, the resulting costs that fall on the manufacturer will force its profits down below those of the other manufacturers. Thus, for example, manufacturers may guarantee that the product is free from defects caused by faulty workmanship, something the manufacturer is in the best position to know, but the consumer takes responsibility for dangers arising from the way the product is used, which is under the consumer's control, and for consequential damages such as loss of earnings, since the plaintiffs are in a much better position to know what they earn than manufacturers and can thus more easily and accurately insure against such losses.[4]

But it is not clear how the return to privity argument works in cases in which the plaintiff is not a buyer of the product but a recipient of a gift or, more significantly, a bystander.[5] If there is no exchange between the plaintiff and the defendant, there can be no straightforward application of the theory of comparative advantage. Bystander victims, including those injured by drugs taken by their parents, cannot influence the allocation of risk and are not engaged in a bargaining process.

In addition, even if one considers only buyers of the product, there are problems with the return of privity approach. First, the producer may be a monopolist or oligopolist, in which case the process of competition leading to an efficient sorting out of responsibilities may never happen. Secondly, buyers may not reach optimal bargains with suppliers and producers because of lack of information, especially the difficulty of understanding

3   Eg P Huber *Liability: The Legal Revolution And Its Consequences* (1988; New York, Basic Books), Schwartz 'Proposals for Product Liability Reform' (1988) 97 Yale LJ 353 and 'The Case Against Strict Liability' (1992) 60 Fordham LR 819, Priest 'A Theory of the Consumer Product Warranty' (1987) 90 Yale LJ 1297.
4   *Cooter and Ulen* at pp 425-430.
5   See *Stapleton* at pp 127-129.

legal technicalities, and because of the apparently inherent tendency for people to underestimate the probabilities of infrequent events[6]

Moral arguments

The moral arguments about product liability flow from two different starting points. One is the idea that to say that someone is under a duty to do something implies a belief that it is possible for the person to fulfill that duty—in other words that ought implies can. The other is the idea that those who take the benefit of an activity should bear the burdens it creates, that receiving creates an obligation to give.

One can derive from the first idea an opposition to liability rules that do not include notions of intention or foreseeability. If the harm caused by a product was impossible to predict, the principle of ought implies can points to no liability. If the defendant could not possibly have foreseen the harm, it makes no sense to say that he ought to have prevented it. It also points to opposition to liability without causation, since under such a rule it is also possible for defendants to be held liable in circumstances in which the defendant could not have prevented the damage—unless, as in the case of insurance contracts, there is some other basis for liability. The same principle also means that one should be suspicious of liability rules that do not allow defendants to claim that precautions were too costly, for although such rules do not strictly violate the principle—it is often physically possible for defendants to have prevented the harm—prohibitive costs of precaution create practical conditions that are close to impossibility.

The second starting point, the benefit and burden principle, leads to very different results.[7] Like the related moral principle that 'the polluter should pay'[8] the benefit and burden principle can justify liability rules that omit both foreseeability and the cost of precautions argument. According to the benefit and burden principle, if a firm profits from selling a product it should accept responsibility for all the harm the product causes regardless of whether the harm was foreseeable or only preventable at great cost. On the other hand, even the benefit and burden principle has difficulty with liability without causation. The application of the principle requires a clear view of what counts as a benefit of what.

Admittedly, in product liability, factual causation is not usually absent, since the connection between the product and the harm and the connection between the product and the defendant are usually clear. But there are cases in which the connections are not clear, for example where an identical product has been manufactured by many different firms.[9] In such cases

---

6   See *Cooter and Ulen* pp 416-17, 425-27, based on D Kahnemann, P Slovic and A Tversky *Judgment Under Uncertainty* (Cambridge; CUP, 1982).
7   See generally *Stapleton* above.
8   See below ch 11.
9   Cf *Sindell v Abbott Laboratories* 26 Cal 3d 588, 607 P 2d 924 (1980).

the benefit and burden principle may be applied by imposing liability on entire industries, on the theory that all firms benefit from the sales of the product. But broader forms of non-causal liability, for example using rules 8 and 9 for collecting together an insurance fund from all firms, starts to shade into arguments that justify not liability but taxation.

Resolving the conflict between these two moral starting points is not easy. Each starting point belongs to its own world of moral argument. The principle that ought implies can sees morality in terms of individuals doing right or wrong. The benefit and burden principle belongs to a world of social obligation in which right and wrong consist of acknowledging or not acknowledging debts owed to other people which have been created by the help they have given one because of the same principle.

Each view has weaknesses from the point of view of the other. The ought implies can principle assumes that obligations arise only out of one's own actions (or inaction) not out of the actions of others or out of an individual's social position. In return, the benefit and burden principle seems to misunderstand the nature of trade—that in a voluntary trade both parties benefit from the exchange, so that it is odd to assume that one side, the producer, should have responsibilities arising out of the gratitude he should feel for the money received in the form of the price, but that the buyer should not equally not accept burdens out of gratitude for having received the product.

Indeed, from the point of view of the benefit and burden principle, ought implies can seems to be saying that the only reason one should help others is to correct a wrong that one has done to them, and that reasons such as social responsibility and gratitude have no place. But from the point of view of the ought implies can principle, the benefit and burden principle seems to be claiming that there is something inherently wrong or unworthy in making a profit.

Neither of these perceptions is accurate. The ought implies can principle is a principle for helping to decide who should be condemned as a wrongdoer, not who in general should pay for whom. Conversely, the benefit and burden principle does not seek to condemn those who benefit, but merely claims that those who benefit should pay for those who suffer.

The problem with tort law, of course, is that it is simultaneously both about condemnation and about who pays for whom. The proponents of liability rules based on the benefit and burden system claim that if such rules were adopted, being found liable in tort will eventually come not to imply moral blame. Opponents say that on the contrary such rules will increase the blame heaped on defendants[10] at the same time as reducing the credibility of tort law as a moral enterprise. Which of these predictions is the more accurate remains to be investigated.

---

10 Cf Lloyd-Bostock 'Common Sense Morality and Accident Compensation' [1980] Ins LJ 331.

Political arguments

All liability rules affect the distribution of wealth. Pro-plaintiff rules, including changes to the burden of proof, shift wealth from the industries concerned, which means their owners, managers and other employees, in favour of consumers. Pro-defendant rules have the opposite effect. Such decisions are the very stuff of politics. Similarly, proposals such as rule 10, under which all entitlements to compensation are entitlements against the government, substantially raise levels of public spending. This is again a central political issue, especially when linked to the consequential issue of how such schemes are funded.[11]

Democratic politics largely consists of balancing the power and import–ance of particular lobby groups, especially producer lobby groups, against the votes of those who will lose if the lobbies prevail. Beyond that, it consists of making decisions about the extent and distribution of public spending and taxation. Product liability brings into very sharp focus both the battle of the producer lobbies to capture or to keep their advantages and the competition for the votes of consumers.

Proponents of rule 10 and other no fault schemes which create entitle–ments against the state funded by general taxation or by levies on the allegedly relevant industries or activities often play down the political content of their proposals and talk about the need for a 'rational' or 'comprehensive' approach to compensation.[12] But any reform that changes the distribution of income and increases the tax burden is not just a technical matter. It is, however, a matter that goes beyond the proper scope of an introductory text.

The law in detail

We are now able to consider the law in detail. We begin with the EC Directive of 1985 before moving to the Consumer Protection Act 1987. Finally we glance back at the common law remedies, all of which are still available but whose use in practice will now be confined to cases to which the statutory remedies do not apply.

The 1985 Directive

The EC Directive 85/474 on product liability took 13 years from initial conception to final approval.[13] Its original objectives were above all political. It was designed to attract more support for European integration by

11 Note for example the reduction in the coverage of the New Zealand scheme as the result of worries about levels of public expenditure. See above ch 1.
12 Eg *Stapleton* at p 3.
13 See *Stapleton* at pp 47-49.

showing that the Community could act for the benefit of ordinary people as consumers and not just for the interests of producer lobby groups.[14] Most member states of the EC followed rules close to the ordinary negligence regime, although some, for example Germany, had introduced a reversal of the burden of proof, and for special cases, for example those concerning pharmaceutical products, there was movement towards even more sharply pro-plaintiff rules.[15] The Directive was also inspired by developments in product liability law in the USA, where state after state had adopted either Section 402A of the American Law Institute's Second Restatement of Torts or near equivalent rules based on the California decision *Greenman v Yuba Power*.[16]

Section 402A of the Second Restatement says that anyone who, in the course of business, sells a product in a 'defective condition unreasonably dangerous to the user or consumer' and which is 'expected to and does reach the user or consumer without substantial change in the condition in which it is sold', is liable to any 'ultimate user or consumer' of the product for personal injury or property damage regardless of whether the seller has 'exercised all possible care.' Section 402A is itself an amalgam of possible rules. The requirement that the product be 'unreasonably dangerous' suggests that the court is to make a judgment about the costs and benefits of the product, but the irrelevance of 'all possible care' suggests something more strict. In practice s 402A represents a relaxation of the foreseeability requirement but the cost of precautions argument, including the benefits of the product for non-consumers, is not ousted. One authoritative commentator on the Second Restatement rule[17] has said that factors relevant to deciding whether the product was 'unreasonably dangerous' include the likelihood and probable seriousness of injury, the usefulness of the product, the availability of substitutes and whether eliminating the defects would impair the product's usefulness or make it prohibitively expensive. In other words, the test is the full test for negligence minus foreseeability.[18]

Even the Californian courts, which initially rejected s 402A's insistence that the product be 'unreasonably dangerous' and required only that the product be 'defective'[19] later came to the view that for cases in which the allegation is that the harm was caused by the product's design, as opposed to the product's performance, the test should be whether the defendant can establish that the 'benefits of the challenged design outweigh the risk of danger inherent in such design', in other words negligence without foreseeability with the balance of proof reversed.[20] In claims for injuries

---

14 See G Borrie *The Development of Consumer Law and Policy* (1984; London, Stevens) at p 101, Dashwood 'The EEC Commission's Proposal on Product Liability' [1977] JBL 202.

15 *Stapleton* at p 47.

16 377 P 2d 897 (1963).

17 John Wade 'On the Nature of Strict Tort Liability for Products' (1973) 44 Miss LJ 825.

18 For other attempts see eg Fischer 'The Meaning of Defect' (1974) 39 Missouri LR 339 and Calabresi and Hirschoff 'Toward a Test for Strict Liability' (1972) 81 Yale LJ 1055.

19 *Cronin v JBE Olson* 501 P 2d 1153, 104 Cal Rep 433 (1972).

20 *Barker v Lull Engineering* 573 P 2d 443, 143 Cal Rep 225 (1978).

caused by the product's performance, the California test is that the product should perform in accordance with ordinary consumer expectations[1]. Although this test is often taken to mean that the cost of precautions rule is excluded (because consumers expect products not to have any foreseeable risks at all), it is at least open to the interpretation that reasonable consumers do not expect safety at any price, and so this rule too may simply require negligence without foreseeability.

More recently, especially with the adoption of the 'state of the art' defence—that at the time the product was supplied the state of knowledge and technology was such that the relevant risk could not have been discovered—even foreseeability has been creeping back into the law of many US jurisdictions.[2] The trend has been strengthened by acceptance of the argument that if the plaintiff says that the product was defective because the defendant failed to warn consumers about the product's risks, the risks have to have been known or at least knowable at the time the product left the control of the defendant.[3]

The starting point for the European Directive, however, was not these later developments but s 402A and the California rule. The Directive begins with the appearance of requiring liability without fault:

'Art 1—The producer shall be liable for damage caused by a defect in his product ...

Art 4—The injured person shall be required to prove the damage, the defect and the causal relationship between defect and damage.'

'Damage' means personal injury and damage to personal property, but not economic loss or damage to commercial or industrial property.[4] 'Product' means any 'movable'—that is all property except land.[5]

But liability for 'defective' products is not the same as liability for 'products'. The crucial definition is that of 'defective'. The Directive adopts a version of the consumer expectations rule:

'Art 6—A product is defective when it does not provide the safety which a person is entitled to expect ...'

But note that this rule, like its Californian equivalent, is unclear. Are people 'entitled to expect' absolute safety at any price—and if not, how much safety are they entitled to expect and at what cost? Are consumers entitled to expect that they will be protected from all risks regardless of the benefits of the product? Or are they entitled to expect only reasonable precautions? Or perhaps consumers are entitled to expect that the dangerousness of the product is outweighed by its utility, but not counting

---

1 Ibid.
2 See eg *Feldman v Lederle Laboratories* 479 A 2d 374 (1984).
3 Ibid.
4 Article 9.
5 Article 2.

as a benefit the resources saved by failing to make the product safer—that is the denial of the costs of precautions argument.

Note further that the Directive does not even necessarily oust foresee–ability. Article 6 continues:

> '[T]aking all circumstances into account, including:
>
> ...
>
> (b) the use to which it could reasonably be expected that the product would be put;
>
> (c) the time the product was put into circulation.'

And it concludes:

> '(2) A product shall not be considered defective for the sole reason that a better product is subsequently put into circulation.'

Consumer entitlements to the expectation of safety are therefore largely to be judged at the time the product was to be put into circulation, not at any later point at which new scientific knowledge or new products or knowledge of the accidents caused by the defendant's product may have changed consumers' expectations.

In addition the Directive gives the defendant a number of defences. First, the defendant can show that 'he did not put the product into circulation', which covers not only cases in which the product is stolen or escapes by accident but also cases where the complaint is about the process by which the product was made and not about the product itself. Secondly, the defendant can show that the defect that caused the damage was probably not present in the product when the defendant put it into circulation—which deals with defects that arise in the course of inter–mediate supply and confirms that the liability is for defects in products not for products themselves. Thirdly, it is a defence that the defendant did not put the product into circulation for 'economic purposes' or 'in the course of a business'—a reflection of the benefit and burden moral principle discussed above but one which, exceptionally, favours the defendant. And fourthly, if the defendant is a components manufacturer, it is a defence to show that defect was attributable to the design of the product or to the manufacturers' instructions rather than to the way the components manufacturer made the part.

Note that this fourth defence, together with a fifth—that there is no liability if the defect results from compliance with the law—constitutes a sort of statutory remoteness rule. It defines the circumstances in which the components manufacturer will be allowed to say that although its making the component was obviously a factual cause of the harm, it should not count as the legal cause. Remoteness issues are also apparently important in Art 8 of the Directive, which says:

> 'The liability of the producer shall not be reduced when the damage is caused both by a defect in the product and by the act or omission of a third party.'

But, confusingly, Art 8 is qualified by the statement that it operates:

'Without prejudice to the provisions of national law concerning the right of contribution or recourse.'

The conclusion must be that the Directive rules out only forms of the reduction or elimination of liability that can leave the plaintiff with no one from whom to recover part of the loss.[6] The producer must be obliged to meet any residual liability not compensated for by anyone else. But as long as any residual loss does not fall on the plaintiff, national rules on the apportionment of damages among different defendants may operate in the usual way.

That one of the most important aims of the Directive is to make sure that victims of accidents caused by products have someone to sue who will mop up any residual liability is visible again in the Directive's definition of 'producer'. This is the most pro-plaintiff provision in the Directive. A 'producer' according to Art 3 means not only the manufacturer of the finished product, the producer of any raw material and the manufacturer of a component part, but also anyone who 'presents himself as the producer' by putting his name, trademark or 'other distinguishing feature' on the product—a provision which catches 'own brand' goods sold by supermarkets—and anyone who imports the product into the EC. In addition, if the producer cannot be identified, every supplier of the product counts as a producer unless he informs the victim who the producer was or who his own supplier was.

But note that the Directive is more favourable to intermediate suppliers than the American rule under s 402A. In s 402A, intermediate suppliers are treated as producers. All are 'suppliers' of defective products. The Directive leaves suppliers with their responsibilities in contract and negligence, but imposes no further liability on them as long as they are not importers or supermarkets selling own brand goods and as long as they reveal the identity of their own suppliers to the plaintiff.

On the other hand, Art 8(2) preserves the possibility of a defence of contributory negligence. It permits both the reduction of damages and the complete disallowance of damages (the former is, in English terms, contrib–utory negligence, the latter remoteness) if the damage is caused both by the defect and by the fault of the injured person.

Finally, the Directive allows, using an opt-out procedure which so far every member state apart from Luxembourg has used,[7] a state of the art or 'development risks' defence. This defence, which large firms—especially in the pharmaceutical industry—lobbied for heavily, is that:

'The state of scientific and technical knowledge at the time when [the producer] put the product into circulation was not such as to enable the existence of the defect to be discovered.'

Thus completely unforeseeable risks are excluded, at least if the reason they were unforeseeable was 'scientific' or 'technical'.

---

6   Eg proportionate several liability. See Howarth 'My Brother's Keeper? Liability for acts of third parties' [1994] LS 88.
7   See *Stapleton* at pp 50-51.

A similar lobbying success appears to have been influential in shaping Art 2, which excludes from the scope of the liability established by the Directive 'primary agricultural products'.[8] The Directive defines 'primary agricultural products' as 'products of the soil, of stock-farming and of fisheries, excluding products which have undergone initial processing'.

There is, however, one more clearly pro-plaintiff provision in the Directive. Article 12 outlaws exemption and exclusion clauses and other attempts to limit liability. It thus rejects the comparative advantage theory of the allocation of risks. It is based on the view that the process of competition and bargaining will not produce optimal results by itself.

The remainder of the Directive contains a somewhat compromised attempt to harmonise the overall exposure of producers to liability. Article 10(1) establishes a common limitation period of three years from the date the plaintiff becomes aware or ought to have become aware of the damage, the defect and the identity of the producer, but the effort is compromised by allowing member states to apply different rules regulating the suspension and interruption ('tolling') of the limitation periods[9] and the only truly common rule is a long-stop limitation date of 10 years from the date the producer put the product into circulation.[10] Moreover, a maximum damages provision[11] providing for a cap on the total damages payable for cases arising out of identical defective products is permissive only. Member states are allowed to adopt such damages caps as long as the maximum figure is greater than 70m ecus but are under no obligation to do so.[12] Given the wide variation in both the theory and the practice of the assessment of damages in the various member states it is therefore doubtful whether the Directive will achieve much in the way of harmonisation.

The 1987 Act

Britain was the first member state to implement the Directive by domestic legislation, one of only three countries to do so before the mandatory implementation date. Subsequently all other member states apart from two, France and Spain, have implemented the Directive. The European Commission has successfully proceeded against France in the ECJ for non-implementation.[13] In any case, because of the *Francovich* case[14] under which individuals may recover compensation from their governments if they suffer

8 States may opt out of this rule and include primary agricultural products within the scope of the law. So far, only Luxembourg has done so.
9 Article 10(2).
10 Article 11.
11 Article 16.
12 Portugal, Greece and Germany have such caps. The other countries that have implemented the Directive have not adopted a cap.
13 *Commission v France* C-293/91, [1993] ECR I-1. This case surely puts an end to suggestions that the EC lacked the legal capacity to pass the Directive. Cf *Stapleton*.
14 *Francovich and Bonifaci v Italy*: C-6, 9/90 [1991] ECR I-5357, ECJ.

because of non-implementation of a directive, citizens of non-implementing member states have a remedy which is if anything more effective than the remedies available in the implementing states.

The 1987 Act, as British statutes usually are, is far more detailed than the Directive, but the basic pattern is the same.

BASIC LIABILITY STANDARD

Section 2 begins with the promise of a pro-plaintiff rule:

'(1) ... where any damage is caused wholly or partly by a defect in a product, every person to whom subsection (2) below applies shall be liable in damages.'

Subsection (2) lists the producer, importer into the EC and own brand supplier as persons responsible under sub-s (1). Subsection (3) adds liability for suppliers, including suppliers of components and wholesalers, who, if it is not reasonably practicable for the plaintiff to identify someone to whom sub-s (2) would apply, fail to identify such a person to the plaintiff within a reasonable period.

The 'producer' includes those who manufacture things, those who win or abstract substances (that is mining, quarrying and oil and gas extraction) and those who process things that are neither manufactured nor abstracted but whose 'essential characteristics' are attributable to an industrial or other process (that is, presumably, producers of spaghetti and sausages but not those who simply wash and pack potatoes or cabbages—the question of the 'essential characteristics' of other produce can however be more difficult—consider, for example, frozen peas—is their frozenness an essential characteristic?).

'Products' are principally 'goods'[15] including 'products' that are incorp–orated into other 'products'. But exactly what will count as 'goods' is unclear. Certainly pure services, giving advice for example, are excluded, but a question is certain to arise about information given not by humans directly but by means of objects. If the defendant publishes a cookery book in which there is a recipe that is dangerously wrong and as a result of eating food prepared according to the recipe the plaintiff falls ill, will the Act apply? Books are 'goods' for they are bought and sold. And so why should not the plaintiff have a claim under the Act? Indeed the Act itself makes words surrounding products relevant by making warnings and instructions relevant to deciding whether the product is defective.[16] But on the other hand the recipe example reverses the relationship between the words and

15 But electricity also counts, presumably in anticipation of cases in which electricity generators make rapid changes to the voltage or other characteristics of the supply with the result that electrical appliances are damaged and, perhaps, people are injured.
16 Section 3(2)(a). See below.

the object. Instructions and warnings are words that deal with how to operate the object. But in recipes the words do not tell readers what to do with the book as a physical object; rather the physical object is the medium by which the words, which are the real product, are delivered. But words themselves are not 'goods'. If they are any sort of property at all, they are intellectual property such as copyright, trademark or patent.

Similar problems arise whatever the medium—a private letter, a video or a tape recording. Computer software may strike some people as different, since the instructions it contains appear to be addressed in the first instance to a machine rather than to a human. But the real difference between software and a recipe in a book is not the addressee of the instructions, for in the end they are both instructions to human users, but simply the ease with which any mistake in the instructions may be identified. After all, computer programs are merely a form of complex recipe. The difference is that a mistake in a recipe will usually be easier to spot than a mistake in a computer program and so contributory negligence or even novus actus interveniens defences will be easier to establish.

A different problem is whether objects that are not normally traded count as 'products'. One example is blood. Although many societies treat blood for transfusions as a tradeable commodity, a commodity that is obtained from the first on a commercial basis, in England blood for transfusion has mostly until now been donated freely and not thereafter traded for money. The argument[17] is that objects that are not normally the subject of commerce cannot be 'goods' and cannot be regulated by comm–ercial law.

The argument may be represented diagramatically thus:

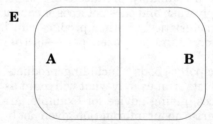

E=All objects; A='Goods' (ie objects that are tradeable); B='Non-goods' (ie objects that circulate non-commercially)

On the other hand, it is noticeable that the definition in the Act of 'supplying' goods[18] includes giving the goods away[19] and that although the Act, like the Directive, spends time on making sure that a distinction is drawn between commercial and non-commercial property damage and between business and non-business producers, it does not bother to make any explicit distinction between commercial and non-commercial products.

17 See P Atiyah *Sale of Goods* (8th ed) (1990) pp 24-5, 51.
18 Section 46(1).
19 Section 46(1)(f).

It is true that one might argue that it is quite compatible with counting only tradeable objects as 'products' that sometimes those objects may circulate in a non-commercial way and also quite compatible with the same position that non-tradeable objects are not 'products' at all.

That is, the following diagram shows a possible state of affairs:

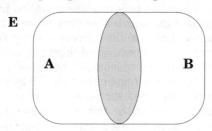

E=All objects; A=Objects that are tradeable; B=objects that may circulate non-commercially. A and B together make up the whole of E. There are no objects that are both not tradeable and which do not circulate commercially. But there are objects that are both tradeable and which do circulate non-commercially.

But compatibility is not the same as necessity. Both positions are internally coherent. The question is rather what good would it do either to bring those who produce non-tradeable objects within the ambit of the Act, or alternatively, what good would it do to exclude them? This question remains to be resolved.

Any person who suffers personal injury or property damage may sue under the Act.[20] Section 5(2), however, excludes from the scope of the Act damage to the product itself, including complaints about the quality of the product. For these the plaintiff has to rely on contract remedies. Furthermore, s 5(3) restricts the range of property to property normally used, or used at least by the plaintiff, for private (that is non-commercial) use, occupation or consumption, and the value of the property has to be more than £275.[1] Pure economic loss is not mentioned, but the orthodox view is that it is excluded. Certainly economic loss suffered by commercial firms must be excluded, since it would be anomalous to allow such claims while the Act explicitly bars claims for damage to commercial property. Moreover, the Directive seems to exclude loss of non-tangible property even by individuals who are not involved in commerce because it refers to an 'item', a reading confirmed by the French text of the Directive, which reads 'dommage causé à une chose ou la destruction d'une chose'. If damage to the non-tangible property of individuals is excluded it would be even more anomalous to include economic loss.

As with the Directive, the crucial provision of the Act is that which defines 'defect'. The Act's definition appears in s 3. A product is defective 'if the safety of the product is not such as persons generally are entitled to

20 Section 5(1).
1 Section 5(4).

expect.' 'Safety' includes the risk of property damage as well as personal injury. Section 3(2) reproduces Art 6 of the Directive. The court is to take into account 'the manner in which and the purposes for which the product has been marketed' (which presumably includes packaging, warnings and instructions), 'what might reasonably be expected to be done with ... the product', and 'the time when the product was supplied by its producer'.

Note that s 3(2) indicates the survival of even more of the foreseeability requirement of negligence than the Directive. As in the Directive, there is a requirement to take into account when judging the consumers' legitimate expectation of safety 'what might reasonably be expected to be done with ... the product'. This seems to suggest that the risks or dangers of the product that arise out of what the user does with it are to be assessed as they would have been imagined at the time of supply.[2] But the Directive's list of factors relevant is supplemented with 'the purposes for which the product has been marketed'. To take into account the 'purposes' for which the product was marketed indicates that the benefits of the product are to be judged as they seemed at the time the product was produced, for that is the point at which its purposes are set.

The requirement to take into account 'the time when the product was supplied' appears in the Act as in the Directive. It may have been intended to cover the obvious point that products deteriorate with age[3] but this cannot be the only intention of the requirement since the question of products that become defective after they have been supplied is covered by its own affirmative defence.[4]

A similar conclusion follows from the statutory enactment of Art 6(2) of the Directive in the final paragraph of s 3(2) of the Act, which says:

> '[N]othing in this section shall require a defect to be inferred from the fact alone that the safety of a product which is supplied after [the time when the product was supplied] is greater than the safety of the product in question.'

That is, the court is not supposed to take into account, or at least to treat as decisive, information about safety and costs that becomes available only after the accident.

The result is that the benefits of the product are to be judged as they appeared at the time of supply and the dangers of the product are to be judged also at the time of supply if they arise from the way the plaintiff used the product. Only risks that arose independently of how the plaintiff

---

2 Admittedly, an amendment to replace 'reasonably be expected' with 'be reasonably foreseen' was rejected in the House of Lords, but only on the ground that the two phrases meant the same thing. See Lord Lucas of Chilworth (Parliamentary Under-Secretary to the Department of Trade and Industry) Official Report (HL) 5th Series vol 483 col 793-5. And those of the contrary view thought that 'foresee' was wider than 'expect'.
3 See Lord Beaverbrook Official Report (HL) 5th Series vol 485 col 844.
4 See s 4(1)(d).

used the product may be judged as at a later date, the time of trial for example.[5]

More controversial still is the Act's stance on the cost-benefit issues. We do know that some sort of balancing of the product's utility against its dangers is intended to be done by the court, since otherwise s 3(2) would be irrelevant. In particular the reference in s 3(2)(a) to the 'purposes for which the product has been marketed' indicate clearly that the product's positive aspects are to be taken into account when judging what persons generally are entitled to expect. Lord Denning, therefore, must have been wrong when during the Parliamentary debate on the Act he said that '[I]f the product is in any way unsafe for people to consume, to eat or to use, there is a defect.'[6] Such an interpretation would mean that the word 'defect' would become meaningless. All products that caused harm would be 'defective' by definition. There would be liability for harm caused by products, not just for harm caused by defective products.

The section does not say explicitly whether or not the cost of precautions argument will be available to the defendant. This is the central point of controversy in the interpretation of the Act. Does the Act mean that consumers are entitled to expect that product safety is incorporated even to the extent that the costs of making the product would rise, so reducing not only the producers' profits but also perhaps the number of willing buyers for the product? Indeed, does the Act mean that consumers are entitled to expect producers to make safety improvements that are so expensive that the product would not in future be produced at all? Or are consumers entitled to expect only the safety that would be reasonable given the cost of precautions and the utility of the product to non-consumers?

The Directive gives no guidance since it also uses the same 'entitled to expect' formula. The Parliamentary debates are, however, more helpful. Ministers implied that the Act is meant to help plaintiffs who are not able to prove negligence.[7] If the cost of precautions argument were available to defendants, given that the Act retains more than half of negligence-style foreseeability and that the product's costs and benefits are still to be weighed by the court, there would be no great difference between liability under the Act and negligence. The only difference would be that dangers not arising out of the way the product was used would be held against the defendant even if they were not discoverable at the time of supply. Such an interpretation would therefore largely frustrate the legislative purpose to leave the plaintiff in a better position than at common law. It follows that the court should deny the defendant at least some part of the cost of

---

5 Cf eg *Stapleton* at 237, claiming that the dangers of the product are to be assessed as they appeared at the time of trial, whereas the benefits of the product were to be assessed as they appeared at the time of supply. This is not quite right, since some dangers are to be assessed as at the time of supply.

6 Official Report (HL) 5th Series vol 483 at col 721.

7 See Mr Michael Howard (Parliamentary Under-Secretary to the Department of Trade and Industry) Official Report (HC) 6th Series vol 115 at col 52, Lord Cameron of Lochbroom (Lord Advocate) Official Report (HL) 5th Series vol 482 at col 1004.

precautions argument. The question is which part? One suggestion, although one that is not likely to find favour with economists, is that the Act intends the defendant to be denied the *AEC v Latimer*[8] argument that it is permissible to take into account the private costs to the defendant of taking extra precautions—that is, the losses to the defendant that would be caused by adding to production costs the costs of taking the extra precautions. The result would be that the court, under the rubric of the product's 'purposes' would balance the product's dangerousness against its benefits to consumers and its benefits to others (eg the benefit to public health of vaccines).[9]

There is a counter-argument that the only intention of the Act is precisely to abolish foreseeability for dangers not arising from mode of use and there is no direct evidence of Parliamentary intent to deprive the defendant of the costs of precaution argument or any part of it. But one has to ask whether those many Parliamentarians who described the liability est–ablished under the Act as 'strict'[10] would have done so had they understood the Act as introducing so small a change in the law?

The best interpretation of the Act, therefore, seems to be that it does exclude the costs of precautions argument. The basic liability it establishes is that if there is any foreseeable risk arising from the way the product is used or any risk foreseeable or not that arises in any other way, the court will judge the product by balancing its overall dangers against its utility, but in judging its utility the court should not take into account the private costs to the defendant of making the product safe for the plaintiff. Its stance is that persons generally are entitled to expect that producers will not trade consumer safety off against their own profits, but they may trade off safety for some against benefits for others.

For example:

* The defendant drug manufacturer markets a drug that cures a wide-spread but sometimes life-threatening disease such as influenza. The drug causes brain damage to one patient in 100,000. Even without the development risks defence[11] the defendant is permitted to argue that the good the drug, which is unique, does for the 99,999 out-weighs the harm to the one. But the defendant may not argue simply that to make the drug safe even for the one would have meant that the drug would have been more costly for the manufacturer.

8 See above ch 3.
9 The possible economic effects of such a rule have yet to be modelled. Prima facie, at least, the effect would seem to be that producers facing inelastic demand curves would have a larger incentive to take precautions than producers facing elastic demand curves. In the former case, most of the loss from having to increase production costs would fall on the producer, and so would be disregarded by the court, whereas in the latter case, most of the loss falls on consumers, and so would be taken into account by the court. In any case, notice that since the Act still requires the court to engage in its own cost-benefit analysis, any process cost advantage that 'strict' liability regimes may have over 'fault' regimes seems not to be achievable.
10 Including the ministers sponsoring the Bill. See above.
11 See below.

*   The plaintiff, as in the famous but mythical case, uses the microwave to dry his poodle, with the obvious consequences. The plaintiff says that producers failed to supply the microwave with instructions saying that one should not put living creatures in the microwave. Result: no liability. The danger arises from the way the product was used, which means that the test is based on foreseeability. The foreseeable risk is zero.

*   The defendant designs a car that explodes on impact from the rear at 30 mph if the car's left indicator light is operating at the time of impact. The defendant says that (1) the fault was not discoverable at the time and (2) the chances of the occurrence of accidents of this type was very small and that the cost of putting the fault right even if it had been discoverable would have been very great. Result: liability. The defect may have been unforeseeable but arises from the state of the product not from an unforeseeable mode of use. The cost of correcting the defect is not relevant. The marginal utility of having one more brand of car on the market is far from overwhelming.

But note the way this interpretation works. Take the drug company example. If the costs of making the drug safe for all 100,000 were so great that the drug would not be produced at all, the losers would be the 99,999 would-be beneficiaries, not just the producing companies. Is the defendant allowed to raise the benefits to 99,999? The above interpretation says yes. But what if the cost of safety meant not that the drug was no longer produced but that, because of the price, the Health Service bought only half as much of it. There are 49,999 losers. Is the defendant allowed in argument to raise their loss? Presumably yes, because if the loss to the 99,999 may be raised, so should the loss of the 49,999. But if so, does this not amount to taking into account the costs of precaution? The answer is that the court may take into account the losses caused to other users or consumers as a result of the higher prices caused by having to make the product more safe but may not take into account the private losses to the producer of having to increase prices and thus, in most, but not all, circumstances, of suffering a reduction in profits.

DEFENCES

We now pass to the defences the defendant has under s 4. There are six defences in all. Their most important feature is that in all of them the burden of proof is on the defendant.

The first defence is that 'the defect is attributable to compliance with any requirement imposed by or under any enactment or with any Community obligation'.[12] In negligence it is for the plaintiff to show fault and if the defendant says that he acted in the way he did because of the requirements of a statute it would be up to the plaintiff to show that the

---

12 Section 4(1)(a).

defendant was wrong in his interpretation of the statute and unreasonable in acting on his wrong interpretation. Under the Act, we may conclude, for this particular aspect of fault, the burden of proof has been reversed. The defendant has to show that his interpretation of the statute was correct.

The second defence under s 4 is that 'the person proceeded against did not at any time supply the product to another'.[13] 'Supply' is defined as selling, hiring or lending the goods, giving them away either as a gift or as a prize, performing any contract for work and materials to furnish the goods, providing the goods in exchange for non-money consideration, and providing the goods in connection with the performance of a statutory duty. Under hire purchase arrangements, which often operate in the rather odd form that the seller sells the goods to a finance house which then hires them out to the buyer, there is a special rule to the effect that there is, of course, a supply, but the supplier is deemed to be not the finance house but the seller.[14] The defence, especially since supplying includes making gifts, is quite narrow and may amount to little more than a quasi-remoteness rule that the defendant is not liable if the goods are stolen either by the plaintiff or by an intermediary.

One further point under the 'no supply' defence is that taxi firms, ship owners and aircraft owners seem to have successfully escaped liability under the Act because of s 46(9), which says that ships, aircraft and motor vehicles do not count as being 'supplied' for the purposes of the Act if the deal with the customers is solely to provide transport services 'for a particular period or for particular voyages, flights or journeys'.

ARE CAR HIRE FIRMS LIABLE FOR DEFECTIVE CARS?

One question which may conceivably arise is the liability of car-hire firms for damage caused by defective vehicles hired out by the firm. If the car-hire firm imports its fleet directly from outside the EC, for example from Korea or the Czech Republic, it will count as the producer of the cars under s 2(2)(c). The question is whether s 46(9) will save the firm from liability.[15] The argument for the plaintiff is that s 46(9) protects the defendant if the only reason for thinking that there was a supply was that the defendant provided services 'consisting in the carriage of ... passengers ... in [a] vehicle'. But the service provided by a car-hire firm is not the carriage of passengers. It is the hirer, that is the driver, who is responsible for the carriage of passengers, if any. The car-hire firm hires out the car for use by the hirer. But the defendant would argue that the subsection also refers to services consisting in the 'use' of the vehicle 'for any other purpose' and that this includes hiring the car to a driver to drive the car anywhere. The plaintiff's response might

---

13 Section 4(1)(b).
14 Section 46.
15 The question arises also directly under s 2(2)(c), which refers to importing the goods in the course of business 'to supply it to another' as well as under the s 4 defence.

be that 'use' of the vehicle refers to use by the defendant not by the person to whom the car was hired.

The argument comes down to whether the purpose of s 46(9) is to differentiate between hiring out a product, which counts as a supply according to s 46(1), and hiring out the services of a driver, ship's crew or air crew who happen to use vehicles in providing the service or to differentiate merely between transport services and other services.

The argument for the first view, which favours the plaintiff in the car-hire case, is that it is arbitrary to single out the transport industry for special protection. The argument for the second view, which favours the defendant in the car-hire case, is that if the intention was to distinguish between personal services that use equipment and just hiring out equipment and to protect the former but not the latter, there are many other forms of personal service using equipment that do not receive an explicit mention in s 46. For example, the plaintiff lives next to a well-appointed office block whose owner hires a gardener to mow the lawn. The gardener proudly brings along the special power mower he has imported from outside the EC. Unfortunately, the mower is defective, goes out of control and injures the plaintiff. There is no equivalent of s 46(9) protecting the gardener from the accusation that he acted as supplier of the mower. Is the office owner liable? The correct view must be that the gardener would not be liable because he had control of the mower at all times and in no sense hired it or lent to the client. If so, s 46(9) makes no sense as providing protection for defendants only in cases in which the vehicle owner retains control of the vehicle, since the defendant has such protection already. It must have a wider effect, namely to protect defendants in the transport business even when they do not have control of the hired vehicle. It would follow that s 46(9) protects car-hire firms.

The third defence is that the defendant was not in business. The defendant has to prove that the only supply of the product was 'otherwise than in the course of [the defendant's] business' and that the defendant is only an intermediate supplier and not the person who made the product or that if he was the person who made the product, he did not make it 'with a view to profit'.[16] Notice that in the case of someone who does make something other than in the course of business but then sells it, a model aeroplane for example, the question seems to be whether the maker intended to sell the object at the time of making it, rather than whether the object is in fact sold at a profit. Notice also that the House of Lords has decided in other circumstances that an activity can be carried on without 'a view to profit' even though profits were made.[17] Intention and purpose are crucial, rather as if we were dealing with a criminal law statute.

---

16 Section 4(1)(c). Technically the defence is not made out if the defendant is an own brand supplier or an importer in the course of business, but in these cases the defendant would anyway probably not have passed the first part of the test that the supply was otherwise than in the course of business.

17 *National Deposit Friendly Society v Skegness UDC* [1959] AC 293.

The fourth defence is that the defect did not exist when the producer, importer or own brand retailer supplied the product (or, if the defendant is an intermediate supplier, when the product was last supplied by a producer, importer or own brand retailer). This defence may seem to be unnecessary given that, according to s 3(2)(c), the time of supply is supposed to be taken into account in judging the degree of safety that people generally are entitled to expect. And it is inapplicable to defects arising from the design of the product which by definition exist from the first. But it may be argued that the function of s 3(2)(c) is only to prevent liability for changes in the product that come about through normal wear and tear, whereas the s 4(1)(d) defence catches all other changes to the product, for example those caused by interventions by third parties. In other words, like the defence under s 4(1)(b), the defence is really dealing with a remoteness issue, that of a novus actus interveniens by a third party or natural process, and the subsection has the effect of preserving the remoteness rule but of reversing the burden of proof.

The fifth defence is that:

'The state of scientific and technical knowledge at the relevant time was not such that a producer of products of the same descript– ion as the product in question might be expected to have discovered the defect if it had existed in his products while they were under his control.'

The 'relevant time' is, again, the time when the product was supplied, or, if the defendant is an intermediate supplier, the time when it was last supplied by a producer, importer or own brand retailer.

This defence is the Act's version of the 'state of the art' or 'development risks' defence. The presence of the defence in the Act was its most controversial aspect and attracted much debate and comment in Parl– iament. Its intention is to reintroduce a fault test for producers of new products, especially pharmaceutical manufacturers. It aims to reduce the adverse effect that it was feared the Act would have on innovation. The name 'development risks defence' rather pre-judges the issue of whether the defence is indeed necessary to protect new product development and whether it will be effective. The preferable name is the more neutral 'state of the art defence', which derives from the fact that the original American versions of the defence consisted of showing that the state of the relevant 'art' at the time was such that the manufacturer could not have known about the defect that caused the product to be unsafe.

The argument against the state of the art defence is that although it encourages new products to come onto the market, it does not encourage extra research into whether or not they will be safe. The 'development risk' is, subject to a fault test, transferred to the victims. And yet the victims are far less able to carry out research into the safety of the product than the producers.

In countries such as Britain that have universal state-provided health care, the main burden of caring for the victims of the unanticipated side-effects of new drugs, which is what the state of the art defence is mainly about, falls on the taxpayer. The effect of the defence is to transfer risks from the producer to the state. It is therefore a kind of subsidy for innovation. But the victims of new products also lose because of the defence. They lose to the extent that tort damages would have compensated them for their future lost earnings whereas state benefits on the whole do not. A state subsidy for innovation may be justified. A subsidy from victims is perhaps less so.

But before making any further comment on the desirability of the defence, it is worth noting its field of operation. As we have seen, a drug that has great beneficial effects for a great number of people, but has adverse side-effects for a few, is not necessarily a defective product under the terms of the Act. Section 3(2)(a) requires the court to take into account when judging whether the product was as safe as persons generally are entitled to expect the 'purposes for which the product has been marketed'. Those purposes should include the healing of the sick and should be taken into account. Furthermore, 'persons generally' may be entitled to expect only the degree of safety that one would normally find in a new drug that has proven beneficial effects for a great number of people—that is that it may have as yet unknown adverse side-effects. It may be that 'persons generally' are entitled to know whether the drug is a new one, including, perhaps, how recently it was approved by any relevant regulatory agencies, and so the question of adequate warning may arise. But just because the drug has adverse side-effects does not mean that the drug manufacturer will be liable. The state of the art defence applies only to cases in which the drug is found to be defective under s 3. These are cases in which the drug's adverse effects are so serious that they eclipse any beneficial effects that it may have had for other people. For example, if a mild pain killer turns out to cause deformities or death in children born to those who took it, the product's benefits are not enough to outweigh its costs.

The effect of the defence is not therefore to make it very much more likely that very important new products such as treatments for life-threatening conditions will come onto the market. The definition of 'defect' ensures that, except in the most unusual circumstances,[18] such products will not be subject to liability. The defence means rather that manufacturers will be more likely to put onto the market products that do not bring overwhelming benefits but which would be welcome if they do not have adverse side-effects—for example mild pain-killers, sedatives and cures for athlete's foot and heartburn. Whether the loss of such new products that might result from the abolition of the state of the art defence is something seriously to worry about is far from clear.

From the manufacturers' point of view, however, the state of the art defence makes a very big difference. To exclude defects which similar producers could not be expected to have discovered because of the state of scientific or technical knowledge means that in one very important respect

---

18   For example, the product changes the personality of those who use it so that they become mass murderers. Cf *Meah v McCreamer* see above ch 4.

the private cost to the manufacturer of making the product safer becomes relevant again. In science-based industries such as pharmaceuticals, the state of scientific and technical knowledge is not independent of producer activity. The state of the art is often not a preserve of university researchers but of the producer firms themselves. Consequently, the amount of money a producer invests in research may affect the state of scientific and technical knowledge. The state of the art defence allows the defendant to say that even though more investment in research may have pushed the state of knowledge on so far that the defect would have become discoverable, a producer of such products would not have been expected to make such an investment because it would have cost too much.

There are several other points to observe about s 4(1)(e). First, nowhere does it use the word 'reasonable'. The defendant is held to what a producer of similar products 'might be expected' to discover. This has led some commentators to believe that if an industry has low standards, so that observers would expect firms not to do any new research into the scientific and technical areas that were relevant to possible defects even though such research would be easy to do, the defence would succeed automatically. But the better view[19] is that 'might be expected' can only mean 'might reasonably be expected'. The purpose of the defence is to protect innovation not to encourage incompetence.[20]

Secondly, the test is what a similar producer might be expected to discover not what someone in an unrelated field might be expected to discover. The problem with modern scientific knowledge is that there is so much of it that it has become extremely compartmentalised. Scientists have become experts on increasingly small fields of study. There may be cases in which the state of scientific knowledge was such that if someone had made an unusual cross-disciplinary connection, for example from the physiology of a rare monkey to the possible effects of certain substances on human beings in certain environmental conditions, the defect may have become discoverable. But it is not reasonable to expect such connections to be made by the research departments of commercial firms. Similarly, technology is often developed for very particular purposes, so that if a car manufacturer might have discovered a defect if it had used testing equipment developed for the aerospace industry or for the oil industry, it may still be able to make out the defence because a car manufacturer may not be expected to know about the technology used in aerospace or oil.[1]

Thirdly, the defence is established by showing that the defect could not have been *discovered*, not by showing that it could not have been *prevented*. For example, a manufacturer may put on the market a new car made out of a new very light material. The car is thus extremely fuel efficient and fast. But the new material turns out to fail after a year or so of hard driving

19 See *Stapleton* at p 242.
20 Cf Lord Lucas of Chilworth Official Report HL 5th Series vol 483 at col 841: 'Neither will it necessarily be of any use to that producer if he shows that he manufactured the products to an accepted national or international safety standard.'.
1 Cf C Wright *Product Liability* (London; Blackstone, 1989) at p 63.

and many people are injured as a result. The question posed by the state of the art defence is whether, given scientific and technical knowledge at the time, the tendency of the new material to fail after a year's use could have been discovered. It is not whether there was any other material that could successfully have been used as a substitute.

And fourthly, although the private costs to the producer of investing in further research are relevant to establishing the defence, the cost of applying that knowledge is not. Section 4(1)(e) says that there is a defence if a relevant state of knowledge prevents the defendant from discovering the defect, not if the expense of applying that knowledge prevents the defendant from discovering the defect. Thus, in the case of the car manufacturer who could have discovered the defect if it had used testing equipment developed for the aerospace industry, the reason for the failure to use the aerospace industry's equipment has to be that car manufacturers in general do not know about aerospace equipment, not that such equip–ment, although known about, was more expensive than the equipment used in the car industry. [2]

The sixth and final defence under s 4(1) is one that is available principally to producers of components. Where the product has been 'comprised' in another product, which as a consequence was found to be defective, it is a defence to show that the defect in the component was 'wholly attributable to the design' of the main product or that the defect was 'wholly attributable ... to compliance by the producer ... with instruct–ions given by the producer of the [main] product'. The intention is clearly to prevent manufacturers from shifting responsibility onto their component makers when the component makers had only been following orders. But note that the defect has to be 'wholly attributable' to the design or specifications of the component. Plainly, where the component manu–facturer has made an error in manufacturing the defence is not available. But what about cases in which the component manufacturer should have realised or could reasonably have discovered that the design or the specifications would result in an unsafe product? In such a case is the defect 'wholly attributable' to the design or the specifications, or is it also 'attributable' to the component manufacturer's failure to take preventative action? If the defence is not available to component manufacturers who could have discovered that the product would be unsafe, the sixth defence becomes in practice a defence that the defendant acted entirely without negligence, so that for component manufacturers who avoid errors in manufacturing, the applicable liability rule under the Act is negligence with the burden of proof reversed.

One significant aspect of the sixth defence is that it contains the only explicit reference in the Act to design defects, and constitutes the only

---

2   Cf Lord Lucas of Chilworth, Official Report HL 5th Series vol 483 col 841: 'It will be of no help to the producer to plead how difficult or how expensive it had or might have been for [the defendant] to have found the answers to that defect. If other producers of products of that type had the knowledge available to them, then the defence is of no use to the producer of the product.'.

special rule in the Act for design defects. In the US, several jurisdictions have developed special rules for design defects which purportedly hold the producer to a less stringent test than that used in cases about errors in manufacturing. Such special rules are not necessary in English law since liability for all defects is not very strict to begin with. The Californian rule, for example, is to allow the defendant to argue the social benefits of the product in a design defect case. Since the Act appears to allow defendants to bring into argument their products' social benefits in all cases, there is no need for such a rule in England.

REMOTENESS AND CAUSATION

What causation and remoteness rules operate under the Act? It is clear from s 2(1) that factual causation operates in the normal way. But note that the damage has to be 'caused' by 'the defect' not by the product or by the defendant. That is, the plaintiff has to show that if the product had been as safe as persons generally are entitled to expect, the damage probably would not have happened. This formulation leads to a difficulty if the product is so unsafe that the only way to avoid the danger is for it not to have been marketed at all. In such a case the product itself, or rather its supply, causes the harm, not a defect *in* the product, for that would imply that there was a version of the product without the defect that the defendant could have supplied. The Act could have read 'where any damage is caused by the supply of a defective product' or it could have repeated the usefully imprecise formula in the Directive that the plaintiff has to show a 'causal relationship between defect and damage'. That the Act failed to do so will provide the courts with a tricky problem of re-interpretation to avoid the clearly undesirable result that inherently dangerous products are to treated more leniently than products that are not inherently dangerous but just happen to be dangerous in the form they took in the events leading up to the accident.

The remoteness rules in operation in the Act also present difficulties. As we have already seen, several of the s 4 defences deal with remoteness issues—s 4(1)(d) with defects caused by subsequent interventions by third parties, s 4(1)(b) with supply brought about by third parties, s 4(1)(f) with defects caused by activities prior to manufacture by a third party—namely design and specification and even s 4(1)(a) on compliance with a statutory requirement is in one sense a remoteness defence since its force is that although the defendant made a defective product the real responsibility lies with the legislature. The important point about these defences is that the burden of proof is on the defendant, unlike in negligence in which the plaintiff has to show that the damage was not too remote.

But it is not clear whether any other form of remoteness argument is permissible under the Act. Remember that Art 8 of the Directive prohibits the reduction of liability where the damage is caused 'both by the defect and by the act or omission of a third party'. The Act, however, does not explicitly re-enact Art 8. Instead it does two things. First it says that there is liability when the defect 'wholly or partly' causes damage, and secondly, s 2(5) declares that where 'two or more persons are liable by virtue of this Part [of the Act] for the same damage, their liability shall be joint and several'. Whether this combination of provisions produces the same result as that intended by the Directive remains to be seen. Certainly joint and several liability means that each defendant is liable for the full amount of the damage (subject, of course to the overriding principle that the plaintiff can only recover to the extent of the total damages awarded). But why does the third party have to be 'liable by virtue of this Part'? What if, for example, the third party is a supplier who negligently failed to prevent the supply of the product but who is not liable under the Act because he was willing to inform the plaintiff who his supplier was?

One way of reading the statute is that the 'wholly or partly' rule displaces all ordinary remoteness rules about third party intervention, leaving the defendant with only the s 4(1) defences. If this is correct, the intervention by the negligent supplier would make no difference to the defendant's liability for the full amount of the loss. The defect existed before the product reached the supplier, and so s 4(1)(d) does not apply and none of the other defences is relevant.

The other way of reading the statute is that 'wholly and partly' refers only to factual causation and 'joint and several' is meant only to deal with the problems of multiple defendants under the Act. In consequence, all remoteness arguments not explicitly removed by the Act or turned into affirmative defences are still available to the defendant.[3]

The first way of interpreting the Act explains the presence in the Act (and the Directive) of so many remoteness rules in the form of affirmative defences. If the defendant may use novus actus arguments under the rubric of causation, when the plaintiff has the burden of proof, why bother to make some remoteness arguments affirmative defences with the burden on the defence?

On the other hand, the presence of the remoteness based defences may be the result of an anxiety on the part of the drafters of the Directive to make sure that, regardless of the varying rules on causation and remoteness in the many EC countries, defendants will have at their disposal at least some remoteness arguments. Moreover, the second way of interpreting the Act has the considerable merit that it allows room for a sensible disposition of cases which, although rare, may eventually occur. For example, the plaintiff buys a car which has the defect that the brakes occasionally lock. The car is clearly not safe. The plaintiff, however, is not the victim of a crash. Instead, the locking of the brakes causes the plaintiff to stop safely at the side of the road. The plaintiff gets out of the car but is immediately struck by a car being driven recklessly by a third party. In factual terms, the defect caused the damage. If the brakes had not locked, the plaintiff would not have been in the wrong place to be hit by the reckless

---

3 Stapleton, for instance, following Hart and Honoré, implies that many remoteness arguments are inherent in the word 'cause' itself. see at pp 121-122 and 171.

third party. But in terms of remoteness, the third party's reckless driving is an independent supervening cause, a novus actus, which relieves the defendant of responsibility.

Furthermore there is a difference between the Act and the Directive that ceases to be troublesome only if the second interpretation is adopted. The Directive speaks of cases in which the damage is caused by the defect and a third party, whereas the Act speaks of all cases in which the defect is 'wholly or partly' the cause of the damage. There seems to be a difference between the Directive and the Act in the treatment of cases in which the accident is caused partly by the defect and partly by a natural event. The Directive makes no mention of such cases. It refers only to human interventions. The Act, however, seems to include natural intervening causes in the 'wholly or partly' rule. For example, what if the plaintiff in the example just mentioned, instead of being hit by a reckless driver, is struck by lightning. The lightning is an overwhelming and independent cause which, following the ordinary rules of remoteness, would relieve the defendant of responsibility. But if the ordinary rules of remoteness are excluded by the Act, the effect would be that the defendant would be liable in the lightning case, something there is no evidence for believing the Directive requires. If, on the other hand, the courts adopt the second interpretation, there is no problem.

Furthermore, Art 8 of the Directive uses different terms when regulating the acts of third parties and the acts of the plaintiff. Article 8(1) prohibits the 'reduction' of liability when the damage is also caused by the act or omission of a third party, but when Art 8(2) speaks of the contributory fault of the plaintiff it does so in terms of whether liability may be 'reduced or disallowed'. The difference between 'reduce' and 'reduce or disallow' is that the latter but not the former concerns the complete denial of liability. It seems to follow that Art 8(1) regulates only reductions of liability not the complete denial of liability and therefore does not regulate the application of English remoteness principles which, at least until now, have concerned not the partial reduction of liability but its complete denial. Since the Act is not clear it is legitimate to use the Directive as a guide to its meaning, and here that guidance seems to be in the direction of the preservation of the ordinary rules of remoteness.

Another oddity of the Act is that although the Directive explicitly allows member states to apply their own contribution rules, the 1987 Act does not, in terms, apply the Civil Liability (Contribution) Act 1978. It may be that the 1978 Act applies anyway, since it is drafted very broadly,[4] so broadly that unlike the Law Reform (Contributory Negligence) Act 1945 there is no need, for example, to deem the liability under the Act to count as 'fault'. But it is at least arguable that when s 2(5) establishes 'joint and several liability' it is restoring the common law position that each defendant is liable for the full damages and that it is the right of the plaintiff, not of the court, to decide how much each defendant must pay.

4   'Any person liable in respect of any damage suffered by another person may recover contribution from any other person liable in respect of the same damage' (s 1(1)).

CONTRIBUTORY NEGLIGENCE

Article 8(2) of the Directive allows the preservation of the contributory negligence defence and includes 100% contributory negligence, a concept allegedly excluded from English law.[5] The Act brings in contributory negligence via s 6(4) and (5), which deem the liability created by the Act to be based on 'fault' at least for the purposes of the 1945 Act. Section 6 does not, however, anticipate the discovery that the 1945 Act does not allow 100% contributory negligence, so that in order to comply with the Directive, either the courts have to adopt the idea (suggested below) that where the 1945 Act does not apply, the old common law rule that contributory negligence was a complete defence still applies, or they will have to bring in the remoteness rule that wholly unreasonable acts by plaintiffs break the chain of causation.

Contributory negligence applies to the 1987 Act in the normal way. Although some aspects of the fault test may have been relaxed for the plaintiff's case against the defendant, the fault test still applies in full in any attempt to reduce the damages because of the plaintiff's unreasonable behaviour.

Differences between the Act and the Directive

One very noticeable aspect of the 1987 Act is that in several respects it does not follow precisely the course laid down by the Directive. In several instances, for example the questions of remoteness and economic loss, the Directive can be used fairly simply to clear up an ambiguity or fill in a gap in the Act. But there are several more serious divergences between the Act and the Directive. In these cases, it may be possible for aggrieved citizens to sue the British government for monetary compensation for the its failure properly to implement the Directive.[6]

AGRICULTURAL PRODUCTS

The Directive allows states to leave agricultural products beyond the scope of the legislation. But what are agricultural products? Article 2 of the Directive says that they are:

> 'Products of the soil, of stock farming and of fisheries, excluding products that have undergone initial processing.'

5   See below ch 15.
6   The degree to which the principles of the *Francovich* case (*Francovich and Bonifaci v Italy*: C–6, 9/90 [1991] ECR I-5357, ECJ) will extend from failure to implement a directive to imperfect implementation of a directive awaits the decision of the ECJ in two cases, viz *Brasserie du Pêcheur* and *Factortame (No 3)*.

But the Act, in s 1(1)(2) and s 2(4) says that they are:

> '[A]ny produce of the soil, of stock farming or of fisheries ... [unless] it had not undergone an industrial process.'

When challenged in Parliament about the difference between 'initial processing' and an 'industrial process', ministers said that 'initial' and 'industrial' were the same thing.[7] But this is plainly not the case. Frozen peas and beans undergo an 'initial' process, but surely that process is not 'industrial' in the same way that making pork pies is 'industrial'?

Furthermore, if the produce has undergone an 'industrial process' it seems that liability would fall on the processor not on the farmer, whereas the Directive envisages that the farmer would be liable.[8]

'PURPOSE' IN S 3

Another major divergence between the Directive and the Act concerns the definition of 'defect'. In s 3 of the Act, the court is instructed to take into account when deciding whether the product was defective the 'purposes for which [it] has been marketed'. The Directive makes no mention of such purposes.

It is possible to argue that since both the Directive and the Act instruct the court to take into account 'all the circumstances', the only difference between the Directive and the Act is that the Act makes explicit consideration that the Directive keeps implicit in the phrase 'all the circumstances'.

On the other hand, the effect of taking into account the product's 'purposes' is potentially very great. Using it, the court can say that a product, especially a pharmaceutical product, was not defective because the benefits that it brought to other users (and to non-users in the case of vaccines against infectious diseases) outweighed the harm it did to victims. The Act does seem to deny the defendant the argument that further precautions would have been costly to the defendant itself. But, because of the purpose clause, it may not deprive the defendant of the argument that the product's benefits to others outweighed its costs.

The Directive, in contrast, has no such clause. It is possible to interpret this omission as deliberate and therefore that the Directive intends that the whole of the cost of precaution argument is to be unavailable to the defendant. Liability under the Directive would then come much closer to the type of liability described by Lord Denning,[9] that is that unless the harm resulted from an unforeseeable use or from the effect of normal wear and tear, the very fact of harm would indicate that the product was defective. If the ECJ interprets the Directive in this way, and it would

---

7   See Lord Lucas of Chilworth above.
8   See *Stapleton* at p 54.
9   See above.

probably make more economic sense than the hybrid test for liability apparently adopted by the Act, there would be a considerable number of cases in which the Directive would point in the direction of liability and the Act would point against liability.

'DID NOT SUPPLY' VS 'DID NOT PUT IN CIRCULATION'

Another divergence between the Directive and the Act is that whereas the Directive talks of the supplier 'putting the product into circulation', the Act talks simply of 'supplying' the product. Some writers[10] allege that since the word 'supply' in other contexts in English law has a technical meaning according to which the person receiving the goods has to get some kind of ownership or possession in the goods, the Act is much narrower than the Directive.

On the other hand, the Act in s 46 explicitly defines 'supply' at great length, something that other statutes, for example the Sale of Goods Act 1979, the Supply of Goods and Services Act 1982 and the Consumer Credit Act 1974 all fail to do. One might conclude that the Act intends to rule out the technical meaning of 'supply' so that the courts will find little difficulty in keeping in line with the Directive.

Moreover, in most of the cases in which it is doubtful whether there is a technical supply (allowing supermarket shoppers to use trolleys free of charge for example) the plaintiff would be interested only in suing the manufacturer, who almost certainly will have supplied the product at some stage.

STATE OF THE ART

Finally, and most notoriously, there is a substantial difference in the terms of the state of the art defence in the Act and in the Directive. In the Directive, the defence is that:

'The state of scientific and technical knowledge at the time when [the producer] put the product into circulation was not such as to enable the existence of the defect to be discovered.'

In contrast, the defence in the Act is that:

'The state of scientific and technical knowledge at the relevant time [ie at the time of supply] was not such that a producer of products of the same description as the product in question might be expected to have discovered the defect if it had existed in his products while they were under his control.'

10 Eg *Stapleton* at p 322-23.

The Act's version is an easier defence to establish in two important respects. First, the Directive talks generally about the discoverability of the defect, whereas the Act specifies that the question is whether a producer similar to the defendant could have discovered the defect. This means that producers, although they are held to reasonable standards within their own industry,[11] are not held to the standards of the best scientific knowledge available. In other words, the standards are industrial standards not scientific ones. Although sometimes these standards will not be different, sometimes they will be very different.

Secondly, the Directive implies that it is necessary for the producer to be unable to discover the defect, whereas the Act talks about what the producer might not have been expected to discover. There will be cases in which the defect will have been discoverable by making more than reasonably to be expected efforts. In these cases the Directive will not allow the defence but the Act will allow it.

It is sometimes claimed[12] that there is no rational position which requires more than reasonable efforts to discover the defect but which still gives the defence some practical scope of operation. The claim is that if one expects more than reasonable efforts, it will always be possible to say that the producer could have done more and more, including new ground-breaking basic research, that would have ensured that the defect would have been discovered. This might be literally true, but it is not clear whether it is so in practice. For example, reasonableness itself depends on a judgment of the seriousness of the risk. In a normal negligence case, that risk is assessed as it would have appeared at the time. But if foreseeability is removed, the relevant risk will be the risk as it appears now, which may be a much greater risk. The effort expected of the producer would be greater, although not necessarily infinite, if the court's judgment is based on what we now know to be the seriousness of the risk, not what the seriousness of the risk would have appeared to be at the time. Similarly, if the burden of proof is on the defendant, as it is in the state of the art defence, more will be required of defendants than if the burden were on the plaintiff.

Common law liability

The combination of the 1987 Act and the possibility of further recourse to the Directive where the Act does not measure up will cover most cases of product liability that are likely to occur in practice. But in view of the exclusion from the coverage of both the Act and the Directive of primary unprocessed foodstuffs and the exclusion of damage to commercial property, it is worth stating briefly the common law remedies that are still available to plaintiffs.[13]

11 See above.
12 *Stapleton* at p 242.
13 The Act also excludes economic loss, but so does the common law: see above ch 6. See eg *Muirhead v Industrial Tank* [1986] QB 507.

Donoghue v Stevenson[14] establishes that ordinary negligence principles govern product liability cases at common law. There is no legal significance as far as negligence is concerned in the presence of contracts between manufacturer and wholesaler, wholesaler and retailer, and retailer and customer, and the absence of contracts between the manufacturer and the customer and between the customer and anyone to whom the customer gives the goods. The central question is whether the manufacturer behaved reasonably in the circumstances. If the manufacturer did not behave reasonably, anyone who suffers harm that is not too remote can sue in negligence for compensation. Customers can sue, donees can sue and so can mere bystanders.[15] The same obligation to take reasonable care applies as much to those who repair goods as those who make them.[16] Intermediate suppliers, such as wholesalers and retailers, are judged on exactly the same principles, although in their case, much turns on whether it is faulty for the wholesaler or retailer not to have inspected the goods before selling them on. It is, for example, reasonable to expect second-hand car dealers thoroughly to inspect the cars that they sell, and those injured in accidents that would have been prevented had a second hand car dealer bothered to inspect a vehicle before selling it will usually find that they have a claim.[17]

A number of questions that occurred repeatedly in common law products liability are worth mentioning. But note that in all of them the answers depend purely on the application of already familiar negligence principles.

Intermediate inspection

In *Donoghue* the product reached the victim in a sealed opaque bottle and Lord Atkin referred in his speech to there having been 'no reasonable possibility of intermediate inspection'. But suggestions that there would only be liability in cases in which the goods arrived in sealed packages were soon dismissed.[18] The mere possibility of or opportunity for inter–mediate inspection was held to be irrelevant.[19] And Lord Atkin's words were reinterpreted as meaning a 'reasonable probability' of intermediate inspection rather than a 'possibility'.[20]

What these cases really stand for is that ordinary principles of fault and remoteness apply.[1] If the defendant reasonably expected that someone else would sort the goods into safe and unsafe examples, or if the defendant reasonably thought that, because he had given an adequate warning to

---

14 [1932] AC 562.
15 See eg *Stennett v Hancock* [1939] 2 All ER 578 (passer-by injured when wheel flew off lorry).
16 *Stennett v Hancock* [1939] 2 All ER 578; *Haseldine v Daw* [1941] 2 KB 343.
17 *Andrews v Hopkinson* [1957] 1 QB 229.
18 *Grant v Australian Knitting Mills* [1936] AC 85.
19 *Herschtal v Stewart & Ardern* [1940] 1 KB 155.
20 *Haseldine v Daw* [1941] 2 KB 343.
1 Cf Lloyd LJ in *Aswan v Lupdine* [1987] 1 All ER 135 at 153f.

test or check the goods, no one would be endangered by them, the court may decide that there was no fault, or that the real fault lay with someone else, in comparison to whose fault the defendant's part in the events paled into insignificance. Thus, where a manufacturer had warned retailers and teachers to test a chemical before classroom use and they had both failed to do so, the manufacturer was not liable to a school child who suffered injuries when the chemical caused an explosion.[2] And where a second hand car dealer tells a buyer that the car may be defective and the car then crashes, injuring the plaintiff, the fault of the buyer in not having the car inspected and repaired may break the chain of causation The plaintiff is left with an action against the buyer.[3] But where the intervening act was entirely predictable and the defendant did nothing about it, the remoteness argument may fail in the ordinary way.[4]

Similarly, even if the plaintiff has an opportunity to inspect the goods before use, the liability of the defendant is not affected unless the plaintiff acted unreasonably in continuing to use the product, in which case there is contributory negligence. If the plaintiff was utterly unreasonable in how he dealt with the product, there will be a break in the chain of causation and no liability at all. Sometimes, the plaintiff will be held to be contributorily negligent, but sometimes the circumstances will have given the plaintiff no real option.[5]

Proving fault

One of the obvious difficulties facing a plaintiff who accuses a manufacturer of negligence is that it is difficult to find out precisely what happened and, more to the point, what should have happened instead. Two lines of argument have emerged from this obstacle. One, the *Daniels v R White Ltd*[6] line, says that if the defendant can show that the system used in manufacturing the goods was practically foolproof, there will be no liability. Whatever went wrong, it must have been nothing to do with the defendant. The other, the *Grant v Australian Knitting Mills* line, is that if the plaintiff can show that it is unlikely that anything that happened to the product after it left the manufacturers' control made it dangerous, the court should conclude that the defect must have arisen during manufacture. Furthermore, if the defendant's system is foolproof, the fact that a defect occurred shows that someone must have acted at least carelessly.

There is something to be said for both approaches. The *Daniels* approach is not popular even with judges,[7] but it does have the merit that since in

2   *Kubach v Hollands* [1937] 3 All ER 907.
3   Cf *Hurley v Dyke* [1979] RTR 265.
4   Cf the Canadian case *Good-Wear Treaders v D & B Holdings* (1979) 98 DLR (3d) 59.
5   See eg *Rimmer v Liverpool City Council* [1984] 1 All ER 930, *Targett v Torfaen Borough Council* [1992] 3 All ER 27.
6   [1938] 4 All ER 258.
7   See eg *Hill v James Crowe* [1978] 1 All ER 812, [1978] ICR 298, in which McKenna J disapproved of *Daniels* and refused to extend its influence into the related field of the liability of employers towards their employees for accidents at work.

many cases no one will know exactly what happened and why, it does make use of the best evidence available, that is the system the manufacturer used. The *Grant* approach has the paradoxical effect that the better the manufacturer's system of work, the more likely the manufacturer is to be found liable. The defendant's best chance is to show that it had a reasonable but not foolproof system which it operated reasonably.

On the other hand the *Grant* approach follows the commonsense intuition that if nothing went wrong after the product left the defendant's hands, something must have gone wrong while it was still in the defendant's control. It also draws on the argument that if a product is not up to the defendant's usual standards, there must have been something the defend–ant could have done about it. But there is an obvious counter-argument that as long as one accepts that there can be mistakes that are not negligent, it is not the case that the existence of a sub-standard item proves that someone must have been at fault.

On the whole, the *Daniels* approach seems more coherent. The excuse often given for the *Grant* approach was that it produced a form of strict liability. Since the effect of the 1987 Act is to reform products liability in the direction of a slightly more strict test, the reasons for clinging to *Grant* have disappeared.

Plaintiffs are in a slightly better position if they need to prove not that the defendant manufactured the product badly but that the defendant designed the product badly. Although they do not have the argument that the very fact that the product did not come up the manufacturer's own standards suggests that something has gone wrong, they have instead the examples of other products of a similar type. The defendant's own particular manufacturing processes may be difficult to reconstruct, but the design process is well known. Indeed, if the defendant consciously decides to accept a risk of causing serious injury or death to reduce costs, the court has a clearer choice than in cases in which it is not clear exactly what has happened or why.[8]

Design defects, of course, are likely to be more expensive to prevent than simple manufacturing errors. To build in an extra safety feature into the design entails extra costs on every unit, whereas simple manufacturing errors are one-offs prevented by paying more attention. But on the other hand, some errors caused by the manufacturing process, as opposed to simple human errors of judgment or attention, can also entail expensive changes affecting every unit made. Moreover, courts in some common law jurisdictions have been willing to say that failure to engage even in very expensive exercises in the recall of defective products, once the defectiveness of the design has become apparent, can be faulty if the risk of harm is more than trivial.[9]

8   See eg *Wyngrove v Scottish Omnibuses Ltd* 1966 SC (HL) 47; cf the *Ford Pinto* case, above ch 3.
9   Eg *Nicholson v John Deere* (1986) 34 DLR (4th) 542.

Employers' liability

In this section we look at the liability of employers for accidents to their employees. The treatment of this very important practical subject will be brief, since it is a specialist topic which lies beyond the scope of most introductory courses in tort. It is also an area in a state of transition while the consequences of the EC Framework Directive on Health and Safety[10] work their way through the legislative process. The Framework Directive aims to unify health and safety standards across the European Community. Its implementation requires the reworking of the whole of health and safety at work law. General regulations, the Management of Health and Safety at Work Regulations 1992,[11] set up procedures and lay down general principles of behaviour both for employers and employees. With one exception,[12] these regulations are not enforceable in the civil courts. There is also a mass of detailed regulation, first about matters that affect nearly all workers—workplaces, equipment, safety equipment[13]—and then regulations about increasingly detailed aspects of work or pieces of equipment.[14] These more detailed regulations will normally be enforceable in the civil courts.

For the moment, as these regulations are brought into effect, and new regulations made and old ones amended, it is not worth attempting to describe the statutory position in detail. The rest of this section will concentrate, therefore on the common law position, which will remain in the background of the new standards, and on the one general statute that remains, the Employers' Liability (Defective Equipment) Act 1969.

Common law

The common law liability of employers for accidents to their employees has three aspects—the contract of employment, vicarious liability for the torts of other employees and the personal duties of the employer. For the first, readers are referred to specialist works on employment law, for the second to chapter 14 below. We will here be concerned with the third aspect, the personal responsibilities of employers, beyond the specific requirements of contract, to protect their employees from accidents.

---

10 Council Directive 89/391. See generally I Smith, C Goddard and N Randall *Health And Safety: The New Legal Framework* (1993; London, Butterworths).
11 SI 1992/2051, amended by SI 1994 /2865.
12 Paragraph 13A(1).
13 Workplace (Health, Safety and Welfare) Regulations 1992 (SI 1992/3004), Provision and Use of Work Equipment Regulations 1992 (SI 1992/2932), Personal Protective Equipment at Work Regulations 1992 (SI 1992/2966) amended by SI 1993/3074,.
14 Manual Handling Regulations 1992 (SI 1992/2793), Health and Safety (Display Screen Equipment) Regulations 1992 (SI 1992/2792), Control of Substances Hazardous to Health (Amendment) Regulations 1992 (SI 1992/2382 and 2966), and Control of Asbestos at Work Regulations 1992 (SI 1992/3068).

It is worth noting how such an odd category of legal obligation developed. After all, a 'personal' duty is not what one might expect employers, most of whom are companies not people, to have. And a tort obligation sitting alongside a contract on which the whole relationship between the parties rests is usually the kind of arrangement the law tries to avoid.

The origin of the personal duties lies in three doctrines of the nineteenth century that excluded employees' accident cases almost entirely from the civil courts. The doctrine of common employment (otherwise known as the 'fellow servant' rule) began with Lord Abinger's much misunderstood judgment in *Priestley v Fowler*.[15] It claimed that employees impliedly contracted not to sue their employer for risks arising from their employment, including the negligence of other employees. Lord Abinger only said that he did not see why the master of a household should be liable for a coach accident caused by one of his servants that harmed another servant when the master knew nothing about driving coaches but the coach driver did. In other words, he was questioning the idea of vicarious liability when the employer knew absolutely nothing of the employee's job, a thought that arises periodically in vicarious liability cases before being pushed down again.[16] But the second doctrine, volenti non fit injuria, the defence of consent, intermingled itself with Lord Abinger's remarks and the idea of the contract of employment as a bargain and produced an almost impregnable barrier to liability. For those cases that might have got through these defences, there was always contributory negligence, then a complete defence, to mop up.

To counter these doctrines, other courts developed techniques through the use of which employees could nevertheless win actions against their employers for accidents at work. One such, discussed in the last chapter was the development of breach of statutory duty as a separate tort. But the main technique was the 'personal' duties of the employer in tort, building on Lord Abinger's comment in *Priestley v Fowler* that '[The master] is no doubt bound to provide for the safety of his servant in the course of his employment, to the best of his judgment, information and belief.' These duties escaped the clutches of the common employment rule because they were not obligations of fellow servants and they were nothing to do with the contract of employment. Volenti also did not apply for similar reasons, leaving only contributory negligence, which by itself was not so much of a barrier.

The common employment doctrine itself was abolished by the Law Reform (Personal Injuries) Act 1948, but by then there was already a fully working system 'personal' duties, so that the abolition was little more than an exercise in tidying up.[17] The locus classicus of the employers' liabilities

---

15 (1837) 3 M & W 1.

16 Cf Byles J in *Clarke v Holmes* (1862) 7 H & N 937, 'If a master's personal knowledge of defects in his machinery be necessary to his liability, the more a master neglects his business and abandons it to others the less he will be liable.'.

17 Note that, however, now that the threat of common employment has gone, there is a growing tendency to treat the employers' common law duties about safety as contractual duties (derived from implied terms) rather than tort duties—see *Johnstone v Bloomsbury Health Authority* [1992] QB 333 and now *Morris v Breaveglen Ltd (t / a Anzac Construction Co)* [1993] ICR 766, [1993] IRLR 350.

was *Wilsons and Clyde Coal Co v English*.[18] The plaintiff was injured while working at the defendant's coal mine. He was crushed by haulage mach–inery as he was travelling through the pit at the end of a shift. The haulage equipment should have been turned off during travelling time. The defendant employer's case was that they had effectively fulfilled any duty that they were subject to by employing a competent and qualified manager, as they were obliged to do by the Coal Mines Act 1911. The House of Lords, on appeal from the Court of Session, found for the employee. Lord Wright said:

> '[The employers'] obligation is fulfilled by the exercise of due care and skill. But it is not fulfilled by entrusting its fulfilment to employees, even though selected with due care and skill. The obligation is threefold, "the provision of a competent staff of men, adequate material and a proper system and effective supervision".'

To Lord Wright's list one should add, although there is an obvious overlap with occupiers' liability, the provision of a safe place of work.

Lord Wright went on to distinguish between a breach of these 'personal' obligations and 'casual negligence' of the managers, foremen or other employees, although he admitted that it would be difficult often to tell which was which.

Note that the sense of a 'personal' obligation, which sits ill in a case where a corporate employer can only act through human agents, means precisely that the obligation 'is not fulfilled by entrusting its fulfilment to employees' or indeed to anyone else. It is a 'non-delegable' duty[19] but not because it cannot be delegated, for all the duties of companies have to be delegated, and in *Wilsons and Clyde Coal* there was even a statute telling the company how and to what sort of person it should delegate, but because delegation in itself to a competent person does not discharge the obligation. In fact, 'non-delegable' usually means that the employer is responsible for the mistakes of others whether the others are employees, independent contractors or anyone else. But, as Lord Wright says, the obligation is fulfilled by the exercise of due care and skill. 'Personal' or 'non-delegable' does not mean 'strict'. As long as everyone who affects the employee's safety acts reasonably, there is no liability, even if the employee is injured.

Competent fellow workers

In the days of the common employment rule, the obligation to provide safe fellow employees was central. It undermined the common employment doctrine's central point, that there could be no liability for the negligent acts of other employees. Its utility in the post-common employment era is

18 [1938] AC 57.
19 See below ch 14.

to provide another possible route for liability when vicarious liability fails to work, for example where the other employee has harmed a fellow employee intentionally and the court holds that the employee's tort was not in the course of employment.[20]

In order to prove a breach of the duty, it is insufficient, however, to show that the employee was unsafe or incompetent on the one occasion of the accident. The plaintiff has to show that the employer should not have hired the person in the first place or that there was a course of conduct which the employer should have noticed was incompetent or unsafe and which called for action, action which may include dismissal although not it does not have to.[1]

Safe place of work

Most of the rules here are no different from the general rules of occupiers' liability and require no further comment. Note however, that the employer is in principle responsible for the safety of the workplace even when the employee is working off-site.[2] The standard of reasonable care, however, applies in the normal way, and the employer need not bring the business to a halt by carefully inspecting every site before sending employees to them. If the information about the particular dangers of a site is easily available, however, for example when the site has been used on previous occasions, the employer may be liable unless it takes reasonable steps to eliminate the risks.[3]

The other point of some divergence between straightforward occupiers' liability and employers' liability is that consent, warnings and notice are less likely to be effective arguments for the defence in employers' liability cases for the obvious reason that because of the contractual relationship and the fear of dismissal, employees are not entirely free to refuse their employer's requests.[4]

Safe equipment and materials

The common law liability here is again simply for lack of reasonable care. There is no need for the employer to use the latest materials and tools, only reasonable materials and tools given the risks.[5] Statute, however,

---

20 Eg *Hudson v Ridge Manufacturing* [1957] 2 QB 348. See below ch 14.
1 *Hudson* above; cf *Smith v Crossley Bros* (1951) 95 Sol Jo 655, *General Cleaning Co v Christmas* [1953] AC 180.
2 *Wilson v Tyneside Window Cleaning Co* [1958] 2 QB 110.
3 Ibid.
4 *McCafferty v Metropolitan Police District Receiver* [1977] 1 WLR 1073, cf *Smith v Austin Lifts* [1959] 1 WLR 100.
5 *Toronto Power Co v Paskwan* [1915] AC 734.

looms large here in the form of the Employers' Liability (Defective Equipment) Act 1969.

The problem the 1969 Act set out to solve was raised by the House of Lords in *Davie v New Merton Board Mills*.[6] A particle of metal chipped off a chisel (technically a 'drift') the plaintiff was using and hit him in the eye. The plaintiff's employers had bought the chisel from reputable suppliers, who in turn had bought a consignment of them from the makers. They had appeared to be in good condition when they were sold. But after the accident, a metallurgical analysis revealed that the metal of which the chisel was made was too hard, and the fault was traced to the negligence of the manufacturers.

The House of Lords decided that since the tool was, to all appearances, in good condition, the employers had discharged their duty by buying from a reputable supplier. The defect was not discoverable by reasonable inspection. But the crucial question was whether the employer should be held responsible, as part of the personal duty, for the manufacturer's fault. The House of Lords held that the personal duty did not stretch that far. Purely commercial transactions of buying and selling could not amount to 'delegating' the employer's duties.

The plaintiff succeeded, however, against the manufacturer, but there was a clear risk that there would be cases in which it would prove impossible or pointless to sue the manufacturer.

The eventual legislative response was the 1969 Act. Section 1 of the 1969 Act provides:

> 'Where after the commencement of this Act
> (a) an employee suffers personal injury in the course of his employment in consequence of a defect in equipment provided by his employer for the purposes of the employer's business; and
> (b) the defect is attributable wholly or partly to the fault of a third party (whether identified or not),
> the injury shall be deemed to be also attributable to negligence on the part of the employer...'

Notice that the effect of the Act is only to make employers vicariously liable for the fault of manufacturers or other third parties. It does not make it any easier to prove fault against manufacturers. Contributory negligence is a defence in the normal way, but any agreement to exclude or limit liability is void.

The main problem to arise in the case law about the 1969 Act is what counts as 'equipment'. In *Coltman v Bibby*[7] the House of Lords decided that a ship could count as equipment. The ship in question, *The Derbyshire*, had sunk with all hands. One of the allegations was that the shipbuilders had been negligent in both design and construction. The courts were asked

6   [1959] AC 604.
7   [1988] AC 276.

whether, if that allegation were proved, the employers would be liable under the Act. The Court of Appeal said that the word 'equipment' meant something ancillary to the employees' work and not something that amounted to the workplace itself. The House of Lords disagreed. The Act itself mentions vehicles and aircraft and it was not much of a leap to include ships.

At the other end of the scale, in *Knowles v Liverpool City Council*[8] the House of Lords had to decide whether a flagstone should count as equipment. The plaintiff was employed by the appellant as a labourer. He injured his finger when a flagstone he was handling broke. The flagstone was unusually weak because of a manufacturing defect. The defendant said that the flagstone was not 'equipment' because it was not a tool but just part of the employer's stock in trade. But the House of Lords decided that the 1969 Act should be interpreted widely and 'equipment' included everything of whatever kind used by the employer for the purposes of his business.

The 1969 Act has not been particularly successful simply because it did nothing to reduce the plaintiff's difficulties in proving fault. But, possibly unintentionally, the situation has been changed by the Consumer Protection Act 1987. The 1969 Act defines 'fault' as including 'breach of statutory duty or other act or omission which gives rise to liability in tort'. As long as one accepts that liability under the Consumer Protection Act is 'tort' liability, any liability arising under that Act counts as fault under the 1969 Act. This means that the test for whether equipment is defective under the 1969 Act is now effectively the same as the test for defectiveness under the Consumer Protection Act, namely whether the safety of the product was not such as persons generally are entitled to expect. Whatever the difficulties of the test for defect,[9] it may well be easier for employees to prove that the tool was defective than that the manufacturer was negligent.

Effective supervision and a safe system of work

The duty to provide a safe system of work, including effective supervision is the most flexible of the *Wilsons and Clyde Coal* categories and the reason why, although there is no restriction on expanding the categories of the duty, no need to do so has arisen. The employer must both devise a safe system of work and then, through effective supervision, make sure that the system operates in practice.[10] This means that merely issuing instructions without following them up will often not be enough for the employer to escape liability.[11] On the other hand, a reasonable employer does take into account the experience and trustworthiness of the employees in

8   [1993] 4 All ER 321, [1993] 1 WLR 1428, 91 LGR 629, [1994] 1 Lloyd's Rep 11, [1994] ICR 243, [1993] IRLR 588.
9   See above.
10 Lord Reid in *General Cleaning Contractors v Christmas* [1953] AC 180.
11 *Thompson v Smiths Ship Repairers* [1984] QB 405.

question,[12] and the courts ought to take into account the costs of excessive supervision not just in monetary terms but in terms of stifling initiative and spreading distrust. With inexperienced or inattentive employees, however, the employers' duty may begin to approach a duty to make sure that employees follow safety regulations.[13]

12 *Baker v T Clarke* [1992] PIQR P262.
13 *Boyle v Kodak* [1969] 1 WLR 661

Chapter 9

Intentional torts—
(1) physical interference

The purpose of this chapter is to look at the protection in tort of physical interests from intentional harm. It is usually said the torts protecting such interests do not follow a unified theory and that they still await their *Donoghue v Stevenson* to rationalise them into a single theoretical whole. But as we shall see, all the material necessary to construct a general tort is already in place. For the time being, however, we shall keep to the traditional classification of these torts as separate causes of action. The torts dealt with are trespass to land, trespass to goods, assault and battery and false imprisonment.

Trespass to land

The two fundamental torts dealing with intentional interference with physical interest are trepass to land and trespass to the person (that is, assault and battery and false imprisonment). We begin with trespass to land.

To have one's property invaded and occupied by another is not only, as one might think, an interference with one's property rights, it is also a threat to one's privacy, peace of mind and, in extreme cases, one's rights to freedom of conscience and to the fulfillment of one's basic need for shelter. It is not surprising, therefore, that some of the cases that establish the tort in its modern form are in reality civil liberties cases. In *Entick v Carrington*[1] for example, the defendants, purporting to act in accordance with a warrant issued not by a judge but by a government minister, entered the plaintiff's property in order to seize both the plaintiff and his books and papers, which included pamphlets the government objected to. They stayed on the plaintiff's property for several hours before bundling the plaintiff and his papers off to the minister's law-clerk. The plaintiff later sued for trespass. The defendants claimed that they were protected by the warrant from the minister. In the Court of Common Pleas, Lord Camden

1   (1765) 19 State Tr 1029.

LCJ declared the warrants illegal and allowed to stand the jury's award of massive damages. In the course of his judgment he said:

> 'The great end for which men entered society was to secure their property. That right is preserved sacred and incommunicable in all instances ... By the laws of England, every invasion of private property, be it ever so minute, is a trespass. No man can set foot upon my ground without my licence, but he is liable to an action.'

But the tort does also protect property from other private individuals who may be in great need of shelter themselves. In *Southwark London Borough Council v Williams* homeless people decided to squat in empty property belonging to the plaintiff local authority. The defendants said that they had a defence of necessity, that they had no alternative but to try to get shelter for themselves in some way. But this defence of private necessity met with the same stern response as the state's plea of necessity in *Entick v Carrington*. Lord Denning said:

> 'If homelessness were once admitted as a defence to trespass, no one's house could be safe. Necessity would open a door which no man could shut. It would not only be those in extreme need who would enter. There would be others who would imagine that they were in need, or would invent a need, so as to gain entry. Each man would say that his need was greater than the next man's ... [The courts] must refuse to admit the plea of necessity to the hungry and the homeless; and trust that their distress will be relieved by the charitable and the good.'

Trespass to land both protects the citizen from the state and protects those who have from those who have not.

Intention

In most cases of trespass to land, the defendant knows what he is doing or at least suspects as much. As in nuisance, even if the defendant starts out not knowing about the plaintiff's claim of right, he soon finds out. And yet there are two kinds of case in which the intention or otherwise of the defendant may become relevant: first, in cases of temporary trespass where the plaintiff's aim is not to get rid of the trespasser but to obtain compensation for the damage caused when they were on the land; and secondly, where the defendant says that there is no trespass because the defendant's right to occupy the land is better than the plaintiff's right.

In the second type of case, the trespass action is often being used as a land law action, as a simple way to find out who has what rights to the land. This cannot be done if all the parties can simply say that they honestly believe theirs to be the better right. And so the courts have often expressed the view that lack of the intention to trespass is not relevant.[2] All that is necessary is that the defendant acted consciously in entering the disputed land.[3] But, in cases where no question of an assertion of a superior right arises, and the plaintiff simply seeks compensation for damage done and, perhaps, an injunction against future incursions, courts may say that there is no trespass without fault of some kind by the defendant. Thus in *League Against Cruel Sports v Scott*[4] the plaintiffs complained of trespass by the defendants' staghounds in the course of hunting (to which, of course, the plaintiffs objected) Park J thought that the owner of the hounds could only be liable if he had intended them to trespass or was careless in allowing them to trespass.

One formal way to reconcile the cases is to say that trespass in person requires only that the conduct be voluntary, but trespass through an object or an animal requires fault. But that would be to look only at the surface of the cases. A better underlying distinction would be that trespass accompanied by a claim of right or justification needs only to be conscious, but in other forms of trespass there has to be intention to violate the plaintiff's rights or at least reckless disregard of those rights. Negligence, despite *League Against Cruel Sports*, should not be enough, but should be left to the tort of negligence itself to deal with.

Interference

As *League Against Cruel Sports* shows, one can trespass in different ways— not just by stepping on someone else's land, but also by putting objects on or even against someone else's land. 'If a single stone had been put against the wall it would have been sufficient.'[5] As we shall see, there is no trespass if the defendant has permission, but if that permission is withdrawn, or if the defendant acts beyond the scope of the permission, the defendant's continuing presence is a trespass.[6] The same rule applies to objects.[7] If I leave a pile of bricks on your land with your permission, the bricks become trespassory if you withdraw your permission and ask me to take them away.

It is also trepass to dig a tunnel at any depth under my land[8] or to project anything over it, no matter how trivial the crossing of the boundary.[9]

2 *Conway v Wimpey* [1951] 2 KB 266.
3 The classic cases are the Civil War pair *Smith v Stone* (1647) Sty 65 —defendant thrown onto plaintiff's land—not liable in trespass; *Gilbert v Stone* (1647) Sty 72—defendant forced at sword point to enter plaintiff's land—liable in trespass since still the defendant's act though coerced.
4 [1986] QB 240, [1985] 2 All ER 489.
5 *Gregory v Piper* (1829) 9 B & C 591.
6 *Hillen v ICI* [1936] AC 65.
7 *Konskier v Goodman* [1928] 1 KB 421.
8 *Bulli Coal Mining v Osborne* [1899] AC 351.
9 *Kelsen v Imperial Tobacco* [1957] 2 QB 334.

This latter rule means that it is often impossible to carry out major building work in crowded city centres without committing trespass against surrounding occupiers, since the builders' scaffolding and cranes will almost inevitably project over neighbouring land.[10] The occupiers' right, however, does not extend into outer space, and it is not a trespass to fly an aeroplane over someone's land, at least as long as the flight takes place above 'such height as is necessary for the ordinary use and enjoyment of [the plaintiff's] land and the structures on it'.[11] This principle does not, however, rule out nuisance actions. In addition section 76(2) of the Civil Aviation Act 1982 provides that the owner of an aircraft is liable without proof of fault for any damage caused by anything falling off or out of the aircraft. There is no liability if the plaintiff contributed to causing the loss by his own fault. Presumably if the defence is established, the common law position comes back into operation and the plaintiff can sue the owner for ordinary negligence. Otherwise the aircraft owner would be in a better position than at common law in one crucial respect—that contributory negligence would be a complete defence to all claims.

As usual there are anomalous rules about highways. According to the common law view, although the highway is dedicated to public use the 'subsoil' of the highway still belongs to the owners of the land adjoining the highway. Since one can commit a trespass by behaving in a way other than that for which one has permission, the courts have said that it can be a trespass against adjoining owners to use the highway for an improper purpose. Since the only proper purposes recognised by the courts for the use of the highway are 'passing and repassing', that is travelling, this doctrine threatens to make actionable a large number of otherwise unobjectionable activities, especially the activities of protestors. For example, in 1893 the activities of an early hunt saboteur in disrupting a grouse shoot by waving his umbrella at the birds from the highway were said to be a trespass because they were not a proper use of the highway.[12] Similarly in *Hickman v Maisey*[13] the Court of Appeal declared to be a trespass the activities of gatherers of intelligence about race horses who gathered on the highway near to the plaintiff's training gallops for the purpose of spying on the horses. This means, for example, that it is possible for picketing other than at one's own place of work as authorised by section 220 of the Trade Union and Labour Relations (Consolidation) Act 1992 to be actionable by the occupiers of the land adjoining the highway. There is no good reason for the existence of this doctrine. The highway should be regarded as a public space, not private property. The interests of landowners

---

10 Eg *Woollerton and Wilson v Richard Costain* [1970] 1 WLR 411, *Charrington v Simons* [1971] 1 WLR 598, *John Trenberth Ltd v National Westminster Bank Ltd* (1979) 39 P & CR 104, *Patel v W H Smith (Eziot) Ltd* [1987] 2 All ER 569, [1987] 1 WLR 853, *Anchor Brewhouse v Berkley House* (1987) 2 EGLR 173, 38 BLR 82. These cases produce interesting problems about remedies. See below.

11 Griffiths J in *Bernstein v Skyviews* [1978] QB 479. See also Civil Aviation Act 1982 s 76(1).

12 *Harrison v Duke of Rutland* [1893] 1 QB 142.

13 [1900] 1 QB 752.

are adequately protected by the law of nuisance. Perhaps the rule should be that there has to be trespass to the subsoil itself, that is for example by digging through it, before the adjoining owners can sue.

Note that section 263 of the Highways Act 1980 vests 'every highway maintainable at public expense' in the highway authority—that is, for most of England, the county council. The consequence of this section is probably that the highway authority also has standing to sue for trespass at least for activities that interfere with the exercise of its duties to maintain the highway. One might hope that it might also one day be interpreted as meaning that adjoining owners no longer have rights over the subsoil of the highway, so bringing down this entire absurd edifice. But unfortunately the orthodox interpretation of section 263 at the moment is that it vests in the highway authority only so much of the subsoil that the highway authority needs to maintain the road and beneath that lies still the realm of the adjoining owners.[14]

We should mention yet one more old doctrine, namely 'trespass ab initio'. If someone becomes a trespasser by abusing or exceeding his permission, the normal rule is that one becomes a trespasser at that point. But if one entered by authority of law (as opposed to by the permission of the occupier) and after a delay starts to take positive actions[15] that exceed or abuse that authority, the trespass counts as having started as soon as the defendant entered the property. It is, so to speak backdated to the start of the defendant's visit—hence 'ab initio'.

The point of this apparent mumbo-jumbo is to be found in the civil liberties function of trespass. It means that if, for example, the police exceed or abuse the powers given to them in a search warrant, the illegality of their search is backdated to the time of their entry, so making the whole search unlawful, not just the portion of it subsequent to the abusive or excessive acts.

Lord Denning criticised the whole doctrine in obiter dicta in *Chic Fashions (West Wales) v Jones*[16]. He said that it was unfair to backdate any form of illegality. But the usefulness of the doctrine in helping to restrain abuse of power by state officials justifies its continued existence.

Licence, authority and necessity

As mentioned already, it is a defence to trespass that the defendant had the plaintiff's consent or 'licence' to be on the land. But the court will assume unless the parties have expressed the contrary that the defendant's

---

14 See eg *R v Secretary of State for the Environment, ex p Perko* Queen's Bench Division (Crown Office List) 11 May 1994 (LEXIS transcript), *Sussex Investments v Jackson* (1993) Times, 29 July, CA.

15 Omissions do not count. See eg the *Six Carpenters' Case* (1610) 8 Co Rep 146a (not paying for drinks and a meal in an inn not 'trespass ab initio').

16 [1968] 2 QB 299. This did not, however, prevent Lord Denning using the doctrine himself in *Cinnamond v British Airports Authority* [1980] 1 WLR 582.

licence is limited to reasonable purposes. As one judge (who had obviously never organised a children's party) once said, 'where you invite a person into your house to use the stairs, you do not invite him to slide down the bannisters.'[17]

The law presumes that you give permission to people to walk up to your front door and knock on it.[18] The presumption can probably be excluded by putting a prominent enough notice at the boundary of your property saying that nobody is welcome, but the scope of notices that say 'No hawkers, No canvassers' may be open to question, since, for example, charity collectors, religious missionaries and political canvassers might reasonably assume that the notice referred only to commercial callers whereas the householder might have imagined that it meant every type of caller.[19]

People who enter on 'bare' licences, that is without any contractual agreement about the terms of their entry and without any other authority, may have their permission to remain revoked at any time. If that happens, they become trespassers if they refuse to leave or if they fail to leave within a reasonable time.[20]

The position of people who are on the property because of a contract they have with the occupier is often scarcely better than that of bare licensees, since even if they can later sue for breach of contract for the withdrawal of their permission, the revocation is nevertheless usually legally effective and they must leave within a reasonable time or become trespassers.[1] Sometimes however, depending on the intentions of the parties, the licence may count as an 'irrevocable' licence. Licences for specific purposes of definite duration are more likely to be interpreted as intended to be irrevocable than more vague or general licences. For example, in *Winter Garden Theatre (London) Ltd v Millenium Productions Ltd*[2] Viscount Simon said:

> '... a third variant of a licence for value... occurs, as in the sale of a ticket to enter premises and witness a particular event, such as a ticket for a seat at a particular performance at a theatre or for entering private ground to witness a day's sport. In this last class of case, the implication of the arrangement, however it may be classified in law, plainly is that the ticket entitles the purchaser to enter and, if he behaves himself, to remain on the premises until the end of the event which he has paid his money to witness.'

In this sort of case, the occupier has no legal power to remove the visitor except in the circumstances specified in the contract, and an attempt to do so by force may amount to an assault.

17 *The Carlgarth* [1927] P 93.
18 *Dunster v Abbott* [1954] 1 WLR 58.
19 Cf *Christian v Johannesson* [1956] NZLR 664 and *Snook v Mannion* [1982] Crim LR 601.
20 *Robson v Hallett* [1967] 2 QB 939.
1 *Kerrison v Smith* [1897] 2 QB 445. This situation is a good example of a power with duty not to exercise it. See WN Hohfeld *Fundamental Legal Conceptions* (New Haven, Yale University Press, 1964).
2 [1948] AC 173, [1947] 2 All ER 331.

Other than licensees, a number of other people may have authority to enter other people's land. Laying to one side people with private rights of access, such as those who have rights of way, the most important group are the police and other public officers who have such powers either at common law, for example the authority to enter a property in order to prevent a breach of the peace, or from warrants issued under statute, for example under the Police and Criminal Evidence Act 1984 sections 16-18. Errors in the way such warrants are obtained and exceeding their terms may make the entry an unlawful trespass.

The other defence that deserves mention is that of necessity. We have already seen that in *Southwark London Borough Council v Williams* the Court of Appeal refused to allow homelessness to underpin a defence of necessity, and it is also seems clear from cases such as *Woollerton* and *John Trenberth* there is no defence of necessity where one cannot make repairs to one's property without overhanging one's neighbours' property, even to prevent danger. But a defence of necessity did succeed in *Rigby v Chief Constable of Northamptonshire*,[3] where the police fired a CS gas canister into the plaintiff's gunsmith's shop to try to force out a dangerously psychopathic gunman who was holed up there, with the result that the building burned down. Although the police lost the case on negligence, they succeeded on trespass.

Who can sue

Trespass protects, above all, possession of land rather than ownership. Possession means physical control of the property on one's own behalf (that is not as an agent for someone else) combined with the intention to 'exclude the world at large from interfering'[4] with the land. This means that even someone in possession of the land under a defective title or even under no title at all can sue for trespass those who challenge his possession.[5] Trespassers cannot defend themeselves by saying that the plaintiff has no right to be in possession in the first place. That is, there is no defence of 'jus tertii'. Even trespassers themselves can get possession if the previous person in possession acquiesces in their expulsion and delays trying to get back in.[6]

The possessor's right prevails against everyone except someone with a better entitlement themselves, the owner with an immediate right to take possession, for example.[7] An owner with a right to immediate possession and intending to regain it can sue. It is then up to the defendant to show that his right to occupy the land is consistent with the plaintiff's ownership (for example that he is a tenant).[8] If the owner has a right to immediate

---

3   [1985] 1 WLR 1242.
4   F Pollock and R Wright *An Essay on Possession in the Common Law* (Oxford 1888).
5   *Graham v Peat* (1801) 1 East 244.
6   *Browne v Dawson* (1840) 12 Ad & El 624.
7   *Delaney v Smith* [1946] KB 393.
8   *Portland Developments v Harte* [1977] QB 306.

possession and does indeed enter the land to exercise that right, the owner is deemed to have had possession since he acquired the right to immediate possession and thus is able to sue anyone who has been on the land unlawfully in the meantime. This legal fiction is known as 'trespass by relation.'

But owners who are out of possession are not otherwise protected. If someone trespasses on land that you have leased to me, only I have the right to sue for trespass, not you.

Remedies

Trespass to land is actionable per se, that is the plaintiff can succeed even though no particular injury can be proved. Nevertheless, plaintiffs may obtain compensation for any actual damage caused to their property by the defendant. Even where the defendant caused no actual damage, compensation will still be payable for unauthorised use of the property, as measured by the letting value of the land. Where the plaintiff did not have possession but regained it and sues for trespass by relation, the damages for unauthorised use are known as 'mesne profits'.

A recent example of an action for damages for unauthorised use is *Ministry of Defence v Ashman*.[9] The second defendant was a Flight Sergeant in the Royal Air Force and the first defendant was his wife. After they separated she stayed on in the married quarters which they had occupied together. The property was owned by the Ministry of Defence. On going into occupation, the second defendant had signed a document saying, first, that he was entitled to occupy the property only so long as he remained a serving member of the Royal Air Force, and secondly, that his family would have to leave the accommodation if he ceased to live with his spouse. But when the couple separated, the wife and children, having nowhere else to go, stayed on in the property, even after being served with a notice to quit. The plaintiffs obtained a possession order, and, after some difficulty, Mrs Ashman was offered accommodation by the local district council whereupon she and her family moved out.

The question, however, was what was the proper measure of damages? The Court of Appeal knew that, according to *Swordheath Properties v Tabet*,[10] the landlord was entitled to recover 'the proper letting value of the property' for the relevant period. In the ordinary case this meant the value to the trespassers of its use, that is the market rent for the property that they would otherwise have had to pay. But in this case, the property was not normally let on the open market, and the trespasser only remained in possession because she was in no position to move anywhere else. The Court of Appeal faced three options. The plaintiffs said that the measure of damages should be the market rent, but the problem with that was that

9   (1993) 66 P & CR 195, [1993] 40 EG 144, 25 HLR 513.
10   [1979] 1 WLR 285.

all the evidence was that if the plaintiffs had regained possession they would have again let it to an RAF family at a subsidised rate. The second option was to set damages at what the court thought the plaintiff had lost, namely the heavily subsidised rent at which such properties were let to service families. The difficulties with that course were (1) that in other cases the courts had said that there was no need for the plaintiff to show that it intended to let the property at all, so that actual loss was not relevant, and (2) that Mrs Ashman, who was not entitled to be there, could not have obtained an alternative suitable property for such a low rent, and so would be making a profit out of committing the tort. The third option was to measure the damages not by what the plaintiff lost but what the defendant gained. In this case, the defendant had gained the amount of rent she would have had to have paid for the least expensive suitable alternative accommodation. (The Court of Appeal assumed that this would have been the rent for a three-bedroomed council house—but since there was evidence that at the time she could not have been allocated such a house it is not clear that this is correct. The correct amount on this measure should have been the amount of rent, less housing benefit, that she would have had to pay on the open market.) The snag with the third option is that it is plainly a restitutory remedy; that is the plaintiff is getting what the defendant gained from using the property without authorisation not what the plaintiff lost. Restitutory damages are possible in tort, especially in the guise of exemplary damages,[11] but the orthodox view is still that a plaintiff has to choose between suing in tort and suing in restitution, the so-called 'waiver of tort' doctrine.[12] Furthermore, a well-known, though much criticised, nineteenth century case, *Phillips v Homfray*,[13] holds that restitutory remedies are not available in trespass to land.

One judge in the Court of Appeal, Lloyd LJ, held out for the orthodox view. Tort damages were about loss to the plaintiff, not gains to the defendant. The actual loss to the plaintiff was probably the rent they would have obtained from another service family. The plaintiff cannot claim restitutory damages because of *Phillips v Homfray*.

But only Lloyd LJ took the orthodox view. Hoffman LJ goes for the third, restitutory option, and does so by simply ignoring *Phillips v Homfray*. Hoffman LJ says:

'It is true that in the earlier cases it has not been expressly stated that a claim for mesne profit for trespass can be a claim for restitution. Nowadays I do not see why we should not call a spade a spade. In this case the Ministry of Defence elected for the restitutionary remedy. It adduced no evidence of what it would have done with the house if the Ashmans had vacated. In my

---

11 See below ch 13.
12 See Birks 'Civil Wrongs, A New World' in *Butterworth Lectures 1990-91* for justified criticism of the old doctrines and the artificial boundary between 'tort' and 'restitution'.
13 (1883) 24 Ch D 439. Cf the remarkable US case *Edwards v Lee's Administrators* 96 SW 2d 1028 (1936).

judgment such matters are irrelevant to a restitution claim. All that matters is the value of benefit which the defendant has received.'

The third judge, Kennedy LJ, also opts for the third, restitutory, option, but instead of saying that the plaintiff had opted for restitution and should, *Phillips v Homfray* notwithstanding, receive just that, he says that it just so happens that the correct measure of damages in trespass to land is the benefit obtained by the defendant. The plaintiff receives, according to Kennedy LJ, a remedy which is 'somewhat analogous' to restitution.

Although Hoffman LJ's approach appears at first sight to be the more revolutionary of the two majority judgments, it is Kennedy LJ's judgment that is the most far-reaching in its implications. Hoffman LJ maintains the orthodox view that the plaintiff has to elect between tort damages and restitutory damages. The effect of such a choice may be that if there has been damage to the property, the plaintiff may sue either for compensation for that damage or for the benefit to the defendant but not both. Kennedy LJ's view, on the other hand, allows for the accumulation of damages, with compensation for actual injury added to recovery of the benefit to the defendant. Kennedy LJ's judgment threatens completely to break down the wall between tort and restitution.

Damages, however, are not the usual remedy for trespass to land. As in nuisance, plaintiffs usually want not compensation but instead for the violation of their rights to stop—in other words, plaintiffs want an injunction.

The fundamental rule that the English courts follow in trespass, just as they do in nuisance, is that if the plaintiff establishes that the defendant is committing the tort, the plaintiff is entitled to an injunction no matter how trivial the incursion and how inconvenient for the defendants. Any other rule, the courts believe, would amount to authorising an expropriation of the plaintiff's property.

The most striking application of the principle that plaintiffs are entitled to injunctions is in the overhanging crane and scaffolding cases. In *Anchor Brewhouse v Berkley House*,[14] for example, where the plaintiffs complained about overhanging cranes from the building of the Docklands development, the plaintiffs' case, except in one minor respect, was not based on any actual or apprehended damage to their respective proprietary interests. The plaintiffs sought injunctions simply because they were owners of their properties and that trespass had been committed and was threatened to be continued. The defendant, after losing on whether overhanging cranes that caused no damage were a trespass at all, argued that it ought not to be subjected to injunctions restraining the use of the cranes, (1) because they were doing no actual damage to the plaintiffs and (2) because their use was virtually essential for the commercial development of the site. The defendant said that the plaintiffs should be left to a damages remedy. The court disagreed and granted the injunctions. Scott J said that the cases had established beyond doubt that:

14 (1987) 2 EGLR 173, 38 BLR 82.

'The ownership of property entitled the owner to license or refuse to license the use of it by others. If he is asked to license the use of it by others, he can charge whatever he chooses for the licence. The law will recognise and protect the monopoly that his ownership carries with it.'

Walton J in *John Trenberth Ltd v National Westminster Bank Ltd*,[15] a case about overhanging scaffolding, said, along the same lines:

'[I]t is perfectly clear that the actual damage, apart from any question of aggravation, caused by the mere trespass, both by oversailing the front of the plaintiffs' property and by actually resting upon the rear of the plaintiffs' property, is comparatively slight; so slight that if an action were brought for it, it would hardly command the smallest coin the the realm. But so far from that being a reason why an injunction should not be granted, it has been said in many of the cases to which Mr Munby drew my attention that the fact that any damage would be trifling is the very reason why an injunction should be granted. People are not to infringe the property rights of others and then say, "And I am entitled to go on doing it because I am really doing you no tangible harm, and fivepence will amply compensate you for that harm".'

Scott J in *Anchor Brewhouse* did, however, express dissatisfaction with the rule, the philosophy behind which he called 'a robust Victorian approach which might, perhaps, find less sympathy now' and went on to say:

'It would in many respects be convenient if the court had power, in order to enable property developments to be expeditiously and economically completed, to allow, on proper commercial terms, some use to be made by the developers of the land of neighbours.'

Whether this is a good idea depends on the same considerations as those discussed below about whether the court should ever order damages without an injunction in nuisance. Considerations of economic efficiency point in the direction of not doing so and of letting the parties settle the price of any necessary permissions between themselves, but considerations of fairness point in the opposite direction. Certainly in situations such as that in *Anchor Brewhouse* and *John Trenberth,* where there is no real inconvenience either short or long term for the plaintiff, it is likely that the developer puts a higher value on the entitlement than the neighbours. But the problem is that there are no obvious obstructions to bargaining between the parties. They all know who one another are and any agreement they might make is fairly easy to monitor and enforce. The only possibility is that one of the neighbours may seriously over–estimate the profits the development offers the developer and may overplay its hand in a 'holdout'. But where all the neighbours are bargaining for pure gains—there are no

15   (1979) 39 P & CR 104.

inconveniences for them for which they are seeking compensation, it is unlikely that any such holdout would take place. And it is even more unlikely any judicial process would save time compared with negotiations. Any case for intervention therefore has to depend on arguments about the distribution of wealth between the parties, but there are no reasons to believe that developers will always be richer than neighbours or that neighbours will always be richer than developers.

Although, contrary to Scott J's view, there is probably no reason for general change, there may, however, be individual cases which should go the other way, cases in which, for example, there is evidence of a serious barrier to bargaining or, perhaps, evidence of a holdout by a person who is plainly insane. The technique that is available to the courts in such situations is to suspend the injunction. In *Woollerton and Wilson v Costain*,[16] Stamp J decided to suspend an injunction in a straightforward crane case, and was rightly criticised in later cases for doing so.[17] But where there truly are special circumstances, suspension may be justified, although only if accompanied by damages.

Trespass to goods

In *Entick v Carrington* the agents of the Secretary of State also interfered with the plaintiff's papers and books. This amounted to the tort of trespass to goods, a parallel tort to trespass to land, whose civil liberties function, although now fallen somewhat into disuse, is to protect the citizen from unwarranted search and seizure.[18]

Trespass to goods, now governed by the Torts (Interference with Goods) Act 1977 and one of the torts now known collectively as 'wrongful interference with goods', is not a tort blessed with much certainty about its scope and requirements. It is not clear, for example, whether intention is required, although it ought to be, or whether it is actionable per se, although again it ought to be, at least when the interference is deliberate.[19] As late as 1951,[20] it suffered from confusion with negligence, largely as a consequence of its use in collision and other road traffic cases, and from the assumption that 'trespass' meant strict liability for direct damage, or at least that the burden of proof was reversed and the defendant had to prove absence of fault. These days, physical harm to goods can be sued for in negligence and the only proper gap for trespass to goods to fill is for intentional or recklessly caused harm, if that is a gap at all.

16 [1970] 1 WLR 411.
17 Eg *John Trenberth* and *Anchor Brewery*.
18 Now governed by the Police and Criminal Evidence Act 1984 ss 8-22.
19 *Wilson v Lombank* [1963] 1 WLR 1294.
20 *National Coal Board v Evans* [1951] 2 KB 861.

On the other hand, trespass to goods can be seen as a lost opportunity. Just as French law, for example, created strict liability for traffic accidents out of Art 1384 of the Code Civil, which did not at first sight appear to concern itself with such matters,[1] so it was possible to have created a largely no fault regime for traffic accidents out of the common law trespasses and so to have satisfied one of the later aspirations of the Pearson Committee.[2] This, perhaps unfortunately, never happened.

The rules of trespass to goods are in principle similar to those of trepass to land. Possession is protected, rather than ownership. This gives rise to problems when people hand their goods over to others for safekeeping or use or repair. These 'bailments' have a number of special rules of their own which are largely beyond the scope of this book, but one should note that while the receiver ('bailee') always has possession, if the lender (bailor) has an immediate right to possession he is treated as having possession itself. On the whole employees do not have possession of their employers' goods (but only 'custody')[3] and things attached to land are possessed by the landowner.[4]

At common law, again in the same fashion as trespass to land, jus tertii was no defence. But s 8 of the 1977 Act now allows a defendant to show that a named third party had a better right than the plaintiff.

Assault and battery

The next intentional tort to consider is assault and battery. Assault is 'an act that causes another person to apprehend the infliction of immediate, unlawful force on his person'.[5] Battery is 'the actual infliction of unlawful force on another person'.[6] It is also a crime. Indeed, summary criminal proceedings for assault, as long as there has been a hearing on the merits and whether they result in a conviction or an acquittal, are a bar to any subsequent civil action.[7] But the main function of assault and battery as a tort is to bring to court, in proceedings in which the prosecution authorities have no power to interfere, assaults and batteries by public officials, especially those by police officers. Like most of the intentional torts discussed in this chapter, the most important function of the tort of assault lies in the field of civil liberties.

---

1 *Jand'heur* Cass 21.2.1927 D.1927.I.97 S.1927.I.137 and Cass Ch Réunies 13.2.1930 D.1930.I.57 S.1930.I.121.
2 Vol 1 Paras 995 ff.
3 But see *Meux v Great Eastern Rly* [1895] 2 QB 387.
4 *South Staffordshire Water v Sharman* [1896] 2 QB 44.
5 *Collins v Wilcock* [1984] 1 WLR 1172.
6 Ibid.
7 Offences against the Person Act 1861 ss 42-45. Plaintiffs may preserve their right to sue by the expedient of starting their civil action before the criminal trial is heard.

Technical requirements

Notice that there can be assault without a battery (the blow does not land) and battery without assault (the defendant hits the plaintiff from behind). In assault, the threat of force must be immediate. There is no assault for threatening gestures from a distance or from behind bars or at people well protected by being inside moving motor vehicles.[8] But the test is whether a reasonable person would apprehend being struck, so that pointing an unloaded gun at someone is an assault if the victim reasonably believed it to be loaded.[9] If the defendant moves threateningly towards the plaintiff, there can be an assault even if the defendant is intercepted or the victim escapes.[10] Words by themselves cannot constitute an assault, but they can transform the situation by turning otherwise ambiguous gestures into threats.[11] Words can also turn an act which would otherwise be an assault into an innocent act, as in the famous case *Tuberville v Savage*[12] in which the defendant put his hand on his sword and said, 'If it were not assize time, I would not take such language from you.' But words such as 'If you don't get out I'll break your neck' accompanied by menacing movements is certainly an assault because the words do not take away the threat but rather reinforce it.[13]

Batteries do not have to involve personal bodily contact between the defendant and the plaintiff. Throwing something that hits the plaintiff, grabbing something from the plaintiff's grasp, getting the plaintiff's horse to throw him, pulling a chair away so that the plaintiff falls on the floor and most other 'practical jokes' are all batteries.[14] The old law required the harm to be caused 'directly', which would seem to rule out some other 'practical jokes' such as giving the plaintiff a bar of soap containing black dye—but they will be caught in any case by the *Wilkinson v Downton* tort.[15] This would also cover spiking the plaintiff's drink or preventing the plaintiff from receiving medical treatment. It is unclear whether deliberately giving someone a disease is a battery or the *Wilkinson v Downton* tort. Presumably, it is a battery to give someone a disease by direct physical contact (handshaking, kissing) and close equivalents of the same (spitting).

Traditionally, battery was said to be 'touching of another in anger'[16] and the Court of Appeal in *Wilson v Pringle*[17] said that the contact had to be

8   *Thomas v National Union of Mineworkers* [1985] 2 All ER 1.
9   *R v St George* (1840) 9 C & P 483.
10   *Mortin v Shoppe* (1828) 3 C & P 373, *Stephens v Myers* (1830) 4 C & P 349.
11   There is some disagreement on this (compare *Meade's Case* (1823) 1 Lew CC 184 with *R v Wilson* [1955] 1 WLR 493) but in principle, does a reasonable person anticipate assault from words alone without any other movement or physical evidence?
12   (1669) 1 Mod Rep 3.
13   *Read v Coker* (1853) 13 CB 850.
14   See eg *Pursell v Horn* (1838) 8 Ad & El 602, *Green v Goddard* (1702) 2 Salk 641, *Hopper v Reeve* (1817) 7 Taunt 698, *Dodwell v Burford* (1669) 1 Mod Rep 24.
15   See below.
16   *Cole v Turner* (1704) 6 Mod Rep 149.
17   [1987] QB 237.

'hostile'. But in *Collins v Wilcock*[18] and *Re F*,[19] Lord Goff rejected these requirements. They had been adopted to rule out claims for battery for ordinary social contact, for example jostling on public transport, but there were better ways of dealing with such cases. Lord Goff also rejected the alternative theory that there was 'implied consent' to such ordinary contact (a slightly absurd theory in any case—it meant that if I wore a sign on my chest saying 'I withdraw my consent to jostling' when travelling on the Tube I could sue large numbers of fellow travellers). Lord Goff's theory was that there could simply be no liability for 'all physical contact which is generally acceptable in the ordinary conduct of everyday life'. Any sort of contact other than the generally acceptable is unlawful, regardless of hostility or anger (an unwanted kiss for example).

Mental element

The defendant must have (a) acted and (b) intended the act or acts that constituted the assault or battery, but, traditionally, need not have intended to injure the plaintiff. In consequence, if A simply blocked B's path, the courts would usually say that there was no tort because there was no act,[20] but if A struck at B but hits C, C had an action for battery against A because A had intended to act and had acted.[1] But it is far from clear that the second part of this rule is still valid. The famous cases *Fowler v Lanning*[2] and *Letang v Cooper*[3] established, first, that one could not sue simply on the basis that 'the defendant shot the plaintiff' without alleging some form of fault, either intentional harm or negligence, and secondly, that it makes no practical difference to put the word 'trespass' into a statement of claim— one cannot, for example, gain extra time before one's action is time-barred by calling one's negligence action 'negligent trespass'.

At first sight, if the only intention required in assault were the intention to act, it is not clear why the statement of claim 'The defendant shot me' should be ruled out. To say 'X shot Y' seems to imply that X was acting consciously and intended to pull the trigger, although it does not imply that X intended to harm Y. But since 'The defendant shot me' was ruled out in *Fowler v Lanning*, it seems to follow that there must be some more specific intention in assault than just the intention to act. But in *Wilson v Pringle* the Court of Appeal reiterated the traditional view and said that only the intention to act was necessary. The problem with *Wilson*, however, is that it also said that the contact had to be 'hostile', a requirement repudiated by Lord Goff in *Re F*. *Wilson* combined the intention to act test with the 'hostility' bad motive test. If the bad motive element is removed,

---

18 [1984] 1 WLR 1172.
19 [1990] 2 AC 1.
20 *Innes v Wylie* (1844) 1 Car & Kir 257.
1   *Livingstone v Ministry of Defence* [1984] NI 356.
2   [1959] 1 QB 426.
3   [1965] 1 QB 232.

it does not follow that the test is merely the intention to act, but rather suggests that the bad motive test should be replaced with something else, for example an intention to injure test, or, perhaps a test of recklessness as to whether injuries occur or not.

Consent

Consent is a defence to the tort of assault and battery, whatever the position may be in criminal law.[4] It may even be more than a defence, for it is possible that the plaintiff has to prove lack of consent rather than the defendant having to prove that there was consent.[5]

Consent is an issue in three common situations: sports that involve bodily contact, fights and medical cases.

As far as sports are concerned, the normal rule is that there is implied consent to physical contacts that are part and parcel of the game, including some fouls, but not to foul play that goes beyond what a reasonable participant would expect.[6] It is, however, difficult to disentangle real 'consent' from what the court thinks reasonable. In the light of Lord Goff's remarks in *Re F* about ordinary social contacts, it might be better simply to say that there can be no battery where the physical contact is generally acceptable in the ordinary conduct of the sport concerned.

An extraordinary line of cases holds that people who voluntarily involve themselves in fights, especially 'an ordinary fight with fists' cannot sue one another for battery, either because of consent or because of the illegality of the whole activity.[7] The point of these cases is to remove arranged fights from the protection of the law. The defence should not prevent a person who is attacked and defends himself from suing the attacker,[8] at least unless the self-defence went beyond the proportional, in which case the illegality point might apply.[9]

The medical cases are the ones that have produced most difficulty. Medical operations carried out without consent, since 'hostility' is no longer a requirement of assault and battery, are in principle tortious. The problems come with (a) patients who cannot give their consent (b) patients who unreasonably withhold their consent (c) children and (d) patients who give their consent but then say that they would not have given it had the doctor provided them with more information.

As far as patients unable to give consent are concerned, there is no defence of consent, implied or otherwise, and the doctors are protected

4   *R v Brown* [1994] 1 AC 212, [1993] 2 All ER 75, [1993] 2 WLR 556, 157 JP 337, 97 Cr App Rep 44 (consent a defence to assault, but not to grievous bodily harm).
5   *Freeman v Home Office (No 2)* [1983] 3 All ER 589.
6   *R v Billinghurst* [1978] Crim LR 553.
7   *Lane v Holloway* [1968] 1 QB 379, *Murphy v Culhane* [1977] QB 94. Note that *Murphy* also suggests that contributory negligence might be relevant in assault in these sorts of cases.
8   Cf *Beckford v R* [1987] 3 All ER 425.
9   Cf *Lynch v Ministry of Defence* [1983] NI 216.

only by a defence of necessity.[10] If the patient is only temporarily uncon—
scious, the doctor is justified by necessity in carrying out only those
procedures that must be carried out before the patient regains conscious—
ness, and even then must not act in a way that is contrary to the known
wishes of the patient.[11] Mere convenience for the doctors is not enough.[12]
Equally, the defence of necessity justifies procedures necessary to bring
the patient back into consciousness. But where the patient is permanently
unable to consent, necessity, according to the House of Lords, allows the
doctors to intervene in whatever way, including both emergency and routine
operations, strikes them as in the best interests of the patient.[13] The only
constraint on the doctors in this situation is a *Bolam* test of what a
respectable body of medical opinion would support.[14] Disturbingly for those
who object to the practice of eugenics, *Re F* decides that this test applies
even in the case of a mentally handicapped person whom doctors wish to
sterilise. All the doctors have to do is find some other doctors who will
agree to say that sterilisation would be in the 'best interests of the patient'.
The spectre of *Buck v Bell*,[15] the US Supreme Court case in which Holmes
J allowed to stand a Virginia statute mandating the sterilisation of 'mental
defectives' with the words 'three generations of imbeciles are enough', hangs
over the law of England.

Furthermore, *Airedale National Health Service Trust v Bland* decides
that where the patient is in a permanent 'persistent vegetative state' (that
is a coma from which the doctors say the patient will never recover) the
doctors may decide that it is not in the best interests of the patient to
continue to live, and may decide to remove life support systems from the
patient.

Patients who unreasonably withhold their consent are within their rights
to do so.[16] But doctors may evade this rule by claiming that the patient's
very condition makes the refusal invalid. In *Re T*[17] the patient refused to
have a blood transfusion because she was a Jehovah's Witness. The doctors
nevertheless gave her a blood transfusion and successfully resisted an
action for battery by saying that the patient only refused to give permission
because, in her weakened state, she succumbed to the persuasion of her
mother.

Re T, *Re F* and *Bland* all follow a theory of medical paternalism that
may not be sustainable in a society in which people are well-informed on
medical matters and sceptical about the claims to selflessness of
professionals.

---

10 *Re F* above n 19, *Airedale National Health Service Trust v Bland* [1993] 1 All ER 821.
    Contra *Re S* [1992] 4 All ER 671.
11 *Re F* above n 19.
12 Cf *Murray v McMurchy* [1949] 2 DLR 442.
13 *Re F* above n 19.
14 *Re F* above, although nb Lord Mustill's doubts on this point.
15 274 US 200 (1927).
16 *Airedale v Bland* above n 10.
17 [1992] 4 All ER 649.

Children's consent presents special problems. 16- and 17-year-olds are presumed to have the same capacity to consent as adults.[18] The capacity of children under 16 to consent depends, according to the *Gillick*[19] case, on whether the particular child has the capacity to understand what is involved in the particular procedure. Where children cannot consent, parents, or the court under its wardship jurisdiction, may give or withhold consent on the child's behalf.[20] Obvious problems arise when the child does have capacity under *Gillick*, refuses to consent, but parents purport to consent anyway. It appears that even with 16- and 17-year-olds, the parents' consent (and a fortiori the consent of the court) will protect the doctors.[1]

Finally, there is the problem of patients who claim that their consent was vitiated by insufficient information or by deception by doctors. In principle, consent obtained by fraud is ineffective. In criminal law, the courts say that there is still consent if the victim consented to the 'nature' of the act but was simply misled about its consequences. Thus, in *R v Clarence*[2] the defendant successfully claimed, on being accused of giving his wife a venereal disease, she had consented to sexual intercourse. But there is no need for modern tort law to be bound by nineteenth century criminal law decisions. The distinction between the 'nature' of the act and its 'consequences' is not only artificial (why should the 'nature' of an act not depend on its consequences) but also inappropriate to tort law. Plaintiffs claim compensation for the consequences of the defendant's acts, not for their 'nature'. But although *Chatterton v Gerson*[3] suggests that consent in medical cases can be vitiated by fraud or misrepresentation, Lord Donaldson in the Court of Appeal in *Sidaway v Bethlem Royal Hospital*[4] said that the position in tort was 'closely analogous' to that in criminal law, and that the distinction between consent to the nature of the defendant's act and consent to its consequences applies in medical tort cases. It is to be hoped that Lord Donaldson's view does not prevail.

Lawful arrest

Clearly it is a defence both to assault and to false imprisonment that the defendant lawfully arrested the plaintiff. For details of the law on this topic, students are referred to the standard works on criminal procedure and civil liberties.[5] Suffice it to say here that private citizens may lawfully

18 Family Law Reform Act 1969 s 8(1).
19 [1986] AC 112.
20 Eg *Re J* [1990] 3 All ER 930.
1   Eg *Re R* [1991] 4 All ER 177.
2   (1888) 22 QBD 23.
3   [1981] QB 432.
4   [1984] QB 493.
5   Eg J Sprack *Emmins on Criminal Procedure* (5th ed) (London: Blackstone, 1992), S.H. Bailey, D.J. Harris, B.L. Jones *Civil Liberties: Cases and Materials* (3rd ed) (London: Butterworths, 1991), D Feldman *Civil Liberties and Human Rights in England and Wales* (Oxford: Clarendon Press, 1993).

arrest without warrant people who are breaching the peace or whom they reasonably and honestly believe are about to cause a breach of the peace. They may also arrest people who are committing arrestable offences (basically serious offences, including theft) or whom they reasonably believe to be committing such an offence and, as long as someone actually has committed the offence in question, they may arrest someone who has committed an arrestable offence or someone they reasonably believe to be guilty of the offence. The advantages that police officers have over private individuals are (a) magistrates issue warrants to them and (b) they can arrest without warrant someone they reasonably suspect to be guilty of an offence even if it turns out that no such offence has been committed by anyone.[6]

False imprisonment

The fourth intentional tort affecting the plaintiff's physical interests is false imprisonment. False imprisonment is 'The unlawful imposition of constraint on another's freedom of movement from a particular place.'[7] 'False' does not mean 'untrue' but merely 'wrongful', and 'imprisonment' does not need to be in a prison. 'Imprisonment is the restraint of a man's liberty, whether it be in the open field, or in the stocks, or in the cage in the streets, or in a man's own house, as well as in the common gaol.'[8] The civil liberties function of this tort is obvious, but it also has uses in the private sector as well.

Restraint

False imprisonment might have developed into a tort protecting freedom of movement in general. For example, it might have developed so that one could sue not only for being unlawfully kept in, but also for being unlawfully kept out of a place, for example by illegal road-blocks by the police.[9] But, instead, it has remained tied to the notion that only the complete restraint of the plaintiff is actionable. In *Bird v Jones* for example, the plaintiff complained that the defendants had appropriated part of the public footpath across a bridge for seats to view a regatta and had prevented the plaintiff from taking his usual route across the bridge. He sued for false imprison–ment, but failed. He could have used another route across the bridge and several other routes across the river. But the court went further than it needed to go to decide the case and said that there could be no false imprisonment unless the plaintiff was completely restrained in all direct–

6   See *Davidson v Chief Constable of North West Wales* [1994] 2 All ER 597.
7   *Collins v Wilcock* [1984] 1 WLR 1172.
8   *Termes de la ley* 'Imprisonment'.
9   Eg during the miners' strike of 1984-85, the police set up road-blocks to prevent pickets from travelling from pit to pit.

ions. Lord Denman CJ dissented, saying, 'As long as I am prevented from doing what I have a right to do, of what importance is it that I am permitted to do something else?' But the majority of the court refused to expand the scope of the tort.

But Lord Denman raised another point that could not be dismissed so easily. He asked, if complete restraint alone was to count as false imprisonment, what about situations in which the plaintiff could have escaped by some circuitous or dangerous route? Was that imprisonment? These questions remain largely unanswered in the case law to this day. It is assumed that there is imprisonment if the only means of escape are unreasonable, especially if they are dangerous, but exactly how an unreasonable means of escape differs from one which is merely inconvenient has never been made clear.

The question of reasonableness does, however, occur in one of the most controversial false imprisonment cases, *Robinson v Balmain Ferry*.[10] The defendants operated a ferry across a river. The system of payment, as with many ferries and toll bridges, was that there were turnstiles on one side of the river only. Passengers travelling in one direction paid as they entered the defendant's wharf. Passengers travelling in the opposite direction paid as they left the wharf. The plaintiff's story was that he entered the wharf by paying a penny, but found that the ferry had just left and, not wanting to wait 20 minutes or so for the next one, decided to leave. But the defendant's employee at the turnstile refused to let him through unless he paid another penny. The plaintiff, a litigious type, sued for false imprisonment, and the case reached the Privy Council. The Privy Council decided that there had been no false imprisonment. The plaintiff argued that one could not enforce contractual rights by imprisonment, which in general is correct. But the court said that the contractual argument was not relevant. The various notices which told the plaintiff that he would have to pay a penny to get out probably constituted a contract, but the contract did not affect the outcome of the case. Instead, there was no imprisonment simply because the condition of paying a penny to leave was a reasonable one in the circumstances.

Robinson is a much misunderstood case. Indeed even the House of Lords in *Herd v Weardale Steel, Coal and Coke*[11] failed to understand it and claimed, contrary to what the Privy Council explicitly said, that it rested on a contractual argument. But if *Robinson* does not turn on the content of the notices, does it stand for the proposition that it is not false imprisonment to impose conditions on people's exit from one's land as long as the conditions are not onerous? That is, is it a case about the means of escape? The plaintiff could, on the one hand, have paid a penny to leave, and on the other could have waited 20 minutes for the next ferry. Is the court saying that this did not amount to complete restraint and there is therefore no imprisonment? The answer to these questions is also no. If I lock you into a room with a timing device on the lock that will let you out in 20 minutes you are

10 [1910] AC 295.
11 [1915] AC 67.

imprisoned for 20 minutes. If I ask you for £1 to get out in the meantime, you are still imprisoned.

The point about *Robinson* is not the reasonableness of the condition itself, but the reasonableness of the system of operating a ferry that caused the situation to arise at all. If one puts oneself in the position of the employee at the out turnstile when Mr Robinson presented himself, one will see what the case was really about. Who exactly is this Mr Robinson? Is he simply trying to get through without paying, having just used the ferry from the other side? If I let him through without paying, in exchange for his name and address, will I get the sack? From the employee's point of view, demanding that Mr Robinson pay his penny is plainly reasonable.

But the plaintiff will point out that the situation only arises in the first place because of the system of collecting fares on one side of the river only. If there were turnstiles on each side of the river, Mr Robinson could not have been trying to get through without paying and the employee at the turnstile would not have had any reasonable ground for not letting him back out. And so the central question in the case becomes, is it a reasonable way to run a ferry (or a toll bridge) to have both turnstiles on one side of the river, as is the almost universal practice? The answer to this question is probably yes. Reasons of the ease of security arrangements, of the flexibility of the workforce and of supervision largely dictate the standard pattern of operation. The condition on exit in *Robinson* was reasonable because it was a reasonable way to run a ferry. Similarly, the reason why it is not false imprisonment for those running a train service to refuse to make an unscheduled stop, whereas it probably is false imprisonment for a person to be held against their will in a fast moving car from which they cannot escape because the kidnappers will not stop the car, is not because there is a contractual condition on exit or that the conditions put on exit are reasonable in the first case but not in the second, but rather because running a railway, and running it so that trains only make the stops that the timetable requires, is itself reasonable whereas there is no reasonable way of kidnapping someone.

Herd v Weardale Steel is less easy to justify. The plaintiffs were miners, the defendants their employers. The plaintiffs decided that working conditions in the pit were unsafe and demanded to be brought up to the surface. The defendants refused to authorise the lift to be operated until the scheduled time at the end of the shift. The plaintiffs sued for false imprisonment and lost in the House of Lords. The defendants' way of operating a coalmine does not strike anyone now as reasonable. There was no reason at all for not allowing the lift to be used to bring the plaintiffs back up. The defendants were purely exercising arbitrary power to punish the employees for daring to question their employers' judgment about what were safe conditions of work. The House of Lords, however, claimed that the plaintiffs' contracts of employment gave consent to the proposition that the employer need only supply a lift to bring them back to the surface at the end of their shift, and they could not alter that position by breaching their own contracts by refusing to work. It is an extraordinary claim, and one which now would find little judicial support, that one can impliedly contract out of the right to stop work in conditions that are unexpectedly dangerous, especially if the conditions are in breach of health and safety legislation. *Herd v Weardale Steel* should therefore be interpreted as a case that turns purely on the interpretation of a particular contract at a particular time.

Mental element

Most false imprisonment is intentional both as to the act of imprisonment and as to the effect of imprisonment. Clearly intention as to the act is a requirement of the tort, but whether it is possible to commit false imprisonment either when one is only negligent as to the effect of imprisonment or when one is reckless as to that consequence is unclear. By analogy with *Fowler v Lanning* and *Letang v Cooper* one might say that at least recklessness as to the effect of imprisonment is necessary. But Gibson LJ in his judgment in *Weldon v Home Office*[12] left open the question of whether a defendant would be liable who was merely negligent as to the effect of imprisonment. The argument in favour of recognising negligent false imprisonment is that unlike assault and battery, which deal usually with personal injury, negligence itself does not give the victim a remedy for the form of harm caused by false imprisonment. On the other hand, one might argue that since both assault and battery and false imprisonment are actionable per se, it is perfectly understandable and coherent for both of them to be committed in circumstances in which there is no remedy in negligence. The best answer, however, may be for negligence to expand its categories of recognised harm to include imprisonment.

Knowledge of plaintiff

One of the old chestnuts in false imprisonment has recently been cracked. Is it false imprisonment when the plaintiff did not know that he was imprisoned? In *Meering v Grahame-White Aviation*[13] Atkin LJ said that there was no need for the plaintiff to have been aware of the imprisonment. The point of the tort was (a) to deter violations of rights of personal liberty and (b) to prevent ridicule of the plaintiff. The law could only fulfill both functions if the plaintiff's knowledge was immaterial. The result was also consistent with the status of false imprisonment as a tort actionable per se. *Meering*, however, failed to discuss the earlier case, *Herring v Boyle*,[14] in which the court had taken the view that if there was no knowledge, there was no imprisonment. The conflict of authority was resolved in

12 [1990] 3 WLR 465 at 470.
13 (1919) 122 LT 44.
14 (1834) 1 Cr M & R 377.

Murray v Ministry of Defence.[15] Soldiers, who were searching for terrorists, detained the plaintiff in her house, but without telling her that she was under arrest. Although she failed in her action for false imprisonment because the soldiers successfully asserted that they had legal authority to detain her under the Northern Ireland (Emergency Provisions) Act 1978, the House of Lords said that the plaintiff's lack of knowledge of her detention was immaterial. According to Lord Griffiths:

> '[T]he law attaches supreme importance to the liberty of the individual and if he suffers a wrongful interference with that liberty, it should remain actionable even without proof of special damage.'

The point is that the main function of false imprisonment as a tort (this may not be true of false imprisonment as a crime, and perhaps the rule ought to be different there) is to vindicate private citizens in their dealings with the excesses and abuses of state officials. It is not just compensation for hurt feelings that they seek, but an opportunity, outside the control of the prosecuting authorities, to call such officials publicly to account.

Who can be sued?

In *Davidson v Chief Constable of North Wales*[16] the plaintiff's friend bought a cassette tape at a store and, having made the purchase, returned to the counter where the plaintiff was waiting. The two stood talking for a while before leaving the store. A store detective who had observed them gained the false impression that they had left without paying for the cassette and telephoned the police. When two police officers arrived the store detective told them that the plaintiff had taken the cassette without paying and pointed her out. The officers arrested the plaintiff and her friend on suspicion of shoplifting. The friend denied that he had taken anything dishonestly and produced the cassette but was unable to produce a receipt because he had thrown it away. The plaintiff said nothing. The police took the plaintiff and her friend to the police station but two hours later released them after they had received a message from the shop assistant who had served the friend confirming that he had paid for the cassette.

The plaintiff sued the store detective's employers for false imprisonment. The police themselves were protected because police officers are allowed to arrest on reasonable suspicion both that an offence has occurred and that the person arrested had committed the offence. But the store detective, as a private citizen, did not have the same protection, since for a private citizen's arrest to be lawful, a crime actually has to have taken place.

15 [1988] 1 WLR 692.
16 [1994] 2 All ER 597.

Reasonable suspicion is not enough.[17] The defendants said that although their store detective did not have the protection of lawful authority, there should be no liability because the arrest, and thus the imprisonment, had been the work of the police.

The store detective had merely given information to the police. The plaintiff's argument was that the police were not the active parties, but had arrested the pair at the instigation of the store detective, who should count as the real culprit.

The Court of Appeal decided in favour of the defendants. Sir Thomas Bingham MR, after an extensive review of the case law, said that the test was 'whether the defendant has merely given information to a properly constituted authority on which that authority may act or not as it decides or whether he has himself been the instigator, promoter and active inciter of the action that follows.' The evidence in the case was that on the one hand one of the police officers had said:

> 'We arrested them because of what the store detective said. It was Constable Walker who actually arrested them. We were acting on the information received. We act on information that we receive. If we are not satisfied with it we don't act upon it. We take the responsibility for an arrest that we make on information. The store detective did not say directly to us, "go and arrest them"; we don't take orders from her; we are not her agents. The information that she gave us led me to believe that an offence had been committed; we were acting on it.'

On the other hand the store detective had said that she expected information given by a store detective such as herself to carry weight with police officers. She intended and expected the police officers to act upon it. They had always done so in the past. She had never known of any occasion when they had failed to do so and accordingly she regarded the arrest as made on her behalf or for her.

In the circumstances, Sir Thomas Bingham said that the test was:

> '[W]hether there was information properly to be considered by the jury as to whether what [the store detective] did went beyond laying information before police officers for them to take such action as they thought fit and amounted to some direction, or procuring, or direct request, or direct encouragement that they should act by way of arresting these defendants. He decided that there was no evidence which went beyond the giving of information. Certainly there was no express request. Certainly there was no encourage–ment. Certainly there was no discussion of any kind as to what action the police officers should take.'

Exactly what might constitute a 'request' or, what is more difficult, 'encouragement' remains to be decided.

---

17 See above.

Prisoners' rights

At one stage it seemed that false imprisonment was not only to be of use against the police but also against the prison authorities. A theory developed that even prisoners had a 'residual liberty' and that violations of the Prison Rules by the authorities, including forcing prisoners to live in inhuman conditions, would mean that the authorities had exceeded the scope of their statutory defences to false imprisonment and that they would be liable in tort. But in the jointly heard appeals in *R v Deputy Governor of Parkhurst Prison, ex p Hague* and *Weldon v Home Office*[18] the House of Lords declared that, because of the terms of s 12 of the Prison Act 1952, which protects the governor and anyone acting on the governor's behalf from suit, prisoners had no such right to 'residual liberty'. Prisoners did have remedies in public law, and in negligence and assault, but the only opportunity for the use of false imprisonment would be where an individual officer (or perhaps a fellow prisoner) acted so far outside his authority that he could no longer be considered to be acting on behalf of the governor.[19] An example would be an officer who goes beserk and kidnaps a rich and famous prisoner, holding him to ransom in part of the prison. In particular, prison conditions themselves cannot constitute false imprisonment, although if a prisoner falls ill because of bad conditions, there may be an action in negligence.

Defences

The defences to false imprisonment are essentially the same as those to assault—consent, necessity and lawful authority.

Malicious prosecution

A plaintiff successfully makes a claim for malicious prosecution when (1) the defendant prosecuted the plaintiff; (2) the prosecution ended in favour of the accused plaintiff; (3) there was no reasonable and probable cause for the prosecution; (4) the prosecution was actuated by 'malice'; and (5) the plaintiff suffered damage. Again the civil liberties function of this tort is obvious. Note also that there is a civil law equivalent of malicious prosecution called 'malicious abuse of process' for which the elements are the same except that the plaintff needs to prove 'special' damage beyond mere harm to his reputation.

This is one of the most difficult torts to prove, with the odds stacked heavily against the plaintiff in almost every element apart from damage. A desire to keep criminal law and civil law proceedings separate plays a

---

18 [1992] 1 AC 58.
19 But nb now on the possibility of vicarious liability: *Racz v Home Office* [1994] 2 AC 45, [1994] 1 All ER 97, [1994] 2 WLR 23.

large part in the policy of the law to make malicious prosecution a plaintiff's graveyard.

Prosecution

Under what circumstances will the law treat a person as having instigated a prosecution? Is any attempt to have the plaintiff prosecuted by the authorities to count, or is it only when the defendant signs the charge sheet or takes some other official action?

The only authoritative answer to this question in England is the Court of Appeal case *Martin v Watson*.[20] The defendant deliberately lied to the police that the plaintiff had indecently exposed himself to her. The plaintiff was prosecuted, but just as the case was coming to trial, the prosecution discovered the truth, offered no evidence at the hearing in the magistrates' court and the charge was dropped. The plaintiff sued for malicious prosecution. The defendant's only realistic argument was that she was not the instigator of the prosecution, since all she had done, albeit maliciously and mendaciously, was to have supplied information to the authorities. The police and the Crown Prosecution Service, exercising independent judgment had seen fit to believe her story and had themselves started the prosecution.

The trial judge found for the plaintiff, on the ground that the maliciousness of the accusation, especially in the context of an offence where the accuser would be the only witness, meant that in reality it was the defendant who had instigated the prosecution. The Court of Appeal, however, by a majority, reversed and ordered judgment for the defendant. The court acknowledged that they were not bound by authority and that the most commonly cited test in the existing cases and texts, that 'the law must be shown to have been set in motion by the defendant,'[1] or 'any person who makes or is actively instrumental in the making or prosecuting of such a charge is deemed to prosecute it and is called the prosecutor'[2] are not determinative.

Ralph Gibson LJ and Hobhouse LJ said that the decision depended ultimately on whether to protect witnesses and those who gave information to the police from the threat of civil action if the criminal prosecution failed. Hobhouse LJ pointed in particular to the line of cases that decides that there can be no civil action for perjury—that is for lying in court—or even civil actions for other torts whose success depends on proving that the defendants lied in court.[3] The control of whether people should suffer for lying in court should rest solely with the public authorities. Hobhouse

---

20 [1994] QB 425, [1994] 2 All ER 606, [1994] 2 WLR 500.
1 *Clerk and Lindsell.*
2 *Halsbury's Laws of England.*
3 See eg *Marrinan v Vibart* [1963] 1 QB 234, [1962] 1 All ER 869.

LJ does not go into why one should exclude private rights of action for perjury, but there are in reality two grounds: to prevent the multiple litigation of the same facts and, more importantly, to make sure that various methods, deals and arrangements used by the police and the prosecuting authorities—entrapment, undercover work, 'co-ordination' of evidence, plea bargains, and so on—are not exposed to too much public examination. The test for who is the prosecutor for the purposes of malicious prosecution should therefore, according to Hobhouse LJ, sharply distinguish between prosecutors and witnesses.

The discretion of the police and the prosecution service to prosecute based on their own assessment of the evidence was crucial. The plaintiff argued that the police and prosecution service's judgment had been impaired by the malicious lies of the defendant and therefore should not count as their own voluntary judgment. But the majority rejected that view, saying that it confused the defendant's malice with the objective question of who in reality was the prosecutor,

McCowan LJ's dissent, however, has considerable force. His central point is simply this:

> 'There can surely be no wish to encourage citizens to make deliberately false charges against a fellow-citizen to the police. That can hardly be described as law enforcement. It is a perversion of the law and deserves no protection. I see no justification for the view that it would be harmful in those circumstances for such a false accuser to be sued for malicious prosecution. On the contrary, I think it would be very regrettable if the law were that a complainant could deliberately concoct an allegation of crime against an innocent man and persuade a police officer, in the absence of any other evidence against the man, to lodge a charge against him, knowing it to be false and malicious, but escape liability for malicious prosecution because the officer and not the complainant had laid the information.'

Ended in the plaintiff's favour

The plaintiff must have won the criminal case. Otherwise the malicious prosecution suit will be nothing but a rerun of the criminal trial with the prospect of a confusing contradictory verdict at the end of it. But since avoiding contradiction is the main aim of the requirement, it does not matter how the plaintiff won. A win on a technical point is enough, and so is a win on appeal.[4]

---

4 *Herniman v Smith* [1938] AC 305. This case also shows that the fact that the plaintiff lost at trial is not evidence of reasonable and probable cause either, since the conviction could have been procured by perjury.

No reasonable and probable cause

The plaintiff has to convince the judge that there was no reasonable and probable cause for the prosecution[5] has to convince the jury, if there was objectively reasonable and probable cause, that the defendant nevertheless did not honestly believe in the case.[6] There is reasonable and probable cause if a reasonable person in the position of the prosecutor would have thought that the plaintiff had a case to answer.[7] That is usually an insurmountable hurdle for the plaintiff. It is insufficient, notice, for the plaintiff to show that the prosecution would probably fail.[8] However, to bring some relief to the plaintiff, the prosecutor's honest belief must be in the guilt of the plaintiff, not just in the proposition that there is a case to answer. Thus a prosecutor with a plausible case but who knows that the plaintiff is not guilty does not have reasonable and probable cause.[9]

Malice

Malice for the purposes of malicious prosecution means having any other motive apart from that of bringing an offender to justice.[10] Spite and ill-will are sufficient but not necessary conditions for a finding of malice. On the other hand anger and revenge may be proper motives if channelled into the criminal justice system.[11]

Malice has to be proved as well as the other elements, not instead of them.[12] And the lack of objective reasonable and probable cause is not evidence of malice.[13] But lack of honest belief is evidence of malice.[14]

Damage

Malicious prosecution is not technically actionable per se. Historically it was an action on the case, not a trespass. But the position in practice is very much more favourable to the plaintiff than it might appear to be, because the plaintiff is not confined to suing for the costs of having to defend himself and lost income for any periods of incarceration. The plaintiff is also allowed to sue for the very fact of imprisonment, as in false

5   *Dallison v Caffrey* [1965] 1 QB 348, *Tempest v Snowden* [1952] 1 KB 130.
6   *Dallison v Caffrey* above n 5.
7   *Glinski v McIver* [1962] AC 726.
8   Ibid.
9   Cf *James v Phelps* (1840) 11 Ad & El 483.
10 *Glinski v McIver* above n 7.
11 *Brown v Hawkes* [1891] 2 QB 718.
12 *Martin v Watson* above n 20.
13 *Turner v Ambler* (1847) 10 QB 252.
14 *Brown v Hawkes* above n 11.

imprisonment, and, as in defamation, harm to reputation. Furthermore, harm to reputation is presumed to follow from having been charged with a serious criminal offence.

A general tort?—*Wilkinson v Downton* to *Khorasandjian v Bush*

The defendant tells the plaintiff, in what he seems to have thought of as a practical joke, that her husband has been smashed up in an accident and is lying in a public house at Leytonstone with both his legs broken. It is all false. The plaintiff, previously known to be a woman of ordinary fortitude and not prone to nervous disorders, goes into shock and suffers from a mental illness as a consequence. She sues the plaintiff for the shock, and for 1s 10$\frac{1}{2}$d rail fares incurred by the plaintiff on sending people to Leytonstone to find out her husband's condition.

These are the facts of the famous case *Wilkinson v Downton*.[15] The problem for the court at the time was that although the 1s 10$\frac{1}{2}$d was recoverable under the tort of deceit, the nervous shock was not recoverable in assault because some considered it to be 'indirect' damage. Still partly in thrall to the old forms of action, the system of pleading officially abolished by the Supreme Court of Judicature Act 1873 under which liability was linked to following strictly specific named procedures and documents, some lawyers believed that 'indirect damage' could not be pleaded in a 'trespass' action, only in an 'action on the case', but on the other hand, 'intentional harm' could not be pleaded in an 'action on the case', only in 'trespass'. This would have meant that intentional but indirect damage would have no home and as a result would not be actionable. The court in *Wilkinson v Downton* swept such superstitions aside, and said:

> 'The defendant has ... wilfully done an act calculated to cause physical harm to the ... plaintiff, ie to infringe her legal right to personal safety, and has thereby caused physical harm to her. That proposition, without more, appears to me to sate a good cause of action, there being no justification for the alleged act.'

To the arguments that the damage was not intended and was too remote, Wright J said that (1) it was sufficient that the defendant was reckless as to the consequences and (2) the effect was not an unnatural consequence of the plaintiff's act.

The judge entered judgment for the plaintiff.

Subsequently in *Janvier v Sweeney*[16] the Court of Appeal approved of and followed *Wilkinson v Downton* in a case where the defendant private detectives, to try to obtain letters belonging to her mistress, had put the

---

15 [1897] 2 QB 57.
16 [1919] 2 KB 316.

frighteners on the plaintiff, by saying that they would denounce her fiancé, a German citizen, as a spy. As Duke LJ said:

'This is a much stronger case than *Wilkinson v Downton*. In that case there was no intention to commit a wrongful act; the defendant merely intended to play a joke upon the plaintiff. In the present case, there was an intention to terrify the plaintiff for the purpose of attaining an unlawful object.'

Although the scope of *Wilkinson v Downton* is controversial, it should be seen as, first, a gap-filling intentional tort—that the intentional doing of any act where the act is intended to do physical harm to the plaintiff, or where the defendant is reckless as to any harm to the plaintiff, gives rise to liability and, secondly, as, in inchoate form, a general tort of the intentional or reckless infliction of physical harm.

The various torts discussed in this chapter may have some technical differences in detail. For example, malicious prosecution and (possibly) *Wilkinson v Downton* are not actionable per se whereas the other torts are; and trespass to land needs no proof of specific intention, at least when it is being used to settle a dispute about who has the better right to the property, whereas, probably, some form of specific intention or recklessness is required in all the others. But they have much in common, including the fact that they all support actionability when there is intention or recklessness and they all have a civil liberties function.

The need for a general tort of the intentional or reckless infliction of physical harm is clearly visible in cases such as *Khorasandjian v Bush*[17], in which the plaintiff complained about the defendant's continual harassing telephone calls. To construct liability in such situations out of nuisance, which is what the courts did, meant that actionability got tangled up with questions of the interests people have in land, plainly an artificial exercise. It would be much better to proceed from an area of the law that already deals with the same kind of harm.

---

17 [1993] QB 727, [1993] 3 All ER 669, [1993] 3 WLR 476, 25 HLR 392, [1993] 2 FCR 257, [1993] 2 FLR 66, [1993] Fam Law 679. See below ch 11.

Chapter 10

Intentional torts—
(2) economic and moral interests

We now turn to the intentional torts whose main concern is the plaintiff's economic interests. As we saw in the chapter on economic loss in negligence, there is no clear differentiation between property interests and economic interests. The distinction taken here is between those torts where the plaintiff mainly objects to physical intrusion, including intrusion in personal liberty (see the previous chapter), and those in which the plaintiff mainly objects to the defendant's expropriation of the plaintiff's wealth, including the value of present and future contracts, which will be dealt with here. The result is that the torts dealt with in this chapter do not have the same significance for civil liberties as do the torts discussed in the previous chapter. But distinctions of this sort are always arbitrary. Some aspects of trespass to land, mesne profits for example, could easily sit in this chapter, and a tort such as conversion, which deals with interference with goods, could easily sit in the previous chapter.

Note that this chapter could also include the whole of the law of intellectual property—of trademarks, copyrights and patents and the tort of passing off—since it also concerns interference with property rights. For reasons of space and pedagogy, rather than logic, it does not. Readers are referred to specialist works on those topics.[1]

Conversion

The original economic tort consists of dealing with somebody else's goods without their permission. Thus, where the defendant deals with the plaintiff's property in a way that amounts to denying the plaintiff's rights, which includes asserting a right over the goods inconsistent with the plaintiff's rights, the defendant commits a tort known as 'conversion'. Conversion goes further than trespass to goods. Trespass to goods is mere

1 Eg W Cornish *Intellectual Property: Patents, Copyright, Trade Marks and Allied Rights* (London: Sweet & Maxwell, 1981 (1987 reimpr)).

interference in the goods as a physical act. Conversion is a denial of the plaintiff's rights whether by taking and using the goods or, more clearly, by disposing of them, especially by selling them. Conversion is the civil equivalent of theft, although without the necessity to prove dishonesty.

Unlike trespass to goods, conversion protects ownership as well as possession. Liens and equitable titles also count, but, crucially, contractual rights to the goods are not protected.[2] This is the space into which the interference with contract torts moved in the mid-nineteenth century. But like trespass, at least at common law, what counts is the relative title of the parties to the action. If I find a gold watch in the street and take it to a jeweller for repair, I can sue the jeweller for conversion if she refuses to give the watch back even though nobody knows to whom the watch really belongs. The jeweller's title is no better than mine and since it derives from mine (I gave her the watch) it is inferior.[3] But now s 8 of the Torts (Interference with Goods) Act 1977 allows a jus tertii defence, so that if the real owner of the watch becomes known, the jeweller could join him as a party and defeat my claim.

Conversion, however, does have some of the characteristics of the trespass torts in their traditional form. There is no need to prove an intention to produce the effect of interference with the plaintiff's title, only an intention to do the act which objectively has that effect. But there needs to be an act rather than an omission. Allowing someone else to steal the plaintiff's car is not conversion.[4]

Acts which do constitute conversion do, however, come in many forms, although they have to amount to a denial of title, not just a physical interference. The obvious cases are variations on taking someone else's goods and selling them. But there are a number of less obvious cases. A bailee who refuses to restore goods to the bailor when properly requested is guilty of conversion.[5] Abusing one's otherwise lawful possession of the goods is conversion. For example, if I change the character of the goods bailed to me[6] (eg turning cloth into clothes, melting down silver coffee pots) that is conversion, because I have treated the goods as not belonging to the bailor. Deliberately destroying something of which one has already taken possession is the act of an owner, and also amounts to conversion (although destroying something still in the owner's possession is not conversion but either negligence or trespass). Even using a hire car for smuggling has been found to be conversion, on the ground that the smuggler knew (or rather was deemed to know) that the car would be seized by the customs authorities if they discovered the smuggling.[7]

As in criminal law, where receiving stolen goods is a crime in itself, receiving goods can also amount to conversion, but again without the

---

2   *Roger v Kennay* (1846) 9 QB 592.
3   Cf *Armory v Delamirie* (1722) 1 Stra 505.
4   *Ashby v Tolhurst* [1937] 2 KB 242. But see now 1977 Act s 2.
5   For a spectacular conversion of this sort—arising out of a fear of industrial action—see *Howard Perry v British Railways* [1980] 1 WLR 1375.
6   See *Philpott v Kelley* (1835) 3 Ad & El 106.
7   *Moorgate Mercantile v Finch* [1962] 1 QB 701.

requirement of a finding of dishonesty.[8] If the defendant receives goods obtained by fraud but does not know that they were obtained by fraud and generally acts in good faith in selling them on, it is still conversion. To receive and sell the goods is an act inconsistent with the real owner's title, even though there was no intention to convert.[9] These cases usually concern two innocent people and a rogue who has absconded, and the court is left the problem of which of the innocent parties should suffer. Usually, it is the recipient rather than the original owner who suffers. But when the recipient does nothing more than keep the goods for a person he honestly believed was entitled to them and then hands them back, there is no conversion. Blackburn J in *Hollins v Fowler* said:

> 'One who deals with the goods at the request of the person who has actual custody of them, in the bona fide belief that the custodier is the true owner, should be excused for what he does if the act is of such a nature as would be excused if done by the authority of the person in possession, if he was a finder of the goods or intrusted with their custody ... A warehouseman with whom goods have been deposited is guilty of no conversion by keeping them or restoring them to the person who deposited them with him, though that person turns out to have had no authority from the true owner.'

Along the same lines an 'involuntary bailee' is not guilty of conversion. An 'involuntary bailee' is someone who receives other people's goods without asking for them.[10] For example in *Lethbridge v Phillips*[11] the plaintiff lent a miniature painting to someone who then sent it to the defendant, in whose house it was damaged. There was no conversion by the defendant. Involuntary bailees do not have to be particularly careful about what is thrust upon them. In a case that is a terrible warning for all aspiring writers,[12] a theatrical producer received an unsolicited manuscript from a playwright. The producer lost the manuscript. There was no liability. The only obligation of the involuntary bailee is not deliberately to destroy or damage the thing. There is no conversion even if the recipient happens to know that the person thrusting the goods on him is not the owner.

There are several other acts that, perhaps surprisingly, do not count as conversion. For example, to make a contract of sale for someone else's goods is not conversion until the goods are delivered.[13] And merely declaring that the goods do not belong to the owner is not enough. There has to be some kind of act.[14]

---

8   *McCombie v Davies* (1805) 6 East 538. See also Torts (Interference with Goods) Act 1977 s 11(2) (receipt of goods as a pledge a conversion when the delivery of those goods is a conversion).

9   *Hollins v Fowler* (1875) LR 7 HL 757.

10 See now also Unsolicited Goods and Services Act 1971.

11 (1819) 2 Stark 544.

12 *Howard v Harris* (1884) 1 Cab & El 253.

13 *Douglas Valley Finance v Hughes* [1969] 1 QB 738.

14 1977 Act s 11(3).

Note that by s 11(1) of the 1977 Act contributory negligence is no defence to conversion (except in relation to banks[15]) although, of course, consent is a defence. It is also a defence that the goods were trespassing on the defendant's land.[16]

Damages for conversion are that the plaintiff recovers the market value of the thing plus special damages. The 1977 Act allows in the alternative, an order to anyone liable in conversion to hand the goods back, again plus special damages.[17] This is subject to a set-off for improvements made in the goods by the defendant if the defendant honestly thought that he was entitled to the goods.[18] (Note that if the defendant does not have the goods so that restoration of the goods under the Act does not apply, it may be possible to recover for the improvements in restitution instead.[19]) There are various provisions in the Act to prevent double recovery and to ensure equity among multiple defendants.[20] Note, finally, that payment in full of damages without an order to restore the goods extinguishes the plaintiff's title to the goods.

Inducing a breach of contract and interfering with contract

Conversion does not cover the plaintiff's contractual rights. If I act in a way incompatible with your contractual rights with a third party, you have to look elsewhere for protection in the law of tort. In this section and the next two, the main interest of the law is in protecting the plaintiff's contractual rights, and, sometimes, the plaintiff's prospective contracts.

Protection first arrived in the form of *Lumley v Gye*.[1] The plaintiff had a contract with an opera singer, Johanna Wagner, to sing in a series of concerts at his theatre. The defendant, by offering a higher fee, lured the singer away to sing in his theatre instead. The plaintiff sued, pointing out that the defendant was aware of the contract between the plaintiff and the singer and knew that if she sang in the defendant's theatre she would be unable to fulfill her engagements with the plaintiff.

The Court of Queen's Bench found in favour of the plaintiff. Crompton J, with whom Wightman J agreed, decided the case on grounds confined to

15 Banking Act 1979 s 47.
16 This is called 'distress damage feasant' and only applies to goods doing damage. See also Animals Act 1971 s 7(1).
17 Section 3.
18 Section 6.
19 See *Lipkin Gorman v Karpnale Ltd* [1991] 2 AC 548, [1991] 3 WLR 10, *Richmark Camera Services Inc v Neilson-Hordell Ltd* [1981] FSR 413, *Associated Dairies Ltd v Pierce* (1981) 43 P & CR 208, 259 Estates Gazette 562, [1981] EGD 409, *Groves-Raffin Construction Ltd v Bank of Nova Scotia* [1976] 1 Lloyd's Rep 373. The plaintiff cannot sue for restitution and for damages in tort at the same time, but must 'waive the tort'. Why the law should not be unified in this field, and in others, is a mystery. See Birks 'Civil Wrongs: A New World' in *Butterworth Lectures 1990-91*.
20 Sections 7 and 8.
1 (1853) 2 E & B 216.

enticing away 'servants', as employees were then known. But Erle J, in terms eventually supported by the House of Lords in *Allen v Flood*,[2] gave more general grounds:

> 'The procurement of the violation of a right is a cause of action in all instances where the violation is an actionable wrong ... He who maliciously procures a damage to another by violation of his right ought to be made to indemnify, and that whether he procures an actionable wrong or a breach of contract ... The remedy on the contract may be inadequate, as where the measure of damages is restricted; or in the case of non-payment of a debt where the damage may be bankruptcy to the creditor who is disappointed but the measure of damages against the debtor is interest only; or in the case of the non-delivery of the goods, the disappointment may lead to a heavy forfeiture under a contract to complete the work within a time, but the measure of damages against the vendor of the goods for non-delivery may be only the difference between the contract price and the market value of the goods in question at the time of the breach. In such cases, he who procures the damage maliciously might justly be made responsible beyond the liability of the contractor.'

The decision in *Lumley v Gye* and its adoption in *Allen v Flood* did not meet with universal approval. As noted in chapter 6, the reasoning of the courts that the plaintiff needs a remedy against the inducer in addition to his remedy in contract against the third party is far from convincing.[3] In all the examples given by Erle J, the plaintiff's difficulties are his own doing. Restrictions on the level of damages in the contract action must have been agreed by the plaintiff. The risk of a cashflow disaster because a debtor does not pay is just one of the risks that those in business have to take. That the deal in question put the plaintiff in risk of bankruptcy is the plaintiff's own doing as well. And the lack of an action for consequential damages caused by the plaintiff's having to miss deadlines and breach contracts with other people is also a matter for negotiation with the third party. If the plaintiff gives notice of these other onerous contracts with third parties to the third party, he can negotiate with the third party for extra compensation in case of breach by the third party. The only relevant rule of law, the rule in *Hadley v Baxendale*,[4] is that if the plaintiff does not bother to tell the third party of the other onerous contracts in circumstances in which their terms would not be obvious, the plaintiff may not in case of breach of contract obtain consequential damages from the third party for his having to breach the onerous contracts. In other words, if the plaintiff failed to tell the third party of the onerous contracts in the first place, it is the plaintiff's choice and the plaintiff's responsibility.

2   [1898] AC 1.
3   See Sayre 'Inducing Breach of Contract' 36 Harv LR 663.
4   (1854) 9 Exch 341.

These grounds for doubting the wisdom of *Lumley v Gye* are still valid today and should be borne in mind whenever an extension of *Lumley v Gye* liability is proposed.

Although *Allen v Flood* approved of *Lumley v Gye* it did stop its development in one particular direction. In *Allen v Flood,* the defendants ordered a strike in protest at an employer's temerity in employing non-union labour. The defendants demanded the dismissal of the new workers. At the time, it was possible for people to be employed 'at will', that is, they could terminate their contracts of employment at any time without notice apart from working to the end of that day, and the employer could dismiss them at any time without notice. The defendants said that this meant that there were no breaches of contract involved either in going on strike or in dismissing the new workers. The House of Lords (consisting of nine law lords and advised by the puisne judges) decided that there was no liability on these facts. In the absence of unlawful means, there was no tort. In addition, Lord Herschell made it clear that there was no liability either for persuading striking workers not to go back to work—that is, there was no liability for preventing the formation of new contracts. For *Lumley v Gye* to apply there has to be interference with a pre-existing legal right of the plaintiff. Expectations or moral obligations were not enough.

Subsequent cases also established that the plaintiff will fail if the contract with the third party is invalid, for example if it is illegal or in restraint of trade.[5]

On the other hand, there have been several important extensions of *Lumley v Gye* since *Allen v Flood*. First, there is 'indirect' inducement to breach contracts. In *DC Thomson v Deakin*[6] unions again objected to the use of non-union labour by an employer. This time, the union had no members employed by the employer concerned. They decided to help put pressure on the employer nevertheless by instructing their members who worked for one of the employer's crucial suppliers to refuse to work on orders for the employer, a tactic known as 'blacking'. The supplier ceased to supply, causing the employer great difficulties. The employer sued the organisers of the 'blacking'. The Court of Appeal decided in favour of the defendants, but on the sole ground that the supplier had not asked its employees to work on orders for the plaintiff, and so there had been no breach of contract by the employees. If there had been such a breach, the union organisers would have been liable for 'indirect' inducement to breach contracts. This would have worked as follows. The defendants persuade the employees to breach their contracts of employment with the supplier. This in turn causes the supplier to breach its contract with the plaintiff. The defendants have therefore 'indirectly' procured a breach of the commercial contract between the supplier and the plaintiff. There is liability for this indirect procure–ment, said the Court of Appeal, if the means used to bring it about were themselves unlawful. Such unlawful means would

5   *Joe Lee v Dalmery* [1927] 1 Ch 300, *De Francesco v Burnum* (1889) 43 Ch D 165, *Grieg v Insole* [1978] 1 WLR 302.

6   [1952] Ch 646.

include committing the *Lumley v Gye* tort against the supplier. The defendants in *Thomson v Deakin* were thus saved only because they had not in fact, by luck more than by judgment, committed the *Lumley v Gye* tort.

Where the defendant did use unlawful means, therefore, as in *Stratford v Lindley*[7], the tort was made out. More expansion came in cases such as *Merkur Island Shipping v Laughton*[8] in which the plaintiffs were further down a contractual chain than the plaintiff in *Thomson*. In *Merkur Island*, in effect, the defendant organised a boycott by the employees of a supplier who supplied another supplier who supplied the plaintiff. The boycott had a domino effect on the contracts and caused a breach of the final contract of supply, on which basis the plaintiff sued and won.

Notice that in the original *Lumley v Gye* tort the defendant had to do something directly to bring about a breach of contract, such as persuading the third party to act inconsistently with the contract or 'informing' the third party of facts that everyone knows mean that the third party will face penalties if it does not do what the defendant wants.[9] In the indirect form, however, the breach of the contract between the plaintiff and the supplier is simply caused by the unlawful means. The breach does not happen because of direct persuasion by the defendant of one of the parties to the contract.

The second expansion of *Lumley v Gye* was to situations in which the 'direct' tort did not produce a technical breach of contract because of a clause in that contract exempting the supplier from performance in the circumstances concerned. In *Torquay Hotel v Cousins*[10] the defendant union official persuaded (by means of unspoken threats of a strike—but in the event nothing turned on that point) suppliers of fuel oil to the plaintiff's hotel to stop supplying it. There was a clause in the contract of supply that exempted the supplier from performance if prevented by a labour dispute. But the Court of Appeal said that the tort was made out if the defendant interfered in the *performance* of the contract. One might object that the contract had been performed according to its terms, since the supply of oil was not required in the circumstances of the case. But Lord Denning said that the union officials could not take advantage of an excuse from performance in the contract the invocation of which they themselves had caused.

Torquay Hotel v Cousins went even further. Lord Denning said, in a passage which clearly contradicts Lord Herschell's view in *Allen v Flood*, that the *Lumley v Gye* tort had also been committed when the union officials turned their attentions to another supplier of fuel oil, appropriately named Alternative Fuels Ltd, and told it not to enter into further contracts for

7   [1965] AC 269.
8   [1983] 2 AC 570.
9   *Torquay Hotel v Cousins* [1969] 2 Ch 106, *Stratford v Lindley* [1965] AC 269. It is also enough for the defendant to persuade the third party simply to enter into a contract with the defendant that is incompatible with the third party's contract with the plaintiff. Cf *Lumley v Gye* itself and *British Motor Trade Association v Salvadori* [1949] Ch 556.
10 [1969] 2 Ch 106.

the supply of oil to the plaintiff. This amounts to saying that it is a tort to prevent the formation of contracts.

It is possible that such a tort might have been a useful development, at least where the defendant is exercising monopoly power. The point has been left open by the Court of Appeal[11]. Also, in *Nagle v Feilden*[12], before the days of sex discrimination legislation, a woman who was refused a licence to train horses allegedly on grounds of her sex obtained a declaration that this was unlawful because the defend–ants were engaged in restraint of trade. But now that this field is occupied not only by domestic law on discrimination, restrictive practices and trade union closed shops but also by European competition law there would seem to be no pressing need for it. The authority of Lord Denning's extension of *Lumley v Gye* is therefore much in doubt.

Two other extensions of *Lumley v Gye* should be mentioned. First, in *Prudential Assurance v Lorenz*[13] inducing a breach of fiduciary duty was declared to be a tort along the same lines as inducing a breach of contract.[14] And in *Meade v Haringey London Borough Council*[15] the Court of Appeal said that it was possible for there to be a tort of inducing a breach of statutory duty. In that case, the union persuaded the local education authority (who probably did not need much persuading) to close down all their own local schools in support of a strike of caretakers that the union had called. Lord Denning thought that this action may have put the council in breach of its statutory duty to provide education and would have allowed parents of affected children to sue the union. Similarly in *Barretts & Baird v Institution of Professional Civil Servants*[16] Henry J thought it was possible such a breach of statutory duty could be founded on obligations in European Community law as well as in domestic British law.

But in *Law Debenture Trust Corpn plc v Ural Caspian Oil*,[17] the Court of Appeal decided that the *Lumley v Gye* tort did not extend to actions taken by defendants to reduce or evade the *consequences* of breaches of contract. The first defendants in *Ural Caspian Oil* had induced a breach of contractual obligations with the plaintiffs to pay over to them a share of compensation payments paid by the Russian government in 1990 for the expropriation of the Russian oil industry during the Bolshevik revolution 70 years earlier. The second defendants were accused by the plaintiff of helping the first defendants to reduce or evade the remedies available to the plaintiff by taking part in a scheme to transfer shares from the first defendants to the second defendants. The second defendants said that since the plaintiff had not at the time obtained judgment against the first defendants, there was no obligation on the plaintiff not to take part in such a scheme. The Court of Appeal agreed.

11 *Hadmor v Hamilton* [1981] 2 All ER 724 (reversed on other grounds [1983] 1 AC 191).
12 [1966] 2 QB 633.
13 (1971) 11 KIR 78.
14 But nb *Metall und Rohstoff v Donaldson Lufkin & Jenrette* [1990] 1 QB 391 in which the Court of Appeal said that it was not a tort to procure the breach of a constructive trust.
15 [1979] ICR 494.
16 [1987] IRLR 3.
17 [1995] 1 All ER 157.

Two questions, however, have always been unclear in *Lumley v Gye*. First, what is the relevant intention or purpose and state of knowledge that the defendant must have had to be held liable? Does the defendant have merely to intend the act that causes a breach of contract, or does the defendant have to intend and want the contract to be broken? Or is it something in between such as recklessness as to the consequences? And second, under what circumstances can the defendant justify his actions? Are defendants allowed to say, for example, that the purpose of their actions was merely to further their own ends rather than to do down the plaintiff? The two questions are related.

The Court of Appeal has confirmed that the state of the law on these two questions is uncertain. In *Millar v Bassey*[18] the defendant, the singer Shirley Bassey, was alleged to have contracted with the plaintiff record company to produce a new album. After negotiations had been completed, and a producer, studios and background musicians and singers hired, the defendant decided to pull out of the contract, causing an immediate breach of contract between the producer and the record company. The plaintiff emphasised that the defendant had unique talents and there was no possibility of hiring a substitute to take her place. The plaintiff said that by breaching her own contract in such circumstances the defendant had forced the producer to breach its contract with the plaintiff and should be liable in the *Lumley v Gye* tort at least in its indirect *Thomson v Deakin* form.

The case produced an extraordinary division of opinion in the Court of Appeal. Beldam LJ began by saying:

'I find difficulty in understanding the distinction drawn between "inducing and causing" [the producer] to break its contracts with the appellants and "procuring" those breaches.'

That is, Beldam LJ found difficult the distinction between the 'direct' tort and the 'indirect' tort. For him it made no particular difference whether the plaintiff actively persuaded the third party to break the contract or just caused them to do so.

He went on, referring to 'intention' as 'that equivocal vocabulary which has given rise to such difficulty' to discuss the necessary mental element in the tort:

'The respondent may not have wished, nor may it have been her primary purpose, to induce or cause [the producer] to break its contracts with the appellants but unless she fulfilled her obligations to [the producer] it was inevitable (not just likely or foreseeable) that [the producer] could not fulfil its obligations to the appellants. This distinction is important and I notice that it was one drawn by Rose J in his judgment in *Edwin Hill & Partners v First National Finance Corpn plc* [1988] 3 All ER 801, [1989] 1 WLR 225 at 228.

18 (1993) Independent, 26 August, LEXIS Transcript 12 July 1993.

> Moreover, in most cases of "inducing" or "procuring" a breach of contract of which *Lumley v Gye* (1853) 2 E & B 216 and *Bowen v Hall* (1881) 6 QBD 333 may be regarded as examples the tort–feasors have been acting primarily to secure their own commercial advantage though they could only achieve it by causing detriment to the plaintiffs.'

That is, for Beldam LJ an inevitable result is the same as an intended one, whatever the defendant may say about what she wanted to happen. The plaintiff argued for a test that the defendant should be taken to have intended the probable consequences of her actions, but Beldam LJ stuck to his 'inevitable' test.

The defendant argued that the only relevant intention was a specific motive of harming the plaintiff. She pointed to *Bowen v Hall*,[19] in which the defendants' intention was to secure for themselves the services of a brickmaker who had contracted to work for the plaintiff. The brickmaker knew about a secret process that the defendant wanted to have knowledge of. Brett LJ said:

> 'We were of opinion that the act of the defendants was done with knowledge of the contract between the plaintiff and Pearson, was done in order to obtain an advantage for one of the defendants at the expense of the plaintiff, was done from a wrong motive, and would therefore justify a finding that it was done in that sense maliciously.'

He then said:

> '[T]he act of the defendants which is complained of must be an act wrongful in law and in fact. Merely to persuade a person to break his contract may not be wrongful in law or fact ... But if the persuasion be used for the indirect purpose of injuring the plaintiff, or of benefiting the defendant at the expense of the plaintiff, it is a malicious act which is in law and in fact a wrong act, and therefore a wrongful act, and therefore an actionable act if injury ensues from it.'

But Beldam LJ said that *Allen v Flood* had explained away *Bowen v Hall*. In *Allen v Flood*, Lord Watson said Brett LJ had only meant to say that there would be liability when the defendant had 'procur[ed] an illegal act' and 'malice' included a 'successful persuasion to break a contract'. Lord Watson added:

> 'The root of the principle is that, in any legal question, malice depends, not on evil motive which influenced the mind of the actor, but upon the illegal character of the act which he contemplated

19 (1881) 6 QBD 333.

and committed. In my opinion it is alike consistent with reason and common sense that when the act done is, apart from the feelings which prompted it, legal, the civil law ought to take no cognizance of its motive.'

Beldam LJ's conclusion was that when the defendant's act was in itself unlawful, a specific intention to injure the plaintiff was not necessary. Proof of such an intention is only necessary when the act is in itself lawful. But, says Beldam LJ, a breach of contract is to be regarded as unlawful and a legal wrong.

Beldam LJ went on to say that, on the basis of *Thomson v Deakin*, there is 'no valid distinction between persuading a man to break his contract with another and making his performance of it impossible by depriving him in breach of their contracts of the services of his employees'. If that is so, Beldam LJ says, there should furthermore be no distinction between persuading someone to breach a contract and 'the deliberate refusal to perform irreplaceable services in breach of contract knowing that such refusal will inevitably make the performance of another's contract impossible'.

Furthermore, Beldam LJ cited *South Wales Miners' Federation v Glamorgan Coal Co*,[20] in which the union had called stoppages not to harm the plaintiff employers but to restrict production so as to keep up the price of coal and thus, under the terms of a collective agreement, to keep up also the employees' bonus payments. The House of Lords held that this was no justification. It was no defence to an action for inducing or procuring a breach of contract that it was done without malice or ill-will to the plaintiff. More recently, Beldam LJ pointed out, in *Edwin Hill & Partners v First National Finance Corpn plc*[1] Stuart-Smith LJ had rejected a submission that the necessary intention to interfere with a contract is not established unless the defendant's conduct is aimed at the plaintiff and there is a desire to injure him. Finally, Beldam LJ rejected the argument[2] that unless there was a rule requiring specific intent to injure in some form, the *Lumley v Gye* tort would have the effect of enforcing contracts on third parties who were not parties to them. Citing the House of Lords in *Rookes v Barnard*,[3] although he could equally have cited *Torquay Hotel v Cousins*, he said that the *Lumley v Gye* tort could be committed even where there was no technical breach of contract, so that the tort was not about the enforcement of the contract but about the wrong done by the defendant.

On the other side in *Millar v Bassey*, Peter Gibson LJ put the more orthodox case that there could not possibly be liability under *Lumley v Gye* merely for the consequences of one's own breach of contract. He rejected the submissions that cases such as *South Wales Miners' Federation v Glamorgan Coal Company* and *Edwin Hill & Partners v First National*

---

20 [1905] AC 239.
1 [1988] 3 All ER 801, [1989] 1 WLR 225.
2 See eg Hobhouse J in *Rickless v United Artists Corpn* [1986] FSR 502.
3 [1964] AC 1129. See below.

Plc forced the conclusion that there was no need to prove a specific intent to injure the plaintiff. In the former case, for example, Peter Gibson LJ pointed out that although it was said in the House of Lords that, 'It is … a principle of the law, applicable even to the criminal law, that people are presumed to intend the reasonable consequences of their acts', in the very next sentence the Lord Chancellor said it was not necessary to have recourse to that presumption in that case. And as for *Edwin Hill & Partners v First National Plc*, Stuart-Smith LJ's remarks were obiter, he had misunderstood the effect of *Thomson v Deakin* and assumed that a case from 1909, *Smithies v National Association of Operative Plasterers*,[4] was binding authority when it was no such thing.

Peter Gibson LJ said that it was a necessary element of the tort that the defendant's conduct must have been directed against the plaintiff 'in the sense that the breach of his contract or the interference with his interests was intended, rather than being merely what probably would result from his conduct.'

Peter Gibson LJ pointed to an number of authorities for his view. In *Quinn v Leathem*,[5] for example, Lord Lindley said:

> '[T]he principle involved in [*Lumley v Gye*] cannot be confined to inducements to break contracts of service, nor indeed to inducements to break any contracts. The principle which underlies the decision reaches all wrongful acts done intentionally to damage a particular individual and actually damaging him.'

And in *DC Thomson & Co Ltd v Deakin*, Jenkins LJ, contrary to Beldam LJ's view, distinguished between direct interference and indirect interference. He said *Lumley v Gye* was authority for the following proposition:

> 'Direct persuasion or procurement or inducement applied by the third party to the contract breaker, with knowledge of the contract and the intention of bringing about its breach, is clearly to be regarded as a wrongful act in itself, and where this is shown a cause of actionable interference in its primary form is made out.'

But in other forms of the tort, including interference in the performance of a contract (as in the later case *Torquay Hotel v Cousins*) and the indirect tort (as in *Thomson* itself), the requirements were more onerous:

> 'First that the person charged with actionable interference knew of the existence of the contract and intended to procure its breach;[6] secondly, that the person so charged did definitely and unequivo-

---

4   [1909] 1 KB 310.
5   [1901] AC 495.
6   In fact, recklessness may be enough: *Emerald Construction v Lowthian* [1966] 1 WLR 691.

cally persuade, induce or procure the employees concerned to break their contracts of employment with the intent I have mentioned.'

Peter Gibson LJ accepted that Jenkins LJ did not expressly refer to there being a requirement that the defendant's conduct should be directed against or intended to injure the plaintiff, although by emphasising knowledge of the contract and intention to procure its breach he got very close. Jenkins LJ also approved of Upjohn J's comment at first instance that a breach of contract which was merely the probable consequence of the interference was not sufficient for the tort.

Peter Gibson LJ's most direct authority was *Rookes v Barnard* where Lord Devlin said that inducing a breach of contract had the following requirements:

'There must be, besides the act of inducement, knowledge by the defendant of the contract in question and of the fact that the act induced will be a breach of it; there must also be malice in the legal sense, that is, an intention to cause the breach and to injure the plaintiff thereby and an absence of justification; and there must be special damage, ie, more than nominal damage, caused to the plaintiff by this breach.'

Peter Gibson LJ also emphasised why, apart from authority, the law ought to put such restrictions on the *Lumley v Gye* tort. Unlike Beldam LJ he accepted that it is a problem with *Lumley v Gye* that it gives a right of action for failure to comply with the terms of a contract against a person who is not a party to the contract, contrary to the principle of privity of contract. Furthermore, unless there is a requirement of specific intention, 'freedom of action would be unduly restricted by liability for incidental consequences'.[7] He went on:

'Interference with contracts may flow from competition and is the normal and expected consequence of industrial action. It would not be right for the law to discourage competition by encouraging actions by unsuccessful competitors or to allow tort actions by those who suffer only incidentally from another person's activities.'

The casting vote in *Millar v Bassey* fell to Ralph Gibson LJ. Although sympathising more with Peter Gibson LJ's view than Beldam LJ's view, he pointed out that the technical issue in the case was whether the plaintiff's view should be struck out as 'unarguable'. In his opinion:

'The tort under consideration remains a comparatively new tort of which the precise boundaries should be established from case to case. One of those boundaries is concerned with the nature of the

---

7   Citing J Fleming *The Law of Torts* (7th ed) (1987) p 656.

intention which is required to satisfy the requirement that the conduct be "directed against" the plaintiffs.'

Although one might think that it is fairly odd to describe a tort established 140 years ago as 'comparatively' new, one can have more sympathy with Ralph Gibson LJ's conclusion:

'In my judgment, the authorities cited to this court do not provide a clear decision upon the point here under consideration.'

He therefore allowed the plaintiff's appeal and directed that the case should proceed to trial.

Note that the issues left open or contested by *Millar* include not only whether there has to be a specific intention in the indirect tort (both sides agreed that there does not have to be such an intention in the direct tort) but also: (1) whether breach of contract itself, as opposed to a tort or crime, can amount to 'unlawful means' for the purposes of the indirect tort and (2) what might amount to 'justification' of the defendant's action—raising prices was not enough in *South Wales Miners' Federation v Glamorgan Coal*, but in *Brimelow v Casson*[8] a defence of justification succeeded where the defendants said that they had instigated industrial action in favour of a pay rise among a group of chorus girls because otherwise the chorus girls would have been forced by poverty into prostitution. In addition there is possibly a defence when the alleged interference consists of enforcing one's own contractual rights if one acquired those rights either before the plaintiff acquired its rights or before the time one knew about the plaintiff's contract.[9] Another question is that if Beldam LJ is correct, is he also correct to limit his rule to cases in which the consequential breaches of contract are 'inevitable' or should the plaintiff's view in *Millar* prevail that 'probability' would suffice?

For what it is worth, the view of the author of this book is that: (1) *Lumley v Gye* was wrongly decided and so were all cases that subsequently have approved of it and extended it, since, without proof of misrepresentation or fraud in the contracts or in the information that led to the contracts' formation, there is no reason to give the plaintiff remedies beyond its contractual remedies; but (2) since it is now too late to correct that mistake, *Lumley v Gye* should not be extended, especially in cases, such as *Millar v Bassey*, where the plaintiff could easily have protected itself by negotiating a clearer deal with the defendant in the first place that would have protected it from consequential loss.

Conspiracy

The second 'economic' tort developed in the late ninteenth century and early twentieth century, mainly in the context of industrial action cases,

8 [1924] 1 Ch 302.
9 Cf Lord Devlin in *Rookes v Barnard* [1964] AC 1129 at 1206ff.

was conspiracy. Following various attempts snuffed out by statute to deem strikes to be criminal conspiracies,[10] in *Allen v Flood, Quinn v Leathem*[11] and, eventually, *Crofter Hand Woven Harris Tweed Co v Veitch*[12] the courts faced attempts by employers to establish a tort of conspiracy under which it would be actionable for employees to combine in a union in order to injure the employer's interests. The main obstacle to the establishment of such a tort was *Mogul SS Co v McGregor Gow*[13] in which the defendant shipping companies had formed a cartel to drive the plaintiff out of the China tea trade. The defendants had run the whole gamut of monopolistic behaviour, including 'predatory' pricing (offering concerted special rates to suppliers that the plaintiff could not match in the short term) to tying arrangements and exclusive supply deals, under which rebates were offered to those local suppliers who would undertake not to deal with the plaintiff. But the plaintiff's claim failed. As long as the defendants used means that were themselves lawful, that is they did not resort to force or fraud or, indeed, committing the *Lumley v Gye* tort, there could be no action against them. As Bowen LJ said in the Court of Appeal:

'[T]he defendants have done nothing more against the plaintiffs than pursue to the bitter end a war of competition waged in the interest of their own trade.'

In *Allen v Flood* the specially augmented House of Lords applied the same principle to labour disputes. The defendants had not used unlawful means of any kind, so they could not be liable in tort.

However, Bowen LJ had also said in *Mogul SS Co v McGregor Gow* that:

'A combination may make oppressive or dangerous that which if it proceeded only from a single person would be otherwise, and the very fact of combination may shew that the object is to do harm, and not to exercise one's own just rights.'

In *Quinn v Leathem* the House of Lords said that there could therefore be a tort of conspiring to do harm to the plaintiff, rather than to further their own 'legitimate' interests, even without the use of unlawful means, and that such a tort could be committed by the trade union organisers of a boycott against a non-union employer. The decision is difficult to justify on its facts, since it is not easy to see how the unions could be said to be doing anything else than advancing their own interests, and the only way of characterising these interests as not 'legitimate' would be to contradict *Allen v Flood* and to say that the law should treat competitive activity by labour organisations differently from the way it treats the same activity by traders. But the House of Lords was bound by a jury finding that the

10   See *R v Bunn* (1872) 12 Cox CC 316 and the Conspiracy and Protection of Property Act 1875.
11   [1901] AC 495.
12   [1942] AC 435.
13   (1889) 23 QBD 598; affd [1892] AC 25.

defendants had indeed intended to harm the plaintiff rather than to advance their own interests.[14]

In *Sorrell v Smith*,[15] however, the House of Lords said that 'malice' was necessary, and that 'malice' meant not just that the defendant wanted to do harm to the plaintiff, but that the defendant's interest in doing harm to the plaintiff outweighed their interest in advancing their own interests.

Finally in the *Crofter* case, the House of Lords said that the test for what advanced the interests of the defendants was subjective—all that was required was that the defendants honestly believed that they were advancing their own interests, not that the court believed that their belief was reasonable. In *Crofter*, the plaintiffs marketed cloth woven by Outer Hebridean crofters but using yarn imported from mainland Scotland. Yarn was also produced locally by mills whose employees were members of the Transport and General Workers' Union. The union asked for higher wages for the mill workers, but the employers said that they could not pay more because they had to compete against the imported yarn. To cure this defect in their argument, the union instructed some of its other members who were dockers in the main Outer Hebridean port to boycott the plaintiff's supplies and products. It is difficult to see what benefit the dockers could derive from this action, but the House of Lords accepted that there was no actionable conspiracy to injure the plaintiff because the union organisers and members honestly believed that they were acting in their own collective interests. Honest belief in collective interests also justified Musicians Union officials who organised a boycott of a Wolverhampton ballroom believed by them to be excluding patrons on the grounds of race.[16] The interest of the defendant does not, said the Court of Appeal, have to be a financial or tradable one.

Conspiracy to injure was once successfully invoked against a defendant union official who acted purely out of personal animosity towards the plaintiff[17] but the tort rarely succeeds because of the nature of the opportunity for justification. The tort has made several appearance in the two massive litigations launched by the Lonrho company against its enemies the oil companies who busted the Rhodesian sanctions[18] and the Fayed brothers, who beat it in the takeover race for the then owner of

14 One of the effects of *Quinn v Leathem* was that, on a change of government, in 1906 Parliament passed a Trades Disputes Act which gave immunity from tort to unions and from certain specific torts for those who acted 'in contemplation or furtherance of a trade dispute'. Over the years plaintiffs' lawyers have stretched the torts discussed in this section and the next two largely to get round these immunities, and the immunities have been changed in response to the cases. At present, the immunities, much reduced in recent years, are to be found in s 219 of the Trade Union and Labour Relations (Consolidation) Act 1992. For detailed discussion the reader is referred to the standard texts on labour law.

15 [1925] AC 700.

16 *Scala Ballroom v Ratcliffe* [1958] 1 WLR 1057.

17 *Huntly v Thornton*.

18 See eg *Lonrho v Shell (No 2)* [1982] AC 173.

Harrods, the House of Fraser.[19] None of these cases expands the scope of the tort, and some of them doubt the reasons for its existence. The most recent in the line, *Lonrho v Fayed (No 5)* confirms that there is no tort unless the defendant's sole or predominant motive was to injure the plaintiff, and also that it is actionable only on proof of damage. In particular, it decides that a plaintiff may not recover damages for lost reputation, business or otherwise, in a conspiracy to injure action, but must take its chances in a defamation action.

Mogul SS Co v McGregor Gow did not rule out the actionability of a conspiracy when the defendants have used unlawful means—force, fraud or the *Lumley v Gye* tort, for example, and the House of Lords has confirmed several times that combining to use unlawful means to injure the plaintiff is a tort.[20] The unlawful means serve as a substitute for the need to prove that the predominant purpose was to injure the plaintiff[1]. Furthermore, justification is not available to the defendant.[2] The main use of conspiracy by unlawful means is, however, to widen the range of possible defendants for the purposes of the broader tort of interference in trade by unlawful means, to which we now turn.[3]

Interference in trade or business by unlawful means

In *Allen v Flood* the defendants escaped liability because their actions caused and involved no breaches of contract. In that context, Lord Herschell said that it was not tortious to persuade people not to contract with the plaintiff. In *Mogul SS Co v McGregor Gow* the Court of Appeal had held that a conspiracy to prevent the making of contracts by the plaintiff was not actionable unless unlawful means were used. It will be noticed at once that what these cases did not cover was the situation where a person *using unlawful means* persuades or induces others not to contract or trade or deal with the plaintiff. In addition, these cases do not decide whether it is tortious to use unlawful means to induce someone to do something lawful that is nevertheless to the plaintiff's detriment.

In *Rookes v Barnard* the House of Lords faced the second of these questions. The plaintiff was an employee of an airline. He resigned from his union because he disagreed with several of its policies. The union had

---

19 Eg *Lonrho v Fayed* [1992] 1 AC 448 and *Lonrho v Fayed (No 5)*[1994] 1 All ER 188, [1993] 1 WLR 1489.

20 *Lonrho v Shell (No 2)* [1982] AC 173, *Lonrho v Fayed* [1992] 1 AC 448.

1   *Lonrho v Fayed* [1992] 1 AC 448.

2   *Metall und Rohstoff AG v Donaldson Lufkin & Jenrette Inc* [1990] 1 QB 391, [1989] 3 All ER 14, citing Lord Denning in *Lonrho v Shell (No 2)* (1981) 125 Sol Jo 255 (CA). See also Evershed LJ in *Greenhalgh v Mallard* [1947] 2 All ER 255.

3   On the parallel question of who can sue, see now s 235A, Trade Union and Labour Relations (Consolidation) Act 1992 which allows anyone to sue a union for industrial action that affects the supply of goods and services to them if there is anyone anywhere who has an action in tort against the union.

an informal arrangement with the airline that only union members would be allowed to work for the airline in the kind of job done by the plaintiff. Three union officials, two of whom were also employees of the airline, informed the airline's management that a union meeting had resolved that if the plaintiff was not dismissed, there would be a strike. The airline gave in and first suspended the plaintiff and then dismissed him, but by allowing him the correct period of notice in accordance with his contract, the airline did not breach the plaintiff's contract. On the other hand, the union members who had threatened to go on strike were threatening to breach their contracts of employment, especially because, so they conceded, their contracts of employment incorporated an agreement by the union not to go on strike.

The House of Lords decided that on these facts all three officials had committed a tort called 'intimidation'.[4] If someone threatens violence, libel or some other tort, in order to force someone to act lawfully to the detriment of the plaintiff, the person making the threat commits, according to the House of Lords, a well-established (though second order) tort against the plaintiff. The question before the House of Lords, therefore, was whether threatening a breach of contract to achieve the same object also amounted to a tort. The Court of Appeal had said that, on the contrary, only violence gave rise to an action for intimidation. The House of Lords, however, decided for the plaintiff. Lord Reid, for example, said:

> 'So long as the defendant only threatens to do what he has a legal right to do he is on safe ground. At least if there is no conspiracy he would not be liable to anyone for doing the act, whatever his motive might be, and it would be absurd to make him liable for threatening to do it but not for doing it. But I agree with Lord Herschell (*Allen v Flood*) that there is a chasm between doing what you have a legal right to do and doing what you have no legal right to do, and there seems to me to be the same chasm between threatening to do what you have a legal right to do and threatening to do what you have no legal right to do. It must follow from *Allen v Flood* that to intimidate by threatening to do what you have a legal right to do is to intimidate by lawful means. But I see no good reason for extending that doctrine. Threatening a breach of contract may be a much more coercive weapon than threatening a tort, particularly when the threat is directed against a company or corporation, and, if there is no technical reason requiring a distinction between different kinds of threats, I can see no other ground for making any such distinction.'

Lord Devlin agreed. He said that the essence of the case was coercion. If the defendant coerced the intermediary then the plaintiff should have an

---

4 The union official who was not an employee could, strictly, only have committed a tort of conspiracy by unlawful means, but this point was not taken up.

action, regardless of whether the coercion was by threat of a criminal offence, a tort or a breach of contract.

Lord Devlin said that it was also tortious to intimidate someone directly, that is to threaten to do something unlawful to induce someone to do something lawful but to their own detriment. Even if this is so, however, it is not clear that threatening to breach a contract should count as adequate unlawful means for the purpose of this 'two-party' version of the tort.[5] If it did, threatening to breach a contract would be a tort in itself, and would allow the plaintiff to evade many of the rules of contract law that limit the plaintiff's damages. On the other hand, the effect of *Lumley v Gye* itself is not much different—since the plaintiff can sue the defendant for damages that he could not obtain from the third party in contract. And it would certainly be the effect of the *Lumley v Gye* tort if the view of Beldam LJ in *Millar v Bassey* were to prevail, for the plaintiff would presumably then be able to recover from Miss Bassey damages that would have been beyond his grasp in contract. It is submitted, however, that these effects are already unfortunate, and the two-party version of the tort should not admit the threat of breach of contract as unlawful means.

The defendants in *Rookes v Barnard* did not raise the possibility of a justification defence to the tort of intimidation. Conventional wisdom is that justification is not permitted in unlawful means torts, although, as we have seen, the situation in inducing a breach of contract is confused.[6]

The first question left over from *Allen v Flood*, whether it is tortious to use unlawful means to prevent people from contracting with the plaintiff, came before the House of Lords in *Hadmor v Hamilton*.[7] Hadmor, the plaintiff, was an independent producer of television programmes that used freelance staff. The defendant was an official of the union ACTT whose policy was to oppose the use by television stations of programmes made by such companies. Hadmor made a series of 15 programmes, the first two of which Thames Television, then a television station, bought and transmitted. The local union branch announced its intention to 'black' any future programmes. Faced with the threat of industrial action if they did not cooperate, Thames told Hadmor that it would be buying no more of the programmes. Hadmor sued the defendant, claiming that it was a tort to interfere in its business using unlawful means. The only serious disagreement among the courts that heard the case was whether it was likely that the union official would probably succeed in establishing a defence based on the immunities from suit granted since 1906 to those who organise industrial action. All the courts held that there was a serious case to be tried on the tort itself. The union was either inducing or threatening to induce Thames employees to breach their contracts of employment by refusing to obey lawful and contractually backed instructions to transmit programmes of Thames' choice. This was the unlawful means. The inter-

---

5   Carty 'Intentional Violation of Economic Interests: The Limits of Common Law Liability' (1988) 104 LQR 250.

6   See above.

7   [1983] 1 AC 191.

ference in business was preventing further contracts between Hadmor and Thames.

The decision in Hadmor was confirmed in *Lonrho v Fayed*.[8] The Secretary of State for Trade and Industry referred the plaintiff's proposed takeover of House of Fraser to the Monopolies and Mergers Commission and required the plaintiff to give an undertaking not to acquire more than 30% of the company's equity. While that undertaking was still in effect, blocking the plaintiff's takeover of House of Fraser, the defendants moved to acquire the same company. The defendants' bid was not referred by the Secretary of State to the Commission. The defendants succeeded in their bid. A few days later the plaintiff was released from its undertaking. The plaintiff sued the defendants and their advisers, alleging that they had induced the Secretary of State not to refer the defendants' bid to the Commission by false and fraudulent misrepresentations about themselves, their commercial background and the source of their finance for the acquisition. The plaintiff's case was that the defendants had thus interfered in the plaintiff's business by unlawful means. Their alleged misrepresentations constituted the unlawful means and the failure of the Secretary of State to refer the defendants' bid to the commission and to lift the undertaking was the interference.

The Court of Appeal, uncontradicted by the House of Lords in the subsequent appeal, accepted the existence of the tort and that it arguably had been committed by the defendants. The Court of Appeal, furthermore, decided that it was unnecessary, as it is unnecessary in intimidation, that there should have been a complete tort committed by the defendant against the intermediary. The Fayeds (the defendants) were accused of deceiving the Secretary of State, but the Secretary of State would have had difficulty in establishing the tort of deceit since it is not clear what damage the Secretary of State suffered.

Moreover, the Court of Appeal declared that there was no need to show in this tort that the defendant's 'predominant purpose' was to harm the plaintiff. As with conspiracy by unlawful means, the unlawfulness of the means supposedly removes the need to show that the predominant purpose was to injure. All that was necessary was that the unlawful act 'was in some sense directed at the plaintiff'. But note that as *Millar v Bassey* shows in relation to the *Lumley v Gye* tort, it is unclear exactly what constitutes the required intention and what exactly 'in some sense directed at the plaintiff' means.

The effect of *Lonrho v Fayed* has been to confirm the view of those who said that 'interference with business by unlawful means' is a general or 'genus' tort of which intimidation, conspiracy by unlawful means and possibly the indirect form of inducing a breach of contract are 'species' or types. It is alleged that not only breaches of contract, threatened breaches of contract and torts from assault to deceit can constitute unlawful means for the purposes of the 'genus' tort, but also crimes that are not themselves actionable and other breaches of statutory duty not themselves actionable.

8   [1992] 1 AC 448.

It is also alleged the interference can be in not only business and trading relationships, present and future, but also in the plaintiff's capacity to fulfill statutory duties.

As far as unlawful means are concerned, there is no question that all torts count—including trespass and nuisance.[9] *Lonrho v Fayed* indicates that deceit counts as well.[10] Contempt of court probably does not count.[11] But it is doubtful whether crimes that are not otherwise actionable in tort should count.[12] It is true that sometimes the reasons that the courts give for refusing private rights of action on a criminal statute are unsatisfactory.[13] But the reasons discussed in chapter 8 should give pause for thought. If allowing an action on the criminal statute would create a strict liability tort or a tort in which damage not recoverable in negligence would be recoverable, or would interfere with a contractually agreed distribution of risk, it would at least indicate that caution needs to be exercised in allowing breach of the same statute to count as unlawful means for the purpose of creating a related tort.

Finally, threatening to breach a contract is unlawful means for intimidation and breaching a contract is unlawful means, probably, for the indirect *Lumley v Gye* tort. Whether breach of contract should count as unlawful means for the 'genus' tort is another question. We have already discussed the difficulties in counting threatening a breach of contract as unlawful means for two-party intimidation. But if Bedlam LJ is right in *Millar v Bassey*, and the two-party intimidation tort can be committed by threat of a breach of contract, both of which, it is submitted, would be a mistake, the next step would be to make someone liable for interference by unlawful means if they breached their contract intending or knowing that it would be inevitable that the plaintiff would not be able to make a contract or engage in a business or receive a benefit (or fulfill a statutory duty). Although such liability has long been foreshadowed,[14] it would have the interesting effect of allowing a straightforward action for third party benefits in contract.

As for interference with statutory duties, as opposed to the normal commercial interests, *Associated British Ports v Transport and General Workers' Union*[15] shows that it is possible for liability to arise. The plaintiff employers complained that the defendant union was organising a strike which was tortious because (a) the employees were in breach of their statu-

9 *Messenger Newspapers v National Graphical Association* [1984] IRLR 397, *Norbrook Laboratories v King* [1984] IRLR 200, *News Group v Society of Graphical and Allied Trades 82 (No 2)* [1987] ICR 181, *Department of Transport v Williams* (1993) 138 Sol Jo LB 5, (1993) Times, 7 December (CA).
10 See also *National Phonograph v Edison Bell* [1908] 1 Ch 335.
11 *Chapman v Honig* [1963] 2 QB 502, but cf *Acrow (Automation) v Rex Chainbelt* [1971] 3 All ER 1175.
12 See Lord Diplock in *Lonrho v Shell (No 2)* [1982] AC 173 and, for different reasons, Sales 'The Tort of Conspiracy and Civil Secondary Liability' [1990] CLJ 491.
13 Above ch 8.
14 Weir 'Chaos or Cosmos: *Rookes, Stratford* and the Economic Torts' [1964] CLJ 225.
15 [1989] IRLR 305.

tory duties under the old dock labour scheme and (b) there was interference in the employers' ability to fulfill its obligations under the scheme. The House of Lords eventually said that the case was one of contract rather than of statutory duty, and the statutes merely followed the contractual position. But the underlying arguments were allowed to stand. In *Department of Transport v Williams*,[16] in which the Department of Transport sued the protesters who, by means of a mass trespass, were preventing the building of a motorway across Twyford Down, it was conceded that interference in activities authorised by statute by the unlawful means of trespass established the tort.

Breach of confidence

The last topic to consider in this section is the protection not of goods or contracts but of information. As mentioned above, we will not consider copyright, patent, trademarks or passing off. But we can consider the most obvious legal protection for information, namely breach of confidence. Breach of confidence is an enormous topic well beyond the scope of an introductory tort law text, and only a sketch of the law will be given here. But it should be regarded as an integral part of the law, especially as, in an age of information, conventional forms of wealth are supplemented by the more fleeting attractions of data and their control. This section also replaces the conventional section in tort textbooks about the so far non-existent tort of breach of privacy. It is more useful to know a little about a right that exists than to know much about a right that does not exist.

The development of the protection of confidential information can be traced back at least to the nineteenth century in cases such as *Prince Albert v Strange*[17] but its modern development began perhaps with *Saltman Engineering Co Ltd v Campbell Engineering Co Ltd*[18] and especially *Duchess of Argyll v Duke of Argyll*.[19] In *Argyll v Argyll* an ex-wife succeeded in stopping her ex-husband from disclosing information given to him by her when they were married and concerning her private affairs. Since then, breach of confidence has grown to encompass many situations in which someone comes into possession of confidential information.[20]

According to Lord Goff of Chieveley in *A-G v Guardian Newspapers (No 2)*,[1] a duty of confidence arises when:

> '[C]onfidential information comes to the knowledge of a person (the confidant) in circumstances where he has notice, or is held to have agreed, that the information is confidential, with the effect that it

16 (1993) 138 Sol Jo LB 5, (1993) Times, 7 December.
17 (1849) 2 De G & Sm 652.
18 (1963) 65 RPC 203.
19 [1967] Ch 302, [1965] 1 All ER 611.
20 See Jones (1970) 86 LQR 463, Cripps (1984) 4 OJLS 361, [1985] CLJ 35, [1983] PL 600 [1985] LQR 506, Tettenborn [1992] PL 200.
1 [1990] 1 AC 109, [1988] 3 All ER 545.

would be just in all the circumstances that he should be precluded
from disclosing the information to others.'

'Notice' includes actual knowledge and where the confidant 'deliberately
closed his eyes to the obvious'.[2]

These circumstances often concern contractual obligations and trade
secrets of various types that employees or ex-employees attempt to use in
their new jobs.[3] But there is also a form of breach of confidence that does
not depend on contract. These are cases where, again to quote Lord Goff:

> '[A] third party receives information from a person who is under a
> duty of confidence in respect of it, knowing that it has been disclosed
> by that person to him in breach of his duty of confidence, but also
> to include certain situations, beloved of law teachers—where an
> obviously confidential document is wafted by an electric fan out of
> a window into a crowded street, or where an obviously confidential
> document, such as a private diary, is dropped in a public place,
> and is then picked up by a passer-by. I also have in mind the
> situations where secrets of importance to national security come
> into the possession of members of the public.'

It was previously thought that no duty of confidentiality could arise
without an identifiable prior relationship between the parties.[4] But Lord
Goff's remarks make this view untenable.[5] Obligations of confidentiality
may arise out of particular relationships, or as a consequence of the
relationship between the plaintiff and a third party, but they can also arise
without such relationships.

The obligations on which breach of confidence is based are said to arise
'in equity', although it is unclear whether that means 'an obligation of
conscience arising from the circumstances in or through which the information was communicated or obtained',[6] or whether it means that confidential information is a form of property.[7] In any case, on the basis of
comments of this sort, breach of confidence is usually excluded from books
on tort law because tort is supposed to be a 'common law' topic and to deal
with 'common law' remedies whereas 'equity' is something different. This
demarcation is, however, largely pure superstition. Tort law deals with
'equitable' remedies, such as injunctions, all the time. The division of substantive and remedial law into 'common law' and 'equity' is an anachro-
nism that should be ignored. If confidential information is considered to

2   Lord Goff ibid.
3   See eg *Faccenda Chicken v Fowler* [1986] 1 All ER 617.
4   Eg *Kaye v Robertson* [1991] FSR 62 per Bingham LJ at p 70.
5   See *Shelley Films v Rex Features* LEXIS transcript (Chancery Division) 10 December
    1993.
6   See *Moorgate Tobacco Co Ltd v Philip Morris Ltd (No 2)* (1984) 156 CLR 414, 438, Deane
    J. See also *Seager v Copydex Ltd* [1967] 1 WLR 923, 931, per Lord Denning.
7   See F Gurry *Breach of Confidence* (Oxford: 1984), and P Birks *An Introduction to the
    Law of Restitution* (Oxford 1985).

be a form of property, interference with it or misappropriation of it is as much a tort as trespass to goods, conversion or trespass to land. If it is 'an obligation ... arising from the circumstances' it is a tort in the same way as negligence is a tort.

To return to the law, Lord Goff in *A-G v Guardian Newspapers (No 2)* kept open the question whether detriment to the plaintiff is an essential ingredient of an action for breach of confidence. Although in most cases the issue will not arise since the plaintiff will not sue unless there is some actual or potential loss, there are some cases in which there will be no loss in the ordinary sense (for example family and personal information where the harm is in the outrage and embarrassment the plaintiff feels rather than in any monetary loss or any lost opportunity). Lord Goff indicated in *A-G v Guardian Newspapers (No 2)* that the best way forward was probably to give 'detriment' a wide meaning in breach of confidence, in the same way perhaps that 'damage' has a wide meaning in such torts as malicious prosecution.

Lord Goff also identified in *A-G v Guardian Newspapers (No 2)* three 'limiting principles' that should apply to keep breach of confidence within manageable bounds.

The first is the principle that 'confidentiality only applies to information to the extent that it is confidential'. That is, information can become so generally accessible that it cannot be regarded as confidential. This rule, which is usually stated as the rule that when information reaches the 'public domain' it cannot be protected by confidentiality, is clear conceptually, but rather unclear in application.

The second limiting principle is that 'the duty of confidence applies neither to useless information, nor to trivia'. This principle obviously interacts with the question of detriment and recognised types of loss.

The third limiting principle is that, the public interest that confidences should be preserved and protected by the law may be outweighed by a countervailing public interest in favour of openness. The court has to carry out a balancing operation, weighing the public interest in maintaining confidence against a countervailing public interest favouring disclosure.

Finally, one should note two other methods of maintaining confidentiality by legal action, namely copyright and, in the case of children, wardship proceedings. Copyright protects the content of written material. Wardship is where children come under the protection of the court and as part of the court's very broad powers to protect its wards, it is possible for the court to prohibit the publication of information detrimental to them.[8]

---

8 See *Re X* [1984] 1 WLR 1422

Chapter 11

Nuisance and *Rylands v Fletcher*

The law of nuisance has a much longer history than the law of negligence,[1] but the more junior tort seems in the last century or so to have eclipsed it. Indeed, some writers believe that nuisance is now merely a form of negligence.[2] Other writers, more reasonably, maintain that parts of the law of nuisance belong in negligence but other parts constitute a separate and important field of law.[3]

In essence, nuisance protects the enjoyment of land from unreasonable interference by others. It is an environmental tort in the sense that what interferes with the enjoyment of land is invariably an interference with the environment more generally—noxious fumes and gases, noise, smells and vibration are common examples. But, traditionally, to be able to sue in nuisance, one has had to have had an interest in land. Many people who might have expected to be able to sue in nuisance have found that their interest in the land was insufficient, including licensees (those who have only a contractual right to occupy)[4] and members of the owner's family.[5] Although more recently there has been a controversial decision by the Court of Appeal that it may be actionable nuisance to harass a non-owner in her home,[6] the underlying historical justification for the tort of nuisance has not been the protection of the environment generally but the protection of the right to enjoy one's own private property and through the protection of that right, the protection of the value of property.

Many nuisance cases are neighbour disputes, in which one neighbour accuses the other of carrying on some noxious activity. Indeed, economists

---

1   See Newark 'The Boundaries of Negligence' (1949) 65 LQR 480; Winfield 'Nuisance as a Tort' [1932] CLJ 189.
2   G Williams and Hepple *Foundations of the Law of Tort* (2nd ed) (London; Butterworths, 1984) pp 123ff.
3   Gearty 'The Place of Private Nuisance in a Modern Law of Torts' [1989] CLJ 214.
4   See *Street v Mountford* [1985] 2 All ER 289.
5   *Malone v Laskey* [1907] 2 KB 141.
6   *Khorasandjian v Bush* [1993] QB 727.

tend to see nuisance as the law that regulates disputes about incompatible land uses.[7] Residential uses and industrial uses of land often do not sit happily together. Nuisance law is one way (along with land use planning) of settling disputes that arise from such incompatible uses. Moreover, civil law systems tend to classify nuisance cases as part of property law rather than as part of tort law. But nuisance is wider than neighbour disputes. Although plaintiffs have to have an interest in land, defendants need not have such an interest. A person who stands on the street outside and makes a loud noise that disturbs local householders is just as likely to be liable in nuisance as another householder who makes the same noise.

One aspect of nuisance that does, however, set it apart from negligence and most other torts is the remedy that most plaintiffs seek. Although most plaintiffs make a claim for compensation for past annoyance, most are really interested in whether they can make the defendants stop their noxious activities, activities which are continuing during the legal action. Plaintiffs therefore almost invariably seek injunctions. This is important not because injunctions are technically a discretionary remedy, for, as we shall see, it is extremely rare that an English court finds a defendant liable and then refuses to grant an injunction, but because it removes from the field of necessary inquiry any question of whether the defendant is acting intentionally as opposed to negligently or innocently. In most nuisance cases, the issue is not about how the alleged nuisance started but whether it should stop. By that time the defendant will be fully aware of what is happening to the plaintiff. The defendant's case cannot be that there is no intention to harm the plaintiff or that there is no foreseeable harm. The harm is self-evident, as is the fact that the defendant could remove the source of the harm at any time. The issue in most nuisance cases is therefore simply whether the plaintiff's interest in the enjoyment of property should outweigh the defendant's interest in the activity complained about.

This relative lack of importance of intention or foreseeability in most nuisance cases means that the court's attention focuses on the consequences of the defendant's activities (and on what would be the consequences of the stopping of those activities) rather than on the behaviour of the defendant. Commentators sometimes say that nuisance is about the degree of interference rather than the fault of the plaintiff. This is not strictly true. It would be better to say that in most cases the court can and must decide the issue of reasonableness without reference to foreseeability or intention because all the parties know all the relevant facts. The test is effectively not whether a reasonable person in the position of the defendant would have started out on the course of action that the defendant took, but whether it would be reasonable to continue with that activity now, knowing what we now know about its consequences.

---

7   See Cooter and Ulen *Law and Economics* (Glenview Ill; Scott Foresman, 1988) pp 168ff; and most famously, Coase 'The Problem of Social Cost' (1960) 3 JLE 1.

Who ought to win nuisance cases?—an economist's view

One of the more remarkable results in the economic analysis of law is that if there were no costs of transacting in one important sense it does not matter who wins. The Coase theorem holds that the party that values the right more[8] will end up with it whether or not the court awards the right to that party to begin with. If the owner of a polluting factory makes more money out of the factory than the combined price that all the affected residents would accept to move out (or would accept to stay but with compensation), it will be worthwhile for the factory owner to buy out the affected residents and carry on with the activities of the factory. If on the other hand the residents thought that the effect on them was worth more than the factory owner's price for going elsewhere, the residents could buy the factory out. Thus, whichever party values the right more highly will get it, either by decision of the court or by negotiation after the trial.

But note two important corollaries of the Coase theorem. First, the theorem only says that the same party will end up with the right. It does not say how much the party who obtains the right has to pay for it. Obviously, if the court awards the right to the party who values it most, the whole of the benefit of the right goes to that party. But if the court awards the right to the party who does not value it most, the other party will have to pay the winner for the right, so sharing the benefit between the parties. The person who values the right most gets the right, but the other person gets money in exchange for the right. Technically, the court's decision does not affect the allocation of resources (who has the right) but it does affect the distribution of wealth (who gets what for the right).

Secondly, the unimportance of which side wins applies only where there are no transactions costs, that is no costs of drawing up agreements, monitoring them and enforcing them. Where, as in real life, there are transactions costs, if the court awards the right to the party who does not value it as much as the other party, there is a danger that because of the costs of transacting, the parties will make no deal and the right will remain where the court puts it. In consequence, the allocation of resources will be, in the sense usually employed by economists, inefficient.

Another related problem is that the parties, or their lawyers, may think it improper to buy and sell injunctions in the way envisaged by Coase, on the ground, for example, that the parties should obey formal orders of the court and not seek to evade them by side deals. If lawyers do think in this way (there appear to be no empirical studies of practice in this area) and treat injunctions as not tradable, the situation becomes lopsided. If the court awards an injunction to the party that does not value the right most, the right will inevitably stay where it is. But if the court refuses an injunction, the losing party retains the option of buying out the winner.

The net result of economic analysis of these aspects of nuisance law is that if the court wants to pursue goals of economic efficiency it should decide the case by looking to see which of the parties values the right

8   See above ch 1.

more, since such a choice minimises the costs of the parties' having to reallocate the rights themselves, if such a reallocation is possible at all. But note that goals of fairness and worries about the distribution of income may point in the opposite direction. Allocating the right to the party that values it least means that the value of the right is more likely to be shared between the parties, especially if the party who values the right most does so merely by dint of having a larger income in the first place. But the costs of allocating the right to the party that values it least are first the costs of transferring the right to the other party and secondly the risk that if transactions costs are too high the right will not be transferred at all and the resource represented by the right will not have reached its most valued use.

Another possibility is to award damages. As we shall see,[9] in England the near universal practice of the courts is only to award damages where they issue an injunction. This means that in England damages in nuisance cases represent compensation only for past harm and the consequences of past harm rather than for harm that may arise in the future. The court assumes that the defendant will obey the injunction and will cause no further harm, so that there is no need for compensation for future harm. But in other jurisdictions, especially in the USA, courts award damages in lieu of injunctions. This happens where the court cannot face the consequences of issuing an injunction, often because the defendant is a local factory which employs large numbers of people who may lose their jobs if the injunction is enforced. Furthermore, where there are large numbers of plaintiffs, for example where a factory pollutes the whole of a town, the chances of the defendant being able to buy off the claims of the all the victims are low. One problem is the high transactions costs of finding and dealing with each individual victim who may be able to enforce the injunction and of trying to ensure that the deals worked out are enforceable against newcomers to the area. Another is the hold-out problem, the fact that the last person to hold out against the factory is in a very strong bargaining position and can hope to extract the whole of the factory's remaining profit. But hold-outs can often be wasteful in terms of bargaining costs, and miscalculations are possible so that the hold-out goes too far and begins to reduce the viability of the factory itself. In cases with these facts, which are similar to those in the leading New York case *Boomer v Atlantic Cement*[10], there is a temptation not to issue an injunction. But on the other hand, the court can see that the plaintiffs are suffering substantial interference in their enjoyment of land, even to the extent of dangers to health. US courts, therefore, reach the compromise of refusing an injunction but grant permanent damages to compensate not only for past harm but also for future harm.

Damages without an injunction are a redistributional device. The point is that the court wants to produce the distributional result that flows from granting the right to the party that values the right less, that is that the

9 See below. For criticism see Tromans 'Nuisance—Prevention or Payment' [1982] CLJ 87.
10 26 NYD 2d 219, 257 NE 2d 870 (CA NY 1970).

parties share the benefits. But the court does not believe that left to themselves, given the transactions costs, the parties will produce that result. And so the court jumps straight to the end of the process and, in effect, orders the parties to exchange the right to pollute for money at a price chosen by the court. The defendant gets the right to pollute, but the plaintiffs take some of the defendants' benefits in compensation.[11]

An even more remarkable result came out of the Arizona Supreme Court in *Spur v Del Webb*[12] in which, in exchange for an injunction, the plaintiff had to compensate the defendant. The defendant owned a cattle ranch in what used to be a rural area. The plaintiffs were developers who gradually built a city for retirees called Sun City around the site of the ranch. Eventually, the ranch found itself no longer in a rural area but in a suburb. The suburban dwellers complained that even the mere smell of the ranch was unacceptable and the plaintiff found it increasingly difficult to sell its properties. That the ranch got there first was no excuse, since the area was now undoubtedly a suburban one and the ranch was a nuisance. On the other hand, it seemed unfair to force the ranch to relocate at great expense just because the plaintiff had built a city around it. The ranch may have been able at some earlier point to buy out the developer but matters had by then gone too far. The court resolved the dilemma by granting the injunction against the ranch but making the operation of the injunction dependent on the plaintiff's paying the defendant's relocation costs.

Spur is the converse of *Boomer*. The right goes to the victim of pollution that the pollution should stop, but the court sets a price for obtaining that right which it obliges the victim to pay the defendant. The value of the relief from pollution is shared between the parties and the defendant is able to keep its business going somewhere else.

The conclusion we might reach is that it is possible for both sides to win a nuisance case, or at least for neither side to lose outright. This result can be reached either by negotiation, which is the route that English law seems to rely on, or by court imposed prices in the form of damages.

What is a nuisance?

The most obvious question about nuisance is also the most difficult. When is the defendant's interference with the plaintiff's enjoyment of land great enough to be actionable?

The basic test is that of unreasonable interference. **A nuisance is an unreasonable interference with the plaintiff's enjoyment of land.** As ever, the central question is how does one judge reasonableness?

It is often said that in nuisance the conduct of the defendant is irrelevant, since what matters is the degree of interference. This would imply universal

---

11   See generally Calabresi and Melamed 'Property Rules, Liability Rules and Inalienability: One view of the cathedral' 85 Harv LR 1089 (1972).

12   494 P 2d 700 (Ariz 1972).

and absolute standards by which one could measure interferences. One would measure noise in terms of decibels, air and water pollution in terms of microns per milligram, light pollution in terms of candelas and so on, and define nuisance solely in terms of limit values. Indeed, local authorities who have to enforce the regulatory equivalent of nuisance, statutory nuisance,[13] often adopt such an approach and, moreover, objective measurements are relevant and admissible evidence in private nuisance cases. But private nuisance does not operate according to fixed measurable standards. It operates instead using a balancing test similar to that used in negligence to decide fault.

The key judicial texts are the following:

- 'If a man lives in a town, it is necessary that he should subject himself to the consequences of the operations of trade which may be carried on in his immediate locality, which are actually necessary for trade and commerce, and also for the enjoyment of property and for the benefit ... of the public at large.'[14]
- 'It is the standard of the ordinary man, and the ordinary man, who may well like peace and quiet, will not complain for instance of the noise of traffic if he chooses to live on a main street in an urban centre, nor of the reasonable noises of industry, if he chooses to live alongside a factory.'[15]
- 'A rule of give and take, live and let live.'[16]
- 'The effect is that, if the user is reasonable, the defendant will not be liable for consequent harm to his neighbour's enjoyment of his land; but if the user is not reasonable, the defendant will be liable, even though he may have exercised reasonable care and skill to avoid it.'[17]
- 'An inconvenience materially interfering with the ordinary comfort ... of human existence, not merely according to elegant or dainty modes of living, but according to plain and sober and simple notions among the English people.'[18]

The central point of these remarks is that unreasonable interference means interference that a reasonable person would object to. It does not matter that the defendant took reasonable care to try to avoid the interference if the interference is too much. On the other hand, a reasonable person does not object to trivial interferences and is not excessively sensitive. Furthermore, reasonable people take into account the value to others of the activities undertaken by the defendant and do not believe that commerce and industry should stop merely for their own convenience.

The test of unreasonable interference can be broken down further into the following elements: the degree of the interference (intensity and

---

13 See eg s 92(1) Public Health Act 1936.
14 Lord Westbury in *St Helens Smelting v Tipping* (1865) 11 HL Cas 642.
15 Veale J in *Halsey v Esso Petroleum* [1961] 2 All ER 145, [1961] 1 WLR 683.
16 Bramwell B in *Bamford v Turnley* (1862) 3 B & S 66.
17 Lord Goff in *Cambridge Water Co v Eastern Counties Leather* [1994] 1 All ER 53, [1994] 2 WLR 53.
18 Knight Bruce VC in *Walter v Selfe* (1851) 4 De G & Sm 315.

duration), the purpose and value of the defendant's activity (including the relevance of malice), and reasonableness of the plaintiff's expectations (including the effect of the locality, the type of harm and abnormal sensitivity on the part of the plaintiff). Finally, there is the vexed question of the place of fault (or lack of care) in nuisance liability.

The degree of interference

Although it is not as decisive as some people think, the starting point for all nuisance cases is the degree of the interference. The degree of interference itself has two aspects: intensity and duration. To some extent these two aspects can be traded off against one another. An intense interference of a short duration is the equivalent of a less intense interference for a long duration.

The courts do not lay down formal thresholds based on scientific measurements of the intensity of the interference and often stress the impossibility of laying down strict rules for deciding the question of reasonableness. In *Bone v Seale*,[19] for example, the defendant attempted without success to persuade the court that no action for nuisance arising out of bad smells could succeed unless the smell was so bad that 'it so nauseated the smeller that he vomited'. But it is clear that the louder the noise, the stronger the smell, the greater the vibrations, the more intense the light, the greater the chance that the court will decide that the interference was unreasonable.

Equally, there are no strict rules about the duration of the nuisance. The longer the disturbance goes on the more likely it is to be counted as a nuisance. The courts may dismiss short-lived inconveniences as trivial.[20] But even temporary interference, such as building work, can be a nuisance if it is of sufficient intensity.[1] At the far extreme, even one-off events such as noxious material being blown over into the plaintiff's land[2] can count as nuisances, at least if the one-off event arises from a continuing state of affairs for which the defendant is responsible.[3] It does not matter that the alleged nuisance was the first occurrence of the one-off event as long as there was an underlying state of affairs because of which further occurrences might occur.[4] Indeed, some judges say in such circumstances that the nuisance is the continuing state of affairs itself rather than the damage caused by the isolated incident.[5]

19 [1975] 1 All ER 787, [1975] 1 WLR 797.
20 See *Cunard v Antifyre* [1933] 1 KB 551 per Talbot J at 557, *Harrison v Southwark and Vauxhall Water Co* [1891] 2 Ch 409.
1   *Matania v National Provincial Bank* [1936] 2 All ER 633.
2   Cf *British Celanese v Hunt* [1969] 2 All ER 1252.
3   *SCM v Whittall* [1970] 1 WLR 1017.
4   Cf *Spicer v Smee* [1946] 1 All ER 489, *Midwood Ltd v Manchester Corpn* [1905] 2 KB 597.
5   Eg *Spicer v Smee* above n 4.

The purpose of the defendant's activity

Sometimes writers say that the public benefit to be derived from the defendant's activity is no defence.[6] But this is too extreme a position. The rule of give and take between neighbours, that a reasonable person in the position of the plaintiff would not complain about reasonable activity despite the interference in his enjoyment of the land, can quite easily incorporate the benefits of the defendant's activity. Indeed, in the absence of absolute scientific standards of interference, it is difficult to see how the rule of give and take could operate without some at least implicit consideration of the defendant's purposes. If, for example, one were to say that there is no liability for the inconvenience caused by the normal operation of a household, that rule has to incorporate not only a view of what counts as a normal household but also the idea that the purposes served by the normal operation of a household are important enough for the law to protect them from legal action in nuisance.

The position seems to be analogous with that in products liability under the Consumer Protection Act 1987,[7] in which there is liability not for all damage caused by products but only for damage caused by 'defective' products, and 'defective' means that the product was not as safe as a consumer 'would be entitled to expect'. At first sight, this formula excludes the utility of the product, because it seems to concentrate on the product's safety, but on further examination the product's benefits are possibly relevant because a reasonable consumer would take them into account when judging how safe he might expect the product to be.

Nevertheless, when Lord Denning attempted to say that cricket playing could not be a nuisance for those living near to the ground into whose property cricket balls would periodically fly, because of the pleasure derived from cricket and its social utility in keeping village communities together, he found himself in a minority.[8] The majority considered that the social utility of cricket could not justify a substantial interference in the plaintiffs' enjoyment of their land. Similarly, the utility of a fish and chip shop to local poor people could not justify its presence in a fashionable street.[9] Serious pollution of a river meant injunctions against a water company that seriously and expensively interfered with its ability to deliver its service.[10] And in one Irish case, the court even held in the middle of a national housing crisis that the only cement factory in the country was a nuisance.[11]

Perhaps the best description of the present law is that where it is not clear whether the interference is substantial enough to count as a nuisance, the purposes and benefits of the defendant's activity will count, but not otherwise; or that the utility of the defendant's conduct is relevant, but

6   See eg *Jones* at 219.
7   See above ch 8.
8   *Miller v Jackson* [1977] QB 966.
9   *Adams v Ursell* [1913] 1 Ch 269.
10 *Pride of Derby and Derbyshire Angling Association v British Celanese* [1953] Ch 149.
11 *Bellew v Irish Cement* [1948] Ir 61.

only as long as the damage is not too great, and that there comes a point at which, whatever the loss to society, the degree of interference is so great that the plaintiff ought to win.[12]

This rule sounds odd, but it may have a justification. Granting an injunction when the most valuable use is that of the defendant, which is what ignoring the benefits of the defendant's activities may amount to, risks economic inefficiency—for the transactions costs of buying out the injunction, if injunctions can be bought out at all, may prevent the right from falling into the hands of the party who produces most value. But if the degree of interference is very great, the redistribution of wealth between the parties in favour of the defendant that would result from allowing the interference to continue might be too unfair to be tolerable. Hence, at that point, whatever it is, the court grants the right to the plaintiff in the expectation that the distribution of wealth will favour the plaintiff whether or not the parties go on to trade the right to enforce the injunction for money, and perhaps in the hope that further negotiations between the parties will result in the right ending up in the right hands.

The best illustration of this principle at work is the way the courts treat evidence that the defendant acted with malice. In *Hollywood Silver Fox Fur Farm v Emmett*[13] the plaintiff company bred silver foxes. The company was involved in a bitter feud with the defendant, who owned adjoining land, about a notice on the plaintiff's land. The defendant sent his son out to shoot his gun near to the plaintiff's vixens' pens, with the intention of frightening and disturbing the creatures so that they could not breed. The shooting of guns in the countryside is not an unusual event and to some extent part of the way of life. On the other hand, firing very close to the boundary of the plaintiff's farm caused substantial disturbance. In normal circumstances it would have been difficult to decide whether the shooting constituted a nuisance. But since the defendant's purpose, as the court found, was not to carry on the normal business of the countryside but specifically to disturb the plaintiff's foxes, the balance tipped in favour of the plaintiff. It is not so much that malice weighs against the defendant so much as it represents the absence of any benefit for anyone in the defendant's activities. In a marginal case, this absence of a good reason for the defendant's action tips the balance in favour of liability. Similarly, in *Christie v Davey*[14] the defendant, annoyed by the plaintiff's piano playing, deliberately set out to make the plaintiff's life intolerable by making loud noises. The plaintiff secured an injunction. Noise is an inevitable result of ordinary domestic life. But where the noise does not arise from the ordinary business of life, it is less justified.

These cases are usually contrasted with *Bradford Corpn v Pickles*[15] in which the House of Lords allowed the defendant, who was annoyed that a neighbour, the plaintiff, had not offered a high enough price to buy his

12 See eg Bohlen *Studies in the Law of Torts*.
13 [1936] 2 KB 468.
14 [1893] 1 Ch 316.
15 [1895] AC 587.

land, to continue deliberately and maliciously to extract water from a well on his land to reduce the amount of that reaching his neighbour's land. It is usually said that *Bradford v Pickles* shows either that the exercise of property rights cannot be unlawful or that malice makes no difference to whether an activity constitutes a nuisance where the benefit was only prospective, as opposed to a benefit that was already present. But if the former were true, how come there is a law of nuisance at all? And the second is only a different way of saying that the plaintiff had no legitimate expectation of receiving the water, so that failing to receive it is no loss. In contrast, according to *Chasemore v Richards*,[16] where the water flows in defined channels instead of just percolating through underground rocks, neighbours do have such a legitimate expectation. Whether or not the distinction between percolating water and water flowing in channels makes any sense, the result of the distinction is that there is liability where there is loss, and no liability where there is no loss. Thus, one can explain *Bradford v Pickles* without reference to malice or intention. Where the type of loss is not recognised, it does not matter how or why the defendant caused the loss.[17]

Reasonableness of the plaintiff's expectations

The treatment of malice leads on to one of the most important elements of the test for whether an interference with the enjoyment of land counts as a nuisance, namely whether the plaintiff's expectations of non-interference are reasonable. Nuisance is about balancing the plaintiff's interest in non-interference with the defendant's interest in carrying on their activities. If the plaintiff's expectations of non-interference are unreasonable, there will be no nuisance.

Locality

The first and most important rule is that of locality. It is unreasonable to expect the same degree of peace and quiet in the middle of a city as in the countryside. On the other hand, it is unreasonable to expect the countryside to be free of farmyard smells, but not the city. Judges have even tried to distinguish between different districts of the same city. Thus Thesiger LJ in *Sturges v Bridgman*[18] said:

---

16 (1859) 7 HL Cas 349.
17 See *Langbrook Properties v Surrey County Council* [1969] 3 All ER 1424, *Stephens v Anglian Water* [1987] 3 All ER 379. Note also *Home Brewery v William Davis* [1987] 1 All ER 637 in which the defendant was the downstream owner whose actions to prevent the percolating water getting onto its land caused flooding upstream. *Held*: no nuisance as long as the defendant acted in accordance with normal practice (ie not maliciously).
18 (1879) 11 Ch D 852.

'What would be a nuisance in Belgrave Square would not necessarily be so in Bermondsey.'

These rules tend to protect the differences in property values between districts. Thus the residents of Belgrave Square, who live in very expensive houses, are protected against inconveniences of smell and noise that the inhabitants of unfashionable Bermondsey have to put up with. The result is that Bermondsey stays unfashionable and Belgrave Square stays expensive.[19]

The locality rule is perhaps a better explanation of the case[20] in which the court said that a fish and chip shop was a nuisance in a fashionable street than the alleged irrelevance of the utility of the defendant's activities. The court simply decided that it was reasonable for those living in a fashionable street to expect to be free of the smell of fish and chips (and, one suspects, of the type of people who eat fish and chips).

Nevertheless, if the degree of interference is excessive even for Bermondsey, the plaintiff may still win. The use of printing presses at night can be a nuisance even in a printing district.[1] The noise and smell of an oil distribution centre could be excessive even for a district on the border between a residential district and an industrial district.[2]

Notice that as a result for example of land use planning decisions by the local council, the nature of a district may change.[3] If this happens, the situation will be judged as it is now rather than as it once was. This may mean that uses which were not nuisances may become nuisances without any change in the character, duration or intensity of the smells, noise or vibrations caused by the defendant. If a town grows up around a ranch, the ranch may become a nuisance, even though nothing has changed in the way the ranch operates.[4] The defendant will argue that the plaintiff 'came to the nuisance', but that is no defence if the district is now one in which the plaintiff's type of use predominates. 'Coming to the nuisance' is only an effective argument when the plaintiff comes into, for example, an industrial district and expects it to be as quiet as a residential area. Indeed, although Lord Denning was of the contrary view in his dissent in *Miller v Jackson*,[5] it is still the law that even if one chooses to occupy the part of one's property nearest to the potential nuisance causer, so that the degree of interference effectively increases, coming to the nuisance is not an excuse as long as the character of the district justifies the plaintiff's expectation that the defendant's activity is inappropriate.[6]

19 See also eg *Thompson-Schwab v Costaki* [1956] 1 All ER 652—setting up a brothel in a 'good-class residential street' is a nuisance.
20 *Adams v Ursell* [1913] 1 Ch 269.
1   *Rushner v Polsue & Alfieri* [1906] 1 Ch 234, criticised in Ogus and Richardson 'Economics and the Environment—A Study of Private Nuisance' [1977] CLJ 284.
2   *Halsey v Esso Petroleum* [1961] 2 All ER 145, [1961] 1 WLR 683.
3   *Gillingham Borough Council v Medway (Chatham) Dock* [1993] QB 343, [1992] 3 All ER 923.
4   *Spur v Del Webb* above.
5   See above.
6   *Sturges v Bridgman* above n 18.

There is one important exception to the locality rule, namely that where the defendant's activity causes physical harm to the plaintiff's property, as opposed to interfering with the enjoyment of that property, locality is not relevant. This rule appears to date back to *St Helens Smelting v Tipping*[7] in which fumes from the defendant's factory damaged trees and crops on the plaintiff's nearby estate. The defendant said that the district was industrial. Lord Westbury announced that while the locality rule applied to most nuisance cases, it did not apply where there was physical damage to the plaintiff's property.

The reason behind the physical harm exception to the locality rule is a puzzle. A number of explanations have come forward, including the idea that physical damage to property is inherently worse than interference with enjoyment (although how this can be true when interference with enjoyment can amount to a public health hazard is unclear) and the claim that damage to property is more easily quantifiable than interference with enjoyment (although how this would affect the locality rule is also unclear). There are better explanations. First, the House of Lords in *St Helens Smelting* faced a choice between two lines of cases, one of which had favoured the locality rule and the other of which had opposed it.[8] Instead of choosing between the two, the House of Lords distinguished between them on the ground that the line that favoured the locality rule concerned interference with enjoyment, whereas the other line concerned physical damage. The second,[9] which explains why the distinction just mentioned between the two lines may make sense, is that the physical damage to property cases would now count merely as negligence cases, whereas there might be some difficulty in redefining the interference cases as negligence since it would be unclear whether interference in the enjoyment of property is a type of loss for which the law of negligence gives compensation.[10]

That is, Lord Westbury meant that anything which certainly amounted to property damage in the sense of reducing the value of the property should be actionable regardless of locality. But what is left is the sort of interference that will not necessarily affect the value of the property, for which the locality rule does apply, a type of loss that seems to fall somewhere between personal injury, unrecoverable mental distress and property damage.

Even this second explanation does not throw very much light on why the distinction affects the applicability of the locality rule in cases of physical interference which are still argued in nuisance. In addition, the view of a number of judges[11] that there is no need to show negligence in cases of nuisance by physical injury to property stands in the way of the assimilation of this type of nuisance with negligence.[12] But there is a third

7   (1865) 11 HL Cas 642.
8   *Hole v Barlow* (1858) 4 CBNS 334, *Bamford v Turnley* (1862) 3 B & S 66.
9   QV *Gearty*.
10 Note that there is a third type of loss in nuisance, namely interference in easements and other servitudes regarding land, for which see standard textbooks on land law.
11 Eg Veale J in *Halsey v Esso* above n 2.
12 Foreseeability of type of harm may nevertheless be required. See below.

explanation. Note that Lord Westbury in the *St Helens Smelting* case drew his distinction between interference with enjoyment and 'sensible injury to *the value* of the property'.[13] Physical damage to the property will affect the value of property in the sense that it may affect the productivity of the soil or the usefulness of the location for a factory or it may simply destroy or disfigure something of value that is on the land.[14] Admittedly, if the property is residential or used for shops, long term interference with enjoyment would most certainly also reduce the value of the land. Who would pay the same for a smelly house as for a non-smelly house? Who would want to patronise a shop that suffered from vibrations and noise if there was an equivalent shop without the vibrations and the noise? And so, why should it make a difference to the application of the locality rule that the injury to the value of the property is 'sensible', that is physical? The answer is that physical damage will reduce the value of property regardless of its locality, but interference with enjoyment will only reduce the value of the property if it is more than that usually experienced in the neighbourhood. The market price of the land will already have taken into account the usual degree of interference in enjoyment.

The pertinence of the third explanation is confirmed by the fact that physical interference does not automatically mean liability in nuisance. If, exceptionally, the degree of physical interference is so low that, contrary to the usual assumption, there will be no damage to the value of the property, there may be no liability. For example, minor subsidence may not be actionable if it results in no 'appreciable harm'.[15] And if the harm is not significant, the court may even implicitly bring back the locality rule to finish off the plaintiff's case, as in *Stearn v Prentice Bros*[16] in which the plaintiff complained that the defendant had, by making a large pile of manure, caused rats to multiply and to eat the plaintiff's crops. The case was one of physical damage but it was dismissed on the ground that the plaintiff had used his land reasonably in the circumstances. Note that it would be very doubtful that the same activity would be reasonable in a town.

Type of loss

The alleged difference in treatment between physical damage and interference in enjoyment leads naturally into a general discussion of the types of loss that are recoverable in nuisance actions. Clearly, anything that reduces the value of the property is actionable. Sometimes the plaintiff can show an exact sum by which the value of the property has fallen, but it is not necessary for the plaintiff to do so. The court will presume that

13 Italics added. 'Sensible' here means 'something that one can sense or feel' rather than 'having or pertaining to good judgment'.
14 Cf *Halsey v Esso* above n 2.
15 *Mitchell v Darley Main* (1884) 14 QBD 125; on appeal (1886) 11 App Cas 127.
16 [1919] 1 KB 394.

the value of the property has been affected if there has been a substantial interference in enjoyment.[17]

But what about other forms of loss such as damage to other property, personal injury and economic loss?

Damage to other property belonging to the plaintiff is apparently recoverable,[18] thus providing the property owner with a convenient form of strict liability where otherwise there would only be negligence.

Whether personal injury is recoverable is, however, more doubtful. No English court has ever allowed it, even as incidental to damage to the value of property. On the other hand, there is no authoritative statement that personal injury is not recoverable. Cases that might have settled the question have been resolved using other points.[19] All we know is that the measure of damages for interference with enjoyment by noise and smells, that is the more personal interference, is not the same as it would be if the case were one of personal injury.[20] There is not much help either in the most closely associated areas of law, namely the rule in *Rylands v Fletcher*[1] and statutory nuisance. In the former, personal injury is probably not recoverable, but the point remains technically open.[2] In the latter, which is part of the criminal law, compensation orders that take personal injuries into account have been disapproved of.[3] Straying further afield, personal injury damages may be recoverable in the anomalous (and oddly named) tort of public nuisance,[4] but that is not a particularly useful guide. The safest view is that personal injury is not recoverable in nuisance.[5]

Whether personal injury nevertheless should be recoverable in nuisance is an even more difficult question. One might argue that it would be unfair to extend the protection of the stricter liability afforded by nuisance to landowners when other victims of accidents have to make do with negligence and the fault standard. On the other hand, in theory, strict liability works best where there is not much that the plaintiffs can do to make themselves safer, that is where there is unilateral causation of the damage,[6] and in many nuisance cases there is indeed little that the plaintiff can do to reduce the risk of personal injury.

The position on economic loss is more favourable to the plaintiff. In *British Celanese v Hunt*[7] metal foil strips escaped from the defendant's factory and landed in an electricity sub-station, where they caused power cuts. The power cuts affected production in the plaintiffs' factories. The

17 *Halsey v Esso* above n 2.
18 Ibid.
19 Eg *Dunne v North Western Gas Board* [1964] 2 QB 806, [1963] 3 All ER 916.
20 See *Bone v Seale* above.
1 See below.
2 Ibid.
3 *Herbert v Lambeth London Borough Council* (1991) 13 Cr App Rep (S) 489, 156 JP 389, 24 HLR 299, 90 LGR 310.
4 See above. See eg *AB v South West Water Services Ltd* [1992] 4 All ER 574.
5 Contra *Devon Lumber v McNeill* (1988) 45 DLR (4th) 300.
6 See above ch 1.
7 [1969] 1 WLR 959.

plaintiffs succeeded. The parallel with *Spartan Steel v Martin*[8] is striking, but the result is rather different. Moreover in *Ryeford Homes v Sevenoaks*[9] a court said that economic loss was 'probably recoverable' in nuisance.

Indeed, there is a strong case in favour of the recoverability of economic loss in nuisance, but one must take care to avoid double counting. The main function of nuisance is to protect the value of property. Economic loss in relation to nuisance will usually be about contracts from which the nuisance prevents the plaintiff from profiting. But the value of land, at least of commercial land, is itself determined largely by the value of what can be achieved on that land. This itself shows why there is a strong case for the recoverability of economic loss. But it also shows why there has to be care about double counting, for the loss of particular contracts may already have been counted indirectly in damages for the loss of the value of the property. If, however, the nuisance was short-lived and it has proved impossible to measure the loss in terms of a reduction in the market price, the one-off losses caused by the interference in the contracts may be counted without double counting.

There are other types of interference that may be too trivial for the law of nuisance. One is interference with the view from the plaintiff's land. Conventionally, interference with the view[10] is not actionable,[11] although one might wonder whether this should be so, since the market value of land, especially residential property, responds to the pleasantness of the view as to the quietness of the neighbourhood. Trivial interferences of all sorts are not actionable, but why should not substantial interferences of all sorts equally be actionable? The objection to allowing claims in nuisance for spoiling a view is that whether a view is pleasant or unpleasant is more difficult to decide, or more subjective, than noises or smells. But one might overcome this objection by restricting claims for spoiled views to cases in which the plaintiff can demonstrate a reduction in the value of the property.

Another type of interference that some judges have said is not recoverable because it is too trivial is interference with television and radio reception. In *Bridlington Relay v Yorkshire Electricity Board*[12] Buckley J said that it was not a substantial enough interference for a nuisance action to lie when the defendants' electricity cable interfered with the plaintiff's radio and television reception. There were, however, some special circumstances in *Bridlington Relay*, most importantly the fact that the plaintiff supplied a sizeable cable network of television and radio subscribers and so, according to Buckley J, the plaintiff had an unusually vulnerable business which fell foul of the rule, discussed below, that to be actionable the interference has to be such that it would be an unreasonable interference for a normal plaintiff. In addition, Buckley J did not say

8   See above ch 6.
9   (1989) 46 BLR 34, 16 Con LR 75.
10 Note that interference with a right to light is different. It may amount to a nuisance by interference with an easement.
11 *McVittie v Bolton Corpn* [1945] 1 KB 281.
12 [1965] Ch 436.

that interference with television or radio reception could never be an actionable nuisance. He said only that interference with the plaintiff's' recreational activities was not as important as interference with their health and physical comfort and would be less likely to be counted as a nuisance.

Nevertheless, most commentators[13] have said that *Bridlington* does not reflect modern reality and the importance of television in daily life (and thus its importance to the value of property). Indeed, not only have the Canadian courts refused to follow it[14] but also there is now an English first instance decision that favours the plaintiff. In *Hunter v Canary Wharf Ltd*[15] Judge Richard Havery ruled that it is arguable that plaintiffs suffer an actionable nuisance when the defendants' high buildings prevent normal television reception.[16]

Unusual sensitivity

The rule in negligence that defendants take plaintiffs as they find them does not apply in nuisance. If the harm the plaintiff suffers comes about partly because of the unusual susceptibility of the plaintiff, there is no liability unless the harm that a plaintiff who was not unusually susceptible would have suffered would itself count as an actionable nuisance. Thus, in *Robinson v Kilvert*[17] the plaintiff, who carried on a warehousing business, stored paper on one floor of a building while the defendant carried on a manufacturing business on the floor below. The process the defendant used produced much hot dry air which damaged some very sensitive paper the plaintiff happened to have had in store. The court refused to grant the plaintiff an injunction because the damage only arose because of the special sensitivity of the paper. And in *Heath v Brighton Corpn*[18] the plaintiff, a minister of religion, failed to obtain an injunction against the operators of a slightly noisy electricity generator because the noise, although annoying to the plaintiff, would not have disturbed ordinary healthy people. But in *McKinnon Industries v Walker*[19] although the plaintiff was carrying on an unusually sensitive business, namely growing orchids, the noxious fumes emanating from the defendant's factory would have harmed even a more robust business, for example growing ordinary flowers. The defendant was therefore liable for the full extent of the plaintiff's loss.

Note that the rule on unusual sensitivity interacts with the locality rule. What counts as unusual sensitivity in the country may not count as such in the town, and vice versa. In *Sturges v Bridgman*,[20] for example, a

13 See *Jones* at p 218, see also Kidner [1989] Conv 279, and Ogus and Richardson [1977] CLJ 284.
14 *Nor-Video Services v Ontario Hydro* (1978) 84 DLR (3d) 221.
15 See (1994) Press Association Newsfile 5 September, Estates Times 16 September.
16 At the time of writing, a Court of Appeal judgment in this case is still awaited.
17 (1889) 41 Ch D 88.
18 (1908) 98 LT 718.
19 (1951) 3 DLR 577.
20 See above.

doctor set up a surgery at the bottom of his garden next to the premises of the defendant. The defendant was a confectioner who used noisy machinery for grinding up his materials. The noise disturbed the plaintiff's practice and he sued successfully for nuisance. The doctor's practice was not an especially sensitive use for the area. But if the area had been devoted entirely to heavy industry, the answer might have been different, either because of the locality rule itself or because the plaintiff's use might have appeared to be unusually sensitive.

Fault

The last important question in the test for nuisance is that of the relevance of the defendant's conduct. Does the defendant have to have been at fault for there to be liability? In most cases, of course, the question does not arise, because the alleged nuisance is continuing to occur, with its results known to the defendant. In these cases, the court asks itself not whether the defendant should be condemned to pay compensation for having started the nuisance, but rather should the nuisance be allowed to continue? But not all cases concern injunctions for continuing nuisances. Some concern instead claims for compensation for past nuisances. It is in these cases that the court has to answer the question of fault.

As we saw in chapter 8, there are many possible tests for liability in tort, of which the test of reasonable care used in negligence is but one. Some tests use a foreseeability rule, some do not. Some allow the defendant to escape liability if the costs of preventing the harm were greater than the costs of the accident. Some break down the costs of precaution that the defendant may point to and allow the defendant to use only the knock-on costs to others of preventing the accident—not the costs that would be borne by the defendant. Some put the burden of proof on the plaintiff, some on the defendant. Some allow the defendant to win if the damage is too remote, others do not. There are a great number of different rules and combinations of rules. As a consequence it is probably best to try to avoid using sweeping categories such as 'fault' and 'strict liability' and to stick with the particular elements of the rule that the courts use.

This approach is especially useful in nuisance, in which the place of 'fault' as against 'strict liability' has caused considerable confusion and difficulty. While it is dangerous to attempt a summary of this vexed area, the following is a rough guide:

(1) **Foreseeability is required in the sense that there is liability only for foreseeable types of harm, but foreseeability is not required of the extent of the damage or the way in which the harm came about.**

(2) **The cost of precaution argument is available in the sense that the test for unreasonable interference includes some consideration of what would be lost, by the defendant or by others, if the defendant could no longer carry on with the activity in**

question. The court itself sets the standard, that is it decides whether the degree of interference outweighs the interests of the defendant. But the cost of precaution argument loses its relevance if the degree of harm crosses a loosely defined threshold at which the distributional effects of allowing the defendant to continue to harm the plaintiff become too great.[1]

(3)   There are remoteness rules specific to nuisance. The foreseeable and preventable acts of trespassers and the foreseeable and preventable consequences of natural occurrences do not break the chain of causation, but, on the other hand, the defendant is not responsible for damage that flows from the plaintiff's extra vulnerability.

Authority for most of these assertions is to be found in the important recent case *Cambridge Water Co v Eastern Counties Leather.*[2] In the *Cambridge Water* case, the defendant was an old-established leather manufacturer which used a chemical solvent in its tanning process. In the course of the process, before a change of method in 1976, regular small spillages of the solvent onto the concrete floor of the tannery took place. The total spillage over a period of years was at least 1,000 gallons. The solvent, which was not soluble in water, seeped through the factory floor into the soil below and kept seeping until it reached the bedrock. It then slowly percolated outwards until it reached the strata of rock from which the plaintiffs, a water company, extracted water. The plaintiff did not discover the presence of the solvent until 1983, when, because of EC mandated standards brought into effect in 1982, it started to test for such pollutants. The tests showed unacceptable levels of the solvent. The plaintiff considered various methods of removing the solvent, including massive dilution, but had to reject them all on technical grounds. Instead, it moved its pumping station a long way upstream, at a cost of £1m. The plaintiff then brought an action against the defendant claiming damages in negligence and nuisance and under the rule in *Rylands v Fletcher.* The judge dismissed the plaintiff's claims in negligence and nuisance on the same grounds: that the defendant could not reasonably have foreseen at the time that repeated spillages of small quantities of solvent would enter the underground strata or that, having done so, they would pollute water supplies.[3] Furthermore, the relevant standards about pollution by solvents were not in force at the time of the spillages. The Court of Appeal, in contrast, held that the defendant was liable in nuisance regardless of foreseeability and that the relevant standards were those when the pollution was discovered not those when the defendant caused it.

In the House of Lords, Lord Goff, with whom the other judges agreed, found for the defendant. On the nuisance point,[4] he said:

1   That is, the point at which to allow the defendant to continue to harm the plaintiff becomes unfair regardless of the benefits the defendant's activities bring. See above.
2   [1994] 1 All ER 53, [1994] 2 WLR 53, [1994] 1 Lloyd's Rep 261.
3   The action under *Rylands v Fletcher* also failed at first instance. See below.
4   The nuisance point did not strictly arise for decision in the House of Lords since the plaintiff had abandoned it. But Lord Goff said that he needed to discuss nuisance in order to reach his conclusions on the only technically live isuue, namely *Rylands v Fletcher.*

'Although liability for nuisance has generally been regarded as strict, at least in the case of a defendant who has been responsible for the creation of a nuisance, even so that liability has been kept under control by the principle of reasonable user—the principle of give and take as between neighbouring occupiers of land, under which "those acts necessary for the common and ordinary use and occupation of land and houses may be done, if conveniently done, without subjecting those who do them to an action": see *Bamford v Turnley* (1862) 3 B & S 66 at 83, [1861-73] All ER Rep 706 at 712 per Bramwell B. The effect is that, if the user is reasonable, the defendant will not be liable for consequent harm to his neighbour's enjoyment of his land; but if the user is not reasonable, the defendant will be liable, even though he may have exercised reasonable care and skill to avoid it.'

That is, the court reserves the right to say that the defendant is liable in nuisance even though the costs of preventing the nuisance outweigh the costs of allowing it to continue as long as the degree of interference is so substantial that it would be unjust to make the victim bear the burden. He went on:

'But it by no means follows that the defendant should be held liable for damage of a type which he could not reasonably foresee; and the development of the law of negligence in the past 60 years points strongly towards a requirement that such foreseeability should be a prerequisite of liability in damages for nuisance, as it is of liability in negligence. For if a plaintiff is in ordinary circumstances only able to claim damages in respect of personal injuries where he can prove such foreseeability on the part of the defendant, it is difficult to see why, in common justice, he should be in a stronger position to claim damages for interference with the enjoyment of his land where the defendant was unable to foresee such damage.'

The point, which is surely correct, is that the fact that nuisance law, when the degree of interference crosses a threshold, denies the defendant the cost of precaution argument does not mean that foreseeability has to be abandoned as well. The test could be, for example, that if some damage of the type that occurs is foreseeable, the defendant is liable regardless of the cost of precaution argument, but if no damage of the relevant type was foreseeable at all, then there should be no recovery. The advantage of such a rule is that, like the state of the art defence in product liability, it limits the defendant's liability in cases which are purely about what has happened in the past to types of harm about which the defendant could actually have done something. It does not threaten companies who innovate with massive and essentially unpredictable compensation costs if their innovation turns out, contrary to any expectation at the time, to interfere with someone else's enjoyment of their land. On the other hand, again like the state of the art defence, it provides no incentive for companies to do research to find out what the environmental effects of innovations might be.

Lord Goff then discusses the judgment of the Privy Council in the *Wagon Mound (No 2)*[5] in which Lord Reid had also said, although in slightly unclear terms, that foreseeabililty is an essential element of nuisance, Lord Goff concludes that Lord Reid meant to restrict his remarks to the foreseeability of the type of harm:

> 'It is unnecessary in the present case to consider the precise nature of this principle; but it appears from Lord Reid's statement of the law that he regarded it essentially as one relating to remoteness of damage.'

That is, the point of a foreseeability requirement in nuisance is to import *Wagon Mound* remoteness rather than a full negligence test. Originally, of course, *Wagon Mound* remoteness may have been intended to unite the tests for fault and remoteness, but as it turned out[6] it did not require foreseeability of the exact way in which the harm came about or foreseeability of the exact extent of the harm. All it requires is foreseeability of the type of harm, a category perhaps easier to pin down in nuisance— where the relevant type of harm is interference in the enjoyment of land— than in negligence.

Nuisance has some other remoteness rules that distinguish it from negligence, even apart from the divergence between the unusual sensitivity rule and the thin skull rule. To begin with, it seems if anything easier for the defendant in a nuisance case to be held liable for the acts of trespassers or other third parties than in negligence. In negligence,[7] the presumption is that even if an intervention by a third party is foreseeable, if it is wrongful and calculated to exploit the situation created by the defendant's actions, the chain of causation will be broken. In nuisance, defendants are responsible not only for nuisances they create themselves but also for the nuisances created by third parties, even by trespassers, which the defendant should have known about and could reasonably be expected to have prevented, that is, if the defendant knowingly or carelessly 'continued' the nuisance.[8] A similar rule applies to nuisances that arise out of the operations of nature. In *Goldman v Hargrave*[9] lightning struck a tree on the defendant's land and caught fire. The defendant chopped the tree down but it continued to smoulder. The defendant thought the smouldering would eventually stop. Instead the tree burst into flames again. The fire spread to the plaintiffs' land. The Privy Council decided that the defendant should be liable if he had been careless. And in *Leakey v National Trust*[10] the Court of Appeal said that the same rule applied where the danger arose from the operations of nature on the land itself as well as where the danger

---

5   [1967] 1 AC 617, [1966] 2 All ER 709.
6   See above ch 4.
7   See *Topp v London County Bus* above ch 4.
8   *Sedleigh-Denfield v O'Callaghan* [1940] AC 880.
9   [1967] 1 AC 645.
10 [1980] QB 485.

arose from such operations on things on the land. In *Leakey*, a mound on the defendant's land suffered from subsidence, a fact known to the defendants. Eventually the subsidence caused a land slip that damaged the plaintiff's property. The land slip would not have happened had the defendant taken preventative action. Indeed the defendant had told the plaintiff that if the plaintiff paid for the remedial action, the defendant would allow the plaintiff to carry it out.

One oddity of *Goldman* and *Leakey* is that both endorse the view that instead of applying the ordinary standard of carelessness, the court should take into account the resources, including organisational and mental resources, available to the defendant. In other words, poor defendants will be in a better position than rich ones. The ordinary rule in negligence, that if one cannot afford to do something safely, one should not have tried to do it at all, does not apply. There appears to be no reason for this rule apart from the notion that natural disasters are sometimes thrust onto landowners of limited means. But this amounts to little more than a thinly-disguised preference for land ownership over other types of property ownership and for the idea, popular in the 1980s, that people should be encouraged to own property that they cannot afford. Nevertheless, in *Page Motors v Epsom and Ewell Borough Council*[11] the Court of Appeal decided that the resources available to the defendant should also be taken into account in cases involving nuisances created by trespassers.

Finally, there is apparently a very useful rule from the point of view of environmental protection that if the defendant's activities only amount to unreasonable interference when combined with the results of the activities of others, the defendant is still liable, as are all the others,[12] although it may be that there has to be some element of a joint venture or at least that each defendant was aware of the activities of the others.[13] Even if one of the activities amounts to an unreasonable interference by itself, and one might expect on the basis of remoteness arguments in negligence that the court might say that other activities pale into insignificance, all the defendants may nevertheless be liable.[14]

Parties to the action

Who can sue and who can be sued for nuisance? The easier question to answer is who can be sued. The answer is anyone who creates a nuisance or anyone who occupies land from which a nuisance emanates who continues or adopts the nuisance is liable. Creating a nuisance means taking positive action that causes it. An occupier continues a nuisance if,

11 (1981) 80 LGR 337.
12 *Thorpe v Brumfitt* (1873) 8 Ch App 650; *Blair and Sumner v Deakin* (1887) 57 LT 522.
13 *Lambton v Mellish* [1894] 3 Ch 163.
14 *Pride of Derbyshire Angling Association v British Celanese* [1953] Ch 149 (three defendants, two causing large amounts of pollution, merely aggravated by activities of third defendant—all three defendants liable).

'with knowledge or presumed knowledge of its existence, he fails to take any reasonable means to bring it to an end though with ample time to do so.'[15] And adopting a nuisance means taking advantage of it, even though one may not positively want it to continue.[16]

Contrary to what many people seem to believe, it is not necessary for the defendant to be the occupier of neighbouring land. Private nuisances can be created from the street or from other people's land.[17] The fact that the defendant has no right to go back to the place where he created the nuisance to stop it is irrelevant.[18] The only special rule about the occupiers of land is that they may be held liable not only for their own nuisances but also for other people's or even nature's that they continue or adopt.

Occupiers are also responsible for nuisances created by their employees, on the ordinary principles of vicarious liability.[19] But, beyond those ordinary principles, occupiers may also be liable for nuisances created by independent contractors. Where the nuisance arises inevitably out of the nature of the work that the defendant has asked the independent contractor to carry out, the occupier will be liable.[20] The defendant cannot escape liability in nuisance by getting someone else to engage in activities that would also have been an unreasonable interference if done by the defendant personally. But if the cause of the nuisance is plainly the way in which the contractor has freely chosen to carry out the work, so that the defendant could not have expected that any nuisance would arise from the work that he ordered to be carried out, the defendant may escape liability (though, of course, the contractor will be liable).[1]

Occupiers may even be liable for nuisances created by trespassers. In *Sedleigh-Denfield v O'Callaghan*[2] the plaintiff's field was flooded because of a blockage in a pipe that had been laid on the defendants' land not by the defendants but by the local authority. The local authority had acted without permission, and were thus technically trespassers. The defendants were held liable not only because they had made use of the trespassing pipe themselves, thereby 'adopting' the nuisance, but also because the defendants knew or ought to have known about the nuisance and could reasonably have done something about it. In *Page Motors v Epsom and Ewell BC*[3] the defendant failed to remove from its land trespassers and squatters who caused mayhem in the neighbourhood. The defendant was held liable because it could reasonably have removed the trespassers in good time and had adopted the nuisance by deciding not to move them out because it feared that they would only immediately occupy another similar

---

15 Fox LJ in *Page Motors v Epsom and Ewell Borough Council* (1981) 80 LGR 337, LEXIS Transcript 1977 P 3315.
16 Ibid.
17 See eg *Southport Corpn v Esso* [1954] 2 QB 182.
18 *Thompson v Gibson* (1841) 7 M & W 456.
19 See above ch 14.
20 *Matania v National Provincial Bank* above.
1   *Dalton v Angus* (1881) 6 App Cas 740.
2   [1940] AC 880.
3   Above.

site. Occupiers are also liable for nuisances created by natural processes if they could and should reasonably have prevented it.[4]

It is not clear to what extent occupiers of land are responsible for nuisances created by people who are lawfully visiting their property but who are not contractors (eg house guests), but since it is clear that an occupier may be responsible for the nuisances created by trespassers if the occupier could reasonably have removed or prevented the nuisance, there seems no reason why nuisances created by lawful visitors should not be the responsibility of the occupier on similar terms.

The only slightly surprising rule about who can be sued is that landlords of unruly tenants cannot as a rule be held liable for nuisances committed by tenants. The tenants are responsible, not the landlord. But there are some exceptions where landlords are liable: (a) where the landlord explicitly authorised the nuisance; (b) where the landlord implicitly authorised the nuisance by letting the property to someone who, as the landlord knew, would use it to do something that ordinarily would be a nuisance, for example quarrying;[5] (c) where the nuisance had already been created before the letting and the landlord knew or ought to have known of its existence;[6] (d) where the nuisance arises from an aspect of the property that is still under the control of the landlord even after the start of the lease (eg where under the lease the landlord is responsible for structural repairs, or even where the landlord merely has the power to enter the property to make repairs).[7]

The serious problems start when one turns to the question of who can sue for nuisance. Nuisance has traditionally protected interests in land, and the traditional rule is that only those with property interests in the affected land may sue. But this rule is coming under increasing pressure and may be in the process of being relaxed slightly. If the courts eventually relax the restriction even more, nuisance may become a general, imperial tort in the style of negligence. It could mean, for example, a general tort of unreasonably interfering with someone else's rights. Whether the development of such a tort would be a welcome development is not an easy question to answer—do we really want the courts to be telling people constantly that they have to pay compensation because they have upset someone's enjoyment of life?

The traditional restrictive point of view appears in *Malone v Laskey*[8] and many subsequent cases.[9] It is that the plaintiff needs to have an interest in the land before being able to sue. The legal right to possession is enough, not just ownership, so that tenants can sue but visitors and even contractual licensees have no rights in nuisance.[10] There are disputes about whether

---

4   *Goldman v Hargrave, Leakey v National Trust* above.
5   *Harris v James* (1876) 45 LJQB 545; *Tetley v Chitty* [1986] 1 All ER 663.
6   *Brew Bros v Snax* [1970] 1 QB 612.
7   See also Defective Premises Act 1972 s 4 above ch 8.
8   [1907] 2 KB 141.
9   Eg *Nunn v Parkes* (1924) 59 L Jo 806, *Cunard v Antifyre* above, *Metropolitan Properties v Jones* [1939] 2 All ER 202. See *Kodilyne*.
10 See eg *Street v Mountford* [1985] 2 All ER 289. Licensees may, of course, have contractual rights against the licensor.

particular interests in land created by statutes should be protected,[11] but the test should presumably be whether the party has the kind of interest in the land that could be sold for valuable consideration, that is the kind of interest that would suffer in terms of value if the defendant could proceed with its activities. If the interest cannot be sold in some way, it is not protected by nuisance in its traditional form which essentially protects land values.

But recently the traditional view has come under attack in *Khorasandjian v Bush*.[12] In *Khorasandjian* the defendant was a 21-year-old man, the plaintiff a 16-year-old woman. They met in 1990 and became friends. Afterwards, their friendship collapsed and the plaintiff told the defendant she did not want to see him again. In late 1991 and early 1992, the defendant assaulted the plaintiff, threatened her with violence, behaved aggressively when he saw her and followed her around shouting abuse. He also pestered her with repeated telephone calls to her parents' house and at her grandmother's house. As a result of stealing the plaintiff's handbag 'as a momento' in March 1992 the defendant was arrested, charged and given a 12-month conditional discharge. He made further threats to the plaintiff and in May 1992 was jailed for threatening to kill her. The telephone harassment led to charges, convictions and fines under the Telecommunications Act 1984. But the aggressive behaviour, pestering and harassment continued, including the persistent telephone calls aimed at the plaintiff herself, her mother, her boyfriend and his mother. The plaintiff obtained an interim injunction restraining the defendant from using violence to, harassing, pestering or communicating with the plaintiff in any way. The defendant appealed against the injunction.

The defendant said, inter alia, that the injunction about the telephone harassment amounted to an injunction for private nuisance that had been obtained by someone who had no property interest in the land. According to *Malone v Laskey* such an injunction was impossible. The plaintiff conceded that the basis of the action was nuisance but challenged the traditional restriction of the right to sue in nuisance to plaintiffs with property interests. By a majority, the Court of Appeal agreed with the plaintiff. Speaking for himself and Rose LJ, Dillon LJ said:

'To my mind, it is ridiculous if in this present age the law is that the making of deliberately harassing and pestering telephone calls to a person is only actionable in the civil courts if the recipient of the calls happens to have the freehold or a leasehold proprietary interest in the premises in which he or she has received the calls.'

He went on:

---

11 For example the rights of spouses under the Matrimonial Homes Acts.
12 [1993] 3 All ER 669. A previous attempt to produce a similar result by inventing a new tort of 'harassment' ran into a brick wall of disapproval in the Court of Appeal. See *Thomas v National Union of Mineworkers* [1986] Ch 20; disapproved *News Group Ltd v Society of Graphical and Allied Trades '82 (No 2)* [1987] ICR 181.

'I apprehend that it is correct, historically, that the tort of private nuisance, which originated as an action on the case, was developed in the beginning to protect private property or rights of property, in relation to the use or enjoyment of land. It is stated in *Clerk & Lindsell on Torts* (16th edn) paragraph 24-01 that "the essence of nuisance is a condition or activity which unduly interferes with the use or enjoyment of land".'

But, citing with approval the Canadian case *Motherwell v Motherwell* [13] in which the wife of the property owner was recognised as having a sufficient interest to sue in a similar case of telephone harassment, and in which the court said that it would be 'absurd' if occupancy of the matrimonial home was insufficient to ground an action for nuisance, Dillon LJ went on:

'The court has at times to reconsider earlier decisions in the light of changed social conditions ... If the wife of the owner is entitled to sue in respect of harassing telephone calls, then I do not see why that should not also apply to a child living at home with her parents.'

Peter Gibson LJ, however, dissented on this point. He took the traditional line:

'I know of no authority which would allow a person with no interest in land or right to occupy land to sue in private nuisance. Given that the purpose of an action in nuisance is to protect the right to use and enjoyment of land (see *Salmond and Heuston on the Law of Torts* (1992) (20th edn) 67), it seems to me to be wrong in principle if a mere licensee or someone without such right could sue in private nuisance.'

Note that Dillon LJ does not say exactly why and how 'changed social conditions' mandate change in the range of plaintiffs in nuisance. It could be that he is referring to the change in the position of women in society and that he is saying that the old law came out of the view that men owned both property and wives and that the protection of the interests of wives could only be achieved through their husbands. But if so, the adoption of the modern position on the emancipation of women does not explain why children, even daughters, should have more rights in nuisance. Although the legal position of spouses about property rights in the matrimonial home has changed dramatically over the last 90 years, the property rights of children have not improved in the same way.

It is not clear, therefore, whether Dillon LJ wants merely to say that the interests of legitimate family occupiers of land should be protected in nuisance, because the property interests of the family as a whole should be treated as one, or whether he wants to say more, for example that the

---

13   (1977) 73 DLR (3d) 62.

rights of all legitimate occupiers of land should attract protection regardless of whether they are saleable or transferable or otherwise have a market value. He may even want to go further and take the shackles completely off the tort of nuisance and to free it from its connection with land values and the occupancy of land.

The fate of the doctrine in *Khorasandjian v Bush* remains to be decided. Certainly at first instance in *Hunter v Canary Wharf Ltd*[14] the court in effect refused to follow it and disallowed claims by non-owners such as children and grandparents for the nuisance of unreasonable interference in television reception.

Defences

Although a large number of arguments are sometimes put forward as 'defences', some of which are said to be effective and others not, most of them are simply applications of rules that we have already discussed. For example, it is sometimes said that there is a 'defence' of absolute ignorance, as in *Ilford UDC v Beal*[15] in which there was no liability when the defendant's construction activities damaged a previously unknown or unidentified sewer belonging to the plaintiff. This case is best seen not as establishing a defence but as an application of the requirement that there has to be foreseeability of the type of harm. There are however two true defences, other than general defences such as volenti and contributory negligence, that are peculiar to nuisance and which deserve more discussion.

Prescription

It is an aspect of many if not all legal systems that, in certain circumstances, property rights can be gained by the passage of time even though the property was illegitimately or irregularly acquired to begin with. In English law, the rule is that property rights can be acquired by long possession, usually 12 years, as long as the possession was open, not maintained by force, and not by the permission of the real owner. Acquiring rights in this way is known as prescription.

Property rights include not only ownership but also rights over other people's property, such as rights of way. These rights, known as easements or more generally servitudes, can also be acquired by prescription on the same terms as other property rights, with the exception that the required period is 20 years. The relevance of this to nuisance is that some kinds of nuisance are capable of becoming property rights because they can count as easements or servitudes. Although cases in which this defence succeeds

---

14 See above.
15 [1925] 1 KB 671. See *Markesinis and Deakin* p 439.

are very rare, there are judicial pronouncements to the effect that the right to commit several forms of nuisance can come within this category, including the right to divert rain water onto one's neighbour's property, the right to annoy one's neighbour by smoke, smells or noise and the right to cause vibrations.[16]

One reason that the defence of prescription rarely succeeds is that time runs not from when the defendant first started the activity, but from when it first became a nuisance to the plaintiff. Thus, in *Sturges v Bridgman* the confectioner had been operating his machinery for 20 years, but the noise and vibrations it made did not become a nuisance until the doctor built his surgery next door. Thus time started to run only from when the vibrations and noise started to interfere with the doctor's work and the previous 20 years did not count.

Statutory authority

The other distinctive defence to nuisance is that the defendant had the authority of a statute to carry on its activity. But, just as it is no defence to negligence that one was acting under a statutory power when it is possible to exercise the power either negligently or non-negligently, so statutory authority is only a defence to nuisance when the only way to exercise the statutory power is to cause unreasonable interference. Thus, in the classic nineteenth century case *Metropolitan Asylum v Hill*[17] a statute authorising the defendants to build a hospital for the poor did not authorise them to build a smallpox hospital that local residents thought would put them in danger.

Much, of course, depends on the meaning of the statute. In *Allen v Gulf Oil Refining*[18] the defendant had obtained a private Act of Parliament that authorised it to acquire land by compulsory purchase for the purpose of building an oil refinery. The Act authorised the building of the refinery, but, oddly, did not explicitly authorise operating it. The House of Lords decided, by a majority of 4-1, that the Act must also have authorised the operation of an oil refinery, since otherwise it would have had the absurd effect of authorising the building of an oil refinery to stand idle. Since the alleged nuisances arose from the ordinary operation of an oil refinery, and not from any extraordinary activities or behaviour of the defendant, the plaintiffs' claims failed.

Some writers[19] criticise the result of *Allen* because they think that it is wrong that the plaintiffs should go uncompensated when normally, where there is a great interference in enjoyment, the benefits and purposes of the defendants' activity are irrelevant. They suggest as a compromise that

16 See *Hulley v Silversprings Bleaching* [1922] 2 Ch 268, *Waterfield v Goodwin* (1955) LJ Ch 332, *Khyatt v Morgan* [1961] NZLR 1020, *Sturges v Bridgman* (1879) 11 Ch D 852.
17 (1881) 6 App Cas 193.
18 [1981] AC 1001.
19 Eg *Markesinis and Deakin* p 441.

the court should have ordered damages but at the same time should have refused an injunction.[20] But this suggestion ignores the way that private Acts of Parliament come about. The whole point of the procedure followed for private Acts of Parliament is that it forces the promoters of the bill to negotiate with objectors to it. The time for compensation to be arranged is during the committee stage of the bill. Indeed, Parliament only passes the bill if it is satisfied with the compensation arrangements that the bill puts in place. This means that the Act authorises not only a set of activities but also a set of compensation settlements. It would therefore be contrary to the intention of Parliament to order damages in a case in which the court is saying that the activity complained of can continue.

Another important problem of statutory authorisation is the relationship between nuisance and planning law. Does the granting of planning permission by a local authority (under its own statutory powers) inoculate the recipient against claims in nuisance? The short answer to this question is no. In *Allen v Gulf Oil*[21] the private Act of Parliament did not exempt the oil company from the need to get planning permission, but the fact that they did get permission did not help them in their defence.[1] On the other hand, planning permission, and more especially local plans, structure plans and planning briefs, all of which may have the effect of guiding particular sorts of development to particular areas, may be relevant to the locality test. Whether an area is Bermondsey or Belgravia may depend to some degree on what the local planning authorities say it is.

Remedies

There are three remedies available to plaintiffs in nuisance: an injunction, damages and self-help (known as 'abatement').

Injunction

The most important and most usually sought remedy is an injunction. The court orders the defendant, on pain of an unlimited fine or imprisonment, to desist from the activity.

In strict theory, injunctions are discretionary remedies. The court does not have to grant an injunction if it thinks that it would be inequitable to do so. But in practice, the remedy follows the right.[2] If the court decides that a nuisance is being committed and that it is not certain whether the nuisance will stop of its own accord, the court will go on to grant an injunction. Occasionally the court will delay the start of the operation of the injunction to allow further negotiations between the parties, but the

20 Cf *Boomer* above.
21 Above.
1 See now *Wheeler v JJ Saunders* (1995) Times, 3 January.
2 *Shelfer v City of London Electric Lighting* [1895] 1 Ch 287.

English courts do not follow the American courts into refusing injunctions while awarding damages (or even granting injunctions conditional on the plaintiff compensating the defendant).[3]

In *Miller v Jackson*,[4] however, a majority of the Court of Appeal were prepared to go the American route, and only failed to do so because one of the judges who supported that course of action, Lord Denning, also found that there was no nuisance in the first place. The case concerned residents of a new housing estate who complained about the playing of cricket on a neighbouring village green. The newcomers had therefore not only come to the nuisance but also their legal action threatened an activity of high social value. Although only Lord Denning wanted to overturn the traditional rules that neither of those matters is decisive in a nuisance action, Cumming-Bruce LJ was at least prepared to take them into account when deciding on whether to grant an injunction or just damages.

But in *Kennaway v Thompson*[5] a similar line of argument in support of a plaintiff who organised power-boat racing was rejected outright. The Court of Appeal reasserted the traditional doctrines. If there is an actionable nuisance, the plaintiff should win an injunction. If the plaintiff received damages but not an injunction, it would amount to compulsory purchase of the plaintiff's right at a price not determined by agreement between the parties but by the court, an arrangement the English courts find objectionable.

Whether the courts are right to follow their traditional view is not clear.[6] If transactions costs are low and the parties can carry on negotiating after the granting of the injunction, the traditional view usually has the effect only of shifting the distribution of income and wealth in the direction of the victims of nuisance, which may not be too bad a thing. But if transactions costs are high, and especially if, because of cultural taboos, injunctions are not tradable at all, along with the shifting of the distribution of income and wealth in favour of victims will come considerable efficiency losses. If the transactions costs are low and the trading of injunctions possible, if a polluting factory could adequately compensate all the victims of the pollution and still make a profit, that is what will happen. But if transactions costs are high, especially if injunctions are not tradable, even if the factory could compensate the victims and carry on profitably, unless the factory manages quickly to innovate and reduce its level of pollution, it will have to close down. For the factory to close when it could have compensated the victims and still have made a profit is to waste resources. In these circumstances, it may be better for the court to make a guess at how much the victims would have accepted in exchange for their rights and to allow the defendant to continue with its activities as long as it pays the price. The question is whether the efficiency losses that will occur because the courts will inevitably get wrong the amounts that the victims would

3   See above.
4   [1977] QB 966.
5   [1981] QB 88.
6   See Markesinis and Tettenborn 'Cricket, Power Boat Racing and Nuisance' (1981) 131 NLJ 108, Tromans 'Nuisance—Prevention or Payment' [1982] CLJ 87.

have settled for in compensation still outweigh the likely losses if the injunction leads to the closure of a factory which, but for the transactions costs and cultural taboos, could have traded its way around liability and back into production.

The answer to this question is not clear. On the one hand it seems likely, though in need of further research to confirm it, that although transactions costs themselves are not high (the parties know one another so that search costs are low and in straightforward nuisance by noise and smell, monitoring is straightforward) cultural taboos about buying and selling injunctions may exist, so that the approach of all or nothing injunctions may have disadvantages. On the other hand, the damages-only approach assumes that the damages paid reflect the true loss suffered by the plaintiff and also, if it is to result in the defendant's activity bearing all the costs that it causes, that the actions of all the plaintiffs added together reflect the harm caused by the activity. The first must be uncertain, since ex hypothesi, the court has replaced the victim in deciding what is sufficient compensation, and there must be doubts also about the second, especially in pollution cases in which large numbers of people suffer small amounts of harm so that very few people bother to sue. In addition, longer term environmental damage, the alleged effects of global warming for example, would not figure at all in the total damage awards.

Damages

Because the assumption is that if there is a nuisance the court will issue an injunction, and that because of the injunction the nuisance will cease, damage awards in English nuisance law are exclusively compensation for past losses (or, more accurately, for losses that have already been caused— it is possible that harm the plaintiff suffered in the past will have effects in the future even if the nuisance itself stops).

If the plaintiff can demonstrate that the nuisance reduced the value of his property permanently by a specific amount, so much the better, but it is not necessary for the plaintiff to prove that any such specific sum has been lost. Instead, the courts look, within the limits set by the foreseeability of type of harm test, to the expenditures the plaintiff may have had to make to eliminate or to avoid the nuisance,[7] estimates of lost business,[8] or, failing these, to fairly arbitrary sums to compensate for the annoyance. The sums paid are not to be calculated with reference to the sums given for loss of amenity in nuisance (eg very loud noise equals temporary deafness) but instead appear to follow a rather lower scale.[9]

7   See eg the £1m cost of moving the borehole in the *Cambridge Water* case.
8   See *Halsey v Esso* above.
9   *Bone v Seale* above.

Abatement

The most obvious remedy for a nuisance is self-help, for example where the victim of the nuisance physically removes the cause of nuisance. When can victims 'abate the nuisance' themselves in this way?

Most of the cases concern the very stuff of the consumer advice columns in the newspapers—neighbour disputes about loud music, trees growing over a neighbour's fence, roots encroaching into one's garden and so on. The dilemma they produce for the courts is that these disputes are trivial and it wastes the courts' time to have to decide every single one of them—why not let the victim have a go and then perhaps allow the defendant to complain if the victim goes too far. On the other hand, trivial neighbour disputes may erupt into disorder or even violence if the parties are allowed to destroy each other's property without formal authorisation.

On the whole, the courts have erred on the side of avoiding disorder and have allowed abatement only a fairly restricted scope. As Eyre CJ said in the eighteenth century:[10]

> 'Abatement ought only to be allowed in clear cases ... where the injury is apparent at the first view of the matter.'

Furthermore, if, as often happens, the victim can only remove the nuisance by entering the nuisance-maker's land, the victim must give notice to the nuisance-maker before entering (although how much notice is not clear).The rule is otherwise if there is an emergency, and it may be that notice is not necessary where the occupier of the land personally created the nuisance.[11]

Another limitation may be that abatement may only include removal of the nuisance (for example hacking off an overhanging branch or cutting off encroaching roots). It may not include entering someone else's land to take positive counter-measures such as putting up a fence on the nuisance-maker's land—unless the victim has a right to such as an easement which would allow it.[12]

Finally, the abatement must be the minimum necessary to stop the nuisance and should not interfere with other property belonging to others.[13] Thus, if you are having a loud outdoor party and I, having given you notice, enter your garden to get you to turn the music down, I might be within my rights to turn the volume of your music down myself but I would not be allowed to destroy your sound system.

---

10 *Kirby v Sadgrove* (1797) 3 Anst 892. See also *Burton v Winters* [1993] 1 WLR 1077.
11 See eg *Jones v Williams* (1843) 11 M & W 176; *Lemmon v Webb* [1895] AC 1; *Lagan Navigation v Lambeg Bleaching* [1927] AC 226.
12 *Jones v Pritchard* [1908] 1 Ch 630, cf *Campbell Davys v Lloyd* [1901] 2 Ch 518 (nb this is a public nuisance case and not necessarily relevant to private nuisance).
13 *Roberts v Rose* (1865) LR 1 Exch 82.

If the victim abates the nuisance, that automatically removes any possibility of obtaining an injunction on the same facts.[14] Equally, if the victim has asked a court for an injunction and the court has refused it, the victim may not abate.[15] But abatement does have one peculiar advantage. Unlike injunctions and damages, the victim does not have to wait until actual damage occurs but can abate as soon as it is clear that damage will be done.[16] Thus, for example, where roots are crossing into my property from your property, I do not have to wait until the roots do any damage before I may remove them. But note that a victim of overhanging branches, although permitted to cut them off, may not keep the branches themselves.

Rylands v Fletcher

In *Rylands v Fletcher*[17] the owners of a mill contracted with engineers to construct a reservoir. Unknown to anyone, beneath the reservoir lay disused mine workings that connected to the plaintiff's working mine. Water from the reservoir burst into the disused workings and thence into the working mine. The court accepted that the defendant owners had not been negligent either in conceiving the project to build the reservoir or in choosing the contractors. The contractors had been negligent and should have noticed and blocked the disused shafts, but since the contractors were not the direct employees of the defendants[18] the contractors' negligence could not affect the defendants. The plaintiff lost at first instance but won on appeal. In the Court of Exchequer Chamber, Blackburn J said:

> 'We think that the true rule of law is that the person who, for his own purposes, brings on his land, and collects and keeps there anything likely to do mischief if it escapes, must keep it at his peril, and, if he does not do so, he is prima facie answerable for all the damage which is the natural consequence of the escape. He can excuse himself by showing that the escape was owing to the plaintiff's default, or, perhaps, that the escape was the consequence of vis major, or the act of God.'

On further appeal to the House of Lords, Lord Cairns LC upheld the decision in favour of the plaintiff and said:

> 'The principles on which this case must be determined appear to me to be extremely simple. The owners, treating them as the owners or occupiers of the [property] on which the reservoir was

14 *Burton v Winters* above.
15 Ibid.
16 *Smith v Giddy* [1904] 2 KB 448.
17 (1866) LR 1 Exch 265; affd (1868) LR 3 HL 330.
18 See below ch 14.

constructed, might lawfully have used that [property] for any purpose for which it might, in the ordinary course of the enjoyment of land, be used, and if, in what I may term the natural user of that land, there had been an accumulation of water, either on the surface or underground, and if by the operation of the laws of nature that accumulation of water had passed off into the [property] occupied by the plaintiff, the plaintiff could not have complained that that result had taken place ....

On the other hand, if the defendants, not stopping at the natural use of their [property], had desired to use it for any purpose which I may call a non-natural use, for the purpose of introducing into that [property] that which, in its natural condition, was not in or upon it ... and if in consequence of their doing so, or in consequence of any imperfection in the mode of their doing so ... [then] that which the defendants were doing they were doing at their own peril.'

There are two fundamentally different views of what *Rylands v Fletcher* stands for. One, the dominant and orthodox view recently reaffirmed by the House of Lords in *Cambridge Water Co v Eastern Counties Leather*[19] is that it deals with a special sub-category of nuisance. It combines the features of *British Celanese v Hunt*, where there was a one-off escape, *Leakey v National Trust*, where the nuisance was caused by a natural substance and *Matania v National Provincial Bank*, in which independent contractors working for the defendant cause an especially annoying nuisance. The rule in *Rylands v Fletcher*, according to the dominant view, is that there is 'strict' liability for one-off escapes of non-natural substances from one's land following an accumulation of something dangerous by the defendant.

The second, unorthodox view, is that *Rylands v Fletcher* reaches well beyond nuisance cases and stands for an attempt to establish 'strict' liability for the harmful results of inherently dangerous activities. This view of *Rylands v Fletcher* was taken up in many US jurisdictions, with the result that the Second Restatement of Torts reads as follows:

'§519 GENERAL PRINCIPLE
(1) One who carries on an abnormally dangerous activity is subject to liability for harm to the person, land or chattels of another resulting from the activity, although he has exercised the utmost care to prevent the harm.
(2) This strict liability is limited to the kind of harm, the possibility of which makes the activity abnormally dangerous.

§520 ABNORMALLY DANGEROUS ACTIVITIES
In determining whether an activity is abnormally dangerous, the following factors are to be considered:

19 See above.

(a) existence of a high degree of risk of some harm to the person, land or chattels of others;
(b) likelihood that the harm that results from it will be great;
(c) inability to eliminate the risk by the exercise of reasonable care;
(d) extent to which the activity is not a matter of common usage;
(e) inappropriateness of the activity to the place where it is carried on; and
(f) extent to which its value to the community is outweighed by its dangerous attributes.'

On one interpretation, the Restatement rule says only that it is possible that an entire activity, and not just the way the defendant practised it, can count as faulty.[20] If the activity is still dangerous despite reasonable care and the activity's dangers outweigh its 'value to the community', the position is precisely that it is negligent to engage in the activity at all. But the Restatement rule must go beyond such an interpretation if its self-description in §520(2) as 'strict liability' is to make any sense. The usual interpretation of the rule is that those who engage in activities that are risky to others beyond a certain threshold are not able to invoke the argument that the costs of precaution would have outweighed the costs of the accident. The rule is therefore similar to that in nuisance[1] and its justification is also similar, namely that to allow the defendant to impose the costs of its activities on the plaintiff is unjust even if the benefits of the defendant's activities outweigh its costs. The difference is that instead of seeking an injunction remedy to prevent future harm, in this kind of liability, the plaintiff seeks damages for past harm. The point is therefore that if the defendant can compensate the victims of its risky activity and still make a profit, it will stay in business and the activity will continue, but the distribution of wealth will not have been shifted away from victims and towards defendants.

On the other hand, although the rule does not envisage post-injunction negotiations between the parties, its operation would involve transactions costs. The parties have to negotiate compensation amounts and if they fail, or if they disagree about the application of the rule in the first place, they may have to go through the extremely expensive process of legal action. It is possible, therefore, for the rule to cause more harm than good, and for that reason for its application to be restricted to cases involving losses so high that the transactions costs pale into insignificance.

The American view of *Rylands v Fletcher*, however, has not been accepted in England. In *Read v J Lyons*,[2] the defendants ran a munitions factory during the Second World War. One day, without any negligence by the defendant, there was an explosion that injured the plaintiff, who was working in the factory. The House of Lords declined the opportunity to

---

20 See §519 Comment b.
1 See §519 Comment c.
2 [1947] AC 156.

accept the Restatement doctrine as the law of England.[3] *Rylands v Fletcher*, according to the House of Lords, applied only to cases in which the noxious substance had escaped from the defendant's land and caused harm on someone else's land. In the *Cambridge Water* case, Lord Goff went further:

'I have to say, however, that there are serious obstacles in the way of the development of the rule in *Rylands v Fletcher* in this way. First of all, if it was so to develop, it should logically apply to liability to all persons suffering injury by reason of the ultra-hazardous operations; but the decision of this House in *Read v J Lyons & Co Ltd* [1947] AC 156, [1946] 2 All ER 471, which establishes that there can be no liability under the rule except in circumstances where the injury has been caused by an escape from land under the control of the defendant, has effectively precluded any such development. Professor Fleming has observed that "the most damaging effect of the decision in *Read v Lyons* is that it prematurely stunted the development of a general theory of strict liability for ultra-hazardous activities" (see *Fleming on Torts* (8th edn) (1992) p 341). Even so, there is much to be said for the view that the courts should not be proceeding down the path of developing such a general theory. In this connection, I refer in particular to the Report of the Law Commission on Civil Liability for Dangerous Things and Activities (Law Com no 32) 1970. In paras 14-16 of the report the Law Commission expressed serious misgivings about the adoption of any test for the application of strict liability involving a general concept of "especially dangerous" or "ultra-hazardous" activity, having regard to the uncertainties and practical difficulties of its application. If the Law Commission is unwilling to consider statutory reform on this basis, it must follow that judges should if anything be even more reluctant to proceed down that path.'

One might point out that the Law Commission was not in a position to consider the 1977 Second Restatement of Torts, which attempts to overcome the criticisms of the First Restatement echoed in the Law Commission's report. In particular, the Second Restatement accepts the criticism that it is not possible to provide a concise definition of 'abnormally dangerous' or 'ultrahazardous' and instead puts forward a list of relevant factors. The list itself is admittedly open to the criticism that by allowing 'value to the community' to outweigh the activity's dangerousness, regardless of how dangerous the activity is, it undermines the whole point of the rule. Moreover, from an economic point of view, whether to adopt a rule of 'strict' liability (or more accurately a rule that denies the cost of precaution argument to the defendant) depends on (1) whether the damages rules

---

3   But Viscount Simon LC pointed out that the defendants would still have won under the doctrine as it then existed because the defendants were acting not for their own benefit but because of the direction of the state.

mean that plaintiffs receive precisely the right amount of compensation that leaves them indifferent between the injury and the compensation and (2) whether reasonable care by the victim significantly affects the dangerousness of the situation.[4] Nevertheless, the rejection of the American approach in the *Cambridge Water* case seems precipitate and insufficiently argued. Indeed one might argue that the move in the direction of allowing nuisance claims to people who do not have proprietary rights in *Khorasandjian v Bush*[5] indicates simultaneous movement in precisely the opposite direction.

One might also note that the position in French law is even more advanced than the American Second Restatement. Article 1384 of the Civil Code has been interpreted since the 1930s[6] as meaning that people are responsible for the risks created by things that they have 'in their keeping', including now both things that they bring onto their property and the property itself.[7]

There are also specific aspects of the way the rule in *Rylands v Fletcher* has been applied that suggest that the idea that the rule deals simply with a subset of nuisance cases must be too narrow. For example, although Widgery J thought otherwise in *Weller v Foot and Mouth Disease Research Institute*,[8] most courts that have turned their mind to the question believe that, unlike in nuisance, plaintiffs in *Rylands v Fletcher* do not need an interest in land to be able to invoke the rule. In *Halsey v Esso*,[9] for example, the plaintiff recovered under the rule not just for the damage the defendant's pollution caused to his land but also for damage to his car parked on the highway. Furthermore, there still remains doubt about whether the rule extends to straightforward personal injury cases. Lord Macmillan in *Read v J Lyons* said, obiter, that it did not, but until then the general assumption had been that it did.[10] Certainly in *Hale v Jennings*[11] a tenant of a fairground stall recovered for personal injuries caused when the defendant's fairground ride broke up and various parts of it flew through the air and hit the plaintiff. The plaintiff in *Hale* might be also 'an occupier' in the sense that there may have been a property right in the stall, but the action was explicitly for personal injury not for harm to the value of property resulting from personal injury. Moreover, the Court of Appeal in *Perry v Kendricks*[12] and *Dunne v North Western Gas*[13] declined to take Lord

---

4 See above ch 1.
5 See above.
6 See the Jand'heur litigation culminating in the decision of the Chambres Réunis of the Cour de Cassation of 13.2.1930, D.1930.I.57, S.1930.I.121.
7 Of course, there are some restrictions on this liability, for example that it can be excluded by express agreement between landlord and tenant—see eg Cass 3e Chambre Civ,1 dec 1993. Arret no 1902 (Pourvoi no 91-16.197).
8 [1966] 1 QB 569.
9 Above. See also dicta in *Miles v Forest Rock Granite* (1918) 34 TLR 500, *Perry v Kendricks* [1956] 1 WLR 85 and *British Celanese v Hunt* [1969] 1 WLR 959.
10 See eg *Shiffman v Order of St John* [1936] 1 All ER 557.
11 [1938] 1 All ER 579.
12 Above.
13 [1964] 2 QB 806.

Macmillan's pronouncement in *Read* as a definitive statement of the law. Therefore, whatever the present formal position in favour of the restrictive view, the elements of a broader approach are in place should the courts ever decide to change direction.

It remains, however, to examine some remaining aspects of the orthodox interpretation of *Rylands v Fletcher* in more detail.

'Strict liability'

As stated elsewhere in this book, 'strict liability' is a vague term. In particular, one must distinguish between rules about foreseeability (that is, as at what point in time does the court judge the defendant's conduct, the time of the defendant's actions or now?) and rules about the availability to the defendant of the 'cost of precautions' argument.

On foreseeability, the matter is settled by the *Cambridge Water* case. Lord Goff admits that there were early cases that appeared to say that foreseeability was not necessary in *Rylands v Fletcher*. For example, in *Humphries v Cousins*,[14] *West v Bristol Tramways Co*,[15] and *Rainham Chemical Works Ltd v Belvedere Fish Guano Co Ltd*[16] courts, including the House of Lords, denied that foreseeability was necessary in a *Rylands v Fletcher* case. Lord Goff, however, says that the remarks of the House of Lords in *Rainham* were obiter dicta and that the other decisions are not binding on the House of Lords in the *Cambridge Water* case. He goes on to decide the issue himself as if he were unencumbered by precedent. After noting that, 'the point is one on which academic opinion appears to be divided: cf *Salmond and Heuston on Torts* (20th edn) (1992) pp 324-325, which favours the prerequisite of foreseeability, and *Clerk and Lindsell on Torts* (16th edn) (1989) para 25.09, which takes a different view,' and arguing that 'the historical connection with the law of nuisance must now be regarded as pointing towards the conclusion that foreseeability of damage is a prerequisite of the recovery of damages under the rule,' he goes on to say:

> 'Having regard to these considerations, and in particular to the step which this House has already taken in *Read v Lyons* to contain the scope of liability under the rule in *Rylands v Fletcher*, it appears to me to be appropriate now to take the view that foreseeability of damage of the relevant type should be regarded as a prerequisite of liability in damages under the rule. Such a conclusion can, as I have already stated, be derived from Blackburn J's original statement of the law; and I can see no good reason why this prerequisite should not be recognised under the rule, as it has

14   (1877) 2 CPD 239, [1874-80] All ER Rep 313.
15   [1908] 2 KB 14, [1908-10] All ER Rep 215.
16   [1921] 2 AC 465, [1921] All ER Rep 48.

been in the case of private nuisance ... It would moreover lead to a more coherent body of common law principles if the rule were to be regarded essentially as an extension of the law of nuisance to cases of isolated escapes from land, even though the rule as established is not limited to escapes which are in fact isolated.'

That is, just as in nuisance, foreseeability of the type of harm is a necessary condition of liability under *Rylands v Fletcher*. But note that this does not mean that foreseeability of the extent of the harm or of the exact way in which the harm comes about has to be foreseeable. On the other hand, the foreseeability requirement imposed by the *Cambridge Water* case probably supersedes older alleged defences to *Rylands v Fletcher* such as 'act of God'. 'Act of God' means an event which human foresight could not provide against or prevent,[17] that is, in the French phrase, an event that is 'imprévisible et irrésistible'. If such an event is truly beyond human foresight, there will be no liability under *Rylands v Fletcher* anyway.

But what about the cost of precaution argument? *Rylands v Fletcher* itself is quite clear. The defendant 'acts at his peril'. If the rule applies, the court should not take into account the social benefit of the activity. There is, however, an important qualification on that position. Building on Lord Cairns' pronouncements in *Rylands,* the courts have declared that the rule only applies where the defendant's use (or 'user') of its land was 'non-natural'.

Any straightforward reading of *Rylands* would say that Lord Cairns' only intention in referring to 'non-natural user' was to say that there was no liability for damage caused by the combination of ordinary natural causes, such as rain, and the laws of nature, such as gravity. There had to be some human intervention. Subject to the qualification that naturally caused nuisances may be the responsibility of the occupier if the occupier knew or ought to have known about them and could reasonably have prevented the harm,[18] this is trite law. But subsequent cases built the requirement for non-natural user into the equivalent of asking whether the defendant's activity was reasonable or of benefit to the community. Thus, for example, in *Read v J Lyons*[19] the House of Lords thought that it would be unlikely to say that the manufacture of bombs in wartime could be construed as a 'non-natural user', even though nothing more artificial or man-made is imaginable. Quite remarkably, even the very kind of accumulation declared to be non-natural in *Rylands,* namely of water, turned out to be 'natural' in the context of a domestic central heating system.[20]

The *Cambridge Water* case has, however, moved the position back towards the original position. Lord Goff said:

---

17   See eg *Tennent v Earl of Glasgow* (1864) 2 M 22 (HL).
18   *Leakey v National Trust* see above.
19   Above.
20   *Rickards v Lothian* [1913] AC 263.

'If the words ["non-natural user"] are extended to embrace the wider interests of the local community or the general benefit of the community at large, it is difficult to see how the exception can be kept within reasonable bounds.'

In the context of the *Cambridge Water* case itself, Lord Goff added:

'Indeed I feel bound to say that the storage of substantial quantities of chemicals on industrial premises should be regarded as an almost classic case of non-natural use; and I find it very difficult to think that it should be thought objectionable to impose strict liability for damage caused in the event of their escape.'

Lord Goff's position is that the courts have used non-natural user to make up for the alleged absence of a foreseeability requirement in *Rylands v Fletcher*, but that once foreseeability comes back in, it becomes easier to deny the defendant the cost of precaution argument.

'It may well be that, now that it is recognised that foreseeability of harm of the relevant type is a prerequisite of liability in damages under the rule, the courts may feel less pressure to extend the concept of natural use to circumstances such as those in the present case; and in due course it may become easier to control this exception, and to ensure that it has a more recognisable basis of principle.'

Escape

The requirement that there must be an 'escape' of material from the defendant's control to a place which the defendant does not occupy or control is as irrational as it is well established. It forms the reason for the decision of the House of Lords in *Read v J Lyons*.

Note, however, that the requirement is that the material escapes from the defendant's control, not that it escapes from land in which the defendant has a proprietary interest. Escape from the defendant's control on the highway into the plaintiff's property will suffice.[1] Moreover, the material that escapes need not be the dangerous substance accumulated by the defendant. If the defendant carries on a quarry blasting business, as part of which it accumulates on site a large amount of explosives, and the blasting operations occasionally lead, as they inevitably do, to quantities of rock travelling much farther than anticipated, the escape of the rock is sufficient.[2]

---

1   *Rigby v Chief Constable of Northamptonshire* [1985] 1 WLR 1242.
2   *Miles v Forest Rock Granite* (1918) 34 TLR 500. The formalistic approach to 'escape' as the way to solve such blasting cases contrasts sharply with the US blasting cases, the arguments in which formed the basis of the original Restatement rule of strict liability

Accumulating dangerous things

It is odd that the reason given by Lord Goff for not adopting the American rule is that it is too difficult to define 'ultra-hazardous' or 'abnormally dangerous' when the orthodox rule itself includes a requirement that the defendant has accumulated something dangerous, or at least in Blackburn J's phrase, something 'liable to do mischief if it escapes'. In any case, the word 'dangerous' is not to be taken literally. Plainly dangerous things such as explosives and gas come within the rule,[3] but so have slightly dangerous things such as oil and electricity[4] and fairground equipment[5] and even for things that would not immediately appear to be dangerous at all, such as flag poles, rusty wire and vibrations.[6] The rule even apparently covers people liable to do mischief as well as things, as in *A-G v Corke*[7] where the court said that the rule could apply to gypsies previously encamped on the defendant's land.[8]

The 'accumulation' requirement is not onerous. It serves only to exclude from the operation of the rule cases in which the danger was caused not by the defendant's intervention but by natural causes, for example the seeds of weeds that the wind has blown onto the defendant's land.[9] As such it would have no separate function if the idea of 'non-natural' came to be understood once again in its original sense of 'resulting from human intervention'.

Remoteness

Although we have already seen that *Wagon Mound* remoteness, in the form of a requirement that the type of damage be foreseeable, applies to *Rylands v Fletcher*, there is still the question of ordinary remoteness, or breaking the chain of causation.

---

for ultra-hazardous activities. See eg *Colton v Onderdonk* 69 Cal 155, 10 P 395 (1886), *Whitman Hotel Corpn v Elliot & Watrous Engineering Co* 54 F 2d 510, 511 (CA 2, 1931), *FitzSimmons & Connell Co v Braun* 199 Ill 390, 396-97, 65 NE 249 (1902).

3 *Rainham Chemical v Belvedere Fish Guano* above, *Batcheller v Tunbridge Wells Gas Co* (1901) 84 LT 765.

4 *Mulholland and Tedd v Baker* [1939] 3 All ER 253, *National Telephone v Baker* [1893] 2 Ch 186.

5 *Hale v Jennings Bros* [1938] 1 All ER 579.

6 *Shiffman v Grand Priory* [1936] 1 All ER 557, *Hoare v McAlpine* [1923] 1 Ch 167, *Crowhurst v Amersham Burial Board* (1878) 4 Ex D 5.

7 [1933] Ch 89.

8 Cf *R v Shorrock* [1994] QB 279, [1993] 3 All ER 917 (public nuisance) and *Page Motors v Epsom and Ewell Borough Council* (1982) 80 LGR 337, [1982] JPL 572 (private nuisance).

9 *Giles v Walker* (1890) 24 QBD 656.

Act or state of the plaintiff

The same rule that over-sensitive plaintiffs cannot recover probably applies in *Rylands v Fletcher* as much as in nuisance,[10] and contributory negligence applies in the same way as it does generally. But an unusual feature of *Rylands v Fletcher* liability is that where one of the occupants of a building suffers harm from the escape of a dangerous material held on the premises for the benefit of all the tenants, gas or water for example, the plaintiff has no action, apparently on the ground that the accumulation was for the plaintiff's benefit and the plaintiff is therefore deemed to have consented to carry the burden of the risk as well.[11] In *Dunne v North Western Gas Board*[12] Sellers LJ suggested an extraordinary extension of this idea by saying that he thought that it should apply to the relationship between the providers of utilities such as gas, water and electricity and all of their customers. He also doubted whether any nationalised industry could ever be liable under the rule since nationalised industries (supposedly) acted in the interests of all, not just in the interests of their owners. Such an extension approaches the view that the government should always win because it represents everyone, a view that not many people would subscribe to.

The privatisation of the utilities in Britain has reduced the practical importance of the point, but in any case the so-called 'common benefit' rule of consent should in principle apply only in cases of specific consent to endure the risk of specific dangers, and in particular only where the consent has contributed to the existence of the danger. Governmental immunity should not extend beyond the same restricted defence of statutory authority that applies in nuisance. There should be immunity only if the only way to obey the statute is to accumulate a dangerous thing so that it might escape without negligence by the defendant. For example, where a statute requires a water company to keep the water at a particular pressure, any escape of the water that arises because of the statutory pressure levels should not count as actionable. The defendant would have a statutory immunity.[13] But if the pressure was higher than the statutory minimum, or if there was no statutory duty in the first place, the immunity would not apply.[14]

Third party interventions

As in nuisance, the chain of causation can be broken by third party interventions but if the defendant could reasonably have prevented the

---

10 *Eastern and South African Telegraph v Cape Town Tramways* [1902] AC 381, but contra *Hoare v McAlpine* above n 6.
11 *Carstairs v Taylor* (1871) LR 6 Exch 217.
12 Above.
13 *Green v Chelsea Waterworks* (1894) 70 LT 547.
14 *Charing Cross Electricity v Hydraulic Power* [1914] 3 KB 772.

intervention, there is no break in the chain. In *Rickards v Lothian*[15] a
third party deliberately blocked the defendant's lavatory, with the result
that the plaintiff's premises were flooded. The intervention was unforeseeable and could not have been prevented by reasonable care. Thus there
was no liability.

It seems that whether the intervention was deliberate or negligent or
innocent makes no difference. What matters is whether the defendant
could have controlled what the third party did. Thus, there was no liability
where the plaintiff suffered injury after children threw a lighted match
into the petrol tank of a vehicle parked on the defendants' premises.[16]

On the other hand, there is liability under *Rylands v Fletcher* not only
for the acts of one's employees and agents but also for the acts of independent contractors, visitors and guests.[17] Indeed, the defendant is
responsible for the acts of so many types of third party that the cases in
which the defendant is not so liable are often referred to as cases of 'acts of
a stranger'.

Several writers[18] say that it would be unfair to hold a defendant liable
for the act of a casual visitor who, for example, leaves gates open or leaves
taps on. But the whole point of *Rylands v Fletcher* liability is that defendants
take responsibility for having the risky material on their property at all.
Unless it escapes in a completely unforeseeable way because of a third
party intervention, the defendant is responsible for the harm that it does.

Special cases—fire and nuclear incidents

Finally, there should be mention of the regimes that govern cases in which
the defendant causes very particular forms of harm namely fire and nuclear
incidents.

Fire

Clearly, if I negligently start a fire, or negligently allow one to spread I
will be liable to anyone the fire harms. Equally, as in the blasting cases, if
I bring onto my land things that are dangerous because they are likely to
catch fire I can be liable under *Rylands v Fletcher* if they do catch fire and
the fire spreads.[19] The argument that the dangerous things themselves do
not escape, but only the fire, ignores (a) that the fire is itself a dangerous
thing and (b) that liability under *Rylands v Fletcher* is for the consequences

---

15 [1913] AC 263.
16 See *Perry v Kendricks* [1956] 1 WLR 85.
17 *Balfour v Barty-King* [1957] 1 QB 496, *Hale v Jennings* above.
18 Including *Salmond and Heuston* and *Markesinis and Deakin*.
19 *Mason v Levy Auto Parts* [1967] 2 QB 530.

of accumulation of dangerous things and for the escape of its consequences from the control of the defendant.[20] Finally, if a fire starts on my land because of natural causes or the act of a third party for whose acts I am not otherwise responsible (eg employees and, possibly, independent contractors), I am liable in nuisance if it spreads and damages my neighbour's property unless I could not reasonably have prevented its spread, taking into account the resource at my disposal.[1]

There is also an eighteenth century statute, the Fires Prevention (Metropolis) Act 1774 (which, despite its name applies to the whole of England and Wales) s 86 of which appears to say that there can be no liability for fires unless there is fault in the way the fire began. But s 86 has been interpreted as not affecting liability where the fire began without fault but spread because of the defendant's negligence,[2] as not affecting liability for fires started deliberately which then spread without any further fault and, most significantly, as not affecting liability under *Rylands v Fletcher*.

Nuclear radiation

The modern equivalent of the Fires Prevention (Metropolis) Act is perhaps the Nuclear Installations Act 1965. The problems associated with liability for incidents involving nuclear power stations are intractable. The period over which harm may manifest itself is likely to be very great, rendering ordinary limitation periods oppressive for victims. Problems of proof of causation are very difficult. The national security aspect of civil nuclear power means that proving carelessness is almost impossible. The scale of the disaster if one happens (a Chernobyl for example) is so immense that it borders on the absurd to call on the courts to pronounce on the balance of costs and benefits of the nuclear industry for the purposes of assigning blame.

The 1965 Act addresses some, but not all, of these problems. Under s 7(1), operators of nuclear installations, such as power stations, are under a duty to 'secure that no [incident] involving nuclear matter ... causes injury to any person or damage to the property of any person.' The duty is a duty of result, that is, if the result to be secured does not occur, the defendant is liable regardless of how or why the result was not secured. This is strict liability in terms both of foreseeability and of the cost of precautions argument. The only complete defence is that the incident occurred because of hostile military conflict. There is even liability if the incident comes about because of a natural disaster. Moreover even contributory negligence does not operate in the normal way. Plaintiffs' damages are reduced only if they intentionally or recklessly injure

---

20 See *Miles v Forest Rock* above (liability in blasting cases for escape of rock, not of explosives).
1 *Goldman v Hargreaves* above.
2 *Filliter v Phippard* (1847) 11 QB 347.

themselves. Finally, the limitation period is 30 years from the date of the incident.

The Act, however, does not help plaintiffs with their problems of proof of causation[3] and it does not cover economic loss. As a result in *Merlin v British Nuclear Fuels plc*,[4] in which a nuclear incident at Sellafield made the plaintiff's house unsaleable, instead of saying that the loss was property damage (since there were high radioactivity readings at the property) or personal injury (since the reason the property was valueless was the risk of cancer) the court decided that the loss was purely economic and denied recovery.

---

3   For the difficulties of proof of causation in nuclear cases, see *Reay and Hope v British Nuclear Fuels plc* (1993) Independent, 22 November.
4   [1990] 2 QB 557 [1990] 3 All ER 711

Chapter 12

Defamation

The law of defamation—libel and slander—seeks to protect people's reputations. Reputation is a crucial asset in social and economic life. People with reputations for dishonesty, for example, or for not keeping their promises, cut themselves off from all but the most simple or anonymous market transactions. People with reputations for disloyalty disqualify themselves from most high-ranking jobs. And people who others think have communicable diseases can find themselves shut out from all social interaction. Indeed, reputation may be a more important method by which people control one another than the law itself. Those who are beyond the control of reputation are dangerous and often wicked. It is no accident that Shakespeare makes his most notorious and unrepentant villain claim that, 'Reputation is an idle and most false imposition, oft got without merit and lost without deserving.'[1] But for the vast majority who are still in thrall to it, the wrongful loss of reputation can be an injustice almost without parallel.

Perhaps unusually, in disputes about reputation what is efficient for society is also what is just for individuals. People in general have an interest in accurate information about others, information that will help them to decide how risky it is to trade with or interact in some other way with others. And individuals cannot in justice expect more or less than that any information about them that is relevant to how risky it is to trade or otherwise interact with them will be strictly accurate. Perhaps people are also entitled to expect privacy about confidential matters that will probably not affect the risks that others may face in dealing with them[2] but that is a different question. Accuracy is both efficient and just.

But defamation does raise difficult issues. Reputations are not pure matters of undisputed fact. There will be disagreements not only about what particular people have done and whether what they have done indicates that they are inherently inclined to act in the same way again, but also about how to interpret those actions and what moral judgments

1   Iago in *Othello* at 2.iii.262 (Wells and Taylor ed, OUP, 1987).
2   See above ch 10.

to make about them. Legal regulation of the debate about reputation is therefore a restriction on freedom of speech and like all such restrictions reduces the chance of finding the truth if there is a truth to be found and prevents people from coming to their own conclusions if there is no truth to be found. If the courts were infallible in their judgments not only about the facts but also about their meaning and their moral significance, there would be no problem. The law would only root out error and would leave alone truth and true judgment. But the courts are not infallible and defamation law is itself a threat to the dissemination of accurate information and to the possibility of informed debate. In the American phrase, the very existence of legal control of information about reputation will have a 'chilling effect' on the exchange of views.

The tension between the plain fact that accurate information about reputation is both useful and just and the equally plain fact of the limitations and disadvantages of using the courts as a means of ensuring such accuracy explains much of the existing law. Moreover the difficulties of dealing with that tension explain why the law of defamation seems permanently to be under fire for its various defects and deficiencies. It might help if English law contained constitutionally entrenched guarantees of freedom of speech, as does US law, so that at least the courts would have consistent guidance about how to decide the most difficult cases. At the moment the European Convention on Human Rights does have some influence, but technically only in interpreting British statutes when they are ambiguous.[3] But even a constitutional provision can only indicate to the courts the general direction that they should take and the presumptions they should use about the relative importance of freedom of speech and court-mandated accuracy about reputation. It could not say precisely where the balance should lie in each individual case.

Malicious falsehood, economic loss and reputation

Two preliminary matters merit attention. The first is the relationship between defamation and the protection of economic interests.

One must, for example, distinguish between the tort of defamation and the related but different tort of malicious falsehood. A defendant is liable for malicious falsehood when the defendant intentionally harms the plaintiff's business by telling untruths. The main aim of malicious falsehood is the protection of economic interests from intentional and malicious harm. Unlike defamation, it requires proof of specific intention to harm the plaintiff. Malicious falsehood is at once wider than defamation, because it protects more than reputation, for example it applies where I lose you business by telling people that you do not open your shop at weekends, and narrower than defamation in that it only protects reputation if the loss of reputation has caused some other, more specific loss, usually a loss of business.[4]

3   *Rantzen v Mirror Group Newspapers (1986) Ltd* [1994] QB 670, [1993] 4 All ER 975, [1993] 3 WLR 953.
4   See *Joyce v Sengupta* [1993] 1 All ER 897.

Because of the rule of the English legal aid scheme that no public financial assistance is available in defamation actions but such assistance is available for malicious falsehood actions, a trend has begun to attempt to conflate the two actions. At the same time, with *Spring v Guardian Assurance*,[5] negligence has muscled in on a field formerly left entirely to defamation.

But the fundamental approach of the courts to loss of reputation is still that laid down by the Court of Appeal in *Lonrho v Fayed (No 5)*,[6] where the plaintiffs failed in an action for the intentional economic tort of conspiracy to injure and the alleged damage was loss of reputation. The protection of reputation is treated by the law as quite distinct from the protection of economic interests. As Dillon LJ said:

'In my judgment, if the plaintiffs want to claim damages for injury to reputation or injury to feelings, they must do so in an action for defamation—not in this very different form of action. Injury to reputation and to feelings is, with very limited exceptions, a field of its own and the established principles in that field are not to be side-stepped by alleging a different cause of action. Justification— truth—is an absolute defence to an action for defamation, and it would, in my judgment, be lamentable if a plaintiff could recover damages against defendants who had combined to tell the truth about the plaintiff and so had destroyed his unwarranted reputa- tion. But that would be the consequence if damages for injury to reputation and injury to feelings could be claimed in a "lawful means" conspiracy action. To tell the truth would be wrongful. I see no difference in this regard between general reputation and commercial or business reputation. To prove loss of orders and loss of trade is another matter; that is recognisable pecuniary dam- age.'

The House of Lords in *Spring* confirmed this approach. There is no recovery in negligence for loss of reputation itself. As Lord Goff said:

'[I]n ... a simple case of the defendants having negligently made a statement damaging to the plaintiff's reputation ... I do not see how there can be a liability upon the defendants in negligence consistently with the policy of the law established in the law of defamation.'

Of course, some overlap is inevitable, especially because defamation damages are allowed to reflect plaintiffs' upset feelings that they have lost their reputation, not just their objective loss of reputation,[7] as Lord Woolf said in *Spring*:

5   See above ch 5.
6   [1994] 1 All ER 188, [1993] 1 WLR 1489.
7   See Lord Diplock in *Cassell & Co Ltd v Broome* [1972] AC 1027, 1125: 'The harm caused to the plaintiff by the publication of the libel upon him often lies more in his own feelings, what he thinks other people are thinking of him, than in any actual change made manifest in their attitude towards him. A solatium for injured feelings, however innocent the publication by the defendant may have been, forms a large element in the damages.'.

'In the case of defamation the primary head, but not the only head, of damages is as to the loss of reputation. In an action for negligence, on the other hand, the subject of the reference will be primarily interested in and largely limited to his economic loss.'

In addition, as the next section shows, defamation law can protect 'commercial' reputations as opposed to specific commercial or economic interests. The difference is that commercial reputation is more general than pure economic loss—which explains both the great ease with which the essentials of the tort of defamation can be established and the existence of the many defences to it.

Who can have a reputation?

The second preliminary matter is the question of whose reputation the law of defamation protects. Obviously, the law protects ordinary individuals. But what about companies, clubs, trade unions and the government?

From the time of the earliest modern legislation allowing the formation of limited liability companies, the law of defamation has protected at least the trading or business reputation of companies.[8] Unincorporated bodies such as clubs have not been so lucky. The courts have excluded them because they have no 'legal' existence. Even more unlucky are trade unions. Although unions have the right to sue and be sued apparently without restriction, because of traditional fears dating back to the *Taff Vale* case,[9] unions do not have corporate status.[10] In *Electrical, Electronic Telecommunications and Plumbing Union v Times Newspapers*[11] O'Connor J used this fact to deny that a union could sue in defamation.

As for the government, it would seem extremely dangerous to give any branch of the state standing to sue for defamation in its own right. One does not have to think about the criminal offences of the old Soviet bloc of 'slandering the state' or even of the past abuses in Britain and America of the idea of sedition to realise that the reputation of the state means little more than the reputation of the ruling party and libel actions by organs of the state are likely to be motivated by a desire to silence political opponents. Even in local government, most of which lacks direct police powers and can claim to have a need to protect its reputation for financial probity at least at those times when it is permitted to raise money directly from the capital markets, striking the right balance between the need for accuracy and the dangers of the suppression of debate about matters of controversy will usually mean that defamation has to give way to the rough and tumble

---

8   *Metropolitan Saloon Omnibus v Hawkins* (1859) 4 H & N 87.
9   *Taff Vale Rly v Amalgamated Society of Railway Servants* [1901] AC 426.
10 Section 10 Trade Union and Labour Relations (Consolidation) Act 1992 (formerly s 2(1) Trade Union and Labour Relations Act 1974).
11 [1980] QB 585.

of political disputation. This is not to say that individual politicians and officials should receive no protection, but only to say that the state itself should not receive protection.

Thus, in *Derbyshire County Council v Times Newspapers*[12] in which the defendant had published articles questioning the propriety of dealings in the plaintiff council's pension fund, the House of Lords said that the council itself, although a body corporate, was not capable of having a reputation that the law of defamation could protect.[13] Lord Keith rejected any analogy between a governmental body and a commercial company:

> 'There are, however, features of a local authority which may be regarded as distinguishing it from other types of corporation, whether trading or non-trading. The most important of these features is that it is a governmental body. Further, it is a democratically elected body, the electoral process nowadays being conducted almost exclusively on party political lines. It is of the highest public importance that a democratically elected governmental body, or indeed any governmental body, should be open to uninhibited public criticism. The threat of a civil action for defamation must inevitably have an inhibiting effect on freedom of speech.'

He went on:

> 'In the case of a local authority temporarily under the control of one political party or another it is difficult to say that the local authority as such has any reputation of its own. Reputation in the eyes of the public is more likely to attach itself to the controlling political party, and with a change in that party the reputation itself will change. A publication attacking the activities of the authority will necessarily be an attack on the body of councillors which represents the controlling party, or on the executives who carry on the day to day management of its affairs.'

But of course,

> 'If the individual reputation of any of these [councillors or officials] is wrongly impaired by the publication any of these can himself bring proceedings for defamation.'

What is defamatory?

A plaintiff may recover for defamation if the defendant publishes defamatory material about the plaintiff and the defendant cannot claim

12 [1993] AC 534.
13 Note that *Derbyshire* overrules the older case *Bognor Regis UDC v Campion* [1972] 2 QB 169.

the benefit of any of the various defences. The obvious questions are
therefore: what makes material defamatory? what counts as publishing
it? how does one decide whether the material is about the plaintiff? and
what are the defences?

We begin with 'what makes material defamatory'?

Three tests

There are three alternative ways in which material may count as
defamatory. The first is when it tends to **'lower the plaintiff in the
estimation of right-thinking people generally'**.[14] The second is that
the statement holds the plaintiff up to **'ridicule, hatred and contempt'**.[15]
The third is that the material tends to cause people to **'shun or avoid'**[16]
the plaintiff. Material is defamatory if it meets any of the tests, even though
it may not meet the others. For example, to say of someone that he is
bankrupt is probably to lower him in the estimation of right thinking people
generally, but not necessarily to cause people to hold him up to ridicule
hatred or contempt or to shun or avoid him. To say of people that they
have a communicable disease may cause others to shun and avoid them,
but it may not lower them in anyone's estimation or hold them up for
ridicule, hatred or contempt. Nevertheless, both these statements are
defamatory.

The context within which words appear is relevant. If the plaintiff quotes
selectively, the defendant may fill in the gaps to show that the words would
not, in context, have had a defamatory meaning. Also relevant is the words'
cumulative effect as opposed to just their meaning phrase by phrase.[17]

Notice that none of the tests makes any reference to the truth or falsity
of the statement. Although some writers say that defamatory material is
'presumed' to be untrue, it is less confusing to say that the legal meaning
of 'defamatory' is different from its ordinary meaning and that in law a
'defamatory' statement means one which, *if believed*, would lower one in
the estimation of right thinking people or cause them to hold the plaintiff
in contempt or cause them to shun or avoid the plaintiff. That is, in law, a
statement can be both defamatory and true.

Notice also that the intention of the defendant is not relevant. What
matters is what others would understand by the words. As Lord Mansfield

---

14 *Sim v Stretch* (1936) 52 TLR 669.
15 *Thorley v Lord Kerry* (1812) 4 Taunt 355, 3 Camp 214n, *Parmiter v Coupland* (1840) 6 M
   & W 105.
16 *Youssoupoff v Metro Goldwyn Mayer* (1934) 50 TLR 581 per Slesser LJ; *Esslemont v
   Chief Constable of West Midlands Police* Court of Appeal LEXIS Transcript 10 November
   1992. See also *Post Pub Co v Peck* 199 F6 (Circuit Court of Appeals, First Circuit 1912),
   De Meo v Community Newspapers Inc 47 Misc 2d 822, 263 NYS 2d 244 (SCNY 1965); S
   346, Western Australia Criminal Code, *Mirror Newspapers Ltd v World Hosts Pty Ltd*
   (1979) 141 CLR 632 (High Court of Australia).
17 See eg *Liberace v Daily Mirror* (1959) Times, 17/18 June.

said: 'Whatever a man publishes he publishes at his peril.'[18] Thus, in *Cassidy v Daily Mirror*[19] the defendant newspaper innocently said that a Mr Cassidy was about to be married to a particular woman (the paper published a picture of the couple and described Mr Cassidy as 'Mr Corrigan', a pseudonym he used). This, understandably, upset Mr Cassidy's existing wife, the plaintiff, who claimed that readers who knew her as his wife would assume that she had been lying about whether she was married to him. The newspaper's complete ignorance of these circumstances could not prevent the story from being counted as defamatory.

Finally, notice that a statement can still be defamatory even if, in fact, no-one believed it. The test is not whether, for example, the statement did in reality lower the plaintiff in the estimation of right thinking people but whether it would have done so if it had been believed.[1] The number of believers may be relevant to the extent of the loss, but not to whether there was defamation at all.

Judge vs jury and the 'meaning' of words

Defamation is one of the few civil law actions in which jury trial is still a common event.[2] As a result, much of the law consists of what judges should say to juries and what tasks the judge has as opposed to the jury. In deciding whether the words were defamatory, technically, first, the judge decides whether the words were capable of a defamatory meaning, and then the jury decides whether they really were defamatory.[3]

The position is further complicated by the ruling in *Lewis v Daily Telegraph*[4] that if the words are capable of bearing several meanings, the judge must rule on whether each meaning is capable of being defamatory, and only the defamatory meanings are put to the jury. The jury then has to decide (a) whether the meaning of the words was one of the meanings ruled capable of being defamatory and (b) whether that meaning was indeed defamatory.

There are fundamental problems with the division of labour between judge and jury and with the role of the jury. The central problem is that if defamation concerns the loss of reputation, if the ordinary people assembled in the jury believe that the defendant's statement adversely affects the

---

18 *R v Woodfall* (1774) Lofft 776. See Holmes J in *Peck v Chicago Tribune* 214 US 185 (US SCt 1909).
19 [1929] 2 KB 331.
1   *Morgan v Odhams Press* [1971] 1 WLR 1239.
2   But note that the Lord Chancellor has proposed further reforms of defamation law under which more cases will be decided by county court judges and some cases will be weeded out for summary disposal by a preliminary hearing before a judge alone.
3   The jury's right to a final say on whether the material was defamatory is supposedly guaranteed by Fox's Libel Act 1792, although technically that Act covers only criminal libel.
4   Otherwise known as *Rubber Improvements v Daily Telegraph* [1964] AC 234.

plaintiff's reputation, the fact that the judge believes that the words are not capable of a defamatory meaning is irrelevant. Indeed, the very fact that the jury disagrees with the judge shows the judge to be wrong.[5] Judges have to resort to notions of what words and phrases 'really' mean—but to do so is to adopt a theory of meaning not only of dubious intellectual value but also of quite the wrong sort for judging harm to reputation. If people think that 'to prevaricate' means 'to waste time' rather than 'to be evasive and mislead people', it is in reality much less harmful to call someone 'a prevaricator' than 'a liar'. It does not matter from the point of view of the harm done to a person's reputation that the 'proper' or dictionary definition of 'to prevaricate' is 'to mislead'. Equally, to say of someone that he 'decimated' the profitability of a company is to say something worse about him than one would guess from the dictionary and historical meaning of 'decimate' which is 'to reduce by a tenth'.

One can only speculate about the real reasons for the judge's power to use the capacity of words to bear a defamatory meaning to prevent cases from reaching the jury. One obvious possibility is the fear that in some cases the jury will be biased against the defendant. Another possibility is that, if the area of life the case concerns is obscure or uses technical language, the judge fears that the jury will not understand the evidence. Yet another possibility is that the judge believes that the jury may respond to popular prejudices, for example against foreigners or homosexuals, that should not form part of the law even if the reality is that they do affect people's reputation.

A related problem is about the role of the jury. Is it the job of each member of the jury to say whether he or she believes personally that the words used mean that the plaintiff is a less worthy person, or are members of the jury supposed to ask themselves whether other people would think less of the plaintiff as a result of hearing the defendant's words? Are members of the jury respondents to an opinion poll of a dozen randomly selected adults, or is it a small polling organisation being asked to guess what the results of a real opinion poll would be if one were carried out? In cases such as *Cassidy v Daily Mirror*,[6] where the words are claimed to be defamatory because some people, knowing facts that others would not know, would interpret the defendant's statement in a particular way, the jury seems to have a pollster role:[7]

> 'It was for the jury to say whether those people [who knew the background facts] could reasonably draw the inference that the so-called Mrs Corrigan was in fact living in immoral cohabitation.'

Moreover, the three tests for defamatory meaning ('lower the plaintiff in the estimation of right thinking people generally', 'ridicule hatred and

5 See eg *Capital & Counties Bank v Henty* (1882) 7 App Cas 741 (circular claiming that bank insolvent led to run on bank—held circular not capable of defamatory meaning, but if so, how come there was a run on the bank?).
6 Above n 19.
7 Per Scrutton LJ.

contempt' and 'shun and avoid') are usually phrased to emphasise what people generally might think, rather than what the individual juror might think.

On the other hand, except in cases in which the defamatory meaning only comes out if one knows certain extraneous facts, it is not the usual practice for the parties to lead evidence of what people in general make of the allegedly defamatory statement. The question is left to the jurors themselves as the epitome of 'ordinary reasonable' people.[8]

Temporal change, minority opinions and the virtuous few

Two kinds of defamation case frequently present difficulties for the courts. In the first, accusations that once were thought to be seriously defamatory lose their force because of changed social attitudes. Should the court rule that the words are no longer capable of bearing a defamatory meaning, on the grounds that there might be a rogue jury or that the courts would look out of date if the judge ruled that the words could be defamatory. The second, into which the first kind of case shades, is whether it can be defamatory to say something of someone that a minority of people would think defamatory but which most people think is harmless?

As for temporal change, there is little doubt that it would be difficult now to obtain judgment for the plaintiff in defamation where the defendant said that the plaintiff was 'a papist',[9] 'a German'[10] or 'Czech'.[11] To call someone a 'communist' might still be actionable on the grounds that it is holding the plaintiff up to ridicule, but it certainly does not have the force it had during the Cold War.[12] But note that in all these cases, behind the immediate accusation lies a meaning that would be defamatory even now, namely that the plaintiff was guilty of treason or disloyalty. Papists in 1683, Germans during the First World War and even Czechs during the Cold War will have appeared at the time to be enemies of the state.

But more profound changes are possible. In *Shaw v Akram*[13] an accusation that the plaintiff had insulted the Muslim faith was held to be defamatory. In previous centuries, an English court may have thought that insulting the Muslim faith was a praiseworthy act, and even more recently doctrinal disputes among Muslims would have seemed to be a matter of indifference to the right-thinking English Christian. But Lawton LJ said that such attitudes were no longer part of the law:

> 'It seems to me that, in the year 1976, the ordinary member of the public, even if he had no religious views of his own or no strongly held views, would not approve of anyone insulting the religious

8   *Lewis v Daily Telegraph* above n 4. See now also *Charleston v News Group* (1995) Times, 31 March, HL.
9   *Row v Clargis* (1683) T Raym 482.
10 *Slazengers v Gibbs* (1916) 33 TLR 35.
11 Per Lord Denning in *Linklater v Daily Telegraph* (1964) 108 Sol Jo 992.
12 See eg *Remington v Bentley* 88 F Supp 166 (SDNY 1949).
13 [1981] LS Gaz R 814, LEXIS Transcript 15 June 1981.

beliefs of others; and anyone who did insult the religious beliefs of other people would, in my judgment, be lowering himself in the estimation of right thinking people. We live in an age ... when it is the desire of right-thinking people to get rid of age-old religious disputes and all that so frequently follows when religious disputes get out of hand. History, I hope, has taught many of us and certainly has taught right-thinking people that one of the ways of causing trouble is to cast slurs and insults on the religious beliefs of others.'

It seems, therefore, that although some changes over time are matters only of surface appearance and that underneath the same age-old categories of defamation continue—treason, untrustworthiness and disloyalty for example—there are other changes in attitudes that are genuinely new and the law of defamation should keep up the changes.

One particularly difficult area, however, is sexual morality. One example will suffice. When male homosexuality was still criminal, before the Sexual Offences Act 1967, to say that someone was a practising homosexual was plainly defamatory, since it was an accusation that the plaintiff was committing criminal offences. But widespread disapproval of homosexuality survived the decriminalisation of homosexual acts between adults in private. In 1975, therefore, Stephenson LJ could still say that despite the 1967 Act, if a defendant argued that to call someone a homosexual was not capable of being defamatory, the defendant would be 'bound to fail'.[14] But by 1992, the situation was starting to change. In the action brought by Jason Donovan, an actor and singer, against *The Face* magazine, Drake J told the jury that it 'may not be defamatory' any more to call someone homosexual and that the issue was 'very debatable'.[15] Even so, Mr Donovan won his case, possibly because of his other claim that since he had previously and publicly denied that he was homosexual, regardless of whether homosexuality in itself lowers one's reputation, the defendant was accusing him of hypocrisy and lying.

The problem of temporal change is closely linked with the problem of minority views. Is it defamatory to make statements about people which are to their discredit only in the view of a small number of people? The problem is particularly acute when the statements would be to the positive credit of the plaintiff in the rest of the world. In *Byrne v Deane*,[16] for example, the defendant denounced the plaintiff for giving away to the police the fact that the club to which they both belonged was engaged in illegal gambling. Within the club, such an accusation of disloyalty would be very damaging to the plaintiff's reputation, and might have substantial consequences, for example exclusion from the club. But as far as the community outside the club is concerned, loyalty taken to the extreme of covering up criminal offences goes too far. The Court of Appeal decided that the denunciation could not be defamatory. Right-thinking people could

14 *R v Bishop* [1975] QB 274.
15 See (1992) Guardian, 9 April p 38, Daily Telegraph, 4 April p 2.
16 [1937] 1 KB 818.

not possibly think less of someone for reporting crimes to the police, even if in doing so the person was being disloyal.

But in principle, if the statement is one about which most people would be indifferent but which a small group of people would react to strongly, the plaintiff has lost reputation and should be able to recover. That the average person or the majority of people would be in the indifferent group should not matter, especially if the small group that reacts strongly is a group on whom the plaintiff depends. Most people, for example, would not find advertising by doctors or lawyers particularly shocking, but within those professions, advertising except within certain very strict limits, is forbidden and strongly disapproved of. An accusation of unwarranted advertising against a doctor or lawyer would not be defamatory if the test were what the average person thought or what the majority thought, and yet such an accusation would be a very serious matter for the doctor or lawyer concerned. One can accept *Byrne v Deane* on the basis that it means, quite reasonably, that the opinion of criminals is not something that the law can easily recognise, but the test should be, as Holmes J said in *Peck v Chicago Tribune*,[17] that there should be liability 'if the [statement] obviously would hurt the plaintiff in the estimation of an important and respectable part of the community'. As Holmes J continued, 'Liability is not a question of majority vote.'

Admittedly, in *Lewis v Daily Telegraph* Lord Devlin said that the test ought to be the effect of the words on the 'ordinary' person, which suggests taking the median or majority view, but the thrust of Lord Devlin's remark is not so much that minority views should not count but rather that one has to assume that in understanding the defendant's statement, one should look to how ordinary people will interpret the statement not the way a lawyer or an exceptionally clear thinking person would interpret it.

Note, however, that often the problem of minority views can be overcome by translating the statement into more general concerns, for example a concern for hypocrisy rather than sexuality, or for intolerance rather than the details of Islamic theology. This is the way, for example, that it is possible to say that it is defamatory to say of a member of one political party that he or she was a member of another party. It would be difficult to persuade a court that, for instance, it should say that it was defamatory to call someone a Conservative. But it is possible that there is an implied accusation of disloyalty or betrayal which everyone would accept as defamatory.

Lying behind all of these problems is the phrase 'right-thinking people'. The question is how seriously to take this phrase. Ultimately the question is whether it is just to deny plaintiffs recovery because, although they have certainly suffered a loss in reputation, the court disagrees with the people who think less of the plaintiff? One line of cases says that what matters is how people really react, and compensates plaintiffs for their loss of reputation even though that loss is the result of less than enlightened attitudes from those who hear or read the message. In *Youssoupoff v*

17 Above. See also *Kelly v Loew's Inc* 76 F Supp 473 (1946).

Metro Goldwyn Mayer,[18] for example, the plaintiff complained of the way she was portrayed in a film, *Rasputin the Mad Monk,* that the defendants had made. In the film, Rasputin rapes the character representing the plaintiff. Doubtless even in 1934 right-thinking people would have nothing but pity for someone who had suffered in the way the character representing the plaintiff had suffered. But the Court of Appeal, recognising that a very great number of people are not 'right-thinking' about such issues and would treat the plaintiff as somehow defiled, held that the plaintiff could succeed nevertheless. As Learned Hand J once said:[19]

> 'We do not believe ... that we need say whether "right-thinking" people would harbor similar feelings ... It is enough if there be some ... who do feel so, even if they would be "wrong-thinking" people if they did.'

On the other hand, *Byrne v Deane* shows that another line of cases exists in which the court takes the opposite view, that there are popular judgments about reputation that the law should not endorse or approve of or use.

One particular problem is whether the judge will allow the jury to decide a case in which people with very suspicious minds would see the defamation but other people would not interpret the words in the same way. For example, the defendant, a newspaper, writes a story which says that the police have started to investigate the plaintiff for fraud. A right-thinking person might say that since people are innocent until proven guilty, and since investigation is not even the same as accusation, such a story would not affect the plaintiff's reputation at all. But less scrupulous people might say to themselves that there is no smoke without fire. The Learned Hand approach would say that what matters is the real effect on the plaintiff, and if people really do think that there is no smoke without fire, the plaintiff has a claim. The *Byrne v Deane* approach, in contrast, would say that the law of defamation should not endorse any view of criminal investigation that diverges from the strict official view. In the event, the case in which these facts arose, *Lewis v Daily Telegraph,* produced a messy compromise. Lord Devlin said that one cannot expect people to be logical, and that it is possible that they will think that an investigation means that there are good grounds for the investigation, and that known grounds for suspicion mean that there is probably guilt. But Lord Devlin goes on to say that to jump from the fact of an investigation to thinking that a plaintiff is guilty is to go too far. 'Two fences have to be taken instead of one.' The test, apparently, is not so much what the right-thinking person would think, but what an 'ordinary sensible person' would think. Subsequently, in *Hartt v Newspaper Publishing*[20] the court attempted to put more detail into the test and came up with the reaction of the 'hypothetical reader who is not

18 (1934) 50 TLR 581.
19 *Grant v Reader's Digest* 151 F 2d 733 (2nd circuit 1945).
20 (1987) Independent, 27 October.

unduly suspicious, but who can read between the lines. He might think loosely, but is not avid for scandal, and will not select one bad meaning where other non-defamatory meanings are available.'[1]

One should remember that all these tests are used to decide whether the case should go to the jury in the first place. The closer the test gets to the actual thought processes of jurors the more pointless it becomes, but the further away it is from the ordinary thought processes of jurors the more it needs to be justified. In any case, the point of defamation is to protect people's actual reputations in the real world, not the reputations they ought to have in an ideal world. Learned Hand's approach is therefore probably better than the confused approach taken presently, perhaps with an exception for the reputation of criminals among criminals for competence in criminality which should not be protected whatever the facts.

Vulgar abuse

Mere abuse of the plaintiff, although perhaps upsetting, is not actionable. Insults can end up as defamation only if they include specific accusations that would, if believed, adversely affect the plaintiff's reputation and even then, if it is obvious that no one would believe the words to be meant as anything but abuse, the judge may rule that the words are not capable of defamatory meaning.[2] Some writers say that the difference lies in the intent of the defendant, but this cannot be literally so, since the defendant's intention is not relevant in defamation. What is relevant is what an observer would have understood by the words. The relevance of intention is to be found in what the observer would have thought that the defendant meant. The real point is that abuse and insults are not accusations but merely expressions of anger.

On the other hand, remember that exposing the plaintiff to hatred, ridicule and contempt is also defamatory. Certain types of caricature can therefore quite easily cross the line between abuse and defamation.[3]

---

1   Is it defamatory to say of someone that there are untrue rumours that he is committing adultery? In view of *Lewis* one might have thought not, since the hurdles to be jumped include believing that when people say that there is an untrue rumour, they are really saying that it is a true rumour. This may be possible if the publication in question has developed an elaborate coded language in which saying that 'X has denied that he has done Y' is used as a formula to accuse X of Y, but in an ordinary magazine surely Lord Devlin's ordinary sensible reader would not jump to such a conclusion. On the other hand, it may be that one can analyse the case into two elements (a) repeating a libel (X is committing adultery) and (b) adding a comment to the effect that the rumour is untrue. On this analysis, to repeat the rumour is to commit the tort, whatever the effect of the comment. (See Steve Platt 'Sue, grab it and run the country' (1993) Independent, 8 July p 29).

2   *Parkins v Scott* (1862) 1 H & C 153; *Goodstein v Chalfonte Hotel* 101 NYS 2d 851 (1950); *Fields v Davis* [1955] CLY 1543.

3   *Dunlop Rubber Co v Dunlop* [1921] 1 AC 367.

True and false innuendo

Frequently, a statement will appear to be quite innocent on its face, but, if one knew other facts about the situation or about the plaintiff, the statement turns out to be far from innocent. Defamation of this sort is known as 'innuendo'.

In *Tolley v Fry*,[4] an amateur golfer complained about a newspaper advertisement that portrayed him as endorsing the defendant's products (he had not in fact done so). Since there was nothing discreditable about the product itself and nothing else about advertisement that was prima facie defamatory about the plaintiff, what was the defamation? The plaintiff's case was that the very fact that he had been seen to endorse a product at all threatened his amateur status. Amateur sportsmen did not endorse products and would be disgraced if they did so. The plaintiff said that anyone who knew that he was an amateur and who knew the implications for his amateur status of the advertisement would think less of him. The jury heard evidence from golfers about the implications of amateur status and found for the plaintiff. The Court of Appeal said that the judge should not have allowed the case to go to the jury at all because the advertisement was not capable of a defamatory meaning. But the House of Lords restored the jury's verdict. In *Cassidy v Daily Mirror*[5] only by knowing that the plaintiff was holding herself out as Mr Cassidy/ Corrigan's wife would one think that there was anything discreditable about her in a picture portraying her husband and another woman as a recently engaged couple. The judge told the jury that the test was whether the picture would discredit the plaintiff in the mind of a reasonable person who knew the circumstances. The defendant's challenge to the judge's direction failed in the Court of Appeal.

An important procedural consequence of a case being based on an innuendo is that the extrinsic facts that make the statement defamatory must be pleaded specifically by the plaintiff and proved. Indeed, if the plaintiff's case depends on a claim that only members of a specific group of people would have known the extrinsic facts that made the statement defamatory, the plaintiff must show that the statement was published to members of that group.[6] The idea is that if the plaintiff's case for saying that the statement is defamatory is not obvious, the defendant deserves some notice of what the plaintiff is going to claim and to be given some chance of showing the opposite. It is this point that has given rise to arguments about so-called 'false' or 'popular' innuendoes, that is cases in which there are no extrinsic facts on which the plaintiff's case depends but nevertheless the meaning of the statement on which the plaintiff depends is not immediately obvious. Unlike 'true' innuendoes, 'false' innuendoes are simply inferences that can be drawn from the statement itself. In a 'true' innuendo case, the plaintiff may have a cause of action

4   [1931] AC 333.
5   Above.
6   *Fullam v Newcastle Chronicle* [1977] 3 All ER 32.

based on the words themselves and another cause of action based on the innuendo.[7] In 'false' innuendo cases, the only cause of action is that based on the words themselves. There is no doubt that such inferences can ground a case in defamation. The question in false innuendo cases is simply whether plaintiffs should have to plead the inferences and meanings on which their case depends. *Lewis v Daily Telegraph* explicitly left the point open. But *Allsop v Church of England Newspaper*[8] decided that where the plaintiff relies on meanings and inferences that go beyond ordinary established meanings, the plaintiff should plead those meanings and inferences.

Another difference between true innuendoes and false innuendoes is that in true innuendoes there is a defence under s 4 of the Defamation Act 1952. Where the defendant's words were not defamatory on their face and the defendant did not know of the circumstances which made them defamatory, and in addition the defendant exercised all reasonable care in relation to the statement and, if the defendant is not the author of the statement and the author was not motivated by malice, the defendant may offer the plaintiff by way of amends a correction and an apology. As long as the correction offered is 'suitable' and the apology 'sufficient' the defendant has a defence to any subsequent defamation action. This defence (whose scope is, admittedly, restricted by the requirement that the defendant prove that there was no negligence) is not available in false innuendo cases since in such cases it is not 'circumstances' that make the words defamatory but interpretation of the words themselves.

Reference to plaintiff

The second requirement of the tort of defamation is that the defamatory comment should refer to the plaintiff. Clearly, if the tort protects reputation, to be actionable the defendant's statement must have been capable of harming the plaintiff's reputation as opposed to the reputation of other people. If I make a defamatory statement but no one knows that I am referring to you, there can be no harm to your reputation.

The problems of reference are: what counts as a sufficient reference; what happens if the defamatory statement seems to refer to someone to whom the defendant could not possibly have meant to refer; and can one defame an entire group of people?

7   Note that because the innuendo is a cause of action in itself, extrinsic facts that come to light only after the publication of the statement cannot be relied upon by the plaintiff. The innuendo is not about what the words could have meant but about what they did mean given the extrinsic facts: *Grappelli v Derek Block* [1981] 1 WLR 822. If no innuendo is pleaded, the plaintiff is not permitted to argue that the words would have meant different things to different people, but must claim that a 'fair-minded reader' would have understood the words in their defamatory meaning : *Charleston v News Group* (1995) Times, 31 March.

8   [1972] 2 QB 161 (plaintiff accused of being 'bent'—held not to be understandable without explanation).

An objective test—the loose-thinking man on the Clapham omnibus

The test for whether a statement has sufficiently referred to the plaintiff is not what the defendant intended nor whether the plaintiff reasonably believed that the statement referred to him. The test is whether reasonable observers would have believed that the statement referred to the plaintiff. But again, as with defamatory meanings, the reasonable observer is no paragon of the intellect. It does not matter if the identification of the plaintiff depends on a certain amount of 'loose thinking' and inattentiveness. In *Morgan v Odhams Press* Johnny Morgan claimed that he had been defamed by a story in the (pre-Murdoch) *Sun* newspaper which said that one Margo Murray had been kidnapped by a gang involved in fixing greyhound races because she was threatening to give the gang away to the police. In fact, Miss Murray had been staying quite freely at the plaintiff's flat. The plaintiff claimed that the article would have made reasonable people think that he was a kidnapper and a fixer of greyhound races. The case depended on extrinsic facts such as Miss Murray's having stayed with the plaintiff during the relevant time, which the plaintiff could prove. The plaintiff also produced various witnesses who, having seen Miss Murray in the company of the plaintiff at the time, assumed that the plaintiff was indeed a kidnapper. The House of Lords by a majority decided that the story was capable of a defamatory meaning. The view of three of their Lordships was that the judge was right to instruct the jury that the question was whether readers who knew of the circumstances would reasonably have understood the article as referring to the plaintiff. There was no requirement that the article itself should contain some kind of pointer to the plaintiff. Lord Reid said that the test is whether 'ordinary sensible people' who knew the extrinsic facts would have been unreasonable in thinking that the article referred to the plaintiff. But he went further and said that one had to allow the 'ordinary sensible' person 'a certain amount of loose thinking', that is that 'ordinary' people did not apply the principles of inference with absolute precision and would believe that statements referred to the plaintiff even when that was only one of several possibilities.

Unintentional defamation

The problem with using a test for reference that is objective (although allowing for loose thinking by the observer) is that it means that there will be occasions when the defendant will be liable even when the defendant could not have known that readers possessed of certain knowledge would understand the statement to refer to a person of whom the defendant has never heard. But this appeared to be the position at common law. In the notorious case *Hulton v Jones*,[9] the plaintiff, who gloried in the name of Thomas Artemus Jones, complained of an account of a motor festival in

9   [1910] AC 20.

Dieppe in which the writer described the antics of an 'Artemus Jones' who was 'with a woman who is not his wife, who must be, you know—the other thing!' Besides the unusual name, none of the description of the Artemus Jones in the article particularly fitted the Artemus Jones of real life. The character in the article was, for example, supposedly a church warden and lived in Peckham. The real Artemus Jones was none of these things. Indeed, he had not even been to Dieppe. But the plaintiff led evidence from witnesses who had read the article and thought that it referred to the plaintiff. The defendant newspaper denied liability saying that it had not known of the plaintiff and had not intended to refer to him. The defendant's account was not particularly convincing, since the plaintiff had himself written articles for the defendant's newspaper for 12 years and was known, if not to the writer of the Dieppe story, at least to the editor. Nevertheless, the House of Lords decided that even if the defendant was telling the truth there would still be liability since what mattered was how the words would be understood, not what they meant in the minds of the writer and the publisher.

Similarly, in *Newstead v London Express*[10] the defendant newspaper had a story that said that 'Harold Newstead, a 30-year-old Camberwell man' had been convicted of bigamy. A different approximately 30-year-old Harold Newstead of Camberwell sued for defamation. The defendant said that there was no intention to defame the other Mr Newstead and that one could not be accused of defaming one person when one had clearly intended to refer to another person about whom the statements were true. But the Court of Appeal accepted neither of these points and found for the plaintiff.

Discontent with these decisions, which put a very heavy burden on newspapers and indeed novelists to make sure that references to villains of various sorts could not be understood as referring to innocent people, led to the insertion in the Defamation Act 1952 of the defence of 'unintentional defamation', a defence that we have already mentioned in relation to innuendo. Section 4 of the Act also extends to cases in which, although the statement was defamatory on its face, the defendant did not intend to refer to the plaintiff and did not know of any circumstances that might make people believe that the statement referred to the plaintiff. The same conditions of the absence of negligence, and of malice by the author if the defendant was not the author, apply in the same way as in innuendo cases, as do the requirements that the correction offered must be suitable and the apology sufficient.

One might note, however, that it is far from clear that s 4 would have saved the defendants in *Hulton v Jones* and *Newstead v London Express* from liability. In *Newstead* one might question whether, by not giving more identifying details of the real bigamist, the newspaper had failed to exercise all reasonable care. And in *Hulton* there is not only a question mark against the reasonableness of the defendant's conduct in not noticing the connection between the articles and Mr Jones, but also there is the question of possible malice by the article's author.

10 [1940] 1 KB 377.

Group libel

Is it possible to defame a large group of people or an entire type or class of person? The answer is no. Groups without corporate personality have no legally protected reputation.[11] But can individual members of groups sue for defamation of the entire group? The answer depends on whether the familiar 'ordinary sensible person' would think that the statement referred to individual identifiable members of the group. In the traditional example the statement 'all lawyers are thieves' is not actionable by lawyers because the court should rule that it is not capable of referring to individual lawyers but is only general insult.[12] But if the words or the words plus the circumstances point to a particular member or members of the group or the group is small enough that the words plausibly refer to all of its members, there can be liability.[13] According to Lord Porter in *Knupffer v London Express*, in which the House of Lords held that a defamatory statement about a small international political party with a few thousand members was not actionable even by the leader of its small, 24-strong, British branch, 'Each case must be must be considered according to its own circumstances,' but relevant factors would include: '[T]he size of the class, the generality of the charge and the extravagance of the accusation'. In *Braddock v Bevins*[14] the defendant implied that an MP 'and her friends in Abercromby' were Communists. Three of the plaintiffs claimed to be one of the MPs 'friends in Abercromby', but the court decided that the words were not capable of referring to the plaintiffs. Nevertheless, the court should assume and tolerate the same degree and methods of inference by readers, logical or otherwise, as that expected elsewhere in the law of defamation, with the result that it is possible for judges to allow the jury to decide whether a statement about a very large organisation referred to the leader of that organisation if the surrounding circumstances make such an inference not unreasonable. Thus, in *Orme v Associated Newspapers*[15] Comyn J agreed that an article attacking the Unification Church was capable of referring to the head of the Unification Church in England, even though the article made no mention of him and was mainly an attack on the Rev Moon, the Church's worldwide leader. The plaintiff, however, had witnesses who said that they believed that the article referred to him. Comyn J said:

> '[A]n approach via identifiability and generality is the right one; and ... one must ask in every case, not primarily questions about class, but primarily whether the alleged offensive material reason— ably refers to the plaintiff in the minds of those who know him and the broad circumstances.'

11 See above.
12 Willes J in *Eastwood v Holmes* (1858) 1 F & F 347.
13 Cf *Le Fanu v Malcolmson* (1848) 1 HL Cas 637, *Browne v DC Thomson* 1912 SC 359, *Foxcroft v Lacy* (1613) Hob 89.
14 [1948] 1 KB 580.
15 (1981) Times, 4 February, LEXIS Transcript 28 January 1981.

Applying that approach, Comyn J concluded:

> 'The plaintiff has given evidence that he felt each and every word
> attacked him personally, but his is, if I may say so, a "l'état c'est
> moi" attitude and is not perhaps as powerful as others. He has
> called witnesses who say that they believed it referred to him.
> Well, if the matter goes to the jury it will be for the jury to weigh
> up whether in fact they accept that evidence at its face value,
> whether in fact the article does refer to him. But, above all, I have
> seen and considered the article in isolation and in its context, and
> I have taken into account all the facts that I have mentioned earlier,
> including the close liaison with America, the photographs of English
> property, the reference in the article to English assets, and Mr
> Orme's appearances as Leader. I have come to the conclusion in
> the end that the article is reasonably capable of referring to the
> plaintiff that it must go to the jury to decide on a fair and common
> sense approach "yes" or "no" whether it in fact does.'

The jury agreed that the article referred to Mr Orme, but went on to find
that the article was true.

'NO REFERENCE INTENDED TO ANY PERSON LIVING OR DEAD'

At the end of films or at the start of novels one often sees a notice saying
something like 'This is a work of fiction. Any resemblance between any
of the characters and any person alive or dead is purely coincidental.'
What is the effect of such a notice in English law? The answer appears
to be very little. Reference is decided from the point of view of the
ordinary sensible observer. The intention of the defendant is not decisive.
It may be that an ordinary sensible person would take the disclaimer
into account when deciding whether there was a reference to the plaintiff,
but if the evidence of reference, perhaps a thinly-disguised portrayal of
a famous person, was very strong, the disclaimer would be of no avail
for the defendant.

If the reference was thus established the defendant may have a s 4
defence, but only if there was no negligence. Checking names in all the
phone books of the world and then checking for similarities and allusions
is a very big task, and the court may say that the precautions taken
were reasonable given the costs of further checking. But a string of
similarities and allusions which homed in on a particular well-known
person would be very difficult to explain away as resulting from
reasonable behaviour.

Choosing a very common name for a character, for example 'John
Smith' reduces the chances of the jury deciding that there was a reference
to the plaintiff. And even if the jury believes that there was a reference,
the difficulties of looking up every John Smith in the world make it

difficult to say that the plaintiff was negligent. But, on the other hand, the court might be invited to say that in choosing such a name in the first place the defendant was bringing difficulties on itself and that therefore the defendant had not taken all reasonable care.

Publication

Since defamation protects the plaintiff's reputation with other people, the defamatory statement is not actionable unless it is published to someone other than the defendant or the plaintiff.[16]

Oddly, publication to the defendant's spouse does not count as publication though publication to the plaintiff's spouse does count.[17] Supposed explanations in terms of the fiction that husband and wife count as one do not work, because otherwise publication to the spouse of the plaintiff would not count as publication. The rule must simply reflect an unwillingness of the courts to pry into private conversations, but note that unlike the similar position under the defence of qualified privilege, proof of malice is irrelevant and no common interest or duty between husband and wife has to be proved.[18] Another oddity is that if I dictate a defamatory letter to a secretary, I publish the defamation to the secretary, but if the secretary reads the letter back to me, the secretary is deemed not to have published the defamation.[19] More obviously, if the recipient of the information could not possibly have understood it, for example because the recipient does not speak the language, there is no publication.

A number of other problems merit brief attention, namely what is the position if the defendant did not mean to publish to any third party, what is the position of those who pass or republish defamatory material, is there any defence for those who, for example, sell magazines without knowing what is in them, and finally how does the requirement of publication work in the context of new information technologies and in particular the Internet?

Standard of care

If the defendant intends merely to let the plaintiff know his opinion of him, but the statement accidentally falls into the hands of a third party, is there a publication to the third party? The answer depends on whether the defendant knew or ought to have foreseen that the statement would fall into a third party's hands.

In *Theaker v Richardson*[20] the defendant wrote a defamatory letter to the plaintiff, a fellow member of a district council. The plaintiff put the

16 Note that in criminal libel, publication to the person defamed does suffice.
17 *Wennhak v Morgan* (1888) 20 QBD 635, *Theaker v Richardson* [1962] 1 WLR 151.
18 See below.
19 *Osborn v Boulter* [1930] 2 KB 226, *Eglantine Inn v Smith* [1948] NI 29.
20 [1962] 1 WLR 151.

letter in an envelope of the sort then used for distributing election addresses and wrote the plaintiff's name on it. The plaintiff's husband, thinking that the envelope contained an election address, opened it, saw the letter and read it. The judge asked the jury whether the husband's reading the letter was a natural and probable consequence of what the defendant did. The jury found for the plaintiff. The Court of Appeal dismissed the defendant's appeal. Pearson LJ approved of the question put to the jury. If the husband's conduct was not out of the ordinary and reasonably to be anticipated and was something which could quite easily happen in the normal course of events, the defendant was responsible for publishing the defamatory letter to the husband. Although one cannot say that spouses always read one another's mail, in the circumstances of the case, given the envelope and so on, the jury's decision was unassailable.

In contrast in *Huth v Huth*[1] the defendant sent his wife a letter in an unsealed envelope suggesting that they were not properly married and that their children were illegitimate. Before the Law Reform (Husband and Wife) Act 1962, there was an extraordinary rule that a wife could not sue her husband in tort. But there was no rule prohibiting children from suing their father, and this is what happened in *Huth v Huth*. On the issue of publication, the plaintiff's case was that the family's butler said that he had looked at the contents of the letter before delivering it to the wife. The defendant said that the butler had no business reading the letter. The plaintiff's response was that since there was a presumption that postmen read postcards, even though they have no business doing so, the same presumption that someone would read the contents ought to apply to unsealed envelopes. The plaintiff lost both at trial and on appeal. Lord Reading CJ in the Court of Appeal emphasised that, 'Fortunately, it is no part of a butler's duty to open letters.'

Lord Reading went to say that there was no publication because the defendant had not intended to publish to a third party. That cannot be right as it stands. Swinfen Eady LJ said, however, that:

> 'There was no publication, because there was no evidence that, to the defendant's knowledge, a letter addressed to his wife and enclosed in this envelope, but unsealed and not fastened down, would in the ordinary course be likely to be opened by the butler, or by any other person in the employ of the mistress.
>
> When the cases which were referred to are looked at it will be seen that in each case the defendant, who must be taken to have intended the natural consequences of his own act in the circum–stances of the case, must on that footing have intended the publication which in fact took place.'

That is, although the court uses the language of intention, because the judges include with intention 'the natural consequences' of the defendant's act, the test is fairly close to saying that the defendant would have been

1   [1915] 3 KB 32.

liable if he had known that the butler would read the letter or, given his knowledge of life, he ought to have realised that the butler might read the letter.

If, therefore, the defendant writes a defamatory letter to someone in business, since everyone knows that most people in business have secret–aries, the letter counts as having been published to the secretary. It may be enough for the defendant, however, to have written 'Personal' or 'Strictly Private' on the envelope, since the common practice has been for secretaries to pass on such envelopes unopened, but if the practice has changed, so will the answer to the question of publication.[2] Note also that Lord Denning claimed in one case[3] that if an employee discloses a defamatory statement to another employee of the same employer, the employer cannot be vicariously liable in defamation since from the employer's point of view it has published to itself, but the majority of the Court of Appeal said that communications between employees were of course publications of the statement. They may attract the defence of qualified privilege[4] but they are still publications of defamatory material.

Republication

To what extent is the original publisher of a defamatory statement responsible for subsequent republications of the statement? And what is the position of those who republish defamatory material merely by passing it unchanged on to others, for example those who sell books and magazines?

The answer to the first question is, or at least ought to be, that voluntary republications by third parties count as intervening acts and break the chain of causation. Where the republication is not fully voluntary because, for example, the person repeating the statement was under a legal or moral duty to do so, the republication should not break the chain. But otherwise, except perhaps where the republication was what the defendant intended, the defendant should not be held responsible for the consequences of republication. But in *Slipper v BBC*[5] the Court of Appeal, although confirming that republication was a question of the effect of intervening acts, seemed to say that if the 'further publications' were foreseeable, natural and probable consequences of the original publication, the defendant could be held responsible for them. In *Slipper*, the plaintiff, a senior police officer, claimed that a BBC film about his unsuccessful attempts to secure the extradition of Ronnie Biggs, the Great Train robber, defamed him, and he further claimed that by showing the film in the usual way in preview to TV critics, the BBC had caused wide repetition of the allegations against him in the TV columns of the newspapers.

---

2   See *Pullman v W Hill* [1891] 1 QB 524.
3   *Riddick v Thames Board Mills* [1977] QB 881.
4   See below.
5   [1991] 1 QB 283.

The defendant's attempt to strike out the part of the claim for damages that referred to the harm caused by the newspaper columns failed.

On the second question, the answer is that every time the statement is published, a new cause of action arises against whoever published it.[6] This means that in principle everyone in the distribution chain who publishes the libel, from the author, through the editor, publisher, printer to the bookseller is potentially liable. The defendant may be able to invoke the defence of 'innocent dissemination'[7] but the burden of proof in the defence lies on the defendant not on the plaintiff.

In *Goldsmith v Sperrings*[8] the international business tycoon Sir James Goldsmith sued the satirical magazine *Private Eye* and all of its distributors. The plaintiff alleged that the magazine had published a series of defamatory articles about him. Some of the distributors settled out of court, agreeing with the plaintiff no longer to sell *Private Eye*. In his negotiations with the magazine and the other distributors, the plaintiff offered to release the distributors who had already settled from their obligation not to sell *Private Eye* as long as the magazine met his terms. The defendants claimed that the plaintiff's tactics were an abuse of the process of the court, and that the plaintiff was maintaining his actions against the distributors not to vindicate and protect his reputation but to destroy the magazine. Lord Denning MR delivered an extraordinary judgment, based, he said, on his own research rather than on the argument of counsel, in which he attempted to overturn the established doctrine that secondary distributors counted as publishers of the libel. Lord Denning's arguments would have moved English law in the direction of the position throughout the USA where distinctions are made between three types of publishing. A primary publisher, which includes someone who consciously and deliberately republishes the defamation, is held liable in the ordinary way. But a secondary publisher, defined by the Second Restatement of Torts as 'one who only delivers or transmits defamatory matter published by a third person' is subject to liability only if, again in the words of the Restatement, 'he knows or has reason to know of its defamatory character.'[9] Some jurisdictions go further and limit the liability of secondary publishers to cases in which they have changed the communication. A third category is the 'common carrier' of information, such as the public telephone network, which, because of the importance of rapid public communications which would become impossible were the telephone company under any sort of duty to check the contents of phone calls and fax messages, may disseminate even material that it knows to be defamatory.[10] The majority of the Court of Appeal in *Goldsmith*, however, declined to follow Lord Denning in his adventure, and the orthodox position in English law remains that

6   *Truth New Zealand v Holloway* [1960] 1 WLR 997.
7   See below.
8   [1977] 1 WLR 478.
9   §581. Note that the rule does not apply to television or radio broadcasters, who are liable as if they were primary publishers.
10   §621.

everyone involved in the publication of the defamatory material is potentially liable.[11]

One further point is worthy of note. The Second Restatement says:[12]

> 'One who intentionally and unreasonably fails to remove defamatory matter that he knows to be exhibited on land or chattels in his possession or under his control is subject to liability for its continued publication.'

This is probably also the law of England. The point is illustrated by *Byrne v Deane*. The allegedly defamatory statement about the plaintiff in that case appeared in the form of an anonymous note on a notice board. The defendant was responsible for the note because he could very easily have had it removed at any time.

Innocent dissemination

The rigour of the orthodox rule that the majority of the Court of Appeal affirmed in *Goldsmith v Sperring*, that each link in the chain of distribution counts as a publisher of the defamatory statement, is subject to a specialised defence of 'innocent (or 'mere') dissemination'.

Those in the position of the American 'second tier' publishers can escape liability if they can prove not only that they did not know that the publication contained a libel but also that there was no reason for them to suspect that the publication contained a libel and that their failure to find out that the publication contained a libel was not due to their own negligence. The defence is more onerous on defendants than the American Restatement position because (a) the burden of proof is on the defendant and (b) the defence fails if the defendant should have suspected the publication must contain defamatory material and should reasonably have investigated it.[13] What degree of inspection the defendant is expected to carry out is not clear. But it is unreasonable to expect newsagents to check the contents of every publication they sell. But note that the test would seem to exclude from the protection of the defence newsagents who sell without checking magazines that are notorious for losing libel actions, for

---

11 One consequence of this position is that publications often have to give indemnities to their distributors against libel actions and may find that their distributors settle actions generously in the knowledge that the publishers will have to pay the amount agreed in the settlement. This happened in the case between John Major and *New Statesman and Society* (see Steve Platt 'Sue, grab it and run the country' (1993) Independent, 8 July p 29). The distributors settled for £48,500 (see (1993) Facts on File World News Digest, 22 July) but the plaintiff settled the principal case against the magazine itself for only £1,000.

12 §577.

13 *Viztelly v Mudie's Select Library* [1900] 2 QB 170.

in such a case there is a plausible argument that there would be reason to suspect that any edition of the publication might contain a libel.

NEW MEDIA—DEFAMATION ON THE INTERNET

The law of defamation has to adapt every time the technology of communication improves. The problems caused, for example, by the advent of radio and television are mentioned below with regard to the distinction between libel and slander. But those problems are now themselves old hat as we move into the era of world wide computer communication and the Internet.[14]

The Internet is a network of computers communicating via a mixture of ordinary telephone lines and dedicated data lines. It began as a way of combining US Defence Department computers so that they would be less vulnerable to attack. Various universities and research institutions then added themselves, followed by government departments, large commercial organisations, specialist providers of information and finally thousands of individuals in all parts of the world Through the Internet flows information of almost every kind. It is also a mail system, with thousands of electronic mail messages going from person to person every hour. The Internet and some of its more or less associated commercial information services also provide electronic bulletin boards and oppor-tunities for general discussion (by electronic mail) of virtually any subject under the sun.

There is not one kind of communication on the Internet but many. There is one-to-one communication, similar to the private letter. E-mail is usually supposed to be confidential, but, like ordinary mail, can be intercepted or stolen. There is also one-to-many communication, equiva-lent to notice-boards but with potentially enormous readerships. And there is many-to-many communication, the electronic equivalents of newspapers and newsletters. Sometimes the one-to-many and many-to-many communications are edited or 'moderated' by people other than their authors, but much of the time they are not.

The Internet also allows the republication and the forwarding of messages at an astonishing rate, because people are able to pass on instantly to others the information that comes to them.

Clearly, it is possible to defame someone electronically. The e-mail message or posting to an electronic bulletin board is just another form of written communication. It is not on paper (until someone decides to print it out, which may never happen) but it is still in permanent form stored on the hard disks of various computers. In the Australian case

---

14 See gen Arnold-Moore 'Legal Pitfalls in Cyberspace: Defamation on Computer Networks' (forthcoming) Jo of Law and Information (also available on the World Wide Web at http:/www.kbs.citri.edu.au/law/defame.html).

Rindos v Hardwick[15] the defendant posted a message to an electronic bulletin board of some 23,000 users. The message accused the plaintiff, a fellow anthropologist, of paedophilia and of advancing his academic career by bullying others rather than by proper anthropological research. This outrageous libel produced a legal action in which liability was not in dispute,[16] but Ipp J took the opportunity to confirm that there was no problem in principle with libel actions for statements made in electronic form.

The difficult problem in electronic defamation, however, (apart from the potentially mystifying consequences of multiple litigation in practic–ally every country in the world) is the position of the various people responsible for transmitting or storing defamatory messages posted by others.[17] The post office is not liable for delivering defamatory letters or even defamatory postcards that have been read by post office workers, and so, presumably, e-mail providers are not liable for merely trans–mitting electronic mail. But what about the one-to-many and many-to-many communications? The culture of the Internet is that those who organise and maintain bulletin boards, newsgroups and conferences intervene as little as possible in what can be written and read, and in practice, although such people can 'kill' messages if they have to, once a message gets out into cyberspace, there is very little anyone can do to stop those who have received from sending it on and on.[18]

Nevertheless the important legal question is whether defendant organisers of bulletin boards will be able to claim the benefit of the defence of innocent dissemination. In the US, operating under rules similar to those in the Restatement, the United States District Court for the Southern District of New York decided in *Cubby v CompuServe*[19] that the publisher of a bulletin board the contents of which it had no opportunity to review and for which others took full responsibility, was in a position between that of a secondary publisher and a common carrier and should not count as having published the defamatory statement unless it knew or had reason to know in advance that the material would be defamatory. Leisure J said:

15 Unreported, WA S Ct, AGIS-NO: '94/3397 (VOL 40:2). See (1994) Australian Financial Review, 4 May. See also *Arnold-Moore*.

16 The issue was the measure of damages. The plaintiff argued successfully that the court could take into account the full size of the potential readership of the bulletin board, ie 23,000 people, rather than, for example, the number of subscribers who could be proved to have seen the libellous message. The court awarded A$40,000—'the largest damages award for four years in a defamation action in Western Australia' according to the Australian Financial Review.

17 See Becker 'The Liability of Computer Bulletin Board Operators for Defamation Posted by Others' 22 Conn L Rev 203 (1989), Charles 'Computer Bulletin Boards and Defamation: Who Should be Liable? Under What Standard?' 2 J Law & Tech 121 (1987), E Jensen 'An Electronic Soapbox: Computer Bulletin Boards and the First Amendment' 39 Fed Comm Law J 217 (1987), Donaldson and Kennedy 'Are Electronic Bulletin Board System Operators Liable For Their Users' Libelous Statements?' Legal Bytes Winter 1992-93, Vol 1, Number 1.

18 Cf *Arnold-Moore*.

19 776 F Supp 135 (1991) LEXIS 15545; 19 Media L Rep 1525.

'CompuServe has no more editorial control over such a public–
ation than does a public library, book store, or newsstand, and
it would be no more feasible for CompuServe to examine every
publication it carries for potentially defamatory statements than
it would be for any other distributor to do so.'

But there are two points to make about *Cubby*.[20] First, it did not discuss
the possibility that although the provider of a bulletin board may not be
liable for the instantaneous postings of defamatory messages, the
remains the question of a duty to remove the defamatory messages from
the bulletin board in the same way as there is a duty under *Byrne v
Deane* to remove defamatory messages from physical noticeboards under
one's control. And secondly, under the English rules of the defence of
innocent dissemination as they survived *Goldsmith v Sperring*, the
burden of proof is on the defendant to show that it acted reasonably in
not finding out about the messages before they were posted—for example,
defendants will have to fight off the suggestion that they should institute
a short delay between the sending of the message and its publication so
that it can be checked for libel. The defendant would point to the sheer
volume of traffic on the Internet and the vast expense of employing
hundreds of libel lawyers to do the checking, not to mention the sacrifice
of an important aspect of the culture of the Internet, namely its
preference for freewheeling and unregulated debate. But it is not a
forgone conclusion that an English court would decide *Cubby* in the
same way.

Slander

Defamation comes in two kinds, libel and slander. Libel is, typically, defamation in written form, whereas slander is spoken defamation. More
broadly, libel is defamation in any 'permanent' form, which, after much
confusion and uncertainty, is defined by statute to include theatrical performances and radio and television broadcasts (including cable
broadcasting).[1] It can also include non-verbal forms of permanent exhibi-
tion, such as pictures or even waxworks.[2] Some authors[3] claim, with the
support of some rather odd remarks by Slesser LJ in *Youssoupoff v Metro
Goldwyn Mayer*, that to be libel rather than slander, the statement has to
be visible. Slesser LJ referred to 'permanent matter to be seen by the eye'.
But why this distinction between the visual and the non-visual should
matter is difficult to discern. The distinction between libel and slander is

---

20 See *Arnold-Moore*.
1 Defamation Act 1952 ss 1 and 16(1), Cable and Broadcasting Act 1984 s 28, Theatres Act
1968 s 4(1).
2 *Monson v Madame Tussauds* [1894] 1 QB 671 (plaintiff's wax effigy placed in Chamber
of Horrors with effigies of notorious murderers).
3 eg *Street on Torts, Salmond and Heuston*.

difficult to justify in the first place[4] without having to explain why words spoken on a near indestructible CD are slander whereas words on flimsy newsprint are libel. And this is before one even reaches the legendary disputes about the status of sky-writing by aeroplanes or words taught to talking parrots.[5]

In reality, the distinction between libel and slander is not very important. The only consequence of classifying the defamatory statement as slander as opposed to libel (apart from the consequence in criminal law that only libels can support a prosecution for criminal libel) is that the plaintiff has to prove 'special damage'. Libel, in contrast, is actionable per se, that is, the plaintiff does not have to prove any loss in order to win the case— although, of course, if one has suffered no loss, one should not expect much in damages. But, the exceptions to the rule that the plaintiff in slander has to prove special damage are so far reaching that they nearly swallow up the rule itself. The exceptions are:

(1)   where the defamation consists of an accusation that the plaintiff has committed a criminal offence.[6] It may be, however, that crimes not immediately punishable by imprisonment do not count,[7] but to say of someone that they are a 'convicted person' is apparently enough;[8]

(2)   where the defamation consists of saying that the plaintiff has a contagious disease.[9] Some writers seem to want this category to fall into disuse by saying (without any authority) that there is a fixed list of diseases, most of which people no longer suffer from, to which the rule applies. In the era of AIDS, a disease that causes the victim to be shunned and avoided if ever there was one, it ought to be clear that this should not be so. The policy of the courts in any case should be to reduce the differences between libel and slander, which implies in turn expanding the exceptions to the special damage rule whenever possible;

(3)   where the defamation is an 'imputation of unchastity or adultery' against any woman or girl. This sexist rule was created by the Slander of Women Act 1891.[10] It should, perhaps, also apply to men;

(4)   where the defamation consists of disparaging the plaintiff in his or her 'office, profession, calling, trade or business'.[11] Section 2 of the Defamation Act 1952 gets rid of the old rule that the statement had

---

4   Note that the Faulks Committee recommended the abolition of the distinction: Cmnd 5909 para 91.
5   See further *Chicken v Ham* (the 'notorious Gramophone Libel case'), in A P Herbert *Uncommon Law* new ed (London; Eyre Methuen, 1979).
6   Eg *Gray v Jones* [1939] 1 All ER 798.
7   *Ormiston v Great Western Rly Co* [1917] 1 KB 598. It is not sufficient either that the crime is punishable by a fine and non-payment of a fine may lead to imprisonment.
8   *Gray v Jones* above.
9   *Bloodworth v Gray* (1844) 7 Man & G 334.
10   See eg *Kerr v Kennedy* [1942] 1 KB 409—but the suggestion in this case that 'unchastity' includes lesbianism has to be read nowadays in the light of the possibility that it is no longer defamatory in the first place to say that someone is homosexual. See above.
11   *Foulger v Newcomb* (1867) LR 2 Exch 327 (gamekeeper accused of poisoning foxes).

to be about the plaintiff's specific activities on the job, as opposed to accusations that would more generally harm his reputation in his work or calling. The same section it is submitted also got rid of the distinction between offices of profit and offices of honour, on the basis of which statements about the plaintiff's competence or fitness for an unpaid office had additionally to be sufficient to justify removing the plaintiff from the office. The section now speaks of '*any* office'. The belief that the old rule has nevertheless been retained is sheer antiquarianism.[12]

In addition 'special damage' includes not only monetary loss but also loss of marriage prospects and loss of consortium.[13]

Thus, there is not much slander left for which people might want to sue that is not actionable in exactly the same way that libel is. In the vast majority of cases, the plaintiff will have been disparaged in his business or job or accused of a criminal offence or have suffered actual loss. Accusing a man of adultery seems to be the worst slander one can probably get away with, and even there is a good case for reform and that the rule ought to be that men and women should be treated alike.

Defences

We have already considered the defences of unintentional defamation and innocent dissemination. Here we move on to the other defences to defamation.

Truth or justification

The first and most important defence to defamation is that the defamatory statement was true. Even if the defendant has found and published the facts out of sheer spite or in the hope of financial gain or for any other disgraceful or malicious motive, the defence of truth (or 'justification') still works. The only exception is that under the Rehabilitation of Offenders Act 1974, ex-offenders are entitled after the passage of time to have their conviction disregarded, and if a defendant maliciously refers to such 'spent' convictions, truth is not a defence to defamation.[14]

On the other hand, the defendant's honest belief that what he or she said was true is insufficient. The burden of proof is on the defendant to show that the accusation really was true, not just that the defendant believed it to be true. The risk of saying something that 'everyone knows' but for which no proof can be found, or the risk of publishing stories obtained

12 Contra virtually every other writer on the subject, mostly relying on *Robinson v Ward* (1958) 108 L Jo 491.
13 *Speight v Gosnay* (1891) 60 LJQB 231, *Lynch v Knight* (1861) 11 ER 854.
14 Section 8.

from informants who will not repeat their stories in court, falls on the defendant.[15]

The sting of the libel and context

The defendant does not have to prove the literal truth of every word of the defamatory statement. In this respect, as in many others, the law is less legalistic than the public at large. The defendant only has to prove the 'sting of the libel', that is the substance of the charges and in particular the aspect of them that tends to discredit the plaintiff.[16] If the defendant said that the plaintiff was imprisoned for three weeks for not paying a fine and the truth was that the plaintiff had only been imprisoned for two weeks, the defence nevertheless works.[17] On the other hand, where the defendant called the plaintiff a 'libellous journalist' the court said that the defence of justification was not made out just by showing that the plaintiff had one conviction for criminal libel, for the sting of the accusation, according to the court, was that the plaintiff was in the habit of committing libel, not that he had done so once.[18]

But, although the rule seems simple, extraordinary tactical battles between the parties, centred on the pleadings, have broken out around it. The main reason is the further rule, in s 5 of the Defamation Act 1952, that:

> 'In an action for libel or slander in respect of words containing two or more distinct charges against the plaintiff, a defence of justification shall not fail by reason only that the truth of every charge is not proved if the words not proved to be true do not materially injure the plaintiff's reputation having regard to the truth of the remaining charges.'

This provision is supposed to mitigate the effect of the common law rule that the defendant had to prove the substance of each charge to be true. But everything depends on what the plaintiff chooses to complain about. If the plaintiff chooses only to complain about the one untrue statement in the book, the section does not allow the defendant to bring in all the true allegations to show that the effect on the margin of the untrue allegation is very small. The section only allows the defendant to use the truth of an allegation about which the plaintiff has complained to offset the effect of not being able to prove the truth of another allegation about which the plaintiff has complained.[19] To that extent the rule still stands that, although

---

15 See Lord Keith in *Derbyshire City Council v Times Newspapers* above.
16 *Edwards v Bell* (1824) 1 Bing 403.
17 *Alexander v North Eastern Rly Co* (1865) 6 B & S 340.
18 *Wakley v Cook and Healey* (1849) 4 Exch 511.
19 *Plato Films v Speidel* [1961] AC 1090, *Polly Peck v Trelford* [1986] QB 1000.

the plaintiff cannot prevent the defendant from trying to show that an isolated statement was not defamatory in the first place by referring to its context, if the statement is defamatory, the defendant does not achieve proof of its truth by showing that other passages in the book or article are true.

But the pleading battle does not end there. Defendants have established that where several defamatory statements have the same 'sting' they are entitled to plead whatever facts from whatever part of the document, complained about or not, that are relevant to establishing the truth of that 'common sting'. Also, defendants have successfully argued that where the words could have any one of a number of meanings, they do not have to stick to the meanings put forward by the plaintiff but may attempt to show the truth of any of the meanings that a properly directed jury might find to be the real meaning of the words.[20] That is, although to some extent the plaintiff can control the debate by choosing the words on which the case will centre, the plaintiff cannot control the debate about what those words might mean. The quid pro quo, however, is that the defendant has to plead the meanings of the words that he or she intends to justify.[1]

'It is alleged that'

Contrary to popular belief it is not possible to inoculate oneself from a defamation action by adding 'allegedly' or 'people say that' in front of the defamatory statement. In *Truth (New Zealand) Ltd v Philip North Holloway*[2] the Privy Council approved a direction to the jury that included the instruction:

'[I]t is not a defence at all that a statement that might be defamatory is put forward by way of report only.'

Conclusiveness of convictions

Section 13 of the Civil Evidence Act 1968 lays down that proof of a conviction of a criminal offence is to be taken as conclusive proof that the defendant really did commit the crime. The common law position before the Act was that since the criminal justice system was fallible, it did not follow from the fact that a person had been convicted of a crime that the person was guilty of that crime. In consequence at common law if the defendant claimed that the plaintiff had committed a criminal offence, it was not a good defence to show merely that the plaintiff had been convicted of that offence. The defendant had to show that the conviction was correct.

---

20 *Prager v Times Newspapers* [1988] 1 WLR 77.
1 *Lucas-Box v News Group* [1986] 1 WLR 147.
2 [1960] 1 WLR 997.

The common law rule was abolished because it allowed people who had been convicted of crimes to relitigate their trials in the civil courts. But the statutory rule was only possible because of a remarkable degree of complacency about the accuracy of the work of the criminal courts. After the revelation in the 1990s of several serious defects in the system, defects that led to wrongful convictions in a number of very high profile cases, one might start to wonder whether the common law rule was not the right one after all. To call someone a terrorist on the basis of a conviction in the late 1970s would seem, were it not for the protection of s 13, a foolhardy thing to do.

There is uncertainty about whether the common law rule ever applied to disciplinary hearings and similar domestic tribunals such as the governing bodies of colleges and internal appeals panels in local govern-ment. Greer LJ in *Cookson v Harewood*[3] suggested that it did not, but there is no reason in principle why it should not have applied. If it did apply, the 1968 Act did nothing to abrogate it, since the Act refers only to criminal convictions.

The issue may become a live one since the increased prominence that some domestic tribunals are achieving, especially in the field of sport. If a tribunal set up by the governing body of a sport decides, for example, that an athlete has cheated by taking drugs, does a reporter have a defence if he refers to the athlete as a 'cheat' who has been 'found out' when all the reporter can show is that the tribunal has found the athlete guilty?

Fair comment

The defence of fair comment is, according to many judges, an important part of the protection of freedom of expression in England. In his dissent in *Telnikoff v Matusevitch*[4] Lord Ackner collected together the following collection of judicial pronouncements on the subject:

> 'In *Lyon v Daily Telegraph Ltd* [1943] KB 746 at 752, [1943] 2 All ER 316 at 319 ... Scott LJ said:
>
>> "the reason why, once a plea of fair comment is established, there is no libel, is that it is in the public interest to have free discussion of matters of public interest."
>
> Towards the end of his judgment Scott LJ added ([1943] KB 746 at 753, [1943] 2 All ER 316 at 320):
>
>> "It [the right of fair comment] is one of the fundamental rights of free speech and writing which are so dear to the British nation, and it is of vital importance to the rule of law upon

3   [1932] 2 KB 478.
4   [1992] 2 AC 343.

which we depend for our personal freedom, that the courts should preserve the right of 'fair comment' undiminished and unimpaired."

In *Slim v Daily Telegraph Ltd* [1968] 2 QB 157 at 170, [1968] 1 All ER 497 at 503 Lord Denning MR said:

"... the right of fair comment is one of the essential elements which go to make up our freedom of speech. We must ever maintain this right intact. It must not be whittled down by legal refinements."

In the Report of the Committee on Defamation (Cmnd 5909 (1975)) under the chairmanship of the late Faulks J it is stated (at para 151):

"the very wide breadth of the main criterion for the defence of fair comment (could an honest albeit prejudiced person have expressed such an opinion?) has stood for over a century. It is generally regarded as a bulwark of free speech.'"

The reason for the importance of the defence of fair comment is quite simple. Most human conversation is not about facts but about opinions. Indeed the whole of libel law is not really concerned with facts but with evaluations and conclusions about people's characters. If the only defence to libel were truth, a vast amount of ordinary everyday talk would become unlawful—not because its content is unreasonable but because it is unprovable, or at least unproven. Questions of morality and ethics are notoriously difficult to achieve consensus about. It is possible that there are right and wrong answers to moral questions, but it is unlikely that we can ever be very certain about what they are. If the law were to require libel defendants to convince a jury of the rightness of their opinions to the same degree as they have to demonstrate the truth of any factual allegations they make, it is unlikely that many juries would ever find in favour of the defendants.

The elements of the defence are (a) that the defendant convinces the judge that the statement is capable of being seen as a comment rather than as a statement of fact, and the jury that it was a comment not a statement of fact; (b) that enough of the factual assumptions underlying the comment are true; (c) that the comment was about a matter of public interest; and (d) that the comment was fair. The plaintiff can, however, defeat the defence if he shows that the comment was malicious.

Comment vs fact

Much confusion has arisen around the question of whether a statement is capable of being regarded by the jury as a comment as opposed to a statement of fact. The problem is that if a statement of fact is to be regarded as defamatory, which it must have been if we are onto the stage in the case of considering defences, it cannot be simply a matter of fact. The fact must have been judged capable of reducing the plaintiff's reputation. This has led most commentators to say that one cannot really say in general or abstract terms what is the difference between fact and comment and that everything depends on the circumstances. But although there are cases where the distinction is difficult to make, in many, even most, cases there is a fairly easy test that can be applied. If the statement puts forward the defendant's own conclusions and evaluations, the statement is comment. If, on the other hand, the statement simply assumes that listeners or readers will draw the obvious conclusions for themselves, it is fact.

So, for example, in *London Artists v Littler*[5] one of the questions was whether an accusation that the plaintiffs were 'plotting' was an accusation of fact or a comment. The court concluded that it was an accusation of fact, first because even the defendant had treated it as such in the pleadings and when giving evidence, and second because one can 'plot' either for good or bad purposes, so that the statement was not an evaluation of the plaintiffs in itself. The allegation of 'plotting' became defamatory only when understood in the context of what the defendant claimed the plaintiffs were plotting to do, namely to close down a West End play. But the question of the plaintiffs' purposes was itself one of fact, because it is obvious that plotting to close a show is a bad thing. The statement is not about the defendant's own opinion of the plaintiffs but an invitation to others to draw their own conclusions.

In contrast, in *Dakhyl v Labouchere*,[6] the defendant described the plaintiff, who claimed to be a medical specialist, as 'a quack of the rankest species'. The words state the defendant's own conclusions about the plaintiff and evaluation of him. They do not merely present facts from which others are invited to draw the obvious conclusions. The House of Lords decided that the defendant was entitled to put his fair comment defence to the jury.

Thus, if the defendant says of the plaintiff 'X is a convicted thief' it is a statement of fact. If the defendant says 'Y is a bad person' that is a comment. And if the defendant says 'W has stolen things and is therefore untrustworthy' it is both a statement of fact and a comment. Note that 'factual' accusations occur where there is moral consensus (eg stealing is bad) whereas 'comments' occur where there is much less agreement (eg one act of dishonesty makes one unworthy of trust forever).

One particular source of confusion has been the doctrine that if the facts on which the alleged comment is based are not obvious the statement counts as a statement of fact and must be justified.[7] This is why *Winfield and Jolowicz* says that 'A is a disgrace to human nature' is a statement of fact.[8] But this sentence is clearly a comment. The doctrine itself uses the

5   [1969] 2 QB 375.
6   [1908] 2 KB 325.
7   See *Kemsley v Foot* [1952] AC 345.
8   *On Torts*.

device of a legal fiction to provide an incentive for people to show their reasoning more. It consists of saying that a comment is a statement of fact even when everyone knows that it is really a comment as a way of punishing those who over-generalise and fail to show how they reached their conclusions. And in any case, the rule is reduced in its effect by the decision in *Kemsley v Foot* that it is often possible to infer the underlying allegations of fact from the words themselves.[9]

Even if the judge decides that the statement was capable of being comment, there is still one more problem that has arisen. It concerns the material the jury should be allowed to take into account when deciding whether the statement was one of fact or comment. In *Telnikoff v Matusevitch*[10] the plaintiff wrote an article in the *Daily Telegraph* which the defendant considered to be racist and anti-semitic. The defendant wrote to the newspaper saying so and the letter was published. The plaintiff sued the defendant for libel. The plaintiff's case was that the defendant had claimed in his letter that the plaintiff had made certain claims and proposals that he had not actually made, so that the statement was a statement of fact. The defendant's case was that if one read the letter alongside the plaintiff's original article, it would be obvious that the defendant was making comments, that is drawing inferences and conclusions from the plaintiff's text, not quoting it directly. But the plaintiff argued successfully that since readers of the letter would not necessarily have seen the original article, the letter had to stand by itself.

The decision in *Telnikoff* leaves the law with the curious anomaly that both for deciding whether the statement was defamatory and for deciding whether it referred to the plaintiff, the jury is permitted to look at the whole context, including material referred to in the allegedly defamatory words.[11] But the same jury is not permitted to look at the same material to help decide whether the words were comment or fact. This is both inconsistent and artificial.

But even more damaging for the position taken by the majority in *Telnikoff* is the central point made by Lord Ackner in his dissent. It is worth quoting Lord Ackner's argument in full.

'If the criticism of an article published in a newspaper on a subject matter of public importance is to be confined to passages actually set out in the criticism, then the freedom to comment on a matter of public importance becomes, from a practical point of view, illusory or non-existent. The ability of a defendant to comment should not depend on whether or not the reader is aware of the material which

9   In *Kemsley v Foot* the plaintiff, Kemsley, complained that the defendant had published an article criticising a third party for being 'lower than Kemsley'. The defendant was permitted to plead fair comment even though no factual basis for the claim appeared in the article. The general idea that the comment had to do with the conduct of the Kemsley Press was adequately indicated in the words themselves. See also *Control Risks v New English Library* [1990] 1 WLR 183.

10   Above n 4.

11   See *Gatley on Libel and Slander* (8th edn) (1981) p 55, para 102 and *Hayward v Thompson* [1982] QB 47.

is the subject of the comment. As pointed out in terms by Woolf LJ, the defence of fair comment is based on the principle that a citizen should be entitled to comment on a matter of public interest and the fact that the publication is limited does not affect the public interest ....

In my judgment the defence of fair comment is not based on the proposition that every person who reads a criticism should be in a position to judge for himself. It would be absurd to suggest that a critic may not say what he thinks of a play performed only once, because the public cannot go and see it to judge for themselves. The defence of fair comment is available to a defendant who has done no more than express his honest opinion on publications put before the public. It is sufficient for him to have identified the publication on which he is commenting without having set out such extracts therefrom as would enable his readers to judge for themselves whether they agreed with his opinion or not. Were the law otherwise it would be necessary or at the very least forensically expedient to set out, ipsissima verba, the entire contents of the article upon which as a matter of public importance the citizen is entitled to comment honestly. In the result the important con– tribution to public discussion on matters of public importance arising out of the publication in the press of correspondence would be seriously curtailed. Yet a free and general discussion of matters of public interest is fundamental to a democratic society.'

The response of the majority to Lord Ackner's point is merely that writers should have to take reasonable care to differentiate in what they write between statements of fact and comments and should take reasonable care to ensure that comments are supported by identified facts. But, with respect, just as Lord Donovan once said[12] that the ordinary sensible reader of the newspapers does not analyse them using the methods of a Fellow of All Souls, so the ordinary writer of letters to the newspapers does not, and should not be expected to, edit them with the same care as an American law professor preparing an article for the Harvard Law Review.

Public interest

The comment must be on a matter of public interest. Fortunately for the editors of tabloid newspapers, according to the leading exposition of what this requirement involves, what is in the 'public interest' is approximately the same as 'what the public is interested in'. In *London Artists v Littler*, which concerned alleged shenanigans in the theatre, Lord Denning said:

'I would not myself confine [the public interest] within narrow limits. Whenever a matter is such as to affect people at large, so

12   In *Morgan v Odhams Press* [1971] 1 WLR 1239.

that they may be legitimately interested in, or concerned at, what is going on; or what may happen to them or to others; then it is a matter of public interest on which everyone is entitled to make fair comment ... Here the public are legitimately *interested*. Many people are interested in what happens in the theatre. The stars welcome publicity. They want to be put at the top of the bill. The producers wish it too. They like the house to be full ... When three stars and a satellite all give notice to leave at the same time—thus putting a successful play in peril—it is to my mind a matter of public interest on which everyone, press and all, are entitled to comment freely.'

Note that the question of whether the comment was on a matter of public interest is a question of law for the judge alone.[13]

Basis in truth

Although the defendant does not have to prove the truth of his opinion, he does have to show that his comment was adequately rooted in fact. If the defendant has based his comments on allegations that are not true, for example if he has called the plaintiff dishonest because he thought that the plaintiff had been convicted of theft when the plaintiff has no such conviction, the comment cannot be fair.[14]

But the defendant does not have to prove that every detail of the underlying facts is true. Section 6 of the Defamation Act 1952 says that a defence of fair comment shall not fail by reason only that the truth of every allegation of fact is not proved 'if the expression of opinion is fair comment having regard to such of the facts alleged or referred to in the words complained of as are proved'. The requirement is only that enough of the underlying facts are true that the comment can still count as fair. It is to the topic of fairness that we now turn.

Fairness of the comment

The Faulks Committee[15] recommended that the defence of fair comment should be renamed 'comment', on the ground that the test for fairness was, or at least should be, so easy to pass that it should not count as a major feature of the test. The function of the defence as a bulwark of free

13 See Lord Denning MR in *London Artists v Littler* above.
14 There is one exception, namely where the statement was privileged (see below). In these circumstances, the comment can be fair even though it was linked to a statement of fact that turned out to be untrue. *Addis v Odhams Press* [1958] 2 QB 275, *Brent Walker v Time Out* [1991] 2 All ER 753.
15 Paras 171-74.

speech would be undermined if the law allowed only comments that judges or juries agreed with.

The test for the fairness of the comment is indeed far from onerous. As recently confirmed by the House of Lords in *Telnikoff v Matusevich* the test is merely:

> 'Whether any man, however prejudiced and obstinate, could honestly hold the view expressed by the defendant.'

That is, the view the defendant expresses has to be so extreme, either in its content or in the way it deals with the evidence, that the ordinary sensible person would conclude that anyone who claimed to hold that view must be lying. Admittedly, if the ordinary sensible person has led the ordinary sheltered life in which one avoids or simply does not come across people who hold views very different from one's own, the test could become rather restrictive, but it ought to be applied broadly, so that if any ordinary sensible person could believe that someone somewhere could honestly hold the view in question, the comment is fair.

Many older cases apply more restrictive tests than the *Telnikoff* test. Courts have said, for example, that abuse and invective or personal attacks not relevant to the subject-matter of the comment cannot be fair.[16] Nineteenth and early twentieth century cases said that one could not impute base or wicked motives to another person unless such a conclusion would be reasonable in the circumstances.[17] But all of these cases, to the extent that they are incompatible with *Telnikoff* must be regarded as unsound. Older cases also seemed to require that the opinion could be held by a 'fair-minded' person.[18] *Telnikoff* confirms that the test is rather whether *any* person could honestly hold the view in question, fair-minded or not.

Note that for the comment to be fair the defendant does not have to show that he himself really believed it, but merely that someone somewhere could honestly believe it. 'The defendant who relies on a plea of fair comment does not have to show that the comment is an honest expression of his views.'[19] It also follows that if the defendant publishes the opinion of another person (for example, publishes a letter in a newspaper) the defendant does not have to show that the writer honestly held the view.[20] The plaintiff's protection against unfairness and dishonesty is to be found in the require-ment of absence of malice rather than in the content of the comment itself. This is important because the burden of proof in showing malice shifts back onto the plaintiff.

16 *Turner v Metro-Goldwyn-Mayer* [1950] 1 All ER 449, *McQuire v Western Morning News* [1903] 2 KB 100.
17 *Campbell v Spottiswoode* (1863) 3 B & S 769, *Hunt v Star Newspaper* [1908] 2 KB 309.
18 Eg *Peter Walker v Hodgson* [1909] 1 KB 239.
19 *Gatley on Libel and Slander* (8th edn) (1981) p 348, para 792, cited by Lord Keith of Kinkel in the House of Lords in *Telnikoff v Matusevich*.
20 *Lyon v Daily Telegraph* [1943] 1 KB 746.

Absence of malice

If the defendant shows that the comment was fair, the plaintiff may still defeat the defence by showing that the comment was made with malice. For the purposes of fair comment, 'malice' means that the defendant's dominant motive was to harm the plaintiff.[1] Evidence that the defendant did not really believe the statement will be strong evidence of malice, but is not a necessary condition of malice.

Absolute privilege

We now move on to the defences to defamation which arise not from the content of the defamatory statement but from the circumstances of its publication or the identity of the publisher. These are the 'privilege' defences. 'Qualified' privilege is where the privilege defence can be defeated by proof of malice. 'Absolute' privilege is where proof of malice makes no difference.

We begin with the situations that attract absolute privilege.

Parliament

Conveniently for members of Parliament, Art 9 of the Bill of Rights 1688, which says, 'the freedom of speech and debates or proceedings in Parliament ought not to be impeached or questioned in any court or place out of Parliament' supposedly protects anything said in Parliamentary debates, committees and other proceedings, including letters by MPs to ministers or officers of the House, from civil actions for libel or slander.[2] In *Church of Scientology v Johnson-Smith*[3] the privilege was extended to exclude the use of words used in Parliament to show that defamatory words used outside Parliament were prompted by malice.

Parliamentary papers, that is reports, papers or proceedings published by Parliament, also have absolute privilege,[4] although extracts from such documents have only qualified privilege.[5]

---

1   See *Telnikoff v Matusevitch* in the Court of Appeal [1991] 1 QB 102, [1990] 3 All ER 865.
2   *Ex p Wason* (1869) LR 4 QB 573, *Re Parliamentary Privilege Act 1770* [1958] AC 331, *Rost v Edwards* [1990] 2 All ER 641. The privilege covers members of Parliament and people giving evidence to Parliamentary committees. It does not, however, cover letters to MPs by constituents: *Rivlin v Bilainkin* [1953] 1 QB 485.
3   [1972] 1 QB 522.
4   Parliamentary Papers Act 1840 s 1.
5   Ibid s 3.

PUBLIC FIGURES AND POLITICIANS

It is, of course, extraordinary that a privilege enjoyed by members of Parliament on the ground that it protects freedom of speech should not extend to protect ordinary citizens from libel suits by politicians. In the USA and other jurisdictions a form of qualified privilege defence has developed called the 'public figure' defence.[6] In the words of the Second Restatement:[7]

> 'One who publishes a false and defamatory communication concerning a public official or public figure in regard to his conduct, fitness or role in that capacity is subject to liability, if, but only if, he:
> (a) knows that the statement is false and that it defames the other person, or
> (b) acts in reckless disregard of these matters.'

The Australian case *Theophanous* does not go so far. It only covers politicians, including present and prospective members of Parliament—as opposed to any 'public figure'—and requires the defendant to show, in addition to absence of actual knowledge of the falsity of the statement or recklessness about it, that the publication was 'reasonable in all the circumstances'. But its grounding in concerns for free political debate is just as firm.

One might consider the extension of the public figure defence to apply to cases brought by people other than those able to claim Parliamentary immunities to be excessive. After all, why should election to the parish council remove one's right to a reputation? If there were to be a public figure defence even for cases brought by such lowly political figures it would be better if it was to be on the Australian basis that the defendant has to prove that it was not negligent. But the absence from English law of such a defence with regard to members of Parliament, whose immunities from suit are absolute, is an injustice that needs to be remedied.

Courts

Defamatory statements made during judicial proceedings also receive absolute privilege. The privilege extends to judges, lawyers, witnesses and the parties. It applies in all courts and tribunals, both superior courts and inferior courts, and even includes domestic tribunals such as the

6 See *New York Times v Sullivan* 376 US 254 (1964), *Theophanous v Herald and Weekly Times* (High Court of Australia 14-16 September 1994 FC 94/041).
7 § 580A.

disciplinary tribunals of the professions, at least those exercising public law functions.[8]

The alleged justifications for the rule are (a) that the law should prevent the relitigation of disputes—although that would be more convincing if the common law had recognised evidence of a criminal conviction as evidence that the person convicted had actually committed the crime; and (b) to prevent actions against people who are 'merely discharging their duty'.[9] That is, lawyers have to say what they are instructed to say, witnesses have to say what they think is the truth even if it turns out not to be the truth and judges have to give the verdict they believe to be right. The idea is, for example, that in the court room a witness is under an obligation to blurt out what she thinks is the truth, even when in the outside world, in the light of her uncertainty, she would stay silent.

Absolute privilege does not, however, apply to hearings that the courts think of as essentially administrative rather than judicial (even though that distinction is no longer a particularly useful one in administrative law). As a result, the licensing hearings—about public entertainments and the sale of alcohol—by both local authorities and magistrates do not attract absolute privilege.[10] Planning appeals also seem to count as administrative rather than judicial.[11]

But even if the proceedings are administrative rather than judicial, it may still be possible for them to attract an immunity equivalent to absolute privilege if it is in the 'public interest' that they do so. In *Hasselblad v Orbinson*[12] for example, the Court of Appeal said that a letter of complaint to the European Commission alleging violations of European competition law was not part of judicial proceedings and did not technically qualify for absolute privilege. Nevertheless, because to allow its use to ground a libel action would seriously impede the Commission in its duties, the court excluded the letter and its contents from the evidence, so effectively establishing an absolute privilege.

The immunity does not apply to statements on matters that are entirely unconnected with the hearing, but if some connection can be made with the proceedings the statement will be protected.[13] If, for example, the defendant says in a criminal trial 'I am on trial only because I am being persecuted because I know that X is guilty of Y', it seems that the defendant is protected from civil liability.[14]

8   *Addis v Crocker* [1961] 1 QB 11. For the criteria of what counts as a sufficiently judicial proceeding, see *Trapp v Mackie* [1979] 1 All ER 489.
9   Fry LJ in *Munster v Lamb* (1883) 11 QBD 588.
10 *Royal Aquarium v Parkinson* [1892] 1 QB 431, *Attwood v Chapman* [1914] 3 KB 275.
11 *Richards v Cresswell* (1987) Times, 24 April.
12 [1985] QB 475.
13 *More v Weaver* [1928] 2 KB 520, *Seaman v Netherclift* (1876) 2 CPD 53. See also *Sirros v Moore* [1975] QB 118 (a judge can be liable for defamation if has no jurisdiction to hear a case, but only if the judge knows about the lack of jurisdiction).
14 For a notorious example, see (1976) The Economist, 7 February p 18 and 14 February p 14.

Fair and accurate media reports of judicial proceedings are protected by the same absolute privilege as long as (a) the proceedings were in public, (b) the proceedings were in the United Kingdom, and (c) the report was published contemporaneously.[15]

It is unclear whether absolute privilege for judicial matters extends to communications between lawyers and their clients.[16] It is possible that the privilege is qualified only, in the normal way of private communications.

Civil service

Most books claim that communications between 'officers of State' attract absolute privilege. The reason is that *Chatterton v Secretary of State for India*[17] decided that what is now called 'public interest immunity' applied to written communications between high officials of state and that the plaintiff could not even introduce other evidence to show what the document contained. The limits of this protection are set therefore by the rules of public interest immunity rather than by any separate rule of the application of absolute privilege in defamation actions. Were advances made towards freedom of information, the scope of the protection would correspondingly contract.

In any case, there is some doubt about whether, even now, such immunity attaches to communications other than policy advice at the highest level (for example senior civil service advice to ministers).[18]

Qualified privilege

More important in practice than absolute privilege are the forms of privilege that can be defeated by malice.

Reports about matters of public interest

Fair and accurate accounts of judicial proceedings not otherwise protected by absolute privilege[19] and of Parliamentary proceedings other than those published by Parliament itself,[20] together with fair and accurate extracts from Parliamentary papers all attract qualified privilege.[1]

15 Law of Libel Act 1888 s 3, Broadcasting Act 1990 Sch 20 para 2, *McCarey v Associated Newspapers* [1964] 1 WLR 855.
16 Pro: *More v Weaver* above; Maybe: *Minter v Priest* [1930] AC 558.
17 [1895] 2 QB 189.
18 See eg *Szalatnay-Stacho v Fink* [1946] 1 All ER 303, *Richards v Naum* [1967] 1 QB 620, *Merricks v Nott-Bower* [1965] 1 QB 57.
19 See above. *Kimber v Press Association* [1893] 1 QB 65.
20 *Wason v Walter* (1868) LR 4 QB 73.
1   Parliamentary Papers Act 1840 s 3.

In the case of reports of Parliamentary proceedings, 'fair and accurate' means not only, for example, that the words attributed to members of Parliament were really said by them but also that any surrounding material inserted by the reporter does not distort the meaning of the words. Subject to that restriction even humorous Parliamentary 'sketches' attract privilege, although one might question whether a Parliamentary sketch that is not malicious is of much journalistic value.

In the case of reports of judicial proceedings, privilege only applies to hearings in public and does not extend to obscene material[2] or to statements whose publication the court has forbidden.[3] The fairness and accuracy of the report are matters for the jury.[4] In addition, reports of proceedings in foreign courts are privileged only if there is a legitimate and proper interest in the case in the United Kingdom,[5] although whether such a bizarrely nationalistic rule is appropriate in the era of global communications is questionable. What, for example, would be the legitimate peculiarly British interest in the trial of OJ Simpson?

Finally, s 7 of the Defamation Act 1952[6] extends qualified privilege to media reports of the proceedings of a variety of other public or semi-public bodies, from the parliaments of commonwealth countries and the meetings of international organisations of which the United Kingdom is a member to committees of local authorities and the proceedings of professional associations. The privilege is restricted to reports of matters 'of public concern' the publication of which is 'for the public benefit'.[7] The section distinguishes between bodies reports of whose proceedings are privileged 'without explanation or contradiction' and bodies reports of whose proceed–ings are privileged 'subject to explanation or contradiction'. The difference is that if the defence is subject to explanation or contradiction, the privilege is lost if the plaintiff has asked the defendant to issue a reasonable explanation or correction and the defendant has not done so.

Matters of private duty and interest

In *Harrison v Bush*,[8] Lord Campbell CJ giving the judgment of the Court of Queen's Bench said:

> 'A communication made bona fide upon any subject matter in which the party communicating has an interest, or in reference to which

2   This was true even at common law. See *Re The Evening News* (1886) 3 TLR 255.
3   *Brook v Evans* (1860) 29 LJ Ch 616.
4   *Kingshott v Associated Kent Newspapers* [1991] 1 QB 88.
5   *Webb v Times Publishing* [1960] 2 QB 535.
6   See also Broadcasting Act 1990 s 166(3).
7   These are also jury questions—see *Kingshott v Associated Kent Newspapers* above n 4. The withdrawal of privilege from publications that are 'prohibited by law' raises a question for the judge, however.
8   (1856) 5 E & B 344 at 348.

he has a duty, is privileged, if made to a person having a corr–
esponding interest or duty, although it contain criminatory matter
which, without this privilege, would be slanderous and actionable.'

This form of privilege can be analysed in a number of different ways,
but one convenient way is to look first at those cases in which the defendant
had a duty to give the information and secondly cases in which the
defendant had an interest in giving the information.

The duty to make the statement can be a legal, moral or social duty.
The recipient, in turn, can have either a duty or a legitimate interest in
receiving the statement.[9] Obvious examples include helping the police when
they ask for information about suspicious behaviour and responding to a
request for information about a former employee. Other examples have
included passing on information to the Law Society about alleged
misconduct by solicitors.[10]

But the test for whether the defendant was under such a duty is unclear.
It seems that the decision is for the judge rather than for the jury,[11] which
makes sense when the defendant claims that there was a legal duty, but
makes less sense when the claim is that there was a social or moral duty
to supply the information. This question ought to be for the jury to decide.
Instead, some judges say that the judges themselves just have to apply
their own view of what moral and social duties people have[12] whereas others
have said that judges should ask themselves, in effect, what a jury might
think people's duties are.[13]

The leading case, *Watt v Longsdon*, itself turns on the suspiciously old-
fashioned notion that unless you have very strong evidence, there is no
duty to tell a man's wife that you suspect him of immorality, drunkenness
and dishonesty but there is a duty, in exactly the same circumstances, to
tell his manager at work and the chairman of the company. The idea that
it is perfectly all right to ruin a man's career with unsubstantiated stories
but not to upset his marriage is at once attractive and repellent—attractive
because it seems to say that family life is more important than work, and
repellent because it smacks of paternalism. Other cases seem to suggest,
for no obviously good reason, that replies to requests for information from
trade protection societies and credit reference agencies are not privileged
if the body requesting the information is being run at a profit.[14]

Note that although it may be slightly harder to convince a court that
the defendant ought to count as being under a duty when the defendant
volunteers the information than when a third party asks the defendant

---

9   *Watt v Longsdon* [1930] 1 KB 130, *Beach v Freeson* [1971] 2 All ER 854.
10 *Beach v Freeson* [1971] 2 All ER 854.
11 *Stuart v Bell* [1891] 2 QB 341.
12 Lindley LJ in *Stuart v Bell*.
13 Scrutton LJ in *Watt v Longsdon* (the judge should try to ascertain what the 'great mass'
     of people would think).
14 *Macintosh v Dun* [1908] AC 390.

for the information, it is still perfectly possible for the occasion to be privileged even in the former case.[15]

The recipient of the information must have at least a legitimate interest in receiving it. The more people the statement is published to the more difficult the defence is to sustain, since the defendant must show that every publication was privileged. But there are cases when publication to quite large groups is privileged, and it is possible to envisage cases in which publication to the public as a whole is privileged.[16] The recipient must have an objective interest in the information. It is not enough for the defendant to believe, erroneously, that the recipient had an interest.[17]

Moving on to cases in which the defendant does not have a duty to send the information but does have an interest, there are two distinct kinds of case. In the first, the sender and receiver of the information have a common interest in it. In the second, the senders of the information are trying to protect their own interests.

In the former case, employees who communicate in the course of their employer's business have a common interest, or at least are treated as if they had such an interest [18] (so, for example, protecting the dictation of letters to secretaries[19]) as do a tenant and a landlord in the behaviour of people employed by the landlord to look after the property or lodgers brought into the property by the tenant.[20] There may be a common interest between a local councillor and local electors in the affairs of the council.[1] *De Buse v McCarthy*[2] says that councillors have no interest in comm— unicating allegations against council employees to the electorate before their investigations have been completed and that electors have no interest in receiving information about the internal workings of the council, only in definite proposals for action. One might question, however, whether this case remains entirely valid in the light of recent legislation that requires rather more open access to local authority papers than was customary 50 years ago.[3] Matters relating to disciplinary action against individual employees are still exempt from the requirement to release information, but it is surely no longer possible to make sweeping statements about the public having no interest in the internal workings of the authority.

The second case is where defendants acted to protect their own interests, rather as one might have a right of self-defence.[4] This looks anomalous, for it seems that there is no requirement for the recipient of the information

15 *Beach v Freeson* [1971] 2 All ER 854.
16 *Chapman v Ellesmere* [1932] 2 KB 431 (whole of public interested in racing has an interest in knowing that a person has been banned fron racing). *Blackshaw v Lord* [1983] 2 All ER 311.
17 *Beach v Freeson* [1971] 2 All ER 854.
18 *Edmondson v Birch* [1907] 1 KB 371.
19 *Bryanston Finance v de Vries* [1975] QB 703.
20 *Toogood v Spyring* (1834) 1 Cr M & R 181 , *Knight v Gibbs* (1834) 1 Ad & El 43.
1   *Cutler v McPhail* [1962] 2 QB 292.
2   [1942] 1 KB 156.
3   See Local Government (Access to Information) Act 1985.
4   *Turner v Metro-Goldwyn-Mayer* [1950] 1 All ER 449.

to have a duty or an interest to receive it. But in fact, such a requirement still operates. In *Osborn v Boulter*,[5] for example, the plaintiff, a publican, attacked the quality of the defendant's beer. The defendant replied that the plaintiff was probably watering down the beer. The defendant published his retort to his own employees. The court said that the publication to the employees was privileged. The publication was in the ordinary course of business to someone with a common interest or even a duty to receive it. In *Somerville v Hawkins* the defendant informed his employees that they should not associate with a former employee who had been dismissed for dishonesty. The other employees' interest was that they were being told the reasons behind a legitimate instruction from their employer.

Malice

All forms of qualified privilege may be defeated by proof of malice. In this context, malice means (a) having any motive, including harming the plaintiff or any other improper purpose, other than fulfilling one's duty to communicate the information or protecting one's own interests or the interests of the recipient of the information, or (b) not believing the truth of the accusation or being reckless as to its truth or falsity. Some writers add a third form of malice, namely the publication of the statement to a wider range of people than necessary to fulfill one's duties or protect one's interests, but (i) the examples of publication beyond those with an interest are not privileged anyway and (ii) such publication is evidence, but no more, of an ulterior motive to harm the plaintiff.

But honesty is the test not competence. Even if the defendant has come to his belief in his case through unreasoning prejudice or through negligence, stupidity and sloppy thinking, as long as the defendant really believes what he said, there is no malice.[6]

Note that the effect of malice is personal to particular people. If one person's defence of privilege (or, probably, fair comment[7]) is defeated by malice, other people who were involved in the publication of the same defamatory statement do not lose their own protection as long as they, personally, were not malicious.[8]

Consent

Finally, although it is not a defence peculiar to defamation, we should mention that if the plaintiff consents to the publication of the defamatory

5 [1930] 2 KB 226.
6 *Horrocks v Lowe* [1975] AC 135, *Clark v Molyneux* (1877) 3 QBD 237. But nb the possibility of a negligence action if the statement causes actual loss. See *Spring v Guardian Assurance* [1994] 3 All ER 129, [1994] IRLR 460, [1994] 3 WLR 354.
7 Sutherland 'Fair comment by the House of Lords?' (1992) 55 MLR 278, *Telnikoff v Matusevich* above.
8 *Egger v Viscount Chelmsford* [1965] 1 QB 248.

statement, and in particular if the plaintiff republishes the defamatory statement, there is no liability.[9]

Remedies

Plaintiffs in libel actions generally want one or more of the following: a retraction or apology, an injunction against repetition of the libel and compensation. English law has no way of ordering an apology, although apologies or the lack of them may sometimes be relevant to the level of damages.[10] Injunctions against repetition of the libel pose no difficulty for the courts after the full hearing of the case, but there are problems associated with interlocutory injunctions. As for damages, they are in the hands of the jury, and controversy rages about what the jury should or should not be told and be allowed to do.

Injunctions

This is not the place to rehearse the law relating to injunctions. Suffice it to say that if there is any prospect of the repetition of the libel, the court will respond favourably to a plaintiff's request for a permanent injunction to be issued against the defendant, breach of which will be a contempt of court and grounds for imprisonment, fines and sequestrations. But usually the plaintiff will be more interested in an injunction before the trial, to prevent the repetition of the alleged libel for the time being. Here, the normal rule is that the court decides whether to grant an injunction by asking whether either party is likely to suffer irreparable harm and if both will suffer irreparable harm, which will suffer the most harm. This test, the 'balance of convenience' test is however not applied in defamation cases where the defendant intends to plead justification. In such cases, because prior restraint is thought to be a much worse invasion of the right of freedom of speech than awarding damages after publication, no injunctions should be awarded. Even when the plaintiff's complaint falls within the one exception to the rule that truth is a defence to defamation, namely s 8 of the Rehabilitation of Offenders Act 1974, the court will still not issue an interlocutory injunction unless there is evidence of malice.[11]

Damages

One might have thought that since the point of defamation is to protect reputation, compensation for defamation ought to be restricted to provable

---

9 See eg *Chapman v Ellesmere* above.
10 See below. In addition a little used procedure under the Libel Acts 1843-5 allows the defendant in cases where the libel was published in a newspaper without malice or gross negligence to publish a full apology and to pay an amount into court by way of amends.
11 *Herbage v Pressdram* [1984] 1 WLR 1160.

monetary loss flowing from the lost reputation, both past and future. But in fact, damages for defamation are 'at large'—that is, one need not specify exactly what one is claiming for but one can mention not only specific losses but also such imponderables as the plaintiff's desire to be vindicated, injury to the plaintiff's feelings and the anxiety suffered during the course of the litigation.[12] Moreover, since the level of damages is set by the jury, the award does not have to be broken down into various heads. It is usually just one lump sum to cover everything. Even where the jury states its awards under different heads, including punitive or exemplary damages, the traditional stance of the appellate courts was to refrain from interference with the award unless it was so manifestly wrong (either too big or too small) that no sensible jury properly instructed could have reached that figure.[13] In the very rare cases where the court came to the conclusion that the jury was manifestly wrong,[14] the appellate court did not substitute its own figure but merely sent the case back for a new trial by jury.

In the late 1980s, however, a series of extraordinary awards by juries, culminating in an award of £1.5m in a case between Lord Aldington and Count Tolstoy and an award of £600,000 in a case between Sonia Sutcliffe, the wife of the 'Yorkshire Ripper', and *Private Eye*,[15] prompted change. The contrast between these defamation awards and the relatively small amounts recovered by personal injury plaintiffs, especially in cases in which children had been killed, became too sharp. Section 8 of the Courts and Legal Services Act of 1990 provided

'(1) In this section "case" means any case where the Court of Appeal has power to order a new trial on the ground that damages awarded by a jury are excessive or inadequate.

(2) Rules of court may provide for the Court of Appeal, in such classes of case as may be specified in the rules, to have power, in place of ordering a new trial, to substitute for the sum awarded by the jury such sum as appears to the court to be proper.'

And, indeed, a new order, Ord 59, r 11(4), has appeared. It provides:

'In any case where the Court of Appeal has power to order a new trial on the ground that damages awarded by a jury are excessive or inadequate, the court may, instead of ordering a new trial, substitute for the sum awarded by the jury such sum as appears to the court to be proper.'

---

12 Per Lord Hailsham in *Cassell v Broome* [1972] AC 1027.
13 *Cassell v Broome* [1972] AC 1027. Exemplary or punitive damages are possible when the defendant deliberately set out to make a profit out of the violation of the plaintiff's rights.
14 Eg *Lewis v Daily Telegraph* [1964] AC 234.
15 *Sutcliffe v Pressdram* [1991] 1 QB 153. The Court of Appeal struck down the award and ordered a new trial. The parties thereupon settled for £60,000.

The first major case to be decided under the new dispensation was *Rantzen v Mirror Group Newspapers*.[16] The facts were that the plaintiff, a successful television presenter and the founder and chair of 'ChildLine', a charity for sexually abused children, sued the defendant newspaper publishers for claiming that she had protected a teacher who had helped her to expose sexual abuse at a boys' school by keeping secret the fact that he was himself an abuser and that she had lied to the newspaper by saying that the story would hamper police inquiries into the matter. The defendants pleaded justification and fair comment. The jury found for the plaintiff and awarded her damages of £250,000. The defendants appealed, saying that the award was excessive.

The defendant complained that the judge had failed to give sufficient guidance to the jury about the financial implications of their award. In *Sutcliffe v Pressdram Ltd*[17] Lord Donaldson MR had said:

'In the instant case I cannot believe that the jury appreciated the true size of the award which they were making. This is understand–able. Despite the inflation which has occurred in the postwar years, sums of money of £100,000 or more, and in many cases less, still lack the reality of the £1 coin or the £5 note. In the lives of ordinary people they are unlikely ever to intrude except in the form of the nominal sale or purchase price of a house ... What is, I think, required, is some guidance to juries in terms which will assist them to appreciate the real value of large sums. It is, and must remain, a jury's duty to award lump sums by way of damages, but there is no reason why they should not be invited notionally to "weigh any sum which they have in mind to award." Whether the jury did so, and how it did so, would be a matter for them, but the judge could, I think, properly invite them to consider what the result would be in terms of weekly, monthly or annual income if the money were invested in a building society deposit account without touching the capital sum awarded or, if they have in mind smaller sums, to consider what they could buy with it.'

The trial judge in *Rantzen* told the jury that he was not allowed to indicate what damages would be appropriate but had just said:

'The figure you come up with, if you get to that point, must be a fair and reasonable one. It must not be miserly otherwise the suspicion will linger. On the other hand, the figure must not be wildly excessive. Be reasonable. Keep your feet on the ground. In so arriving at a figure you are entitled to take into account the value of money, what it can buy—a house, a car or a holiday.'

On appeal, the defendant complained that the judge did not direct the jury's attention to the fact that a large sum of money could produce an

16 [1994] QB 670, [1993] 4 All ER 975.
17 [1991] 1 QB 153.

income which could be enjoyed while the principal sum was left intact. Neill LJ, however, said:

> 'In our judgment ... the judge gave sufficient guidance to the jury by telling them to take into account the value of money and to relate it to its purchasing power by reference to a house, a car or holiday. He might have gone further but we are satisfied that this suggestion of misdirection is not made out.'

The defendant's second complaint was that the judge had failed to take into account *Pamplin v Express Newspapers Ltd (No 2)*.[18] In that case the Court of Appeal had pointed out that although there was no such thing as a defence of partial justification, since the defendant had to prove the truth of all the libellous stings to succeed on liability, the facts proved by the defendant to be true may be important on the issue of damages. But again, the Court of Appeal in *Rantzen* said that the judge had given the jury sufficient guidance by saying:

> 'You are entitled to bear in mind that the defendants have sought to justify and say that what they wrote in part was true in substance and in fact. Here of course you must be careful. You may well find that they have justified part of what they wrote against her in substance and in fact and that it was true, and in so far as they have succeeded obviously she is not entitled to any award at all. But where they have sought to justify and they have failed she is entitled to compensation and the fact that it has taken your verdict to nail the lie and prove their justification plea was misfounded. Your award can reflect that fact.'

The defendant's next complaint was that the judge had misdirected the jury by saying that the jury could take into account in assessing damages the fact that the defendants had not apologised to the plaintiff. The defendant argued that a failure to apologise can only aggravate damages where the defendant pleads justification or fair comment dishonestly. The defendant pointed out that Lord Guest said in *Morgan v Odhams Press Ltd*:[19]

> 'Failure to apologise is not evidence of malice ... By parity of reasoning it cannot increase the damages.'

But the Court of Appeal distinguished *Morgan* by saying that since the defence there was that the words did not refer to the plaintiff and could not be understood to refer to him, the absence of an apology was explicable. Neill LJ continued, 'In other cases, though the absence of an apology may be no proof of malice, it can increase the injury to the plaintiff's feelings.'

18 [1988] 1 WLR 116 (Note).
19 [1971] 1 WLR 1239, 1262.

Neill LJ also cited Lord Hailsham LC's speech in *Cassell v Broome*[20] in which he included 'the absence of an apology, or the reaffirmation of the truth of the matters complained of, or the malice of the defendant' as factors relevant to the measure of damage.[1] Neill LJ therefore concluded:

'In the present case the judge told the jury that they were entitled to take into account the fact that there had been "no apology throughout." In the context of the present case we do not regard that as a misdirection.'

The defendant also claimed that the judge had wrongly directed the jury that they could take account of the fact that the defendants had persisted in a plea of justification. Neill LJ commented:

'It has often been said that the fact that a defendant persists in a plea of justification or fair comment is no evidence whatever of malice unless the plea has been put forward mala fide. It has also been said that the persistence in such a plea should not be taken into account in aggravation of damages. It may merely show that the defendant, though mistaken, has a firm and honest belief in the strength of his case. On the other hand, if one looks at the matter not from the point of view of the state of mind of the defendant but for the purpose of assessing the injury to the plaintiff's feelings, it is easy to see that a contest which involves justification or fair comment may increase the injury and add greatly to the anxiety caused by the proceedings which the plaintiff has had to bring to clear his name.'[2]

But the defendant had more success when it came to the direct consequences of the 1990 Act. The Court of Appeal took into account the effect of the guarantees of freedom of expression in the European Convention on Human Rights and took encouragement from the way the House of Lords has recently been using the Convention not only to resolve ambiguities in British statutes but also to guide the courts in the exercise of their own discretions.[3] The Court of Appeal was particularly impressed with the US concept that defamation law can have a 'chilling effect' on free expression and with the words of the Convention that restrictions on fundamental freedoms should only be allowed in so far as they are 'necessary in a democratic society' or 'justified by a pressing social need.' As a result, Neill LJ

---

20   [1972] AC 1027.
1   See also Nourse LJ in *Sutcliffe v Pressdram* [1991] 1 QB 153, 184: 'The conduct of a defendant which may often be regarded as aggravating the injury to the plaintiff's feelings, so as to support a claim for "aggravated" damages, includes a failure to make any or any sufficient apology and withdrawal'.
2   See also Lord Diplock in *Cassell v Broome* [1972] AC 1027, 1125.
3   See *Derbyshire County Council v Times Newspapers* [1993] AC 534 and *R v Secretary of State for the Home Department, ex p Brind* [1991] 1 AC 696.

concluded that the test for when an appellate court should intervene in a jury decision in libel cases should change:

> 'If one applies these words it seems to us that the grant of an almost limitless discretion to a jury fails to provide a satisfactory measurement for deciding what is "necessary in a democratic society" or "justified by a pressing social need." We consider therefore that the common law if properly understood requires the courts to subject large awards of damages to a more searching scrutiny than has been customary in the past. It follows that what has been regarded as the barrier against intervention should be lowered. The question becomes: "Could a reasonable jury have thought that this award was necessary to compensate the plaintiff and to re-establish his reputation?"'

Although the Court of Appeal refused to endorse explicit comparisons between personal injury awards and defamation awards and it also refused to rule out the possibility that defamation damages could be used to 'vindicate' the plaintiff, the new test itself led the court to reduce the award from £250,000 to £110,000.

Bad reputation

The only important question about damages in defamation that *Rantzen* does not touch on is the defendant's argument that the plaintiff had such a general bad reputation to begin with that the libel would not have had much effect and that damages should be reduced accordingly. The legitimacy of the argument was established in *Scott v Sampson*[4] and although questioned by Viscount Simonds in *Plato Films v Speidel*[5] there is little doubt about its status.

Because the argument depends on starting from what the plaintiff would lose by the particular libel at hand, the defendant can refer only to the plaintiff's actual reputation, not to the reputation he or she ought to have had. In addition, the defendant may lead evidence only of the plaintiff's reputation in general terms, not start a series of mini-trials by launching into the details of the plaintiff's personal history.

4   (1882) 8 QBD 491.
5   [1961] AC 1090

Chapter 13

Damages

The principal aim of damage awards in English tort law is to compensate successful plaintiffs by putting them in a position equivalent to the one they enjoyed before the accident, at least as far as money can do this. Occasionally, the courts award exemplary or punitive damages[1] and some torts which are actionable per se have the peculiarity that the court can award damages even though the plaintiff has proved no harm to the principal interest that the tort supposedly protects.[2]

There is, however, a fundamental difficulty in deciding the level of compensation. The aim, put bluntly in the language of economics, must be that the plaintiff should be indifferent between the state of having suffered no harm and the state of having suffered the harm and receiving the compensation. But there are two very different ways of trying to achieve this state of indifference. One is to ask how much money the victim would have paid to avoid having the harm happen. The other is to ask how much one would have to pay the victim for the victim to volunteer to suffer the harm. Most people would nominate a much higher amount in response to the second question than the first. The reason is that in the first way of asking the question there is a natural upper limit to the amount the victim could nominate, namely the whole of the victim's wealth. In the second way of asking the question, there is no such natural upper limit. The victim can ask for any sum, no matter how large. The first way of asking the question is therefore more realistic, although it does have the disadvantage of awarding higher amounts in damages to richer people just because they have more wealth to offer in exchange for safety. Indeed the tension between realism and equality lies at the heart of the law of damages and explains the existence on the one hand of damages for lost earnings and on the other standard amounts, regardless of the victim's income, for 'losses of amenity' such as no longer being able to see, hear or walk.

By calling the damage award 'compensation' the law unfortunately calls to mind the second way of asking the question and prompts the response

---

1   See below.
2   Eg in libel, damages are payable for mental distress even if the only people who knew about the libel did not believe it.

that money can never be an adequate compensation for certain injuries.[3] Who would ever volunteer to suffer horrible injuries, no matter what the money compensation? But the first way of asking the question is something that most people act on every day. We decide whether to take risky jobs, we decide whether to risk our health by living in a city rather than the countryside, we decide what to eat and drink and whether to smoke. We do, both implicitly and explicitly, place quite precise values on our willingness to pay to avoid harm.

Another problem is that one obvious way of measuring loss in a personal injury case is to add the expenses that the accident caused to the victim to the reduction in earnings that the victim will suffer in the future. But this measure of loss may underestimate the willingness of the victim to have paid more than the amounts lost to have avoided the harm, for the victim would have had the whole of his or her lifetime income to use to avoid the harm. Thus, pure lost earnings approaches, or 'human capital' approaches, lead to undercompensation.[4] One rather crude way of making up for the difference is to add in amounts for 'pain and suffering'—that is, an attempt to represent the amount the victim would have been willing to pay to avoid the harm over and above expenses and lost income. But talk of 'pain and suffering' has the distinct disadvantage of implying the use of the second way of asking the basic question, of asking 'how much in exchange for subjecting yourself to this pain?'

Unfortunately, to base damage awards on realistic assessments of what the plaintiff would have paid to avoid the harm in question, including assessments of the victim's own risk-avoiding or risk-preferring behaviour, is a long way off. But it is reasonable at least to judge the existing law against the levels of damage award that such an approach would imply.

Types of damages awarded

The traditional classification of damages awarded by the courts is, in order of increasing magnitude, as follows:

Nominal damages

In torts that are actionable per se, that is without proof of any actual loss, and the plaintiff proves no loss but nevertheless wins the case, the court may choose to award the plaintiff a purely nominal sum, £1 for example. The danger for the plaintiff in such cases is the system of paying money into court. At any stage of the litigation defendants can pay into court an amount of money for which they are willing to settle the action. They do not have to tell the plaintiff how much they have paid in. If the plaintiff

---

3   Cf *Alcock v Chief Constable of South Yorkshire* [1992] 1 AC 310.
4   See 'The Price of a Life' (1993) Economist, 4 December p 103.

chooses to carry on with the action and the amount of damages awarded turns out to be less than the amount paid in, the plaintiff, although technically successful, has to pay all the costs, including the defendant's costs, from the time the money was paid in. This means that plaintiffs who just want to have their day in court, or who really want above all else to humiliate the defendant in public, have to pay for the privilege.

Even worse than nominal damages are contemptuous damages. The court, or more usually the jury in a libel trial, decides that the plaintiff was technically in the right but so disapproves of the merits of the plaintiff's case (including in libel cases a disdain for the plaintiff's entitlement to any reputation) that it awards the lowest possible amount—that is, now, one penny. In addition, the famous English costs rule, that the loser pays the winner's costs, is not really a firm rule at all but merely the way in which the court usually exercises its discretion under s 51 of the Supreme Court Act 1981 and Ord 62 of the Supreme Court Rules. It is open to the judge in an appropriate case to refuse to order the defendant to pay the plaintiff's costs.

General and special damages

One of the most confusing aspects of the terminology of the law of damages is that the contrast between 'general' and 'special' damages refers to two very different distinctions. In the first distinction, 'general damage' is what torts actionable per se are about, for example loss of reputation in libel. Such damage is presumed to occur and does not need to be pleaded. In contrast, 'special damage' is what one has to plead when the tort is not actionable per se. If damage is 'the gist of the action', as it is in negligence, nuisance and breach of statutory duty, the plaintiff must allege and be able to prove that some recognised loss has occurred.

But in the second contrast between 'general' and 'special' damages, the starting point is precisely that the action is one where there is no liability without proof of loss but the question is how to classify losses. Some losses are fairly easy to calculate in money terms. Expenses that the plaintiff has incurred, the cost of replacing or repairing damaged property, lost earnings until the time of trial—all these are 'special' damages, whereas less easily pinned down amounts, including future loss of earnings, pain and suffering and loss of amenity, are all 'general damages'. The distinction does not matter much, except that special pecuniary damages receive a higher interest rate than that applicable to other forms of damages and it is payable on the whole period from the time of the accident to the date of trial.

Aggravated damages

Aggravated damages are awarded where the court believes that because of the way in which the defendant has behaved, the plaintiff has suffered more than the normal degree of anguish and loss of dignity that being the victim of a tort entails. The court therefore orders an enhanced level of compensation. Examples have included: a particularly arrogant trespass by an 'insolent' defendant private investigator,[5] unlawful forcible injection of a remand prisoner with tranquilliser (the 'chemical cosh');[6] a particularly vicious and humiliating sexual assault;[7] an outrageous attempt by a union to close down an employer's business by trespass and nuisance;[8] and an embarrassing and nasty commercial fraud involving the sale of shares by someone who did not own them.[9]

On the other hand, the courts do not use aggravated damage awards when it is more straightforward simply to award more for physical pain and suffering.[10] Moreover, anger and indignation by themselves cannot ground a claim for aggravated damages in most torts since they are not recognised heads of damage for which any compensation is payable at all.[11]

There are two conceptual problems with aggravated damages. First, it is very difficult to keep separate the idea of enhanced compensation for extra distress and the idea of punishing the defendant for being bad, which is properly the function of exemplary or punitive damages. Secondly, it is difficult to justify awarding damages for extra mental anguish when in most torts, defamation being an exception, mental anguish by itself is not actionable.

In the *South West Water* case, the Court of Appeal said, moreover, that since injury to feelings was recoverable in any case in defamation, there is no need to classify damages for humiliating the plaintiff as 'aggravated' damages since the court is doing no more than awarding the appropriate amount under the appropriate head. At the same time, since pain and suffering are generally actionable and the courts say that it is preferable to classify physical harm as pain and suffering as opposed to aggravated damages, it is hard to see what role is left for aggravated damages to play. Either mental anguish is not recoverable in the tort in question, in which case aggravated damages are not payable at all, or it is recoverable, in which case the damages are no more than those that are normally paid, and is therefore not classifiable as 'aggravated damages' either.

The effects of the *South West Water* case on aggravated damages may be more far-reaching than the Court of Appeal realised. The reasoning in the case is a challenge to the very existence of the category of aggravated

5   *Jolliffe v Willmett* [1971] 1 All ER 478.
6   *Barbara v Home Office* (1984) 134 NLJ 888.
7   *W and D v Meah* [1986] 1 All ER 935.
8   *Messenger Newspapers v National Graphical Association* [1984] IRLR 397. Several writers complain that since companies can have no feelings of dignity or pride, the award of £10,000 aggravated damages in this case was wrong. One can perhaps justify it, however, as a case in which the corporate veil was rightly pierced because of the personal animosity shown by the union to the owner of the company, Mr Shah.
9   *Archer v Brown* [1985] QB 401.
10   *Kralj v McGrath* [1986] 1 All ER 54.
11   *AB v South West Water Services* [1993] QB 507, [1993] 1 All ER 609.

damages. Whether future cases draw back from this radical position remains to be seen. The position that *South West Water* approaches is, for example, seemingly at odds with what Lord Devlin said in *Rookes v Barnard*[12] about aggravated damages, namely that:

'[I]t is very well established that in cases where the damages are at large the jury (or the judge if the award is left to him) can take into account the motives and conduct of the defendant where they aggravate the injury done to the plaintiff. There may be malevolence or spite or the manner of committing the wrong may be such as to injure the plaintiff's proper feelings of dignity and pride. These are matters which the jury can take into account in assessing the appropriate compensation.'

Exemplary or punitive damages

Exemplary or punitive damages go beyond 'aggravated' damages and compensation. We are here concerned with the explicit use of tort damages either to punish or to deter the defendant. For reasons that remain obscure, the English courts are far more reluctant to make awards of punitive damages than, for example, the courts in the United States. The principles of the law were laid down in two House of Lords cases in the 1960s and 1970s, namely *Rookes v Barnard* and *Cassell v Broome*.[13] Before *Rookes*, surprisingly, the question of exemplary damages had not arisen for decision in the House of Lords.

In *Rookes*, Lord Devlin said:

'Exemplary damages are essentially different from ordinary damages. The object of damages in the usual sense of the term is to compensate. The object of exemplary damages is to punish and deter. It may well be thought that this confuses the civil and criminal functions of the law ... Indeed, when one examines the cases in which large damages have been awarded ... it is not at all easy to say whether the idea of compensation or the idea of punishment has prevailed.'

Lord Devlin then goes on to say:

'[The] authorities convince me of two things. First, that your Lordships could not without a complete disregard of precedent, and indeed of statute, now arrive at a determination that refused altogether to recognise the exemplary principle. Secondly, that there are certain categories of cases in which an award of exemplary

12 [1964] AC 1129.
13 [1972] AC 1027.

damages can serve a useful purpose in vindicating the strength of
the law, and thus affording a practical justification for admitting
into the civil law, a principle which ought logically to belong to the
criminal.'

He then put forward two categories of case in which the law should allow
exemplary damages[14] and three general considerations for the courts to
bear in mind when making exemplary awards.

The first category is 'oppressive, arbitrary or unconstitutional action by
the servants of the government'.[15] This is a category derived from the
eighteenth century civil libertarian cases such as *Wilkes v Wood*[16] in which
the courts used the law of torts to resist such abuses of power as the general
warrant. But Lord Devlin stuck to the classical liberal view that the state
is in a category of its own when it comes to oppression in going on to say:

> 'I should not extend this category ... to oppressive action by private
> corporations or individuals. Where one man is more powerful than
> another, it is inevitable that he will try to use his power to gain his
> ends; and if his power is much greater than the other's, he might
> perhaps be said to be using it oppressively. If he uses his power
> illegally, he must of course pay for his illegality in the ordinary
> way; but he is not to be punished simply because he is the more
> powerful. In the case of the government it is different, for the
> servants of the government are also the servants of the people and
> the use of their power must always be subordinate to their duty of
> service. It is true that there is something repugnant about a big
> man bullying a small man and very likely the bullying will be a
> source of humiliation that makes the case one for aggravated
> damages, but it is not in my opinion punishable by damages.'

Lord Devlin's second category was 'Cases in the second category are
those in which the defendant's conduct has been calculated by him to make
a profit for himself which may well exceed the compensation payable to
the plaintiff.' Lord Devlin explained:

> 'Where a defendant with a cynical disregard for a plaintiff's rights
> has calculated that the money to be made out of his wrongdoing
> will probably exceed the damages at risk, it is necessary for the
> law to show that it cannot be broken with impunity. This category

14 In fact, as Lord Devlin soon remarks, there is a third category—namely cases in which
the award of exemplary or punitive damages is explicitly mandated by statute.

15 This phrase includes the police—see Lord Reid in *Cassell v Broome*. For recent examples
of exemplary damage claims against the police, prison officers and other officers of the
state, for false imprisonment, misfeasance in public office, malicious prosecution, assault
and so on, see eg *Racz v Home Office* [1994] 2 AC 45, [1994] 1 All ER 97, *Holden v Chief
Constable of Lancashire* [1986] 3 All ER 836, *A-G (St Christopher) v Reynolds* [1980] AC
637.

16 (1763) Lofft 1.

is not confined to moneymaking in the strict sense. It extends to cases in which the defendant is seeking to gain at the expense of the plaintiff some object—perhaps some property that he covets—which either he could not obtain at all or not obtain except at a price greater than he wants to put down. Exemplary damages can properly be awarded whenever it is necessary to teach a wrongdoer that tort does not pay.'

Lord Devlin's three considerations were:

'First, the plaintiff cannot recover exemplary damages unless he is the victim of the punishable behaviour. The anomaly inherent in exemplary damages would become an absurdity if a plaintiff totally unaffected by some oppressive conduct which the jury wished to punish obtained a windfall in consequence.

And then:

'Secondly, the power to award exemplary damages constitutes a weapon that, while it can be used in defence of liberty, as in the *Wilkes* case, can also be used against liberty. Some of the awards that juries have made in the past seem to me to amount to a greater punishment than would be likely to be incurred if the conduct were criminal; and moreover a punishment imposed without the safe–guard which the criminal law gives to an offender. I should not allow the respect which is traditionally paid to an assessment of damages by a jury to prevent me from seeing that the weapon is used with restraint. It may even be that the House may find it necessary to follow the precedent it set for itself in *Benham v Gambling*, and place some arbitrary limit on awards of damages that are made by way of punishment. Exhortations to be moderate may not be enough.'

And finally:

'Thirdly, the means of the parties, irrelevant in the assessment of compensation, are material in the assessment of exemplary damages. Everything that aggravates or mitigates the defendant's conduct is relevant.'

In *Cassell v Broome* the House of Lords reaffirmed most of what Lord Devlin had said in *Rookes*. The only cause for dissent was that Lord Reid found that he now disapproved of the idea that exemplary damages could be used to 'vindicate' the legal process. Nevertheless, in the face of argument that Lord Devlin's categories should expand, so that, for example, the first category should include oppressive behaviour by private individuals not just by the state, and that the second category should include any case of malice or spite rather than just cases where the defendant has worked out that it could pay the compensatory damages and still make a profit out of disregarding the plaintiffs' rights,[17] the House of Lords stuck to Lord Devlin's narrow categories.

Lord Reid admitted in *Cassell v Broome* that the cut-off points that the law has chosen are not entirely logical and that they have an element in them of drawing the line merely where it preserves the authority of the maximum number of old cases rather than on the basis of clear principle. Unfortunately, this admission seems recently to have prompted the Court of Appeal to believe that the courts should apply any arbitrary rule that comes to hand to restrict the scope of exemplary damages as long as it technically preserves the old precedents. In *AB v South West Water*, the defendants accidentally spilled about 20 tonnes of aluminium sulphate into the drinking water system at their treatment works at Lowermoor, Camelford in Cornwall. The plaintiffs drank the contaminated water and suffered a variety of ill effects as a result. They claimed for product liability under the Consumer Protection Act 1987, public nuisance, breach of statutory duty, negligence, *Rylands v Fletcher*, breach of contract and breach of EC law. The defendants admitted liability for breach of statutory duty and admitted their liability to pay compensatory damages. But the plaintiffs also claimed exemplary and aggravated damages because of what happened after the initial contamination. They alleged that the defendants' employees acted in an arrogant and high-handed manner when they complained and deliberately misled them by sending them a circular asserting that the water from Lowermoor treatment works was safe to use and drink when the defendants could not have possibly known one way or the other about the safety of the water because they had carried out no tests at the time. Subsequently, the defendants allegedly failed to give any proper information about what could be done to minimise the ill effects of drinking the water and failed to close down the plant and supply fresh water by other means.

The defendants said, however, that the plaintiffs could not obtain exemplary or punitive damages because (1) nuisance is not a cause of action that can found a claim for exemplary damages; (2) the case was not within either of the categories laid down by Lord Devlin in *Rookes v Barnard*; (3) in any event this was not an appropriate case for exemplary damages because it was a claim for damages for personal injuries and is therefore unlike any case in which exemplary damages have been awarded.

The case really should have turned only on the second point. The first and third points represent the kind of formalism that brings the law into disrepute. The interesting question was whether a nationalised industry (now a privatised but licensed and regulated monopoly water supplier) should count as part of the state for the purposes of Lord Devlin's strict but troublesome distinction between state and private sector oppression. The question is not only an important one for exemplary damages cases, but also for the application of EC law (especially the scope of application of Directives). It is even an important question for political philosophy, for if

---

17 Cf the *Ford Pinto* case above ch 3.

one accepts, as Lord Devlin seemed to do in *Rookes*,[18] the classical liberal distinction between state and non-state oppression, which in turn is based on a conception of equality under which the state is under an obligation to treat all citizens with equal concern and respect but individuals are under no similar obligation to one another, one has to say where the limits are, to ask where private power relies so much, directly or indirectly, on the power of the state, that it crosses the line and becomes the equivalent of action by the state. Sadly, however, Stuart-Smith LJ found the arguments on this point, in particular the extremely important EC arguments, 'difficult to follow'. Instead he devoted most of his judgment to attempting to establish the quite extraordinary proposition that *Rookes v Barnard* and *Cassell v Broome* had decided that there could be no exemplary damages in any case that concerned a tort in which no court had awarded exemplary damages before 1964 (the date of *Rookes*). Given that *Rookes v Barnard* itself was about whether to recognise the brand new tort of intimidation[19] and that not one of the law lords thought it relevant when discussing the issue of whether there could be exemplary damages in this new tort to mention the lack of any precedent about exemplary damages, the absurdity of this line of reasoning should have been more apparent to the Court of Appeal than it was. They were led astray by dicta in the judgments of a minority of the court in *Cassell v Broome*, namely Lords Hailsham and Diplock. Lord Hailsham, for example, said:

> 'I do not think that [Lord Devlin] was under the impression either that he had completely rationalised the law of exemplary damages, nor by listing the "categories" was he intending, I would think, to add to the number of torts for which exemplary damages can be awarded. Thus I disagree with the dictum of Widgery LJ in *Mafo v Adams* [1970] 1 QB 548 at 558, [1969] 3 All ER 1404 at 1410 (which, for this purpose, can be treated as an action for deceit) when he said: "As I understand Lord Devlin's speech, the circumstances in which exemplary damages may be obtained have been drastically reduced, but the range of offences in respect of which they may be granted has been increased, and I see no reason since *Rookes v Barnard* why, when considering a claim for exemplary damages, one should regard the nature of the tort as excluding the claim." This would be a perfectly logical inference if Lord Devlin imagined that he was substituting a completely rational code by enumerating the categories and stating the considerations. It is true, of course, that actions for deceit could well come within the purview of the second category. But I can see no reason for thinking that Lord Devlin intended to extend the category to deceit, and counsel on both sides before us were constrained to say that, though it may be paradoxical, they were unable to find a single case where either

---

18 Note that Lord Devlin appears to take a very different view in his famous book *The Enforcement of Morals* (Oxford: OUP, 1968).
19 See above ch 10.

exemplary or aggravated damages had been awarded for deceit, despite the fact that contumelious, outrageous, oppressive, or dishonest conduct on the part of the defendant is almost inherently associated with it.'

But to say that this means that there is an arbitrary cut-off point of 1964 for torts in which exemplary damages can be awarded is to mis–understand what Lord Devlin was doing in *Rookes*. Notice, first, that in the example that Lord Hailsham gives, deceit, it is very unlikely that a case would come within Lord Devlin's categories because (1) this is a private sector, indeed financial sector, tort par excellence and (2) damages for deceit, because they include all the direct consequences of the tort, including all the intended consequences and not excluding unforeseeable consequences,[20] are both extensive enough and uncertain enough that the courts already have enough discretion to remove any profit from the defendant's grasp. The point of Lord Devlin's second category is to allow damage awards that remove all financial incentives to commit the tort. This is the point of such awards in libel cases where newspapers may calculate that a sensational but untrue story will increase circulation so much that they will be able to settle the libel action and still make money. It is also the point in *Bell v Midland Railway* in which the defendant blocked access to the plaintiff's premises to capture the plaintiff's business. And again it is the point of the award of exemplary damages in a case such as *Guppys (Bridport) Ltd v Brookling, Guppys (Bridport) Ltd v James*[1] in which landlords attempt to harass tenants out of their flats in order to make a large profit by redeveloping the building. As Professor Birks has pointed out,[2] there are circumstances in which the measure of damages should be the degree to which the defendant profited, or enriched himself, from his wrong, for only then is the policy of the law that such events should not happen at all. It should matter little whether the label given to such circumstances is 'tort' or 'contract' or 'restitution' (or even 'criminal law').[3] The important question is the opposite of the one normally asked, namely why, and if so in what circumstances, should the defendant be allowed to retain any residual profit from the wrong?[4]

Secondly, what Lord Devlin was doing in *Rookes* was to extract principles which as far as possible explained the existing authorities. If those

20 See eg *Doyle v Olby* [1969] 2 QB 158.
1 (1983) 14 HLR 1.
2 'Civil Wrongs: A New World' in *Butterworth Lectures 1990-91*.
3 For another example of the penetration of restitution damages into tort see *Ministry of Defence v Ashman* (1993) 66 P & CR 195, [1993] 40 EG 144, 25 HLR 513, discussed above ch 9.
4 One example may be where A promises to sell a widget to B for £x. B would have paid up to £2x for the widget, and so is pleased with the deal. But before delivery C offers A £3x for the widget. If A reneges and sells the widget to C, A can pay B £x , so that B is no worse off than he would have been had the deal gone through, and keep £x. The alternative would be to force A to pay £2x to B, but that would mean that in practice B gets the widget and if C does not find and deal with B, C will be worse off without A or B being any better off. This explains why ordinary contract damages are not restitutory.

principles then mean that some cases no longer quite fit, that some cases in which there is liability should no longer support liability and some cases in which there used to be no liability should now have liability, that is precisely how the common law works. It is incremental change supported by principle which in turn comes from the constant rationalisation and re-rationalisation of the cases. It can never be a complete and final rational–isation of the law, but, that does not mean that thought has to stop, arbitrarily, in 1964. That is how, in a case about plainly new law, namely discrimination law,[5] May LJ could say coolly, in a passage inadequately dismissed as obiter dicta in *South West Water* but supported in *Wileman v Minilec Engineering Ltd*[6] and assumed to be correct in principle in *Bradford Metropolitan City Council v Arora* that:[7]

> 'In so far as exemplary damages are concerned, counsel for the plaintiff submitted that in some racial discrimination cases it would be appropriate to award these as well as compensation including aggravated damages. In the instant case, however, exemplary damages were not asked for in the court below and counsel did not ask for an award of such damages from us. Nevertheless, provided that the facts of a given case fall within the principles applicable, in essence those laid down in the two well-known decisions of the House of Lords in *Rookes v Barnard* and *Cassell & Co Ltd v Broome* to which I have referred, I see no reason why an award of exemplary damages could not be made in a racial discrimination case.'

But *AB v South West Water* is already having a doleful effect on the law and in *Deane v Ealing London Borough Council*[8] the Employment Appeal Tribunal accepted meekly that there could be no exemplary damages in discrimination cases merely because there was no anti-discrimination law before 1964.

Heads of compensatory damages

In most tort cases the plaintiff claims compensation for a variety of losses. There will be expenses the plaintiff has incurred, such as medical expenses, travel expenses and the replacement of damaged property. There will be claims for lost income, including wages lost because of non-attendance at work, lost overtime, and lost business in the case of the self-employed. There will be claims for future lost earnings or lost capacity to earn, claims for future expenses, claims for pain and suffering, both in the past and in the future, claims for loss of physical capacity (known as 'loss of amenity') and claims for other property and economic losses.

5   *Alexander v Home Office* [1988] 2 All ER 118 at 123, [1988] 1 WLR 968 at 976.
6   [1988] ICR 318.
7   [1991] 2 QB 507, [1991] 3 All ER 545.
8   [1993] ICR 329.

The effects of lump sum compensation

Before looking at some of these possible claims in more detail, one should note that each damage award in England is dealt with, with a few exceptions, by ordering a lump sum to be paid at once in settlement of all claims. This practice has a number of important consequences for the way English litigants behave and for how English courts calculate awards.

Wait and see

The first problem for the litigant in a once and for all lump sum system is when to sue. If one moves too early, the full consequences of one's injuries may not be obvious at the time of trial and one may end up uncompensated for a disability that appears only later. With very few exceptions, the plaintiff has only one legal action for each wrong done,[9] so that the plaintiff may not at common law come back later with a second action for recently noticed injuries. It may be possible to start a second action if the new damage is of a completely different type. For example, there is a motor accident after which the plaintiff brings an action for damage to his car. After that action is won, the plaintiff gets symptoms of a back injury caused by the original crash but not noticeable until then. Assuming that he can overcome the obvious causal fade problem, the plaintiff may, exceptionally, be able to start a second action.[10] But the normal situation at common law is that the plaintiff needs to make sure that all the relevant injuries and harms are provable before proceeding. The problem for plaintiffs without great financial resources is that they may find that such a wait is beyond them, and they are therefore prey to aggressive bargaining by defendants.

The situation has become slightly more flexible since 1982 with the insertion of s 32A of the Supreme Court Act 1981 and the associated Ord 37 of the Rules of the Supreme Court. This enables the court to award provisional damages in cases where there is a chance that as a result of the tort, the plaintiff will at some time in the future develop a serious disease or suffer serious deterioration in physical or mental health. If this is the case, the court first awards damages on the assumption that the plaintiff's condition will not worsen, and then, if the condition develops as feared, the plaintiff comes back for an increase in the award. The usefulness of s 32A has been limited, however, by *Willson v Ministry of Defence*.[11] In *Willson* the court held that the progression of arthritis to the stage where it requires surgery and consequently the plaintiff's employment prospects

---

9 *Fetter v Beale* (1701) 1 Ld Raym 339. Note, however, that in continuing torts such as nuisance, each time damage occurs the plaintiff gets a new cause of action (*Darley Main Colliery v Mitchell* (1886) 11 App Cas 127). In trespass to land, a new cause of action arises every new day.

10 See *Brunsden v Humphrey* (1884) 14 QBD 141.

11 [1991] 1 All ER 638.

tumble did not count as a serious deterioration for the purposes of the Act because it was just the ordinary progression of the disease, something that the court thought that it could deal with satisfactorily in advance as part of the lump sum. Furthermore, that the plaintiff's condition may cause the plaintiff to suffer a further serious accident does not come within the section either. The section covers only 'clear, severable' risks of the development of specific diseases or conditions.[12]

Two other devices also help to reduce the inflexibility of the all at once lump sum system. First, it is possible to split a trial into a liability phase and an assessment of damages phase, so that the liability issues are dealt with as quickly as possible and the plaintiff receives interim payments until the trial of the assessment of damages hearing. The second is that if there is an appeal, some changes in circumstances between the trial and the appeal may be taken into account at the appeal.[13]

Lump sums, interest rates and the art of prophecy

Awarding a lump sum to cover all past and future losses means (a) that the court is guessing about what would have happened in the future and (b) the plaintiff is usually in a position to invest the money so that it brings in a return.

Both of these points are used by judges to reduce the amounts they give in damages. The so-called 'vicissitudes' argument is that we do not know whether the plaintiff would have lived very long anyway, or that the plaintiff would have had a job, or been healthy. The court therefore deducts amounts from the award to reflect these possibilities.

The vicissitudes argument has not been sufficiently examined by the courts. It is, for example, inconsistent on the one hand, to be hostile to 'loss of a chance' damages and to impose deductions for vicissitudes.[14] 'Lost chances' are merely positive vicissitudes. In any case, why count only the negative vicissitudes? What about the chance that the plaintiff would have been promoted in his job, switched into his own business and made millions, had it not been for the accident? The defendant would say that the plaintiff should not be able to claim for unlikely events. But if so, the plaintiff's damages should not be reduced because of unlikely disasters such as redundancy or illness. It is noticeable that the vicissitudes argument and discounting in general applies only to future pecuniary losses, such as extra expenses and lost earnings, and not to pain and suffering and loss of

---

12 It seems that s 32 only helps victims. It does not assist dependants to be able to protect themselves from the problem of the delayed fatal accident. See above and *Middleton v Elliott* (1990) Independent, 16 November.

13 Eg *Mulholland v Mitchell* [1971] AC 666, *Lim Poh Choo v Camden and Islington Area Health Authority* [1980] AC 174.

14 See above ch 4.

amenity. If the courts took the vicissitudes argument seriously they would be applying it to all forms of loss which carry on into the future.

The courts should instead be aiming simply at their best guess—no more and no less—of the plaintiff's future prospects, both financial and otherwise, without giving undue weight either to unlikely windfalls or unlikely disasters.

The argument for reducing the lump sum is on much firmer ground when it comes to the possibility of investing the money and living off the interest. If the plaintiff receives so large a sum that by the time he would have retired from work he still has a large nest egg, the plaintiff has been over-compensated, for one does not expect to make such a profit on life. The aim of the lump sum award, therefore, must be to bring the plaintiff to the position he would have been in at the time of his retirement—some savings, and a pension, but not enough capital that he need not have worked in the preceding years. Thus, the court awards a lump sum in the expectation that the plaintiff will invest it and spend the income and some of the capital every year so that some of the lump sum is used up every year.

The next question, however, is what interest rate to apply. The traditional view was, and now is once more, that the court should assume that the plaintiff will be able to obtain a return of around 4 to 5 per cent.[15] There was no need to take inflation into account since interest rates and asset values would rise automatically to take inflation into account leaving a stable 'real' interest rate over inflation for the plaintiff to spend. During the 1970s, however, extraordinary economic and political conditions started to shake the traditional view. Inflation grew to record levels, reaching 27% in August 1975 and, after falling back to a mere 7.4% in June 1978, rose rapidly again to reach 22% in May 1980. Interest rates, however, failed to keep pace. The returns on long-term UK government stock remained between 11 and 17% for the entire period. This meant that between 1975 and 1980, except for 1978, interest rates were often effectively negative. If one invested money, inflation reduced its value more quickly than interest payments could restore it.

The result for tort plaintiffs was that their lump sum awards seemed far too low. They claimed that instead of reducing the lump sum to take into account interest rates, since real interest rates were now negative, the courts should be awarding additional amounts to offset inflation. Although plaintiffs appeared to be on the brink of making some progress in *Cookson v Knowles*[16] when Lord Fraser said that 'In exceptional cases ... it might be appropriate to allow for future inflation' the House of Lords eventually decided that there was no evidence that the inflationary bursts of the 1970s would be permanent and decided to sit tight and maintain the traditional rule. Thus, in *Lim Poh Choo v Camden and Islington Area Health Authority* Lord Scarman said:

15 *Auty v National Coal Board* [1985] 1 All ER 930.
16 [1979] AC 556, [1978] 2 All ER 604.

'It is pure speculation whether inflation will continue at present, or higher, rates, or even disappear. The only sure comment one may make on any financial prediction is that it is as likely to be falsified as to be borne out by the event ...

The correct approach should be, therefore, in the first place to assess damages without regard to the risk of future inflation. If it can be demonstrated that, on the particular facts of a case, such an assessment would not result in a fair compensation (bearing in mind the investment opportunity the lump sum award offers) some increase is permissible. But the victims of tort who receive a lump sum award are entitled to no better protection against inflation than others who have to rely on capital for their future support. To attempt such protection would be to put them in a privileged position ...'

Lord Scarman's words have been borne out by experience. In the rest of the 1980s inflation varied between 2.4% and 8% whereas government long-term stock returns did not fall below 9% and even reached 18.8%. Real interest rates were often back in the 4-5% range, although at times they were very much higher. In July 1981, for example, the return on long-term stock was 10% higher than the inflation rate. The use of interest rates by government as its principal tool of macro-economic policy, especially when it was aiming to achieve low inflation through keeping exchange rates high, has meant, if anything, that the 4-5% range has been on the low side. But just as the inflation of the 1970s was no reason to change the policy of the courts in the direction of increasing awards, so the high interest rates of the 1980s are no reason to change in the opposite direction. As Lord Oliver said in *Hodgson v Trapp*, [17] predicting 'future political economic and fiscal policies requires not the services of an actuary or an accountant but those of a prophet.' Probably wisely, in 1972 the Court of Appeal in *Mitchell v Mulholland (No 2)*[18] declined to accept evidence from economists about the future rate of inflation. Given the violent changes in both world conditions and government policy in the 20 years after *Mitchell*, the court's refusal to listen to the economists was almost certainly an act of kindness, for it saved the economists from the extreme embarrassment of having their predictions recorded for posterity.

Another problem that the events of the 1970s highlighted was that of tax rates. *British Transport Commission v Gourley*[19] decided that the plaintiff should receive compensation according to his net future earnings rather than his pre-tax earnings. Such a rule is correct in principle, since the plaintiff should not receive more than his actual loss. Some writers complain that the rule means that the state suffers an uncompensated loss, since the defendant does not have to pay the tax authorities the amount

---

17 [1988] 3 All ER 870.
18 [1972] 1 QB 65.
19 [1956] AC 185.

that would have been raised from the plaintiff.[20] But the obvious retort is that the Revenue's loss is plainly relational economic loss, and there is no one better placed to spread the loss than themselves. But great care has to be taken in applying the *Gourley* principle. At any particular time, the lump sum award itself may or may not be taxed, the income from the lump sum may or may not be taxed, and if it is taxed it may be taxed at a rate higher, lower or the same as the tax rates on the income the plaintiff would have earned, and tax rates themselves may change. Predicting future changes in tax policy is, of course, as difficult as predicting future inflation rates, and unless there is some very specific reason to think otherwise (an increase or reduction already announced, for example) the court can probably do no better than assume that the present arrangements will continue. This means that, in all probability, the award will turn out to be either too much or too little, but that is a feature of every aspect of a lump sum award, not just of the consequences of changes in tax rates.

Thus, in *Hodgson v Trapp*[1] the House of Lords decided that there should be no additional lump sum award to take into account the possibility of the return of that other feature of the mid and late 1970s, the extra tax on investment incomes. Predicting future election results is an even more uncertain business than predicting inflation rates.

But some problems remain even if the court assumes a continuation of present rates. In particular, if, as now, the lump sum itself is not taxed but the income from it is taxed, it will take much careful juggling of the figures to ensure that the net amount the plaintiff is expected to have available to spend each year, which combines the taxed income and a part of the untaxed lump sum, is correct.[2]

Avoiding the lump sum—structured settlements

The lump sum system has a number of advantages. The defendant, or rather the defendant's insurer, knows exactly how much there is to pay. The plaintiff knows that the money is already under his own control and does not have to worry about the possibility that future payments will not arrive. Most of all, there is no need for continuing (and expensive) monitoring by the court or the defendant of the plaintiff's health and well-being. Nevertheless, it is true that the lump sum method, especially as practised by the English courts,[3] is a very crude attempt at calculating compensation and is often, as things turn out, too generous or not generous enough. If the plaintiff recovers or finds that he is after all employable, or just dies young, the plaintiff ends up over-compensated, even if the court

---

20　See Bishop and Kay 'Taxation and Damages: The Rule in *Gourley's Case*' (1987) 105 LQR 366.

1　[1989] AC 807.

2　See *Thomas v Wignall* [1987] QB 1098 and Burrows (1987) 105 LQR 366 for discussion.

3　Especially the 'multiplier method' as described below.

has taken the vicissitudes into account. But if another condition develops or the injuries turn out to be worse than diagnosed or the plaintiff would have been promoted, the plaintiff will have been under-compensated.

The alternative to lump sum payments is some form of periodic payment. Periodic payments can more accurately reflect the exact consequences of the tort for the plaintiff by being open to revision. If the plaintiff's condition turns out to be worse than expected, payments can rise. If the plaintiff dies, payments stop. But this flexibility is bought at a price. There is more uncertainty about the defendant's exposure, uncertainty about which the insurance company will want to be compensated for. There are also potentially great costs involved in going back to the court for new orders, including possibly the costs of tracking down a reluctant defendant or dealing with the problem of a bankrupt defendant. The experience of the courts and now the Child Support Agency with maintenance payments for children of divorced parents is not a happy precedent.

Nevertheless, largely because of a tax concession, parties have begun to negotiate settlements that provide in part for periodic payments. These 'structured' settlements involve a lump sum for losses suffered before the trial and periodic payments afterwards.[4] The structured settlement is not, however, a full periodic payment system. The defendant secures the periodic payments for the plaintiff by buying, with a lump sum, an annuity. The income from the annuity is then paid to the plaintiff in accordance with an agreement between the parties. The only flexibility in the structured settlement is therefore that which the parties build in at the start. If the injury turns out to be worse or better, the payments can only increase or decrease if the agreement allows for such a change. Since the defendant has to buy the annuity from a lump sum, this is not possible, unless one can find an annuity provider willing to gamble on the exact state of the plaintiff's health, as opposed to on the plaintiff's life span, on which all annuity providers are effectively betting, and willing to bear the expense of checking up on the plaintiff. The only flexibility that is usually possible is in the speed and timing of the payments, but nothing that will affect the price the defendant has to pay for the annuity. Indeed the need to negotiate in advance the possible contingencies and different timings of payments together with the set-up costs of the annuity mean that structured settlements are usually not suitable for small damages claims.

The structured settlement does overcome the problem of the plaintiff who lives much longer than expected or who dies young. Indeed where the parties disagree radically about the plaintiff's life expectancy, the struct–ured settlement is often the only way to reach a settlement.[5] The annuity can carry on until the plaintiff dies (or for some other period) whenever

4   See eg Lewis 'Pensions Replace Lump Sum Damages: Are structured settlements the most important reform of tort in modern times?' (1988) 15 JLS 392, 'Legal Limits on the Structure of Settlement of Damages' [1993] CLJ 470, Law Commission Consultation Paper no 125 (1992) and Final Report no 224 (1994) on Structured Settlements and Interim and Provisional Damages.

5   Braithwaite 'Bottom up—settling the unsettleable' (1994) 144 NLJ 638.

that is. Annuity companies make their living by using actuarial tables about how long people live, and they are willing to bear these kinds of risk. It also puts the cost of managing the capital onto the annuity company (and, thus, on to the defendant) instead of on the plaintiff.

The main reason for the growth of structured settlements is, however, the tax break that they receive. Like lump sum awards, there is no tax on buying the annuity for the plaintiff in the first place. But, better than the position under the lump sum, there is no tax either on the income paid out of the annuity. This means that, in effect, by setting up a structured settlement, the defendant can pay out less and the plaintiff receive more (both at taxpayers' expense) than in the equivalent lump sum settlement.

Tax concessions are a very uncertain basis for decision and a very unsatisfactory means for implementing policy. The courts have therefore been wary of structured settlements and have not sought to dispel the impression that the judges have no power to order the parties to settle in such a way.

In its final report of structured settlements,[6] the Law Commission supp–orted the continuation of the existing voluntary system. The Commission recognised the value of structured settlements for many plaintiffs and defendants, but declined to recommend that courts should have the power to oblige parties to structure a damages award in the same way, largely because there were too many practical problems about when the power should be exercised and what happens if the structure fails. It recommended some technical and administrative changes that would make structured settlements easier to administer (for example allowing the annuity provider to pay the money directly to the plaintiff instead, as now, having to go through the defendant or the defendant's insurer).

Loss of earnings

In personal injury cases in England, where the National Health Service pays for most people's medical costs, lost earnings, both before the trial and in the future, often loom larger than the other types of loss that plaintiffs claim for. In this section we look at the calculation of loss of earnings damages.

THE SIGNIFICANCE OF LOSS OF EARNINGS DAMAGES AND A RADICAL THOUGHT

One should note that the recoverability of lost earnings is the clearest illustration of the commitment of the law to the full compensation of the victim even if the application of that principle means that rich people

6   See above n 4.

may receive higher compensation than poor people.[7] Note also that lost earnings can be a form of relational loss,[8] for the plaintiff is complaining that his relationship with a third party, the employer, has become less valuable. But it is recoverable relational loss because having to earn a living is not something one can opt out of, so that the relationship is not fully voluntary, and there is no question about the plaintiff's being the right plaintiff and the defendant's being the right defendant.

But one might bring together the point about the rich receiving higher damages and the point about the relational nature of the loss and suggest that, just as there is an argument that damage to expensive but vulnerable property, such as expensive cars, should not be recoverable because such damage is just a risk that one takes when buying such an object, so losses which flow from the plaintiff's having chosen to take a high paying job in which non-performance means no pay may equally count as the result of the plaintiff's own choice. Instead of ordering damages at a rate that reflects the plaintiff's actual loss, the law could be that damages for lost earnings should be set at the national average rate of pay, which would preserve the same overall deterrent effect of the law, or, even more radically, at the subsistence rate represented by income support levels.

Lost earnings before trial

The plaintiff's lost earnings before trial are usually easy to calculate. Personal injuries often lead to time off work, which may have financial consequences for the plaintiff. Some plaintiffs are in jobs in which non-attendance at work results in no pay at all. These may claim the full amount of their lost pay. Others may have been paid at reduced rates in the form of sick pay under their contracts. They are entitled to the difference between their normal pay and what they received. Others may receive some payments at the full rate, but then lose their jobs altogether because of their non-attendance. They are entitled to compensation at the full rate for the period after they were fired.

As we have seen, it is pay net of tax that counts. Pension contributions are dealt with by taking the rate of pay to be that after the deduction of the pension contribution but then counting loss of pension rights as a separate claimable loss.[9]

Contractual benefits such as company cars and subsidised meals also count as lost earnings. If the plaintiff is self-employed, or earns overtime beyond the requirements of his or her contract of employment, such lost earnings can still be recovered as long as they can be proved on the balance of probabilities to have occurred.

7   But note that some rich people, those who live the proceeds of their wealth, are not entitled to loss of earnings awards.
8   See above ch 6.
9   *Dews v National Coal Board* [1987] 2 All ER 545.

Lost future earnings

The calculation of lost future earnings is, however, obviously more difficult to estimate. The variables include: the level of earnings the plaintiff would have attained if there had been no injury, including the plaintiff's prospects for promotion or recruitment by another employer at higher pay; the prospective length of the plaintiff's working life; the effect of recessions, redundancies, restructuring and economic growth; the plaintiff's prospects for remunerative employment despite the injuries; and the plaintiff's prospects of recovery or deterioration. The degree of uncertainty about these factors is, if the courts are honest, very great and getting greater. There always has been uncertainty in many cases about whether the plaintiff would recover or not, and so about what kind of work the plaintiff might be able to find. And the effect of economic growth on the overall level of earnings has always been so uncertain that the courts, somewhat unfairly from the plaintiff's point of view, have refused to take it into account. But now, as the patterns of people's working lives change, so that fewer people can expect to have a steady predictable 'career' within one large organisation or to train for one job and to work in that job for their entire working lives, the plausibility of guesses about how much people would have earned, and in what jobs, over a 20- or 30-year period is going down rapidly. All that one can really do is to assume, for lack of any better information, that the plaintiff will maintain his or her relative position in the income distribution and that the pattern of the plaintiff's lifetime earnings (whether, for example, they will rise with age or whether they reach a plateau at an early stage) will be similar to that presently experienced by people in a similar position in the distribution. One might try to add in guesses about the prospects in a rapidly changing world for people of different educational attainments. The educational attainments of children are, for example, already used in assessing the lost future earnings of children and young people.[10]

Note that if a student suffers brain damage as a result of a tort, there are no lost earnings in the past and no present employment from whose rates of pay to estimate future loss. But the student has suffered lost future earnings. Similarly, if the plaintiff suffers injuries which mean that he is unlikely to get another job at the same pay as his present one, but his employer has so far kept him on at his old rate of pay out of sympathy, there are no lost earnings yet, but there must be a prospect of loss in the future if and when the employer changes its mind.[11]

In these cases, the plaintiff receives compensation for 'lost earning capacity'—that is, lost future earnings that have not yet begun and may never begin but which probably will occur at some stage. Such awards may edge into the highly speculative especially when the courts start to

10 Eg *Housecroft v Burnett* [1986] 1 All ER 332. In *Hughes v McKeown* [1985] 3 All ER 284, [1985] 1 WLR 963 even the educational attainments of the plaintiff's siblings were taken into account.
11 Cf *Moeliker v Reyrolle* [1977] 1 All ER 9.

discuss the future earnings capacity of children,[12] but the concept is a useful one. Indeed, in the circumstances of great flexibility and change in the labour market, earning capacity may become a more useful concept than lost future earnings.

One area in which social change must at some stage have an effect is in the treatment of the earnings prospects of women. In *Harris v Harris*[13] Lord Denning said that in cases where the plaintiff was an unmarried young woman damages under the head of lost future earnings should be reduced to take into account the possibility that she will get married and drop out of employment, albeit temporarily, to have children. On the other hand, young women plaintiffs should, according to Lord Denning, also receive a sum under the head of loss of amenity for loss of the prospects of getting married and thus enjoying the economic support of a husband. Lord Denning's approach was challenged by Leonard J in *Hughes v McKeown*.[14] Leonard J's approach was to say that a woman who left her employment to have children would still be working, for she would be working in the home and her husband would be taking advantage of her work. Even though the husband would not be paying her in money but rather would be paying in kind, in terms of food, shelter, clothes and so on, it would be entirely wrong to treat the woman as not earning during those years. There should therefore be no deduction of the prospects of the interruption of employment by child-rearing. On the other hand, the loss of prospects of marriage head of damage should include only an amount for the non-pecuniary element of the loss—loss of the prospect of companion-ship and emotional support[15]—and not an amount for lost financial support from a husband.

In *Housecroft v Burnett*[16] the Court of Appeal endorsed the *Hughes* approach in general terms, but at the same time declared it to be compatible with *Harris* because of the distinction between the emotional and the financial aspects of marriage. But the question is whether any discount is made, and the Court of Appeal appears in *Housecroft* to endorse the view that a small discount would be in order where an amount for lost prospect of marriage has been included in the loss of amenity head. With respect, this cannot be right, for the loss of companionship damages that *Hughes* envisages are quite separate from the lost income damages If the court admits that the value of support from the husband during the years of child-rearing should be counted as roughly equivalent to the earning from employment the plaintiff would have received over the same period, there is no reason to deduct anything from the lost earnings damages. The *Hughes*

12 See eg *Cronin v Redbridge London Borough Council* (1987) Times, 20 May. The best approach in the case of children is not, as some suggest, to award a moderate conventional amount, but to assume, unless there is evidence to the contrary, that the plaintiff would have reached national average levels of income over a national average working life.
13 [1973] 1 Lloyd's Rep 445.
14 [1985] 3 All ER 284, [1985] 1 WLR 963.
15 This is something which, of course, men can claim for too—see *Oakley v Walker* (1977) 121 Sol Jo 619.
16 Above n 10.

approach is more consonant with modern notions of equality between the sexes and in so far as *Harris* is inconsistent with it, it should be overruled.

A word is necessary about the rather odd mechanics of the court's calculation of the lump sum to award for loss of future earnings. One might have imagined that courts would draw upon the expertise of actuaries in estimating life expectancies and taking into account the effect of interest rates. Instead, the courts have attempted to calculate loss of future earnings by working out how much per year the plaintiff will lose (the 'multiplicand') and then multiplying it by a number of years (the multiplier). The multiplier starts out as the number of years during which the plaintiff will experience the loss (that is, in many cases, the number of years until retirement) but it is then progressively reduced to take into account the 'vicissitudes' and the interest payments the plaintiff will receive if the lump sum is invested. Multipliers, it seems, rarely exceed 18 regardless of how young the victim is.

As a leading actuary has remarked:[17]

> 'From an actuarial perspective this choosing a "multiplier" is no more than a crude amateur approximation to the calculation of an annuity value using mortality and rates of interest as appropriate.'

But judges have usually excluded actuarial tables and advice from the court room, treating them as a form of crib that may be used to check answers arrived at by other means but no more.[18] This insistently anti-scientific and intuitive, one might even say romantic, attitude has come in for severe criticism by the Law Commission.[19] The Commission strongly advises that courts should allow into evidence at least the government actuary's official life expectancy tables (the 'Ogden' tables), which counsel, and indirectly the courts, have been relying on unofficially for years.

The lost years

One particular problem in the assessment of lost future income damages is the so-called lost years question. If the plaintiff's injuries mean that, probably, the plaintiff will die sooner than he or she otherwise would, can the plaintiff claim lost earnings for the years when, but for the accident he or she would be alive and working but now, because of the injuries, probably will be dead already? In 1962 the Court of Appeal said that no damages could be recovered for these 'lost years'.[20] The argument was that the plaintiff could not really say that he was making a loss because of the lost years because whereas it is true that he would have earned in those years,

---

17 Carroll 'Compensation: a UK actuarial view' (1994) 144 NLJ 507.
18 Per Edmund Davies LJ in *Mitchell v Mulholland (No 2)* [1972] 1 QB 65, 77.
19 Report no 224, above n 4.
20 *Oliver v Ashman* [1962] 2 QB 210.

it is also true that he will now have no outgoings for those years either. The key to understanding the lost years issue is simply that the dead have no living expenses. The trouble with the rule in *Oliver v Ashman* was that it had harsh results for the dependants of plaintiffs. Dependants would have received support during the lost years from the plaintiff. If no award is given they lose. There is no prospect either for the dependants to make a claim under the Fatal Accidents Act[1] because the victim would still for the time being be alive, and there is no claim under the Act if there has been an action between the victim and the defendant which has been won by the victim, settled out of court or run out of time, one of which reasons would almost certainly apply to the defendants. The House of Lords therefore overruled *Oliver* in *Pickett v British Rail Engineering.*[2] *Pickett* said that the plaintiff could recover loss of earnings for the lost years but the court would deduct from the claim an amount to represent the personal living expenses of the plaintiff, so leaving over an amount for the depend-ants. If the plaintiff has no dependants and no prospect of acquiring any, the lost years award should be zero. If the plaintiff is very young, so that, except in the case of child movie stars,[3] he or she has no dependants, the court also often awards nothing for the lost years[4] on the ground that any award would be too speculative. They mean that if the plaintiff is now unlikely to have any dependants because of the injuries sustained in the accident, it seems odd to give the plaintiff damages for the support of non-existent dependants for the years when the plaintiff will probably be already dead.

In order to prevent further complications[5] s 4 of the Administration of Justice Act 1982 restricted the right to sue for the lost years to living plaintiffs and, reversing the effect of *Gammell v Wilson*, said that the right to sue for the lost years would not survive the death of the plaintiff and devolve onto the plaintiff's heirs—unlike other parts of a negligence action.

Collateral benefits

Tort law is not the only system of compensation for personal injury or illness. As we saw in chapter 1[6] social security payments play an important role, somewhat larger than tort though of the same general magnitude in money terms, in compensating victims of accidents. There is also private first party insurance, that is insurance policies taken out by potential victims of accidents and illness to cover, for example, loss of earnings for periods when they are unable to work because of sickness or injury. In

1   See below.
2   [1980] AC 136.
3   See *Gammell v Wilson* [1982] AC 27.
4   *Croke v Wiseman* [1981] 3 All ER 852, *Connolly v Camden & Islington Area Health Authority* [1981] 3 All ER 250.
5   See *Gammell v Wilson* above n 3.
6   Above .

very high profile accident cases, such as the Zeebrugge ferry disaster and the King's Cross fire, there may even be charitable donations to the victims. How does the law deal with these benefits that flow to the plaintiff because of the accident? In particular, are they deducted from the plaintiff's claim?

In the case of social security benefits, the law was radically reformed in 1989. The position now[7] is that, in effect, specified social security benefits are deducted in full from any damages paid in respect of a maximum of the first five years after the accident or injury, but that the defendant has to pay the equivalent amount to the state. The mechanics are that damages are calculated without taking the specified social security payments into account at all, but instead of paying the full amount to the plaintiff, the defendant deducts the social security payments element and sends a cheque for that amount to the government. The defendant then sends another cheque to the plaintiff, plus a certificate saying how much the defendant paid to the government, for the remainder. Note that specified benefits payable beyond the five-year period are not deducted at all. Moreover, the payment of compensation, if before the end of the five-year period, itself brings the relevant period to an end, so that there can be no deduction in respect of future social security payments.

In theory, this scheme applies not just to damage awards but also to settlements, including structured settlements and payments into court. All people making compensation payments are under a duty to report the fact to the Department of Social Security. The plaintiff is under a similar duty if he or she has received any of the specified benefits. From this, one should be able to see that the main purpose of the recoupment provisions is, like that of the Child Support Act, to reduce government expenditure on social security.

The recoupment scheme applies to most of the major social security benefits (including income support, unemployment benefit and their successors, sickness benefit, statutory sick pay, family credit and all the disability, mobility and injury benefits). The scheme does not, however, apply to a small number of benefits, some of which, housing benefit for example, could amount to large sums.[8] It is not entirely clear what should happen to these benefits. Probably they should be deducted in full, since that was the direction in which decisions were moving for benefits not specified under the scheme that preceded the 1989 Act.[9]

The scheme also does not apply to compensation amounts below £2,500. In these cases, the old pre-1989 scheme applies, under which half the

---

7   Social Security Administration Act 1992, Pt IV.
8   Some writers point out that child benefit is not covered by the scheme, but this is unlikely to be of practical importance in many cases since child benefit is payable regardless of means on proof of parenthood. The cases in which the plaintiff has had more children as a result of the tort are very rare—but see *Thake v Maurice* [1986] QB 644, [1986] 1 All ER 497, [1986] 2 WLR 337, CA, *Udale v Bloomsbury Area Health Authority* [1983] 2 All ER 522, [1983] 1 WLR 1098, *McKay v Essex Area Health Authority* [1982] QB 1166, [1982] 2 All ER 771, [1982] 2 WLR 890, CA, *Allan v Greater Glasgow Health Board* (1993) 17 BMLR 135 Court of Session (Outer House). See below.
9   *Hodgson v Trapp* above, *Nabi v British Leyland* [1980] 1 WLR 529, *Westwood v Secretary of State for Employment* [1985] AC 20.

amount paid in the specified benefits was deductible for five years and thereafter the specified benefits were not deductible at all, but all non-specified benefits were deductible in full. The law could do without such immense complexity, especially for such small sums.

Finally, just in case anyone might have thought otherwise, the 1989 scheme does not apply where benefits are fully deductible anyway, for example in damages under the Fatal Accidents Act, Criminal Injuries Compensation Board payments and compensation payments ordered by the criminal courts.

Other collateral benefits are not subject to the same degree of statutory regulation. The questions are largely ones of common law. Payments under the plaintiff's own private insurance are, perhaps surprisingly, not deducted.[10] The nineteenth century judges who were the first to consider the problem were of the view that the plaintiff was entitled to the extra benefits of the insurance policy because he had paid for them by his payments of insurance premiums. Furthermore, the defendant should not, they thought, be allowed to escape paying damages just because the plaintiff had been careful and cautious.

The rule applies to occupational pensions that are triggered by the plaintiff's becoming incapacitated as well as straightforward insurance policies.[11] The House of Lords also decided that it did not matter whether the contributions to the pension were paid by the employee or directly by the employer. This must be right, despite criticisms from some quarters, because there is no real difference between that part of an employee's pay that comes in the form of cash and that which, as with pension contrib-utions, comes in deferred payments or in kind. The plaintiff has effectively bought insurance cover in the form of a pension with deferred payments from the employer. If private insurance is to be exempt from deduction, so should payments under such a pension. This view was confirmed by the House of Lords in *Smoker v London Fire and Civil Defence Authority*.[12] It is anomalous, however, that if the plaintiff receives sick pay under his contract of employment, the sums are deducted from his lost earnings (or rather his lost earnings consist of the difference between his normal pay and his reduced sick pay) and the position is the same even though the employer pays the employee out of the proceeds of an insurance policy taken out by the employer against the possibility of the employee's falling ill.[13] The distinctions being used here are very fine, perhaps too fine. First there is a distinction between a deferred payment triggered by the plaintiff's illness and an immediate payment triggered by the plaintiff's illness; and secondly, there is a distinction between insurance against the consequences of illness or injury to oneself and insurance against the consequences to oneself of injury and illness occurring to someone else.

The basic rule on first party insurance is nevertheless odd anyway, since it encourages people to take out first party insurance for situations where

10 *Bradburn v Great Western Rly* (1874) LR 10 Exch 1.
11 *Parry v Cleaver* [1970] AC 1.
12 [1991] 2 All ER 449.
13 *Hussain v New Taplow Mills* [1988] AC 514, *McCamley v Cammell Laird* [1990] 1 All ER 854.

the liability rule already encourages other people to take out third party insurance. This seems wasteful.

A similar rule applies to charitable donations to the plaintiff. They are not deducted. The justification this time is that the courts want to avoid discouraging such charitable giving, which, they fear would be the case if the rule were that donations were deductible. Donors would be put off because, in effect, their donations would be relieving the defendant's burden rather than the plaintiff's burden.[14]

Expenses

The plaintiff is entitled to claim for any expenses that arise as a result of the tort and which it is reasonable to incur. Both past and future expenses are claimable.

The most obvious type of expense incurred by the plaintiff is medical expenses in personal injury cases. The National Health Service takes care of the medical care itself and the cost of medication, so that the enormous claims possible in the USA for medical expenses do not usually appear in Britain. But there are costs that the NHS or local authority social services departments do not cover, for example travel costs to and from treatment centres, some forms of the adaptation of the plaintiff's house for use by someone with a disability[15] and Court of Protection fees for plaintiffs rendered mentally incapacitated.

On the other hand, if the plaintiff is completely incapacitated, the plaintiff may, either temporarily or permanently, become in effect resident in a hospital. If the hospital is maintained at public expense and the plaintiff saves on living expenses by being in hospital, s 5 of the Administration of Justice Act 1982 provides that the amounts saved by the plaintiff can be set off against the damages. If the plaintiff saves in a similar way by staying in a private nursing home, the same rule applies, but not by virtue of the statute but by virtue of *Lim Poh Choo v Camden & Islington Area Health Authority*.[16]

What happens if the plaintiff chooses non-NHS care? Although there are no private accident and emergency units, many private hospitals offer, for example, rehabilitation units. Can the plaintiff claim for the costs of private care even though there is a perfectly good NHS alternative? By a political compromise enacted as s 2(4) of the Law Reform (Personal Injuries) Act 1948 the answer is yes. The plaintiff is not to be treated as having acted unreasonably by reason only of having used private medical care when he or she could have used the NHS. But if the plaintiff does use the NHS, there will be no expenses and nothing claimable.

14 See A Burrows *Remedies for Torts and Breach of Contract* (London: Butterworths, 1987) p114.

15 Although any enhancement of the capital value of the house will be offset against the cost: *Roberts v Johnstone* [1989] QB 878.

16 Above.

Mitigation

The private health care cases raise the general question of the mitigation of loss. If the plaintiff acts unreasonably in dealing with the injury, whether or not the plaintiff's acts amount to contributory negligence or a break in the chain of causation,[17] the court may refuse to allow the plaintiff to recover the extra damage attributable to the plaintiff's own unreasonable act. If the plaintiff could get to his hospital appointments by ordinary taxi, but chooses to hire a Rolls Royce for the purpose, the extra cost of the Rolls Royce is not recoverable. But that is not to say that the plaintiff must use the cheapest available methods. Everything depends on what the court considers to be reasonable. To use a taxi when one could have used a bus will not be thought to be unreasonable, for example.

More serious examples of plaintiffs who refuse to take reasonable steps to keep their losses down not just in the sense of the cost of the expenses incurred by the plaintiff but instead the nature of the injury itself start to shade into remoteness issues. For example, if a plaintiff refuses medical treatment, so that the injuries become far more serious than they otherwise would be, the court may decide that the plaintiff has acted in an utterly unreasonable way, thus breaking the chain of causation. Although there is a case[18] which seems to imply that an ordinary unreasonableness test would apply, it seems better to stick to the more stringent remoteness test for this type of case, and to reserve the reasonableness test for cases about the immediate monetary cost of the expenses incurred by the plaintiff.

Expenses of others

One of the more controversial questions in the law of damages is whether claims can be made for the costs of care where relatives offer their services for nothing but in doing so incur costs themselves. The argument for allowing them to do so is that cost is not just immediate monetary cost, but includes opportunity cost, that is what had to be given up to do what was done. The argument against is that the plaintiff should only claim for losses that he himself has suffered. Losses incurred by others are (a) their business and (b) relational and therefore probably not recoverable.

The latest case to consider this issue is *Hunt v Severs*.[19] In *Hunt v Severs*, the plaintiff suffered severe injuries in an accident when she was a pillion passenger on a motor cycle driven by the defendant, who was her boyfriend. She was discharged from hospital and started to live with the defendant. The couple were married three years later. The plaintiff's injuries were so

---

17 See above ch 4.
18 *Selvanayagam v University of the West Indies* [1983] 1 WLR 585, PC. This case is also wrong to suggest that the burden of proof in mitigation cases is on the plaintiff. It is on the defendant. See *Steele v Robert George* [1942] AC 497.
19 [1994] 2 All ER 385, [1994] 2 WLR 602, [1994] 2 Lloyd's Rep 129.

serious that she had lost all chance of working and there was a chance that her condition would get worse.

At the trial, the defendant[20] admitted liability. The issue was that the plaintiff claimed £77,000 as the value of the care that the defendant himself had given and would give the plaintiff. The judge awarded the £77,000 and the defendant appealed, saying that the award amounted to saying that the defendant pays twice, once in the care itself and once in money.

The Court of Appeal dismissed the appeal, and the defendant appealed to the House of Lords. The House of Lords, however, found for the defendant.

Lord Bridge, however, began his judgment by reaffirming that in general, the plaintiff can recover damages for the costs to a third party of rendering free caring services:

> '[A] plaintiff who establishes a claim for damages for personal injury is entitled in English law to recover as part of those damages the reasonable value of services rendered to him gratuitously by a relative or friend in the provision of nursing care or domestic assistance of the kind rendered necessary by the injuries the plaintiff has suffered.'

But it is necessary to understand why the plaintiff may receive such damages:

> '[I]t is ... important to recognise that the underlying rationale of the English law, as all the cases before *Donnelly v Joyce* demonstrate, is to enable the voluntary carer to receive proper recompense for his or her services.'

Donnelly v Joyce[1] said instead that the rationale was that 'The loss is the plaintiff's loss' and that 'The question from what source the plaintiff's needs have been met' is not relevant. It is simply a matter of estimating the cost of the services rendered. Lord Bridge said of this point of view:

> 'I cannot accept that the question from what source that need has been met is irrelevant. If an injured plaintiff is treated in hospital as a private patient he is entitled to recover the cost of that treatment. But if he receives free treatment under the National Health Service, his need has been met without cost to him and he cannot claim the cost of the treatment from the tortfeasor. So it cannot, I think, be right to say that in all cases the plaintiff's loss is "for the purpose of damages ... the proper and reasonable cost of supplying his needs".'

20 Or rather, the defendant's insurance company. If it was not for the insistence of the insurance company, of course, such a case would never come to trial. The whole point of the action is really a dispute between the defendant and his insurance company rather than a dispute between the defendant and the plaintiff.

1 [1974] QB 454, [1973] 3 All ER 475.

But what of the argument that the carer's loss is relational and should not be recoverable? Lord Bridge cites the judgment of Megaw J in *Wattson v Port of London Authority*.[2] In that case, the plaintiff's wife gave up her work and consequently lost earnings in order to look after her injured husband. Megaw J held that the wife's loss was properly included in the husband's damages. The defendant argued that there had been no contract between husband and wife caring for the husband. Megaw J retorted:

> 'That is not how human beings work and it would, in my judgment—and I say this because I think it ought to be said—be a blot on the law if the law were to be such that a wife who in these circumstances had held her husband to make a contract to repay her should he recover damages for that amount; but if she behaves like an ordinary decent human being and does not put construction upon the act of that service, there is financial disadvantage to the plaintiff as a result.'

Although Lord Bridge does not say so explicitly, the clear implication here is that the argument against relational loss does not apply where people act out of a sense of social obligation or moral duty. The wife's caring for the husband is not a fully voluntary act in the sense that a commercial contract is. The closest analogy is relational nervous shock, where the court accepts that in certain close family relationships, psychiatric illness caused by injury to a loved one is not the outcome of some voluntary choice by the plaintiff but a natural and inevitable result of a natural and inevitable relationship.

Once it is established that the real purpose of allowing the plaintiff to recover the costs to the carer of supplying the care is to compensate the carer, according to Lord Bridge two consequences flow. The first is that if the carer is the defendant, the rule should not apply, for there is no reason to compensate the defendant with the defendant's own money. The reality of the situation that the money is in fact the insurance company's money should not be allowed to interfere with the principle that it is absurd to compensate the defendant for putting right that which he caused to go wrong in the first place.

The second is, contrary to *Donnelly v Joyce*, that any money recovered by the plaintiff under this head of damage should be handed over to the carer, and for that reason the sum involved should be regarded as held on trust by the plaintiff for the carer.

Wrongful conception

The next problem to deal with under the rubric of damages for the expenses the tort causes the plaintiff to incur is the problem of so-called 'wrongful

2   [1969] 1 Lloyd's Rep 95.

birth', that is the problems associated with the birth of children. The main question is whether parents can sue for the expense of bringing up unwanted children. But to understand the answer to that question one has to know the answers to two other questions: first, can children sue for harm sustained before they were born; and secondly, can children sue for being born with disabilities?

The first problem is regulated by statute.[3] The Congenital Disabilities (Civil Liability) Act 1976 says that if a child suffers injury before it is born, as long as it is eventually born alive it can sue those who caused the harm. If the injury was effectively caused before conception, for example by exposure to radiation, the Act provides in effect that if either of the parents knew of the risk, the chain of causation is broken.

The second problem concerns not injuries suffered by the unborn, but rather whether a child born with severe disabilities can sue if it can be shown that if the defendant doctors had informed the parents in time of the disabilities the parents would have had an abortion and the child would not have been born and would not have suffered. In *McKay v Essex Area Health Authority*[4] the Court of Appeal decided that for the child to recover damages for the pain and suffering of being alive at all was against public policy. Whatever the truth of the matter, the law should not be seen to endorse the idea that death can sometimes be better than life. In any case, *Rance v Mid-Downs Health Authority*[5] suggests that many of the abortions that the plaintiff's case in *McKay* envisages would be illegal.

But does any of this mean, for example, where the plaintiff's case is that, for example, the defendant doctors carried out a sterilisation operation so carelessly that she became pregnant again, that the plaintiff cannot recover for the pain and suffering of the birth itself and the costs of bringing up a child? The argument against recoverability in these cases is that (a) any harm caused to the baby can be covered by an action under the 1976 Act, (b) the plaintiffs' case depends on complaining that it would be better that the child had never been born so that (c) no useful purpose would be served by allowing the action. In addition, defendants argue that the birth of a child is a joyous event that should offset all the damages.

But in *Thake v Maurice*,[6] *Emeh v Kensington and Chelsea and West-minster Health Authority*[7] and *Gold v Haringey Health Authority*[8] the Court of Appeal rejected the arguments against liability in these 'wrongful conception' cases. Although there may be some discount to take into account the joys of the birth and life of a healthy child, the parents were entitled to

---

3   For children born before 23 July 1976, the common law still applies, but according to *Burton v Islington Health Authority* [1992] 3 All ER 833, [1992] 3 WLR 637, 10 BMLR 63 the common law was very much like the statute anyway.

4   [1982] QB 1166.

5   [1991] 1 All ER 801.

6   [1986] QB 644, [1986] 1 All ER 497, [1986] 2 WLR 337, CA, *Udale v Bloomsbury Area Health Authority* [1983] 2 All ER 522, [1983] 1 WLR 1098, *McKay v Essex Area Health Authority* [1982] QB 1166, [1982] 2 All ER 771, [1982] 2 WLR 890, CA, *Allan v Greater Glasgow Health Board* (1993) 17 BMLR 135 Court of Session (Outer House).

7   [1985] QB 1012.

8   [1988] QB 481.

compensation for the ruination of the family finances. Moreover, the pain and suffering of childbirth is not entirely offset by joy at a new birth and should be recoverable to some degree.[9]

Pain and suffering

Courts often award considerable amounts as compensation for 'pain and suffering'. There appears to be no general guidance about how they should set these amounts. All that is clear is that both past and future pain and suffering can be taken into account[10] and that any type of pain may qualify. Even some forms of purely mental anguish may qualify, for example that caused by the knowledge that the accident has shortened one's life expectancy.[11] Pain and suffering damages are supposed to reflect the subjective suffering of the plaintiff, so that if, for whatever reason, the plaintiff is unconscious or in a coma no pain and suffering damages are payable.[12] But it is impossible really to know how much another person is suffering and a degree of conventionality must be involved in setting amounts for pain and suffering. There was an interesting suggestion in the nineteenth century that the richer the plaintiff is the less the pain and suffering award should be, since rich people are in less need and have more available offsetting pleasures.[13] But the thought was squashed by Lord Morris in *West v Shephard*. Pain and suffering is not completely subjective.

Loss of amenity

One of the fundamental problems with the full compensation principle that English law follows is that often high income plaintiffs will receive higher damages than low income plaintiffs, even though the injury was the same. Loss of amenity damages attempt to redress the balance, although not by very much. The idea is to concentrate on the impact of the plaintiff's physical injuries on the plaintiff's capabilities and capacities for enjoyment of various aspects of life.[14] The capacities of people of different income levels to enjoy life are the same[15] so that, with a small amount of leeway to reflect different tastes and pursuits, the courts should make similar awards for similar injuries. Since loss of capacity is supposedly

9   *Thake* and *Allan* above n 6, but cf *Allen v Bloomsbury Health Authority* (1993) 13 BMLR 47, [1993] 1 All ER 651.
10   *West v Shephard* [1964] AC 326.
11   Administration of Justice Act 1982 s 1(1)(b). NB s 1(1)(a) abolished the old head of damage for loss of expectation of life itself.
12   *Wise v Kaye* [1962] 1 QB 638, *West v Shephard* [1964] AC 326.
13   *Phillips v London and South Western Rly Co* (1879) 5 CPD 280.
14   See eg *Cook v JL Kier* [1970] 1 WLR 774.
15   *Fletcher v Autocar* [1968] 2 QB 322.

objective, loss of amenity damages are still payable if the plaintiff is in a coma.[16] The damages represent 100% loss of amenity.[17]

The result is a kind of tariff system—so much for an eye, so much for losing the sense of smell, so much for no longer being able to run. The tariff can move, both in absolute terms and relatively, but movement is relatively slow. Since the awards are the same for people of different income levels, loss of amenity awards tend slightly to offset the inequality inherent in lost income awards. But the amounts involved are relatively low. In *Hunt v Severs*, for example, doctors described the plaintiff's injuries as 'the worst paraplegic case they had come across'. And yet loss of amenity damages and pain and suffering added together were set at £90,000—compared to more than £400,000 for future lost income.

Property damage

The basic rule for the measure of property damage is the same as that for personal injury—to restore the status quo ante as far as that is possible by money. The obvious measures are therefore that if an item of property has been destroyed completely the defendant must pay what it would take to obtain a similar item. If the item of property is productive machinery which has been damaged so that it no longer works, the obvious measure of damage is the cost of repair, including the cost of hiring a substitute in the interim. If the item of property is something that the plaintiff had for the purpose of selling, the measure of damage should be the fall in the item's market value.

The courts do not quite conform to these principles but they are close enough. Damages for complete destruction of the property are measured by the property's market value at the time of its destruction. This may not, of course, be the cost of replacing it as of the date of trial, but it is often close enough.[18] Costs of hire of a substitute may be recoverable as well as long as the costs are reasonable—but if hire charges are very much higher than the costs of buying a substitute, hiring the substitute may be adjudged unreasonable.[19] Lost profits are also recoverable if the plaintiff has been denied the use of an income generating asset, but, of course, such losses can only be reasonable for as long as it is reasonable not to have obtained a substitute.[20]

Damages for all types of damage to goods short of destruction have been fixed at the cost of reasonable repair.[21] Unreasonable repair would include over-elaborate or meticulous repairs for everyday items. Borderline cases include meticulous repair of objects of great sentimental value. If the costs

---

16 *West v Shephard* above n 10.
17 *Lim v Islington & Camden Health Authority* above.
18 See *Moss v Christchurch RDC* [1925] 2 KB 750 for a case where the two values differed sharply. The market value prevailed.
19 *Liesbosch v Edison, The Edison* [1933] AC 449. See above ch 6.
20 *The Edison* above n 19.
21 See *Dodd Properties v Canterbury City Council* [1980] 1 WLR 433; *The London Corpn* [1935] P 70.

of repair are, however, so great that they could not be recovered by selling the object even in its repaired state, the measure will be the reduction in the object's market value.[22] If, as is often the case[1] the object simply because it has been subject to repair, will never attain its previous market value, the plaintiff will be able to claim both the cost of repair and the final net diminution of value.

The only kind of property to which the diminution of market value seems to be the rule is land or buildings, although the plaintiff may be justified in using repair costs instead if the property is the plaintiff's home and there is no reason to expect the plaintiff to move.

In cases of the negligent valuation of property, *Hayes v James and Charles Dodd*[2] holds that if the transaction would still have taken place but on different terms, the disappointed buyer can only get the difference in value, not the cost of repairing the defect the valuer failed to find.[3]

Interest

Successful plaintiffs are entitled to interest on their awards. The rates of interest, however, tend to be very low and different rates apply to different sorts of damages. The table summarises the position.

Head of damage	Rate of interest	Starting date
Special pecuniary damages before trial	half special investment rate for money paid into court	accident
Future loss (pecuniary and non pecuniary)	none	none
Non-pecuniary loss before trial (personal injury cases)	2%	service of writ
Non-pecuniary loss before trial (non personal injury cases)	none	none

These differences are largely the result of historical accident and it is not worth even attempting a rationale.

22 *Darbishire v Warran* [1963] 1 WLR 1067. There may be an exception where the object is unique and does not have a conventional market value: *O'Grady v Westminster Scaffolding* [1962] 2 Lloyd's Rep 238.
1   See eg *Payton v Brooks* [1974] RTR 169.
2   [1990] 2 All ER 815.
3   *Banque Bruxelles Lambert v Eagle Star* (1995) Times, 21 February on the other hand suggests that where the transaction would not have taken place at all if the valuation had been correct, the plaintiff can recover all of the loss on the deal, including any fall in market value.

Other sources of compensation

Two non-tort but also non-social security sources of compensation for accident victims are worth mentioning.

The Motor Insurers Bureau

One of the larger problems of uncompensated loss through accidents is the problem of motor vehicle accidents in which the culprit either was (illegally) uninsured or drove off without being identified. To provide cover for these situations all the insurance companies involved in motor vehicle insurance are obliged to join the Motor Insurers' Bureau, technically a private company but in fact a joint creation of the insurance industry and government. The MIB has come to a series of contractually binding agreements with the government that it will step in and act as a kind of insurer of last resort to make sure that victims of traffic accidents find compensation when they have valid claims that they have been injured by the fault of someone who should have been compulsorily insured under the Road Traffic Acts.

Technically, no one apart from the government has any right that the MIB carry out its obligations. Victims of accidents are in the position of third party beneficiaries and have no direct rights. But in practice the MIB operates as if it had duties to victims and simply does not raise the point about privity of contract when victims sue it. The courts allow these fictions to pass with a wry smile.[4]

The present agreements (of 1972, 1977 and 1988) provide MIB cover for:

(1) *hit-and-run drivers*—the MIB acts as if it were the insurer of any hit-and-run driver. There are arbitration procedures if the MIB denies liability. Note, however, that the MIB accepts no responsibility if the evidence is that the driver deliberately drove at the victim.[5] *Gardner v Moore* is sometimes cited to contradict the contention that the MIB is not responsible for deliberate acts, but *Gardner* was not about a hit and run case but about a case in which the driver was known but was uninsured. The point of the case was whether the driver was under an obligation to insure himself against the effects of his doing intentional harm—for if the driver does not have to be compulsorily insured the case falls outside the remit of the MIB. It is in this context that Lord Hailsham said that the requirement to insure was a general one 'arising out of the use of his car'. But this remark does not apply to the Hit-and-Run MIB agreement which explicitly excludes liability for deliberately driving one's car at someone.

(2) *uninsured drivers*—where someone who ought to have been insured causes an accident the MIB again acts as if it were the driver's in-

---

4   See Lord Hailsham in *Gardner v Moore* [1984] AC 548.
5   Clause 1(1)(e) of the 2nd Agreement of 22 November 1972.

surer, and negotiates and litigates accordingly. The MIB's actions do not, of course, alter the driver's criminal law liability.

(3) *invalid insurance*—where the driver did have an insurance policy but it is invalid for some reason—there was misrepresentation for example. The MIB makes good any claim the victim would have had against the insurance company had the policy been valid. The liability of the driver, however, remains.

The Criminal Injuries Compensation Board

The Criminal Injuries Compensation scheme, administered by the Criminal Injuries Compensation Board, provides ex gratia compensation to the victims of violent crime. In 1992-93 alone it made nearly 37,000 awards worth £152m. It was introduced in 1964 under the Royal prerogative, but the courts decided that it was subject to judicial review and they hear a number of cases every year challenging the Board's decisions. In 1988 the CICB was put on a statutory basis and the scheme modified. But the 1988 statutory scheme has not been brought into operation. Instead, in 1993 and 1994, the Home Secretary purported to exercise his prerogative powers radically to modify the scheme by reducing the compensation available. The government failed however to get legislation through Parliament to repeal the 1988 Act and the Court of Appeal decided on a judicial review that the Home Secretary lacked the power to introduce any version of the scheme that differed radically from that authorised by Parliament in the 1988 Act.[6]

The restriction of the scheme to crimes of violence is an important one. Under the prerogative scheme, there is a case-by-case approach to deciding what counts as a crime of violence, largely unchecked by the High Court in judicial review.[7] The 1988 scheme, if it is ever implemented, provides a list of offences to which the scheme applies.

There does not have to have been a criminal conviction for the victim to be able to obtain compensation, but victims endanger their payments if they fail to report the crime or co-operate fully with the police. The statutory scheme also includes provisions, mainly based on CICB practice, to exclude victims with criminal records (including records picked up after the crime), to exclude many victims of domestic violence unless there has been a prosecution and the violent partner no longer lives in the same household as the victim, and to exclude most injuries caused accidentally in the course of the apprehension of an offender or the prevention of a crime.

The present scheme and the 1988 statutory scheme calculate the size of payments in a way very similar to that used in tort, except that there is a cap of 1.5 times average earnings on lost pay, social security and other collateral benefits are deducted in full, and there are stricter rules on

---

6   *R v Secretary of State for the Home Department, ex p Fire Brigades Union* [1995] 2 WLR 1. The House of Lords affirmed the Court of Appeal decision in April 1995.
7   *R v Criminal Injuries Compensation Board, ex p Warner* [1986] 2 All ER 478.

reimbursement of private medical bills. But otherwise the scheme is very much based on tort rules, including awards for pain and suffering, loss of amenity and other expenses. There is also a contributory negligence rule similar to that in operation in tort law.

The scheme that the Home Secretary proposed and which was struck down on judicial review was very different. In effect it set compensation at loss of amenity levels only. No pain and suffering awards would be given and no lost income award. There would be an explicit tariff based on objective physical criteria and no more. The courts in *ex p Fire Brigades Union* considered this scheme to be well beyond the scope of the statutory scheme and therefore the Home Secretary exceeded his powers in trying to impose it without Parliamentary approval.

What emerges from this juridico-political maelstrom remains to be seen.

The Criminal Injuries Compensation scheme is not to be confused with the powers of the criminal courts when sentencing offenders to require them to pay compensation to their victims. Section 35 of the Powers of Criminal Courts Act 1973 authorises such compensation orders in a wide variety of criminal cases. These orders tend not to be made, however, if the offender is sent to prison, which means that the more serious the offence, the less likely there is to be a compensation order. Victims of serious crimes are expected to use the Criminal Injuries Compensation scheme. Awards of smaller amounts of compensation are, however, very common in the magistrates' courts. The compensation order is separate from the sentence for the offence, but such orders are frequently used in combination with both fines and community sentences.

Death and the Fatal Accidents Act

The common law treated tort actions as personal to the plaintiff, with the result that the death of the plaintiff meant that any causes of action died as well. In addition the common law gave relatives no right to sue for the death of someone on whose income they depended for support. This was an extreme application of the principle that relational losses should not be recoverable.

The rule disallowing claims by relatives was relaxed by statute in the nineteenth century.[8] The rules are now laid down by the Fatal Accidents Act 1976. The rule that the action died with the person was relaxed by statute in the twentieth century, by the Law Reform (Miscellaneous Provisions) Act 1934.

Clearly there are problems of double counting damages if there is both an action by a dead plaintiff (through the plaintiff's estate) and an action by his or her relatives claiming for lost financial support. The deceased had only one income and could have spent it only once, either on him or herself or on the dependants. At the same time, there are problems of

8   See above ch 6.

possible under-compensation if the law restricts the rights of the estate or
the dependants too much.

Survivorship actions

Section 1(1) of the 1934 Act declares that all causes of action (except
defamation) both for and against a deceased person survive his death. The
action carries on in the hands of the estate largely as it would have done,
except that certain types of damages are not recoverable by the estate.
They include awards for pain and suffering and loss of amenity referring
to any period after the plaintiff's death,[9] lost income for any period after
the death (which subsumes any 'lost years' claim as well)[10] and exemplary
damages. Even where the death comes about because of the events that
are subject to the action, no account is taken of any gains or losses which
occur because of the death, except that the estate can lodge a claim for
funeral expenses. This means, for example, that life assurance counts as a
non-deductible collateral benefit.

The result of these rules is that it is often not very expensive accidentally
to kill somebody, at least as far as compensation to their estate is concerned,
especially if the person dies instantly. In that case, there will be no lost
income before death or other expenses, because the victim was dead before
any such losses could occur; there will be no pain and suffering award or
loss of amenity award, because none was suffered before death and none
is recoverable for any later period; and no lost income for the future is
payable because of s 1(2)(a). Only funeral expenses are clearly payable in
such a case. In contrast, causing paralysis or even putting the victim into
a coma (for which 100% loss of amenity is payable though not pain and
suffering) can produce damage awards of many hundreds of thousands of
pounds.

Dependency claims under the Fatal Accidents Act

Dependants claiming under the Fatal Accidents Act are claiming not on
behalf of the estate but on their own behalf. What they are claiming is in
effect economic loss—they are claiming the lost financial support that they
derived from the deceased. Note that apart from the award for bereavement[11] economic loss is all that dependants may claim. The Fatal Accidents
Act does not allow dependants to claim for pain and suffering. Note also

---

9   Pain and mental agony in the last few moments before death are, astonishingly, not
    recoverable since they are counted as part of the death itself—for which damages are not
    payable: *Hicks v Chief Constable of South Yorkshire Police* [1992] 2 All ER 65.
10 Section 1(2)(a). This restriction was introduced by the Administration of Justice Act 1982
    in order to avoid double compensation as a result of the lost years rule of *Pickett v British
    Rail Engineering* [1980] AC 136.
11 See above ch 6.

that there is no Non-Fatal Accidents Act. If dependants derive income from a living plaintiff, it is to the living plaintiff, rather than to the courts, that they must turn for their support. This means that if the deceased before he died obtained judgment from the defendants or settled his action, the relatives have no Fatal Accidents Act claim.[12]

To obtain compensation under the Act, a relative of the deceased has to prove four things: that the death was caused by the 'wrongful act, neglect or default' of the defendant; that the deceased would have had a valid claim against the defendant had the plaintiff survived; that the relative is a 'legal' dependant according to the Act; and that the relative was a 'factual' dependant of the deceased.

The first two conditions are, in short, whether the deceased had a valid claim in tort against the defendant. A claim under the Consumer Protection Act is deemed to be a claim based on the 'wrongful act' of the defendant.[13] If not, the relatives have no claim either. If the defendant could have raised a contributory negligence defence against the deceased, the same defence can be raised against the relatives and their damages reduced accordingly.[14]

The third condition is fulfilled if the relative in question can bring him or herself within the list of relationships listed in the Act itself. The list has changed dramatically over the last 150 years to reflect social and attitudinal change. For example the law now recognises not only spouses, children, step-children, parents, grandchildren, grandparents, aunts and uncles and siblings, but also ex-spouses, illegitimate children and the 'cohabitee' —someone who has been living with the deceased in the same household 'as husband or wife' for at least two years before the death and was still living with the deceased at the time of death. Note that if married couples separate or divorce, they still count as legal dependants, but if cohabitees split up, they do not count. Note also that the phrase 'as husband or wife' will probably rule out homosexual couples.

The fourth condition is that the relative has to prove that he or she really was financially dependent on the deceased. If there was no financial support (as often in the case of parents to their middle-aged children for example) there is no action. Lost business opportunities which would have arisen because the relatives worked together are not the same as lost support and, as pure economic loss, are not recoverable.[15] Purely speculative claims about the degree to which children may have supported their parents in later life are rightly treated with scepticism, but where there is a reasonable prospect of support materialising in the near future, a claim may be admitted.[16]

12　See *Pickett v British Rail Engineering* above n 10.
13　CPA 1987 s 6(1)(a).
14　1976 Act s 5. Although the Act does not say so, if the death was partly caused by the fault of a dependant, the damages payable to that dependant are reduced, but not those to innocent relatives: *Mulholland v McCrea* [1961] NI 135, *Dodds v Dodds* [1978] QB 543.
15　*Burgess v Florence Nightingale Hospital* [1955] 1 QB 349.
16　*Taff Vale Ry v Jenkins* [1913] AC 1—16-year-old girl's reasonable prospect of supporting parents. Although note that the award was by a jury.

Calculating the damages

To keep matters straightforward, the deceased's personal representatives are allowed to sue on behalf of all the dependants, with the proceeds being shared out later. But if the personal representatives do not begin an action within six months of the death, individual dependants may sue on their own behalf. Each dependant is entitled to have his or her loss calculated individually, although in practice the court often calculates a global amount that is then divided up between the qualifying dependants

The same lump sum method is used in the damage award as in ordinary damages. Each dependant is entitled to the lost support that they would have expected over their lifetime. The length of the lost dependency of each qualifying relative is estimated (children usually only to the end of expected full-time education—although this is often unrealistically low) and spouses to the end of their lives. Lost dependency until trial is a fairly straightforward calculation,[17] although strictly any amounts should be discounted for the likelihood that the deceased would have died anyway or would have stopped supporting the relative for some other reason. Lost future support is more difficult, since there are large numbers of imponderables, such as exactly how much the deceased would have earned over the relevant period, how much the deceased would have spent on his or her own personal expenses, and how much would have been paid out in support. If the support came in kind (eg housework) the calculation of the loss in money terms is even more difficult, although still perfectly legitimate[18]. The courts tend to assume that present trends will continue unless there is proof to the contrary. They work out an amount for present levels of support per year and multiply it by the expected number of years support, with reductions in the multiplier for the usual vicissitudes point and the advantage of having a lump sum. This is a crude method, but no method can be entirely satisfactory.

In estimating the number of years' support, the courts no longer base the lost support for the widow on guesses about her chances of remarriage, since the judges thought the exercise embarrassing and others thought it offensive. Nevertheless, the courts have to do something of the sort indirectly if there are children, for a new husband for the widow may take on some of the financial support of the children.

By s 3(4) of the 1976 Act (as amended in 1982) all benefits accruing to the dependant as a result of the death either through the estate or otherwise are disregarded. All life assurance payments and so on to the dependants are disregarded and are not deducted. Benefits in kind and benefits which appear in the form of better care by relatives compared to the care supplied by the deceased parent are included within the rule.[19]

---

17 See *Cookson v Knowles* [1979] AC 556.
18 Eg *Hay v Hughes* [1975] QB 790.
19 *Stanley v Sadique* [1991] 1 All ER 529, but cf *Watson v Willmott* [1991] 1 QB 140.

Contribution

If a number of people are or would be liable for the same loss, the plaintiff does not have to sue them all but can sue whichever of them he wants. The plaintiff is entitled to judgment for the whole loss against any of the defendants. It is not a defence to a tort action that someone else is just as liable as you are (although, of course, it is a defence that someone else's wrongdoing broke the chain of causation so that you are not liable in the first place). The plaintiff is, however, only allowed to enforce judgment against the various defendants to the value of the loss. The plaintiff may not recover more than the total loss from the defendants added together.[20]

This system of 'joint and several liability', the purpose of which is to ensure that the plaintiff has the maximum chance of recovering the damages in full[1] has been modified by statute to give defendants rights against other people who may be liable, so that the others are forced to share in the burden of paying the damages. A defendant against whom the court has awarded damages is allowed to bring an action against anyone else 'liable in respect of the same damage' to recover a 'contribution' from them.[2] The amount of the contribution is set by the court according to what the court finds to be 'just and equitable having regard to that person's responsibility for the damage in question'.[3]

The effect of the system of contribution is that the plaintiff still has the maximum chance of recovering the damages in full, for the risk of not being able to find the other people who are liable falls on the defendant not on the plaintiff, but that the burden placed on each defendant does not reflect merely the whim of the plaintiff.

The 1978 Act makes it clear that contribution can be claimed not just from other tortfeasors but also from those in breach of other civil obligations, such as contracts and trusts, as long as they have caused the same damage.

The basis of apportionment is the same as that under contributory negligence.[4] It is a mixture of causation and blameworthiness. Where, however, the damages would have been set at an amount less than the full amount because of contributory negligence, statutory limits or restrictions or a pre-accident agreement with the plaintiff, the court may not require a defendant to contribute more than he could have been obliged to pay in

---

20 There is a technical distinction between 'joint' tortfeasors, where people worked together on a common enterprise to commit the tort or where one person authorised another to commit a tort (including vicarious liability) and 'concurrent and several' tortfeasors where people acted independently to cause the same damage. The only practical difference this distinction now makes is that if the plaintiff 'releases' (ie agrees not to sue) a joint tortfeasor the other joint tortfeasors are released as well whereas a release of one concurrent and several tortfeasor leaves the position of the others unchanged. See eg *Cutler v McPhail* [1962] 2 All ER 474.

1 See Howarth 'My Brother's Keeper' [1994] Legal Studies 88 for suggestions for reform in some cases.

2 Civil Liability (Contribution) Act 1978 s 1(1).

3 Section 2(1).

4 See ch 15.

ordinary damages.[5] Where there is contributory negligence, the contributory negligence is dealt with first.[6] This means that the total amount of the damages is reduced first and then apportionment for the purposes of the Contribution Act is carried out on the basis of the reduced sum. The court is not permitted to say 'they were all equally to blame' and then divide the damages up into equal parts, including a 'part' for the defendant's contributory negligence.[7]

Defendants who settle, as long as the claim against them would amount to a valid legal claim if the facts were proved, retain their right to contribution.[8] Where there are legal doubts, however, the claim to contribution may not be valid, and the case may end up in court not because plaintiff and defendant disagree about liability but because the defendants disagree about the law.

Contribution should not be confused with indemnity, which is a contractual claim right that someone else pay for all or part of your damages. Third party insurance is a form of indemnity. Problems have arisen out of claims that certain types of contract contain implied terms that one party indemnify the other. Most controversially of all, in *Lister v Romford Ice*[9] the House of Lords decided that contracts of employment contained implied terms to the effect that if the employee committed a tort for which the employer is vicariously liable,[10] the employee will pay the employer that amount of the damages. Employers, or rather their insurance companies, do not insist on their rights, however, fearing an industrial relations disaster if they did so.

5   Section 2(3).
6   *Fitzgerald v Lane* [1989] AC 328.
7   Ibid.
8   Section 1(4).
9   [1957] AC 555.
10 See ch 14 below.

Chapter 14

Vicarious liability

The liability of an employer for the tort of an employee regardless of whether the employer has been at fault in any way itself is an established part of English law,[1] much more firmly established than it is, for example, in German law.[2] The justification for making employers so liable is, however, not as obvious as it might seem. Employers do not have physical control over their employees. Employees are not slaves. Furthermore, employers rarely ask or require employees to act negligently or in some other tortious way so that employees are rarely 'authorised' to commit torts in any ordinary meaning of the word. What we are here considering is the liability of employers for torts that their employees committed without asking them.

One explanation of vicarious liability is that it follows from the 'benefit and burden' principle. Employers take the benefit of the employees' work, so that they should take the burden of the wrongs committed by those employees. But if the employee is being paid, why should the employer bear any extra burden?

A related explanation is that the damages that arise in tort cases should count as a cost of the defendant's business. But if so, why require that the employee has committed a tort in the first place? Why not have strict liability for all the acts of one's employees regardless of whether the employee was at fault?

Similarly the argument that the employer is in a better position to know or at least to find out the overall costs of accidents associated with the business proves too much, for, again, it implies liability without fault for all the harmful consequences of the business, not just the ones that result from torts by the employees.

---

1   See *Staveley Iron and Chemical Co v Jones* [1956] AC 627, *ICI v Shatwell* [1965] AC 656.
2   See Markesinis *German Law Of Torts* ch 3. German law did not adopt a full vicarious liability doctrine in the way that English and French law did (for French law see Code Civile art 1384 'Les maîtres et les commettants [sont responsables] du dommage causé par leurs domestiques et préposés dans les fonctions auxquelles ils les ont employés'), but has relied on a mixture of presumptions about negligence in the selection and training of employees and various contractual devices to arrive at approximately the same results.

Another justification is that the employer is in a better position than anyone else to encourage employees to be safe. Vicarious liability allegedly provides an incentive where tort law by itself would not do so. The argument is that employees are often too poor to pay damages themselves and so do not bother to worry about the threat of tort actions too much. All this is possible, but it is not entirely clear either that employees would be little deterred by the threat of tort actions if employers did not have to pick up the bill, or that well-insured employers will be so much more deterred than employees.

A better version of this argument[3] is that vicarious liability gives the employer an incentive to discover which employees are likely to cause harm to others so that the employer can control them and, if necessary, sack them. Vicarious liability thus raises the incentives for employees to be safe, because it makes their jobs depend in part on being safe, and it reduces the overall number of accidents because it tends to remove dangerous people from jobs where they do harm.

Finally, there are two arguments that do not depend on incentive effects of any kind. The first is that it is a rule of honour that social superiors should take the blame for whatever goes wrong in the organisations and households run by those superiors. Thus the old name for the rule that employers should pay for the torts of their employees (or, as it would have been phrased at the time, why masters should pay for the torts of servants) was *respondeat superior.* A similar principle used to apply to cabinet ministers, who used to be expected to take the rap for the mistakes of their civil servants and would resign. As a principle, it probably sounds very out-of-date now. And it is difficult to see large companies as the 'social superiors' of anyone. But it may have resonances yet in the case law.

The other reason is simply a deep pocket argument. Employers are better off than employees and more likely to have liability insurance. They are therefore in a better position to pay compensation. This is true, but cannot explain by itself why the law should pick on the particular employer, as opposed to the richest employer in town, or the government.

Perhaps the honest position is to say that there is no single argument that justifies vicarious liability in its present form, but that it is well entrenched that its removal would be strongly resisted, both by potential victims of accidents and by employees.

As for the present law, figure 1 (page 634) gives a summary. Assuming that the employer has not committed a tort personally (for example in the selection of the employee) and that someone for whom the employer might be alleged to be responsible has committed a tort of some kind, the first question is whether the person committing the tort was an employee of the employer. If the answer is yes, we go on to ask whether the employee committed the tort in the course of employment. If the answer to that question is yes, the employer is liable. If the answer to the question about the tortfeasor's status as an employee was no, assuming that there was some kind of contractual relationship between the tortfeasor and the

---

3   See Denning LJ in *Cassidy v Ministry of Health* [1951] 2 KB 343.

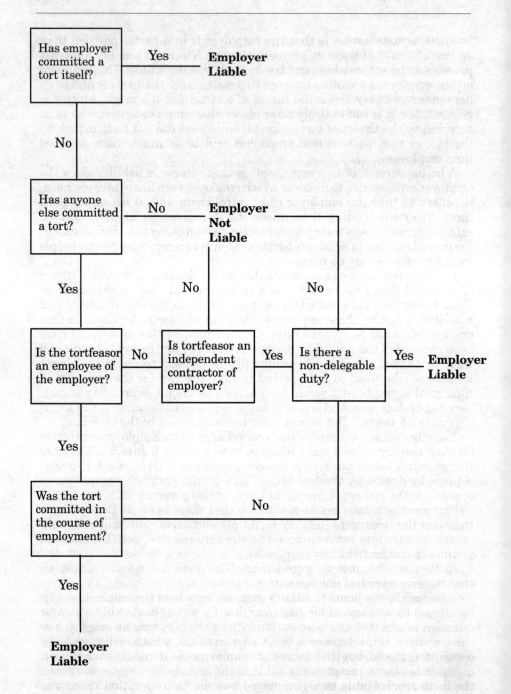

Figure 1 - Vicarious liability flow chart

employer, we then ask whether the situation involved 'non-delegable' duties of the employer. If it does, the employer may still be liable, but if not, not. In addition, if the tort was committed by an employee but not in the course of employment, the employer may still be liable if the situation involved a non-delegable duty.

Let us look at each of the questions in turn.

Has the employer committed a tort itself?

If the employer is a company, which can only act through agents, the question of the employer's committing a tort personally cannot arise in this form. But the same results usually flow from characterising the obligations considered here as non-delegable duties.

Employers are under various common law duties to their employees[4] the breach of which may result in injury to other employees. These duties include the duty to provide a safe system of work, safe fellow employees, a safe place of work and a safe and effectively supervised system of work.[5] In these actions by the injured employees against a human employer, no question of vicarious liability need arise. The employer is liable directly for his or her own default.

Equally, the employer can be liable to non-employees, that is to the rest of the world, for carelessly choosing someone incompetent to do the work, or not training them properly or not supervising them properly. It does not matter whether the person chosen worked as an employee or as an independent contractor if the employer was negligent in the first place in choosing that person.

Has someone else committed a tort?

If the employer has not committed a tort, the question then becomes whether the employer is liable vicariously for someone else's tort. But note that someone else actually has to have committed a tort for which the employer can be held responsible. This may seem obvious but it is often forgotten in the rush to consider more difficult questions such as the meaning of 'course of employment'.

The important point to note is that the vicarious responsibility of the employer for the tort of an employee may be strict, in the sense that the employer cannot escape responsibility by showing that it could not have foreseen the employee's tort or by showing that it could not reasonably have prevented it, but that does not diminish the need to show that someone has committed a recognised tort. If the tort the employee is accused of requires proof of fault, then there must be fault on the part of the employee

4   See above.
5   Ibid.

before the employer can be vicariously liable. If the employee could escape liability by proving a defence, the employer escapes too.

Is the tortfeasor an employee of the employer?

If there has been a tort by someone else, the next question is whether the tortfeasor is an employee of the employer. There are two questions within the main question: is the tortfeasor an employee as opposed to an independent contractor? and, is the employee this employer's employee as opposed to some other employer's employee?

The law about who is an employee as opposed to an independent contractor (or 'self-employed') has been remarkably confused until very recently. One reason is that there are so many disparate reasons why the question is asked. Tort law is perhaps one of the least important reasons why it matters who is an employee. Other reasons include employment rights (eg one has no right not to be unfairly dismissed unless one is an employee), taxation (the taxation of employees and the self-employed is very different) and social security (employee status changes both contributions and benefits). Who should count as an employee really ought to vary depending on the purpose for which the question is asked.[6] But the English courts have insisted that the test should be the same regardless of the context, and cases about social security law and unfair dismissal law are cited freely and without embarrassment in tort cases without regard to the importance of the questions of what social security and tax law are trying to achieve and whom unfair dismissal law is trying to protect. For example, a case that is almost invariably cited in tort books on the question of who counts as an employee for the purposes of vicarious liability is *Ready Mixed Concrete v Minister of Pensions*.[7] But this is a case about national insurance contributions. The purposes of national insurance and tax law are not the same as the purposes of tort law.

Another problem is that the underlying social reality—what goes on in factories and offices—keeps changing. The view of the employment (or 'master-servant') relationship in, say *Priestley v Fowler*,[8] is one of a household, in which domestic servants carry out mundane tasks in the house and on the estate for a master. In domestic service, employment is as much a relationship of status as of contract. Admittedly at that time, millions of people were indeed domestic servants, but already there were also millions working in factories and mines. Moreover, there were, and are, very different types of factory work. The job of the machine minder and the job of the toolmaker were different in almost every respect—in degree of autonomy and of supervision, method of payment and physical conditions of work.

---

6   This is the position in US federal law. *United States v Silk* 331 US 704 (1946). There is some hint of a possibility of future change in England in *Lane v Shire Roofing* (1995) Times, 22 February.

7   [1968] 2 QB 497.

8   (1837) 3 M & W 1.

In the mid twentieth century, there was a trend towards the creation of very large bureaucracies. This brought into organisations people who had always thought of themselves as independent professionals. In Britain, the central example was the creation of the National Health Service. As a consequence thousands of consultants found that they were now employees of a government service. But because of their different histories and statuses, to say that an NHS consultant is an 'employee' is very different from saying that a foundry labourer is an 'employee'.

More recently, there has been a counter-trend, towards contracting-out and reducing businesses to their core functions, making more and more people 'freelance', 'self-employed' and 'consultants' as opposed to employees. But in many cases the same people are still doing the same jobs—except that they are paid in a different way and their jobs are less secure.

The law nearly always fails to keep up completely with these social changes, and the concepts it uses have sometimes been appropriate to what people were doing 20 to 50 years earlier. Furthermore, the views of judges who seemed progressive at the time can be out of date now, but also tests for who counts as an employee that once seemed puzzling can make excellent sense years later.

For example, the case *Yewens v Noakes*[9] is often cited as a case in which the test for who should count as an employee was about 'control'—in the words of Bramwell LJ, a person was a servant, or employee, if he was 'subject to the command of the master as to the manner in which he shall do his work.' But, as the judgment of Baggallay LJ makes clear, the test applied in this case (which, incidentally was a tax case—there would have been a difference in property tax if the person concerned had been a servant) was equally one of social status, for as Baggallay LJ said, the person concerned could not be a 'servant' because, from his job as a senior clerk, he was 'almost a gentleman'.

On the other hand, Lord Denning's favourite test in the 1950s[10] was whether the person is employed 'as part of the business' and whether the person's work 'is done as an integral part of the business' as opposed to independent contractors whose work 'although done for the business, is not integrated into it but is only accessory to it'. This test tended to be attacked as too vague.[11] But beginning in cases of obviously non-standard types of employment relationship, such as the part-time and casual market research interviewers in *Market Investigations v Minister of Social Security*[12] it came back in the form of the question 'Is the person in business on his own account?', that is, when looking at the situation in the round, are we looking at one integrated organisation or two separate businesses? This test is clearly better suited to the modern era of contracted-out freelances and so-called micro-businesses than the 'control test' or any version of it.

---

9   (1880) 6 QBD 530.
10 *Cassidy v Ministry of Health* above n 3, *Stevenson Jordan and Harrison v MacDonald and Evans* [1952] 1 TLR 101.
11 See eg *Ready Mixed Concrete* above n 7.
12 [1969] 2 QB 173.

Fortunately, the 'business on his own account' test has now established itself firmly, first in the Privy Council in a worker's compensation case concerning a skilled but casually employed building worker, *Lee Ting Sang v Chung Chi-Keung*[13] and now in the English Court of Appeal in the income tax case *Hall (Inspector of Taxes) v Lorimer*.[14] *Hall v Lorimer* is especially significant since a major part of the Revenue's case was that the taxpayer, a freelance television mixer and editor, was an employee because the television companies he worked for told him where, when and for how long to work, and he was therefore subject to their control. The Court of Appeal dismissed the argument almost without comment. The Court, furthermore, did not cite the usually ubiquitous *Ready Mixed Concrete* case (which gave priority to control over all the other tests) at all, although it was cited in argument. It may be that *Hall v Lorimer* finally marks the end of the control test for who counts as an employee. For the moment, however, control remains just one factor among many.[14a]

How then do we tell whether the employee is 'in business on his own account'? The courts have identified a number of relevant factors, none of which is decisive. As Mummery J said in *Hall v Lorimer* in the court below:[15]

'In order to decide whether a person carries on business on his own account it is necessary to consider many different aspects of that person's work activity. This is not a mechanical exercise of running through items on a check list to see whether they are present in, or absent from, a given situation. The object of the exercise is to paint a picture from the accumulation of detail. The overall effect can only be appreciated by standing back from the detailed picture which has been painted, by viewing it from a distance and by making an informed, considered, qualitative appreciation of the whole. It is a matter of evaluation of the overall effect of the detail, which is not necessarily the same as the sum total of the individual details. Not all details are of equal weight or importance in any given situation. The details may also vary in importance from one situation to another.'

But the relevant factors include, on the side of tending to show that the person was not an employee, that the person provides his or her own equipment, hires helpers, takes a financial risk (including the risk of bad debts and not finding enough work[16]), has responsibility for investment and management decisions, has an opportunity of profiting from sound management,[17] charges different amounts for different jobs, invoices the employer rather than is paid regularly, sends substitutes to do the work, spends a large amount on the expenses of the work, and is not dependent

---

13 [1990] 2 AC 374, [1990] 2 WLR 1173, PC.
14 [1994] 1 All ER 250, [1994] 1 WLR 209, [1994] STC 23, [1994] ICR 218, [1994] IRLR 171.
14a Another approach is that of *Lane v Shire Roofing* (above n 6) where the Court of Appeal
    said that the control test applied only to unskilled workers.
15 [1992] STC 599 at 612.
16 *Hall v Lorimer* above n 14.
17 Cooke J in *Market Investigations*.

on one or very few clients.[18] On the side of showing that the person was an employee, the factors or 'indicia' include: that the person is engaged to work full time during specified hours for a regular salary, that the employer has the first call on the person's services, and that the person needs the consent of the employer to work for someone else.[19]

The degree of skill and judgment needed for the job is largely neutral since, as Nolan LJ put it in *Hall v Lorimer*, 'A brain surgeon may very well be an employee. A window cleaner is commonly self- employed.' Casual work, and moving from one employer to another on short-term contracts is consistent both with employee and with independent contractor status.[20] The fact that the person supplies labour only services, and not some tangible product, is irrelevant.[1] Barristers, Nolan LJ seemed anxious to point out in *Hall v Lorimer*, were not employees but had no tangible product. Further– more, *Hall v Lorimer* shows that it is not fatal to independent contractor status not to have a place of work other than an office at home. Finally, what the people themselves say that they are is relevant, but, because of the tax implications, never decisive.[2]

Note, however, that at the end of his judgment, Nolan LJ expressed the view that even the 'business on his own account' test was too restrictive. He said:

> '[T]he question whether the individual is in business on his own account, though often helpful, may be of little assistance in the case of one carrying on a profession or vocation. A self-employed author working from home or an actor or a singer may earn his living without any of the normal trappings of a business ... The extent to which the individual is dependent on or independent of a particular paymaster for the financial exploitation of his talents may well be significant.'

Note the relevant differences, therefore, between a casual skilled building worker, who is an employee,[3] and a television technician, who is not an employee[4] are that the television technician is paid much more, keeps proper accounts and gives extended credit to customers. Although a factor not mentioned explicitly, notice also that the television mixer probably had more direct contact with the people in charge of the project than would a casual building worker.

Although the law is becoming clearer, the question remains whether it is right for the purposes of vicarious liability. Much depends on what the

---

18 *Hall v Lorimer* above n 14.
19 Pennycuick V-C in *Fall (Inspector of Taxes) v Hitchen* [1973] 1 All ER 368, [1973] 1 WLR 286.
20 *Lee Ting Sang v Chung Chi-Keung* above n 13.
1   *Hall v Lorimer* above n 14.
2   *Ferguson v Dawson* [1976] 1 WLR 1213, *Massey v Crown Life* [1978] 2 All ER 576, [1978] ICR 590, *Young & Woods v West* [1980] IRLR 201, *Warner Holidays v Secretary of State* [1983] ICR 440.
3   *Lee Ting Sang v Chung Chi-Keung* above n 13.
4   *Hall v Lorimer* above n 14.

justification for vicarious liability is in the first place. If it is merely the deep pocket of the employer, for example, it is difficult to see why there should be more than minimal restrictions on who counts as an employee, if any restrictions at all. If the justification is the responsibility of social superiors for those below them, there is no better test than Sir Richard Baggallay's—was the person (almost) a gentleman or not? But if the justification is, as hinted above, that vicarious liability enlists employers in the task of identifying employees who are relatively unsafe and depriving them of opportunities to cause harm, either by supervising them more closely or by sacking them, is the 'business on his own account' test the right test? The answer may be a qualified yes.

To be able to make accurate judgments about whether a person is particularly safe or unsafe in their job, one has to have extensive information about that person. Sacking or refusing to hire someone on safety grounds when on the whole they are not unsafe is neither just nor efficient. An employer will not have such information about someone who works only for short periods for the employer and who works for many other employers. The record-keeping that employers would need to do to get an accurate picture of such employees would be prohibitive in itself. To the extent, therefore that the 'business on his own account' test requires extended contact between the employer and alleged employee, it is the right test. The emphasis on accounting practice is also interesting since it forms part of record-keeping. Financial records, however, are not necessarily the right records to concentrate on, and the relevance of the method of billing is difficult to see from the tort point of view.

One might also question the treatment of casual workers. Record keeping is even more of a problem for employers using large numbers of casual building workers than it is for employers using television editors. The treatment of casual workers as employees for the purposes of vicarious liability, whatever its merits for the purposes of employment protection, workers' compensation or tax, is therefore probably not wholly justified, unless one is willing to resort to the social status argument. But the issue would probably turn out to be a purely technical one for no doubt if there was no longer vicarious liability for the torts of casual workers, the categories of non-delegable duties would expand accordingly.

The second question under the heading of whether the tortfeasor was the employee of the employer is the question of whose employee the tortfeasor was. Normally, there is no problem here, since most people have only one job and if they have more than one it is usually obvious which one they were doing at the time of the accident. The difficulties come when one employer 'lends' an employee to another. In *Mersey Docks and Harbour Board v Coggins and Griffiths Ltd*[5] the Harbour Board hired out a mobile crane, with an employee to work it, to a firm of stevedores. The contract between the Board and the stevedores said that the employee was for the

5   [1947] AC 1.

time being to become an employee of the stevedores. Because of the employee's negligence there was an accident which injured the plaintiff. The question was which of the two employers should be vicariously liable? Despite the agreement, the court held that the Harbour Board was still the employer. Here the control test still holds sway, but factors such as the duration of the temporary posting and, crucially, who has the power to dismiss are also relevant. The burden on the party arguing that the responsibility should be shifted from the original employer is a heavy one.[6]

In the light of the changes happening in the test of who is an employee at all, it is perhaps surprising that no similar reappraisal has occurred for the question of whose employee the tortfeasor is. The reason is probably that since there is no doubt in such cases that the tortfeasor is an employee, the 'business on his own account' test cannot apply. But certainly a version of the 'integration' test is possible and perhaps is lurking in the background of the cases. The heavy burden on the party alleging that there has been a transfer is perhaps an echo of the idea that the employer with the most information or the best access to information should bear the risk, and the emphasis on the power to dismiss is an echo of the idea that the employer is responsible in vicarious liability because of its power to choose its employees. Furthermore, the courts do not use *Coggins and Griffith* to help decide whether an employer has transferred its employers' liability responsibilities to another employer. In such cases, the contract of employment is what governs liability and unless there is evidence that the 'lent' employee agreed to a variation in that contract, all responsibilities remain with the original employer.[7]

Was the tort committed in the course of employment?

This is the most difficult of the questions to answer in any particular case, although in terms of a general formula the law could not be easier to state:

> '[A] master ... is liable even for acts which he has not authorised, provided they are so connected with acts which he has authorised that they may rightly be regarded as modes — although improper modes — of doing them. In other words, a master is responsible not merely for what he authorises his servants to do, but also for the way in which he does it ... On the other hand, if the unauthorised and wrongful act of the servant is not so connected with the authorised act as to be a mode of doing it, but is an independent act, the master is not responsible: for in such a case the servant is

6 *Bhoomidas v Port of Singapore Authority* [1978] 1 All ER 956 (entire and absolute control of the employee has to be transferred). See *Gibb v United Steel* [1957] 1 WLR 668.
7 *Morris v Breaveglen Ltd (t/a Anzac Construction Co)* [1993] ICR 766, [1993] IRLR 350. For other contractual problems with lending an employee see the contrasting cases, *Phillips v Hyland* [1987] 1 WLR 659 and *Thompson v T Lohan* [1987] 1 WLR 649.

not acting in the course of his employment but has gone outside of it.'[8]

The problem is how to apply this test. The difference between an unauthorised mode of doing something authorised and doing something so unconnected with authorised acts that it should count as an independent act is not always obvious. Some fairly clear landmarks, however, can be erected:

(i) Express prohibition of an act is not enough to take it outside the test. In *Rose v Plenty*,[9] a milkman took a boy on his round with him in his milk cart despite his employer's express instruction not to do so. Due mainly to the milkman's negligent driving the boy was injured. The Court of Appeal nevertheless held the employer vicariously liable. The milkman was still doing his job, he was just doing it very badly. Similarly in *Limpus v London General Omnibus*[10] a bus driver, disobeying an express instruction from his employer, engaged in racing his bus on the street, with the result that the plaintiff was injured. The employer was held liable.[11] On the other hand, employees who do other people's jobs are not just acting against instructions but not doing their job at all, and so there is no vicarious liability.[12]

Indeed, although there is no consistent authority in favour of saying so, to give an employee an explicit instruction not to do something is prima facie evidence that what is prohibited is a wrongful way of doing the job—otherwise why bother to tell the employee not to do it in the first place? Job descriptions, which define the scope of the job, are not usually phrased in terms of prohibitions but in terms of positive instructions and authorisations.

(ii) There can be vicarious liability even for intentional torts. Thus in *Racz v Home Office*,[13] the House of Lords said that a claim alleging misfeasance in public office by a prison officer and holding the Home Office vicariously liable was allowed to proceed to trial. Furthermore, the same general principle, the distinction between not doing your job and doing your job in an unauthorised way, applies.[14]

---

8 *Racz v Home Office* [1994] 2 AC 45, [1994] 1 All ER 97, [1994] 2 WLR 23 quoting with approval *Salmond and Heuston on the Law of Torts* (19th edn) (1987), pp 521-522 and (20th edn) (1992), p 457.
9 [1976] 1 WLR 141.
10 (1862) 1 H & C 526.
11 Contra *Conway v Wimpey* [1951] 2 KB 266—this annoying case can be satisfactorily explained away on the basis that the unauthorised passenger knew he was a trespasser because he must have known from the notices inside the vehicle that the driver had no authority to invite him inside. Before *British Railways Board v Herrington* and the 1984 Act he would have had no rights. Cf *Stone v Taffe* [1974] 3 All ER 1016. The other remarks of Asquith LJ ought to be treated as obiter and wrong—or if necessary, just wrong.
12 *Beard v London General Omnibus* [1900] 2 QB 530 (conductor drove bus—no liability).
13 Above n 8.
14 See also *Heasmans v Clarity Cleaning* [1987] ICR 949.

Thus, even assaults can be in the course of employment if the employee is just doing his job, for example protecting his employer's property, in an over-enthusiastic fashion.[15] But fighting with other employees or customers in work time when the employee is just indulging in personal quarrels will not be held to be in the course of employment.[16] Even where the quarrel arose from the way the employee was doing his job, assaults that are essentially vindications of personal honour are not in the course of employment. Thus in *Warren v Henlys Ltd*[17] the employee petrol pump attendant wrongly accused the plaintiff of attempting to drive off without paying. The employee became abusive so the plaintiff called the police and said he would report the employee to his employer. The employee then assaulted the plaintiff. The employer was not liable.

A similar distinction is that between employment where part of the job is an activity which forms the basis of the tort and employment which merely gives the employee the opportunity to commit the tort. Thus in *Heasmans v Clarity Cleaning*[18] there was no vicarious liability where a cleaner employed by the defendant made unauthorised telephone calls, and ran up huge bills, from the office she was employed to clean. The Court of Appeal remarked that she was employed to clean telephones not to make calls with them.[19]

(iii) There is no need for the plaintiff to show that the employee's act was for the employer's benefit, although if the act was for the employer's benefit it may overcome doubts about what the employee was doing, especially in cases about intentional torts. Thus in *Century Insurance v Northern Ireland Road Transport Board*[20] the employee was delivering petrol from a tanker into a storage tank of a garage. While the petrol was flowing the employee lit a cigarette and tossed the match away with a carefree gesture. In the ensuing blaze, several nearby houses were damaged along with the tanker and a vehicle belonging to the garage owner. In the House of Lords, Lord Wright said that the case was 'too obvious as a matter of common sense to require either argument or authority'. It was not necessary, although it may once have been, to show that the employee's act was for the employer's benefit. It was enough that the employee was generally doing his job at the time of the negligent act as opposed to doing something else.

There are, however, a great number of disputed questions in this area of the law. We will consider three of them.

---

15 *Poland v Parr* [1927] 1 KB 236—it is doubtful whether the language of implied authority used in this case would be necessary nowadays.

16 *Keppel Bus Co v Sa'ad bin Ahmad* [1974] 2 All ER 700.

17 [1948] 2 All ER 935.

18 Above n 14.

19 Cf also *Irving v Post Office* [1987] IRLR 289.

20 [1942] AC 509.

Not doing the job at all

Sometimes it is very difficult to distinguish between someone doing their job in a very neglectful way and someone not doing their job at all. The most notorious recent case is *General Engineering v Kingston Corpn.*[1] The fire brigade of Kingston, Jamaica were in dispute with their employers, the local authority. As a result their union organised a protest the method of which was that the fire brigade would go to fires very slowly, taking frequent breaks on the way. When a fire broke out in the plaintiff's premises, the fire brigade took 17 minutes to get there instead of the expected three minutes. As a result the plaintiff's premises were completely destroyed. The plaintiff sued the local authority as the fire fighters' employers. The case reached the Privy Council where Lord Ackner said that the fire fighters' actions were 'the very negation of carrying out some act authorised by the employer albeit in a wrongful and unauthorised mode'. Lord Ackner's view was that the only accurate description of what the fire fighters were doing was that they were taking industrial action. It would not be an accurate description of their activities to say that they were putting out fires.

But the problem with this decision is that if it is accepted that the point of vicarious liability in general is to put pressure on employers to seek out and control or dismiss employees likely to be unsafe for other people, to allow employers not to have to seek out fire fighters who take very long periods to reach fires seems perverse. The only justification for the finding in *General Engineering* is that since the activity concerned was really a strike, it did not indicate anything usable by the employer about the competence and safety of individual employees. One might argue that employing as fire fighters people willing to go on strike is something of a mistake that the court should be encouraging the employer not to repeat, but the reality, backed by industrial relations law, is often that there is not much in practice that employers can do.

The dishonesty torts

The case in which the House of Lords announced that it was not necessary to show that the employee's act was for the employer's benefit was *Lloyd v Grace, Smith.*[2] In that case, a solicitor's managing clerk deceived a client of the solicitor into transferring property to him. The clerk disposed of the property and pocketed the proceeds. The solicitor was held to be vicariously liable. The House of Lords said that the clerk had used the authority that he actually had to commit the fraud. Lord Loreburn said:

'If the agent commits the fraud purporting to act in the course of business such as he was authorised, or held out as authorised, to

1   [1989] 1 WLR 69.
2   [1912] AC 716.

transact on account of his principal, then the latter may be held liable for it.'

The appearance of the language of the law of agency in this case ('agent', 'principal', 'authorised', 'course of business', 'held out') is the result of the fact that the deceit was perpetrated by means of a contract, so that the courts look at the case as if the problem were whether the employer could be 'bound' by the fraudulent deal. Similar language appears in *Armagas v Mundogas*,[3] also a case in which the employee's alleged tort was a fraud on the defendant. Lord Keith in that case goes as far as to say that there is no difference between the scope of an agent's authority and the 'course of employment' test. The point of this is that the employer will not be liable unless the employee has at least 'ostensible' authority, which only exists where the employee is acting within the usual course of the authority of someone in his position and, crucially, that the employer has done something to make the victim believe that the employee has authority. People cannot make themselves agents for others merely by their own efforts.[4] The effect of bringing agency ideas into cases of this sort is therefore that there is no liability unless there has been some participation, though not necessarily wrongful participation, by the employer in persuading the plaintiff to deal with the employee. But in other cases, there is no such requirement. In the express prohibition cases, for example, there is no requirement that the employer did something to induce the plaintiff to take a lift with the employee. The most one could say is that if the plaintiff knew that the employee was acting in a way that the employer had prohibited, it is possible that the plaintiff's claim would fail.[5] And in *Rose v Plenty*, Scarman LJ said, 'I think one can see how careful one must be not to introduce into a study of this sort of problem ideas of trespass and agency.'

In the Court of Appeal in *Armagas* Robert Goff LJ tried to resolve this tension by saying that agency ideas could come in when the torts committed are those which involve reliance by the plaintiff on a representation by the employee (which would cover *Hedley Byrne* as well as deceit[6]) but not in torts that involve physical damage. This idea resolves the formal problem of reconciling the case, but it is unclear how such a distinction relates to the purposes of vicarious liability. Presumably it is just as much in the public interest that employers are encouraged to root out potential fraudsters who do not have ostensible authority as it is to root out those who do. Perhaps the idea behind the distinction is that one cannot expect employers to keep track of the activities of those employees who do not usually make deals on behalf of the company.

---

3   [1986] AC 717.
4   Although an agent can be clothed with ostensible authority by inaction as well as action by the principal—see *First Energy v Hungarian International Bank* [1993] 2 Lloyd's Rep 194, [1993] BCLC 1409, [1993] BCC 533.
5   *Stone v Taffe* [1974] 3 All ER 1016 per Stephenson LJ.
6   See eg *Kooragang v Richardson and Wrench* [1982] AC 462.

Deviating motor vehicles

One area of particular confusion has been what to do with cases of employees who cause traffic accidents when travelling in the opposite direction from the one the employer was expecting them to go or in areas of town their employer would be surprised to find them. The classic (and classically unhelpful) test is to ask whether the employee was engaged in the employer's business or 'on a frolic of his own'.[7] The field was further confused by the importation of ideas from shipping law about what happens when a ship is lost at a position it would not have been at if it had kept to its original itinerary.[8]

There is, frankly, no way of making sense of all the case law. Lord Lowry has however, produced a synthesis that accounts for as much of it as possible. All one can do is to list some of the more well-known decisions together with Lord Lowry's synthesis.

In *Whatman v Pearson*,[9] the employees were allowed an hour for dinner, but were forbidden to go home, or to leave their horses and carts unguarded. But one of the employees went home for dinner anyway, about a quarter of an hour out of his way. He then negligently left his horse out in the street. The horse ran off and damaged the plaintiff's property. The Court of Common Pleas decided that the employee was still acting in the course of his employment. Byles J said that he was still acting within the 'general scope' of his job, which involved looking after the horse and cart all day.

In *Storey v Ashton*[10] the employees were sent to deliver some wine. On their way back, one of the employees persuaded the other that since it was by then after hours, they should change direction and pay a visit to one of the employee's relatives. On the way there, they negligently ran over the plaintiff, who sued the employer. The Court of Queen's Bench decided for the employer. Cockburn CJ said it was a question of degree how far a deviation from the authorised route would be considered as a 'separate journey'. But in this case it was more than a deviation. It was a 'new and independent journey' which was 'entirely for his own business'.

In *Crook v Derbyshire Stone*[11] a lorry driver was held not to be within his employment as soon as he stopped for a meal break. But in *Harvey v RG O'Dell*[12] a five mile journey to get a meal during working hours was held to be within the scope of the employee's employment. And in *Hilton v Burton (Rhodes) Ltd*,[13] a group of employees who first had lunch in a pub and then travelled eight miles away from their work site for tea were held to be on a frolic of their own when they were involved in an accident allegedly on their way back.

---

7   *Joel v Morison* (1834) 6 C & P 501.
8   *Storey v Ashton* (1869) LR 4 QB 476.
9   (1868) LR 3 CP 422.
10 Above n 8.
11 [1956] 1 WLR 432.
12 [1958] 2 QB 78.
13 [1961] 1 WLR 705.

Finally, in *Smith v Stages*[14] the employees' job was to travel the country installing insulation in power stations. Their employer told them to leave a job in Staffordshire and travel to a power station in Wales for a week, and then come back immediately to Staffordshire. They were paid their hourly rate for the journeys there and back plus travelling expenses, but the mode of travel was not specified. The employees decided to travel together in a car. They finished the work in Wales two days early (by working without sleep) and then decided to drive straight back to Stafford-shire. Not surprisingly, in their state of extreme fatigue they drove into a wall and were both injured. The employee who was the passenger at the time of the crash sued the employee who was driving. He turned out to be uninsured and so the employer was joined as a defendant on the theory that it was vicariously liable for the negligence of the driver. The House of Lords, upholding the Court of Appeal and reversing the trial judge, found for the plaintiff. Lord Goff said that the fact that the men were travelling back early was immaterial since they were still being paid to travel there and back. He also thought that it was significant that they were travelling on a Monday, 'a normal working day' (although in fact it was a Bank Holiday).

This is the case in which Lord Lowry, who thought that the crucial point was that the pair were 'on duty' at the time of the accident, produced his synthesis of the case law. Lord Lowry said that there were six rules in all: (1) commuting to work even in transport provided by the employer is not acting in the course of employment unless the employee's contract of employment requires him to use the employer's transport, he will be acting in the course of employment; (2) travelling between work sites in the course of the day is within his employment; (3) being paid wages for travelling time indicates that the employee is 'on duty' while travelling—but being paid travel expenses does not; (4) travelling 'in the employers' time' from home to a place of work different from the employee's usual place of work is within employment; (5) 'a deviation from or interruption of a journey undertaken in the course of employment (unless the deviation or inter-ruption is merely incidental to the journey) will for the time being (which may include an overnight interruption) take the employee out of the course of his employment'; (6) return journeys have the same status as the outward journey.

Finally, before leaving the topic of motor vehicle journeys, we should mention the rule in *Launchbury v Morgans*.[15]

In a series of cases[16] the courts developed a notion that the owners of cars could be held liable for accidents caused while other people were driving them when the owner had not relinquished the 'right to control' the car and had 'delegated the task' of driving the car to someone else. The liability

14 [1989] AC 928.
15 [1971] 2 QB 245.
16 *Samson v Aitchison* [1912] AC 844, *Parker v Miller* (1926) 42 TLR 408, *Hewitt v Bonvin* [1940] 1 KB 188, *Chowdhary v Gillot* [1947] 2 All ER 541.

did not apply, however, where the owner had given up possession in a bailment.

In *Ormrod v Crosville Motors*[17] the defendant asked a friend to drive the defendant's car from Liverpool to Monte Carlo. The friend had not got very far before he ran into a bus. The friend's wife was injured. At the time, wives could not sue husbands in tort, but if the defendant were held liable, his insurance company would pay up for the harm caused by the friend. The defendant was duly found liable on the theory that the car was being used for the defendant's purposes.

And so we arrive at *Morgans v Launchbury*.[18] The car this time belonged to the defendant's wife, although it was treated as a collective resource of the whole family and the husband often used it for travelling to work and for jaunts to pubs. The husband told the wife that if he got drunk, he would get somebody else to drive him home in the car. Subsequently, he did get drunk and did ask a friend to drive him home. But the friend drove the car at 90 miles an hour into a bus. The husband was killed and the plaintiffs, other passengers in the car, were injured. The plaintiffs, in an attempt to get at the wife's liability insurance, sued the wife on the theory that the previous cases should be rationalised into a general principle that there was vicarious liability, at least in vehicle cases, whenever someone did something of 'concern or interest' to somebody else. In the alternative the plaintiffs argued that there was such a thing as a 'family' car which should be recognised in law. The Court of Appeal found for the plaintiffs. The House of Lords reversed. There was no general principle that there was vicarious liability whenever someone acted in someone else's interest, and there was no clear way to introduce a 'family car' doctrine without causing more confusion. But the previous line of cases up to and including *Ormrod* were not disapproved of. They were said to stand for the proposition that if a person specifically asked someone else to do something for them, including driving a car, there could be vicarious liability on the ground that the task had been 'delegated'. Mere permission to use a car was not enough to trigger this delegation doctrine, but where the car was used with permission for a specific task that was in the owner's interest and specifically envisaged by the owner, there could be vicarious liability.

The 'delegated task' doctrine of *Morgans v Launchbury* is surprisingly undeveloped,[19] possibly because the House of Lords decision stepped so far back from the radical position adopted by the Court of Appeal.

Is the tortfeasor an independent contractor of the employer?

If the tortfeasor is not an employee, there is still a chance of liability through the so-called 'non-delegable duties'. But to make the non-delegable duty argument work there are still minimum requirements for the relationship

17 [1953] 1 WLR 1120.
18 [1973] AC 127.
19 But see *Norwood v Navan* [1981] RTR 457 and *Watkins v Birmingham City Council* (1976) 126 NLJ 442.

between the tortfeasor and the defendant. There is no good name for this relationship. It can be referred to as 'delegation', although, as we have seen, 'delegation' can lead to vicarious liability in another way, and in any case it is confusing to refer to the 'delegation' of 'non-delegable' duties. The other name is the relationship of 'independent contractor', although that is not quite accurate either, since, although in most cases there is some kind of contract between the tortfeasor and the defendant, it is not a formal requirement that there should be a contract, and even if there is a contract the relationship does not necessarily arise.

The one case that explains the requirement is *Davie v New Merton Board Mills*.[20] The plaintiff was hit in the eye by a piece of the chisel (a 'drift' technically) that he was using for his job. The chisel turned out to have been badly manufactured, but there was no way the employer or the retailer could have known that fact. The plaintiff's case against the employer failed. The plaintiff's main argument was that the employer had a non-delegable duty to provide safe equipment which he had chosen to attempt to fulfill by buying the chisel from a retailer and by relying on the skill of the manufacturer. But the House of Lords said that a purely commercial relationship of buying and selling was outside the scope of vicarious liability of any kind. For the non-delegable duty idea to work, the defendant had to have 'engaged' the actual tortfeasor to do some work. The relationship, therefore, has to be one in which the tortfeasor renders some service personally to the defendant.

Is there a non-delegable duty?

Although the phrase 'non-delegable duty' has rightly been criticised as illogical and even fraudulent[1] it is too well established to shift. The idea strictly is that the defendant employer remains responsible to see that a task is carried out with a breach of the duty that is imposed initially on the employer. But it is easier to see it as a description of a list of the circumstances in which there is vicarious liability even for the acts of independent contractors. It is also possible to use the non-delegable duty argument to impose liability on an employer for the tort of an employee when the tort was not committed in the course of employment. If the tort nevertheless put the employer in breach of a non-delegable duty, there will be liability on this, different, ground.[2]

The list of non-delegable duties does not have any particular rationale, and there is a modern tendency for it to grow slowly but without much pattern.[3]

20 [1959] AC 604. Note that the immediate effect of the case was reversed by the Employer's Liability (Defective Equipment) Act 1969.
1 Williams [1956] CLJ 180.
2 *Morris v Martin* [1966] 1 QB 716, *Hudson v Ridge Manufacturing* [1957] 2 QB 348, cf *Harrison v Michelin Tyre* [1985] 1 All ER 918.
3 See McKendrick 'Vicarious Liability and Independent Contractors: A re-examination' (1990) 53 MLR 770. The list of non-delegables also includes an apparently random selection of statutory duties.

Extra-hazardous activities

Where the defendant has engaged someone to carry out operations that are 'inherently dangerous'[4] any duties in relation to the activity will be non-delegable. The duties may be in nuisance[5], *Rylands v Fletcher*,[6] negligence[7] or for the escape of fire.[8] Note that the extra-hazardous nature of the activity does not mean that there is strict liability for any damage caused. There has to be a breach of duty in the normal way for the tort concerned. The effect of the extra-hazardousness is that employers become liable for the torts of independent contractors, not just for employees.

Employers' common law duties

All the common law duties of employers, for safe fellow employees, safe premises, safe equipment and materials and a safe effectively supervised system of work,[9] are non-delegable. This means, in effect, that employers which are companies and cannot have literally 'personal' duties are covered by the same rules as individual employers. There is an argument that the confirmation in *McDermid v Nash Dredging*[10] that the employers' duty to provide a safe system of work, including the duty that the system works, means that there is effectively vicarious liability for all the acts of independent contractors that affect employees.[11] On the other hand, the rule perhaps should be restricted to the provision of effective supervision.

Bailees

A bailee for reward is someone who, for money or other consideration, keeps something in safe-keeping for someone else. The bailee's duty is to make sure that the goods are treated with reasonable care, which includes care that the goods are not lost or stolen as well as not damaged.[12] It is for the bailee to prove that care was taken.

The bailee's duty is non-delegable. The result is that if an employee or an independent contractor steals the goods or damages them, the bailee

---

4   *Honeywill and Stein v Larkin Bros* [1934] 1 KB 191.
5   *Matania v National Provincial Bank* [1936] 2 All ER 633.
6   *Balfour v Barty-King* [1957] 1 QB 496.
7   *Honeywill & Stein v Larkin Bros* above n 4.
8   *Hobbs (Farms) v Baxenden Chemical* [1992] 1 Lloyd's Rep 54.
9   See above ch 8.
10 [1987] AC 906.
11 McKendrick (1990) 53 MLR 770.
12 If there is no payment, the bailee is a 'gratuitous' bailee and the standard of care required is only to take as much care as one does of one's own property.

for reward will usually be liable regardless of whether the wrong was committed in the course of employment.[13]

Public nuisance and the highway

The strange obsession of English law with the highway carries on into non-delegability. In *Tarry v Ashton*[14] the defendant hired a contractor to repair a lamp on his property. The lamp overhung the highway. The lamp fell off and injured a passer-by who successfully sued the defendant. The mysterious category of public nuisance that deals with interference with the highway created a non-delegable duty.[15] But since the reasons for the special protection for the highway are so unclear, the courts accept that the rule is not to be extended uncritically. And so in *Salsbury v Woodland*[16] where work being done near but not on the highway caused an accident on the highway, the duty was declared not to be non-delegable.

'Collateral negligence'

When the wind blew a sub-contractor's tool off a window sill and it fell and hit a passer-by in the street below, the negligence was said to be 'collateral' and not the responsibility of the employer.[17] Such 'collateral' negligence is hard to pin down, but appears to mean that there is no liability on the basis of non-delegability for the sort of act for which there is vicarious liability in a case like *Century Insurance*, namely acts not specifically and immediately related to the task for which the contractor was hired.[18] It is thus a kind of course of employment rule for non-delegable duties but different from course of employment in ways that are not entirely clear.

Although the notion of collateral negligence is widely cited, its basis in authority is thin and its utility questionable. The results it achieves could be reached equally well by more careful consideration of whether the contractor was at fault and whether the employer's duty is non-delegable in the first place.

13 *Morris v Martin* above n 2.
14 (1876) 1 QBD 314.
15 The non-delegability may extend to duties not strictly to do with the highway but in analogous cases of places to which the public has access, eg railway platforms: *Pickard v Smith* (1861) 10 CBNS 470. *Rogers v Night Riders* [1983] RTR 324 seems to go even further and extend the non-delegability to minicab services. *Sed quaere.*
16 [1970] 1 QB 324.
17 *Padbury v Holliday & Greenwood* (1912) 28 TLR 494.
18 Cf *Halliday v National Telephone* [1899] 2 QB 392, *Pickard v Smith* above n 15, Lord Denning in *Salsbury v Woodland* above n 16.

Chapter 15

Defences

In this chapter we consider some of the defences that defendants may try to raise in a range of different cases. Not all the possible defences are discussed here. Some are very specific to particular torts, for example justification in defamation, and are considered with those torts. Others, exclusion of liability by notice, for example, although not entirely specific to a single tort, nevertheless occur so frequently in relation to a particular kind of case, in that instance, occupiers' liability, that they are best considered along with liability in that kind of case. Finally, limitation of action, that is running out of time, is not discussed at all. It is a specialist topic in procedural law, to the standard references in which the interested reader is referred.

A 'defence' is, strictly, an argument that the defendant raises and, if there are disputed facts, has to prove, which if successful means that the defendant wins the case. Thus 'fair comment' is a defence to defamation. But the most common defence, contributory negligence, no longer fits the description in full, since for 50 years it has been only a partial defence whose effect is to reduce the damages the defendant has to pay rather than to exclude liability completely.

Contributory negligence

Before the Law Reform (Contributory Negligence) Act 1945, contributory negligence was a complete defence. The introduction of a partial defence, which had the effect of reducing damages rather than excluding all liability based on the proportion of the responsibility that the court thinks the plaintiff should bear, might be thought to have improved the position of plaintiffs relative to that of defendants. But it is not entirely clear that this was the effect of the Act. One of the reasons for the 1945 Act was that the previous law was so complex. The cause of the complexity was the desire of judges to mitigate the harshness of the old rule by specifying circumstances in which the plaintiff's fault did not affect liability at all.

Most notorious of these rules was the 'last clear chance' rule, which said that contributory negligence did not apply when, after the plaintiff had acted negligently, the defendant still had a chance of averting the danger.[1] The rule became further complicated by the invention of such notions as 'constructive last clear chance' or 'clearest last chance'. In the former, for example,[2] if the defendant did not have a last clear chance because of his own carelessness, he was deemed nevertheless to have had the last clear chance. Thus, if I carelessly wander in to the middle of the road, and you drive into me when going too fast, you may not have had a chance to avoid me, but if you would have had an opportunity to avoid me if you had been travelling more slowly, you are deemed to have had the last clear chance and the defence of contributory negligence fails.

The effect of these rules was that the plaintiff's position under the old rule was not as bad as it seemed. Immediately after the 1945 Act there was some speculation that the last clear chance rules may have survived the reform. But Denning LJ in *Jones v Livox Quarries*[3] announced, 'It can safely be asserted that the doctrine of last opportunity is obsolete.' No case has contradicted Denning's view (which he reiterated in *Lloyds Bank v Budd*[4]) and it is now the orthodox view. But if this is so, notice that a number of plaintiffs who would have received 100% of their damages under the old rules now receive only a part of their damages. In the case in which I wander in to the middle of the street, for example, whereas before 1945 constructive last clear chance would have meant that I would recover my damages in full, now, under the Act, my damages will probably be substantially reduced.

Although it would be wrong to pine with nostalgia for the pre-1945 rule[5] it would also be wrong to assume that the reform was necessarily a great humanitarian measure that automatically helps the victims of accidents.

Proportionality

If one abandons the common law rules, one faces a large number of possible replacement rules. For example, the rule could be the old maritime rule[6] that whenever both sides are to blame and it is impossible to say how much each side was to blame, the damages should be borne equally by the parties (that is, half of each side's losses are paid for by the other side). Another possibility is to keep the all or nothing rule where the plaintiff is more than half to blame, but to have proportional reduction in damages for cases in which the plaintiff is thought to be less than half to blame. But the 1945 Act opts for a thorough going reform under which full proportionality is introduced. Section 1(1) of the Act says:

1   *Davies v Mann* (1842) 10 M & W 546.
2   See *British Columbia Electric Rly Co v Loach* [1916] 1 AC 719.
3   [1952] 2 QB 608.
4   [1982] RTR 80.
5   See further Howarth 'My Brother's Keeper' [1994] Legal Studies 88 at 104.
6   See Maritime Conventions Act 1911 s 1.

'Where any person suffers damage as a result partly of his own fault and partly of the fault of any other person or persons, a claim in respect of that damage shall not be defeated by reason of the fault of the person suffering the damage, but the damages recoverable in respect thereof shall be reduced to such extent as the court thinks just and equitable having regard to the claimant's share in the responsibility for the damage.'

Responsibility, causation, standards and proportionality

The statute refers to the 'claimant's share in the responsibility for the damage'. 'Responsibility' is a difficult word to construe. It is essentially a moral concept, but it also has a sense of causation. But causation (as opposed to our degree of uncertainty about what caused what) is an all or nothing concept. Events can have more than one cause (for example, a fire is caused by the fuel, the presence of oxygen and the flame) but one cannot say that one cause is 'more' a cause of the event than any of the others.[7] They are all equally causes. If, therefore, there is to be proportionality in contributory negligence, it cannot come from the causal meaning of 'responsibility'. It has to come either from our degree of certainty about causation[8] or, more likely, from the moral content of the word. Contributory negligence under the Act is therefore mainly an exercise in deciding relative blameworthiness. The only role of causation is in making sure that the plaintiff's allegedly faulty act made a difference. If it did not, there is no contributory negligence at all.

But note that like causation in liability for negligence, causation in contributory negligence is intimately connected with the required standard of conduct. What matters is not what would have happened had the plaintiff not been there, or if the plaintiff had not acted at all, but what would have happened if the plaintiff had acted properly. For this reason, in some cases there is an in-built or natural proportionality, since what would have happened had the plaintiff acted properly is that the plaintiff would still have been injured, but would not have been injured so badly. For example, if the plaintiff had been driving at the speed limit, the collision would not have been so severe, but it would still have happened. But what if there would have been no injury at all had the plaintiff acted properly? Is there no liability at all in such a case? The answer must be no, for this is precisely the kind of case in which there is more than one cause, and proportionality must be decided on the basis of blameworthiness.

Another issue that arises is a kind of *Wagon Mound* remoteness in reverse. If the plaintiff had acted properly, there would have been no injury, but the injury that happened was not the sort of injury that one would have expected would arise out of the plaintiff's lack of care. The best way

7 This is the' equivalence of conditions' concept of French law. See above ch 4.
8 See above ch 4.

to deal with this point, however, is to ignore it, or rather to incorporate it into blameworthiness. *Wagon Mound* remoteness is largely a matter of blameworthiness anyway[9] and it simply confuses matters to have several categories of blameworthiness to contend with.

Both courts and commentators have had some difficulty with these fairly simple principles, and attempts to apply various notions of causation have collapsed into the inevitable pleas for 'common sense'.[10] But the Court of Appeal found some of the right approach very early in the history of the 1945 Act in *Jones v Livox*.[11] The plaintiff, disregarding his employer's safety instructions, was riding on the back of a slow-moving quarry vehicle known as a 'traxcavator'. One of the employees drove another quarry vehicle into the back of the traxcavator and injured the plaintiff. The employer, the defendant, claimed that the plaintiff had been contributorily negligent. The plaintiff said that his contributory negligence should not count against him because the only foreseeable risk that he had run was being thrown off the traxcavator, not being crushed by another vehicle. He could have been riding on another part of the vehicle and he would have been just as careless, and yet he would not have been injured.

The Court of Appeal said that the plaintiff's argument should fail. Lord Denning said:

> 'Once negligence is proved, then no matter whether it is actionable negligence or contributory negligence, the person who is guilty of it must bear his proper share of responsibility for the consequences. The consequences do not depend on foreseeability, but on causation. The question in every case is: what faults were there which caused the damage? Was his fault one of them?'

As long as one does not take it as laying down how the various shares of responsibility should be measured, this passage is a perfectly workable exposition of the Act. The answer to the questions in this case are (1) the plaintiff was at fault in riding on the outside of the traxcavator and (2) if the plaintiff had acted properly (ie had kept inside the cab of the traxcavator and had not ridden on some other part of the exterior), there would have been no injury. There is therefore contributory negligence according to the Act, and the court should pass onto deciding by how much the damages should be reduced. If the court believes that the plaintiff's conduct was not particularly dangerous, the time to take that into account is in the apportionment stage.

The method the Act calls for can be illustrated further using what must be the most extreme example imaginable of a *Wagon Mound* remoteness problem in a contributory negligence case, namely the old Pennsylvania case *Berry v Sugar Notch*.[12] The plaintiff was a motorman employed by a

9   See above ch 4.
10 Eg Lord Reid in *Stapley v Gypsum Mines* [1953] AC 663.
11 [1952] 2 QB 608.
12 191 Pa 345, 43 A 240 (S Ct Penn, 1899).

tramway company. The tramcars were subject to a speed limit of eight miles an hour within the borough of Sugar Notch. On the road followed by the tram there was a large chestnut tree which, the jury found, the local authority had carelessly neglected. On the day of the accident the plaintiff was running his tram on the same road during a violent storm. As the plaintiff passed by the tree it was blown down. The tree landed on the tram, injuring the plaintiff. The evidence was that at the time the plaintiff was driving the tram at a speed well in excess of eight miles an hour. The defendant local authority said that there was contributory negligence, since the plaintiff was travelling at more than the speed limit and if the plaintiff had been travelling at the right speed, the tram would not have been at the spot on the road where the tree would land on it. At the time in Pennsylvania, contributory negligence was a complete defence, and so the Pennsylvania Supreme Court, commenting that '[the defendant's] argument, while we cannot deny its ingenuity, strikes us, to say the least, as being somewhat sophistical,' said that since no one would have foreseen a connection between the tram's speed and a tree falling on it, there was no causation and thus no contributory negligence. The Court's argument is precisely that argued for by the plaintiff in *Jones v Livox* except in a more extreme case. In *Jones* the plaintiff could have acted just as badly and the accident would not have happened. In *Berry v Sugar Notch* the plaintiff could have behaved even more carelessly, by driving even faster, and the accident would not have happened. But where there is proportional contributory negligence, the correct approach, although one that reaches the same result, is to admit that the plaintiff was careless, and that if the plaintiff had not been careless the accident probably would not have happened, but that in judging the relative blameworthiness of the parties, the court should take into account the fact that driving trams at more than eight miles an hour does not make trees fall over on people, whereas neglecting trees does mean that they fall over on people. The court should then assess relative blameworthiness so that so much of the blame lies on the defendant that the maxim de minimis non curat lex will apply and the plaintiff should receive full damages.[13]

The remains of the old approach, however, infected even the Court of Appeal in *Livox*. Lord Denning said that if the plaintiff had been sitting on the traxcavator and someone had accidentally shot him, the plaintiff's carelessness would not count as a cause of the accident at all, but would be a mere background condition or a 'circumstance' in which the cause operated. This is an odd remark for a judge to make who was so keen to abolish the last clear chance rule.

The point is that if proportionality is possible it is no longer necessary or even desirable to distinguish between causes and mere conditions.

The courts, unfortunately, add to the confusion by referring to the dangerousness of the plaintiff's conduct for the kind of injury that occurred

---

13 *Johnson v Tennant Bros Ltd* [1954] CA Transcript 329, cited in *Capps v Miller* [1989] 2 All ER 333, [1989] 1 WLR 839, [1989] RTR 312 and *Rushton v Turner Bros Asbestos Co Ltd* [1959] 3 All ER 517, [1960] 1 WLR 96.

as its 'causative potency',[14] a tag which suggests, wrongly, that dangerous–ness is being taken into account in deciding whether there was any relevant contributory negligence at all, as opposed to being a relevant consideration at the apportionment phase.[15] The courts also, rather unfortunately but without doing much harm in practice, attempt to distinguish between 'causative potency' and 'blameworthiness', a pointless exercise since, as the courts admit, both are relevant to apportionment and nothing else.[16]

Seat-belts, crash-helmets and causation

It is, however, worth mentioning that the courts have said that when the Act talks of the plaintiff's 'share in the responsibility for the damage', the last three words should be taken literally. It is blameworthiness in causing the damage that counts, rather than, for example, responsibility for causing the accident that caused the damage. In cases, therefore, where plaintiffs fail to wear a seat-belt[17] or a crash-helmet,[18] evidence that their injuries would have been not so bad had they been wearing a belt or a helmet is decisive. It is no excuse that wearing a belt or a helmet would not have prevented the accident.

One suspects, however, that were contributory negligence still a complete defence, the courts would have taken a different view. It would have seemed to be very unfair to deny the plaintiff an action completely because of not wearing a seat-belt or a helmet when the defendant negligently caused the accident. In some US jurisdictions where the 'seat-belt defense' came up while the old contributory negligence defence still applied, the courts adopted the argument that what matters is the cause of the accident, not the cause of the damage. For example, in *Derheim v N Fiorito Co*[19] the Supreme Court of the State of Washington decided that since Washington had not adopted a 'comparative' approach to contributory negligence, it should not allow the 'seat-belt defense'. Even the adoption of a statute making seat-belt or crash-helmet wearing compulsory might not have been decisive in favour of the defence, since the question is framed as one of causation not as one of fault.

It may be, therefore, that the way seat-belt and crash-helmet cases are handled in England is an example of how the 1945 Act has worked to the disadvantage of plaintiffs, who have their damages reduced in circum–stances in which it is quite possible that had the Act not been passed, they would have recovered in full.

14 See eg *Davies v Swan Motor Co (Swansea) Ltd* [1949] 2 KB 291, [1949] 1 All ER 620.

15 A classic example of this near but not quite confusion is to be found in *Stapley v Gypsum Mines* [1953] AC 663 per Lord Reid: 'The "claimant's responsibility for the damage" cannot be assessed without considering the relative importance of [the plaintiff's] acts in causing the damage, apart from his blameworthiness.'.

16 *Davies v Swan Motor Co (Swansea) Ltd* [1949] 2 KB 291, [1949] 1 All ER 620.

17 *Froom v Butcher* [1976] QB 286.

18 *Capps v Miller* [1989] 2 All ER 333.

19 80 Wash 2d 161, 492 P 2d 1030 (1972).

100% contributory negligence

In *Pitts v Hunt*[20] the Court of Appeal announced, to general surprise, that the 1945 Act did not allow a finding that the plaintiff was '100% contributorily negligent'. Previous cases where such findings had been approved by the Court of Appeal itself, for example *Jayes v IMI (Kynoch)*,[1] were ignored. The Court of Appeal's argument was that s 1 of the Act said that it applied 'where any person suffers damage as the result partly of his own fault and partly of the fault of any other person or persons'. This meant that the Act did not apply where the damage was not at least partly someone else's fault. To say that the plaintiff was 100% contributorily negligent was to say that the plaintiff was not partly but entirely to blame and, that by subtraction, the defendant must be 0% to blame, that is not to blame at all. Therefore the Act did not apply.

In formal terms, *Pitts v Hunt* is per incuriam on this point since *Jayes* was not even cited by counsel. But that does not deal with its ingenious, not to say 'sophistical' argument. There is, however, one way past the Court of Appeal's argument in *Pitts*. If the Act does not apply when the plaintiff is 100% to blame, it must follow that the old contributory negligence rule must still be in force for such cases, namely that contributory negligence is a complete defence. This produces the desired result.

Apportionment

In the seat-belt cases,[2] the Court of Appeal, led by Lord Denning, decided that if there would have been no injury at all if the plaintiff had been wearing a seat-belt, damages should be reduced by 25%, but if the injuries would only have been reduced, the figure should be 15%. Lord Denning said, quite correctly, that the assessment had to take into account 'blameworthiness'. But neither he nor any other judge has ever explained how one turns a judgment on blameworthiness into a precise percentage. The problem is often side-stepped by the appellate courts on the ground that apportionment is a decision for the trial judge whose opinion should be respected unless it is obviously wrong.

There are a number of possible approaches the courts might adopt, both in contributory negligence and in contribution, where the problems are similar.[3] One possibility is relative dangerousness—in which the court tries to assess the amount of harm the plaintiff's kind of conduct causes on average in normal circumstances in the absence of the defendant's type of conduct and to compare that with the amount of harm the defendant's type of harm causes on average in normal circumstances in the absence of

20 [1991] 1 QB 24, [1990] 3 All ER 344, [1990] 3 WLR 542, [1990] RTR 290.
1   [1985] ICR 155.
2   Eg *Froom v Butcher* above n 17, *Owens v Brimmell* [1977] QB 859.
3   See Howarth 'My Brother's Keeper' [1994] Legal Studies 88 at 103-104.

the plaintiff's type of conduct. For example, in a seat belt case, one would ask how dangerous it is not to wear a seat belt (serious injuries per person per year might be a crude measure) in accidents in which the other driver was not negligent and to compare that with how dangerous it is to drive carelessly, using the same measure, counting only accidents in which the victims were wearing seat-belts.

This approach has the advantages of sounding like what judges may mean by 'causative potency' and of being capable of applying even to cases where the defendant is accused of breaching a strict liability duty, which might otherwise always count as not blameworthy at all, rather than a negligence duty. But its disadvantages are that it is susceptible to manipulation in setting what counts as the 'type' of conduct (for example, is the 'type' driving at 90 mph or driving at any speed over the limit?) and that it does not capture the aspects of blameworthiness that relate to how difficult it was to act in any other way. Moreover, for many types of behaviour, the relevant information will either not exist or be disputed.

Another possibility is to assume that the defendant and the plaintiff were equally to blame unless one or the other acted in a particularly reprehensible way, for example a defendant who acted intentionally or a plaintiff who acted recklessly. This approach has the advantage of having some moral content, but its disadvantage is that there seems to be no way that it could reproduce the full range of gradations from 10% to 90%[4] contributory negligence that the courts use now.

Standard of care

Lord Denning in *Jones v Livox* said:

> 'A person is guilty of contributory negligence if he ought reasonably to have foreseen that if he did not act as a reasonable, prudent man, he might be hurt himself; and in his reckonings he must take into account the possibility of others being careless.'

The test is the same as that applied to negligence itself. A reasonable person weighs the risk, including the seriousness of the risk, and balances the risk against the costs of taking further precautions. The difference, of course, is that it is more surprising that people do not take reasonable care of themselves than that they do not take reasonable care with the interests of others. Indeed the economic theory of contributory negligence suggests that whatever the contributory negligence rule a legal system adopts, including no rule at all, as long as liability itself is based on fault, victims will still act in the same way—for if they assume, as seems fairly

4   Contributory negligence of less than 10% can apparently, safely be ignored on the grounds that de minimis non curat lex—see *Capps v Miller* [1989] 2 All ER 333 citing the unreported case *Johnson v Tennant Bros.*

sensible, that most people do not act carelessly, no one will be responsible for accidents that affect one other than themselves. And so, even if there is no contributory negligence rule at all reasonable people will take proper care of themselves.

Since the test for fault is the same as in defendant's negligence, there is no particular advantage in going into the question in any great detail. The same consideration of all the circumstances applies, including the effect of emergencies and dilemmas[5].Children are judged according to the standards of 'ordinary' children of their age,[6] although there will always be some dispute about what exactly is to be expected of very young children.[7] Adults who are infirm are given a degree of leeway in some cases,[8] but the correct view is that adults should understand their own limitations, and the reason an infirm 90-year-old is contributorily negligent for shuffling into the path of an incoming vehicle is not that he cannot move as quickly as a fit 20-year-old but because he ought to know that he cannot move that quickly and should know better than to put himself in such a position in the first place.[9] There does seem to be a tendency, especially in older cases, to give the benefit of the doubt to employees in employers' liability cases, but that seems to be a tradition that goes back to the reaction against the nineteenth century trio of absolute defences for employers—common employment, volenti and contributory negligence—and seems anachronistic now. The citation of pre-1945 Act cases in this field must be treated with particular caution.[10] The notion of favouring the employee may be more defensible in the statutory employers' torts, on the ground that since the earliest Factories Acts, legislation in this field has had a paternalistic intent of protecting employees even from their own follies.

Contributory negligence in torts other than negligence

Section 4 of the 1945 Act says that for the purposes of the Act 'fault' in s 1 means 'negligence, breach of statutory duty, or other act or omission that gives rise to liability in tort or would, apart from this Act, give rise to the defence of contributory negligence'. According to Lord Denning in *Murphy v Culhane*,[11] a case about assault, the section clearly intended to extend

---

5 See the infamous *Sayers v Harlow UDC* [1958] 1 WLR 623 (plaintiff stuck in public lavatory—tried to climb out—unreasonable method, but could have been reasonable ones).
6 *Gough v Thorne* [1966] 3 All ER 398 cf *Morales v Eccleston* [1991] RTR 151.
7 *McKinnell v White* 1971 SLT 61 for example seems to expect too much from a five-year-old.
8 *Daly v Liverpool Corpn* [1939] 2 All ER 142.
9 Cf *Baxter v Woolcombers Ltd* (1963) 107 Sol Jo 553.
10 Eg *Caswell v Powell Duffryn* [1940] AC 152 which seems to make too many allowances for the employee's state of fatigue, although the effect on the victim's judgment of great noise and smoke is a valid consideration and should also count as part of the employers' failure to provide a safe system of work.
11 [1977] QB 94—contra *Lane v Holloway* [1968] 1 QB 379.

the scope of contributory negligence to include all torts.[12] This is so whatever the position before the Act.

In *Alliance & Leicester Building Society v Edgestop*,[13] however, Mummery J insisted that contributory negligence was not a defence to deceit, since it had not been a defence before the 1945 Act and since, as Mummery J claimed, the Act had not changed anything. Mummery J argued that when s 4 defines 'fault' it defines it not just for the purpose of saying what 'fault' means in s 1 about the kind of defendant's conduct caught by the Act but also the kind of plaintiff's conduct caught by the Act. This means, according to Mummery J, that there can be no contributory negligence under the Act if the plaintiff's conduct did not constitute a tort against the defendant. But, the learned Chancery judge continued, in deceit cases, the plaintiff's lack of care does not constitute a tort against the defendant. Therefore there is only contributory negligence where it applied 'apart from this Act'. Before the Act there was no doubt that contributory negligence was inapplicable to deceit, and so, Mummery J, concludes, that is still the position.

With respect, Mummery J's argument is entirely wrong. As long ago as 1951, in *Nance v British Colombia Electric Rly*[14] Viscount Simon said that 'contributory negligence is set up as a shield' against the plaintiff's claim, and that it is not necessary for the defendant to have a counter-claim of any kind against the plaintiff. If Mummery J were correct, virtually every contributory negligence case since 1945 would be wrong. Where, for example, is the counter-claim of the defendant against the plaintiff in a seat-belt or crash-helmet case? How does the plaintiff's not wearing a seat-belt constitute a tort against the defendant? As Glanville Williams said also in 1951,[15] if the 'fault' of the plaintiff in s 1 meant that the plaintiff had to commit a tort, the Act would be nonsense. Either the definition of fault does not apply to the plaintiff's fault or 'negligence' in the definition refers purely to carelessness and not the whole tort of negligence.

Volenti non fit injuria or consent

The second general defence to consider is volenti non fit injuria, or consent, sometimes known, though confusingly, as assumption of risk.

We have already dealt with a form of consent in the intentional torts.[16] In trespass to land and even assault, if the defendant has the plaintiff's consent (or 'licence') to walk on the plaintiff's land or carry out a surgical operation on the plaintiff, there is no tort. Consent in these torts includes

---

12 It may also include contract where the contract claim is co-extensive with an independent tort claim—*Barclays Bank Plc v Fairclough Building Ltd* [1995] 1 All ER 289 (CA).
13 [1994] 2 All ER 38, [1993] 1 WLR 1462.
14 [1951] AC 601.
15 *Joint Torts and Contributory Negligence* at pp 318-19.
16 See above.

implied consent, such as the implied consent to walk up the path to someone's front door.[17]

But it would be very dangerous to transfer these ideas of consent from the intentional torts into negligence, especially the idea of implied consent, whose existence in the intentional torts is justified only by the fact that they are mostly actionable per se. Implied consent is one technique of excluding very trivial claims and yet retaining, for cases mainly of official intrusion that does not cause immediate harm, the formal position that these torts are actionable without proof of special damage. Indeed, in *Re F*[18] Lord Goff ended the fiction in the tort of assault and battery of implied consent for small everyday acts of jostling and replaced it with a frank statement that such trivial acts were not actionable.

But in negligence, there is already a mechanism that excludes trivial claims, namely that if there is no damage there is no action.

Furthermore, the idea of implied consent has the potential to undermine the very foundations of the law of negligence. In one sense of consent, people consent to the risk of injury every time they step into the street, and many people consent to the risk of injury every time they go to work. They consent in the sense that they know that the streets and some workplaces are dangerous places. This is the notion of consent which got out of hand in the nineteenth century especially in employers' liability cases.[19] By saying that employees consented to the risks of their jobs when they accepted them, the nineteenth century judges prevented almost every possible negligence claim against an employer.

But with the reaction against the nineteenth century doctrines of common employment and especially the advent of proportionate contributory negligence, the scope of the volenti defence, and especially of implied consent to negligence has started to disappear from the law. Indeed, there is already a venerable tradition that denies that volenti has any place in negligence law at all.[20] But it probably remains for explicit and implied agreements not to sue,[1] and implied agreement is found very rarely, especially outside two particular areas, namely accepting rides in vehicles with patently incapable or drunk drivers and sports. Even in those two areas, as we shall see, the conditions for the application of the defence are strict, or else there are increasing doubts about its applicability at all.

The elements of the defence are now that the plaintiff should have voluntarily agreed with the defendant, in advance of the faulty act, that the plaintiff would not sue the defendant for the negligent act (or breach of statutory duty) that the defendant actually committed,[2] or that the

17 Ibid.
18 Discussed above ch 8.
19 See above. For a short historical account see *Markesinis and Deakin* 654-655.
20 See *Beven on Negligence* (4th edn) at 790 and Diplock LJ in *Wooldridge v Sumner* [1963] 2 QB 43.
1 See Lord Denning in *Nettleship v Weston* [1971] 2 QB 691 esp at 701.
2 Note that those who say that the defence can never properly apply in negligence say that if the agreement is in advance of the accident, the plaintiff cannot really know what he

plaintiff helped to cause the defendant to act in a faulty manner in circumstances in which such an agreement should be inferred.[3]

'Voluntary'

To count as voluntary, the plaintiff's agreement must have been based on full knowledge and not forced by circumstances such as threats or having a choice of evils.[4]

Full knowledge means knowledge of what all the relevant risks of injury are and how serious they are.[5] Moreover, the cases often say that the plaintiff has to be willing to accept that the defendant is negligent, not just that there is a risk of injury.[6] It is submitted, therefore, that the plaintiff's knowledge should have to include knowledge of the difficulties and costs of taking effective precautions against the accidents in question, for otherwise the plaintiff could not fully consent to negligence in the sense of fault or breach of duty.

The plaintiff's knowledge is what he did know, not what he ought to have known.[7] If his thought processes are befuddled by drink he may be found to have not known things that when sober he would have known, or at least would have found out. If this is so, there is no defence.[8]

Voluntariness even in the face of full knowledge can be negatived by economic pressure, including the implied threat of dismissal.[9] It is also negatived in most rescue cases, where the mixture of emergency and social duty operates to make the idea of voluntariness meaningless.[10] And people who are mentally ill do not count as volenti if they kill themselves.[11]

Agreed in advance or causation

In older cases, it was assumed that there is no problem in saying that people voluntarily accept risks that they simply come across, for example

---

or she is consenting to, but if it is after the event, it is a waiver, not volenti. See eg *Dann v Hamilton* [1939] 1 KB 509, cf *Woodley v Metropolitan District Rly* (1877) 2 Ex D 384 (knowledge of likelihood of negligence not enough).

3   Cf Jaffey 'Volenti Non Fit Injuria' [1985] CLJ 87—a very helpful article.

4   *Bowater v Rowley Regis* [1944] KB 476.

5   *Osborne v London and North Western Rly Co* (1888) 21 QBD 220.

6   *Thomas v Quartermaine* (1887) 18 QBD 685, *Nettleship v Weston* above n 1.

7   *Smith v Austin Lifts* [1959] 1 WLR 100.

8   *Morris v Murray* [1991] 2 QB 6, [1990] 3 All ER 801 (but note that the plaintiff was not drunk enough in that case).

9   *Bowater v Rowley Regis* above n 4, *Smith v Charles Baker & Sons* [1891] AC 325.

10 *Baker v TE Hopkins* [1959] 1 WLR 966.

11 *Kirkham v Chief Constable of Greater Manchester Police* [1990] 2 QB 283—note that the test is mental illness, not legal insanity.

dangers at work or on other people's premises.[12] It is not clear, however, that this is still correct.[13] Situations which, like rescues, force themselves on the plaintiff can hardly count as conducive to fully voluntary decision-making.

There are some cases, however, in which an agreement has to be implied. In these cases, however, the point is that for the defence to succeed, the plaintiff has to have done more than wait for something to happen, but rather participates in initiating the danger.

For example, in cases in which people accept lifts from plainly incapable or drunken drivers (a type of case to which, it is important to note, volenti no longer applies because of statutory intervention[14]), volenti does not apply where the plaintiff simply accepted a lift in a car driven by an obvious drunk. In *Dann v Hamilton*,[15] the plaintiff accepted a lift home from a trip to see the Coronation decorations from a man she knew to be, in the words of the judge, 'dead drunk'. Nevertheless, a volenti defence did not succeed.

The defendant in cases of the *Dann* sort is generally left with arguments about contributory negligence (although note that in *Dann* itself, (a) contributory negligence was not pleaded, and (b) if it had been, since the case was before the 1945 Act, the case would have turned on very complex arguments about last clear chances.) But where the plaintiff takes an active part in initiating the danger the volenti defence may succeed, because the court is more willing to infer an agreement not to sue from the facts. In *Morris v Murray*,[16] for example, the plaintiff was said to have consented to be taken on a flight in a light aeroplane piloted by a man who had drunk the equivalent of 17 whiskies, many of them in the presence of the plaintiff. The plane soon crashed and the pilot was killed and the plaintiff injured. The flight was the pilot's idea, but the plaintiff had taken an active part in the event, driving the pilot from the pub to the aerodrome and helping to set the plane up for the flight. A volenti defence succeeded.

And in *ICI v Shatwell*,[17] two brothers who worked for the defendants as shot-firers agreed, in violation of the employer's instructions, to carry out a blast in a very dangerous way, with the result that both were injured. Each sued the employer vicariously for the negligence of the other. The defence of volenti succeeded.

Admittedly there is one sort of case in which the initiation idea does not seem to justify an implied agreement to sue but in which consent sometimes succeeds as a defence, namely in sports accidents involving either comp‒etitors or spectators. In *Wooldridge v Sumner*, for example, the plaintiff, a professional photographer covering the Horse of the Year show, was trampled by the defendant's horse after its rider lost control of it during a

12   *Dann v Hamilton* above n 2.
13   See especially Diplock LJ in *Wooldridge v Sumner* above n 20 as explained in *Morris v Murray* above n 8.
14   Road Traffic Act 1988 s 149 as interpreted in *Pitts v Hunt* [1991] 1 QB 24.
15   Above n 2.
16   Above n 8.
17   [1965] AC 656, distinguishing *Stapley v Gypsum Mines* [1953] AC 663.

competition. The court decided that the photographer could not sue because spectators consent to the normal spills and thrills of the sport, including the obvious fact that some performances are going to be better than others.[18] But subsequent cases about sport have come to the same result without referring to volenti or, indeed, to *Wooldridge v Sumner*. Cases such as *Condon v Basi*,[19] a case about soccer, indicate that it is a better approach to say that events that are normal incidents of the game are not faulty. The 'consent' in a case such as *Wooldridge v Sumner* is consent only to non-negligent behaviour, and is therefore not an application of the volenti defence at all.

Illegality

In *Cummings v Granger*,[20] Lord Denning said:

> '[A]ny thief or burglar who goes on to premises knowing that there is a guard-dog there ... [and] he is bitten or injured he cannot recover. He voluntarily takes the risk of it. Even if he does not know there is a guard-dog there, he might be defeated by the plea, "ex turpi causa non oritur actio."'

'Ex turpi causa non oritur actio' means 'no action arises from a bad cause' or, in Tony Weir's translation, 'Bad people get less'.[1]

It is apparently a defence to a tort action that the plaintiff's injuries arose from his participation in bad behaviour—usually but not necessarily criminal behaviour. There are two alleged reasons for the defence: that the court should not assist plaintiffs when it would be 'an offence to the public conscience'[2] to do so; and that the court would find it impossible to formulate a standard of care for criminal activities.[3] The second reason is in reality a mealy-mouthed version of the first reason, for it is perfectly easy to formulate standards of care for criminal activity, either standards that recognise that there is little public benefit in criminals getting away so that whatever they do is probably faulty, or standards that take into account what the criminals were trying to do, for example to blow up one's accomplices when trying to blow open a safe is careless. The 'impossibility' is only that it is embarrassing to formulate such standards publicly and causes an outcry in the press.

But there is an obvious objection to the defence of illegality. Why should a person lose all of his ordinary rights to personal safety and the protection

---

18 See also *Simms v Leigh Rugby Football Club Ltd* [1969] 2 All ER 923 (rugby player thrown against wall—volenti to risk of injury).

19 [1985] 1 WLR 866.

20 [1977] QB 397.

1 *Casebook* 256.

2 *Euro-Diam v Bathurst* [1988] 2 All ER 23.

3 *Kirkham v Chief Constable of Greater Manchester Police* [1990] 2 QB 283.

of his property just because of his criminal activities? Is it right to recreate the class of outlaws—people who have lost the law's protection because they themselves once broke the law?[4] Perhaps more important, should tort law encourage people to take pot shots at burglars?

These are not imaginary problems. On 2 December 1994, the following report appeared in the *Daily Telegraph*:

> 'A retired miner who shot and seriously injured a burglar trying to break into his allotment shed has been ordered to pay his victim £4,033 compensation. A High Court judge said Mr Ted Newbery, 82, had responded in a "highly dangerous way" to the threat posed by the burglar, Mark Revill, 28, and may have been "disproportionately violent". Mr Justice Rougier, however, ruled that Revill was two-thirds responsible for the incident and reduced his £12,100 award by the same proportion. He also awarded Mr Newbery, of Ilkeston, Derbys, £400 damages for a successful counter-claim against Revill that the burglar had caused the pensioner nervous shock.'

The report went on to say that Mr Newbery had developed a 'siege mentality' after his allotment was repeatedly vandalised and had started sleeping in his shed. When the burglar and an accomplice tried to break into the shed, Mr Newbery fired an unlicensed 12-bore shotgun through a hole in the door. The burglar was hit in the chest and lost most of the use of his right arm, suffered from blackouts and had pellets lodged in his lungs and liver.

The judge, Rougier J is reported to have said:

> 'It was a highly dangerous thing for the defendant to do but, in part, fear had clouded his perception and judgment, although I think he was carrying out a preconceived contingency plan. To place a shotgun through a hole in the door, thereby losing one's ability to see, constitutes negligence amounting to recklessness. But I am trying to balance the blameworthiness and negligence of both parties. The burglar runs many risks, not least being injured by a householder, but, whether through fear or anger, the reaction of the defendant may have been disproportionately violent.'

In the next few days, a public outcry ensued, and a fund was set up to pay Mr Newbery's damages. One MP said of the judgment, 'No ordinary person would have ruled that way. It may be the strict letter of the law but it denies justice.' But another MP, a lawyer, said, 'We can't encourage people just to go around using guns. That way lies anarchy and the law cannot allow it. It is clear the old man was negligent, but what is at issue, I believe, is the level of the compensation. Is £4,000 fair when he was the innocent party?'[5]

4   Cf Hervey (1981) 97 LQR 537.
5   (1994) Sunday Telegraph, 4 December.

One thing Rougier J obviously had not done was to have allowed a defence of illegality. The conscience of the public, or at least what passes for the conscience of the press, was certainly outraged. But the MP who spoke in defence of the judgment had a point. Why should plaintiffs get away with dangerous behaviour just because defendants engage in bad behaviour? Surely that way anarchy does lie.

The case law on the defence of illegality bounces backwards and forwards between the two attitudes—on the one hand the moral populism of the outraged public conscience and on the other the studied classical utilitarianism of the careful calculation of consequences. In *Euro-Diam v Bathurst*,[6] Kerr LJ attempted the following uneasy synthesis:

> 'The ex turpi defence ... applies if in all the circumstances it would be an affront to the public conscience to grant the relief which [the plaintiff] seeks because the courts would thereby appear to assist or encourage the plaintiff in his illegal conduct or to encourage others in similar acts.'

But surely what should matter is not what would 'appear' to be the case but what is the case? Does judgment for the plaintiff in *Revill v Newbery* encourage burglars to burgle as well as discouraging the shooting of intruders? If it does have both such effects (which presumably it would have if burglars were economically rational people who read the law reports) then it may be worth considering invoking the defence. But how do we know what the effect of the use of the defence would be?

In fact, there are two sorts of ex turpi causa case. In one sort, both the plaintiff and the defendant are criminals and the incident arose out of a joint criminal enterprise. In the other, the plaintiff alone was engaged in bad behaviour.

It is in the first sort of case in which the courts usually find the defence of illegality made out. In *Ashton v Turner*[7] for example, the plaintiff was the passenger in a getaway car driven by the defendant. The defendant crashed the car and the plaintiff was injured. The defence of illegality succeeded. In *Pitts v Hunt*[8] the plaintiff encouraged the defendant to get drunk and drive his motorbike around in a reckless and dangerous fashion. While the plaintiff was riding as a pillion passenger, the defendant crashed the bike. The defendant was killed and the plaintiff injured. The defence of illegality succeeded.

In such cases, it is not so much the public that is outraged as the court. In the getaway car cases, the court is, in effect, being asked to divide up the spoils of the crime, and even to help the criminals replace some of the proceeds of the crime that they have lost by getting caught with insurance moneys. Moreover, the defence of volenti almost always is applicable, since the parties will have planned and committed the crimes together. In *Pitts*

6   Above n 2.
7   [1981] QB 137.
8   [1991] 1 QB 24.

v Hunt, of course, volenti did not work because of s 149 of the Road Traffic Act, and so illegality serves as a substitute in cases of joint criminal activity.

But it is much more difficult to make the defence work in cases in which only the plaintiff was engaged in criminality or in which plaintiff and defendant were engaged in different and unrelated criminal acts. In *Farrell v Secretary of State for Defence*[9] for example, the case of a robber who was mistaken for a terrorist and shot dead by a soldier was not affected by the illegality defence. In *Saunders v Edwards*[10] the defendants committed a deceit on the plaintiff who then committed a different deceit on the Revenue. The defence of illegality raised by the first fraudster failed. In these cases, the court is not required to settle disputes about the division of the proceeds of a joint enterprise but simply faces a defence in the form of a negative jus tertii—not so much 'you have no right because a third party has a better right than you' as 'you have no right because you have done a worse wrong to a third party'. Note also that these cases do not raise a parallel defence in volenti. There is no real consent to the defendant's tort. It is often a risk that the criminal takes, but knowing is not the same as accepting or initiating. In these cases, therefore, the illegality point is not a strong one and borders on being irrelevant.

The distinction followed by at least the better decisions is that of Lord Asquith in *National Coal Board v England*:[11]

> 'If two burglars, A and B, agree to open a safe by means of explosives, and A so negligently handles the explosive charge as to injure B, B might find some difficulty in maintaining an action for negligence against A. But if A and B are proceeding to the premises which they intend burglariously to enter, and before they enter them, B picks A's pocket and steals his watch, I cannot prevail on myself to believe that A could not sue in tort.'

In between these two sorts of case are cases of fights, which if they are pre-arranged or happen in circumstances in which either side could easily back off, should count as joint criminal enterprises and the illegality defence should work.[12] But if not pre-arranged and one side or the other really has no option but to fight, the defence of illegality should fail, although, as in all these cases, contributory negligence will be relevant.

Into this second category falls Ted Newbery's shot gun blast, thus vindicating Rougier J in the eyes of the law if not in the eyes of the popular press.[13]

---

9   [1980] 1 All ER 166.
10   [1987] 2 All ER 651.
11   [1954] AC 403.
12   *Murphy v Culhane* [1977] QB 94.
13   On the 'disproportionality' aspect of the case, cf *Lane v Holloway* [1968] 1 QB 379, but *Murphy* is to be preferred on the question of contributory negligence.

Necessity

Necessity is a defence to the intentional torts[14] and, perhaps, intentional examples of *Rylands v Fletcher.*[15] It occurs in cases in which the defendant, faced with a choice of two serious evils, chose the option that produces the least damage to the public generally, but which of necessity harms the plaintiff in the process. The defence is not necessary in negligence because it is built into the decision about fault.[16] Its use in medical cases to justify interventions believed by doctors to be in the best interests of patients who cannot give consent has already been discussed.[17] It has also been used to justify force feeding prisoners on hunger strike,[18] but it is not clear that this is still right—especially since the legalisation of suicide. More easily justified are cases in which the defendant destroyed property in order to save human life.[19]

The defence is established where the decision was reasonable to avoid a substantial and imminent danger, and the actions taken were reasonable and proportionate in the circumstances.[20]

14 See above chs 9 and 10.
15 See *Rigby v Chief Constable of Northamptonshire* [1985] 2 All ER 985; see above ch 3.
16 This explains *Rigby* rather than any technical point about necessity.
17 *Re F* [1990] 2 AC 1; see above.
18 At least this is one explanation of *Leigh v Gladstone* (1909) 26 TLR 139.
19 *Southport Corpn v Esso* [1954] 2 QB 182.
20 *Southport Corpn v Esso* above n 19, *Cope v Sharp (No 2)* [1912] 1 KB 496.

Index